THE PAPERMAC GUIDE TO
CHILD HEALTH

Professor David Hull FRCP DCH

David Hull established the Department of Child Health at the Queen's Medical Centre, Nottingham in 1972, after holding the posts of Consultant Paediatrician at the Hospital for Sick Children, Great Ormond Street, London, and Lecturer in Paediatrics at the University of Oxford Medical School. He is recognized as one of the foremost figures in child health in the United Kingdom, and his department at Nottingham as one of the most advanced in the country.

THE PAPERMAC GUIDE TO
CHILD HEALTH

Edited by
Professor DAVID HULL FRCP DCH

PAPERMAC

EDITED BY

Professor David Hull FRCP DCH
Department of Child Health
University Hospital, Nottingham

ADVISORY BOARD

Dr Peter Barbor FRCP JP
Consultant Paediatrician
University Hospital, Nottingham

Dr Arnon Bentovim FRCPsych
Consultant Psychiatrist
Hospital for Sick Children, Great Ormond Street
and Tavistock Clinic, London

Dr Michael Modell FRCGP MRCP DCH
General Practitioner
The James Wigg Practice
Kentish Town Health Centre, and
Head, General Practice Unit,
University College London

Copyright © Frances Lincoln Limited 1985
Photographs © Anthea Sieveking 1985
All rights reserved. No reproduction, copy or transmission of this publication may be made without written permission. No paragraph of this publication may be reproduced, copied or transmitted save with written permission or in accordance with the provisions of the Copyright Act 1956 (as amended). Any person who does any unauthorized act in relation to this publication may be liable to criminal prosecution and civil claims for damages.

First published as *The Macmillan Guide to Child Health*
in 1985 by Macmillan London Limited

Published 1988 by
PAPERMAC
a division of Macmillan Publishers Limited
4 Little Essex Street, London WC2R 3LF and Basingstoke
Associated companies in Auckland, Delhi, Dublin,
Gaborone, Hamburg, Harare, Hong Kong, Johannesburg,
Kuala Lumpur, Lagos, Manzini, Melbourne, Mexico City,
Nairobi, New York, Singapore and Tokyo

British Library Cataloguing in Publication Data
 The Papermac guide to child health.
 1 Children – Care and hygiene
 I. Hull, David
 613'.0432'0240431 RJ61
 ISBN 0-333-46507-5

Printed in Yugoslavia by Mladinska Knjiga

Project editors	Esther Eisenthal
	Clare Mitchison
Project art editor	Bob Gordon
Text editors	Jo Christian
	Sarah Mitchell
	Lindy Newton
	Steve Parker
Designers	Gill della Casa
	Pauline Faulks
	Patrick Nugent
Editorial assistants	Gian Douglas-Home
	Elizabeth Galfalvi
General editor	Pippa Rubinstein
Art director	Debbie MacKinnon

The Papermac Guide to Child Health was conceived and produced by Frances Lincoln Limited, Apollo Works, 5 Charlton Kings Road, London NW5 2SB

CONTRIBUTORS

Margaret Adcock
Social Work Consultant and Tutor
on the Advanced Course
in Social Work with Children
and Families
Goldsmith's College, London

Professor John Bain MD FRCGP
DCH DObstRCOG
Primary Medical Care, Aldermoor
Health Centre
University of Southampton

Dr Dora Black FRCPsych
Consultant Child Psychiatrist
Royal Free Hospital, London

Dr Charles Brook MD FRCP DCH
Consultant Paediatrician
The Middlesex Hospital, London

Dr Peter Bruggen DRCOG DCH
FRCPsych
Consultant Psychiatrist
Adolescent Unit, Hill End Hospital
St Albans
and Tavistock Clinic, London

Dr Cyril Chantler FRCP
Professor, Paediatric Nephrology
Evelina Children's Hospital and
Guy's Hospital, London

Dr Judith Chessells FRCP
DObstRCOG
Consultant Clinical Haematologist
Hospital for Sick Children
Great Ormond Street, London

Dr Allan F Colver MRCP
Snr Registrar in Community
Paediatrics
Northumberland Health Authority

Dr David Curnock MRCP DCH
DObstRCOG
Consultant Paediatrician
Nottingham City Hospital

Elizabeth Fenwick MA
Medical Editor

Dr J S Fitzsimmons DCH FRCP
Consultant in Clinical Genetics
Nottingham City Hospital

Dr Gillian Forrest MRCPsych
MRCGP
Consultant Child Psychiatrist
Park Hospital for Children, Oxford

Mr Kevin P. Gibbin FRCS
ENT Surgeon
University Hospital, Nottingham

Dr D M B Hall MRCP
Consultant and
Snr Lecturer in Paediatrics
St George's Hospital, London

Dr Stephen Herman FRCP DCH
Consultant Paediatrician
Royal National Orthopaedic and
Central Middlesex Hospitals, London

Eva Holmes
Principal Educational Psychologist
Enfield School Psychological Service

Dr Ruth Holt BChD MSc BChD
Snr Lecturer, Children's Dentistry
Eastman Dental Institute, London

Carol Hull RSCN RCNT
University Hospital, Nottingham

Jenny Jenkins MA
Snr Psychologist
Hospital for Sick Children
Great Ormond Street, London

Dr Sue Jenkins MB MRCP DCH
Community Paediatric Research
Unit, St Mary's Hospital and
Snr Clinical Medical Officer
Paddington and Kensington Health
Authority, North London

Dr Derek I Johnston MD FRCP
DCH
Consultant Paediatrician
University Hospital, Nottingham

Dr Julian Kenyon MD MB ChB
Director, Centre for the Study of
Alternative Therapies, Southampton

Dr Bryan Lask MB MPhil
MRCPsych
Consultant Psychiatrist
Hospital for Sick Children
Great Ormond Street, London

Lady Limerick MA
Foundation for the
Study of Infant Deaths, London

Miss Margaret J Mayell MB ChB
FRCS
Consultant Paediatric Surgeon
Nottingham City Hospital

Dr David Mellor FRCP DCH
Consultant Paediatric Neurologist
Nottingham City
and University Hospitals

Dr Peter Milla MSc, MRCP
Snr Lecturer in Child Health
Institute of Child Health
and Hon Consultant Paediatric
Gastroenterologist
Hospital for Sick Children
Great Ormond Street, London

Dr A D Milner FRCP DCH
Professor of Paediatric Respiratory
Medicine, Nottingham University

Valerie Muter
Snr Clinical Psychologist
Hospital for Sick Children
Great Ormond Street, London

Charles O'Brian
Senior Lecturer in Social Work,
Oxford Polytechnic

Mrs Elsie Osborne BA(Hons) ABPsS
Psychologist
The Tavistock Clinic, London

Diana Parker MPhil
Solicitor in Family Law

Steve Parker BSc(Hons)
Medical Editor

Freda Patton
Community Dietician
Bloomsbury Health District, London

Dr Kathleen N. Pearl MRCP DCH
Consultant Paediatrician
Farnborough Hospital, Kent

Dr Leon Polnay MRCP DCH
Snr Lecturer in Child Health
University of Nottingham

Dr Naomi Richman FRCPsych
Reader in Child Psychiatry
Institute of Child Health
and Hon Consultant
Hospital for Sick Children
Great Ormond Street, London

Margaret Robinson
Co-ordinator, Conciliation Service of
the Institute of Family Therapy and
Lecturer in Social Work
University of Southampton

Dr Nick Rutter MRCP
Snr Lecturer in Child Health
Nottingham University

Debbie Sell
Snr Speech Therapist
Hospital for Sick Children
Great Ormond Street, London

Dr F Spicer OBE JP
Director, Youth Advisory Centre
London

Dr Derek Steinberg MB MPhil
FRCPsych
Consultant in Child and
Adolescent Psychiatry
Bethlem Royal Hospital and
The Maudsley Hospital, London

Mr David Taylor FRCP
Consultant Ophthalmologist
Hospital for Sick Children
Great Ormond Street, London

Helen Utidjian
Health Visitor, Bloomsbury Health
District

Dr Julian Verbov MD FRCP CBiol
MIBiol
Consultant Dermatologist
Royal Liverpool Children's Hospital

Professor C B S Wood
Joint Academic Department of
Child Health, St Bartholomew's
and the London Hospital
Medical Colleges
Queen Elizabeth Hospital
for Children, London

HOW TO USE THIS BOOK

Whether your child is fit and well or has a problem with his or her health, the Macmillan Guide to Child Health can offer you the information, advice and support that you need.

Part One, Care of the child, and Part Two, Care of the sick child, discuss topics of general interest to all parents. Part One outlines how a child develops. It also gives advice on how best to maintain and safeguard a child's health, both physical and psychological, and how to deal with problems such as difficulties at school or tensions within the family.

Part Two is the section to turn to if your child needs nursing at home or in hospital, whether in the short or long term. You will also find advice on when you would be wise to call the doctor.

Part Three, Problems, diseases and disorders, describes all but the rarest of childhood illnesses. If you suspect that your child may have a particular problem, the appropriate entry tells you the signs and symptoms to look for. If you know that your child has a particular problem, the relevant section describes the course of the disease, how common it is, the treatment that you and your doctor can give and the possible complications. Problems are discussed under a colour-banded heading, with the exception of some rare or simple problems which may be grouped and described under a heading in bold type within the text.

Index of symptoms
If you know that your child is ill, but are uncertain of what the problem is, the Index of symptoms at the back of the book will lead you towards a number of possibilities. However, this index is not intended as a guide to self-diagnosis: if you are worried about a symptom that your child has, consult a doctor.

Accidents
If your child has a minor accident that can be treated at home, turn to the section on first aid in **The sick child at home**. This section also advises you on when to ask for medical help. If your child suffers a serious accident, the appendix **Emergency actions** tells you how to cope. The section in Part Two on **Accident and injury** explains how accidental injuries are treated in hospital and how you can help.

Cross-references
Where a word has been italicized, this indicates that a more detailed discussion of the term or problem appears elsewhere in the book. Refer to the index, where you will find the page reference. The page reference in bold type shows the page on which the main discussion or definition appears.

At the end of some sections of text there are boxed references to other sections and this indicates that these sections should be read in conjunction for a more complete picture.

Resources
The appendices aim to tell you what resources are available and to enable you to use them effectively. They also give you detailed information on particular topics such as what drugs are prescribed for certain diseases and the way they work, and what screening measures are carried out and when, in order to help prevent illness. The information in one appendix may complement the information in another: **Who's who in the health service** is relevant to the discussion in **Child abuse**, for example.

The appendix **Support groups and publications** directs you to many other sources of information, advice and support: this is especially important if your child has a long-term or severe illness or problem. You should also refer to this section for useful addresses as necessary when reading the other appendices.

CONTENTS

Editor's introduction   8

PART ONE
CARE OF THE CHILD

Family life   10
The unborn child   22
The newborn child   27
Feeding and diet   36
Day-to-day care   43
Safety   52
Early growth and development   60
Learning and school   72
The older child and adolescent   80

PART TWO
CARE OF THE SICK CHILD

Using the family doctor   88
The sick child at home   94
Hospitals and the sick child   106
Medical procedures   112
Longstanding problems   115
Counselling   119
Alternative therapies   122

PART THREE
PROBLEMS, DISEASES AND DISORDERS

Genetics   126
Problems of the newborn child   134
Accident and injury   145
Infection   151
Allergy   165
Cancer   169
Behaviour and development   179
The eyes   195
The teeth   203
The ears   207
The mouth, nose and throat   215
The lungs   221
The heart and circulation   227
The blood   234
The digestive system   241
The kidneys, bladder and genitals   255
Glandular disorders   266
The bones and joints   274
The skin and hair   282
The brain, nerves and muscles   292
Life and death   306

PART FOUR
APPENDICES: RESOURCES

Who's who in the health service   312
The law and your child   316
Adoption and fostering   318
Child abuse   319
Support groups and publications   320
Drugs and treatments   326
Screening programme   329

Emergency actions   330

Index of symptoms   342
Index   344
Acknowledgements   352

EDITOR'S INTRODUCTION

This book is written primarily for parents, but is intended for anyone who has the responsibilities and therefore the joys of looking after children. Children are dependent on their parents or care-givers: at birth babies are helpless and literally in their parents' hands; as they grow they become increasingly independent, but protection and encouragement are still essential for them if they are to fulfil their potential. Especially during the turbulence of adolescence, young people need someone to look to for standards and security.

As a parent and care-giver you are ideally placed to get to know the individual character traits, behaviour patterns and idiosyncrasies which go towards making your children unique and special. You are the best judge of the subtle changes in behaviour and mood which tell you that something is amiss – whether of a physical, psychological or emotional nature. Thus there is every reason for you to feel confident that *you* are the expert on the subject of your children. You are the one who knows what is in the best short- and long-term interests of your children and family. Only you can decide if you can cope with your children's health problems, whether minor childhood illnesses, such as measles and mumps, or permanent disabilities, such as deafness or Down's syndrome, or whether you need to seek advice or help from professionals. Even when your children are being treated by health professionals you remain of central importance in interpreting for them; providing them with security in strange and perhaps frightening situations; and representing to the doctor what they are feeling or how they are responding to treatment.

And just as you will assess when to seek other people's help in the case of illness, so you will assess what is best in the context of the day-to-day care of your children. You may decide to share some of the tasks with other care-takers, but the ultimate responsibility for making decisions about your children's welfare remains yours.

This guide to child health presents information that will help you make the many decisions involved in parenthood and childcare. If it makes you feel happier and more confident in this activity it will have succeeded.

David Hull
September 1985

PART ONE

CARE OF THE CHILD

FAMILY LIFE

Many parents' first instinct when they have children is to want to make their children's lives as easy as they can. They do not want their children to have to face the stresses they had when they were growing up. The impulse to protect children is strong – and it is very hard to believe that what affected you as a child does not necessarily affect your own children in the same way. But children develop not only through encouragement and example, but also through facing difficulties, overcoming them and learning from their mistakes. Doing too much to protect children can create problems: they need to face challenges to gain a sense of independence and strength. You probably want a great deal for your children and hope they will feel fulfilled and achieve a great deal. You may want them to achieve things you could not or did not achieve. But if they are to feel secure, your love must not be conditional on their achievements and your expectations must be realistic. Every child has his or her own potential and talents, and comparisons with friends and the peer group can lead to a tense relationship between parents and children.

There is no doubt that your love and attention are the most important influences on your child's behaviour, at whatever age. However, it can be difficult for parents to decide how to be both loving and firm. Some parents are afraid of spoiling their children by giving them too much attention. Others fear that asserting their own needs might inhibit their children's emotional development or affect their children's love for them. Try to be firm and consistent in an atmosphere of affection.

When you want to stop your child doing something, make it clear that it is your child's particular behaviour that you disapprove of and not your child himself. Try to stay on your child's side and remember that he wants a loving relationship as much as you do.

At times all parents feel angry and hostile towards their children. These emotions are normal and there is no need to feel guilty about them, but it is best not to act on them. There may be times when your natural reaction to your child's difficult behaviour is to shout at or hit him. This relieves your feelings but may teach your child to behave in this way himself.

Despite their good intentions, most parents do sometimes shout at or smack their children and this may occasionally be a better solution than a long sulk or endless criticism of a child. Whatever your way of coping when tensions rise, remember to make it clear that you still love your child after the storm has passed. It may also help if you decide in advance how you are going to deal with a particular piece of difficult behaviour.

▶**See also** Early growth and development; Counselling; Behaviour and development

THE FAMILY LIFE CYCLE

The traditional family goes through stages in its life, from its creation as a couple, who then become 'expecting parents', parents with a baby, with a toddler, a school-age child, an adolescent, then a young adult and the cycle begins again. Each stage has its special pleasures, its losses and its gains, and its special difficulties. Surmounting them enables the family to move to the next stage.

Babies need plenty of physical contact and loving attention from the people around them. This closeness helps children to feel confident in their own worth and forms the secure base on which they can build their independence. Separation – being alone and finding independence – is a particular struggle during early childhood. It is an enormous temptation to parents to prolong the period of babyish dependence. Yet, without some early separations, going to school can be more

Time spent with other children of the same age and away from the family helps a child develop independence and a sense of self outside the role that he plays within the family.

difficult. Try to make sure your child has opportunities to be independent of you, with babysitters, relatives or friends, to give him confidence in the world beyond his immediate family.

The process of growing up involves loss as well as achievement. Not surprisingly, children sometimes express their confusion by reverting to old habits, such as *bedwetting* or *sleeping problems*. At the same time parents have to suffer the pangs of change and have to move onwards themselves to gain from newly-found freedoms, which can feel empty at first.

The struggle towards independence and self-sufficiency continues as a child grows. From the first days at school a child is subject to new pressures: for example, the need to be respect-worthy to peers and teachers is strongly felt, and may conflict in practice with being love-worthy to parents. Children have to venture out on their own before finding a sense of self and you cannot do this for them, you can only help the process along.

Adolescence can be a particularly difficult time for both parents and children, as it is a period of rapid change that demands flexibility from the whole family. Parents have to acknowledge that they will lose the togetherness and oneness of the early years, although equal satisfaction can be found in the companionship of a teenage or adult son or daughter.

DECISION-MAKING

A parent's role includes making decisions on a child's behalf. It can often be difficult to balance different needs. For example, protecting a child from accidents is a priority for any parent, yet the protection should not be so thorough that the child has no freedom to fall and learn by painful experience. Children need to learn to cycle, roller skate and swing on climbing frames to learn control of their bodies and mastery of movement. Risks can be minimized without removing them entirely by, for example, making rules about where it is safe to cycle and about using stabilizers and helmets. Your responsibility in making decisions is to balance the risks in a thoughtful way, and not to feel guilty when you take a risk. Give your children the message that challenges can be met, and that you can pick yourself up and try again.

In the context of your children's health you must also take risks. There are risks in deciding against treatment, such as the use of antibiotics, or procedures such as *immunizations* or operations – and there are also risks in accepting them. It is important to make decisions on the basis of full information and to listen to the advice of doctors and experts. However, in the end, you have to take responsibility for making the best decision you can and only you can decide on the interests of your children as you see them.

COPING WITH FAMILY PROBLEMS

All families face problems and have to make choices. They have to decide how children are to be cared for, how difficulties in family relationships can be resolved and how each member of the family can best be helped to grow and develop. Whatever choices you make, involve your child without asking him to take responsibility beyond his years.

For example, if you are about to move house or your child is going to change schools, talk about the change, go to look at the new house or school, discuss what the gains and the losses will be. Acknowledge that changes are sad for you, too, and that you will miss neighbours and familiar places. After all, the physical world you live in becomes part of yourself, and losing a familiar room or house sometimes feels like losing a layer of skin. Children feel this even more acutely as they have so little experience of change.

There are some guidelines for coping with problems and decisions:

o Do not try to hide family problems. A child apparently absorbed in play may be listening intently to adult conversation. Always assume that your child has an inkling of everything going on in the family, but that he will not understand it unless you talk about it
o When there is a family problem, find out what your child thinks is going on before you tell him. You may find that he has mistaken your passionate debate for anger. Explain simply and factually what is happening
o Avoid asking a young child's opinions in a way that will make him feel responsible for decisions. On major issues, such as a choice of schools or places to live, make it clear that you would like to know how your child feels, but that you will make the final decision

EVERYDAY STRESSES AND STRAINS

One of the hardest things to grasp about children is that often what it seems they should enjoy and get pleasure from can cause upset and distress. Young children at times find excitement hard to cope with and laughter and tears are very close. The excitement of the party can become too much and tears can infect all the guests. This is why the adults have to control the emotional temperature with calming games, such as 'being quiet as mice' and 'statues', mixed with noisier ones.

Anything new – birthday gifts, clothes, rooms painted, a new house, a new brother or sister, winning – may create a surprisingly heavy, sad and quite depressed reaction as well as giving pleasure. This is because new things are markers of change, such as getting a year older or being an only child. You cannot protect your child from loss and change, but be aware that novelty is not always easy.

SUBSTITUTE CARE

One of the earliest decisions you may have to make affecting your child is whether to look after him yourself as a full-time commitment or whether to arrange some alternative form of care, by a relative, for instance, or a nanny, a childminder or a nursery. Many parents are worried that their infants and toddlers will be deprived if they are not with them for a great deal of the time. Of course it is sad not to share as much of a young child's life as possible, but recent research has not shown that it is in any way damaging if a child does not have a parent's company for the majority of the time, even while the child is very young.

While young children do need stability in their relationships and can be confused by changes of care-takers, they are capable of forming close relationships with several people, not just one. It is the quality of care they receive that determines the strength of their attachment to a particular person rather than the length of time spent with them. The few hours in the evening that a working parent spends with a child can form the basis of a strong and loving bond.

Substitute care-takers can be stimulating, warm, responsive and consistent, and can form excellent relationships with infants and young children. So long as the care-taker is not overstretched by caring for too many children, he or she can provide excellent care. Indeed, such substitute care can help children to manage ordinary stresses such as going to school for the first time.

If you decide to use substitute care for a young child, so that, for example, you can go out to work, the ideal is a care-taker who is not only a responsible person but is also responsive to your child. You should give your child plenty of preparation by familiarizing him with the person who will be looking after him and the place where he will be, and by sorting out a routine of taking and fetching that can be as predictable as possible. Even with a well-prepared child, there may be a period of clinging, *sleeping problems*, occasional *bedwetting*, anger about the arrangements and complaints about other children. Talk through the situation with your child and be patient and sympathetic about his difficulties. If the care-taking arrangement is satisfactory, the problems should gradually resolve.

Playgroups or nurseries can provide a break for a parent at home or regular day-long care to support a working parent. The company of other children may be particularly important to an only child.

Each new child changes the relationships within a family. A second child who becomes the middle sibling of three may find it especially hard to create a new role.

SIBLING RIVALRY

One of the key events in a child's life is the birth of a new brother or sister. The pregnancy itself is an ideal time for children to understand where babies come from and how they are born, and for them to be given the first of many explanations about how they are made. Children have to be very young indeed *not* to understand this.

You can help an older child prepare for the birth by talking through what is going to happen, by going over the facts, using calendars to explain dates, and by listening to your child's fears and expectations. Allow him plenty of time to get used to the coming change and upheaval.

Your child is likely to have mixed reactions to a new brother or sister: excitement at having a playmate, apprehension about being displaced, and often disappointment when the baby does not want to play immediately. However, the fierce battles and rivalry that many parents fear are not inevitable. The temperaments of the particular children and the way that the parents treat their children are the key factors that determine how much rivalry there is between siblings.

Getting the balance right between adapting to a new baby's needs and helping an older child cope with the change is not easy. Try to make sure that older children have some privileges, perhaps staying up later or having special times for your undivided attention, and that younger children are protected from angry, bossy treatment by older, stronger and cleverer siblings.

Squabbling mixed with happy play is a very common pattern between brothers and sisters. It is unreasonable to expect a young child to be fair according to adult standards all the time. It is probably better to reward all your children for not squabbling or to be angry with them all when they do argue than to try to sort out who is right and who is wrong. Although there will inevitably be times when you are fraught and over-react, be careful that one child is not always given support at the expense of another.

▶ **See also** Behaviour and development

THE SINGLE-PARENT FAMILY

Increasingly nowadays the story of two parents bringing up their children to adulthood does not always start or end in a traditional way. More and more children will be brought up by one of their parents alone for at least part of their lives, because their parent has chosen to be alone, because of marital breakdown and divorce or because of the death of a parent. It is estimated that today 1 family in 8 is headed by a single parent, usually a woman.

With help and support a single parent can manage the difficult task of providing for all a child's needs. There are, indeed, tasks which are simpler for a single parent: there is no one to undermine or disqualify attempts to lay down rules, for example. Yet, there are other tasks two adults can perform more easily, such as backing each other up through the crises of illness, work or school difficulties.

Two parents can also help each other to keep a perspective on being with a child, and can help each other to avoid depending on the child to fulfil their needs. This can be seen at each phase of development. During infancy a single mother may have more time to be preoccupied with the baby, yet there may be no one there to pull her away when the infant needs to explore the rest of the world. During the toddler period, growing independence may be a joy and a relief for the single parent, yet the gap it creates can feel considerable and the toddler, sensing his parent's need, can rush to fill it with demands and tantrums. Similar problems are seen in school-age children: the single parent is often relieved at the lessening of the burden while feeling a further awareness of his or her own needs, which the child may meet by clinging and wanting to stay at home. Creating a network of friends and supporters who can help to contradict this sense of isolation is a priority for every single parent.

Adolescence is particularly difficult for a single parent: there are great pleasures in having a more adult companion and friend, yet facing the conflicts while the adolescent struggles to find an independence he may not be ready for can be quite overwhelming and exhausting. Other adults may be essential to help manage an adolescent's rebellion, and testing-out of limits can be demanding and wearing. It can be particularly hard for a mother to manage a boy's challenge of authority or for a father to manage a daughter's rule-testing. Yet, despite the ease of being with someone of their own sex, boys with their fathers miss their mothers and girls miss their fathers.

NEW RELATIONSHIPS

In many single-parent families, particularly those which have established their own ways and habits, the introduction of a possible step-parent is very difficult for the children. While it is important for you to seek your own happiness with new friends and lovers, it is helpful to be as clear and honest as possible with your children about the status of newcomers and to avoid introducing them to too many transient father- or mother-figures. Sexual intimacy with new partners needs to be handled sensitively whether your children are demanding toddlers or inquisitive teenagers.

A new marriage creates a new family group, yet some members of the new family also continue to be part of their original nuclear family group. For some children whose parents are divorced or who have been bereaved of a parent, it is only when a parent remarries that they are able to accept the finality of the situation and can begin to grieve. Some adults expect that the children involved will quickly accept the situation; but in fact it takes time for bonds of affection to develop in the remarried family. These new attachments can be helped or hindered by the attitudes of all the adults involved, and especially by the grandparents and the children's non-custodial parent, if there has been a divorce.

Patterns of behaviour in individual families are never quite the same, but some of the common difficulties that arise as a result of remarriage are those related to eating habits and discipline. However, despite problems, remarriage can often bring emotional enrichment, fresh hope, renewed potential and a real sense of belonging.

DIVORCE

In most Western countries the number of divorces has doubled in recent years. Lifespans are longer; expectations of marriage and family life are higher; and the role of women has changed. It is now more socially acceptable for adults to think of their own needs as well as those of their children. More people feel that the cost of maintaining a togetherness 'for the children's sake' could make a far more damaging, unhappy atmosphere than parting, managing alone or finding a new partner who will meet their needs.

It is estimated that about 1 child in 5 will experience the divorce of his parents. A proportion of these children will experience the remarriage of one or both parents (perhaps more than once) while they are still at school.

In order to minimize the pain and distress children suffer as a result of their parents' separation, it is important that parents try to agree about custody and access arrangements. Part of your decision-making may involve consulting your children (unless they are very young indeed), but remember that they cannot be expected to carry the responsibility for choosing which parent to live with.

During the period of marital breakdown and divorce, the whole family usually goes through a process of intense grief that is similar to mourning. Indeed, the divorce process *is* a bereavement, for future relationships and family interactions are likely to be different. Although children often yearn for their parents' reconciliation for years after a divorce, it does help them cope if the family can talk together about future plans.

About half the children of divorcing parents show clear problems that take a year or so to settle down. In general, the children in single-parent families who tend to suffer least are those who have plenty of contact with their non-custodial parent and whose parents have a co-operative relationship. Children who have

If you are the non-custodial parent, meal-times may be a good opportunity to establish closeness with your children, reminding them that you are still part of the family.

regular contact with their non-custodial parent but whose divorced parents do not have a good relationship usually have some difficulties. The children who are most at risk are those who never see their non-custodial parent.

A child's ability to come to terms with what has happened depends on each parent's attitude towards being a single parent, but particularly the custodial parent's attitude. A child's happiness after divorce depends partly on the way in which both parents, despite their own pain and anger with each other, are able to end their emotional partnership as husband and wife and to develop a new one, based on shared and co-operative parenting. Some divorced parents are able to co-parent in ways that they found impossible to achieve while married to each other. Others seem unable to separate their anger and sorrow over the failure of their marriage from their care and concern as parents. If children see their parents' relationship as a pitched battle, they may feel conflicting loyalties and join with one parent in anger against the other.

You may find it hard to care for your children as well as you would like after a separation or divorce. You may want to cling to your children or you may feel distant from them. However, it is important not to draw them into your anger and, although you may be lonely, it is also important to avoid drawing your eldest child into a surrogate adult role. Remember that your children have to cope with their own feelings which will be related to their age and stage of development. Keeping their environment as stable as possible after a divorce usually helps: moving house, changing schools or losing touch with familiar friends all add to the upset and disruption. It may be possible to defer such changes even if they cannot be avoided altogether.

The first birthdays and other festivals after a separation are always painful occasions. It helps if you are able to agree some suitable arrangements well beforehand so that last-minute arguments and disappointments are avoided. Some parents can continue to share in birthday parties and other feast-days for their children. Another solution might be to hold two celebrations, one with each parent.

CHILDREN'S REACTIONS TO DIVORCE

UNDER 2
Babies primarily react to the feelings of the care-taking parent, usually the mother. Toddlers may generally regress to an earlier stage and persistently ask about the absent parent.

2 TO 5
These children are particularly frightened and confused. They may blame themselves, or have macabre fantasies about the absent parent. They fear being sent away or replaced.

6 TO 8
Children of this age experience pervasive grief. They, too, are frightened of being sent away or of being deprived of essentials such as food and toys. Boys in particular both yearn for and inhibit their aggression towards their absent parent. Children may also be angry with their care-taking parent, but afraid of expressing it.

9 TO 12
These children sometimes appear calm and understanding while in fact being unable to grasp or accept what is happening. Alternatively, they may show clear and well-organized anger which is directed against one or both parents. They may experience a shaken sense of identity. Some children develop psychosomatic symptoms or they may counteract their feelings of powerlessness by energetic attempts at mastery in play and other activities. Relationships with their parents can undergo dramatic changes as they align with one parent against the other. Boys who enjoy good relationships with their fathers suffer particularly if their fathers leave home.

13 TO 18
Young people of this age are often most openly upset and express strong feelings of anger, embarrassment, shame and sadness. The separation forces them to see their parents as individuals with their own sexuality and may evoke vivid sexual fantasies. Many feel the need to disengage themselves from their situation by leaving home and family.

DEATH IN THE FAMILY

Children's concepts of death develop slowly, but by the age of 8 years most children of normal intelligence and experience will understand that death is universal and irrevocable; that they and their family will one day die; and that death is caused by disease, accident, murder, war or old age.

Children as young as 3 or 4 years old may display an amazing understanding of death if they have personal experience of it: someone close to them may have died or they may themselves be suffering from a potentially fatal illness such as *leukemia* and be in contact with others whose disease is more advanced than theirs. However, in general, the concepts of pre-school children are not so well developed. Young children find abstract ideas hard to understand and therefore usually find religious explanations rather confusing. They see themselves at the centre of the world, and have difficulty in understanding cause and effect, with the result that they tend to seek an explanation for the death of a parent or sibling in terms of something they did or omitted to do.

Some children appear unable to express grief. They may do so in time, but if they do not, and if they develop physical symptoms or behavioural problems that persist, professional help should be sought through your family doctor. Most children cope with their loss, helped by family, friends and others, but it may take 2 years or more before they are over the worst. Keeping their lives and routines as stable as possible is important and other changes, such as moving house, are best avoided within the first year. Looking after yourself and allowing others to look after you also helps your children.

Children need permission to stop grieving when they have fully worked through the mourning process. It is difficult for young children in particular to sustain a sad mood over a long period of time, and they should be encouraged to play and be active with their friends, and not to feel bad about being happy. However, it is important to keep open the possibility of talking about the person who has died, and not to regard the subject as closed.

DEATH OF A PARENT

All children who have recently lost a parent will be changed by the experience, and in the long term surviving the experience can be strengthening. Children around 2½ years old and those around puberty often find it hardest to cope.

Children are likely to have difficulties at school for a while and may develop a series of minor illnesses. Young children may be afraid to sleep, likening it to death – an idea often suggested by adult euphemisms for death. They may also become afraid of any illness: they need to be helped to understand that most illnesses are self-limiting and can be healed by the body's defences, aided in some cases by doctors and nurses.

Adolescents may either become suddenly adult in their behaviour or regress to childishness for a while. Older children commonly suffer from the feeling that they have to do everything perfectly and make no mistakes, or they may punish themselves in subtle or not-so-subtle ways.

The structure of the family inevitably changes after the death of a parent. The role of the parent who has died has to be filled, and an older child often steps into this role. This can cause problems if he is burdened with too many responsibilities.

Following the death of a parent most children feel themselves to be very different from their friends, and birthdays and festivals can be particularly sad. Even when the children have grown up they may sorely miss the dead parent on occasions such as their own weddings or the births of their own children.

DEATH OF A SIBLING

Children's feelings towards a sick brother or sister can be very mixed: after all, they are in competition with the sick child for your attention, and they rarely win. As a result children often see the death of a sibling as the granting of a secret wish and this provokes feelings of guilt, triumph and fears of retaliation.

Sibling rivalry continues after the death, in a form that may be particularly hard for the remaining brothers and sisters. The child who has died can never do anything wrong again and parents may idealize the memory of the lost child to a degree that makes it impossible for siblings to compete. They may try to compensate by becoming extremely good or, alternatively, they may become very difficult in order to test out your love.

A baby born after an older sibling has died may feel as he grows that he is a 'replacement', and may become confused as to whether he is really himself or the reincarnation of the dead brother or sister. It is important to make it clear that he is a person in his own right.

If you lose one child, your other children have to cope with your grief, as well as their own losses. Stillbirths and miscarriages can be a particular problem if you are too distressed to explain to your children what has happened. For example, if a child has a fantasy about the baby going down the drain, this may make him avoid using the toilet.

THE SEQUENCE OF GRIEVING

A child who loses a parent or a sibling needs to go through a long period of mourning. Everyone who grieves passes through the same stages of coping with the loss. In the very young, separation alone can trigger grieving and grieving often begins before death if the parent or sibling has been ill.

Grieving involves the following reactions, although these may not always follow a strict sequence:

o The initial reaction is shock and denial: 'it isn't true – you're lying'
o Over the following hours or days, a young child will protest and search: agitated, noisy crying is accompanied by restlessness and searching for the dead parent. Older children express anger and grief
o Next comes sadness, withdrawal, and sometimes depression. Quieter, mournful crying, inactivity, loss of appetite and sleeplessness are common
o Over a period of months, the child is gradually able to emerge from grief to more or less normal functioning, although there will be much movement back and forth between grieving and relative happiness

HELPING YOUR CHILD TO MOURN

Research unequivocally indicates that children who can be helped to cry and talk about their dead parent or sibling recover more quickly and are less likely to have problems later on.

However children often need help with this. In particular, they may have few words, little experience, and may be overwhelmed or frightened by the reactions of others – especially the remaining family. Older children and adolescents may identify so strongly with the 'chief mourner' – the parents or remaining parent – that they are unable to fully experience their own grief.

FAMILY LIFE 21

It may be hard for you to help your child express grief on your own and this is where friends, relatives, priests and doctors can help. Call upon them unstintingly – they all want to help. Sit and look at photos of happier times. Feel free to cry with your children: reassure them that it is the right thing to do. Boys especially may need to be told specifically that, far from being unmanly, crying is the normal way of showing grief. The death needs to be gone over repeatedly, not just once. Children need to be able to talk through their misconceptions about death and you should be aware of the possible confusions.

A photograph album helps you to focus on your loss and to talk over what each of you misses about the person who has died.

Generally it is helpful for all but the very youngest children to go to the funeral of a lost parent or sibling. They should be in the care of a familiar adult who is not directly affected and who will answer their questions.

▶ **See also** Behaviour and development; Life and death; Appendix: Support groups and publications

THE UNBORN CHILD

Pregnancy is timed from the first day of the mother's last menstrual period. The usual duration of pregnancy is 40 weeks, though it may be a couple of weeks more or less. For convenience, pregnancy is often considered as 3 trimesters, or 3-month periods.

By the fifth week, just when you might begin to realize you are pregnant, the fertilized egg has settled in the womb lining and the embryo has already begun to develop the various tissues and organs of the body, such as the heart, brain and muscles. By the end of the second month the embryo is less that 2 cm (¾ in) long, but is recognizably human. Eyes, mouth, ears, hands and feet can all be identified. By the end of the third month the developing baby, now called the fetus, is fully formed and all the major organs, including the sex organs, are present. The heart is pumping blood around the body. The nerves send messages and the muscles contract, but the movements are weak and pass unnoticed.

In the second trimester the baby grows fast. Nails, eyebrows and eyelashes appear, though the eyes remain sealed until about 26 weeks. The mother usually first feels the baby's movements between 18 and 22 weeks. The baby's body becomes covered with fine hair, called lanugo, which is shed just before or soon after the birth; why this happens is not known.

During the last 3 months of pregnancy the baby grows and builds up his energy reserves. He moves more vigorously, sometimes in response to touch or noise. Vernix, a white, water-resistant substance, traces of which can still be seen at birth, appears on the skin. Finally the baby, now fitting fairly tightly in the womb, moves into position for delivery, usually head down.

Nowadays, pregnancy and birth are very safe for both mother and baby. The perinatal mortality rate (deaths at or within the first week of birth) is continually falling, and nearly 99 out of 100 babies are born alive.

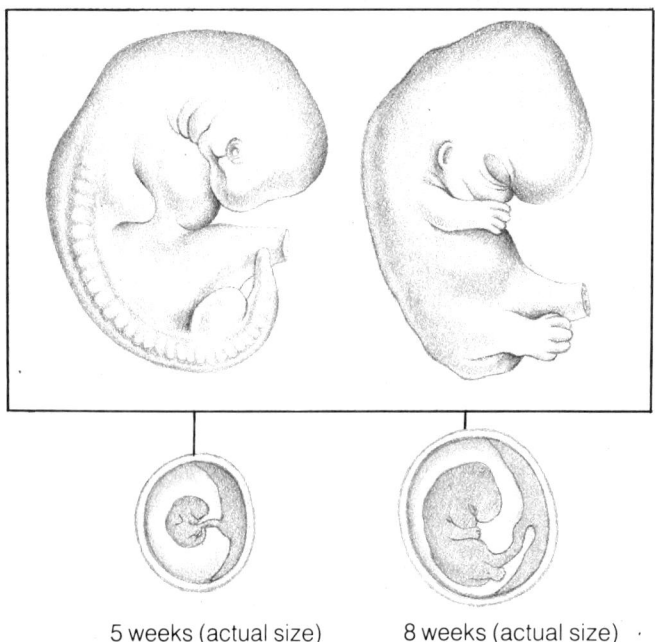

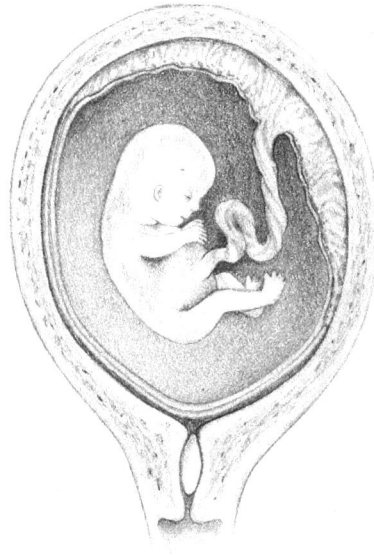

5 weeks (actual size)   8 weeks (actual size)   12 weeks

The placenta

The fetus lies in a sac of watery liquid, the amniotic fluid, which cushions it within the womb. Its life-support system is the placenta, a mass of tissue formed by the fetus in the wall of the womb, containing fetal blood vessels, which lie bathed in the mother's circulation.

The placenta acts as a selective barrier, allowing some substances to pass through while protecting the fetus from other harmful ones. This arrangement protects the fetus from many of the ills that may affect the mother. Oxygen and nutrients from the mother's blood diffuse into the fetal blood vessels, and carbon dioxide and other waste products from the fetus are returned to the mother. Blood passes from the fetus to the placenta and back again through the blood vessels in the umbilical cord.

▶ See also Problems of the newborn child

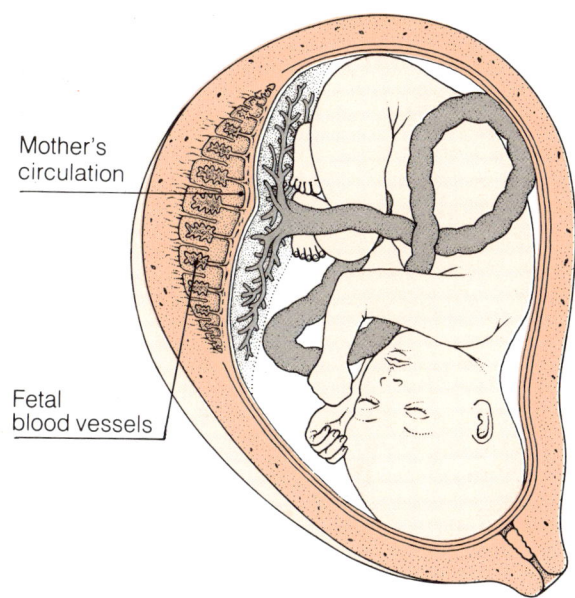

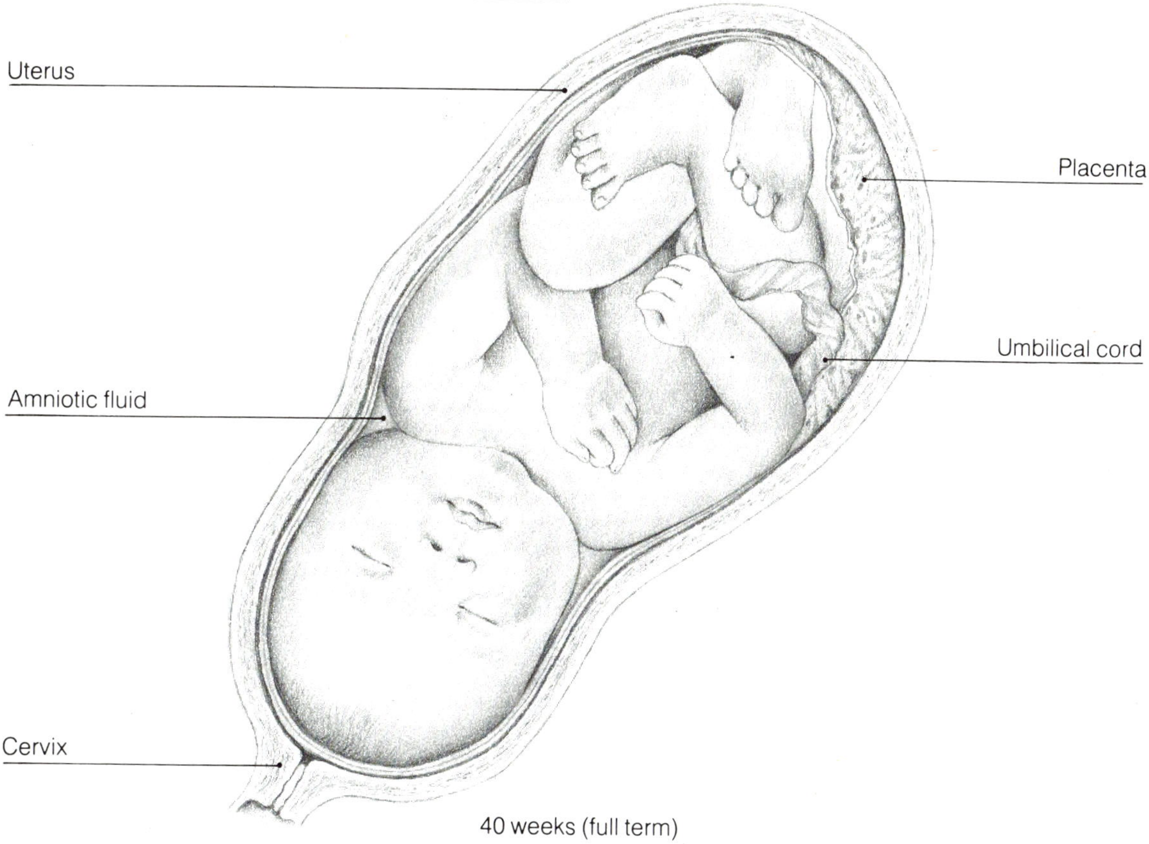

40 weeks (full term)

TWINS

o Most twins are fraternal. They develop from two fertilized eggs and each fetus has a placenta. Identical twins result when a single egg splits after fertilization. In this case there is usually a shared placenta
o The mother will gain weight rapidly early in pregnancy and will be large for her dates
o Her final weight gain will be more than if she had a singleton as not only are there two babies but each has his own amniotic fluid and in some cases his own placenta
o Throughout pregnancy her weight and blood pressure will need careful checking
o Maternal toxemia is an increased risk
o Rest is especially important
o Full term is considered to be 38 rather than 40 weeks but hospital treatment or delivery should be expected from 28 weeks
o Labour is not usually longer than it is with a single baby
o There may be complications depending on the babies' positions: if both are breech they may be delivered by Caesarean section

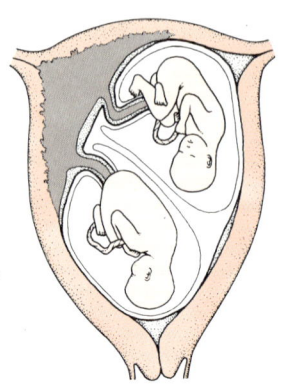
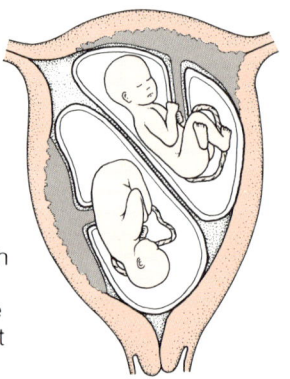

The most common position for twins in the uterus is either both with their heads down, or one head down and the other bottom down (that is, breech).

ADJUSTING YOUR LIFESTYLE

It is in the interests of your baby to adjust your lifestyle before beginning a pregnancy. During the first 12 weeks, when the major organs are formed, the embryo is at its most vulnerable, and at this stage you may not even realize that you are pregnant.

DIET

If you eat a varied and well-balanced diet there is no need to worry about your baby's growth and nutrition. Even if you lose your appetite during the pregnancy or if vomiting is a problem, this does not matter, provided you were generally well nourished when the pregnancy began. The baby's needs can be met from your energy reserves.

A healthy diet contains plenty of fresh fruit, vegetables and cereals, to boost your intake of fibre and vitamin C. Adequate protein and iron are also important. Iron tablets used to be prescribed routinely in pregnancy, and still are by some doctors, but in fact they are unnecessary for the majority of women.

Vitamin supplements should not be necessary either, with the possible exception of folic acid, a vitamin found in liver and fresh vegetables. There is some evidence that folic acid reduces the risk of the fetus developing *spina bifida*, and because it is not stored efficiently by the body it is often prescribed for pregnant women.

ALCOHOL

Alcohol is quickly absorbed into the mother's bloodstream and passes through the placenta to the fetus. There is little doubt that it can have an adverse effect upon the developing fetus. Certainly, women who drink regularly and heavily during pregnancy – 'heavily' implies 1.7 litres (3 pt) of beer or its equivalent per day – run an increased risk of having babies with facial deformities and reduced intellectual capacity. However, not all babies are equally affected. It is heavy drinking during the early weeks of pregnancy that causes most damage.

Whether a little alcohol does any harm has not been established. However, as there is some uncertainty it is best to avoid alcohol altogether, if you can.

SMOKING

There is no doubt that smoking is harmful to smokers and to those around them. It is equally harmful to the fetus. The nicotine and other chemicals inhaled in cigarette smoke restrict the growth of the fetus. Babies of smokers weigh, on average, 200 g (7 oz) less than those of non-smokers. They are more likely to be born prematurely and are more at risk of complications when they are born.

Again, not all babies of smoking mothers are affected, so if you are a smoker you have to make a choice: the immediate benefits to you of smoking against the possible adverse effects on your child. If it can be done, both parents should stop smoking before conception.

DRUGS

Most drugs cross the placenta and, while many are harmless, some can cause congenital abnormalities. If you are pregnant, or trying to become pregnant, you should avoid taking any drugs, prescribed or non-prescribed, except on your doctor's advice. This is especially important during the first 12 weeks.

GERMAN MEASLES (Rubella)

Most adults who catch *German measles* hardly notice that they are ill. By contrast, if the highly infectious virus reaches the developing tissues of the baby during the first 12 weeks of pregnancy it can cause permanent heart defects, mental retardation, deafness or blindness, and even miscarriage. Because of this, rubella vaccination is recommended for every schoolgirl, and abortion is offered to any pregnant woman who does contract the disease during early pregnancy.

Rubella is difficult to diagnose with certainty, as it can easily be confused with other infections. Even if you have been vaccinated, there is a small chance that the vaccine may not have taken. Unless you are sure you are immune, ask for a blood test to see whether or not you should be vaccinated *before* becoming pregnant: vaccination cannot safely be given to anyone who is already pregnant. If you are not immune and have been in contact with the infection, your doctor will arrange blood tests which will show whether or not you have contracted the disease.

ANTENATAL CARE

The physical examinations, blood and urine tests and special investigations such as *ultrasound* that are part of the antenatal care offered to all pregnant women, are intended not only to safeguard the mother's health but also to determine whether she has any problem that might affect the baby.

MATERNAL TOXEMIA (Pre-eclampsia)

Toxemia is a peculiar, ill-understood reaction of the body to pregnancy. If it is allowed to develop untreated it interferes with the supply of oxygen and nutrients to the baby. In extreme cases, it can permanently damage many vital tissues, particularly the brain, and can threaten the baby's life.

The early signs of toxemia – protein in the urine, oedema (swelling of the ankles, hands or face), and raised blood pressure – are nearly always detected in the antenatal clinic, and the mother is carefully monitored to make sure the condition develops no further. Babies whose mothers have toxemia are most at risk during birth, so if all is not well, a forceps delivery or a Caesarean section may be necessary.

POOR INTRAUTERINE GROWTH

Occasionally a baby may not receive quite enough nourishment from the placenta during the final weeks in the womb. At birth, such infants are skinny and wrinkled, but they usually feed well and quickly gain weight.

Sometimes, however, the problem begins much earlier in pregnancy. The baby may not be getting enough food to support his rapid growth, either because the maternal blood supply to the placenta is inadequate or because the placenta itself is disturbed. If the baby is not growing as expected, your doctor may carry out special blood tests to see whether the placenta is functioning efficiently. In severe cases the doctor may suggest an early delivery.

Babies who have been undernourished in the womb for a prolonged period are properly formed but much smaller than they should be. Such 'small-for-dates' babies may need *special care* in the first weeks of life. Most of these babies will eventually catch up and progress normally, but if there are complications then the future can only be gauged after assessing the baby's progress.

MATERNAL DIABETES

Some women have *diabetes* before they become pregnant, others develop the disease during pregnancy. In this case the disease is known as gestational diabetes, and it is usually diagnosed through antenatal urine tests.

Both forms of diabetes can affect the baby. Unless the mother's diabetes is properly controlled, too much glucose will cross the placenta and the baby will grow large and fat, which can cause difficulties around the time of birth. After birth, as a rebound reaction to the period of excess glucose supply, the baby will tend to have too little glucose in his blood and will therefore have to be watched carefully for a day or two. The abnormal size and fatness do not persist and the baby soon reverts to a normal growth pattern.

Because the risks to the baby are greatest in late pregnancy, it used to be common practice to induce the babies of diabetic mothers early. However, careful control of the mother's diabetes greatly reduces the risks to the baby and nowadays most diabetic women carry their babies to term and deliver them normally.

GENITAL HERPES

If you or your partner have, or have had, genital herpes, do tell your doctor. If the virus is present and still active it can infect the baby on the way through the birth canal during labour and can cause serious damage or even death. A Caesarean section may be recommended to avoid this.

COMPLICATIONS OF LABOUR

It is not easy to predict the course of labour, especially a first labour, and it is because of this that most doctors believe it is safest for babies to be born in hospital. Sometimes labour is difficult or prolonged, perhaps because the baby is lying in an awkward position, or has too large a head to pass easily through the mother's pelvis, or because the uterus does not contract forcefully enough. In hospital, careful monitoring will ensure that the baby is getting enough oxygen. If the baby shows any signs of distress, delivery may have to be by forceps or Caesarean section.

Drugs designed to relieve labour pains (gas-and-air and epidural anaesthesia) will not harm the baby. General pain-killing drugs such as pethidine are only used in the first stage of labour; if they are given late in labour they may affect the baby's breathing.

CONGENITAL ABNORMALITIES

Many parents fear that their baby may be born with an abnormality, but in fact this is the case for only about 3 per cent of babies.

The causes of many abnormalities are not understood. There are antenatal tests that aim to identify some abnormalities at an early stage of pregnancy, and there may be effective treatment after birth. In some cases an abortion may be advised. A few babies are born with very severe abnormalities and the best that can be offered to them is a loving environment during their brief lives.

Parents often feel guilty if their child is not perfectly formed. Such guilt is normal but there is rarely any reason for it. Remember, whatever the problem there is always someone who can help.

▶See also Genetics; Life and death; Appendix: Support groups and publications

THE NEWBORN CHILD

The moment of birth results in dramatic changes in the baby's body functions. It is also the beginning of significant emotional adjustments for the mother and father.

As the umbilical cord is clamped and cut, the baby takes on many of the functions which were previously performed by the mother through the placenta. Before birth all the baby's oxygen came from the mother by way of the placenta and umbilical cord, but now the baby's lungs must expand and take in air.

Together with clamping the cord this results in major changes in the pathway of the baby's circulating blood. Previously nutrients arrived across the placenta and waste products were disposed of by the same route – now the baby must start to suck and digest milk, and the bowel and kidneys begin to work. In the womb the temperature was kept constant – now the baby must regulate heat gain and loss. In these and other ways the newborn adapts to the new surroundings.

IMMEDIATE CARE OF THE BABY AT BIRTH

Immediately after birth your baby's nose and mouth will be cleared of mucus, and he will be handed up into your arms.

The cord is clamped and then cut. Babies can quickly become cold, so the wet delivery sheet around the baby is removed and replaced by a warm dry towel.

The baby's condition at birth is assessed by the midwife or doctor using a scoring system devised by an American anaesthetist, Virginia Apgar. The Apgar score is a rating of 0, 1 or 2 for each of five observations: heart rate, breathing, colour, muscle tone and movement, and response to stimulation. The baby's score is usually assessed shortly after birth, but it can be repeated at intervals afterwards if needed. Babies without difficulties usually have a score between 7 and 10.

After the delivery, make sure that you and your partner have some quiet time to enjoy your new baby together. Be prepared for a range of emotions from exhaustion to elation. You may be able to put your baby to the breast before the umbilical cord is clamped or soon afterwards.

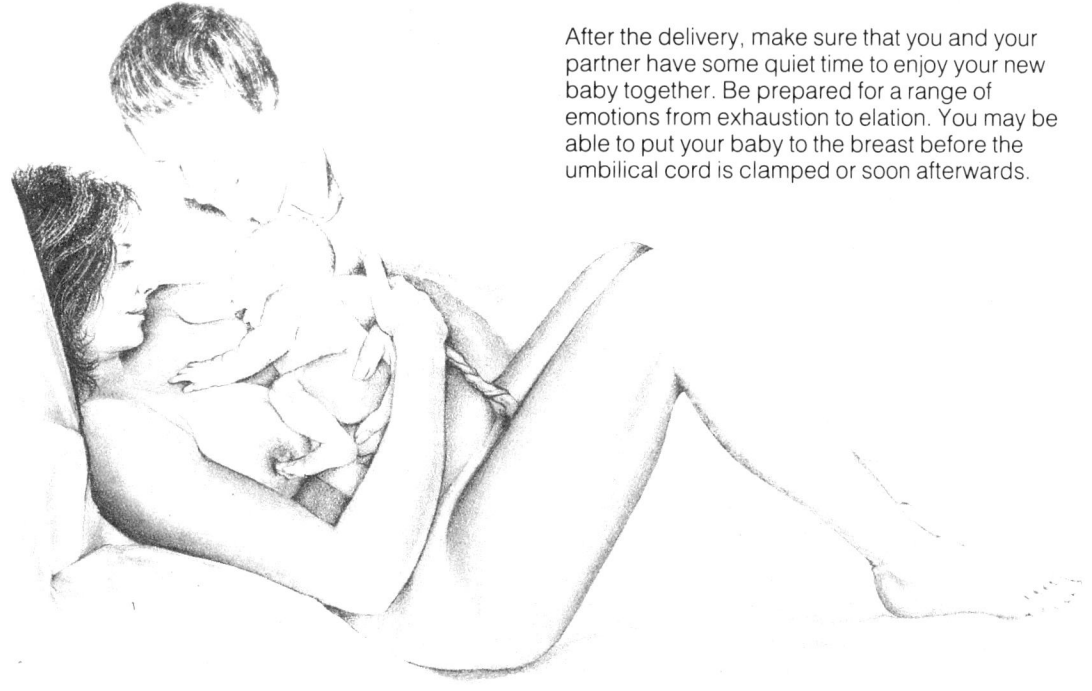

RESUSCITATION

Sometimes a baby has difficulties during the labour or delivery and needs help at birth to breathe normally. When the Apgar score is less than 7, the baby will be lifted up onto a resuscitation trolley, kept warm, often by means of an overhead radiant heater, and given gentle stimulation to breathe while oxygen is directed onto his face. At this point some babies will take their first breaths, and can be brought over to their parents. Others will need more help, and this is given by inflating the baby's lungs by means of a closely applied face mask or by a breathing tube that is passed through the mouth into the windpipe. Most babies rapidly become pink, and after some time begin regular breathing. Some babies, especially those still in a state of shock from the birth, need injections of sugar, alkali and drugs which are often given into the umbilical vein. Although this procedure can seem to take an age to anxious parents, it is in fact very swift, usually taking between 5 and 15 minutes. Babies who are premature or have been born with some abnormality may need to go on from the resuscitation trolley for more care in the *special care baby unit*.

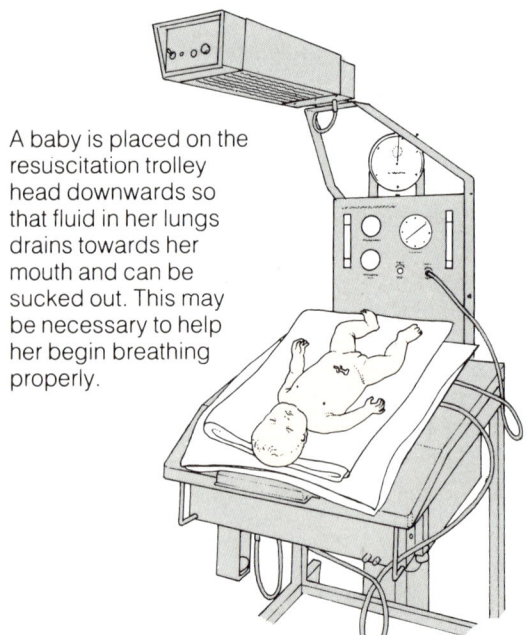

A baby is placed on the resuscitation trolley head downwards so that fluid in her lungs drains towards her mouth and can be sucked out. This may be necessary to help her begin breathing properly.

CARE OF THE UMBILICAL CORD

The cord is clamped with two pairs of forceps and then cut between them with sterile scissors leaving about 4 cm (1½ in) at the navel. The pair of forceps attached to the baby is then replaced with a clamping device to prevent any bleeding. The device may consist of paired elastic bands, or it may be a tensioned plastic clip called a Hollister clamp. The device is left on for a few days as the cord dries and shrivels. The part of the cord attached to the baby's umbilicus can easily become infected and should be kept clean with surgical spirit and an antiseptic cord powder until it drops off. This usually happens after about a week.

FEEDING

Immediately after birth babies are often alert and ready to suck, and will happily breastfeed. Breastfeeding can be satisfying for both you and your baby. It also helps your uterus to contract and expel the placenta: if it is your second or subsequent labour, you may find the contractions painful. Many midwives and mothers feel that putting the baby to the breast soon after birth helps in establishing successful breastfeeding. If you prefer to bottle-feed you will also give the first feed within 4 to 6 hours of your baby's birth.

CLEANING AND WASHING

The skin of the newborn baby is often still covered with *vernix*. Bathing a baby in the first few hours of life may lower the body temperature, so only the face, head and hands are gently cleaned. The first bath can be left until the baby is a few days old.

▶ **See also** Feeding and diet; Day-to-day care; Problems of the newborn child

WHAT DOES A NEWBORN BABY EXPERIENCE?

Contrary to older beliefs, newborn babies can appreciate many of the sights, sounds and smells around them. Moving both eyes together and focusing them on an object are skills that are developed over the early months, but immediately after birth babies can appreciate the colour and shape of a face or brightly coloured object placed near to them, at about 23 cm (9 in). This distance is where a mother's face is positioned when breastfeeding. Within a few days the baby will look directly into the mother's eyes when he is feeding.

A baby also responds to sound. A sudden loud noise can startle a baby, whose head will then jerk back and arms extend briefly. Quieter sounds and voices make the baby suddenly alert with eyes wide open and a change in the pattern of breathing. Sometimes the response is simply blinking the eyes.

A baby also has a sense of smell and each can recognize the particular smell of his own mother's breast milk.

All babies, including premature babies, are very aware of touch. Physical contact between babies and their parents has been found to be a very important factor in development. At birth a baby has a number of reflexes in response to being touched. If one cheek is stroked the baby will turn to that side – the 'rooting reflex'. Touching the hand causes the baby to grasp; stroking the upper surface of the foot results in the baby flexing the leg at the hip and knee – this is the 'placing reflex'. If the back is stroked along one side of the spine the baby bends towards that side.

EXAMINATION AT BIRTH

As the baby is being born the midwife and doctor are assessing the baby's condition. After the birth, the staff check the baby more carefully. They assess whether the facial features and body proportions are normal. The baby is turned over to check for *spina bifida* and that the back is normal. The anus and legs are examined and the fingers and toes checked. The number of blood vessels in the umbilical cord is recorded. Normally there are two arteries and one vein. If there is only one artery there may be another abnormality elsewhere.

The baby is weighed, and the body length and head circumference may be measured. Babies born around the expected time weigh between 2.5 and 4.4 kg (5½-9¾ lb), with an average length of 50 cm (20 in) and head circumference of 35 cm (14 in).

The baby's temperature is checked with a rectal thermometer and the baby warmed if necessary. A suction tube may be passed to the stomach. This checks that the gullet is complete and normal, and allows any swallowed mucus and debris to be sucked out. A thorough examination of the heart and other organs is left until the baby is 24 to 36 hours old, when the mother is in the postnatal ward. This is because the baby could easily become cold during a prolonged examination in the delivery room, and because there can be misleading signs in the hour or so after birth. For example, there may be a *heart murmur* due to changes in the circulation at birth, and the lung fluid, which is present in the chest during pregnancy, may not yet have been absorbed.

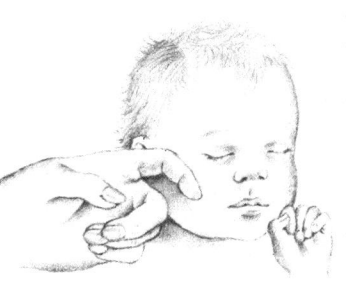

When the baby's cheek touches the breast the rooting reflex helps him find the nipple. You can use your baby's rooting reflex when you breastfeed him. If he needs help in finding the nipple, stroke his cheek and he will turn his face towards you and open his mouth ready to take in the nipple.

SECOND-DAY EXAMINATION

With the baby warm and settled, a thorough examination is made 24 to 36 hours after birth. If you are with your baby for this check you will also have an opportunity to ask questions and to tell the doctor about any worries you have concerning feeding and care generally. There are many different ways of checking the newborn baby but the doctor often starts at the top of the head and works down to the toes.

HEAD AND NECK
The baby's head is often shaped by the mother's pelvis during labour and this 'moulding' returns to normal after several days. The pressure also causes some swelling ('caput') of parts of the scalp which settles down soon after birth. The doctor checks the 'fontanelle', the soft spot on the top of the baby's head. This diamond-shaped area is where several of the skull bones meet and it may not close up until the child is 2 years old.

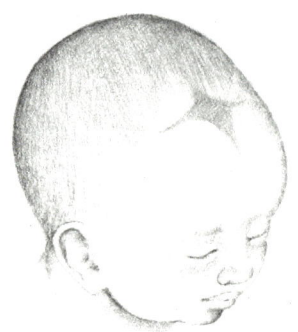

The fontanelle is clearly visible especially when the baby cries.

There may be bruising over the baby's face or head, and marks left by forceps during delivery, for example. The ears, eyes and nose are examined, and the roof of the mouth checked for *cleft lip and palate*. The fold of skin holding the tongue to the floor of the mouth often seems to be short at birth, but the tip of the tongue grows forwards during the first year and there is very rarely any interference with speech. Cutting the fold of skin is an operation which is almost never required.

Most babies do not have teeth at birth, although some babies are born with one or more. Occasionally these are loose or coming through at an unusual angle. Usually they are removed in case they fall out and are inhaled by the baby.

ARMS AND HANDS
The doctor checks the fingers and the palm creases. Most babies have two major creases across each palm. If there is a single crease, the baby may have other abnormalities, such as *Down's syndrome*, which are looked for. The pulse in each arm is felt and a check made for normal movements and strength.

CHEST AND HEART
Male as well as female babies often have enlarged breasts at birth. A little milk may even be secreted from the breasts.

The doctor listens to the heart and lungs. Most of the noises heard immediately after delivery will have gone, but if there is still a murmur this will be noted and checked when you visit the postnatal clinic. A murmur is not uncommon, and does not mean that the baby necessarily has a *congenital heart defect*.

ABDOMEN AND GENITALS
The doctor feels the abdomen gently to be sure that the liver, spleen or kidneys are not enlarged, and checks that the baby has had a bowel action and has passed urine during the first 24 hours.

Boys' testes are checked to ensure that they are properly descended. The foreskin of a newborn boy naturally adheres to the tip of the penis and it is not forced back. The genitalia of a baby girl are checked to ensure that the labia, or genital folds, are not joined together and that the clitoris is normal in size. She may have some white vaginal discharge, which may become slightly blood-stained after a few days as the hormone levels in the baby's body drop. The doctor feels the pulses in the baby's groin and turns the baby over to check the lower spine and anus. There may be a small harmless dimple or pit over the spine just behind the anus which needs no treatment.

THE HIPS

The baby's hips are checked by holding the thighs firmly and moving each hip joint to see whether the head of the thigh bone is unstable or lies outside the hip joint, that is, it is dislocated. In either case the baby will be seen by orthopaedic specialists. *Congenital dislocation of the hip* can usually be effectively treated in the weeks after birth.

The newborn baby's reflexes are instinctive movements. Even though she will not be able to walk until she is about 1 year old, in the few days following birth the stepping reflex makes her attempt to walk when her feet come into contact with a horizontal surface.

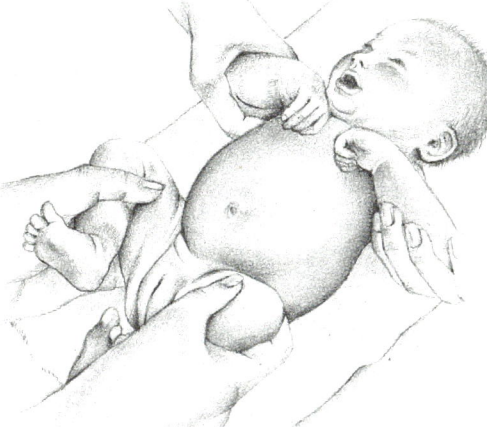

Testing the hips is not painful for the baby though she may cry because of the disturbance of having her legs moved about.

LEGS AND FEET

The baby's legs are examined to see that they are of equal length and size. The ankle joints are sometimes still held in the position they had in the womb with the result that the baby has a *club foot*.

NERVES AND MUSCLES

The baby's nerves and muscles are assessed by putting the arms and legs through a range of movements to be sure that they are not too stiff and not too floppy. The baby's head control is checked, and then the reflexes: sucking, grasping a finger, stepping when lowered to a flat surface, 'placing' when the feet are brought up to a vertical surface, and the startle, or Moro, response, when the baby's whole body reacts to a loud noise.

A newborn baby's grasp can be so strong that she can be lifted into the air when grasping an adult's fingers with both hands.

The Moro reflex is quite a violent movement. If the baby is startled, she will fling out her arms and open her hands.

COMMON PROBLEMS

After the examination the doctor will talk with you about any minor problems such as skin blemishes. You can use this opportunity to ask any questions and to point out anything you have noticed and are worried about.
Sometimes the baby may be seen again by a doctor for a discharge examination. During the first week of your baby's life you will have daily contact with a midwife so that you can discuss any other problems that arise.
Problems of the newborn child in Part Three describes the treatment of more serious problems.

BIRTHMARKS

Marks on a baby's skin are common and there are various types.
Salmon patches, also called stork's beak marks, are pink marks often seen above the bridge of the nose and on the eyelids, and over the nape of the neck. They fade with time.

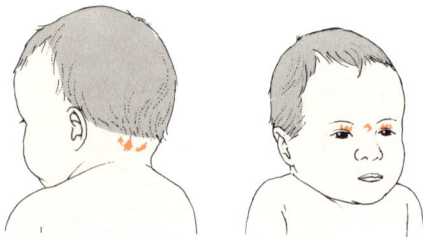

Salmon patches

Port wine stains are darker red with a sharply defined edge. They are dilated capillaries in the skin and are permanent, but can later be covered by masking creams.
Strawberry marks appear as a tiny red dot and are not always obvious at first. They are the result of dilated blood vessels. They grow during the early months of life, becoming red raised lumps, but then begin to shrivel during the child's second year, and disappear before school age without leaving a scar.
Mongolian blue spots are blue discolorations of the skin. They are commonly found on the lower back of Asian or black babies. They fade with time.

MINOR INJURIES

The process of birth may cause minor injuries, especially if delivery has been difficult.
Cephalhaematoma is a bruise on the head that develops as a result of bleeding from one of the blood vessels beneath the tissue covering the bone. The swelling disappears after some weeks, although the edge may be felt for months. It does not require any treatment.

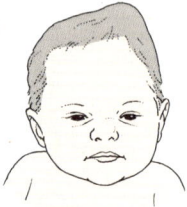

Cephalhaematoma

Scalp bruises occur under the scalp and can spread anywhere across the baby's head. The bruise disappears after a couple of weeks.
Forceps bruises, a result of forceps delivery, usually appear on the baby's cheeks and quickly fade. Babies delivered by the vacuum apparatus, 'ventouse extraction', may have bruising where the suction cup was applied.
Bloodshot eyes are caused by tiny vessels bleeding under the white of the eye as a result of pressure on the baby's head during labour. This can produce dramatic-looking but harmless red marks over the white of the eye. They disappear after a week.

JAUNDICE

Many newborn babies become slightly jaundiced on about the third day of life. *Jaundice* is yellow colouring of the skin caused by the pigment bilirubin. This pigment is formed in the normal process of the breakdown of red blood cells. Before birth most of the bilirubin is removed by the placenta and dealt with by the mother's body but after birth the baby has to deal with it alone and it takes a few days for the liver to increase its own capacity to deal with the pigment. This type of jaundice is not a disease and is called physiological jaundice: it clears spontaneously at the end of the first week. It is important that the baby feeds well and does not become dehydrated.

THE NEWBORN CHILD

MINOR INFECTIONS

Towards the end of pregnancy the baby receives antibodies across the placenta from the mother and these give some protection against infection. For many infections, however, a baby has to build up resistance, and this takes time because the immune system of the newborn is not fully developed. In the first weeks of life, therefore, minor infections of a baby's eyes, mouth, skin and navel are common. Newborn babies normally breathe through the nose rather than the mouth, so when they have nasal colds their feeding may be disturbed. When babies get nasal colds *and* go off their feeds the doctor may prescribe decongestant nasal drops to help.

Eye infections are common because the baby's eyes are often moist, and tears do not drain easily down the tear duct to the nose. If you notice your baby's eyes becoming sticky with pus, you should show this to the doctor, who will prescribe eye drops or ointment. The baby's mouth can be infected with *thrush*: you will notice white patches in your baby's mouth which may be sore. It is easily treated. A baby's skin may become infected with a bacterium called staphylococcus. Creamy-white spots will appear and, if there are only a few, washing the baby with a soap containing a mild antiseptic may keep them in check. If more spots appear, you should consult your doctor for treatment.

In spite of cleanliness and care an infection sometimes develops at the navel. If the surrounding skin looks red or there is an offensive discharge, you should show it to your midwife or doctor.

SPOTS AND RASHES

As well as the occasional infected spots, newborn babies often have other rashes that are generally harmless.

Urticaria are large red spots, each with a tiny red centre, which may appear during the first week of life. Unlike infected spots they disappear after a few hours while others continue to form. They are probably the skin's reaction to being in air rather than in contact with amniotic fluid. They need no treatment and do not recur.

Milia are small white spots mainly on the nose but also elsewhere on the face. They are blocked *sebaceous glands* which are very common and require no treatment.

Heat rash is the name given to small red spots that often appear, especially on a baby's face. They can occur when a baby is over-wrapped and sweaty, but also develop in babies who are not overheated and in cool weather. Apart from trying to keep the baby's clothes and blankets appropriate to the room temperature there is no special treatment. It is best to accept the fact that most normal babies go through 'spotty' phases.

White spots in the mouth may be seen near the mid-line on the roof of the mouth. They are called Epstein's pearls and are harmless cysts, not to be mistaken for thrush.

Cradle cap is a form of *dandruff* of the scalp and consists of thickened white patches which are initially hard to remove. Although there are many proprietary remedies, none of these work well and it is worth discussing the problem and its treatment with your doctor.

Nappy rash can be of three types, or a mixture of them. The most common is ammonia *dermatitis* and is due to contact between the skin and wet nappies. Skin bacteria act on the

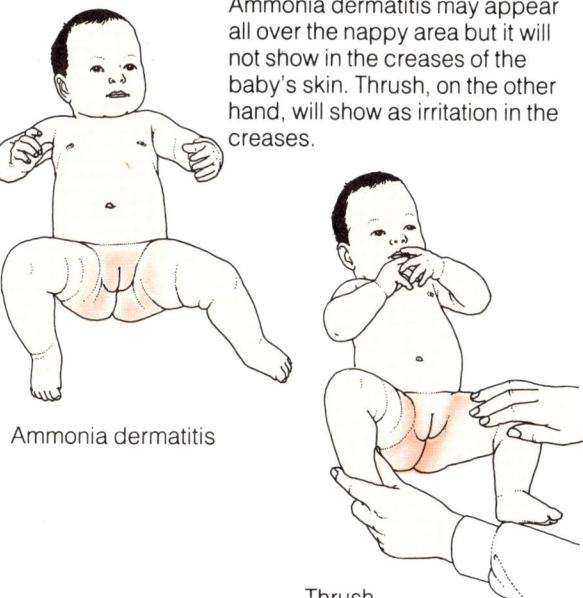

Ammonia dermatitis may appear all over the nappy area but it will not show in the creases of the baby's skin. Thrush, on the other hand, will show as irritation in the creases.

Ammonia dermatitis

Thrush

Even at birth, differences in size and weight, features and personalities make each baby a complete individual.

urine to release ammonia, which 'burns' the skin. It can be treated by changing wet nappies as soon as possible and applying a barrier cream such as zinc and castor oil. A second cause is *thrush*, and in this case the baby's mouth is often also affected. Red areas of irritation can be seen spreading out from the anus. It is treated by a cream containing an anti-thrush agent. Thirdly, nappy rash may be due to *seborrhoeic dermatitis*, a striking red rash which spreads beyond the nappy area.

Dry peeling skin is common when babies are born later than expected and sometimes when they are *small for dates*. Baby oil keeps the skin moist and it improves without treatment.

VOMITING

Many newborn babies bring back part of their feed. This 'possetting', regurgitating a little milk after a feed, is common, and does not need special treatment, provided that the baby is feeding well and gaining weight. Excessive possetting can be improved with feed thickeners. If your baby brings up a large part of the feed, or the vomit is stained with green or yellow bile, then the baby may have an infection and you should consult your doctor.

STOOLS AND URINE

A baby's first bowel actions after birth are of a sticky black material called meconium, which is bile and bowel debris accumulated during the pregnancy. After a couple of days of milk feeds the stools change from black to green and finally to yellow. Seeing these changing stools is important because it proves that the baby's bowel is complete from end to end.

The number of stools passed varies very greatly. Initially breastfed babies may have many loose stools because of the high content of sugar lactose in breast milk. Later, they often have fewer stools because there is so little residue in breast milk, and they may pass stools as infrequently as once or twice a week. So long as the stools are soft this is not *constipation*. Many babies go red in the face and grunt when passing stools: this does not necessarily mean they are constipated. The frequency of stools also varies when a baby is bottle-fed. It may be five or six a day or one every other day. Urine sometimes stains the nappy a faint pink as it dries out. This is due to salts in the urine and is perfectly normal.

CRYING

There are a number of reasons for a baby to cry: hunger, thirst, a wet nappy, heat, cold or discomfort. With time he may cry for company, and many babies cry when tired. Sometimes crying is a reaction to the mother's mood.

You will learn to recognize your baby's different cries and how to cope with them by gentle movements, cuddles, singing and talking. But if nothing works and your patience is exhausted, get someone else to take over for an hour while you have a break.

If the crying seems strange, and especially if your baby is not feeding well, he may be ill and you should contact your doctor or midwife.

SCREENING PROCEDURES

The careful examinations that the baby has after birth are intended to pick up any problem that can be corrected early in life, such as *congenital dislocation of the hip*. There are also several screening tests that are done in the early weeks of a baby's life to detect other treatable conditions.

Two major tests, for *phenylketonuria* (the Guthrie test) and *cretinism*, are both detected from a sample of the baby's blood taken on the sixth day. If the baby suffers from either condition, it can be successfully treated.

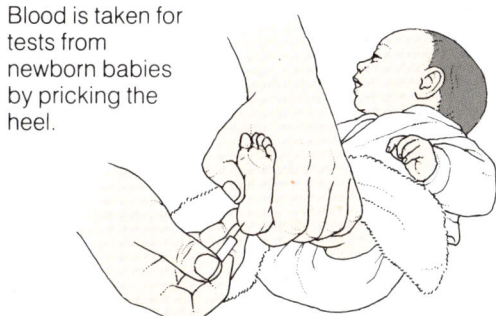

Blood is taken for tests from newborn babies by pricking the heel.

▶See also Early growth and development

THE 6-WEEK EXAMINATION

Babies are routinely re-examined when they are about 6 weeks of age. This examination provides an opportunity to notice any problems that were not apparent at birth. Sometimes a *heart murmur* can now be heard, while other murmurs, present at birth, may have disappeared. The baby's weight gain, length and head circumference are charted to check that growth is normal. Developmental skills acquired since birth are observed. At 6 weeks most babies are smiling responsively and will fix their eyes on a friendly face, following it to either side. They alert to sounds and gurgle happily to themselves.

Immunizations begin a few weeks later and your baby's growth and development will continue to be charted regularly at the child health clinic.

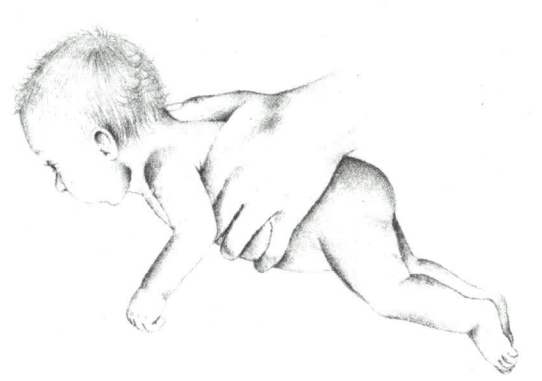

By 6 weeks a baby lying in a position face downwards and lifted upwards will raise her head in line with her body so that she is able to look forwards.

FEEDING AND DIET

Feeding their children, and watching them thrive and develop, is a major concern for parents. From a baby's birth, parents have to adjust their lifestyle to the new infant's demands for food. Ensuring that the child is well fed continues to be an important part of parenting.

Food and emotions are powerfully linked and the connection between food and comfort starts early in life. Whether a baby is breastfed or bottle-fed, parent and baby need to settle comfortably, and the transformation of the baby's hunger into contentment reinforces the bond of love between them.

Unfortunately, eating can also be the source of much anxiety. Most parents have periods of worry about the quality and quantity of food that their children eat. This anxiety is rarely justified: a healthy child will always eat when hungry and most children will eat a balanced diet if they are set a good example and allowed to choose from a reasonable range of food. Tastes and choices can be influenced by advertising, but basic eating patterns are learned in the family during childhood.

In general, our intake of sugar, salt and animal fat needs to be reduced to prevent diet-related disease, so aim for foods that are low in these ingredients. There is no dietary need for refined sugar at all, and there are many other more nutritious sources of sweetness, such as fresh and dried fruits and root vegetables. Choose fresh food in preference to processed and refined food and check labels for artificial colourings, flavourings and preservatives. Although it is worth encouraging your child to eat sensibly there is no evidence that very low fat or other special diets have any long-term health benefits.

Children, in common with adults, can have their feeding patterns upset not only by illness, but also by holidays and family stress. Tensions and hostilities within the family are often played out at meal-times, and can create difficulties. Sometimes a child may mirror a parent's own difficulty with food, seeming to prefer biscuits, cakes, chocolates or sweet drinks to more nutritious food. This can be worrying for parents and it is easy for a system of coercion and reward to be set up at meal-times in order to try to solve the problem. Try to resist doing this.

·It can be worth thinking about your own early experiences and taking stock of any values about food that you may wish to encourage or discourage in your own children. Doing what you can to minimize tension when feeding an infant is an investment, for a pattern of relaxation usually continues happily to the meal-table.

▶See also Behaviour and development

BREASTFEEDING AND BOTTLE-FEEDING

Nutritionally, breast milk is better suited to your baby's need than cow's milk, even cow's milk that has been modified and specially prepared for infants. Luckily, most mothers are able to breastfeed their babies.

During pregnancy, the breasts prepare for feeding. The first feeds from the breast give a baby colostrum, a form of milk that is rich in some minerals, and in vitamins A, B_{12} and E. It contains less fat and sugar than mature milk, making it easier for the newborn baby to digest. There is no need to supplement colostrum. After a few days' transition, mature milk starts to come into the breasts. The breasts become full and tense; the baby feeding relieves the tension and stimulates the production of more milk.

Whether you decide to continue with breastfeeding or switch to bottle-feeding will depend on a number of factors. It will help you to decide if you discuss them with your partner, midwife and doctor.

REASONS FOR BREASTFEEDING	REASONS FOR BOTTLE-FEEDING
o Colostrum and breast milk are the natural food for human babies. A mother's milk changes its composition during each feed and over the weeks to adapt to the baby's changing needs o Colostrum and breast milk contain maternal antibodies that protect the baby's bowel against diseases such as gastro-enteritis o Breast milk is easier for babies to digest than formula milk and is less likely to cause allergic reactions; adjusting your own diet may help to alleviate any problems that do occur o The milk is at exactly the right temperature for the baby o There is no need to sterilize equipment or to prepare feeds. In particular, travelling, going out and night feeds are easier o Apart from the cost of ensuring that you have a nutritious diet, breastfeeding is free o It is rare for a breastfed baby to be overweight	o You may find greater satisfaction and confidence in preparing bottle-feeds than in breastfeeding o You can share feeding with your partner or others close to you and the baby. Remember, though, that if you breastfeed, you can express breast milk in order to give it as the occasional bottle-feed o If you want to return to work very soon after the birth, you may find it easier if someone else can feed the baby o There may be physical problems with breastfeeding. If you are unwell, breastfeeding may prove too great a strain on your reserves or you may need to take drugs, which could pass into the milk and affect the baby. If your baby has a cleft palate, breastfeeding can be very difficult. Premature babies may also have problems in establishing feeding, and twins or triplets present logistic difficulties

ESTABLISHING FEEDING

If you feed on demand, your baby will usually take as much milk as he needs, whether you are breast- or bottle-feeding. As his digestive system matures and his stomach grows, he will feed more efficiently and the intervals between feeds will become more regular.

WHICH MILK?

If you are bottle-feeding or supplementing breastfeeds, you will need to choose a milk. If your baby is under 6 months old, do not use ordinary cow's milk or evaporated milk. The proteins and fats in cow's milk are not appropriate for small babies and the balance of minerals is also unsuitable.

If your baby is over 6 months you may use standard cow's milk, although if the milk is unpasteurized it must be boiled and cooled. It is preferable not to give cow's milk to a baby until he is older than 12 months. You can also use evaporated milk that has been diluted with 1½ parts cooled boiled water to 1 part evaporated milk. If you do not use formula milk, you should give your baby additional vitamins A, B_{12}, C and D.

Never use goat's milk or a soya milk formula without medical advice. Your baby may be allergic to either if he is allergic to cow's milk. Goat's milk is low in vitamins A, C and D, and in folic acid; it also has a high sodium content.

COMMON PROBLEMS

Your baby may not be able to suck easily if his nose is blocked by your breast or your clothes. He may also have difficulty if your breasts are engorged: a warm bath before the feed may help the nipple to stand out and the milk to flow.

A baby may not suck well if offered food when tired rather than hungry, or if he has been crying a lot and is upset.

Infections, including colds, ear infections and oral *thrush*, may make feeding difficult for a few days.

A new baby may suck hungrily at the breast or bottle, then drift into a doze, then suck again. Some babies are naturally more sleepy than others, and may need gently waking to feed regularly. But even the most experienced mothers can find that a newborn baby needs up to an hour for each feed.

BREASTFEEDING

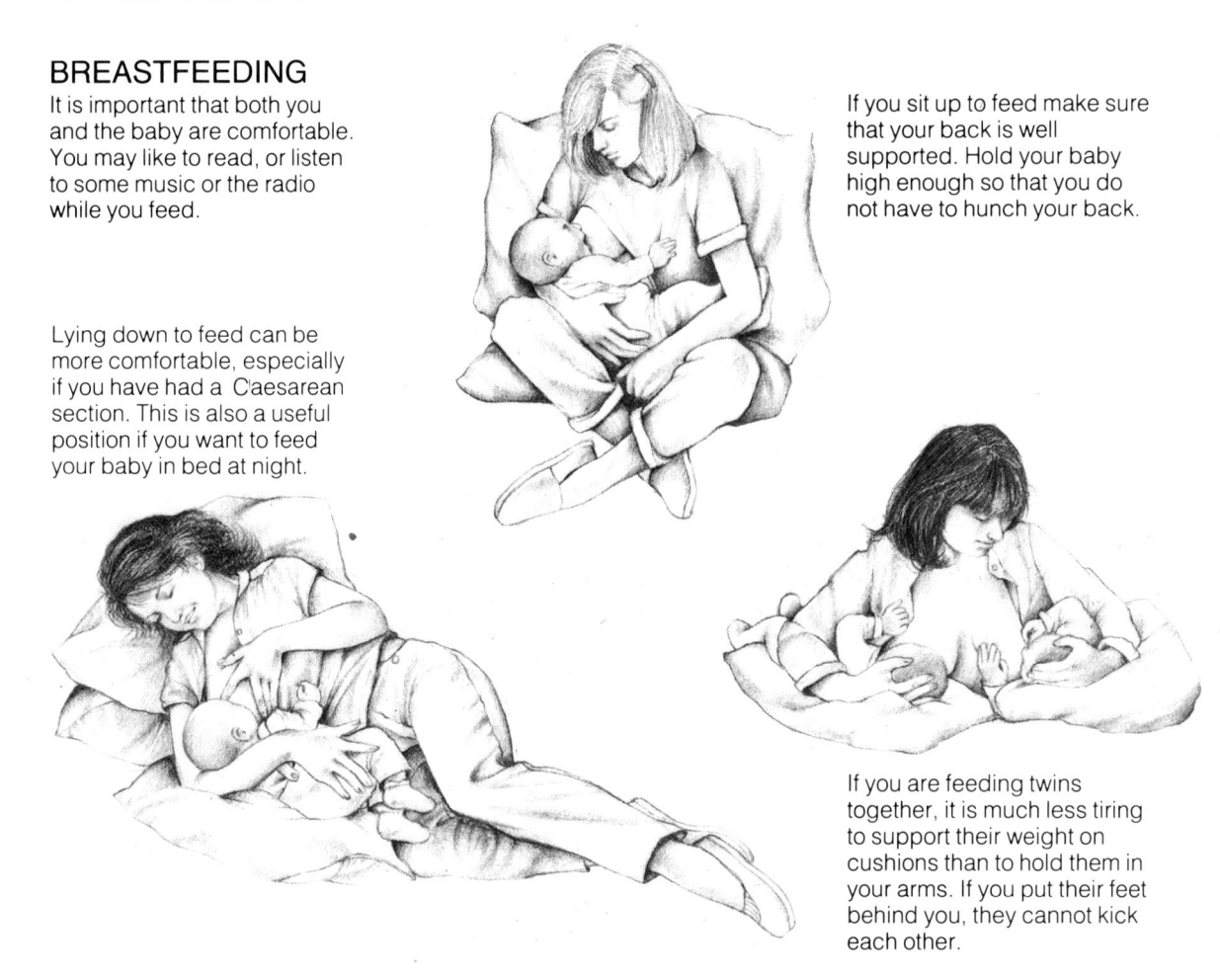

It is important that both you and the baby are comfortable. You may like to read, or listen to some music or the radio while you feed.

If you sit up to feed make sure that your back is well supported. Hold your baby high enough so that you do not have to hunch your back.

Lying down to feed can be more comfortable, especially if you have had a Caesarean section. This is also a useful position if you want to feed your baby in bed at night.

If you are feeding twins together, it is much less tiring to support their weight on cushions than to hold them in your arms. If you put their feet behind you, they cannot kick each other.

If your baby still seems hungry after a feed and you think that you are not producing enough milk, increase the number of feeds. If you are breastfeeding, the more the baby feeds, the more milk you will produce.

Babies may regurgitate large amounts of milk. This may be because they have had too much milk or have drunk too quickly, though this is more common if you are bottle-feeding.

Alternatively, babies may bring up milk with wind bubbles: try feeding in a more upright position, ensure that your baby is not bounced about while feeding and, if you are bottle-feeding, make sure that the hole in the teat is neither so small that the baby has to labour hard to feed nor so large that the baby cannot cope with the flow of milk. Seek advice if your baby regurgitates persistently or if the milk is mixed with blood or bile.

Some babies suffer a colic variously known as evening or 3-month colic. The baby cries and becomes very distressed, usually in the early evening, and is not satisfied by cuddling, extra or different feeds or any other remedy. This is very wearing for parents. A check-up with your doctor can reassure you that your baby does not have any other problem; for infants over 6 months old your doctor may prescribe a drug to relax the bowel.

If you are breastfeeding, you might like to try cutting out dairy products from your own diet, as there is some suggestion that these may contribute to colic.

▶See also The newborn child

MAKING UP BOTTLE-FEEDS

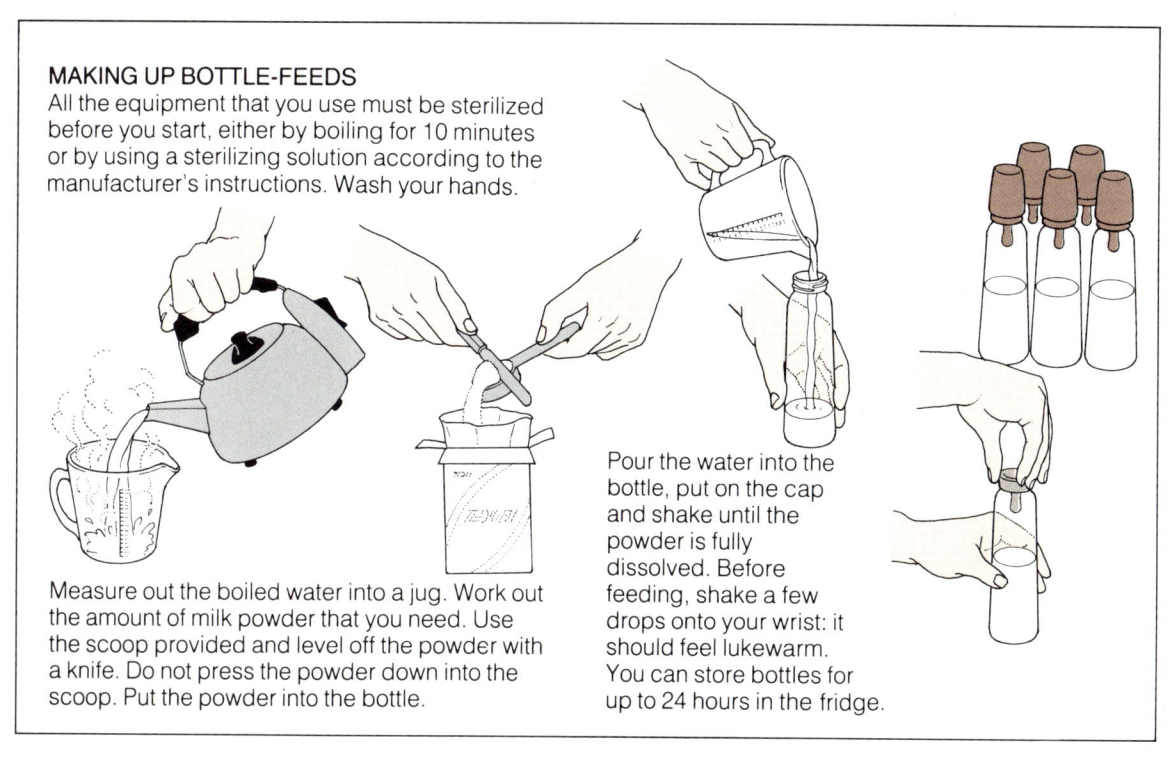

All the equipment that you use must be sterilized before you start, either by boiling for 10 minutes or by using a sterilizing solution according to the manufacturer's instructions. Wash your hands.

Measure out the boiled water into a jug. Work out the amount of milk powder that you need. Use the scoop provided and level off the powder with a knife. Do not press the powder down into the scoop. Put the powder into the bottle.

Pour the water into the bottle, put on the cap and shake until the powder is fully dissolved. Before feeding, shake a few drops onto your wrist: it should feel lukewarm. You can store bottles for up to 24 hours in the fridge.

WEANING

Until the age of 4 months or so, milk is the only food a baby needs. Many babies thrive happily on milk alone for 6 months. Do not add cereals or other solid foods to bottle-feeds for a baby under 6 months old.

As babies develop and become more active, they need extra calories and different nutrients to supplement their milk. When your baby still seems hungry after a substantial breast- or bottle-feed, you can start to think about giving solid foods. Begin by giving small amounts of baby rice or pureed or sieved vegetables or fruit once a day. Offer just enough to cover the tip of a teaspoon, and introduce only one new taste at a time.

Later, you can offer other cereals, custard or yoghurt; or you can sieve or liquidize any home-cooked food that the rest of the family is eating, as long as it is not fried and it does not contain added salt or sugar. Commercially prepared baby food is convenient when you are travelling or away from home. For preference, choose varieties without artificial additives.

Babies enjoy trying different tastes but may not like them all. Let them make their own choice. Gradually, a wider range of foods can be introduced and their texture can be lumpier: by the time your baby is 8 to 10 months old, you can mince or grate food, and by the age of 1 year, your baby will probably be able to manage the same food as the rest of the family. While teething, babies usually enjoy chewing on hard foods such as crusts of bread, scrubbed carrots or peeled apple quarters.

FOODS TO WATCH CAREFULLY

Some foods are more likely than others to cause allergic reactions. The commonest ones are cow's milk, eggs (especially egg white), wheat, cheese, shellfish and pork. Peanuts, tomatoes, strawberries and citrus fruit can also sometimes cause a reaction. Introduce these foods in small quantities and one at a time so that you can pinpoint the source of the reaction if it occurs.

▶ **See also** Allergy

PLANNING YOUR DIET

NUTRIENT	SOURCES	EATING WELL
Carbohydrate There are three types of carbohydrate: sugar, starch and cellulose or fibre. Carbohydrate is necessary for energy and fibre prevents *constipation* and other digestive disorders.	Refined sugar (sucrose) is found in many processed foods, such as sweets, cakes, biscuits, jam, canned fruit and sweetened drinks. Fructose is a simple sugar found in fruit, fruit juices and honey. Starch is found in many foods, especially cereals, pulses and potatoes. Fibre is found in wholemeal flours, wholegrain cereals, fruit, vegetables, nuts and pulses.	Aim to eat a variety of starchy high-fibre foods and keep sugary foods for special occasions. If you allow your child to eat sweets, offer these at the end of a meal, and encourage him to brush his teeth afterwards.
Fat Small quantities of fat are needed to obtain the fat-soluble vitamins. Butter, for example, contains vitamins A and D.	Fats include meat fats, dairy fats (especially butter and cream) and oils from fish and vegetable sources.	Adults may benefit from diets that are low in fat. Starting your child on a relatively low-fat diet will help to set up good eating patterns for later life. However, children under 5 years old should be given full-cream milk.
Protein A supply of protein is needed for growth and for repair of the body. Growing children need a greater proportion of protein in their diets than adults.	Animal protein is found in meat, fish, eggs and dairy products. Vegetable protein is found in whole-grain cereals, nuts, pulses and root vegetables.	Milk is a good source of protein as well as of calcium, so if your child enjoys milk, aim to give 0.6 litre (1 pt) a day from about 1 year onwards.
Calcium Calcium is important in the formation of teeth and bones. Good supplies of vitamin D are required for the absorption of calcium.	The main sources are cheese, yoghurt and milk, tinned fish, white bread, green leafy vegetables, almonds, soya beans and seaweeds.	If your child dislikes milk, make sure that he eats plenty of other calcium-rich foods.
Iron Iron is important in preventing *anaemia*. Vitamin C helps to enable the absorption of iron.	Good sources are liver, meat, eggs, bread, cereals, pulses and green vegetables.	Serve plenty of fruit and vegetables at meals to help your child absorb iron.
Salt All body fluids contain salt: salt is needed to maintain the water balance of the body and to regulate nerve and muscle activity.	Many foods contain salt. There is no need to add table or cooking salt to food, nor to eat especially salty foods.	Avoid adding salt to a young child's or infant's food: this is particularly important for young babies since their kidneys cannot yet excrete excess salt.

NUTRIENT	SOURCES	EATING WELL
Vitamin A This is essential for vision in dim light and for maintaining the health of the skin and linings of the body. It is a fat-soluble vitamin.	Fatty fish, such as herring, sardines and tuna; fish oils; dairy products; carrots, tomatoes, cabbage, spinach and brussels sprouts.	A varied diet usually provides enough vitamin A, but vitamin drops or cod liver oil guard against deficiency. Excessive doses of vitamin A can be poisonous.
Vitamin B Complex This is a group of separate vitamins which are important in the chemical reactions that release energy from food. They tend to occur in the same foods, and are water-soluble and therefore easily destroyed by cooking.	Milk, liver, whole-grain cereals, pulses, eggs, green leafy vegetables, nuts and seeds, yeast extract.	Sunlight destroys vitamin B_{12} so avoid leaving milk out on the doorstep. Vegans should take a supplement of vitamin B_{12}.
Vitamin C Deficiency of vitamin C causes scurvy, or bleeding from the gums and small blood vessels, and prevents rapid healing of wounds. It is important for growth and development of bone. Vitamin C is water-soluble.	Breast and formula milk; fruit and vegetables, especially citrus fruits, blackcurrants, strawberries, tomatoes, potatoes, green leafy vegetables.	Vitamin C is easily destroyed during storage and cooking. Buy your fruit and vegetables as fresh as possible and eat them raw or steam or cook them lightly.
Vitamin D This is necessary for the absorption of calcium. Adolescents need extra vitamin D and should take a supplement in winter. A deficiency of vitamin D can cause *rickets*.	Fish liver oils, fatty fish, dairy products. The body can manufacture vitamin D when exposed to sunlight.	Dietary needs for vitamin D depend on how much sunlight a child is exposed to and the colour of the child's skin: dark-skinned children create less vitamin D from sunlight than light-skinned children. Supplements will ensure that your child is not deficient, but it is important not to exceed the stated dose, as too high a dose can be harmful.
Vitamin E The need for vitamin E in humans is not proven; rats need the vitamin for normal fertility.	Wheatgerm, oats, brown rice and other whole-grain cereals, nuts, seeds, pulses, green leafy vegetables.	A deficiency of vitamin E is unlikely in a normal diet.
Vitamin K Vitamin K is needed for normal clotting of the blood.	Spinach, cauliflower, peas and cereals.	Excessive doses of vitamin K preparations may cause *anaemia*.

EATING FOR HEALTH

Given a varied diet, it is unlikely that your child will suffer from any nutritional deficiency. Children occasionally choose to eat eccentric diets and some basic information about the sources of important nutrients will help you to assess whether or not you need to make adjustments. Remember, though, that while children often pass through faddish phases they usually obtain the nutrients they need in the long term.

VEGETARIANS AND VEGANS

The nutritional value of a vegetarian diet that includes dairy products is very similar to a mixed diet. The calorie value may be lower because vegetarians tend to eat more high-fibre foods and fresh fruit and vegetables. Nut butters, such as peanut butter, are good concentrated sources of calories, protein and B vitamins. If your child has 0.6 litre (1 pt) milk per day, or the equivalent as yoghurt or cheese, this will provide the calcium needed for healthy bones and teeth as well as protein and vitamins.

Vegans eat no food of animal origin at all. A vegan diet can be very healthy, but needs careful planning to ensure an adequate intake of nutrients, especially for children. Ask your doctor or health visitor to check your child's diet. A wide and varied selection of whole-grain cereals, pulses, seeds, beans, fruit and vegetables should give sufficient nutrients. Vitamin B_{12} is found only in animal foods and so will need to be given as a supplement.

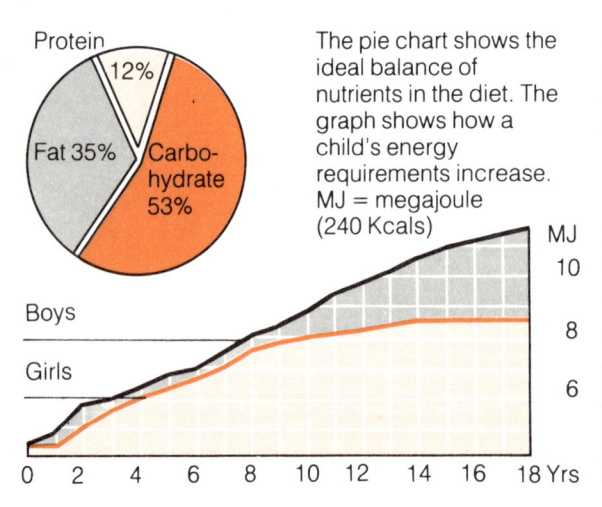

OBESITY

Babies and children become obese for the same reasons as adults: they eat more than they need and the excess energy is stored as fat. Your own common sense will usually tell you whether or not your child is overweight, but body weight charts are also a useful guide.

Children have different energy requirements and one child may gain weight on a diet that contains no more calories than that of a slim child. It is, however, true that overweight children tend to have overweight parents, perhaps because of family eating patterns and perhaps because of hereditary factors in *metabolism*.

Keep a check on your child's weight: it is much easier to prevent obesity than to cure it. But remember that children often go through temporary phases of chubbiness, particularly in babyhood and adolescence. Girls are particularly likely to put on extra fat during puberty. They need help in understanding the reasons for the weight changes and support in avoiding unsound ideas about eating and slimming. The excess fat of adolescence in both boys and girls usually disappears as they grow and as their muscles develop.

Make sure that you do not encourage bad eating habits by your own example or by confusing emotional issues with eating, by making a virtue of cleaning the plate or offering sweets as rewards or consolation, for example.

If your child becomes considerably overweight, you may want to seek help from your doctor. Be aware that your child may be expressing unhappiness about other areas of life. If parents and child are both motivated to reduce the child's weight, a diet and exercise plan may be successful.

The pie chart shows the ideal balance of nutrients in the diet. The graph shows how a child's energy requirements increase. MJ = megajoule (240 Kcals)

▶See also Early growth and development; The older child and adolescent; Glandular disorders

DAY-TO-DAY CARE

There are no hard and fast rules on how you should look after the physical needs of your child. There are few rights and wrongs. The advice of other parents may be helpful at times, but generally it is better to go by your own instinct than to act on other people's ideas. Common sense is the basis of the day-to-day care of your baby, child and even adolescent. Particularly in the first year you are likely to receive conflicting advice from friends, relatives and health professionals, but as a parent you can have the confidence to recognize what your child wants. You will learn to know when your child is tired, hungry or thirsty and therefore needs sleep, food, drink or comfort.

It is also important in the day-to-day care of your child that you look after yourself. Consistency in responding to a child is a good principle, but at times you will be tired or irritable, and therefore inconsistent in your behaviour. So explain to your child from an early age that there are things *you* need, and encourage him to be considerate and to recognize that you have feelings of your own.

Establishing day-to-day routines can help you as well as your child: for example, fixing a specific bedtime will not only give a child security and enough sleep but will also enable you to plan some time for yourself.

Routines do give a sense of security. While home itself provides a firm base from which to explore other environments, and security comes as much from the stable presence of a loved adult as from the environment, children also benefit from the reassurance of familiar patterns in day-to-day living. Even a minimal routine in a generally chaotic home is helpful to a child's sense of security.

It is also worth remembering that attitudes and habits encouraged during childhood can become strongly rooted, and that if you establish routines for bedtime, teeth-cleaning, even meal-times, you will be setting patterns of behaviour for your child as he grows older. Keep a sense of proportion, though: there is no need to feel trapped by rigid routines.

▶See also Behaviour and development

WASHING AND HYGIENE

Your attitudes to your child's hygiene will be very personal and will reflect your own lifestyle. However, a few aspects, such as keeping babies clean and making sure children wash their hands before eating, are important in cutting down the risk of *infections*.

A newborn baby is particularly vulnerable to infections, so regular cleansing of the skin, particularly of the napkin area and navel, is important. As the baby grows, immunity to infection increases, although skin infections are still more common where hygiene is neglected. Teaching children to wash their hands after using the toilet is also important.

When choosing soaps and other cleansing products remember that your child's skin may be sensitive to the perfume or detergent in particular brands. *Dry skin* or skin *rashes* may result, in which case try another brand.

For older babies and toddlers bathtime usually becomes a focus for play, and it can provide a relaxing part of the bedtime routine, calming children down at the end of the day.

By about 3 or 4 years a boy's foreskin is no longer adherent to his penis and you can show him how to retract it when washing.

Aim to wash your child's hair about once a week, although if he hates it, washing it less often will do no harm.

Babies' nails seem to grow very fast and, unless kept short, they can easily scratch. Cut your baby's nails with a pair of safety scissors after a feed, when sleepiness will stop him wriggling around too much. When you cut children's nails, avoid leaving sharp corners and do not cut too close to the skin.

WASHING THE NEWBORN BABY

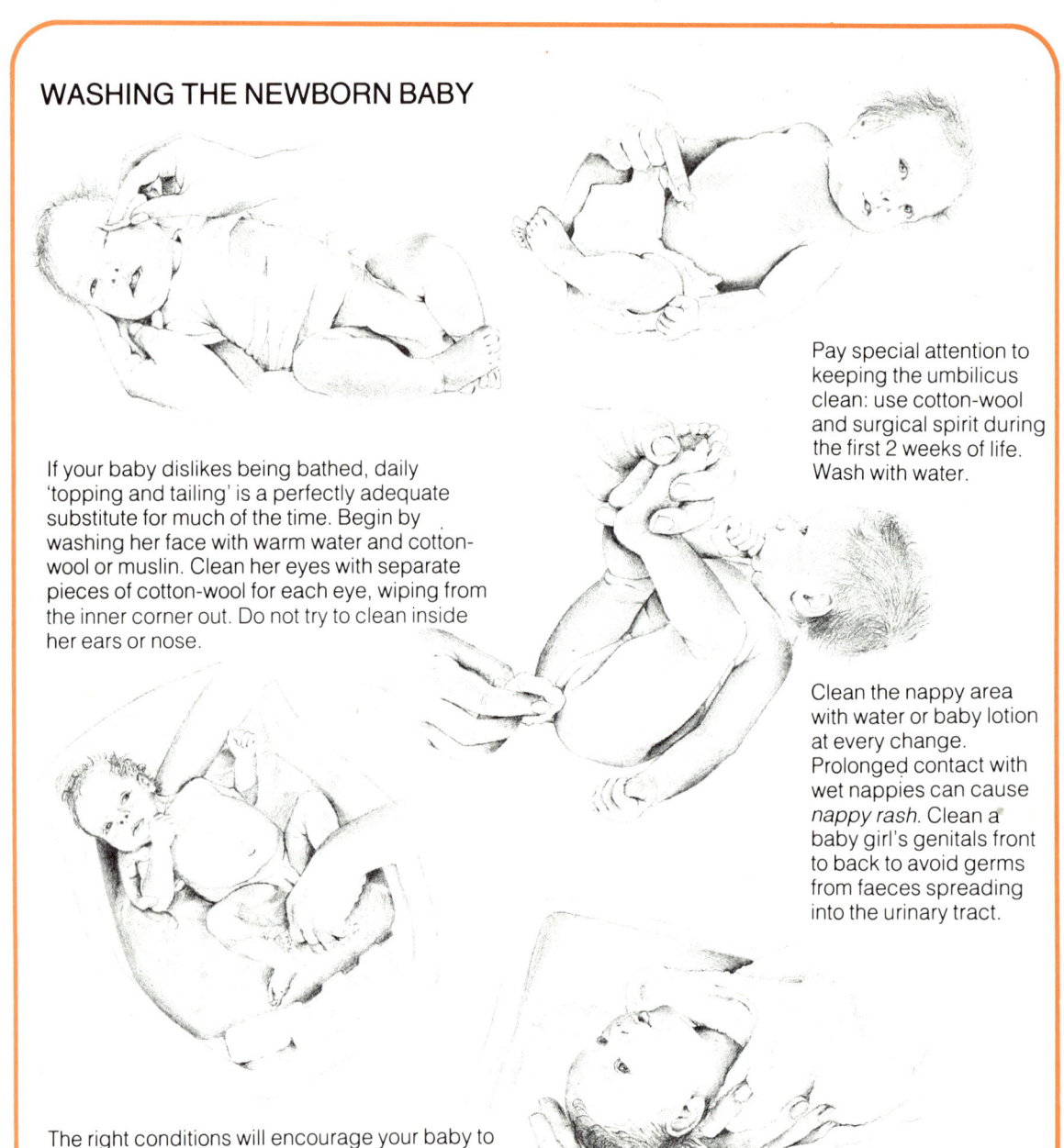

If your baby dislikes being bathed, daily 'topping and tailing' is a perfectly adequate substitute for much of the time. Begin by washing her face with warm water and cotton-wool or muslin. Clean her eyes with separate pieces of cotton-wool for each eye, wiping from the inner corner out. Do not try to clean inside her ears or nose.

Pay special attention to keeping the umbilicus clean: use cotton-wool and surgical spirit during the first 2 weeks of life. Wash with water.

Clean the nappy area with water or baby lotion at every change. Prolonged contact with wet nappies can cause *nappy rash*. Clean a baby girl's genitals front to back to avoid germs from faeces spreading into the urinary tract.

The right conditions will encourage your baby to enjoy a bath. Most babies prefer a bath before feeding. A baby bath is convenient but not essential. The room should be around 18-21°C (65-70°F) and the water about 29°C (85°F). Fill the bath by putting cold water in first, then hot, and test the temperature with your elbow – it should feel warm. Never leave a baby unattended in the bath.

Wash your baby's hair about once a week with water only. Wrap her securely in a towel on your lap, and gently hold her backwards over the water. Support her head with one hand.

Older children will become increasingly responsible for their own hygiene, but at about 10 to 12 years of age they will need your support and advice as their sweat glands alter and body odour from sweating becomes evident. The use of underarm deodorants should not begin until puberty and is, in any case, largely dictated by social and cultural pressures. Vaginal deodorants should be avoided at all times as they can cause allergic inflammation of the sensitive skin lining the vagina. A girl with an offensive vaginal discharge should see her doctor.

BLADDER AND BOWEL CONTROL

In the first months of life babies pass urine at frequent intervals, with short dry periods in between. With increasing age the bladder holds a larger quantity and urine is passed at longer intervals. At about the age of 16 months children may begin to be aware of being wet and may cry to be changed. Usually between about 18 months and 2 years they begin to indicate to their parents that they are passing urine and acquire a word for it. Soon after this they recognize the sensation of having a full bladder and may call out before passing urine. This is normally the cue if you are wondering when to start toilet-training; until your child is aware of the sensation and beginning to get the feeling of control then toilet-training is doomed to failure.

TOILET-TRAINING

By about 2½ years most children are able to tell their parents by word or gesture that they need to pass urine, and are usually able to hang on for a few minutes (but not much longer!). Bowel control is often achieved a little earlier than bladder control. Different children gain bladder and bowel control at different ages, just as they begin to walk and talk over a wide range of time. Girls tend to develop control earlier than boys. When you feel it is time to encourage your child to be toilet-trained it is important to be relaxed about it. Children quickly pick up tensions, and conflict over toilet-training can be counter-productive. Giving praise and encouragement when a child uses the pot or toilet and not fussing or getting cross about accidents usually works best. Let your child run around without nappies on so that the pot can be used without hindrance – but be prepared for some puddles on the floor. The summer is a good time to start toilet-training, as your child can play outside where accidents will not matter.

At 3 years old most children are normally dry during the day, although at this age it is common for children to have accidents, especially when they are concentrating on play. They may occasionally soil their pants.

Constipation can usually be avoided by ensuring a diet with adequate fibre and fluids.

BEDWETTING

Some children become dry at night and during the day at about the same time, but dryness at night more often follows a few months after dryness during the day, usually by about 3½ to 4 years old. All the same, occasional bedwetting is a very common problem in children during the early school years. Children from families where one parent wet the bed after the age of 5, or children who have been slow in some other aspect of their development may take longer than usual to become regularly dry during the night.

A child who is normally dry may wet the bed when ill or upset. Any serious stress, such as the separation of parents or an unexpected separation of a child from his mother, during the years when a child usually becomes dry at night may result in bedwetting. This can continue for quite some time. Sympathy, and not punishment, is the most effective approach to bedwetting. If a child over the age of 5 still regularly wets the bed and does not appear to be improving, it is probably worth discussing the problem with a doctor. Similarly, you should consult a doctor if a child who has been dry at night starts bedwetting when there is no obvious physical or emotional cause.

▶ **See also** The digestive system; The kidneys, bladder and genitals

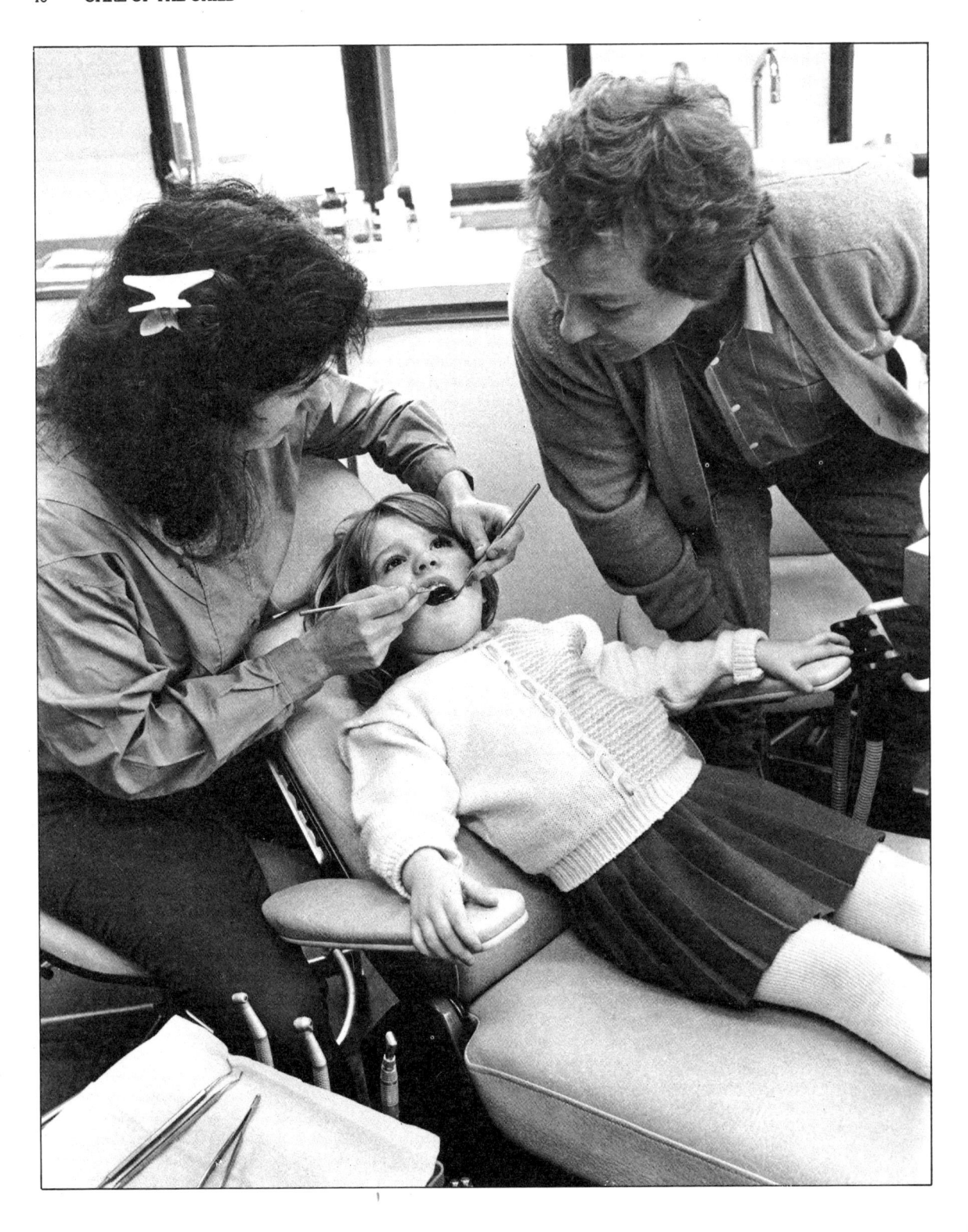

CARE OF THE CHILD

CARE OF THE TEETH

By caring for your child's teeth and gums right from the start you can do a great deal to prevent most dental disease. Restricting sugar in the diet, using fluorides, cleaning teeth and gums and visiting the dentist are all helpful measures to keep teeth and gums healthy.

The most crucial factor in causing tooth decay is eating sugary foods, since sugar gets broken down by bacteria on the tooth surface to form acids which attack the tooth enamel. Frequent sugary snacks, particularly in the form of sticky foods or sweets, can result in acid production over a long period of time (and are therefore more harmful than eating a lot of sugary food at one time).

Baby comforters such as minifeeders or bottles containing sweet drinks can contribute to tooth decay. If you discourage a 'sweet tooth' from your child's earliest days by not adding honey or sugar to feeds or giving repeated sweet drinks, he is likely to develop healthy eating habits. It is just as important for older children and teenagers to avoid frequently eating and drinking sweet things, and habits from early childhood are more influential at this age than parental nagging.

Dentists recommend cleaning children's teeth twice daily after meals, and children from around the age of 6 years can do this for themselves. It is more important to brush all accessible surfaces of the teeth systematically than to use any particular technique. From around the age of 2½ to 3 years regular visits to the dentist at 4- to 6-monthly intervals help to accustom children to having their teeth examined. When treatment becomes necessary at a later age, children are more likely to be calm and co-operative if they are familiar with the surgery.

▶ **See also** The teeth

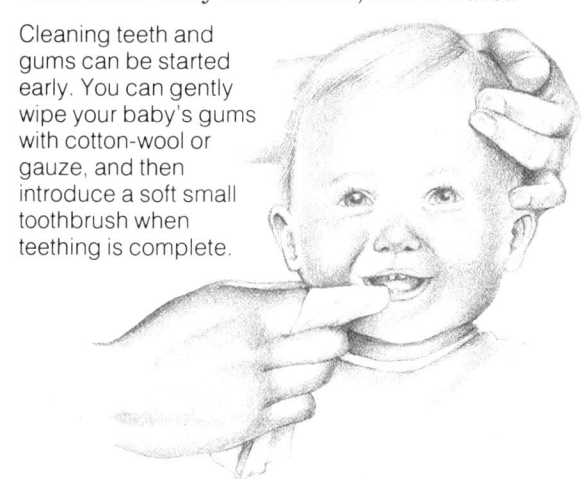

Cleaning teeth and gums can be started early. You can gently wipe your baby's gums with cotton-wool or gauze, and then introduce a soft small toothbrush when teething is complete.

Choose a dentist who is used to treating young children and will take the time to gain your child's confidence.

WARMTH AND CLOTHING

It is difficult for newborn babies especially to keep themselves warm, and so in cold weather watch the temperature carefully. The room in which a baby plays or sleeps should be kept at about 18°C (65°F). It may need additional warmth during the night and a heater with a thermostat is useful. When you go out in cold weather dress your baby warmly with a woollen hat, mittens, bootees and a jacket as well as the usual pram blankets, but remember to take the extra clothing off when you return to warm surroundings: it is as dangerous for a baby to be too hot as too cold.

In general, children's clothes should be warm in winter, cool in summer, comfortably fitting and easily washable. Clothes that are not tight-fitting are much more comfortable, and two or three loose-fitting layers in which the air can circulate are warmer in winter than one thick sweater. Heat is lost from the head, as well as from the rest of the body, so in cold weather dress children in hats or caps when they go out.

Remember that clothes are also a form of self-expression, and many children as young as 3 years have strong preferences for what they want to wear. This may be frustrating for parents, but in most cases is not worth a battle and is a sign of increasing independence of choice.

Ideally, underclothes should be changed every day. Tight nylon pants can cause chafing and sweating with resulting redness. Pants are

48 CARE OF THE CHILD

more comfortable if they are a little loose and made of cotton or with a cotton gusset. Socks, too, get sweaty and should be clean each day. Socks that are too tight can cause constriction and aggravate deformities of the toes, so it is important that they should be long enough and wide enough for your child's feet without being stretched. Remember that some socks may shrink in the wash.

SHOES

Shoes are not necessary until babies can walk unaided, and before this it is best if you leave your baby's feet as free as possible and bare when it is warm. Check frequently that the feet of all-in-one baby suits are still large enough and are not cramping your baby's toes.

The small bones of the feet are continually growing until adolescence and can easily become distorted by being squeezed into shoes that are too tight or ill-fitting. Choose shoes with laces or instep straps, as these support the heel and prevent the foot sliding down to cramp the toes. Leather shoes are preferable to those made of synthetic materials as leather allows the feet to 'breathe' more.

It is important to avoid narrow and ill-fitting styles as your children get older and begin to wear fashionable shoes: adult foot problems such as bunions, crooked toes and painful corns can often, though not always, be traced back to a lack of sensible foot care throughout childhood and adolescence.

SLEEP

Babies' sleeping patterns vary greatly and some sleep much more than others. It can take a newborn baby some time to settle down into a reasonable pattern of being awake at times in the day and sleeping for longer periods at night. The development of a diurnal rhythm – a day and night rhythm, with longer periods of sleep taken at night – occurs over the first few months, with many babies sleeping 6 to 8

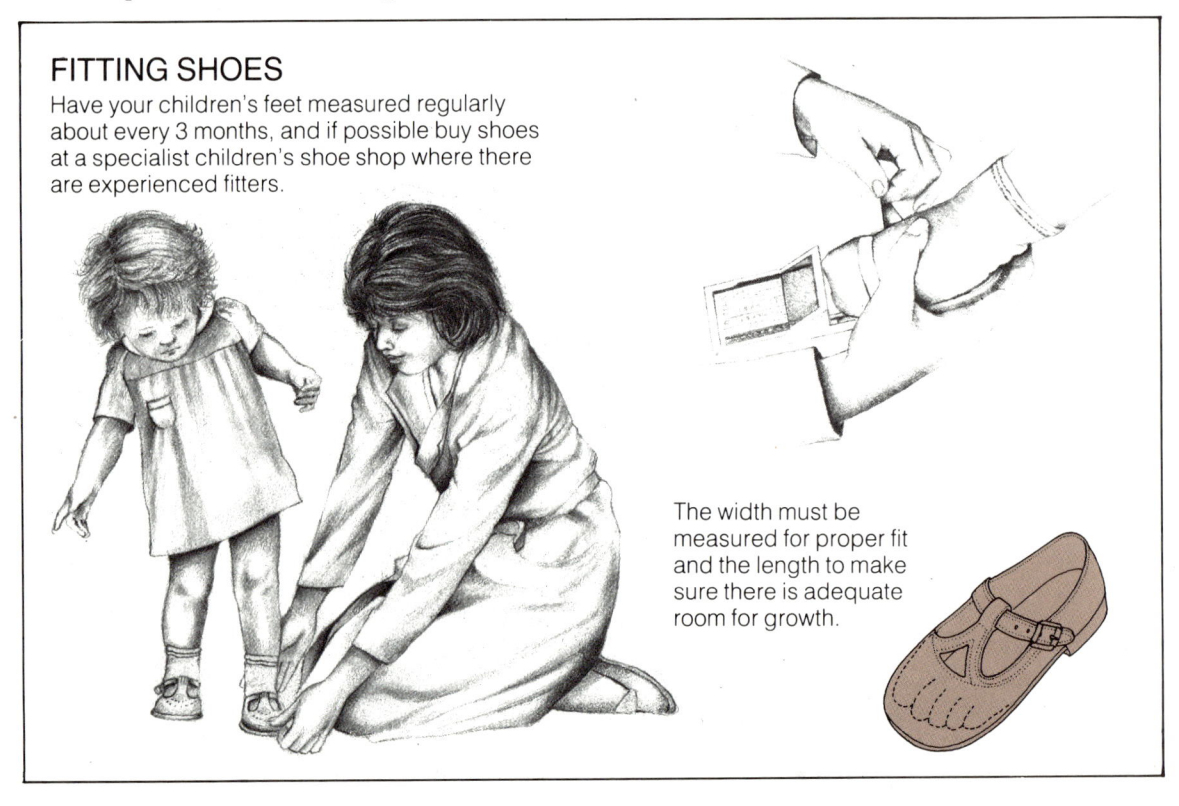

FITTING SHOES

Have your children's feet measured regularly about every 3 months, and if possible buy shoes at a specialist children's shoe shop where there are experienced fitters.

The width must be measured for proper fit and the length to make sure there is adequate room for growth.

hours at night by 3 months and the majority by 4 months. But not all babies develop this pattern by this age. Some are more lively and wakeful than others, often being more difficult to settle and less predictable.

From the first weeks of life let your baby get used to going to sleep with the activities and noises of the household in the background rather than trying to achieve complete silence. As your baby grows it helps to establish a day and night routine by making it clear that daytime is the time for activity, fun and stimulation, with the evenings being calmer and more peaceful. Often a regular bedtime routine, such as supper, bath and a story, helps a child relax at the end of the day and provides a cue to bedtime.

Children's need for sleep varies a lot from individual to individual, and very often children sleep less than their parents expect. The amount of time that babies spend asleep decreases fairly rapidly in the first few weeks of life; newborn babies spend a total of around 17 to 18 hours a day asleep, but by about 4 months the total amount of time spent asleep is, on average, 14 to 16 hours. By 12 to 18 months babies usually sleep 10 hours at night, often with day-time sleeps of 1 or 2 hours as well. Within these averages there is a lot of individual variation, both in the hours and the pattern of sleep, and many babies who are quite healthy may sleep less than this.

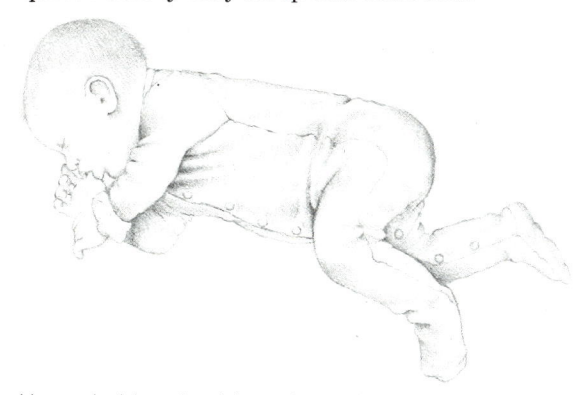

Young babies should not sleep with a pillow, as this might obstruct their breathing. A newborn baby does not move about in his sleep, but stays in whatever position you put him down. Most babies sleep comfortably on their sides.

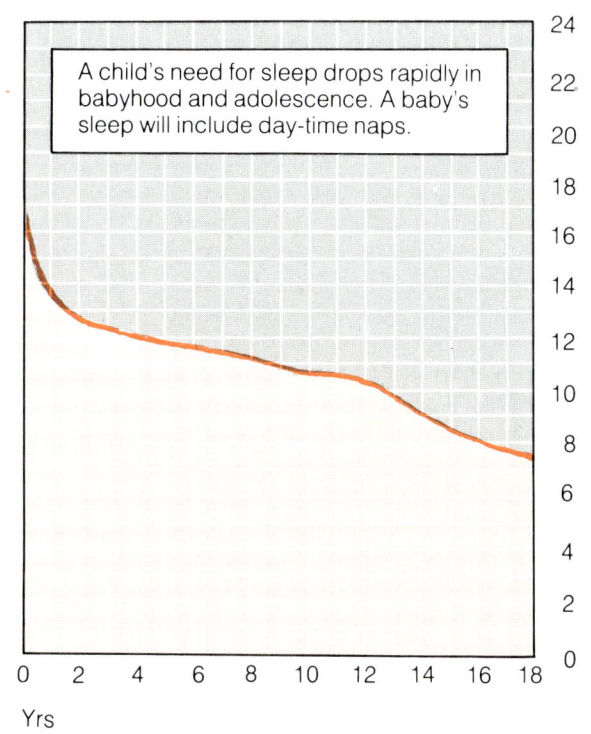

AVERAGE AMOUNTS OF SLEEP

A child's need for sleep drops rapidly in babyhood and adolescence. A baby's sleep will include day-time naps.

COMMON SLEEP PROBLEMS

In the early years of life most children have difficulties in settling to sleep in the evening and they may wake and demand attention during the night. The slightly older child may have nightmares or, less commonly, wake terrified and disoriented.

Many children develop special routines to settle to sleep. They may always need a parent with them, or may only be able to fall asleep on the sofa, and it can then be quite hard to alter these habits. Some children need comforters, such as a piece of blanket or a bottle to suck, until well into school age. There is no evidence that these are harmful and if you try to remove them your child may become quite distressed. The majority of children who need comforters give these up of their own accord by the age of 6 or 7 years, although they may continue to suck their thumbs for some years.

Difficulty in settling at night and night-waking may be symptoms of *anxiety*, for example *separation anxiety*. Children often have difficulty expressing the cause of their anxiety, but if you can get to the root of it you may be able to assure them that all is well and go some way towards solving their sleep problems.

Other factors that can contribute to the development of sleep problems are illness and major changes in routine. Fear of the dark may contribute to waking, in which case it is sensible to provide a night-light for your child, and the problem will be solved.

Ways of coping with sleep problems vary from family to family and if you are happy with your way of coping, which may mean having your child in bed with you every night, then that is the right thing for you: do not be deterred by anyone else's advice suggesting a different strategy. Try to be consistent in your management of sleep problems and, if two parents are involved, agree between you how you are going to cope with a child who wakes or is difficult to settle at night. Children left to cry for a long time on some occasions but taken into their parents' bed on others will be getting conflicting messages, and this will not help solve the problem. Do not hesitate to discuss a sleep problem with your doctor if you feel exhausted or fraught about it.

▶ **See also** Behaviour and development

PLAY AND ACTIVITY

Play and activity are essential ingredients in a child's life and important in normal development. Parents usually play with their babies instinctively right from the start. The functions of play are many: not only is it a way of releasing tension and encouraging relaxation but also from very early on it encourages the development of physical and social skills.

A young baby reaching out to swipe at a hanging toy is learning to co-ordinate hand and eye and to control body movement, as well as developing his visual and tactile senses. Play is also important in language development, and for the emergence of creativity. Children begin to socialize as they grow and play with others. It is through play that concepts of co-operation and competition are eventually learnt.

Organized games and sports at school have been shown to improve concentration on lessons and deskwork.

▶ **See also** Early growth and development

STRESS AND RELAXATION

Stress is a major factor in most people's lives and can contribute to illness and disability. In older people, stress can increase the heart rate, raise the blood pressure, cause digestive disorders (such as *colitis* and *ulcers*) and increase muscle tension, resulting in headache and backache. It also increases the body's susceptibility to infection.

Stress affects children as much as adults, and even small babies will rapidly pick up tensions. They recognize the quality of touch or handling, and will respond to tense and hostile feelings with restlessness and irritability. Tension and stress in children may be expressed in behaviour such as nail-biting, hair-twiddling, plucking at clothes, fidgeting, anxious expression and facial *tics*. Some children may react with disruptive or withdrawn behaviour or *bedwetting*.

Children can be helped to relax at all ages. Apart from plenty of play activities, physical contact is important: cuddling and stroking will calm a tense, upset child. A bedtime routine usually diffuses tensions at the end of the day: a warm bath, warm drink, bedtime story and cuddle are comforting for children of all ages. Physical activities such as running and swimming are relaxing and can involve the whole family. Moving and dancing to music is another good way to encourage relaxation.

Studying and examinations introduce new stresses and tensions. Older schoolchildren and students have to spend long hours at their desks, often under pressure. A few practical details, such as a comfortable chair, a desk at the right height and adequate lighting, can reduce the chance of back- and neck-ache. Regular exercise is a good investment of time:

Children need a balance between indoor play, which may involve considerable concentration and good hand-eye co-ordination, and outdoor play, which tends to use up energy and develop whole-body co-ordination.

it aids concentration so that the hours spent studying are more productive. Regular, balanced meals are also important.

During periods of intense study, before examinations for example, muscle *relaxation techniques* are very helpful. They can be learnt from a physiotherapist if there are no facilities at your child's school or college. They can be adopted at intervals as your child sits at his desk. Deep-breathing techniques can also be learnt and used to calm nervousness immediately before examinations or other tense situations such as job interviews.

▶**See also** Behaviour and development; Appendix: Support groups and publications

SAFETY

More children are killed by accidents than by illness, and road accidents are responsible for most deaths, with the child as a pedestrian, passenger or cyclist.

In general, children up to 5 years old have accidents in the home, with burns, falls and poisonings making up a large proportion. After the age of 5, more accidents occur outside the home, with falls and sports injuries making up the majority, aside from road accidents. Boys are up to 10 times more likely than girls to have accidents, and almost twice as many boys as girls have fatal accidents.

Cycling proficiency tests are designed to encourage good cycling habits. They are a good way of satisfying a child's enthusiasm for cycling while developing his skills.

Most accidents can be prevented and in the short term you are the one best placed to protect your child. It is not easy to remember all the dangers a child might encounter, and the emphasis in this section is on those which you can permanently remove or reduce by carrying out a single action, such as buying a child-seat for the car or fitting a lock to the medicine cabinet.

If you take safety precautions yourself, particularly in the house, your children learn that you attach importance to safety. This influences their own attitudes to safety – now and also in adult life, in the protection they will give their own children.

In this section common dangers are emphasized, as are rare ones that have serious consequences. However, these warnings should not make you too worried about the possibility of accidents. A great difficulty for parents is to know when they are over-protecting their children. Youngsters need a certain degree of freedom, to learn from the experience of taking risks and so develop their own ways of safe living. The time to 'let your child go' will vary with his age and personality, and with the particular danger. But, for each danger think of the sequence: protect, teach, release.

For example, a child should not be allowed onto stairs until he is 10 to 12 months old. Some months then follow when the child should always be accompanied and held or helped up and down the stairs. Then, at about 18 months (the precise age will vary according to the skill and agility of the child), he has to be allowed to manage the stairs alone. The same sequence, with differing time scales, can later be applied when the child learns to cross a road or ride a bicycle.

The sick child at home tells you how to assess the harm done as the result of accidents, and what first-aid you should administer. **Accident and injury** describes the treatment given in hospital. First-aid for serious accidents is outlined in the appendix on **Emergency actions**.

ON THE ROAD

THE PEDESTRIAN
Check pram brakes regularly so that the pram left on a slope does not roll onto the road. Children in prams or pushchairs are vulnerable because you may inadvertently push them beyond a parked car before any oncoming traffic is visible. Check pram and pushchair brakes regularly. Toddlers should have reins; they are impulsive and may suddenly dash across a road. If your front door leads onto a road, make sure that it is self-closing and self-locking.

Crossing the road is a complex skill: children up to 5 years of age should not be allowed to cross roads by themselves. Between 5 and 7 years children can be instructed on quiet roads. Between 7 and 9 they should have achieved competence on quiet roads. Remember that small children will not be able to see over the brow of a hill, and that children with hearing or sight problems are at greater risk.

1 Straps in pushchair
2 Toddler on reins
3 Keep pushchair on kerb until road is clear
4 Older child holds pushchair
5 Self-locking gate

THE CYCLIST
In principle riding a bicycle is fairly safe. Children may be encouraged to ride in parks, gardens and safe-play areas from the age at which they can balance. The main danger is riding on a road. Your first responsibility is to make sure the bicycle is safe and well maintained. Your second responsibility is to make sure your child is a safe rider. On quiet roads you can supervise him to make sure that he can steer, look round and do hand signals without wobbling. A child of 7 may be able to do this but it will be some years before he can manage busier roads.

1 Safety helmet
2 Bright clothing
3 Lights working
4 Reflectors
5 Brakes working
6 Saddle correct height

IN THE CAR
A baby should travel in a carrycot that is strapped onto the back seat of the car; he should never be carried in an adult's arms, because he acts as a cushion for the adult's weight in a collision. Once he is able to sit up, a child should travel belted into a child-seat. When bigger, the child can have a child-harness, perhaps with a booster seat fitted. By the age of 10 most children are big enough to fit into adult safety belts, but until then they should never travel in the front seat of a car. Fit child-proof locks to car doors so that children cannot open them while the car is moving.

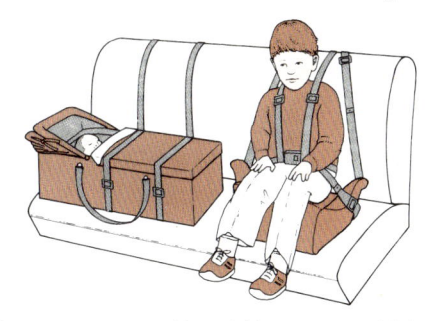

1 Carrycot strapped in   2 Harness on child-seat

IN THE HOME

FALLS

Falls indoors are extremely common. Most are minor but some produce skull or limb fractures, or even kill. Never leave a baby in a bouncing cradle or chair on a table, or he may bounce off the edge. Once a baby is crawling, use a stair-gate to seal off the stairs. Ideally you should have self-closing stair-gates at the top and bottom of the stairs, but one adjustable stair-gate can be moved to the top or the bottom as necessary. Make sure children cannot climb on banisters by boarding over or replacing horizontal rails. Any landing above a stairwell should be fenced off by boarding, or by a balustrade with uprights close enough together to keep a small child from squeezing through.

Windows should have safety locks fitted; if they can be opened, the gap should be too small for a child to fall through.

BURNS AND SCALDS

Burns and scalds are the commonest home accidents and usually the most serious. To avoid them you can take some important safety measures. Every open fire should have a fire-guard, which should be kept in place until children are about 5 years old. Do not leave toddlers in the same room as naked flames, even if these are protected by a fire-guard.

By fitting a cooker-guard and ensuring saucepan handles do not project beyond the edge of the cooker you can prevent a saucepan sliding or being pulled over. If you use a tablecloth in the kitchen, choose a plastic one and pin it to the table so that it cannot be pulled off, bringing hot liquids with it.

Make it a rule never to have hot drinks when holding a baby or toddler as these may spill and cause a tragic accident. Ask friends and relatives to observe this rule as well.

The hanging flex from an electric kettle can easily be pulled by a child, bringing boiling water down on himself. The flex should be securely fixed to the wall, with only a short length left free. Similar warnings apply to irons, which like kettles can still burn many minutes after being switched off.

Domestic fires are rare but often fatal. Cigarette butts are a common cause. Fit smoke alarms to give early warning of fire – and keep matches well out of the reach and sight of children.

LOW-LEVEL GLASS

Low-level glass panels in interior doors or partitions are a great danger. People of all ages can trip or be pushed into the glass, with the risk of severe bleeding or permanently damaged nerves and muscles.

If you do not need the extra light then board up the panel or replace the door. If you really do need the light, the glass can be replaced by laminated, toughened or wire-net glass. Alternatively, you can fit acrylic panels, but a cheaper system is to apply a special transparent safety film to the existing glass.

LIVING-AREA SAFETY

1 Stair-gate
2 Unused sockets covered with blank plugs
3 Fire-guard
4 Hooks fixing fire-guard to wall
5 Cigarettes, matches and ashtray out of reach

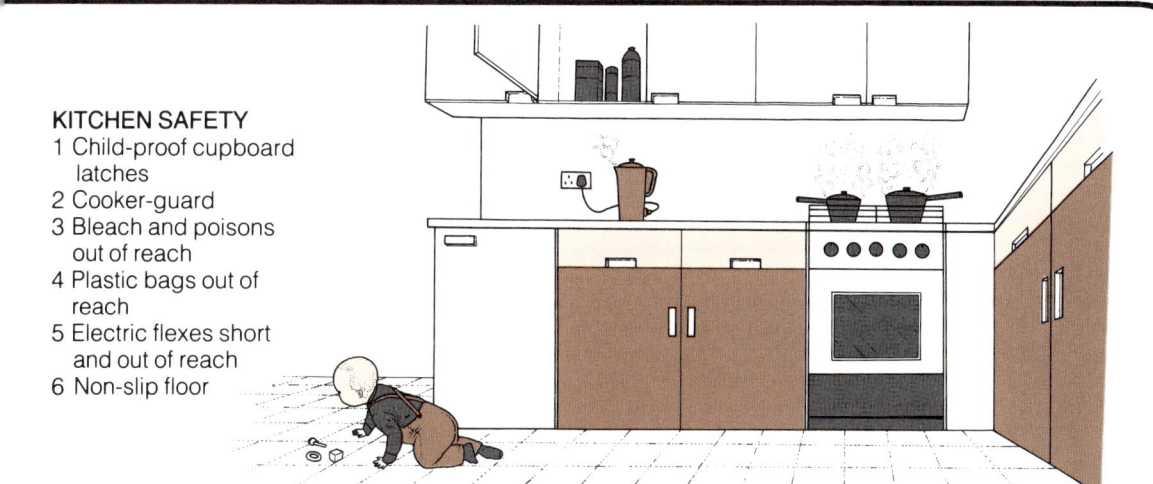

SAFETY

KITCHEN SAFETY
1 Child-proof cupboard latches
2 Cooker-guard
3 Bleach and poisons out of reach
4 Plastic bags out of reach
5 Electric flexes short and out of reach
6 Non-slip floor

ELECTRICITY
Mains electricity is a danger that young children cannot understand. Their curiosity can result in electric shock – or death in seconds. Make sure no electrical appliances or sockets have bare or broken wires, and that all plugs are wired correctly and earthed where necessary. Mains appliances should never be used in the bathroom or near water. Unused sockets are best protected from inquisitive fingers by 'blank' plastic plugs that cost very little.

BATH-TIME
A baby risks drowning even in very shallow water; until a child is at least 3½ or 4 years old never leave him alone in the bath, even for a moment. If the telephone or doorbell rings ignore it or take your baby with you, even if he starts to cry.

SUFFOCATION
Plastic bags can cause suffocation. Colourful plastic bags make tempting hats and helmets for young children, but if they slip they can stop a child breathing and muffle cries for help. Make it a rule that they are either disposed of when brought into the house or put somewhere safe, out of a child's reach.

POISONING
Babies automatically put things in their mouths, as a way of finding out more about them. Toddlers and children may eat or drink something simply out of curiosity or because they mistake it for a sweet. Poisoning can be fatal: even a few adult tablets of paracetamol, aspirin or a tranquillizer can be life-threatening for a baby or toddler. You should throw away old or unwanted tablets and medicines, and ask for new medicines to be supplied in child-resistant containers. All medicines and tablets should be put in a cupboard or drawer that is both out of reach of children and kept locked.

Domestic fluids and powders for washing, cleaning, disinfecting and polishing are highly dangerous. So are chemicals and DIY materials such as turpentine, paint-stripper, weed-killer and caustic soda. Store these items in cupboards with secure child-proof latches, out of a child's reach and tell your child they are dangerous. Label all containers clearly: never use milk or lemonade bottles.

Accidental poisoning is more difficult to prevent when your children visit other people's homes. Ask relatives and friends to use child-proof containers and lock away any poisons.

If you are not sure whether your child has swallowed a poisonous substance it is better to assume that he has.

PETS
Children can gain a great deal from looking after pets - but pets do have their health risks. *Ringworm*, *fleas*, toxocara (a worm) and several other conditions can be caught by handling pets too intimately. A child should not share food with a pet, or kiss it, or dabble in its food, bedding or toilet tray.

OUT OF DOORS

CLIMBING
Falls from trees, walls and other high places can cause *head injuries* and *broken bones*. Children enjoy climbing and will probably do it – whether they are on their own or not, and whether their parents want them to or not. Therefore parents should not discourage climbing, but should supervise it until the child gains confidence and dexterity. The 'training' can begin in your garden on a climbing frame or in a playground where the surface is safe. As your child gets older, if you ask him not to climb on roofs or certain structures in your neighbourhood then he may accept this advice more easily knowing that you permit other types of climbing.

POISONOUS PLANTS
Few children are able to distinguish safe fungi, leaves, berries and other plant products from dangerous ones. Combined with the toddlers' enjoyment of putting things in their mouths, this makes poisoning common. Daffodil bulbs, holly berries, laburnum seeds, laurel, lupin, rhododendron, rhubarb leaves and yew berries are just some of the items that may make a child ill, requiring hospital treatment. Parents should instruct their young children never to eat berries, nuts, leaves (or, indeed, any other foods) unless these have been approved by a knowledgeable adult. Fortunately with prompt treatment fatalities from such poisoning are very rare, and most children recover completely.

PLAYGROUNDS AND FUNFAIRS
Playgrounds offer the opportunity for excitement on climbing frames, swings, slides, see-saws and roundabouts. The equipment should be on grass or a soft artificial surface. Most playground equipment is suitable for supervised children under 5 years old, but a roundabout is an exception because its movement is determined by all the children on it, not just your child. If it revolves too fast, a smaller child can be thrown off and badly injured as the roundabout continues to rotate. Swings should be well distanced from other equipment and you should warn your child not to run near them.

Small merry-go-rounds designed specifically for young children are usually safe. Remember that the more exciting funfair equipment is designed to be frightening and participants need muscular control to stop themselves being thrown around. Such equipment is therefore unsuitable until children are at least 5 years old.

GARDEN SAFETY
1 Climbing frame to practise climbing skills
2 Adult to supervise
3 Fence, hedge or wall
4 No poisonous plants
5 Pond covered over
6 Lockable tool-shed

WATER

Children suffer brain damage or die through drowning. Toddlers can drown in very shallow pools of water, so while your children are small, garden pools and ponds should be drained or covered with strong mesh or securely fenced. Children in a temporary paddling pool should be supervised.

Youngsters risk drowning when they are playing and exploring. Falling into a canal, river, pond or even boating lake in a park can kill a child in a minute if he cannot swim, and if good swimmers are not present. It is therefore most important for your child's enjoyment and safety to encourage him to learn to swim.

ICE

When roads are icy, every aspect of road safety becomes especially important. As a pedestrian, remember that cars may not be able to brake normally. Make sure that your child's outdoor shoes have non-slip soles.

Teach your child never to walk or skate on an ice-covered pond or river, unless the ice has been tested and declared safe.

SPORTS

Sports involve a balance between excitement and safety that children should be aware of. Risks are taken in football, hockey and many other common school sports, but children may also want to do bicycle stunt-riding, junior motorbiking, horse-riding or boxing. All these carry dangers for a child, partly because of the intrinsic risk but also because a child has less well-developed judgement and co-ordination than an adult. For all these activities safety equipment should be worn, children should be supervised by instructors and the element of competition should be discouraged.

STRANGERS

The balance you strike between care and over-protection determines how your child reacts to strangers. Children do face a small risk of being physically or sexually abused by strangers, but the size of the risk of abuse is often exaggerated by newspaper reports of rare but horrifying incidents. A child whose parents convey distrust of all strangers may grow up unnecessarily timid.

Up to the age of 6 or 7 years children should not be allowed to play alone in public places. Between 7 and 11 parents should explain the possible dangers; children can be allowed to talk to strangers, but they should be told never to accept sweets or presents, never to go off with a stranger, and never to get into a stranger's car.

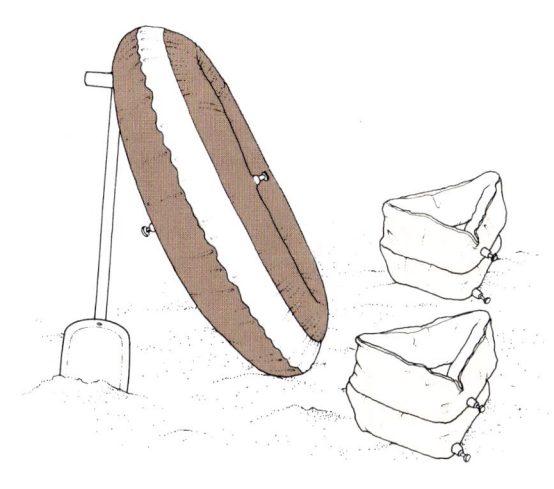

ANIMALS

You may also have to protect your child from other people's pets. Stop him approaching a dog or cat unless you know it will not bite or scratch. Particularly in urban areas, dog dirt can be a real hazard. If your child gets dog dirt on his skin or clothing, wash it off immediately.

FIREWORKS

If children are allowed close to fireworks, even though they do not light them, they may be in danger. Burns may happen if children peer to see if a firework is alight, or hold one in their hands which suddenly goes off. If you arrange a fireworks party, make sure adults light all the fireworks – or let your children enjoy them at a community display.

WATER SAFETY
1 Arm-bands with double air-chambers
2 Swimming ring with double air-chambers

HOLIDAY AND TRAVEL

TRAVELLING
Many children are miserable if they have to endure more than an hour or so in a car, bus or coach. If you are making a long car journey, you can have a brief stop every hour. Choose a place where children can run about safely and where you can easily keep an eye on them. Lay-bys on busy roads are dangerous for stops and picnics.

Travel games may keep children occupied, but avoid games that involve too much reading or writing since these may bring on *travel sickness*.

SUN
Sunburn and *sunstroke* do not come on for some hours after exposure. Protective suncreams can help against sunburn, but must be put on before going out into the sun if they are to be effective. Buy sunscreeen creams rather than suntan lotions for maximum protection. At the start of a holiday children should be encouraged to wear sun-hats, and shirts to cover their shoulders.

If children play in bright sun for more than an hour at a time, there is a risk of sunstroke. For the rest of the day they should play in the shade. The sun is also dangerous for babies left in prams or stationary cars, when overheating can make them seriously ill.

BEACHES AND BOATS
Apart from the general dangers of water, the seaside may present additional hazards in the tides and the strong currents that can quickly carry a child out of his depth. Children should not be allowed out of sight of an adult nor allowed to play unsupervised with floating airbeds because these can drift or be blown out to sea. Remember that swimming on a full stomach can cause *cramp*. Allow time for your child's stomach to empty after a meal for about 1½ hours before he swims.

Families who sail regularly should know all about boating safety and the need for life-jackets. Every person in any boat should have a life-jacket and wear it all the time. Courses on sailing are available for children; every child in the boat should also be able to swim.

A sun-umbrella is useful for protecting children's skin on hot days. It allows them to play out in the open air without risking sunburn and sunstroke.

Instruction in water-safety and handling a boat helps to make a child confident and competent on the water.

FARMS AND FARM ANIMALS
Children should not be allowed near farm machinery unless supervised. Protective shields and guards are often absent or in poor repair, so severe cuts or crushing can occur. Tractors and trailers may look fun but they are high, unsteady

and noisy, and when they start off a child who is clinging on can be thrown to the ground and injured.

Farm dogs may be less friendly than town dogs, while ducks, hens and geese can peck a child who approaches them. Urge caution with all unfamiliar animals until they have proved themselves friendly. In countries where *rabies* is endemic you will need to be particularly careful.

DISEASE AND ILLNESS

Most Westerners do not need additional immunization for travelling in Europe or North America. For other countries it may be necessary to have *typhoid*, *cholera* or yellow fever immunizations. These immunizations are not encouraged for children under 1 year old but may be justified if you are moving abroad. Your family doctor should have information on the current regulations for travel immunization and will know whether they conflict with the standard immunization programme.

If you are travelling to an area where *malaria* occurs, your children should take preventive tablets. In some parts of the world you should be careful of the food your family eats and avoid drinking water unless it is bottled or pre-boiled. Your doctor should be able to advise you.

A DISEASE CHECKLIST

DISEASE	REGION, OR RISK FACTOR	SOURCE OF INFECTION	PRECAUTIONS
CHOLERA	Africa, Asia, Middle East	Contaminated food* or water	Vaccination. Booster every 6 months
INFECTIOUS HEPATITIS	Where sanitation is primitive	Contaminated food*, water, or contact with infected person	Advice from your doctor
MALARIA	Africa, Asia, Latin America	Bite from infected mosquito	Tablets (taken before, during and after visit)
POLIO	Worldwide except for developed nations	Contact with infected person, contaminated food* and water	Oral drops, advice from your doctor
RABIES	Most parts of the world	Bite from infected animal	Advice from your doctor
TETANUS	Areas with poor medical facilities	Contaminated open wound	Advice from your doctor
TYPHOID	Worldwide except for developed nations	Contaminated food*, water or milk	Vaccination. Booster after 3 years
YELLOW FEVER	Africa, Latin America	Bite from infected mosquito	Vaccination. Booster after 10 years

*Avoid uncooked food and cold or re-heated food. In particular: salad, unpeeled fruit, raw shellfish, dairy products, ice cubes

EARLY GROWTH AND DEVELOPMENT

Childhood development always follows the same recognizable pattern. Some stages seem to be essential: all children learn to sit unsupported before they learn to walk. Others are non-essential: a few children learn to walk without ever having crawled. Children all develop at different rates, and the age at which they pass the milestones of development varies widely from one child to another. There are racial differences too. Black babies usually have greater muscular control at birth than white babies, and their physical development remains ahead throughout the first year of life.

Babies sometimes seem to concentrate on mastering one activity before moving on to the next. In fact, the different areas of skill are all interdependent, although they are treated as separate topics in this chapter. Development is not always smooth, and the changes sometimes seem fast and obvious, at other times slow and hard to see. However, overall children are continually acquiring new skills.

Some skills are learned most easily at a particular stage of development and some cannot then be learned at a later date. For example, it is only during the first 6 months of life that the brain can learn to interpret visual stimuli in the normal way. A child who is born with cataracts (which cause opacity of the lens of the eye) which are not removed before the age of 6 months will always be visually impaired, even though there is no physical reason why vision should not be normal. There is a critical stage for learning language, too. Children who are deaf during the first few years of life may never learn to speak properly, even if their hearing returns at some later age.

More controversially, some people believe that there are similar critical periods for learning emotional skills. For example, in some cases it may be true that a child deprived of emotional closeness will have more difficulty in forming close friendships and sexual relationships as an adult.

DEVELOPMENTAL CHECKS

Medical surveillance of children's development includes regular developmental checks by the family doctor or clinic doctor and health visitor, usually at 6 weeks, 7 to 8 months, 18 months, 2 ½ years and before starting school. The term 'developmental checks' makes many parents believe that their child is being tested in some way. But these checks are not examinations to be passed or failed: they are opportunities to discuss any worries that you may have about your child's development and to check that your child has acquired the skills that most children of a similar age have acquired. In addition, your child's sight and hearing will be assessed so that minor impairments and problems are diagnosed and corrected as early as possible.

The doctor or nurse will ask your child to perform a range of activities. These are chosen to demonstrate abilities and reveal disabilities in general physical development, manual dexterity, hand-eye co-ordination, vision, hearing and speech.

These activities will usually include some that most children of that age would not be expected to manage, so do not expect your child to be able to do everything that is asked. Some skills are also very much influenced by experience. A child's ability to manage buttons, for example, depends partly on manual dexterity, but also on whether the child normally wears clothes with buttons, or is more used to zips or Velcro fastenings. If your child does not manage a specific task that you know he does perfectly well at home, you should tell the doctor.

The chart overleaf gives you some idea of the average age range during which new developmental skills are acquired. Growth can be plotted on highly accurate charts, but development, which represents an increase in the complexity of a child's skills, cannot be measured with anything like the same precision. The chart gives only a rough guide: provided your child is alert and happy there is no need to worry if his progress in some areas seems a little slow.

TOILET-TRAINING

Most children begin to control their bowels and bladders from the age of 2 years. **Day-to-day care** discusses these developments.

PHYSICAL SKILLS

The ability to walk and run independently requires normal muscles, bones and joints, and a normal brain and nervous system. Disease of any of these systems can lead to late development of such skills. The acquisition of motor skills is not related to intelligence: if your child walks later than another, he will not necessarily be slower mentally.

Most newborn babies find it difficult to lift their heads. By 3 months the neck muscles have grown strong enough for them to lift their heads right up while lying on their backs. However, they will still need some head support in a sitting position until they are about 5 months old. Between 5 and 8 months most babies learn to sit without support, and most are making vigorous efforts to crawl by 8 months, often beginning by propelling themselves backwards in stunned surprise before mastering a real forward crawl at around 10 months. Some children walk without ever going through the crawling stage, others learn to shuffle around on their bottoms before starting to walk. Bottom-shuffling seems to be a family characteristic and is more common in boys. However, it may also be due to weakness of the muscles themselves in *hypotonia*. By about 6 to 10 months most children can pull themselves into a standing position and between 8 and 13 months learn to cruise or step sideways holding on to furniture.

If your child is not walking by 18 months you should consult your family doctor.

Between 3 and 5 years a child can usually balance sufficiently well to hop on one foot and skip as for hopscotch. Skipping with a rope is a far more difficult skill and is not usually achieved until 8 years. In a vehicle with pedals a 2-year-old child usually scoots along, pushing himself by foot. At some time between 21 months and 3 years he begins to pedal. Most 6-year-olds can bicycle without stabilizers.

▶**See also** The bones and joints; The brain, nerves and muscles; Appendix: Screening programme

DEXTERITY

Children need to learn to dress and undress, to eat in a socially acceptable manner, to use tools and instruments and eventually to write. All this depends on the acquisition of manual dexterity, and on the ability to co-ordinate their hand movements with what they see. Between 6 weeks and 3 months babies learn to bring their hands together and, having 'found' their hands, they usually begin to play with them at around 3 months. At this age babies learn through all their senses, and will see, touch, suck and listen to their hands as they will with any new objects presented to them.

LEFT-HANDEDNESS
○ Until they are about 2 years old most children are ambidextrous; at some point in their third year a preference for one hand emerges
○ Left-handedness may be inherited
○ More boys than girls are left-handed
○ There is no evidence that a left-handed child has more problems than a right-handed child
○ Pressure on a left-handed child to use his right hand may cause stuttering. Otherwise, left-handed children are no more likely to stutter than right-handed ones
○ If your child clearly prefers to use his left hand, do not encourage him to use his right hand
○ If your child is truly ambidextrous you may wish to encourage him to use his right hand

CARE OF THE CHILD

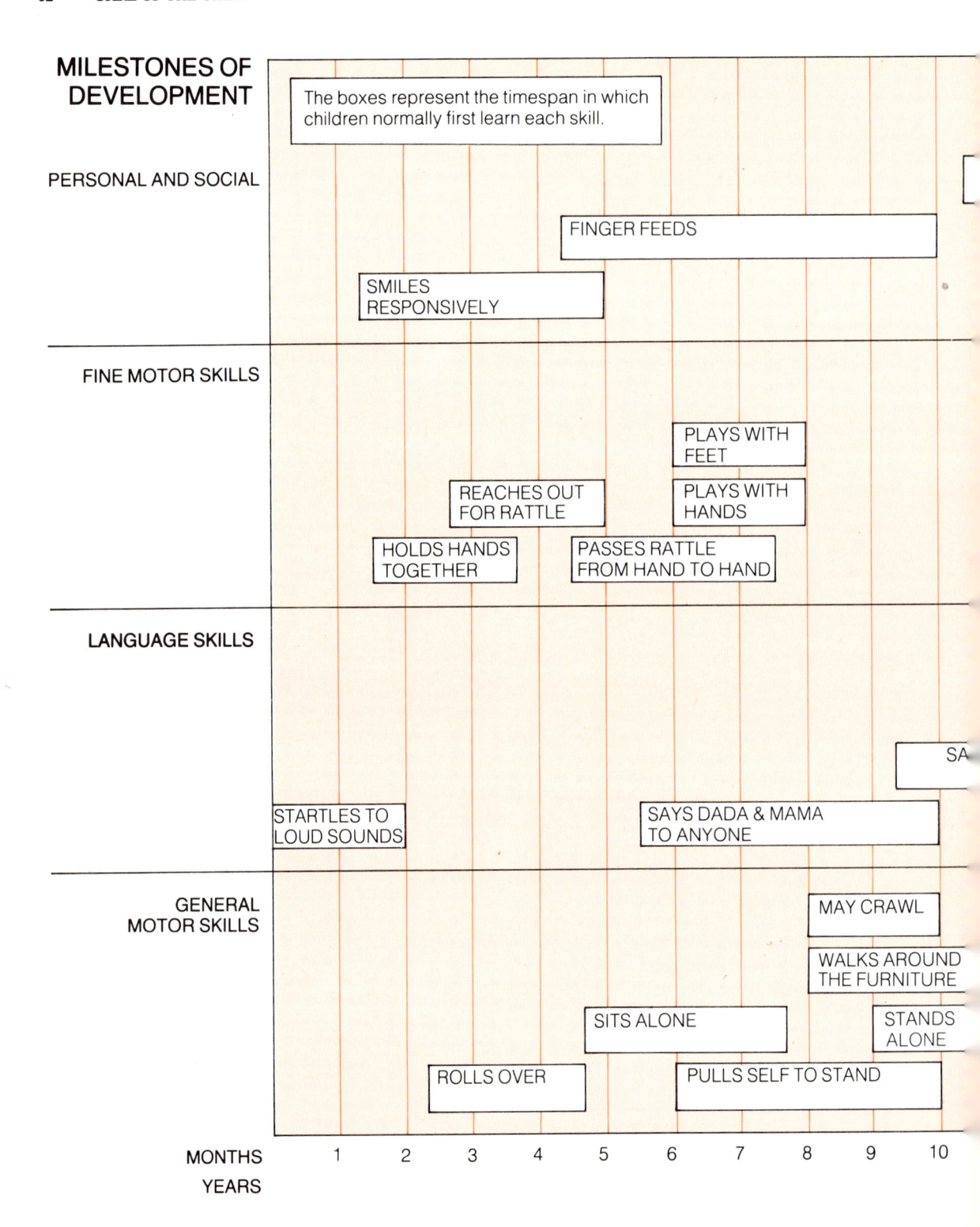

MILESTONES OF DEVELOPMENT

The boxes represent the timespan in which children normally first learn each skill.

PERSONAL AND SOCIAL

- FINGER FEEDS
- SMILES RESPONSIVELY

FINE MOTOR SKILLS

- PLAYS WITH FEET
- REACHES OUT FOR RATTLE
- PLAYS WITH HANDS
- HOLDS HANDS TOGETHER
- PASSES RATTLE FROM HAND TO HAND

LANGUAGE SKILLS

- STARTLES TO LOUD SOUNDS
- SAYS DADA & MAMA TO ANYONE
- SA...

GENERAL MOTOR SKILLS

- MAY CRAWL
- WALKS AROUND THE FURNITURE
- SITS ALONE
- STANDS ALONE
- ROLLS OVER
- PULLS SELF TO STAND

MONTHS   1   2   3   4   5   6   7   8   9   10

YEARS

EARLY GROWTH AND DEVELOPMENT

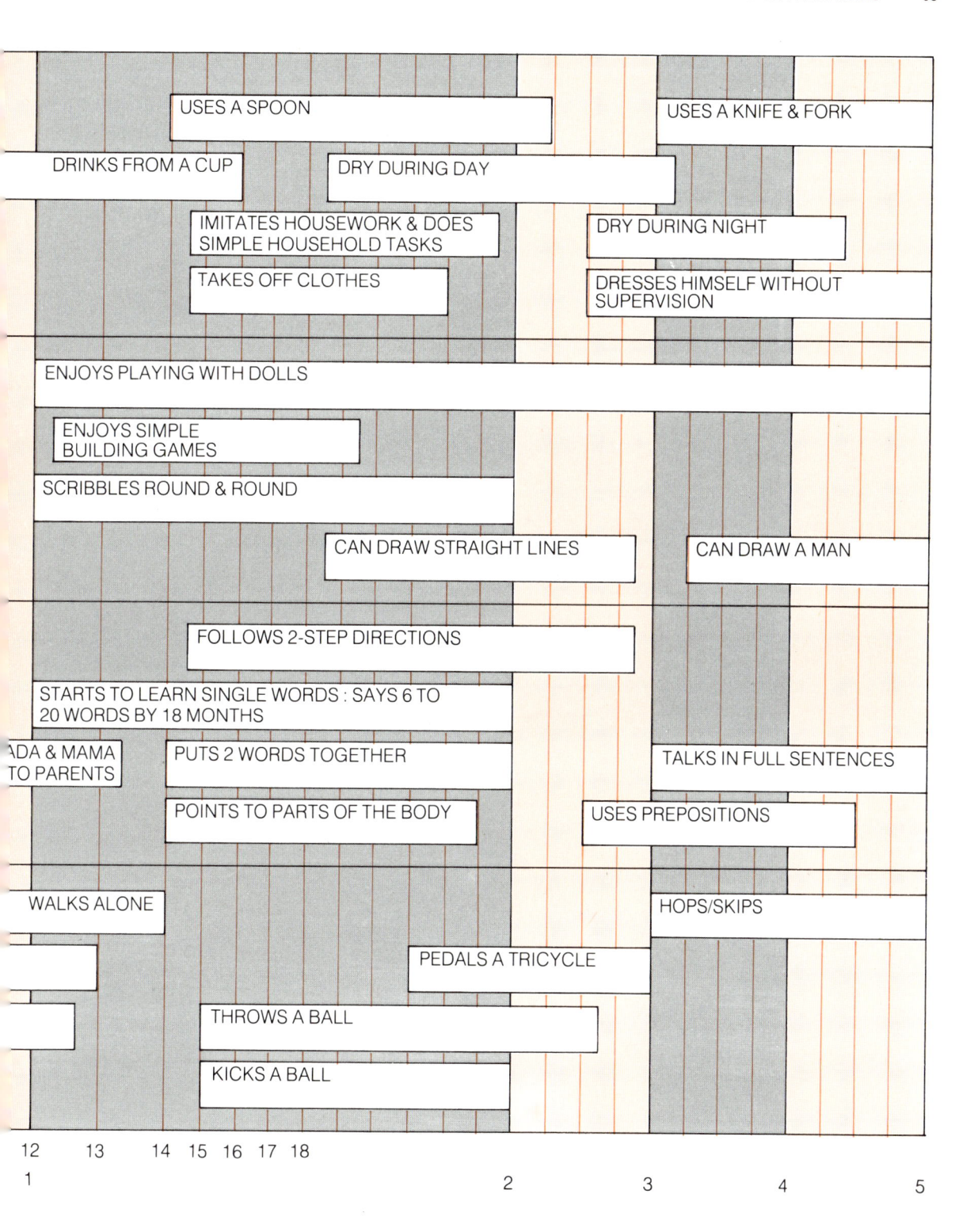

Milestone	Age Range
USES A SPOON	
USES A KNIFE & FORK	
DRINKS FROM A CUP	
DRY DURING DAY	
IMITATES HOUSEWORK & DOES SIMPLE HOUSEHOLD TASKS	
DRY DURING NIGHT	
TAKES OFF CLOTHES	
DRESSES HIMSELF WITHOUT SUPERVISION	
ENJOYS PLAYING WITH DOLLS	
ENJOYS SIMPLE BUILDING GAMES	
SCRIBBLES ROUND & ROUND	
CAN DRAW STRAIGHT LINES	
CAN DRAW A MAN	
FOLLOWS 2-STEP DIRECTIONS	
STARTS TO LEARN SINGLE WORDS : SAYS 6 TO 20 WORDS BY 18 MONTHS	
DADA & MAMA TO PARENTS	
PUTS 2 WORDS TOGETHER	
TALKS IN FULL SENTENCES	
POINTS TO PARTS OF THE BODY	
USES PREPOSITIONS	
WALKS ALONE	
HOPS/SKIPS	
PEDALS A TRICYCLE	
THROWS A BALL	
KICKS A BALL	

12 13 14 15 16 17 18
1   2   3   4   5

HANDLING AND FEEDING

A newborn baby will automatically grasp any object put into the palm of his hand. This grasp reflex fades with time and by 4 to 5 months babies can reach out for objects purposefully and voluntarily, and will explore everything they get hold of by sucking it. However, it is not until 9 or 10 months that they learn to let go of whatever they are holding. At first their grasp is clumsy, but gradually they learn to use their fingers individually and develop a precise grip using the thumb and index finger for small objects. This is particularly important when, at a year or so, they begin to take an interest in pencils and start to scribble. Next they learn to draw circles and vertical lines, and, by about the age of 4, most children can set out to draw a figure that is recognizably a person.

Feeding skills depend very much on practice. Children can feed themselves finger foods by about 10 months. Teacher-beakers or trainer cups are useful for children under 1 year old and some small babies enjoy using a straw. By 12 to 15 months most children can manage a normal cup, although some supervision may be needed to prevent spills. Most 3-year-olds can manage a spoon and fork, and most 4-year-olds can handle a knife and fork, although the knife is still mostly used to push the food rather than to cut with.

DRESSING

Many babies hate being dressed and undressed. However, by 12 months they are usually beginning to take more interest and often hold out an arm or a foot at the appropriate moment. By 14 months children enjoy being allowed to pull off socks, vests and easy garments. The ability to dress independently depends on experience, but also on the sort of clothes that a child usually wears. Clothes with Velcro fastenings and elasticated waists are far easier to deal with than those with buttons, hooks and eyes or zips. Shoes with laces defeat most children until they are at least 5 or 6 years old.

▶ **See also** The brain, nerves and muscles

GROWTH

Growth means increase in size. Different parts of the body grow at different rates. For example, a baby's brain grows very rapidly and its growth is essentially complete by 3 years of age. At birth the skull is already three-quarters of its adult size. On the other hand, growth of the sex organs is slow in early childhood but accelerates with puberty.

The long bones and spine are the major determinants of height. The rate of increase of height, or height velocity, for different ages is not even. Growth in the first years of life is very rapid; most babies double their birthweight in the first 4 months and double their length by the age of 4 years. In the first

BABIES' WEIGHT AND HEAD CIRCUMFERENCE

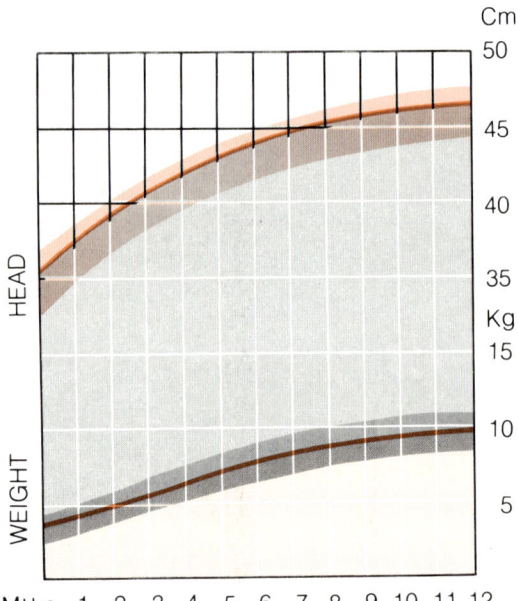

As a baby grows, his weight and head circumference should follow the curve shown on the chart. The heavy line in the centre of each band marks the median or average at any particular age. The coloured band shows the normal range: 94 per cent of babies fall within these limits. Consult your doctor if your baby's weight or head circumference falls outside the tinted band.

year, babies usually have good appetites, but their interest in food often diminishes. Food is fuel for growth, and in the same way that a car driven very fast needs more fuel, a 1-year-old child who grows 12 cm (5 in) a year needs relatively more food for his body weight than does a 6-year-old child growing 6 cm (2 ½ in) in a year.

Predicting height
You cannot make your child grow taller than he is destined to be, and this depends partly on how tall you, his parents, are. Adult size is not directly related to size at birth. However, after the first year of life it is possible to predict a child's adult height from his current height and age, using height and weight charts. This is because most children follow their own particular growth line. For example, a 2-year-old boy with a height of 86 cm (34 in) is exactly on the central or median line on the graph of the normal range of height in boys. This means that 50 per cent of other 2-year-old boys will be taller than him and 50 per cent will be smaller. At 4 years he would be expected to be about 102 cm (40 in) tall.

If at 5 years this boy was 104 cm (41 in) tall rather than the expected 108 cm (42 ½ in), he would be failing to grow as expected. In medical terms, he would be failing to thrive. Children whose height is altogether outside the normal range for their age, or whose rate of growth suddenly slows down should be seen by their family doctor.

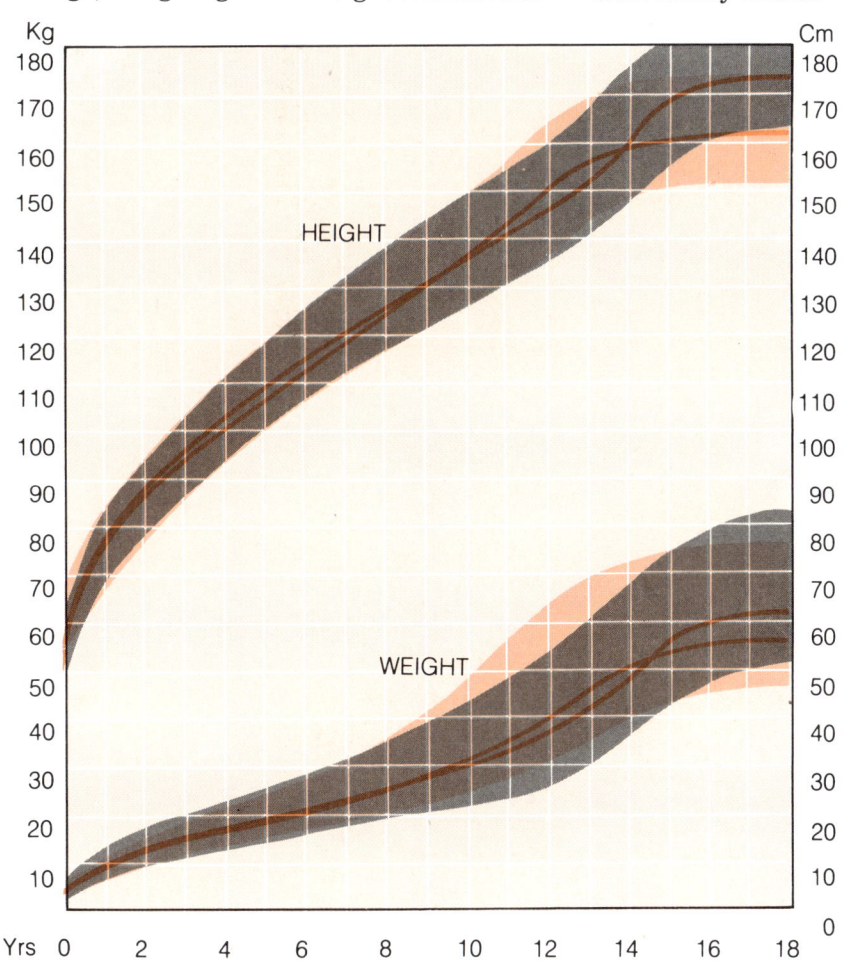

CHILDREN'S WEIGHT AND HEIGHT

The coloured band shows the range of normal height and weight: 3 per cent of children fall below and 3 per cent above each band.

An older child's height can be measured while he stands up; it may be easier to measure a young child by lying him down and stretching a tape measure from his heels to the top of his head. Weigh both babies and children before a meal or feed and without clothes.

Boys
Girls

Monitoring growth

There are many reasons for failure to thrive, and it is important to keep a regular check on your children's growth: poor growth may be the only sign that something is amiss.

Although it is easier to weigh babies than to measure their height, weight is a less reliable index of growth than height. For example, a child who has a minor illness will tend to eat less and will therefore temporarily lose weight, and a baby's weight will be affected by the timing of the last feed and by his clothing.

The weight charts can also be used to make sure that your child is not becoming too fat or too thin. Your child's positions on the coloured band on the weight and height charts should be more or less the same. A child who is at the lower end of the band on the height chart, for example, should also be on the lower end of the band on the weight chart.

Babies are regularly weighed in child health clinics. Measurement of a child's height is usually done as part of annual general health checks in child health clinics or schools. Keep a record of your child's height and age so that you have it if you move, or if the child goes to a different school. Some school health services provide special booklets in which children can keep these records. Otherwise you can easily fill in a standard height chart and this has the advantage of showing very clearly any abnormalities in your child's growth rate.

▶See also Feeding and diet; The older child and adolescent; Glandular disorders

HEARING

Adequate hearing is essential to the development of normal speech and to the child's understanding of the world around him. It is difficult to detect deafness in a child of less than 6 months because until this age even a baby who cannot hear will make a full range of normal sounds. However, methods of testing newborn babies are being evaluated.

You can check your baby's hearing at about 3 months by seeing whether, if you make a loud noise near him when he is crying, he stops and becomes still. At 4 months he should turn his head towards you if you speak quietly or shake a rattle when you are near him but out of his line of direct vision. If he seems quite unaware of the sound, mention it to your family doctor.

Your child will be routinely screened for nerve deafness at 6 to 9 months, and later in nurseries and in schools. If you have a history of deafness in the family or if you are worried that your child does not hear properly, discuss this with your health visitor or family doctor. Remember, though, that a toddler may fail to respond when you speak to him simply because he is absorbed in what he is doing.

▶See also The ears

One hearing test routinely carried out for babies involves making a sudden noise out of the baby's sight to see whether he turns to look.

VISION

Babies can see from birth, although they do not see with the same definition as adults. However, a baby's inability to understand and interpret what he sees is more important than his lack of visual discrimination. Babies begin to recognize their parents by 2 weeks of age, and it is usually this recognition that provokes the first responsive smile. Blind babies tend to smile at a later age.

A baby's vision is tested by assessing his ability to follow a moving object with his eyes. At 3 months he should be able to follow the movement of a toy held about 20 cm (8 in) away from him. An older child will be asked to match shapes or letters with those shown at a distance.

Many babies squint at birth, but any child who continues to squint, either constantly or intermittently, after 6 months or who develops a squint during early childhood should be seen by an eye specialist. If a squint is left untreated the squinting eye will forget how to see properly and may eventually become blind.

Short sight and long sight usually develop during late childhood. If either condition runs in your family, your child should have yearly checks by an optician throughout childhood.

To test her vision, your child may be asked to point to the letter that matches the one that the tester chooses.

▶ **See also** The eyes

LANGUAGE DEVELOPMENT

The essence of language is not noise but communication. Communication is possible without words: we all use facial expression and gesture to communicate. Speech is therefore an important facet of language development, but by no means the only part.

During the first 6 months of life, language development is identical in all babies, of whatever nationality. It begins with the communicative gurgling of the 6-week-old, and goes on to 'babbling' at 3 months, when the baby produces cooing open vowel sounds. Consonants develop later: 'ma' and 'da' are usually the first, though they are not used with any meaning until around the end of the first year. From 6 months onwards this babble becomes increasingly elaborate and expressive, and gradually, between the 10th and 14th month, the baby will start to use particular sounds to identify particular objects.

At this age babies understand many more words than they can say. Children of just over a year can often understand and follow simple commands, and comprehension of spoken language increases rapidly during the second year. By 18 months most children can say between 6 and 20 recognizable single words. At this stage children love nursery rhymes and repetitive rituals that help them develop language skills. By 2 years they are using two-word phrases and by 3 years most are talking well in sentences that include verbs and prepositions, and enjoy chanting nonsense words and rhymes.

Children learn language in a sequence. They use it first to obtain their basic needs, perhaps learning to say 'drink' while pointing to a cup, later to express particular feelings towards a particular person. The use of language to learn comes with the persistent 'what's that' and 'why' of the toddler. Finally, language is used imaginatively to create the make-believe stories which are the precursor of poetry and fictional writing.

Girls tend to learn to talk earlier than boys, but all children's ability to use language will depend more than anything else on how much they are talked to.

There is no evidence that children in bilingual families suffer any significant delay in language development. However, if a child already has a problem with speech, caused by deafness or generally slow development, then living in a bilingual family may compound the problem. The child who is cared for by a succession of foreign care-takers may be slow in talking, too.

EMOTIONAL AND SOCIAL DEVELOPMENT

Parents recognize differences in personality between their children from the moment of birth – one child may be placid, the next demanding and noisy. But the interaction between the child and the family is also an important factor in forming a child's character.

Most studies of infant development have focused on the importance of the mother's responsiveness and style of caring. But it is now widely recognized that fathers can care for their children equally well.

Babies can undoubtedly thrive within a wide range of parenting styles, and the evidence shows that there are few strict guidelines that parents should follow. What does seem to be important is continuity. Even if both parents work, try to make sure that the child has the same familiar care-taker throughout the early pre-school years.

THE EARLY YEARS

The process of mutual attachment, often called bonding, develops throughout infancy. Plenty of physical contact between parent and child helps to establish this early closeness, and there is evidence that it is enhanced if parents and child have a period of uninterrupted time together immediately after the birth.

This strong, early bond seems to create the best basis from which later independence can grow. Over the first 5 years it changes to allow the child more independent activity and freedom to explore. Between 7 months and 1 year, most babies go through a stage of *separation anxiety* when they are reluctant even to let their mothers or care-takers out of their sight. And throughout early childhood the child needs to be able to return quickly at moments of anxiety and stress or, more often, just look from time to time for reassurance.

Children's increasing independence is helped by their intellectual development and use of language. This gives them a better understanding of the world around them and allows them to find new ways of approaching others, of expressing themselves and of keeping some control of feelings and actions.

This greater potential for controlling emotions is not always realized, of course. Anger can explode into tantrums, and fears become unmanageable at times. It is natural, too, that a child's need to assert independence may cause conflict with parents or care-takers. For example, a toddler who is learning to dress himself may resist your attempts to take over when you are in a hurry. All the same, the greater the child's internal resources, the easier it is for the family to help him deal with his own strong feelings.

Games and other play activities provide ways in which aggression and competitive feelings can be channelled into socially acceptable behaviour. Small children enjoy playing alongside other children, but until they are at least 2 or 3 years old they will have little idea about playing *with* them. It is only gradually that children gain an understanding of rules, of taking turns or sharing. Children learn through play, they acquire various skills and they gain an awareness of their own separate identity.

THE SCHOOLCHILD

When your child starts school, the demand for these social and emotional skills is increased. Experience of using play materials and playing games with simple rules encourages the capacity to wait and to tolerate some frustration, to be aware of the effect that he has on others, and to understand the concept of symbols, which is essential for learning to read and write. This experience provides the basis for more formal learning and helps the child form relationships with others.

School may be more demanding than home but it also offers a break from the intimate emotional ties of home, in the form of relationships that are friendly but less intense. At school, links within peer groups can be made and broken on a more equal basis than those between brothers and sisters. Whether or not your child has brothers and sisters, the classroom and playground groups provide opportunities for companionship and for assessing self against others, for self-discovery and the definition of social boundaries. Sometimes, too, these playground groups provide an opportunity for bullying. At this age children can be very cruel and if a child who has previously seemed settled becomes reluctant or unhappy about school, it is always worth considering this possible cause.

Letting off steam is important for toddlers who are constantly frustrated by their own limitations and the limits set on their behaviour by others.

SELF-IMAGE

During the early school years children often swing between quite mature behaviour and returns to babyishness, especially at times of major change, stress or illness. Try to respond to both, encouraging your child's attempts to mature as well as responding to his occasional need to be more dependent.

A sense of achievement can help to compensate for the separation from home that school entails. Although it is important (and inevitable) that children will sometimes experience failure, it is when their achievements outweigh their failures that confidence grows. You can boost this confidence by showing your children that you are proud of their achievements at school. It is normal for children to swing between feelings of mastery and inferiority, but if you can help them to be realistic about what they can and cannot do you will save them from undue humiliation.

Although it is possible to find friendships between boys and girls during the early school years, first friendships are usually between children of the same sex. Whether this is due to social pressures or to natural preference is not at all clear.

RESPONSIBILITY

It can be difficult to decide how much responsibility to give your child, particularly when he is between 8 and 10 years old. Battles often arise because he is eager to do things that you feel are not yet safe. One way of dealing with these is to set targets and assure your child that you will help him achieve them. For example, you might agree that he will be allowed to go fishing with his friends provided he first learns to swim, or that he can cycle to school after he has been on a road safety course. It is then up to you to arrange the swimming lessons or the course.

FRIENDSHIPS

In later childhood it becomes important to children to be able and allowed to do the same things as their friends. You may find that your child increasingly quotes the behaviour of these friends when you are discussing what he should or should not be allowed to do.

There are positive advantages to children in identifying with a group. They feel part of a larger world and learn to put the wishes of others before their own, and this can put a child's own problems into a new perspective.

It is tempting for parents to try to control these friendships, just because they recognize how important they are. In practice, best friends tend to come and go, and membership of various groups fluctuates. Trust your children to manage their own friendships, but be ready to give support and sympathy if a friendship ends, or a friend moves away.

Not all children are equally gregarious. Some are naturally self-sufficient and even outgoing children appreciate occasional periods of solitude. But habitual isolation by choice is very rare. Children who cannot join in or make friends, even when they want to, need help. Your child will be accepted more easily if you let him conform as much as possible to the group: allow him to wear the same kind of clothes and spend his pocket money on the same things, for example.

> ▶ **See also** Family life; Learning and school; Behaviour and development

CHILDREN'S SEXUALITY

Interest in the opposite sex occurs as soon as children discover that there are differences between boys and girls. Usually it gives rise to some exploratory games on the level of simple curiosity, but there may also be an increase in modesty imposed by the children themselves.

Masturbation is common in children of all ages, too – indeed, even tiny infants discover that they get pleasurable sensations from handling their genitals. As a child grows a point to make is that it is a private and not a public activity.

All this behaviour is a normal part of children's sexual development and you should accept and disregard it. You need only be concerned if a child seems to masturbate compulsively and frequently, because it may be that the child is using it as an escape from reality, perhaps because he has some anxiety that needs to be resolved. Explore this possibility, but keep any feelings of horror or anger you have to yourself, or you could stimulate quite needless guilt in the child.

An interest in dirty jokes and a fascination with forbidden words is very general during the early school years. This is not only an expression of interest in the adult world of sex but may also be a means of self-assertion and independence. Such riddles and rhymes have a long history and adults may sometimes be taken aback to rediscover a forgotten part of their own childhood.

The desire of many parents to be more open about sex can sometimes be taken rather too far. An older child may feel uneasy, about sharing bathtime or undressing with his parents, for example, and as adolescence approaches, most children demand privacy and a lock on the bathroom door. Nevertheless, the more open you are with your children, the easier it will be for you to talk to them about sex and sexual relationships. Sex education need not be formal – it is largely a matter of giving truthful, simple answers to the questions your children ask.

> ▶ **See also** The older child and adolescent

LEARNING AND SCHOOL

Intellectual development is built into the human system in much the same way as physical development. However, whereas development of ordinary physical skills is only minimally affected by restriction or encouragement, intellectual development can be greatly affected by either stimulation or deprivation during the early years. Intelligence is partly inherited, but it is also influenced by the child's environment. How much your children eventually achieve will depend not only on their innate ability but also on the mental stimulation and the opportunities to learn new intellectual skills you give them. Children seem to develop most successfully when they are involved with an adult who can structure their joint activity so that it presents a mental challenge that the child can strive to meet but that will not overwhelm him.

Jean Piaget, a Swiss psychologist, was one of the first people to study the intellectual (cognitive) development of children, and to suggest that, like physical development, it progresses in an orderly fashion through certain predetermined stages. Piaget may have sometimes underestimated the ability of children of a certain age to perform certain tasks and, although he believed that development proceeded in a series of separate and clear-cut steps, most people now see it as a continuous process, with new and more complex mental skills acquired gradually through experience. But nevertheless, Piaget's work on the pattern of intellectual milestones still gives a good general guide to development.

LEARNING AND REASONING

An infant is not an entirely blank sheet on which intellect must be printed. It is true that every child learns about the world through his experience of it, but underlying this experience seems to be some pre-programmed knowledge – even extremely young infants will respond to anything that looks like a human face before they have had the time to discover faces through experience. During the first 2 years of life (which Piaget called the 'sensory-motor' stage of development), children gain much of their information about their environment from touching, prodding and poking it. They discover that they are separate from the outside world – they suck their fingers and discover they belong to them, they suck the corner of a blanket and discover it does not. At first, for the young infant, out of sight is out of mind. It is not until they are about 10 months old that babies realize that an object exists even if it cannot be seen and will search for a toy that they have seen hidden under a blanket. Gradually babies learn that their actions have results – they will deliberately shake a rattle because it makes a noise. As they learn to anticipate the results of their actions, they will begin to make choices, to decide that a certain course of action is undesirable and to avoid it.

PRE-SCHOOL YEARS

From about 2 years old until the age of 6 or 7, a child's thinking is dominated by what he sees, hears and feels at that moment, and by the fact that he is entirely egocentric, seeing things only from his own point of view. A child of this age will match objects on the basis of colour rather than form, judging two red objects, for example, however different they are, to be more similar than two identically shaped but different coloured ones. As language develops, so does imagination. A 3- or 4-year-old can think in symbolic terms, pushing his bricks around the floor, for example, as if they were cars. Up to the age of about 6, children learn best by doing, exploring and playing with objects and solving problems that have some basis in reality.

SCHOOL-AGE CHILDREN

As a child learns more about the world around him, he becomes more able to reason logically. While younger children tend to solve problems by trial and error, from the age of about 6 years children begin to adopt a more abstract approach to problems, forming general hypotheses and rules which enable them to reason and apply what they have learnt in one situation to another. They begin to see beyond what lies in front of them, to look at a situation from more than just their own viewpoint and to reconcile these different views. This new way of thinking Piaget called 'concrete operational thinking'. If a ball of plasticine is rolled into a sausage shape a younger child will judge it visually. He may see it as larger, because it is longer, or smaller, because it is thinner. But by the time they are 6 or 7 years old most children are able to 'think backwards' and realize that the same piece of plasticine is involved and that the old shape and the new therefore contain the same quantity.

Memory improves significantly throughout the childhood years. A 6-year-old child, asked to recall a list of 15 words he has been read, will remember about four of them, a 9-year-old five, and an 11-year-old seven words. This may be because memory capacity increases with age, but it is more likely that as children grow older their memories improve because they acquire various stratagies to help them remember. They learn, for example, that if they organize their material into categories (classifying an orange, an apple and a pear as fruit rather than remembering them as three separate objects, for example) they can hold more in memory. They also learn to memorize by 'rehearsing' or repeating things again and again to themselves.

ADOLESCENCE

As they grow older, children's ability to think in abstract terms and deal with hypothetical problems increases. Some intellectual skills – ability at maths and science, for example – do not fully emerge until 15 or 16 years and only then if the opportunity is given to develop them. So it makes educational nonsense to decide a child's educational capability at 11 years old, or even 14 or 15. Teenagers gradually come to accept that other people may hold opinions which, even if different from their own, can be equally valid. They develop a greater awareness of inconsistencies in the world around them and start to question previously held ideas.

MORAL DEVELOPMENT

Do children learn a code of behaviour from their parents and their society, or are they pre-programmed, acquiring a moral sense as a natural part of their development? Psychologists are divided. Piaget noticed that until the age of about 6 years old, children play without any attention to rules. Between the ages of about 6 and 10 they acknowledge the existence of rules – in fact they may be most insistent that other people follow them – but they make little attempt to keep the rules themselves. It is not until the age of about 10 to 12 years that they begin conscientiously to abide by the rules of their games.

Certainly a child's attitude towards right and wrong changes dramatically during childhood. A pre-school child sees things very much in terms of good or bad and will judge an action entirely by its consequences. He will see an accident in which his sister accidentally drops and breaks a cup of tea she was helpfully carrying as worse than his own deliberate knocking over of a glass of water which did not break. However, the school-age child can understand that behaviour should be judged in context, taking into account the intention behind an act, as well as its results. Children of school age have developed a 'conscience' – a set of internal guidelines. If they behave well it is often because they want to, rather than just because they fear punishment. But their ideas of right and wrong are still those they have absorbed from the family or from their peers.

Throughout adolescence children build their own moral code, based partly on what they have been taught, but also on what they have observed from their own experience. Teenage children of immigrant families may find it particularly hard to reconcile the social values of their families and their friends, and need special understanding from their parents.

SCHOOL

By the time they are 3 years old most children are ready to spend 2 or 3 hours a day at a playgroup or nursery school, although they settle more easily if a parent can stay with them for the first few days. Children with some pre-school experience usually have better developed vocabulary and dexterity than children without pre-school experience. They may also find the social adjustment to school easier to make.

Going to school for the first time is a major step for any child. He has been an important member of a small family group and suddenly he has to share the attention of an unfamiliar adult with 20 or 30 other children. It is not surprising that, at first, learning to adjust to this new environment with its new rules of behaviour takes precedence over learning to read and write. Many infant schools help to prepare children by inviting them to visit at least once before they start.

For at least the first few weeks after starting school your child will probably come home tired out and irritable. He may express the strain by being more demanding or clinging at home or he may show his anxiety by crying in school or failing to join in.

Most children are able to settle happily within a couple of months, but about 1 in 10 continues to find it difficult to adjust to school. Often they are children who have always been unable to accept change easily, or who have experienced an exceptional number of changes in early childhood. They may seem to be aggressive and hostile towards the other children or, alternatively, they may seem to be withdrawn or restless.

Modern schools usually welcome parents into the classroom, especially in the early school years. Parent participation helps both to bridge the gap between home and school and to ease the teacher's workload.

▶See also Behaviour and development; Appendices: Who's who in the health service; The law and your child

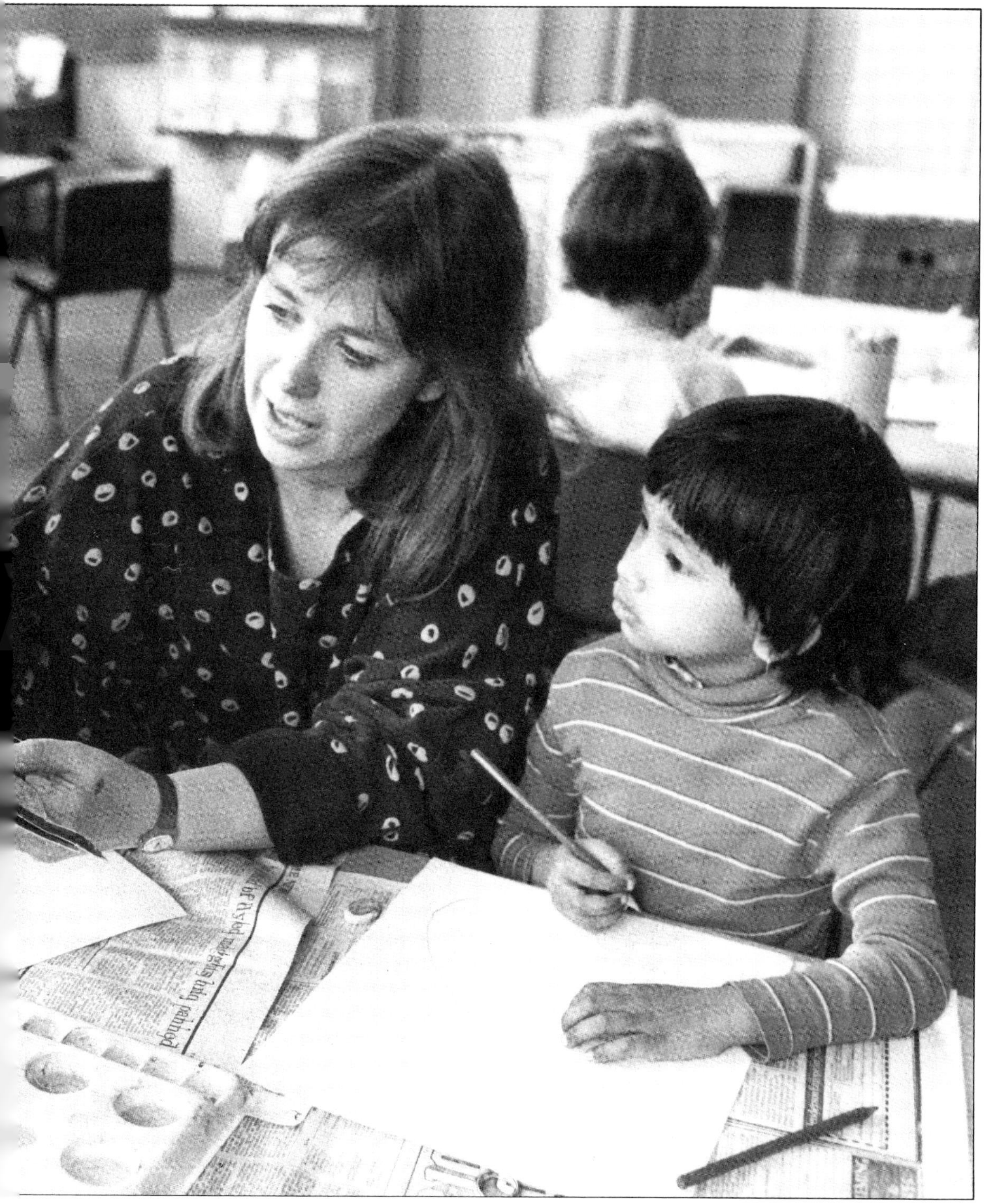

STRESS AT SCHOOL

It is quite usual for all children to express some dislike of school, especially during their first year. Common complaints are about school meals, the toilets, undressing for games, a teacher who shouts or children who bully. You will probably know from your child's behaviour when he is under stress, although it may be more difficult to persuade him to tell you what is wrong. Often there will be something simple you can do to solve the problem. For example, if there are some foods your child really dislikes, tell the school so that he is not forced to eat them, or give him a packed lunch. It is important to discuss these complaints with your child's teacher, who may be unaware that anything is wrong.

Should your child need professional help with a persisting problem, the school can put you in touch with the school's psychologist or a child guidance clinic.

Most children are temporarily anxious at the beginning of the new school year, especially if they are changing schools. The transition to a large and impersonal second school can be particularly difficult. It will help if your child can visit the school and meet the staff in advance, so that they are not completely unfamiliar when he starts school officially. You may need professional help if, as rarely happens, your child's panic about leaving home persists. However, most children adapt well and enjoy the stimulus of new school subjects and interests.

Most difficulties in class between children and staff arise as children grow older and begin to question authority. They may express their frustration by being disruptive or provoking confrontations with teachers. Very occasionally there is a real clash of personalities between a child and a teacher and, if this seems to be the case, you should discuss it at the school.

DIFFICULTIES WITH WORK

Temporary difficulty with new work, dislike of a particular subject, or boredom if work is too easy are also common causes of stress. Homework may cause problems. If it is

COMMON SIGNS OF STRESS
o Reluctance to go to school
o Recurrent physical symptoms such as stomach-ache or headache that have no obvious explanation
o Sleeping difficulties
o Loss of appetite
o Excessive anxiety about minor details
o Panic about homework or examinations

intended to involve new learning rather than consolidating what has been taught in the classroom and your child finds it daunting to face new work on his own, you should give what help you can rather than leaving him to struggle alone. If you can, create a quiet space for your child to work, with his own desk or table. Show an interest in his work and be sensitive about distractions: your child will find it hard to work if the rest of the family are involved in some fascinating project.

Examinations worry many children. Panic about examinations is not related to ability but to temperament, external pressures or ambition. Teachers and parents often put excessive emphasis on examination success, and it is important for your child to know that you are not expecting 100 per cent, that you yourself have failed examinations, and that failure is not final. Give credit for effort, and acknowledge the luck element in tests and examinations.

Writing, reading and arithmetic are not the only skills that a school can teach. Playing an instrument not only develops musical talent but can also encourage social confidence, co-operation and a sense of group achievement.

LEARNING DIFFICULTIES

Children vary in their rate of learning. It can depend on many factors including how long it takes them to settle into their class and how interested they are in a topic.

At least 1 in 5 children experiences some degree of difficulty in learning while at school, and it is not always easy to be sure whether this is only a temporary difficulty that you can help to solve, or whether professional help is necessary. Some children lack self-confidence and start school convinced that they will fail. Sometimes lack of continuity in teaching delays a child's development. Ill-health may also cause problems: apart from any particular health problems your child may suffer, the early school years are the peak period for the minor childhood *infections*, including colds and influenza, which your child will inevitably contract once he starts school.

Sometimes parents and teachers have unrealistic expectations of a child, so that he will appear to fail consistently and may become apathetic or aggressive as a result. Children who have learning difficulties easily feel self-conscious about their failure and need reassurance and encouragement. *Behavioural problems*, especially at second school, are often associated with learning difficulties that have not been fully recognized.

If you think your child is not making adequate progress, arrange to talk this over with the teacher who knows him best. Ask about remedial help, discuss the lessons your child finds particularly difficult and ask about how you can help at home. If there are domestic problems which may be affecting your child's work or behaviour, inform the school. Remember that although you may believe your child to be more capable than the school maintains, this may not necessarily be so. An independent assessment by the school psychologist may be helpful.

It helps children to talk about school problems at home so that they can see them in perspective. They are often surprised and relieved to hear that their parents were also bad spellers, disliked French or were often given detentions.

Most children have mastered the rudiments of reading by the time they are 7 years old. Children who have been slow in talking tend also to be slow readers, and so do those who have had frequent illnesses or changes of school. A very few children read and spell less well than their general level of ability would suggest. This specific reading difficulty is known as *dyslexia*.

READING DIFFICULTIES
The ease with which a child learns to read will depend on various other skills:

o Language development and vocabulary
o Visual discrimination of shapes
o Auditory discrimination of sounds
o Ability to attend and to concentrate
o Motivation and self-confidence

Parents can help by:

o Reading stories
o Encouraging drawing and painting
o Developing vocabulary through conversation and games

ASSESSMENT OF INTELLIGENCE

General intelligence comprises ability to reason, speed of learning, memory and perception of similarities and differences. A child's success at school will be partly determined by his general intelligence. Some children are consistently quicker than others at learning new skills and understanding complex ideas. These differences between children are the result partly of inherited factors and partly of environmental ones.

An educational psychologist can assess how a child learns as well as his level of ability, so that parents and teachers can be given constructive advice on helping children to overcome difficulties. The psychologist will establish the range of skills of which a child is capable, see how he responds to encouragement or to challenge, whether there is a difference between his verbal and non-verbal abilities, and will also assess the child's self-confidence.

Educational psychologists may visit schools regularly and, by arrangement with the head teacher, will talk to parents who want to discuss their child's learning or behavioural difficulties. No psychologist will interview a child without parental consent, or make an assessment of your child without taking your knowledge of him into account. You can also arrange to see a psychologist privately.

INTELLIGENCE TESTS

Modern intelligence tests measure a wide range of abilities, including vocabulary, spatial ability, numeracy, verbal and non-verbal reasoning and memory. The tests provide an 'intelligence quotient' that compares children with others of the same age. If your child is of average ability his IQ will fall between 85 and 115.

Although a high IQ suggests that your child will do well, this isolated score can be very misleading, especially if the child is young. Psychologists prefer to take many other factors into account before predicting a child's academic potential.

A child who finds academic work easy may become bored by classwork unless she is given sufficient new challenges and individual attention.

SPECIAL NEEDS

One in 5 children needs special help at school. This may be because of a physical problem, such as *epilepsy* or a speech impairment, or because of a behavioural or learning problem. Most of these children can stay in ordinary schools with support from specialist staff or advisory teachers. Parents who feel that the school is unable to make adequate arrangements for their child can ask for him to be assessed by an educational psychologist and a doctor.

EDUCATIONALLY SUBNORMAL CHILDREN

About 1 in 50 children needs help in a special school or unit because of the severity or complexity of his difficulties. An assessment of the child's situation is made, taking into account the views of parents, reports from teachers and advice from a doctor and an educational psychologist. Parents are invited to discuss the recommendations for special provisions made and can ask to visit any school or ask for a written description before accepting the recommendations. The child's position is reviewed every year and at $13\frac{1}{2}$ years there is a thorough reassessment in which parents are fully involved.

THE OLDER CHILD AND ADOLESCENT

Adolescence literally means growing up and becoming an adult. It includes all the changes that make a child a fully-grown human being. These changes are physical and sexual, psychological and emotional. Puberty is the time of rapid physical growth and sexual maturation. The events of puberty occur in a set order, but there is a wide variation in their timing. However, girls usually begin and end their pubertal development earlier than boys. Altogether adolescence continues beyond the teens and into the early twenties.

PHYSICAL DEVELOPMENT

Few children enter puberty before they are 9 years old. By the age of 13 most girls, and by 14 most boys, show some signs of pubertal development.

The first visible sign of puberty in girls is usually the growth spurt that begins around the age of 10 or 11 years, with most girls reaching their final adult height at around 14 or 15 years. Breast development begins at about 10 or 11 and the first downy pubic hair usually appears around this time. Underarm hair does not usually appear until 12 or 13 years, and the glands responsible for underarm sweating develop at about this age as well. The girl's hips broaden, and her body becomes more rounded.

Menstruation usually begins late in the sequence of development, about 2 years after a girl's breasts begin to develop and always after her period of fastest growth has been passed. Once a girl has started to menstruate, only about 2 more years of growth remain to her. Although she is menstruating, the girl may not yet be fertile as ovulation does not usually begin until periods become regular, generally about 18 months after they start.

Consult your doctor if your daughter shows no sign of breast development by the time she is 15, or if her periods begin before she is 10 or have not started by the age of 16.

The first signs of puberty in boys are less obvious than in girls. Enlargement of the testicles, with darkening of the scrotal skin

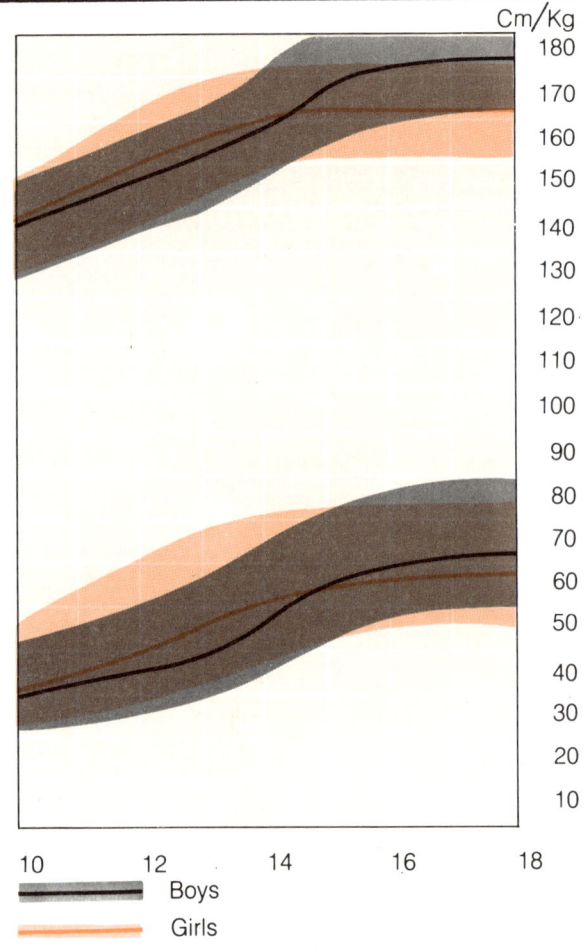

Boys start their growth spurt later than girls. If your child's height or weight falls outside the coloured band, consult your doctor. The central line marks the average course of development.

and the growth of fine pubic hair, usually occurs at about 12 or 13 years. About a year later the penis starts to lengthen and erections become more frequent than in earlier childhood. Although production of semen begins almost as soon as the testes start to enlarge, the first ejaculation usually occurs about 2 years after this. The first ejaculates are clear and contain no sperm.

The growth spurt in boys starts at about the age of 12 or 13 years. It is because boys have about 2 more years of steady growth than girls before their final spurt that their adult height is greater. However, the duration of the growth spurt is rather less than for girls, so they reach their final height only about 1 year later. Boys start to grow underarm, body and facial hair between 13 and 15 years old, and at about this age, too, the sweat glands start to develop. The voice does not usually deepen until the growth spurt is well established, usually at about the age of 14 or 15.

If your son's growth spurt is delayed, so that he is very much shorter than most of his peers, or if his testes have not started to enlarge by the time he is about 14 years old, consult your family doctor.

COMMON ADOLESCENT WORRIES

o Uneven breast development. It is, in fact, quite normal for one breast to begin to 'bud' before the other
o Breast size. Girls may need reassurance that both large and small breasts are attractive
o Temporary swelling of one or both breasts in early adolescent boys. This is not uncommon or abnormal and soon disappears
o Spots, due to the increased oiliness of the skin. Consult your doctor for treatment if your child has severe *acne*
o Weight. Girls may be very self-conscious about their newly-rounded shape. Many try to diet; in some cases over-concern about weight may be a sign of *anorexia nervosa*
o Height. Tall girls and short boys may both feel awkward and need reassurance
o Muscularity or shoulder girth of boys. It is normal for teenage boys to be slighter than adult men and their shoulders continue to broaden until they are about 25 years old

---

ANXIETIES ABOUT DEVELOPMENT

Early maturation is almost always advantageous for boys. Physique is important to boys, and the fact that a boy is bigger, stronger and perhaps has more ability at sport than his peers gives him confidence and tends to increase his popularity. Because he looks grown up, adults may give him more responsibility. Girls who mature early may enjoy being treated by adults as grown up, but they may also be regarded as sexually precocious and put under more sexual pressure than they can cope with.

Late maturers, boys and girls, may lack social self-confidence. They may be teased by their peers, and treated as children by adults. A boy may be at a disadvantage with girls, who are in any case more mature than boys of their own age. A girl may worry if she alone among her friends has not yet started to develop.

Almost all adolescents are self-conscious about their developing bodies and sexuality, and may worry intensely about perfectly normal changes. Try to give them reassurance.

▶ **See also** Glandular disorders

EMOTIONAL MATURITY

Adolescence is often regarded as a time of emotional upheaval for both parents and children. But although parents and teenagers often conflict with and irritate each other, all the evidence is that most families come through this period successfully and that most adolescents manage to remain on good terms with their families.

Mood swings and occasional periods of misery are common in adolescence, although few teenagers suffer from true emotional disorders. Friendships become increasingly important as a child enters adolescence and becomes more independent of his family.

Adolescents also like to push themselves and to experience as much as they can. They may take risks with motorbikes, drugs or sex. Accidents, particularly road accidents, are the commonest cause of death in this age group. Drug-taking is an issue that worries many parents. Find out the facts, so that you can explain exactly why you are worried. Simply forbidding an activity seldom works because, as adolescence progresses, children become less likely to accept authority. However, most children are influenced by their parents and respect their views on important matters.

One of the most dangerous addictive drugs is tobacco, and the most effective way you can persuade your child not to smoke is by not smoking yourself. Similarly, if you want to help your child avoid alcohol abuse, make sure that you yourself do not misuse drink.

DIFFERENCES BETWEEN BOYS AND GIRLS

In their early school years boys and girls are, on the whole, subject to the same expectations and the same pressures. But during adolescence a girl who shows prowess in a traditionally 'male' field – computing or science, for example – may over and over again receive the message 'You have done very well – for a girl'. She may begin to believe that it is unfeminine to be brighter than her male contemporaries or to be assertive. She may also feel that it is unfeminine to play sports. In just the same way, it is socially acceptable for women – but not men – to share tender feelings and to cry. Much adult unhappiness might be avoided if adolescents were helped to understand that some qualities are too valuable to be compartmentalized into 'male' or 'female' attributes. You can point out to your children the losses involved in conforming to these sexual stereotypes. You can also help by encouraging your children to develop several areas of skill instead of focusing exclusively on, for example, schoolwork or sports training.

INDEPENDENCE

One of the ways that adolescents begin their inevitable separation from the family is by testing authority. At least some degree of rebelliousness, however difficult it is for you to accept, is probably essential to the child who is trying to become independent. It is normal, too, for your child to want to create his own 'emotional space' by not sharing as much as he used to with you, and by emphasizing his own individuality and difference from you in his clothes, hairstyle, taste in music or the way he decorates his room.

Remember also that a child's capacity to think logically and in abstract terms grows throughout adolescence. It is probably this new ability, at least as much as rebelliousness, that leads to the questioning, criticism and idealism which are so characteristic of teenagers.

All this can be hard for parents to deal with. Remember that you can supervise your children while giving them the independence

Boys may be pressured by their peers or by their school into avoiding 'feminine' subjects such as domestic science or needlework. A boy who grows up without being able to take care of his day-to-day needs is at a disadvantage.

and privacy they need. Make sure that you could answer the question: 'Where are your children now?' Be clear and consistent in the way you use your authority and about your boundaries and your limits. Be as tolerant as you can, but let your children know what you are not prepared to tolerate. For example, you may feel that they are entitled to keep their own rooms as they like, but that you are not prepared to let them spread untidiness throughout the house. In deciding on your own limits, you may find it helpful to think back to your own adolescence. Negotiation usually works better than confrontation, but hold firm on those issues that affect your children's own health or safety.

It is important to keep the channels of communication open throughout the years of adolescence. If you and your children can talk to each other and discuss the issues on which you feel strongly, you will come to a better understanding.

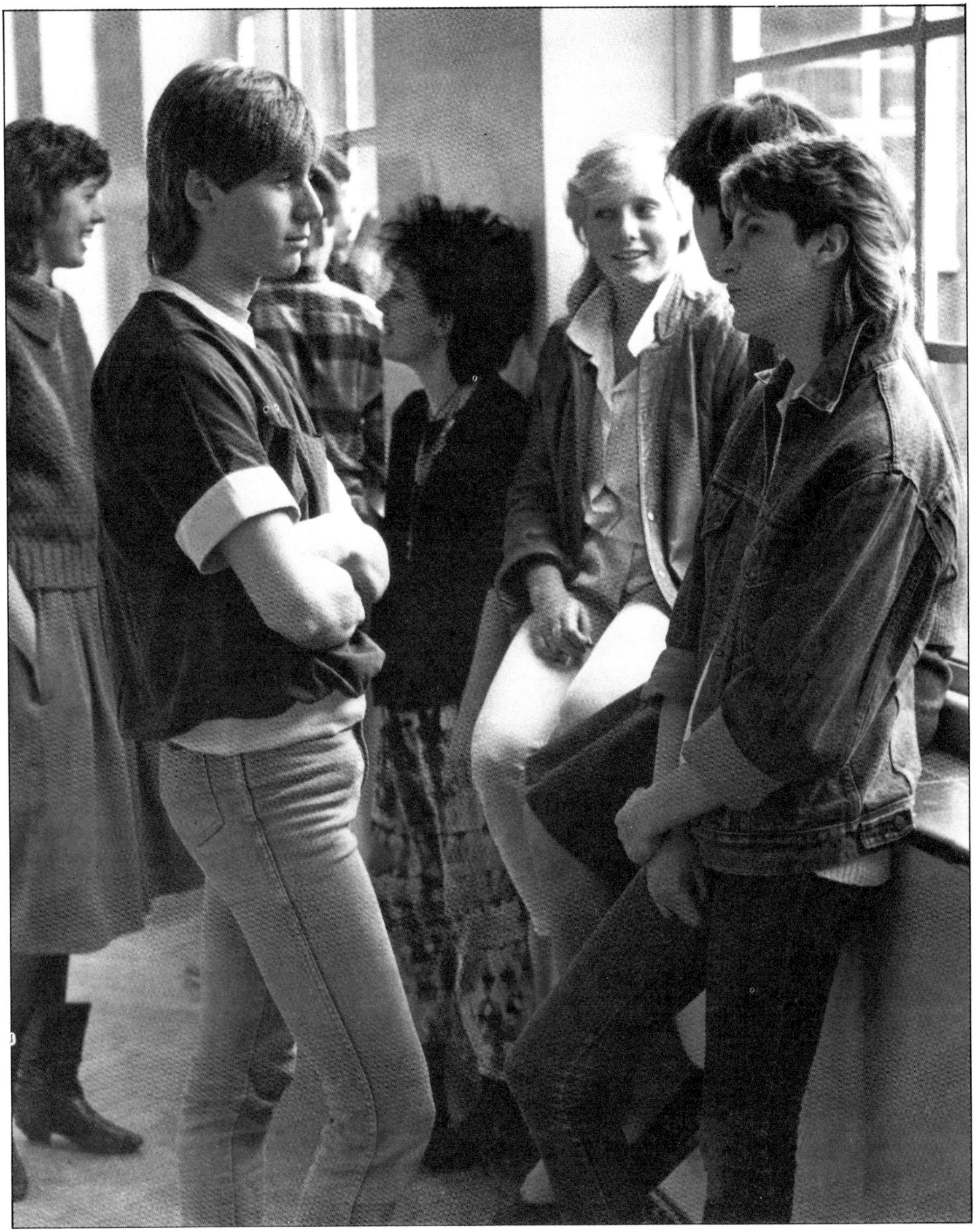

Adolescents need to feel they belong and that they are accepted as part of a group. This identification with a group is one of the ways in which they can express their separation from the family. At first they may tend to conform slavishly to whatever image the group likes to present, but as they grow in confidence they become much less susceptible to group pressures.

It is inevitable that as your children grow up a new relationship will evolve between each of them and you. You may want to be a friend. But it is worth remembering that adolescents do need a supportive parent to turn to and to rely on, however independent they may seem. Although being a parent includes showing some of the qualities of a good friend, a parent also needs to be able to draw limits, which the adolescent can test and accept or reject.

▶ See also Behaviour and development

SEXUAL ACTIVITY

In modern Western society there are fewer rules and more freedom of choice concerning sexual activity than ever before. Boys and girls entering their teens have to make their own decisions about when they should start to have sex and how to handle sexual encounters. Inevitably, parents worry about precocious sexual activity and the risks of *promiscuity*, pregnancy and *sexually transmitted disease*.

Young adolescents usually go about in mixed-sex groups. They may pair off within the group, but these early relationships seldom last long. Very intense attachments to someone of the same sex are quite common, especially if there is little opportunity for meeting people of the opposite sex (for example in single-sex boarding schools), but they rarely involve any overt homosexual activity. Neither do they mean that the child is likely to be homosexual as an adult. Some teenagers, however, will grow up with a sexual preference for their own sex. If you or your child needs support in dealing with this, seek help from a counsellor or support group: your family doctor will be to suggest local sources of help.

Masturbation is a recognized part of sexual development. It is a way in which teenagers can learn about their bodies and about what gives them sexual pleasure. Make sure that you do not communicate to your child the attitude that it is anything to feel guilty about, or that it is an undesirable phase that they will pass through.

Boys and girls usually begin dating and kissing between the ages of 13 and 16 years and by the age of 17 a large number of boys and girls have had intercourse. Boys tend to have a greater number of sexual partners, while girls tend to be more interested in one lasting 'romantic' relationship. But few teenagers are promiscuous in having frequent, casual sex and their partners are usually those with whom they have steady, and occasionally lasting, relationships. Most have several sexual relationships before settling down.

There is nothing unhealthy or abnormal about adolescents experimenting with sex and relationships before settling down with a partner. However, problems may arise if they start to have sex before they are emotionally mature, or ready to take responsibility for their actions and cope with new and overwhelming feelings. They can also find it hard to resist pressure from others.

You can safeguard your children's well-being and help them withstand these external pressures by ensuring that they have sufficient information about the feelings and emotional risks involved in sexual relationships, as well as the physical risks. It is best if they feel free to talk to you about any worries they have. For your part, tell them exactly what your own anxieties are – that they might have sex too soon, or that they will be hurt or hurt their partner, or become involved in something they cannot handle.

SEX EDUCATION AND CONTRACEPTION

All youngsters should know about sex and contraception before they are likely to be sexually active. A substantial number of teenagers have no contraceptive protection the first time they have intercourse. They are usually more likely to ask questions in a private discussion than in a school session on sex education, but if you find it difficult to talk to your children about sex, there are useful books that you and your children can read.

You may feel that it is a reasonable safety measure for your daughter to go on the Pill automatically when she is 16 years old. This is nearly always a mistake. It may put pressure on the girl to have sex before she feels ready for it, either because she thinks you expect it of her, or because she has been deprived of an adequate excuse for refusing sex. It is much better to help your daughter learn how to refuse sex when she does not want it, and to make sure that she knows where to get advice and contraceptive protection when she does want to embark on a sexual relationship. Boys also need advice. A boy should be encouraged never to have intercourse with a girl who is not really willing, and he should be taught to protect his partner against conception by using a sheath, unless he is certain she is using an efficient contraceptive method herself.

The sheath and the diaphragm are both effective if used properly, with a spermicide, although many girls prefer the Pill. The health-risks of taking the Pill are not yet entirely clear: a discussion with your family doctor may help you and your daughter to decide on a method of contraception.

SEXUALLY TRANSMITTED DISEASES

Make sure your teenagers understand that the greater their number of partners, the greater the risk of sexually transmitted, or venereal, disease. They should know that a sheath does give both partners some protection against contracting a *sexually transmitted disease*, but that this is not reliable. It is important that teenagers realize they can visit their family doctor or a doctor at an STD clinic in full confidence, and that they understand the importance of prompt treatment for sexually transmitted diseases.

TEENAGE PREGNANCY

If a girl thinks she is pregnant, it is best if she can discuss this with her parents. Most young girls do turn to their parents first, but some are so scared of their parents' reactions that they turn to someone outside the family, or may even refuse to acknowledge the possibility that they are pregnant.

It is vitally important to confirm a pregnancy, and decide whether there should be an *abortion*, as early as possible. Abortion carries very little risk when the fetus is under 10 to 12 weeks, but becomes more problematic with the passing of each week after this. Pregnancy tests can be arranged through your doctor or family planning clinic, done at a chemist, or carried out using a do-it-yourself testing kit bought at a chemist. If a girl may be pregnant she should have a test 2 weeks after the first missed period. However, a negative result at this early stage can occasionally be unreliable, so if the girl has still not started a period a week or so later, arrange another test.

It is very easy for parents of a pregnant daughter to blame the boy and refuse him any further involvement. But remember that they are probably fond of each other and that, even if he can be of little practical help, he will probably want to do what he can to support her. It is also important for the girl to decide for herself what is to be done, without parental pressure. She should be given adequate time – perhaps 4 weeks – to make the decision. It is often helpful for the girl, and her boyfriend if possible, to talk to a counsellor or doctor.

If the girl does decide to have an abortion, it is essential that those around her give her every possible support. A properly performed abortion is very unlikely to affect her later ability to conceive or to bear children. Her own attitude, and that of those around her, towards the abortion will very much affect the way she feels about it afterwards. Most girls recover rapidly, but some are left with a feeling of sadness or guilt, especially if they were ambivalent about the operation or pressure was put on them to have it. Equally, if the girl decides to continue the pregnancy, she will need all the support of those around her. Practical arrangements will vary according to each family's circumstances, but there are many sources of support and counselling.

▶See also Appendix: Support groups and publications

PART TWO

CARE OF THE SICK CHILD

USING THE FAMILY DOCTOR

When children are ill, it is their parents who have the responsibility of deciding whether to ask for medical help. It can sometimes be difficult to be sure if a child is ill or not, and many parents are uncertain about which symptoms justify sufficient concern to consult a doctor. Whether there is an obvious symptom like diarrhoea or your child just seems off-colour, you will probably want to wait a little while to see whether you need to call for help. If your child is with another care-taker or is at school you may have to make a decision based on information relayed to you over the telephone. The age of the child affects the decision and, in general, the younger the child the more potentially serious is any infection. Whatever the age of the child, the best signs of health are a good appetite and normal energy.

Whatever your situation, once you have decided that there is a problem, the second step is to try to identify what is wrong, and the third step is to work out what to do and how to do it. These three stages are the same steps that a doctor goes through in caring for a sick child: recognition, diagnosis and treatment. This section helps you decide when your child has a problem and whether you need medical help. Part Three tells you how to recognize particular problems and what treatment can be given by yourself and by others.

Another decision that you may have to make as a parent is where and how to find the most appropriate medical help. The following sections in Part Two explain what help is available and how to obtain it. The appendix **Who's who in the health service** tells you how the different parts of the system fit together and describes the role of each health professional.

If your child has a problem that needs urgent attention, you may have a choice between going to your family doctor or your local hospital. Which you choose will depend on a number of factors: how close you are to either, whether it is night or day, whether you have a car and what your relationship with your doctor or local hospital is like. In general, you should go directly to hospital if your child's condition is life-threatening or if you need to make use of hospital equipment or facilities, such as X-rays or anaesthetics. You should go to your family doctor for advice if your child has a problem that can be dealt with at home with the right medical support and advice.

Following are some general guidelines to help you make a decision, but above all trust your common sense.

Consult your family doctor urgently, or if he is not available over a period of hours, ring your local hospital for advice about:

o **Fits; loss of consciousness** following a fall. Contact a doctor urgently in these cases. There is no need to worry about a simple faint
o **Acute pain** in a sick child that does not quickly improve
o **Unusual irritability** in a child who is unwell, particularly if accompanied by severe headache and an aversion to looking at light
o **Persistent wheezing or difficulty in breathing**, particularly in an asthmatic child whose wheeze does not respond to usual treatment. A cough that follows a cold, even if it lasts for 2 or 3 weeks, needs no treatment so long as the child regains normal vigour after the cold
o **Vomiting** in a baby or toddler lasting more than a few hours, with or without diarrhoea. This is important because the child may be losing a lot of fluid that urgently needs to be replaced. An older child with persistent vomiting and diarrhoea should also be seen by a doctor. Single attacks of vomiting in older children are common and need not cause concern; nor should mild diarrhoea in a child who is otherwise in normal health

o **Persistent fever**, 40°C (104°F) or more, which you are unable to bring down by cool sponging, removing most of your child's clothing and giving paracetamol. You should also seek help if your child has had a lower fever for 3 or 4 days, or sooner if the child is under 1 year old. If your child is prone to *febrile convulsions*, consult your doctor as soon as fever develops

> It is important to contact the doctor about any child aged only a few weeks or months who becomes listless or goes off his feeds.

EMERGENCY SITUATIONS

If your child suffers a serious accident, the appendix **Emergency actions** at the back of the book tells you step by step what you should do in each instance. **Accident and injury** in Part Three describes how children are treated in hospital for many of these emergencies. It also describes the support that you can provide during the hospital treatment and the after-care that you can help to give, both in hospital and at home.

The sick child at home in Part Two outlines basic first-aid measures for minor accidents at home.

THE FAMILY DOCTOR

For the majority of people, the family doctor is the most familiar medical person. He usually has a list of about 2,000 people who can ask for help with any problem related to their health. For example, the problem may be a simple illness; or it may arise from the stresses and strains that occur in the family; or it may be that a patient feels below par for no apparent reason. In most cases, doctors prefer to look after the whole family, since problems often relate to family circumstances.

Young doctors now spend at least 3 years in additional training for general practice to enable them to cope better with the wide range of problems that they are likely to encounter. This usually includes experience of sick children, of emergencies, of pregnancy and labour and of emotional problems. This expertise should help to give you confidence in your family doctor, but the ultimate test of a good doctor is that he gives confidence in your own ability to care for your child's health.

The practice

Most family doctors work in groups with three to five or more other doctors. Only about 12 per cent work alone. With other professional workers, such as health visitors and nurses, family doctors make up the primary health care team. The health visitor is a state registered nurse with special training in the health of families with young children; the practice nurse is skilled in many nursing procedures, such as treating wounds and giving injections; and the district nurse is able to help care for the child who needs special nursing at home. Most practices include one trainee doctor, and a few larger groups have two trainees.

The receptionist is one of the most important members of the family doctor's team, and has a difficult and often undervalued role in understanding and reassuring callers who may be upset, tense and sometimes even angry. The receptionist can help you decide whether the doctor should be contacted immediately or whether your child should be given the next available appointment. She can also give advice on whether your problem can best be dealt with by the doctor, the health visitor or the practice nurse. The receptionist will also advise you about when you can contact your doctor on the telephone.

Choosing a doctor

If there is more than one practice in your area, discuss the choice with your friends, neighbours and particularly with other parents. Avoid taking the advice of just one person: their needs may be very different from yours. The health visitor at a local child health clinic can often give valuable information about local practices: how big they are, if patients are seen by appointment, how easy it is to get an emergency appointment if you feel your child is acutely ill and whether any of the local practices run their own child health clinics offering regular health and developmental checks for all children under 5 years old. It may be important to you that your doctor has a special interest in children, or in particular aspects of medicine such as *psychotherapy* or *alternative therapies*. It is not a good idea to register with a doctor if you live on the edge of the practice area as you may be reluctant to make appointments if the surgery is not easily accessible and your doctor may be reluctant to visit your home.

If you register with a large group practice, try to see only one or two of the doctors whom you prefer so that you can get to know each other. Of course, if you request a home visit in the evening, during the night or at weekends then the emergency doctor on duty will see your child rather than your regular doctor.

THE FAMILY AND THE DOCTOR

For your own and your child's sake you need to have a good working partnership with your family doctor and other members of the primary care team. Until recently it was commonplace for doctors to tell their patients the diagnosis of their disease and to recommend a regimen of treatment. Nowadays medical students are being taught that it is no longer acceptable in most cases simply to tell patients what to do: instead they are taught to suggest the course of action that seems most appropriate in the circumstances. The result should be a two-way relationship in which your doctor accepts that you know most about your child and you respect the professional expertise of the physician.

It takes time to build up a good relationship, and you will probably feel most at ease with a familiar doctor who has treated you and your children in the past. Stay with a doctor that you trust, even though you may sometimes disagree with him. Your own role is important: if you treat the doctor as an ally, your child is more likely to do likewise.

Remember that you can change doctors if you are dissatisfied. Equally, if your family doctor feels that the relationship with you and your family has broken down irretrievably, he is entitled to ask you to leave the practice and register elsewhere, although this only rarely happens. If there is more than one doctor in the partnership it is often possible to change to another within the same practice.

Communications between your child and the family doctor will change over the years. You will have to act as interpreter for infants and

It can be quite difficult visiting the doctor if you have to bring more than one child. Many surgeries have some toys available for children, but it may help to bring some of your own. Because of the extra distractions, it is a particularly good idea to write down everything that you want to ask the doctor.

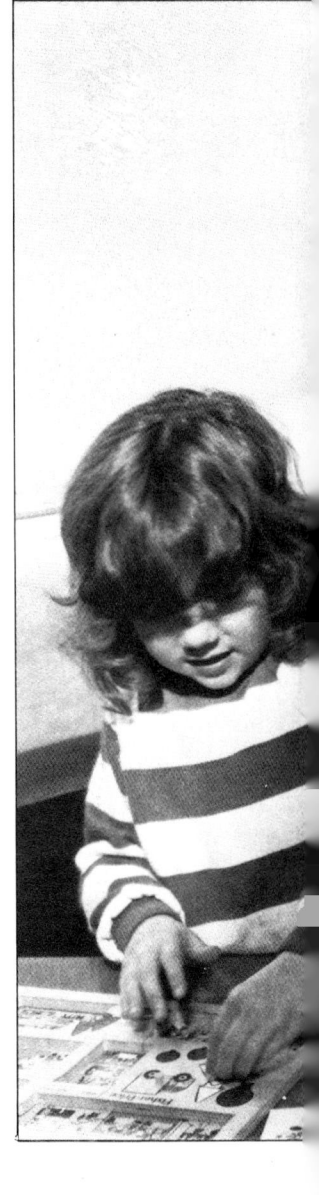

young children, but even children of 5 and 6 years are capable of answering questions themselves if they feel inclined. Older children can usually describe their aches and pains better than their parents. A good doctor will be able to make your child feel at home. You can help by explaining to your child before arriving at the surgery who the doctor is and what is likely to happen. Introduce the doctor to your child when you come into the consulting room.

If your child is going to have an injection or any other treatment, explain what it will involve and warn him just before it happens so that your child knows what to expect. Make sure that your child understands what the doctor is recommending and why.

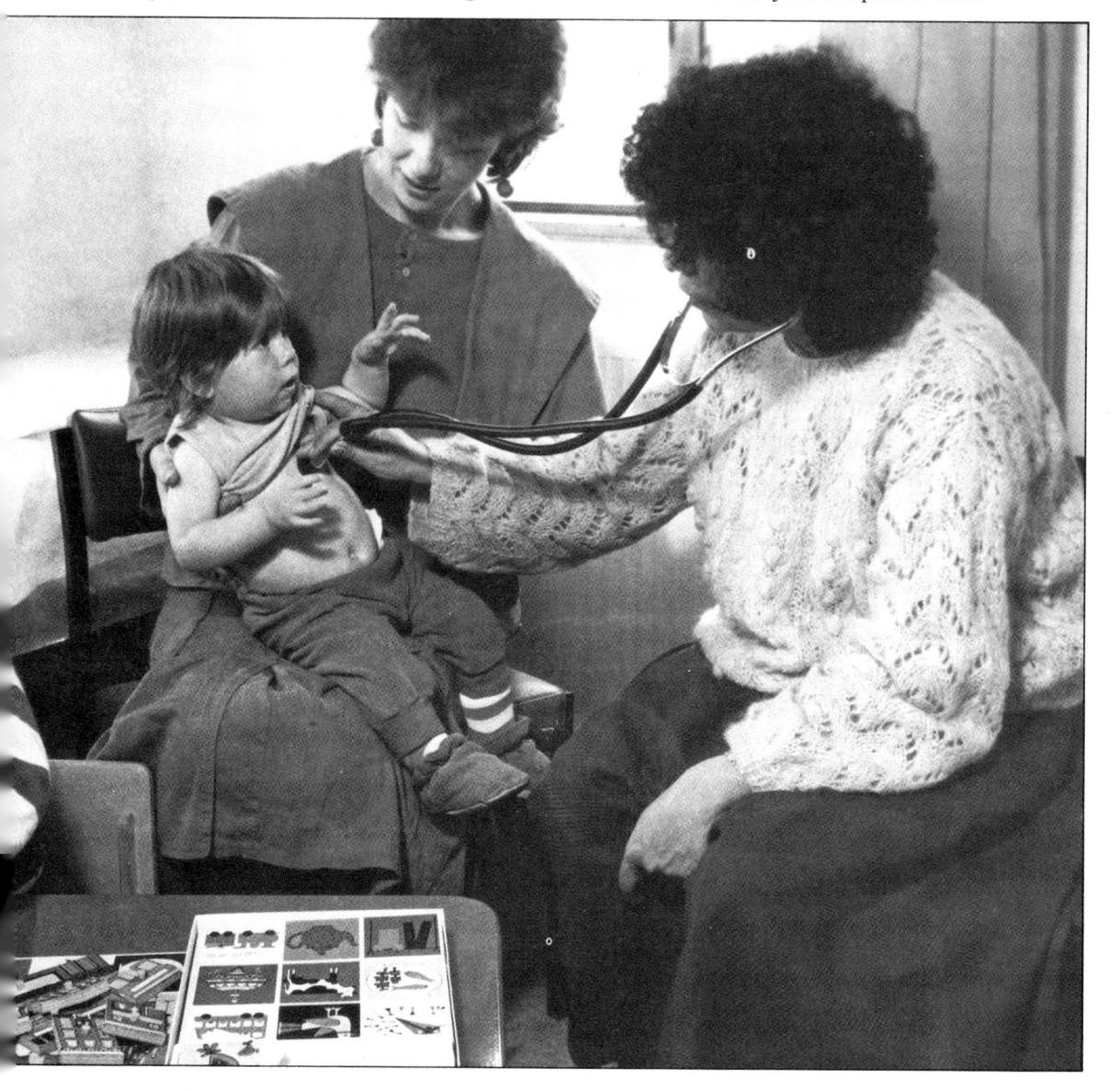

Young teenagers often prefer to see the doctor alone. This may be better even for a 13- or 14-year-old if you think the problem can be resolved without your help. It is then reasonable to ask your doctor to give your teenager a note explaining the diagnosis and recommended treatment. Some adolescents prefer to consult a doctor who does not treat their parents. Most doctors would consider this an acceptable part of growing up. In a group practice it is usually easy for adolescents to see another doctor in the partnership. Girls of all ages, but perhaps particularly in adolescence, may prefer to see a woman doctor. Although only 20 per cent of general practitioners are women, many groups contain at least one female family doctor.

One common fear of adolescents is that the information they give to the doctor will be passed on to their parents. This fear means that the young person may not tell the doctor about an important symptom. Most doctors are aware of this difficulty and consider that confidential consultations are appropriate for teenagers of more than 15 years old and are an essential part of a trusting relationship with young people.

CONSULTING THE DOCTOR

Each practice has its own hours, appointments system and policy on home visits and emergencies. It is important to choose a practice whose hours and appointments system are convenient for you. You should also make sure that you understand how to contact a doctor without an appointment: there may, for example, be a different telephone number for out-of-surgery hours.

HOME VISIT OR SURGERY?

Most doctors enjoy visiting patients at home and feel that it is useful to see something of the background of the family. However, home visits are time-consuming; the doctor could see three or four children in the surgery in the time it takes to visit one child. Also, the facilities for examining patients and carrying out simple diagnostic tests are better in the surgery than at home. If you live near the doctor or have access to a car, a visit to the surgery is unlikely to make your child more unwell. If you save your doctor a home visit by taking your child to the practice it is entirely reasonable to ask the receptionist to arrange for the doctor to see you quickly. Some practices have a small room where sick and potentially infectious patients can wait.

TELEPHONE CONSULTATIONS

Some doctors set aside a certain time during each day when their patients are encouraged to discuss problems with them on the telephone. Unless the problem is very urgent, most doctors prefer parents to leave a number with the receptionist so that their calls can be returned at the end of the surgery session or between consultations.

It is usually up to the parent to decide whether a child needs to be seen by the doctor or not. However, if you can speak to the doctor on the telephone it sometimes becomes clear that an urgent visit is not needed. Many illnesses take time to develop. It is impossible, for example, to tell whether a child has *appendicitis* an hour after starting to develop a colicky tummy ache. A telephone consultation can often clarify what is the most useful time for you to make a visit to the surgery or whether a visit is needed at all.

NIGHT CONSULTATIONS

Many parents are reluctant to contact the doctor in the middle of the night, but if you think that you need medical help urgently you should telephone the doctor at any time. Although any problem seems worse during the night, there are in fact some symptoms that are usually more severe during the night, such as *asthma* and *croup*. If you have doubts about whether to call your doctor, it is worth telephoning during the evening to ask about your child's symptoms. The doctor may prefer to visit you straightaway rather than risk having to come out at night.

Many doctors, particularly in cities, employ a deputizing service for night and weekend visits to ensure that they are able to work properly during the day. The deputizing service arranges for a doctor who is not a member of the practice to answer calls during the night and, if necessary, to make visits. All doctors who work for these services are fully qualified and some are in fact family doctors.

However, it is important to fill in the details of your child's case for a deputizing doctor, as he will not have access to your child's notes.

BOOKING AN APPOINTMENT

If your practice runs an appointments system, it is helpful to let the receptionist know what you need when you book an appointment. Children who are unwell are seen in ordinary surgeries, whilst *developmental checks*, full medical examinations and *immunizations* are often carried out in special child health clinics within the practice.

The doctor will find it difficult to deal with more than one person in the time allowed for one appointment. If you wish to consult about yourself as well as your child, or about two children, ask for double time, and ask the receptionist to make sure that your doctor has both sets of notes.

MAKING THE MOST OF THE CONSULTATION

During the consultation, as well as describing the symptoms, tell the doctor which remedies you have tried. You may find it helpful to note whether your child has been in recent contact with anyone who has been ill, whether there is a past or family history of a similar illness and also which *immunizations* your child has had.

Good communication is essential. If it becomes obvious during the course of the consultation that your doctor has misunderstood you, restate your point. You may find it helpful to make a list of questions that you want to ask before you go to the surgery. If the doctor uses medical jargon that you do not understand, do not hesitate to ask for an explanation. You will ideally want to know what is wrong with your child by the end of the consultation. However, in many instances an exact diagnosis is not possible, though the doctor will usually be able to tell you whether the illness is serious or not.

You will also want to understand clearly the treatment that is suggested. For example, does the medicine prescribed need to be given for a set number of days or only until the child has recovered? Should it be given on an empty stomach or after a meal? Although four times a day is prescribed, does it really matter if it is given three times a day instead? Does the medicine have any side effects? If the treatment is complex or unfamiliar to you, write down the doctor's recommendations or ask for written instructions. At the end of the consultation you will need to know whether you should make another appointment or whether you should contact the doctor again only if your child does not get better within a few days.

PRESCRIPTIONS

Do not expect a prescription at the end of each consultation: the majority of childhood infections are caused by viruses that antibiotics will not affect. Drugs are often unnecessary: half a glass of warm water with a teaspoon of honey is as effective as cough medicine in suppressing a cough. Babies and toddlers with diarrhoea and vomiting need to have lost fluid replaced and should not be given a drug against diarrhoea. Most doctors would rather have their prescriptions questioned by parents than be asked for antibiotics to cure simple colds.

SEEING A SPECIALIST

If your child needs to be seen by a hospital specialist, your family doctor will make the appropriate referral by writing a letter for you to take or send to the hospital. Ask your doctor if there is a choice of specialists, and what their particular strengths are.

The specialist will give advice and may arrange special investigations or treatment. Nonetheless the day-to-day medical care of your child remains the responsibility of your family doctor. If you visit a specialist, your family doctor will receive a letter from him about a week later, and will be able to answer any queries that you may have.

If you are unhappy about your child's progress, discuss whether a second opinion is indicated. Sometimes your general practitioner will persuade you that it is not necessary, but on other occasions it is reasonable to insist on a referral.

THE SICK CHILD AT HOME

The great majority of sick children are cared for at home. If you are a new parent or if you are faced with an illness which is new to you, you may feel unsure of your ability to cope, but in most instances caring for a sick child's needs does not require special nursing skills.

If your child has a simple illness, like a cold or stomach upset, you will probably feel happy to cope at home without seeking further advice. However, with a more serious illness, such as *measles*, you may want to call the family doctor for specific advice about treatment. Home nursing can be even more demanding after your child has been in hospital with a serious illness, when it may be necessary to continue some of the special care he has been receiving.

If you have a choice between nursing a child at home or in hospital, remember that there are many advantages to nursing at home. Your child will feel more secure in familiar surroundings, you can be flexible about times for giving meals, medicines or baths, and your other children can be more easily cared for at the same time. You may worry that you will fail to observe some important change in the way the illness is developing, or that you will miss signs that your child's condition is

GAMES AND ENTERTAINMENT

When your child is confined to bed, she will probably want entertainment. Sick children usually prefer simple favourites well within their abilities, rather than new and challenging games. However, if your child simply wants to drowse or watch television, there is no need for other distractions.

Children appear to recover more quickly than adults, but they do need some time before they are able to resume their normal activities. For older children the key decision is to judge when they are fit to go to school. This will usually be when they feel able to cope, but if they are still easily tired, weepy and irritable, a few more days at home are needed.

Entertaining a child who is ill can be very demanding. Thinking of games that will amuse your child while you are busy can be particularly difficult. You may find the following ideas useful.

For babies:
o mobiles
o rattles
o soft toys, especially ones that squeak
o musical toys or boxes
o a mirror

For toddlers:
o crayons or felt-tip pens
o small blackboard, chalks and duster
o small box or bag containing surprises such as balloons, a small car, a necklace, a small bell
o large-piece jigsaw
o play-dough and biscuit cutters
o plasticine
o small building bricks
o sticky stars and shapes
o bubbles to blow
o a kaleidoscope

For older children:
o card games for one person, such as patience
o writing a diary
o making a scrapbook or stamp album
o making a shell box
o Origami
o modelling with pipe cleaners
o tiddly winks
o easy knitting, crochet or embroidery
o small-piece jigsaws
o string for cat's cradle
o construction kits, such as Lego
o games with marbles, such as solitaire

THE SICK CHILD AT HOME

deteriorating. Even when your child's needs are fairly routine, such as feeding or bathing, you may be afraid of making the illness worse or causing pain. However, nobody knows your child as well as you do, and you, better than anyone, will know when he is not progressing as he should be. Common sense is the best guide to home nursing, but if you are in doubt ask your doctor for advice.

Your family situation

If you and your partner both work, or if you are a single parent, caring for a child who is ill creates special problems. There are obvious adjustments that can be made, such as keeping housework to a minimum, making simple meals and asking friends and other members of the family to help. Taking time off work depends very much on individual circumstances. If it is not possible for you to be at home, the most important factor for your peace of mind is the adequacy of the arrangements that can be made for your child while you are at work.

Younger brothers and sisters will not easily accept the argument that the sick child needs most of your attention. Unless they are very young, they should be given an explanation of what is happening. They can be involved in helping you, or in playing games with the sick child. If possible, try to make some time, however brief, when you can give attention to your other children.

Finally, and perhaps most importantly, if you are to care for your sick child, you must look after yourself. Eating and sleeping sensibly and having time to yourself away from him, even if it is only for an hour are essential for your well-being. Night nursing is particularly tiring, so the simplest plan may be for you to alternate nights 'on duty' with your partner or a friend.

Gentle games and pastimes that involve the imagination fascinate children: you can teach your sick child how to make finger shadows and then she can experiment in making different kinds and performing 'shows'.

Gentle music can be soothing for a sick child of any age. A personal stereo allows your child to take her music with her from room to room. Recorded stories are also often popular.

WHAT TO LOOK FOR

The treatment that your doctor recommends may rest heavily on the story that you tell. However, it can be difficult to put your finger on exactly what is wrong when your child is sick. Making observations about specific aspects of your child's health may help you to assess the illness and also to communicate with your doctor. The following are useful topics to consider.

DROWSINESS AND CONFUSION

It is always worrying when a sick child becomes abnormally drowsy. Likewise, if a child becomes confused or loses normal skills, you should seek help.

MOVEMENTS

Babies, infants and older children commonly make odd twitching movements when they are asleep or feverish. However, if your child makes unexpected or persistent movements which appear to be beyond control you should report this to your doctor. If your child jerks uncontrollably, he may be having a *fit*. Try to remember what happened immediately before and after, as well as during the event. Most of these episodes will turn out to be of no lasting significance, but a clear description will help your doctor advise you.

DISCOMFORT

Young children do not distinguish between the expected pain that follows a fall and the unexpected aches and pains of illness. Sorting out just where the pain is can be a problem, especially in a young child. So it is as well to remember what your child does as well as says when the discomfort occurs. For example, is the pain bad enough to interfere with play, eating or watching television? Is the pain associated with a change of complexion, or with tears or vomiting? How long does it last? Will your child allow you to touch or rub it better? Does a cuddle ease the pain or are you pushed away?

Remember that even young children do not take long to realize that complaining of pain has a dramatic effect on the behaviour of adults and usually results in unexpected rewards. Watching your child's behaviour during an episode of pain or discomfort often helps you to decide the importance and urgency of the problem.

TEMPERATURE, PULSE AND BREATHING

In hospital, nurses regularly record a child's body temperature, pulse rate and rate of breathing. Body temperature gives some information about the body's *metabolism* as a whole, and is used as a guide to infection. Pulse rate is a useful measure of the heart's activity,

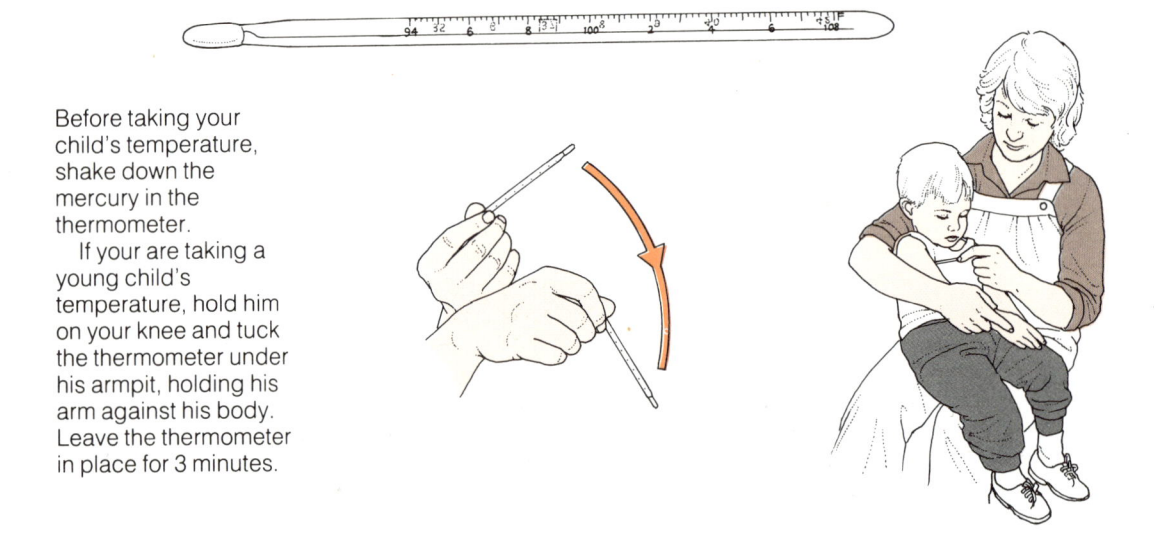

Before taking your child's temperature, shake down the mercury in the thermometer.
If your are taking a young child's temperature, hold him on your knee and tuck the thermometer under his armpit, holding his arm against his body. Leave the thermometer in place for 3 minutes.

and the rate of breathing measures how hard the lungs are working. Both pulse and breathing rate change when the body is challenged by an illness, just as they do when you climb the stairs, or get excited or upset.

You do not usually need to take your child's pulse. It should be enough to measure temperature and to note whether your child is pale or flushed, restless or settled, sweating or dry-skinned.

With a sensible, normal child aged 5 years or more, body temperature can be measured as in adults, by placing a clinical thermometer under the tongue. Normal body temperature taken by this method is about 37°C (98.4°F) but may vary within 0.6°C (1°F). In children under 5 years of age, including babies, the best site for recording temperature is under the arm. Temperature recorded under the arm is about 0.6°C (1°F) lower than in the mouth. Strip thermometers, which are placed on the child's forehead, are far less accurate than clinical thermometers and should be used only as a rough guide. There is no point in measuring temperature under the tongue immediately after a hot or cold drink, or a meal.

You can also observe your child's breathing pattern. At rest, breathing is normally quiet, unstressed and regular, although in babies it is more rapid and can vary in depth and frequency. In sickness, breathing may become more rapid, much deeper, or be accompanied by far more effort, especially if the illness involves the lungs. In severe illness it can become all three: rapid, deep and forced. It is the accompanying noises that can be most worrying. A grunting noise when the child breathes in, called *stridor*, is usually due to narrowing of the upper airways. A high squeaky noise on breathing out, called wheeze, is usually due to narrowing of the lower airways to the lungs.

EATING AND DRINKING

Children often react to illness with loss of appetite or vomiting. It does not necessarily mean anything is wrong with their stomachs.

In some illnesses, it can be important to know how much fluid and food has been taken and how much retained. Estimating the amount vomited back is very difficult, as it often looks far more than it really is. The doctor may ask about the colour and content of the vomit, how often the vomiting occurred, its timing in relation to drinks and meals, whether it caused discomfort and whether it trickled out (effortless vomiting) or shot out (projectile vomiting).

Many doctors recommend against putting a young baby to sleep or lie down on his back as, if he vomits, he could choke or inhale the vomit. This is especially important if your baby has a stomach upset. Instead, lie him on one side, propped up with a rolled towel behind his back, if necessary. Alternatively, lie him on his stomach, with his head turned to one side.

BLADDER AND BOWEL

Just as many acute illnesses affect the appetite and cause vomiting, so they change the habit of the bladder and the bowel. Note when and how often the sick child has a dirty nappy or goes to the toilet and pay attention to what is passed. Does the urine look and smell normal? Is the volume greater or less than normal? Is passing urine associated with discomfort?

Looking at the bowel motion is less instructive. However, if your child has diarrhoea, then it can be important to note whether the stool is watery, whether it contains blood or mucus and whether the action appears to be painful. Stools vary in colour and the different shades of brown and green have no significance.

Constipation can be a sign of dehydration, although a sick child who does not eat much is bound to pass fewer motions than usual.

CARE

If possible keep your home warm enough so that your child can move from room to room with you and stay comfortable in light pyjamas and a dressing gown. Very few children like or need to lie in a darkened quiet room. However, bright lights do irritate sore eyes, and quietness is appreciated by anyone who has a headache. Even if sick children cannot say what they want, they often show what distresses them by their behaviour.

COMFORT AND REST

The first aim is to ensure comfort. A sick child who is comfortable and free from pain will take as much rest as is needed. If your child wants to get out of bed, there is no need to object: the best solution is to provide a comfortable chair or a pile of cushions wherever you are, so that your child can be comforted by your presence and you can keep an eye on him.

If a child has pain in a particular place, with a broken bone or an inflamed joint, for example, then the position that he rests in can be important. A child will instinctively place the painful limb in the position of least discomfort. Plenty of pillows help, for they can both support and surround and thus protect. Often the local hospital can supply equipment that will help keep your child in the correct position while permitting some mobility.

A breathless child will probably be most comfortable sitting supported by pillows. A breathless baby can be put into a reclining baby chair. At night, more pillows than usual will help an older child, or you can raise the head end of the child's bed with a few books.

FEVER

If your child has a fever, remove most of his clothes: light cotton nightclothes are the most that is needed. If the room is very warm, a cooling fan is helpful, but avoid pointing it directly at your child as this can be uncomfortable. If these simple procedures do not lower the fever, a cool wash may help. Wring out a flannel in tepid water and gently run it over your child's limbs, face and neck, leaving a film of moisture on the skin.

PAIN RELIEF

Pain is always worse for children when borne alone in the silence of their own company. Your comforting presence and enough, but not too much, distraction and entertainment play an important role.

There is no reason why any child should be in continuous pain. Painkillers such as paracetamol are usually effective, but reassurance and comforting can also help.

Children, even young infants, can be remarkably brave. Often your acceptance that your child has pain makes the pain much easier to bear. It may also help if you explain how the treatment and care that you give will help to relieve pain or cure the illness. Fear associated with uncertainty makes pain harder to bear. Knowing what is going to happen makes acceptance easier. A simple truthful explanation can help older children who want to know why they are in pain.

A cold compress placed over the forehead can be soothing for a child with a fever and may lessen a headache. Make one by soaking a flannel in ice-cold water and then squeezing out most of the water. Older children may find a covered hot-water bottle a comfort, either hugged close for stomach pain, or against the ear for earache. Hot-water bottles should not be given to babies and toddlers because of the risk of burns.

SKIN CARE AND CLEANLINESS

Many children resent being disturbed for the sake of cleanliness when they are sick. All that is usually necessary is to wash the child's hands and face, although a baby or toddler who is not toilet-trained will need the nappy area washed as well. If your baby or toddler has diarrhoea, change the nappy as soon as it is dirty. Avoid giving a hot bath if your child has a fever because it can make the fever rise even higher. If your child is perspiring give a quick wash all over with a flannel while he lies on a large towel.

Make sure that teeth are cleaned as usual, especially if your child is not eating or drinking, as this can make the mouth dry and sour. Applying lip salve helps to prevent cracked and sore lips.

FLUIDS AND FOOD

Children who are feverish usually have a poor appetite. No sick child should be forced to eat. Usually small frequent snacks are more acceptable than complete meals and it often helps to build the snacks round favourite foods. Drinks are more important than food and adequate nutrition can usually be given in the form of fluids. A teacher-beaker may be useful; alternatively, straws are often popular.

Fever causes sweating, so a fevered child needs to drink more. Small, frequent sips are usually easiest to cope with. Older children may enjoy sucking ice or ice lollies, and they may also enjoy fizzy drinks.

Not uncommonly, sick children develop sore mouths as a result of ulcers or infection. They will find it easier to eat bland foods such as ice cream, yoghurt, bananas, mashed potatoes or scrambled eggs, or food that has been blended. Avoid acidic foods like tomatoes, citrus fruit and citrus juices, and spicy or salty foods.

If your child has been prescribed antibiotics you may like to give yoghurt, as this may help to restore the beneficial bacteria in the gut that the drugs destroy. However, there is no proof that it does, so do not force yoghurt on an unwilling child.

INFECTIONS

Many of the common childhood infections are highly contagious, so if the rest of the family has not already had the disease they will usually catch it no matter what precautions you take. However, friends who have not had the illness should stay away until your child is no longer infectious, which does not necessarily mean until he has recovered.

If your child has a gastro-intestinal infection, the risk of cross-infection can be greatly reduced by a high standard of hygiene, particularly by meticulous hand-washing. Dirty linen and nappies should be washed straightaway. Ask your child to use his own towel and flannel.

▶ **See also** Infection

MEDICINE CABINET

The cabinet should contain:
o Any medicine that has been given by prescription for current illness. Antibiotics should be kept in the refrigerator, but make sure that they are out of a small child's reach or in a childproof container
o Paracetamol for relief of pain and to reduce fever in adult or junior form depending on the age of your child
o A bottle of kaolin mixture for diarrhoea. This should not be given to babies or toddlers
o A few tablets of an antacid such as aluminium hydroxide for minor tummy aches
o A small bottle of Dramamine or Avomine tablets for car- or sea-sickness
o A couple of 5 ml teaspoons from the chemist and a measuring glass for liquid medicines
o Fabric plasters of various sizes and shapes. Avoid waterproof plasters as these make the skin soggy
o A packet of cotton-wool
o A pair of hand scissors
o A pair of tweezers to remove splinters
o A few packets of sterile gauze swabs
o Non-adherent dry absorbent dressing (melolin) for covering burns or wounds
o Bandages of various sizes, including an 8 cm (3 in) crepe bandage for minor sprains
o Adhesive strapping for fastening bandages
o A bottle of liquid antiseptic
o Plain or oily calamine lotion for irritating rashes. Unfortunately, calamine lotion is rather messy and its effect soon wears off
o Aqueous cream, such as Nivea, for minor rashes, and zinc and castor oil cream for nappy rash if you have a child in nappies
o A glass and mercury clinical thermometer

Remember:

o Keep medicines out of children's reach and in childproof containers
o Throw away prescribed medicines after finishing a course
o Check for use-by-dates on medicines

GIVING MEDICINE

Medicines are usually prescribed to be given once, twice, three or four times each day: the time interval depends on how quickly the drug becomes active and how long its effects last. Many drugs are effective only if taken at regular intervals. However, it is rarely necessary to wake your child during the night to give medicine. For example, if a medicine has been prescribed to be given three times a day at 8-hourly intervals, give the first dose on waking and the last just before your child falls asleep, unless he usually wakes for a drink in the night, in which case the last dose can be given at the same time.

Most medicines should be given 30 minutes or so before a meal. This not only aids rapid absorption but also means that should your child become distressed he will settle down before a meal. If the medicine or the attempt to reject it leads to retching, your child is less likely to vomit because the stomach is empty. However, remember to read carefully the directions as some medicines should be given with or after a meal.

It is important that your child finishes a course of antibiotics. If he does not, some of the problem-causing bacteria may remain and may have developed a resistance to the drug.

BY MOUTH

It can be difficult to make sure that your child actually takes the medicine. Your strategy for dealing with this will vary, depending among other things on the age of your child, his temperament and the taste and form of the medicine. Your own attitude is important: try to keep a calm, matter-of-fact approach and disguise your own feelings if you yourself dislike medicine or are a poor pill-swallower. Your youngster may surprise you by taking the medicine easily.

Most toddlers protest initially at having to take medicine, but you can usually get them to take it without too much fuss. It is important to explain why you want the child to take the medicine and that taking it will make him feel better.

If you have to give a spoonful of medicine, transfer it into a small cup and give a little at a time, so that what is spat out can be collected and regiven. It helps to have a favourite drink ready to chase the medicine down, and it may help to offer a treat of some sort as a reward.

Never put the medicine into a large amount of fluid or mix it with food as your child may not take it all. If necessary, tablets may be crushed and added to a teaspoonful or so of liquid. Very sweet medicines, though still generally prescribed, are now frowned upon because they give the child a taste for sugar and if taken for long could encourage dental decay.

Some toddlers cannot be persuaded and a quiet firm approach is needed. You may need help, one person to hold the child and the other to give the medicine. Sit your child on your knee, with one of your child's arms behind your back and the other held by your hand. Then reach out for the medicine, which should be already prepared and lying on a nearby surface, and when your child opens his mouth to protest, pop the medicine in.

Deceiving may get one dose down, but it is a mistake, for it usually only works once and your child's trust is lost.

If you are having difficulties in getting your child to accept medicine, ask your family doctor if the drug is available in an alternative form. A different flavour or texture may be more acceptable to your child.

NOSE DROPS
To give nose drops to a baby, lie the baby across your knee with his neck extended over your left thigh; support his head in your left hand. Place the tip of the dropper just inside the nostril and release the prescribed number of drops. Leave the child in position for a minute.

To give nose drops to an older child, ask the child to blow his nose and to lie down on a comfortable surface with his neck extended over a pillow placed under the shoulders. Give the drops as above.

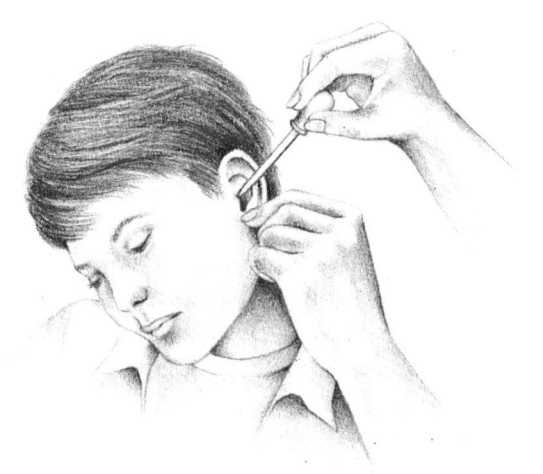

EAR DROPS
Lie the child on one side or tilt his head to the unaffected side. Place the dropper close to his ear and release the drops into the ear canal. Leave your child in this position for a minute or so. Then put a piece of cotton-wool in the ear to prevent any excess fluid running out, but take care not to pack it into the ear so tightly that you cannot get it out.

EYE DROPS
Two people are needed to put drops in the eyes of all but the most co-operative youngsters. A young child can lie on your knee, and an older child should lie on a comfortable surface. Your helper should hold the child's head, while you stand beside the child and hold the dropper in one hand, resting your hand on the child's forehead. Place your other hand on his cheek with your index finger near his lower lid. Ask or encourage him to look up and pull the lower lid gently downwards with your index finger. Lower the dropper so that you can put the prescribed number of drops in the gap between the lower lid and the eye. Take care that the dropper itself does not touch the eye or the lid and hurt the child.

ANAL ADMINISTRATION
Occasionally medicines are prescribed to be given via the anus. Their form and the way that they are administered vary. For each medication, you will be shown the technique and given an applicator by the doctor, nurse or dispensing chemist.

FIRST AID FOR MINOR INJURIES

Every growing child suffers from minor injuries. Without over-protecting your child, you cannot expect to prevent occasional cuts, burns and bruises. Some children seem to be particularly accident-prone: this may be because they are especially adventurous; or because they are unusually *clumsy*; or because they are under greater stress or strain than is normal.

The human body repairs itself very efficiently after everyday cuts, scrapes, grazes, bruises and knocks. Do not encourage squeamishness about minor injuries. If your child wants to see what you are doing, let him. Older children can help with cleaning and dressing their own injuries, and this will give them the knowledge and confidence to tackle such problems when help is not around.

It is important to wash your hands before treating any injury, and to avoid coughing or sneezing over a wound.

This section describes the actions that you can take in the way of first-aid treatment for minor injuries, with advice on when to carry out treatment yourself, when to consult a doctor and when to rush your child straight to hospital.

Emergency actions at the end of the book outlines what you should do in more serious life-threatening situations; **Accident and injury** in Part Three covers hospital treatment for accidental injuries and how you can help.

CUTS AND GRAZES

Interfere with these small wounds as little as possible, beyond cleaning, drying and dressing them. Hold the wound under clean running water to wash away dirt and debris. A dirty graze will be painful so run the water slowly at first, then faster as the child gets used to it. Any dirt that cannot be washed off can be eased off with the corner of a gauze square. Bleeding also helps to wash out the cut. Dry the surrounding skin thoroughly with cotton-wool or paper tissues, dabbing away from the wound's edge.

Small wounds can be covered with plasters. If the wound is on a joint or another awkward site, a sterile dressing held in place with a bandage may be more effective. Specially-shaped dressings are available for difficult places like knuckles and knees. The aim of dressing is to cushion the area from knocks and to keep it clean and dry. Moist skin takes longer to heal and is more prone to infection, so avoid waterproof dressings if possible. Never use a fluffy dressing on the wound – it may adhere and pull away the scab. Creams or ointments of any sort, antiseptic or otherwise, are unnecessary.

If blood soaks through a dressing, put another one on top. Leave the dressing on a wound until healing is well under way, usually 2 to 3 days. If the dressing comes off before this, replace it with a new one.

Seek medical help if a cut does not stop bleeding within a few minutes; or if it shows no signs of healing within 2 to 3 days; or if it becomes yellow and pus-filled. Wounds caused by dirty objects, particularly if rusty or soil-contaminated, should be seen by a doctor since there is a risk of *tetanus*. Your child may need a booster immunization.

A deep, long or jagged cut, or an extensive graze, may leave a scar. Consult your doctor about a wound like this fairly quickly. He may decide that it should be brought together by stitches or special adhesive strips, but once the edges of the wound have started to heal themselves they will not rejoin if stitched.

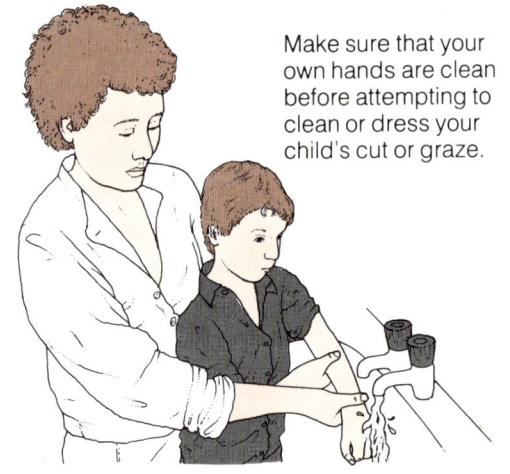

Make sure that your own hands are clean before attempting to clean or dress your child's cut or graze.

BRUISES

A bruise, or contusion, is caused by bleeding from damaged blood vessels beneath skin that remains intact. The blood turns the area red, then blue or black, and then yellow or green as the area heals.

A small bruise needs no treatment. Large or painful bruises may be cooled with a cold compress or ice-pack: low temperatures constrict the small blood vessels and may lessen the bleeding and swelling.

If there is bleeding under a nail, the blood cannot escape and this puts pressure on the sensitive tissues of the injured finger or toe. This may cause severe pain. Take your child to the doctor, who may burn or drill a tiny hole through the nail. This procedure sounds harrowing but it quickly releases the pressure under the nail and relieves pain.

Seek medical help if your child seems to bruise repeatedly or easily. There may be an underlying disorder.

intact. The small ring-pads used for bunions are also useful for blisters; you can put a plaster or pad-plus-bandage dressing on top. After a few days, the fluid within the blister will be reabsorbed and the overlying skin will shrivel and fall away. If a blister does burst, leave the overlying skin as it is and treat as for any small wound.

Seek medical help if the size of a burn is greater than 2.5 cm (1 in); if it is deep; or if it is on a child's face, a joint or any other crucial part of the body. You should also seek help if a blister or small burn becomes infected.

If your child's skin is hot, red and sore as a result of sunburn you can treat this by tepid bathing, applying liberally a soothing lotion such as calamine and giving him paracetamol to relieve pain if necessary. Put on the lightest, softest clothing while the skin is still painful, and do not let him expose the burnt skin to the sun until it is no longer sore. Seek medical help if sunburn is severe and the skin is blistered.

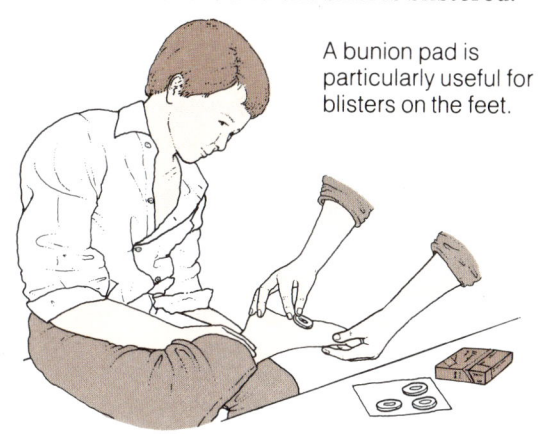

Make an ice-pack by putting several ice-cubes in a plastic bag and sealing the bag.

A bunion pad is particularly useful for blisters on the feet.

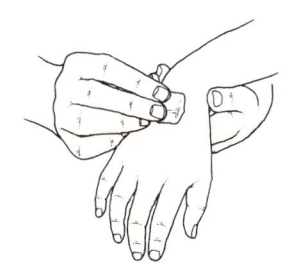

BURNS

A small surface burn caused by electricity may conceal extensive damage in the tissues beneath. A small burn not caused by electricity can usually be treated at home.

Cool the burned skin at once with cold, clean, running water; keep cooling it for 10 minutes. Dry it gently with a clean towel and cover with a non-adhesive dressing. Do not apply any sort of ointment.

Blisters may be caused by burns, scalds, or by friction. They are part of the skin's protective mechanism and should be left

An ice-cube can be used to cool a small burn; you will need a basin or towel to catch the drips.

BITES AND STINGS

Human bites that break the skin should always be shown to a doctor. There is a high risk of infection from the bacteria in the biter's mouth. Small animal bites and scratches rarely have serious consequences although you should wash and dress the wound. However, if the animal was wild or unfamiliar or acting oddly you should seek medical advice, as there may be a risk of rabies – a viral infection of the brain passed on by animals, against which your child can be given a series of vaccinations. Deeper bites from dogs, cats, rabbits and other large animals may become infected and should also be seen by a doctor. Wash and dress the wound first. Do the same for a snake bite; try to remember what the snake looked like so that appropriate anti-venom can be given if necessary.

The best precautions you can take are to make sure your child's and your pet's *immunizations* are kept up to date and to teach your child to handle animals properly and confidently.

The skin's natural reaction to insect bites and stings is to swell, redden and itch. A cold compress or calamine helps to reduce itchiness. Bee and wasp stings can be very painful and the child will need plenty of consolation. If you can see the bee's sting in the skin, you may wish to remove it gently with fine tweezers. Do not try to squeeze it out, as you may push more venom into the skin. The pain of the sting usually fades in an hour or so.

A few children are extra-sensitive to bites or stings and may show signs of *anaphylactic shock* in which case they need emergency help.

If you can see a bee's sting, remove it promptly before the child's skin around the area begins to swell.

SPRAINS AND STRAINS

A sprain happens when a joint is forced past its normal limit of movement and some of the ligaments and other joint tissues are damaged. The main signs are swelling and pain, particularly on movement.

A mild sprain requires little treatment except rest as the child gradually recovers use of the joint. Bandaging may help to restrict movement and provide support for the first day, but you should encourage the child to use the joint as soon as possible.

A strain is caused by over-stretching or over-sudden contraction of a muscle so that some of its fibres are damaged. A strained muscle is also sometimes called a pulled muscle. Treat a mild strain in the same way as a sprain.

Seek medical help for any sprain, strain and similar injury that prevents the child moving the affected part, or causes extreme pain when he does so. It is best not to move the child; call help to the scene instead.

If an originally mild sprain or strain worsens steadily, instead of starting to heal after a few hours, you should consult a doctor.

Your child should start gently using a sprained joint as soon as the sharp pain dies down. She should not force any movement that produces sudden pain.

SUNSTROKE AND HEATSTROKE

Exposure to the sun or to great heat can lead to heat exhaustion when the salt and water balance of the body is upset. The symptoms of mild sun- or heatstroke are weakness, dizziness and fever. Your child should rest in a cool well-ventilated room. Sponge your child's skin with cool water and give him plenty of slightly salted drinks of water. If he has not recovered within a few hours you should consult a doctor.

If your child suddenly develops a high fever and becomes delirious he should be taken immediately to hospital for emergency treatment.

Use cool rather than cold water for sponging. Leave a fine film of water on the child's skin which will cool the child as it dries.

EYE, EAR AND NOSE INJURIES

If your child gets any sort of chemical in his eye, the first priority is to wash the chemical away. It is best to do this with clean tap water. Tilt the child's head to the side of the injured eye and run the liquid over it, making sure that the liquid drains away freely and does not contaminate the skin. Encourage the child to blink. After a few minutes, cover the eye and take the child directly to hospital. To reduce painful eye movements in one injured eye it may help to cover the uninjured eye, since both eyes tend to move in unison.

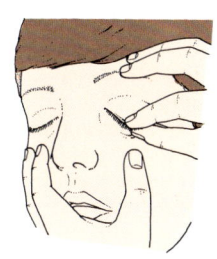

If your child has something in his eye, you should encourage him to cry, as the foreign body may be washed away by tear fluid. Discourage him from rubbing the affected eye. Rubbing the other eye stimulates both eyes to water and may wash out the particle. If the foreign body is not washed out by tears, you can look for it by lifting up each lid in turn and looking at both the surface of the eyeball and the lid lining. Ask an older child to look up, down to the left and to the right. If you can see the particle, remove it gently by picking it up on a twist of cotton-wool or a corner of a tissue.

If you encounter any difficulty, the task is best left to a doctor. You should also take your child to the doctor if there is any risk of there being a splinter of glass or metal in the eye.

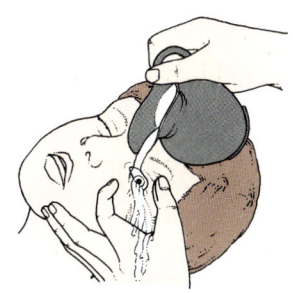

If a child with a chemical in his eye cannot easily open the eye, you may have to gently hold the lids open as you flush the eye with water.

Gently pulling the upper lid down over the lower lid may sometimes be enough to dislodge a foreign body.

A black eye is caused by bruising of the tissues around the eye. The eyeball itself, encased in its bony socket, is rarely damaged. However, if the eye looks odd or the child says his sight is affected in any way, you should consult a doctor.

Small objects such as beads, peas, tissue paper and small pebbles often find their way into children's ears and up their noses. This causes irritation, and clumsy attempts to remove the objects only worsen the situation. Medical advice should be sought.

An insect in the ear canal can frighten a child with its buzzing and movements. A few drops of oil in the canal will usually kill the insect. Take your child to the doctor, as it may be necessary to remove the insect by syringing.

HOSPITALS AND THE SICK CHILD

At some time or another most children have to go to hospital. They may be admitted directly to a ward as the result of an accident or illness. More often they will visit a day-time clinic as an outpatient, referred by the family doctor to see a hospital specialist.

Hospitals can seem frightening places to your child, especially if admission was so sudden that you could not prepare him for it. Try to be as reassuring and calm as possible, even though the experience will probably be equally stressful for you.

▶ **See also** Appendix: Who's who in the health service

HOSPITAL DEPARTMENTS

The names used to describe the various departments within a hospital can be confusing unless your are familiar with them. You may feel intimidated by the terminology unless someone explains to you what it means, and you may have difficulties finding your way around a large hospital unless you can understand the signs. Below are the names of the departments that you might have to visit with your child. Although a paediatrician is most likely to see your child, you may also visit other departments for more specialized advice and treatment.

CARDIOLOGY	Problems of the heart
CHEMICAL PATHOLOGY	Analysis of substances found in samples of blood, urine and faeces
DERMATOLOGY	Problems of the skin
EAR, NOSE AND THROAT (ENT)	Problems of the ears, nose, throat and sinuses
ENDOCRINOLOGY	Problems of the endocrine glands and hormones
GASTRO-ENTEROLOGY	Problems of the stomach and intestines
HAEMATOLOGY	Analysis of blood and bone marrow
HISTOLOGY	Analysis of tissue samples
MICROBIOLOGY	Identification of organisms that cause disease
NEPHROLOGY	Problems of the kidneys
NEUROLOGY	Problems of the brain, nerves and muscles
NEUROSURGERY	Brain and spinal cord surgery
OBSTETRICS	Care of women and babies during pregnancy, birth and the postnatal period
ONCOLOGY	Treatment of cancers
OPHTHALMOLOGY	Problems of the eye
ORTHOPAEDICS	Surgical treatment of bone and joint disorders
PAEDIATRICS	All the health problems affecting children
PSYCHIATRY	Mental illness and emotional disturbance
RADIOLOGY	X-rays and their interpretation
RHEUMATOLOGY	Problems of the joints and surrounding tissues
THORACIC SURGERY	Chest and lung surgery
UROLOGY	Problems of the kidneys and urinary tract
VENEREOLOGY	Venereal disease

OUTPATIENT APPOINTMENTS

The doctor you see in an outpatient clinic will be a specialist in a particular field of medicine. Find out the doctor's name (it may not be the consultant you have been referred to but another member of his team); this is useful for you to know, and means you can introduce the doctor to your child and make the interview seem more friendly and less impersonal for him. Do the same if you have to take your child to see doctors in other departments for special tests or treatment.

Because of the unpredictable nature of the cases that have to be dealt with, it is difficult for hospitals to make outpatient clinics run to time, and so you may have to wait. Ask for information about how long the delay is likely to be and let the staff know if your child is becoming distressed by the waiting.

After examining your child, the specialist may decide that he can treat him in the clinic, with regular outpatient appointments. Alternatively, he may refer him back to your family doctor with the results of the examination and advice on treatment; or he may suggest that your child should come into hospital for further treatment.

DECISIONS ABOUT TREATMENT

You will probably want to know what the treatment will involve, the risks and benefits to your child, the final outcome and long-term effects, and it can be useful to make a written list of questions you want to ask the specialist.

If, after seeing a specialist, you feel in any way worried about the suggested treatment, you could talk about this to your family doctor. It is entirely reasonable for you to seek as much advice as possible about something as important as your child's health.

Although some clinics (especially in children's hospitals) do provide a play area with toys for children, it is wise to take food, drink, toys or books to keep your child occupied.

GOING INTO HOSPITAL

Until they are at least 7 years old, children need a parent with them as much as possible when they go into hospital. Young children tend to be bewildered by strange surroundings and may be terrified of separation from their parents. They may think that they are being punished for something they have done. Older children will have a greater awareness of what is happening, but may still have only a partial understanding of it and may be worried by fantasy-based fears about hospital or illness.

STAYING WITH YOUR CHILD

Most hospitals encourage parents to stay with their children throughout the day, and many have accommodation for one or both parents to stay overnight. However, hospitals vary in the facilities they can offer. Not all can allow parents to stay, for reasons of either policy or space, and of course not all parents can manage to stay because of commitments to work or other children. But if your child is under 7 years old, do try to do so, perhaps taking alternate nights with your partner or another adult to whom your child is close.

Whether you can stay overnight or only during the day, it is important for your child's well-being to spend as much time with him and to do as much for him as you can. He will be reassured and comforted if you can do most of the normal caring for him that you would at home – putting him to bed, getting him up, changing, feeding and washing.

Try to find out the hospital's policy on staying *before* your child is admitted, by asking your doctor or the specialist involved, talking to other parents or, best of all, visiting the ward and meeting the ward sister. You do have a right to be with your child, and most hospitals will make it easy for you to stay.

VISITING

If you cannot stay with your child, you should aim to visit at least once a day if this is possible. Even older children or adolescents still need the reassurance of frequent visits. Hospital life can be especially difficult for adolescents who may feel uncomfortable in a

A DAY IN HOSPITAL

The daily routine in a children's ward is usually fairly flexible, although much depends on the age of your child, how ill he is and whether he needs specialist treatment.

6.00-7.00 a.m. Children are woken; nurse checks each child's condition and temperature; those who are well enough get up.

7.45 Breakfast.

8.30 Ward round by doctor.

9.00-12.00 Play or teaching sessions for children who feel well enough

9.00 Medicine round; dressings, X-rays and physiotherapy for children who need them; baths or washing

10.30 The consultant doctor may make a ward round – he will check each child's chart and condition and talk about any treatment and how they are feeling.

11.30 Medicine round.

12.00 Lunch: children can usually choose from a menu passed round in advance. There are special meals for children on special diets.

12.30 p.m. Mid-day observation by nurse or sister; rest period.

14.00-16.00 Play or teaching sessions.

18.00 Medicine round.

18.00-19.00 Supper.

19.00 Younger children are washed and put to bed. Bedtime observation by nurse or sister. Older children are often allowed to stay up longer.

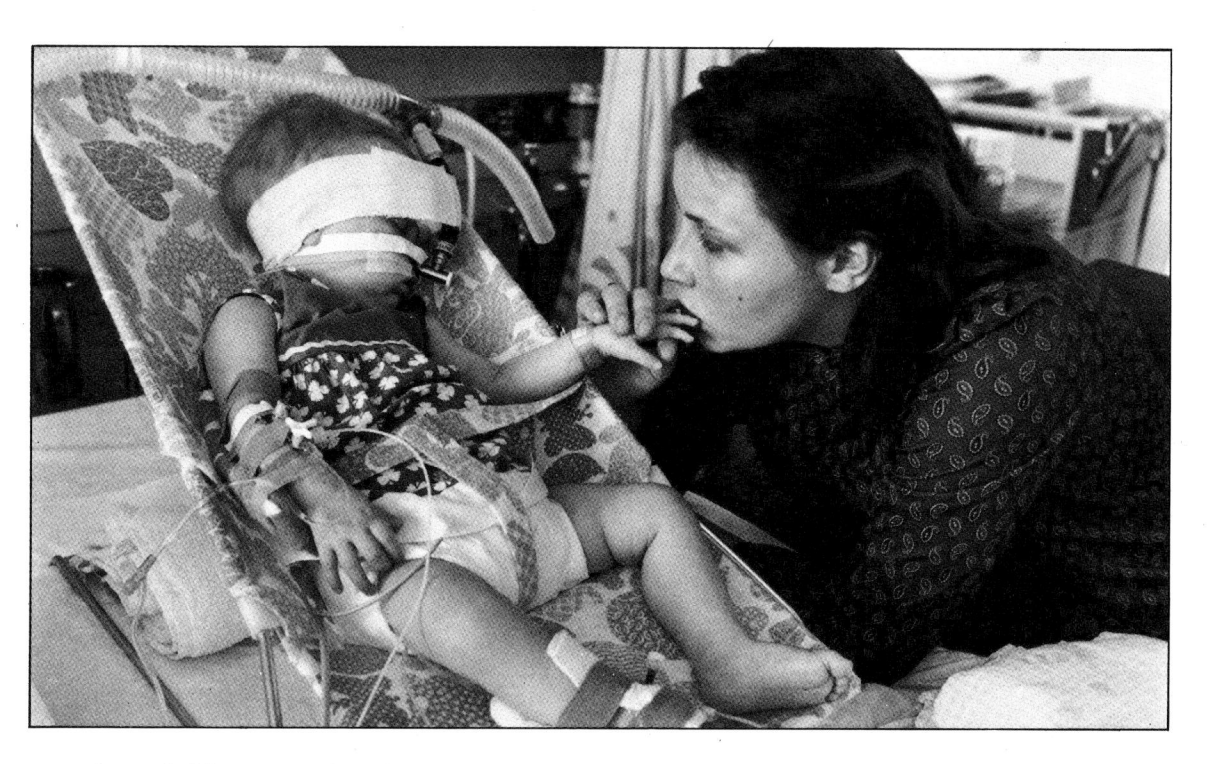

mixed-sex children's ward and yet out of place in an adult ward with elderly and perhaps very sick people.

If his brothers and sisters can visit regularly, your child will feel less isolated from what is going on at home. Ask friends and relatives to stagger their visits, so that your child has someone with him most of the day, rather than a crowd all at once – and you have some relief. If visiting is a real problem talk to the social worker. She may be able to arrange a home help or day nursery place if you have other children who cannot be left. She may also be able to help with the cost of fares or transport if these pose problems for you.

Your child may seem upset when you arrive or leave, but this does not mean that you should restrict your visits, which would indeed make him feel abandoned. He will be crying, not because your visits upset him, but because you are the person to whom he can express his emotions. When you go, say goodbye calmly and tell him (and the ward sister as well, so that she can remind him) exactly when you will be coming back.

Intensive care units can seem frightening places, especially as you are also likely to be tense about your child's condition. Whatever treatment your child is having, she needs to feel your love and presence: physical contact is especially important.

PROLONGED HOSPITAL STAY

It may be difficult to stay continuously with a child who has to spend long periods in hospital. All the same, you should try to be there until he has settled and whenever he is likely to be especially frightened or uncomfortable, for example before or after an operation. Letters or postcards from home will make him feel less isolated. Most wards have a mobile telephone, so that your child can telephone you or, if he is too young to do this, you can perhaps arrange with the ward sister to call him at a prearranged time. Toys from home are also reassuring.

▶ **See also** Appendices: The law and your child; Support groups and publications

WARD LIFE

Discover as much as you can about the normal daily routine of the ward, so that you can explain to your child what will be happening to him. There may be playleaders to guide the younger children in amusing themselves and teachers to help older ones keep abreast of schoolwork when they have a lengthy stay.

Ask whether your child will be able to wear his own clothes; remember that if he does so, the hospital laundry will not wash them. Most important of all, make sure that he takes his favourite teddy bear or cuddly. A young child may like to take in his own plate or cup or something special of yours as well, such as something that you often wear.

If you cannot stay with your child, make sure that the nurses know his routine so that there is as little change as possible. They should know whether he wakes or wets at night, what particular cuddly he needs to sleep with, whether he uses a dummy or is used to a night-time bottle. Even if you feel embarrassed because you think he is too old for these comfort measures, a hospital stay is not the time to persuade him to abandon them. If there are foods he dislikes, check that he will not be expected to eat these, or find out if there is a choice of menu. Tell the ward sister his nickname, if he has one, and any family words he may use – especially those he will use to ask to go to the toilet.

As your child begins to recover, your companionship is important to help pass the time. Most children's wards encourage play and provide some toys.

ASKING FOR INFORMATION

It is important to be as well-informed as possible about what will happen to your child; remember that you are always entitled to information. If you want to talk to your child's doctor, and do not get an opportunity to do so on the ward, ask the ward sister to make an appointment with him. Of course you will be aware of the many pressures on your doctor's time, but it will save misunderstandings if you get all the answers you want as soon as possible. If you do not understand them, ask again until you do.

However worried you may be, it is in the best interests of your child to be calm and co-operative in discussion with hospital staff. If you seem at odds with the medical staff who are looking after your child, this may worry him and shake his confidence in them.

OPERATIONS AND HOSPITAL PROCEDURES

Without frightening him, give your child as much honest information about the procedures he will undergo as you can. Give him a chance to express his feelings and fears about it all. Children's books describing life in hospital and hospital procedures can be useful. A young child may be helped by acting out what will happen to him, with you, with brothers and sisters or at his playgroup. It may help him to feel in control if he acts out the part of the doctor or nurse with you as the patient.

If your child is to have an operation it is especially important for him to know what to expect when he recovers from the anaesthetic. A plaster cast, stitches, dressings, vomiting after an anaesthetic, and, most of all, pain, will be more distressing if he has not been prepared for them. It will help if you can promise to be there when he wakes up. Reassure him that any pain he might have following the operation will not last, and that he will be given medicine to help make it better. You may like to promise that he will have a treat or a special present when everything is over; focus his attention ahead of the operation instead of on it.

HAVING AN OPERATION
Explain to your child what will happen to him on the day of his operation:

o Nothing to eat or drink for at least 4 hours before
o Having a bath
o Exchanging his own clothes for a hospital gown, and wearing a bracelet with his name
o Being given a premedication (premed) – a drug to relax him before the anaesthetic. Find out whether this will be given by injection or by mouth
o Feeling sleepy and thirsty – warn him that he will not be allowed to drink
o Transferring to a bed on wheels to be taken to the anaesthetic room
o Having an injection or a mask over his face, which will send him quickly to sleep
o The next thing he will know will be waking up

AFTER THE OPERATION

Do not be upset if, as he comes out of the anaesthetic, your child seems distressed, is crying or even angry. He will go back to sleep and probably remember nothing of this when he finally wakes.

If your child has had a major operation he may need to spend some days in the intensive care unit, so that his condition can be monitored continuously. He may be given oxygen to help him breathe, and food and medication by intravenous drip. If you cannot be there when he comes round, you may be able to arrange beforehand for him to meet the nurse who will be looking after him.

RETURNING HOME

Children who have been in hospital are often difficult and demanding when they return home. Younger children often regress to more childish behaviour – a child who has been dry may start to bedwet again, for example. Older children may be aggressive, jealous of brothers or sisters who have been at home while they were away, and reluctant to go back to school. It will help if you can reintegrate your child with his school-life before he returns, perhaps by having friends over to play, or arranging a visit from his teacher.

MEDICAL PROCEDURES

From the earliest age children are usually subject to a variety of medical procedures. These may be intended to prevent illness, treat disease or monitor health. For example, injections of vaccine may be given to immunize against *diphtheria*, injections of insulin may be necessary in the treatment of *diabetes* and blood tests may be taken to diagnose diseases.

This section describes procedures which are carried out in connection with a wide range of problems and diseases.

There are other medical and surgical procedures, such as *lumbar puncture* or *biopsy*, that are specific to particular problems or parts of the body. Such procedures are described in the relevant sections of Part Three.

INJECTIONS

Injections can be given in a variety of ways, depending on which drug or vaccine is to be given and what effect is required.

In *immunizations* against diseases such as *diphtheria*, *tetanus*, *whooping cough*, *measles* and *German measles*, a small amount of fluid is injected into the muscle of the thigh and this usually causes discomfort for a few seconds only. The immunization for *tuberculosis* is injected into the skin. Injections of penicillin or other antibiotics are given for the treatment of severe infections such as *pneumonia*. These injections involve a larger amount of fluid that has to go deep into the muscle of a child's thigh. This can be painful and there is usually a dull ache for some time afterwards. Children in hospital who need repeated injections are often given these intravenously (into a vein).

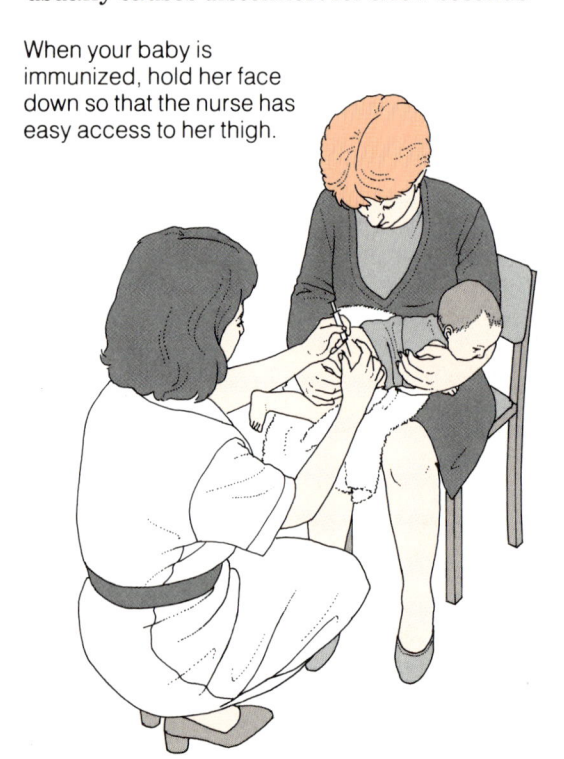

Babies recover quicker from the shock of an injection if they can be immediately comforted with a feed. Give children fair warning of what to expect from an injection: a completely unexpected prick can frighten and anger a child. The promise of a reward afterwards may help a young child, and diverting attention away from the needle by singing or reading a book can also make the experience easier for him. Schoolchildren may still need your presence and comfort to cope.

When your baby is immunized, hold her face down so that the nurse has easy access to her thigh.

BLOOD PRESSURE

Your child's blood pressure may be taken during a check-up by your doctor or in connection with urinary problems. Blood pressure is measured by listening to the blood going along the main artery of the arm, and the reading indicates the strength of the contraction of the muscles of the heart and the elasticity of the arteries. The highest (systolic) and the lowest (diastolic) pressures are recorded. The average for children is lower than adults and increases from $100/60$ at birth to 6 years to $120/70$ at 15 years and older.

BLOOD TESTS

Blood tests are done for a variety of reasons. An analysis may help in the diagnosis of illness. The amount of, for example, *glucose* or *urea* can be measured and the results may be necessary to know whether a child is suffering from *diabetes*, kidney disease or *hepatitis*.

A test may be required to assess how much blood has been lost following an accident; or the identification of your child's blood group may be necessary in order to match blood should a *transfusion* be required during an operation.

Small amounts of blood can be taken from babies and children by pricking the finger or heel with a small disposable blade. When a greater amount is needed it has to be taken with a syringe from a vein usually from the inside of the elbow. Apart from the prick as the needle goes in, the procedure is not painful.

Younger children generally prefer to have their attention distracted while their blood is being taken, but older children may be fascinated by the procedure and want to know what is going on and why.

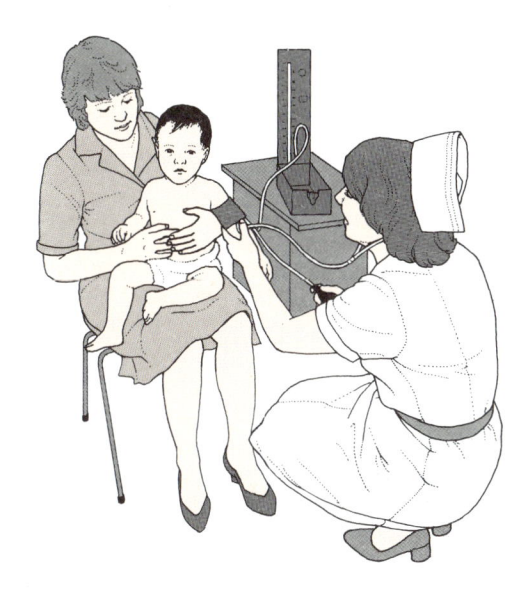

To measure your child's blood pressure, the doctor or nurse will wrap a cuff around his arm and inflate the cuff to form a tight band. This is not painful but does create a sensation of pressure.

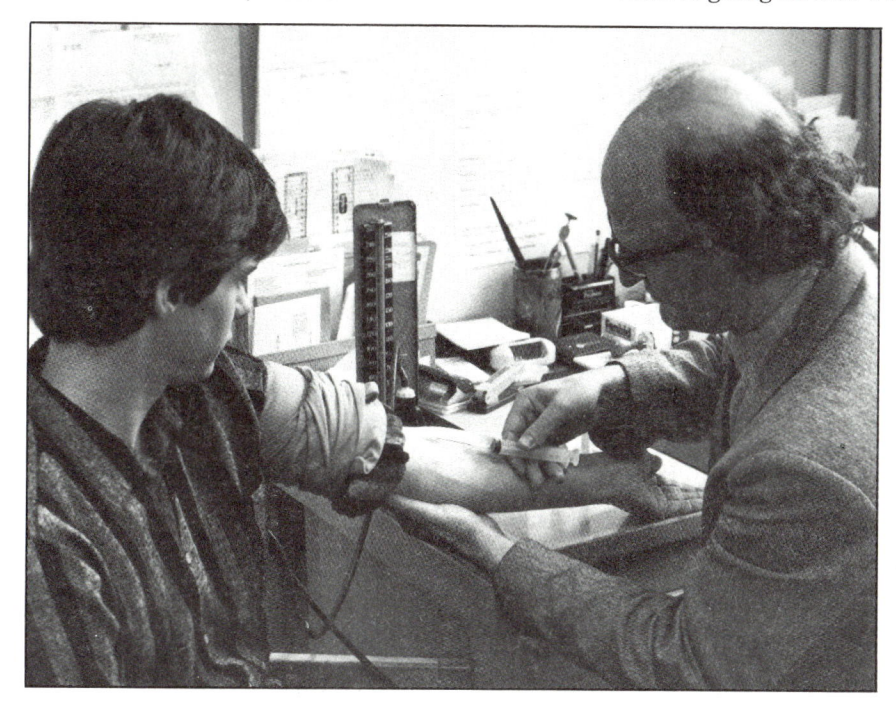

It is easier to see the veins in some people's arms than in others Occasionally a doctor or nurse taking blood for a blood test may need to insert the needle several times before finding a vein.

X-RAYS

Few children reach adulthood without having had an X-ray. This may be needed to check whether a bone has been broken as the result of a fall or accident, or to detect a lung infection when your child has been suffering from a cough or fever for a long time. If your doctor thinks that your child may be suffering from an infection of the kidneys and urinary system he may organize an *intravenous pyelogram*. This involves injecting a dye which will show up on the X-ray. Although in general it is thought that there is no danger to children from the number of X-rays they are likely to have, you may want to question whether an X-ray is necessary if you think the doctor is suggesting it merely as a matter of course.

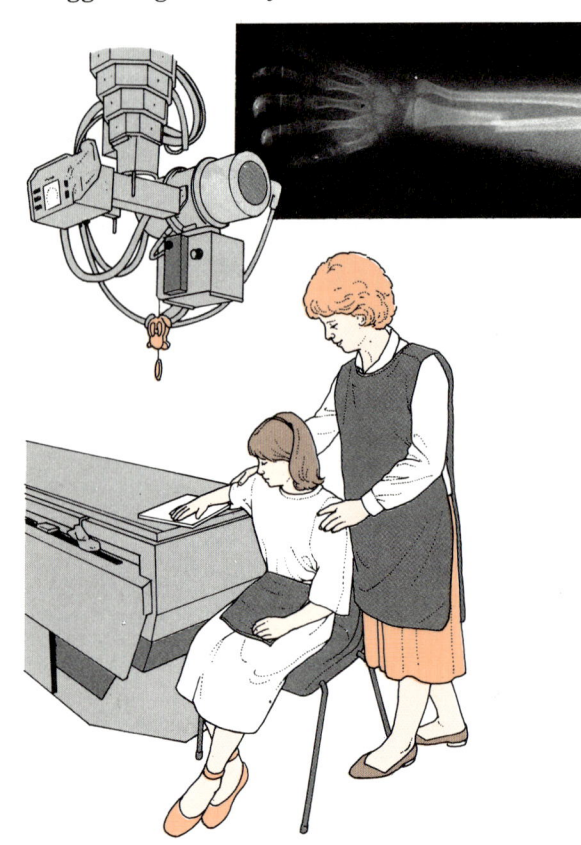

Both you and your child should be given protective clothing to wear while the X-ray is being taken.

The process is painless, but the equipment might prove frightening to younger children. Try to prepare them by showing them illustrations and giving some explanation of what will happen. You should normally be able to stay with your child throughout the X-ray procedure.

URINE TESTS

As well as coughs, colds and *viral infections*, a baby or toddler may have a fever as the result of a *urinary tract infection*. Your doctor will take a urine sample if he suspects this is the case, and when the sample is analyzed in a laboratory, the nature of the infection that your child is suffering from will be known. A sample can also be tested to see if it contains *glucose*, for example. This happens when a child has *diabetes*, and treatment will depend on the amount of glucose found. The urine specimen should not be contaminated by bacteria from around the genitals and anus, so you should wash and dry these areas before collecting the urine. Once a child is toilet-trained all that is needed is a sterile container for him to urinate into on request. Ask for a container from your doctor's surgery.

A special plastic bag has to be placed over the genitals of a baby or toddler and the urine collected is transferred into a sterile container.

Urine left at room temperature soon becomes contaminated by bacteria, so if a sample has to be kept at home for any length of time it should be kept in a refrigerator.

STOOL TESTS

A child with diarrhoea resulting from an infection usually recovers within a few days. If the condition lasts longer than 2 or 3 days, your doctor may want to examine a sample of your child's faeces. This sample is called a stool specimen.

Ask your child to use a cleaned pot and collect the faeces in a sterile container using a disposable wooden spatula. You should be able to obtain both of these from your doctor's surgery. If your child is not yet toilet-trained, spoon the faeces off his bottom with a spatula.

LONGSTANDING PROBLEMS

One in 10 children has a problem that will affect him for many years, if not for life. For some the problem affects general physical health, for example, *asthma*, heart disease or *diabetes*; for others, diseases of the bones and joints or the nerves and muscles affect the ability to move; for yet others, communication is affected, when their hearing, vision or speech is involved. And a number of children have difficulties that affect their behaviour or thinking and learning. Whatever the problem, there are features in common, both for the child and for the child's family.

This section deals only with the general aspects of handicap and longstanding problems, physical and mental. Specific information on individual diseases and disorders is given in Part Three.

> ▶**See also** Appendix: The law and your child

LIMITATIONS

If a child has a disability it may mean that he cannot play, work or display the same degree of independence as other children. This perceived inequality may damage a child's self-confidence and self-image. It may also affect his popularity with other children. So the most positive approach for a parent is to concentrate on the child's potential to develop those abilities which may be on a par with most other children's.

A child with disabilities also has strengths, and by developing these can gain in confidence and a sense of achievement. A 'handicapped child' is, after all, a 'normal child' with a handicap. Such children, encouraged to have a positive attitude towards their achievements, are likely to suffer fewer emotional problems.

A child with a longstanding problem has the same general needs as any other. Recreation and social contact, in one form or another, are craved by every child. Restrictions to protect a handicapped child are best kept to a minimum so that he can grow to independence and can follow as normal a programme at school and at home as possible. You can discuss the risks of specific activities and any restrictions you should impose with your doctor to satisfy yourself that you are not being over-protective.

ADJUSTING AS A FAMILY

To a parent, the thought that your child has a handicap of one form or another comes as a shock. Often you are the first to realize that something is wrong. You may have feelings of guilt, which are normal but unwarranted and which may hinder your acceptance and understanding of the problem. However, in all but the most difficult handicaps you will probably be the main provider of treatment, especially during your child's pre-school years. Family life will have to adapt to incorporate this. Inevitably the degree of flexibility that normally exists in family life will decrease. For some parents routine may be so restricted as to make it impossible to have a moment off unless someone else takes over. Your own needs and those of your other children should not be forgotten, otherwise the quality of life of your whole family will suffer, to the further disadvantage of your handicapped child. Arranging short-term and voluntary help through your doctor or social services is a sound strategy to keep family life as balanced and relaxed as possible. Also, self-help groups provide a great deal of support. These groups make it possible for you to meet others in a similar position to yourself.

Coping outside the family circle can raise difficulties: there is widespread fear and

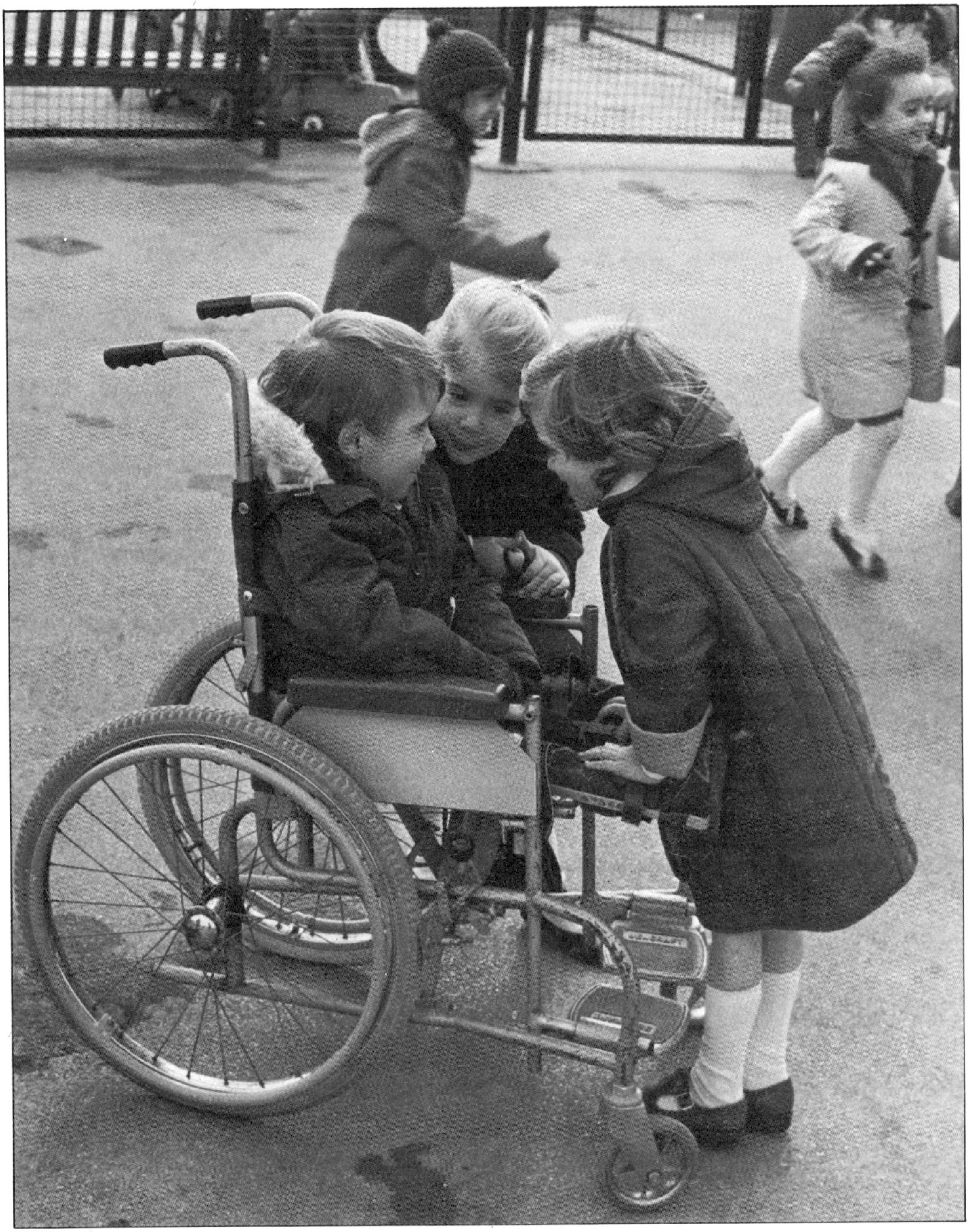

ignorance about handicap which often shows itself in insensitive behaviour or comments. Explaining why your child is unable to react or perform in the normally accepted manner can avoid embarrassment in social situations. Open and sensitive discussion with your other children should help them to come to terms with their sibling's handicap so that they do not feel shamed or embarrassed by it.

ATTITUDES TO TREATMENT

When a child suffers from asthma, diabetes or *epilepsy*, the demands of continuous treatment can be great. Regular treatment to prevent symptoms is very important but it is often difficult for the child to understand this when he feels 'well'. It may complicate social activities since most children are reluctant to appear different. Try explaining to your child, whatever his age, in a manner that will help him explain to friends and classmates why he is unable to participate in various activities. Special diets also emphasize differences. Physiotherapy and other forms of therapy on a daily basis can take up a large part of a child's day, interfering with enjoyable activities like play. It may require extra organizational efforts on your part to keep your child's day as 'normal' as possible, and not to allow treatments and therapies to dominate his life in an oppressive way: there may be the occasion when a social activity should take precedence over a treatment so that life does not appear to lose all its fun.

PROFESSIONAL SUPPORT

For a child with severe or multiple handicaps, care by a team of professionals is necessary. Your family doctor can help you organize this. For the young child, services are likely to be centred around the home and a child development centre. The latter usually provides a comprehensive assessment of the child's needs. A doctor is usually the one who co-ordinates the assessment, but

A handicapped child needs contact with other children just like any other child. Children are often less embarrassed by a handicap than adults.

physiotherapists, occupational therapists, speech therapists, psychologists, teachers and social workers may all be involved, depending on the type of handicap.

Community resources such as day nurseries with special facilities and toy libraries are widely available and can be contacted through your doctor, hospital or support group. Depending on the handicap, later education may have to be at a special school.

Severely handicapped children may need to be cared for in a residential centre or school as they would otherwise be totally dependent on their families throughout their lives.

The decision to have a child cared for in a residential centre is a difficult one for most parents, and can only be arrived at after thoughtful discussion and consideration of what is best for all members of the family. In many cases it is not considered until a severely handicapped child reaches the teenage years and usually becomes much harder to cope with. Where there are good local support services which offer flexible short- and longer-term care – whenever parents need a break – young children even with severe handicaps rarely need full residential care.

GROWING UP

Anxieties are normally experienced by parents and children during *adolescence* and these are likely to be greater when children are suffering from longstanding problems, and especially when they are physically disabled or mentally handicapped. If parents are aware of their children's problems, and know where to turn for advice and support, they will be better able to help their children cope.

Children with chronic problems such as asthma or epilepsy will need to be fully informed about their conditions and how to manage them. Only then will they be able to look after themselves and thus become independent of their parents. However, children with greater disabilities face many more problems. They may have to remain physically dependent on their parents as well as other carers and professional helpers for intimate functions like washing and toileting.

Some thought is needed to enable a child whose mobility is limited to experience the range of normal play. Depending on his degree of handicap, your child may benefit from attending a pre-school group that is specially equipped for children with disabilities.

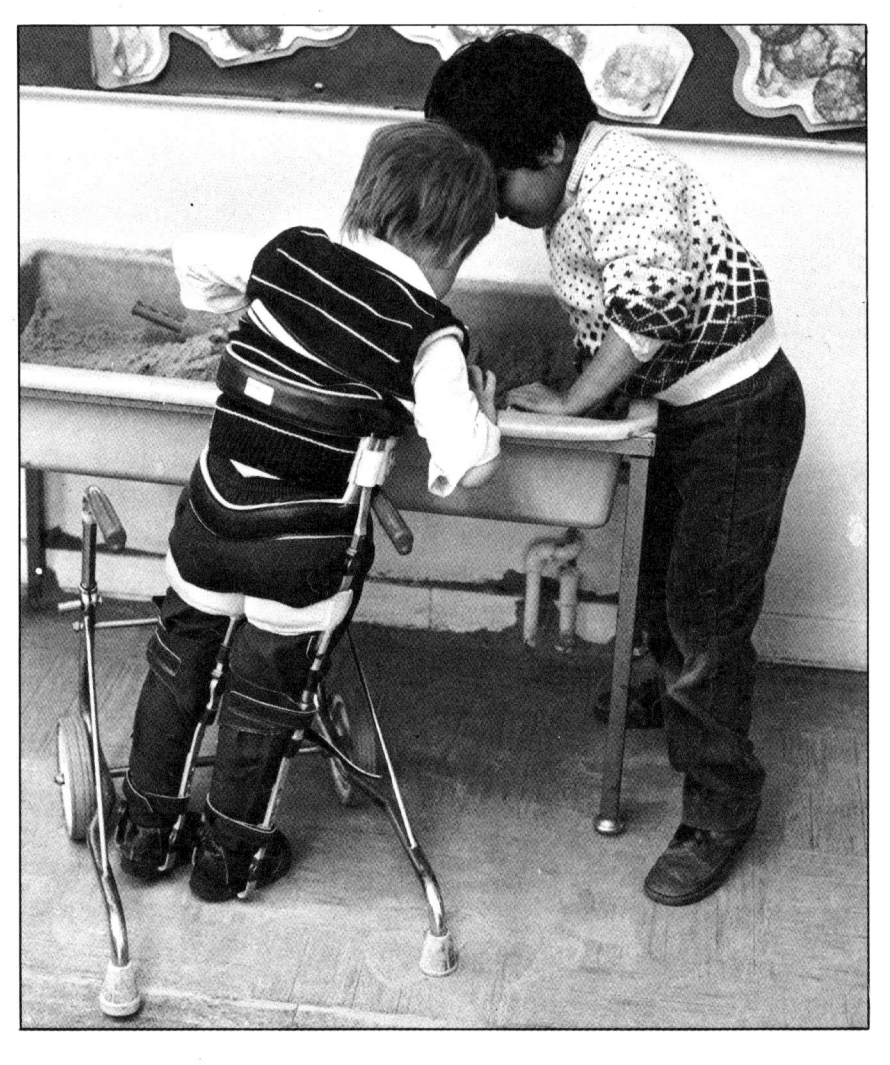

They will be denied the privacy and independence craved by all adolescents. Their mobility may be limited so that opportunities for meeting and mixing with peers will be limited. And if their disabilities affect behaviour and speech this will prove a barrier to forming relationships with others of their own age.

The severely mentally and physically handicapped have feelings and needs just as any other human being. It is often difficult for a parent to recognize these and, for example, to help their adolescent towards greater independence when it might be so much quicker and easier to do everything for him. Coming to terms with a disabled child's sexuality may prove most difficult for a parent. But in the interests of the child it should not be denied and he should receive adequate sex education so that he can cope with his feelings and relationships. Parents can refer to professionals and support groups to help them with this and, when possible, encourage their children to seek advice themselves.

▶See also Appendix: Support groups and publications

COUNSELLING

All children as they grow up go through stages that their parents find difficult, whether because of *sleeping difficulties*, tantrums or other problems. Most families manage to cope, relying on their own resources and on help from friends, neighbours, extended family and health visitors. The family doctor and your child's teachers, once he starts school, can also give support.

However, some families find it very hard to cope with tensions and problems. This may be because of their circumstances: they may be unusually isolated, or they may be suffering from other stresses that reduce their ability to cope. Alternatively, the child may seem unusually hard to cope with, whether because of inherited problems, or difficult experiences in the past.

ASKING FOR HELP

Counselling can be used as an additional support for the family as a whole or for a child who is having particular difficulty. If you are in doubt about whether your child needs help, your doctor, health visitor or your child's teachers can advise you, and can also direct you to the appropriate agency for the sort of help your child needs.

It can sometimes be difficult to know whether your child needs counselling. You should probably seek help:

o If your child's school or doctor suggests that he needs help
o If your child has a problem that interferes with schoolwork or friendships
o If the family's stability and emotional health are threatened by the behaviour of one child
o If you are afraid that your child might physically damage others
o If you are afraid that your child might attempt suicide
o If your child persistently steals or shoplifts or breaks the law in other ways
o Remember that you can also ask for help at any time you feel the need of it

Counselling is carried out in a wide range of settings, including child guidance clinics, probation and social services offices, hospitals and family counselling centres. Counselling centres may be within the health or social services or may be part of voluntary or private agencies. They are staffed by people trained and experienced in specific types of counselling, for example, for bereavement.

Child guidance clinics help with the whole breadth of problems occurring in childhood, including problems of behaviour or learning. They are staffed by teams of professionals with different backgrounds – medical, psychological or social work – who work together.

DIFFERENT FORMS OF HELP

Child psychiatrists are doctors who have specialized in emotional and behavioural disorders of childhood and the family.

Educational psychologists have training in psychology and experience in teaching. Their psychological training gives particular emphasis to the way the normal child grows and functions, as well as to problems of learning and behaviour.

Child psychotherapists do not have medical training but have intensive training in child development and the way relationships develop in the family. They are able to help children understand and work through their problems and anxieties.

Social workers know the way that welfare provisions work in the community. They help parents and families who are having problems relating within the family or within the community.

▶See also Appendix: Who's who in the health service

COUNSELLING AND PSYCHOTHERAPY

The approach of psychiatrists and psychotherapists is often called psychotherapy, while that of social workers and educational psychologists is more usually called counselling. However, the boundaries between psychotherapy and counselling may not always be clearly defined. Some situations demand special skills: working with children who are in particular trouble can be demanding, as well as requiring a high degree of experience and training. If problems are longstanding or if your child grew up with poor relationships due to death, loss or disruption, then he may not have enough inner confidence to tackle new strains in life. Such situations may call for psychotherapy rather than counselling. Counselling is more appropriate for a current crisis that requires short-term help.

SETTING UP SESSIONS

Counselling is usually on a regular weekly basis, whereas psychotherapy can be weekly or even as often as three or four times a week in some instances. Either may continue for anything from a few weeks to several years. Meetings may consist of individual sessions between counsellor or therapist and the child,

Young children may find it easier to communicate with a therapist through play than by talking directly. Play with a 'family' of dolls can often be very expressive.

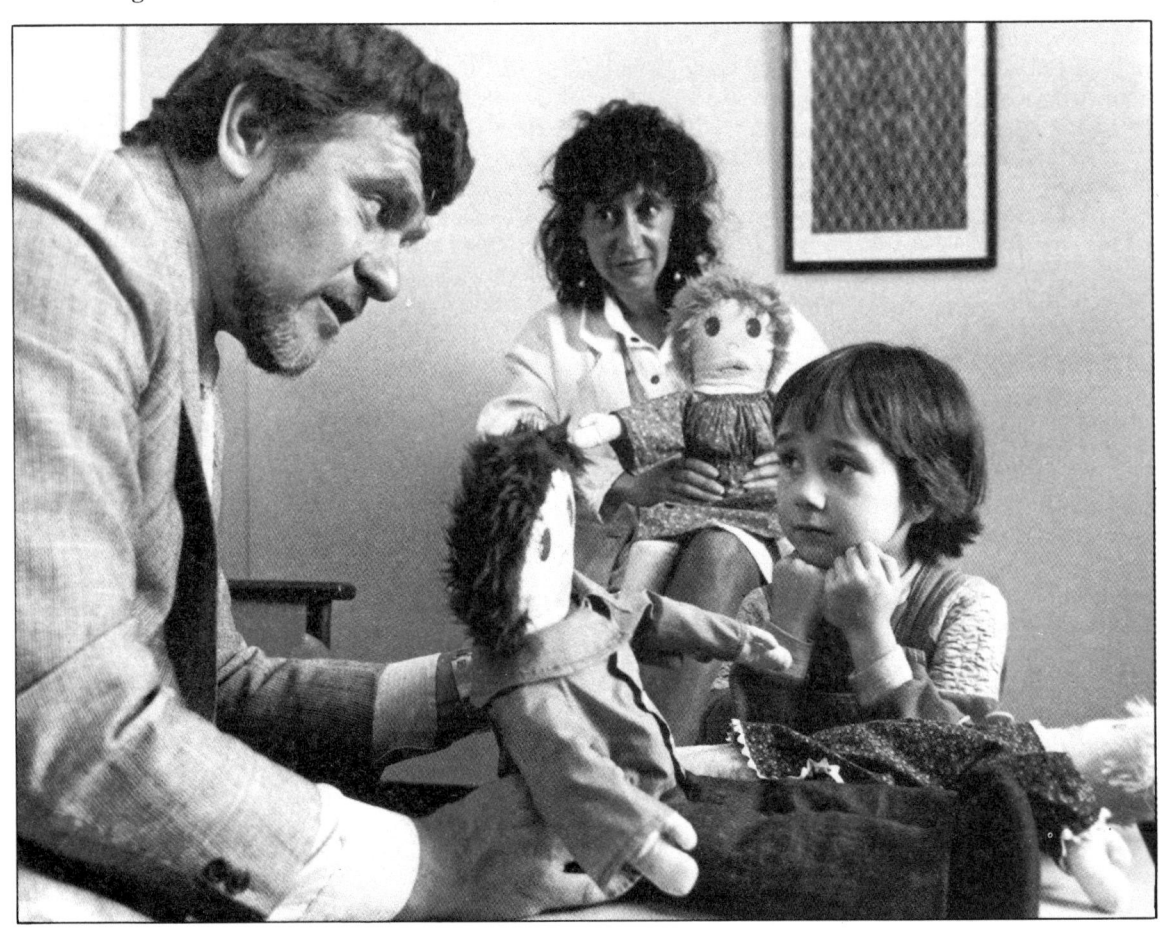

or may also include the parent. In some cases, the child or family may be treated as part of a larger group. Alternatively, family therapy aims to treat the family as a unit, and the therapist sees not only the child who manifests the problem but also those close to the child.

The psychiatrist or psychotherapist will probably encourage your child to take time to talk through problems before offering any response. In family therapy, the therapist may take a much more active part in facilitating the discussions and helping you and your children talk to each other about what is difficult. He may try to change the patterns of interaction in your family by setting you tasks, such as doing something different as a family. He may discover that your complaints about the child who is most noisy and difficult may be a distraction hiding a more serious concern, perhaps a fear about changes in the parents' relationship, or a fear about another child in the family, and will help you face and deal with this.

The essence of counselling or therapy is to have the space and time to be able to explore the issues that concern you with somebody skilled and experienced who is sufficiently removed from your situation to be able to present a balanced view of it. Whatever the form of psychotherapy or counselling, the aim is to give the child or family the resources to do without special help at the end of the course of therapy.

▶See also Behaviour and development

A CASE STUDY

Elizabeth was a 12-year-old, referred by a paediatrician for family counselling. She had been seen for 2 years or so by her paediatrician with a whole range of symptoms – temperatures running without infections, abdominal pains, headaches and so on.

The paediatrician gradually realized that the symptoms were appearing only over school terms and not during the holidays. The doctor felt they were a manifestation of difficulties that Elizabeth had about going to school although, when asked, Elizabeth always said she enjoyed her school.

When the family was seen they seemed very caring and loving towards each other. However, the mother was exasperated by not knowing whether Elizabeth was 'really' ill, or whether the symptoms were an expression of tension. Sometimes she let Elizabeth off going to school and was furious to see her recover within hours. At other times she sent her off to school in the morning, only to have her sent home with a 'real' illness later in the day.

The family shared the fact that Elizabeth had always been very close to her mother and found growing up and growing away quite hard. She had done well in junior school, and had only started her problems when she began to go to senior school.

Elizabeth's mother confided that her own mother had been very strict and unsympathetic and Elizabeth's mother had vowed never to be like this with Elizabeth.

Elizabeth's father commented that when he was around he always knew when Elizabeth was 'putting it on' or was genuinely ill, but that he had to get off to work early and so did not get involved in the decision about whether or not she should go to school.

The counsellor suggested that for the next few weeks Elizabeth's father get special permission to go into work late and that he should decide whether Elizabeth should go to school or not. The counsellor also asked Elizabeth to teach her mother when to be firm by sometimes pretending to feel worse than she did, checking in the evening whether her mother could detect whether she was pretending or not and then putting her right.

When the family were seen 4 weeks later they told us that after a dreadful week when her father almost had to drag Elizabeth to school doubled up in pain, she had got much better. Her mother realized she had been confused about the issue of firmness, and her father had got back to work early. Once Elizabeth faced being grown up, she found that it was not so bad after all.

ALTERNATIVE THERAPIES

Complementary, or 'alternative', medicine has been used for many years as an alternative to conventional medicine. It is an approach to coping with illness which does not rely predominantly on drugs or surgery. Some aspects of complementary medicine are now increasingly being used alongside conventional medicine and are practised by greater numbers of trained doctors.

The aim of alternative therapies is the successful cure of ailments rather than the suppression of their symptoms. Many people believe that drugs such as antibiotics, while invaluable in the treatment of some serious conditions, have been used excessively to treat minor common problems with dangerous and alarming side effects. They see the value of alternative therapies in the treatment of everyday childhood illnesses such as coughs, colds, sore throats, earache, upset stomachs, *virus infections* or the young baby's *colic*. Alternative therapies are often sought for the cure and treatment of chronic conditions such as food allergies, especially when conventional medicine has proven unsuccessful.

Important therapies are homeopathy, a system that uses natural remedies in minute quantities; acupuncture, which involves the insertion of needles into the skin at determined points; and osteopathy, which aims to correct deformations of the skeleton and hence the balance of the body and its functions. There are many others: naturopathy, for example, which is based on the idea that illness is due to the food we eat and the way we live, and clinical ecology, which is concerned with the body's reactions to foods and chemicals in the environment.

Practitioners of alternative therapies are concerned with the whole person and not just the symptoms or disease from which he may be suffering. A consultation will involve questions about lifestyle, environment and family background, for all skilled diagnosticians know that these factors can influence the health of the individual child.

Your family doctor may be able to recommend a practitioner of alternative therapies to you or you can consult the register of the relevant professional body which lists practitioners with recognized qualifications.

Although there is still relatively little scientific proof of the effectiveness of the various therapies, the experience of many qualified practitioners has revealed positive results in the treatment of problems including respiratory, skin, digestive, nervous and psychosomatic conditions.

▶ **See also** Appendix: Support groups and publications

HOMEOPATHY

'Homeopathy' literally means 'similar suffering' and its practice is based on like curing like. This means that the remedy chosen for any particular problem is that which would reproduce in a well person the symptoms of the person being treated. There are more than 2,000 homeopathic remedies. Most of these are derived from plant sources. Their special method of preparation was devised by Samuel Hahnemann about 200 years ago and they are administered in the minutest doses possible to have an effect. Most homeopathic remedies are given in the form of dissolving tablets placed under the tongue. Young children find this easier than taking tablets they have to swallow.

Homeopaths are concerned with the unique picture presented by each patient. When they see your child they will want to know about his mental and emotional as well as physical state. On your visit you will be asked about the exact symptoms that your child is suffering as well as details of physical history and behaviour. He will be observed carefully, as will your interaction with him. A remedy will be prescribed for the individual child, depending on all these factors. Thus the same remedy is not necessarily prescribed for two different children suffering similar symptoms.

Homeopathy has been discovered to be particularly effective in the treatment of many common children's problems such as sleep and feeding problems, colds, *croup*, *asthma*, infectious diseases, headaches, stomach problems including constipation and diarrhoea, eye, ear and skin problems, and nervous and psychosomatic disorders. In some cases remedies may be used alongside conventional medicine. Many medically qualified homeopaths believe that homeopathy is particularly effective in the treatment of children's *eczema* and upper respiratory infections. Homeopaths usually also have a knowledge of diet and the problems caused by various foods and they can advise on these.

You can safely treat your own child with the advice of a practitioner and following the information provided by reputable homeopathic institutions and publications. You can also buy first-aid homeopathy kits that contain remedies for minor ailments as well as common accidents such as burns.

Homeopathic remedies should be kept out of the reach of children. If they should take them by mistake they are unlikely to require emergency treatment, but a homeopath should be contacted at once for an antidote.

ACUPUNCTURE

'Acupuncture', that is 'needle puncture', is part of traditional Chinese medicine, an empirical system that originated some 4,000 years ago. In recent decades its practice has grown in Russia, Western Europe and in the United States. It is based on the theory that there is a balanced flow of energy around a healthy body and that this flow becomes unbalanced in illness. The energy flows through 26 main circuits or lines covering the body, which are known as meridians. Surplus energy is expelled through the skin at certain points on each meridian.

An acupuncturist is able to assess the body's condition by feeling certain pulses and can then tell which meridians require balancing. Depending on the problem some of the points on the meridians may be painful when pressed. Following the assessment the acupuncturist inserts fine needles at the points considered to need treatment. They are inserted to depths depending on the particular point and the problem being treated. The insertion is felt as a mild prick, although points requiring treatment may be tender. They are left in for anything from a few seconds to several minutes. A number of sessions may be necessary.

Acupuncture is known to affect the nervous system and reduce pain. Its anaesthetizing effects are recognized, for example in surgery.

Each meridian is related to different organ or function of the body. The points on the meridian may be treated with a single needle, or with a 'plum blossom' needle consisting of several needles clustered together, with heat or with pressure from a thumb (acupressure) or blunt needle.

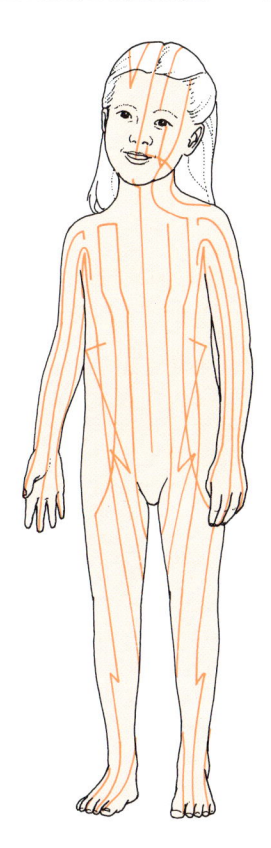

Clinical trials have been carried out on the treatment of headaches and joint pains with acupuncture, but while it can treat the symptom it may not cure the cause of the pain.

Research is still required to judge the precise effect of acupuncture in helping conditions such as *sinusitis*, *hay fever*, *bronchitis* and *asthma*, stomach and bowel disorders and skin problems such as *dermatitis*, *eczema* and *psoriasis*. Nonetheless, children of all ages suffering from these among other conditions appear to benefit from acupuncture. It has been found effective in curing some cases of drug addiction and smoking, but only when the sufferer wants to be cured.

OSTEOPATHY

Osteopathy is concerned with the body's musculo-skeletal framework and the relationship this has with the body's functions. It aims to diagnose and correct problems of the skeleton and muscles. These may be caused by injury or stress and can result in nerve and movement problems. The body's vital organs can in turn be affected.

For older children osteopathy may be used to treat disorders of the spine. As osteopaths believe that the improvement of the mechanical functioning of the spine can lead to the improvement of the functioning of vital organs supplied by nerves from the spine, they hope to treat successfully breathing, digestive and circulation problems. Osteopathy is used in the treatment of chronic disorders such as *migraine* and *asthma*.

A consultation with an osteopath involves a physical examination during which the curvature of the spine, the condition of the joints as well as their movement and the condition of the muscles is noted. The osteopath also needs to know the details of any problems your child is currently suffering, any past injuries and the general condition of health. X-rays may be necessary before treatment can begin.

Manipulation may be aimed at relaxing muscles by 'kneading' and 'stretching' them, easing joints by rhythmical movements or restoring them to normal positions by forceful movements known as 'high velocity thrusts'. These thrusts may be accompanied by loud clicks and the joint treated in this way may be sore for some days afterwards.

Cranial osteopathy is gentle manipulation of the skull and can be practised on children from the time of birth. It may be practised on children suffering from *autism* and to help children who have suffered *birth injuries*.

CLINICAL ECOLOGY

The human body reacts against certain chemicals in foods and in the atmosphere. Some of these may aggravate *sinusitis*, *eczema*, *migraine* or gastro-intestinal problems.

Ecological therapy is initially experimental. A complete fast is often part of the therapy for adults, but this should not be undertaken by children. Certain foods can be systematically eliminated from the diet and if the symptoms from which the child is suffering disappear, the food in question can be avoided and the problem should cease.

A clinical ecologist may test a child's muscle tone before and after eating a particular food. Weakening of the tone indicates that the food should be avoided. This approach is based on the fact that many children who react severely to certain foods do so by collapsing, that is they lose muscle tone. The approach does not involve time-consuming elimination diets.

Osteopathy is often used to treat sports injuries in children and teenagers. A child to whom sports are very important may be tempted to ignore an injury or to go back to playing before the injury has healed. An osteopath will be able to give you advice on how best to speed healing.

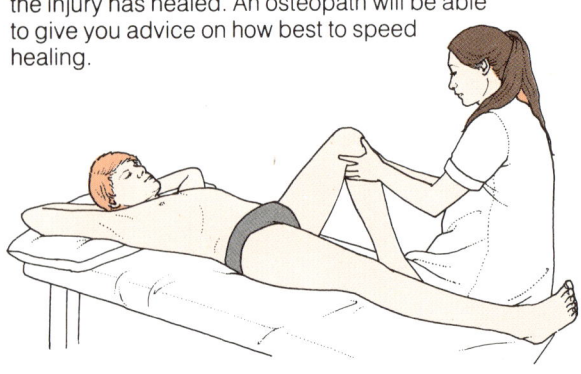

PART THREE
PROBLEMS, DISEASES AND DISORDERS

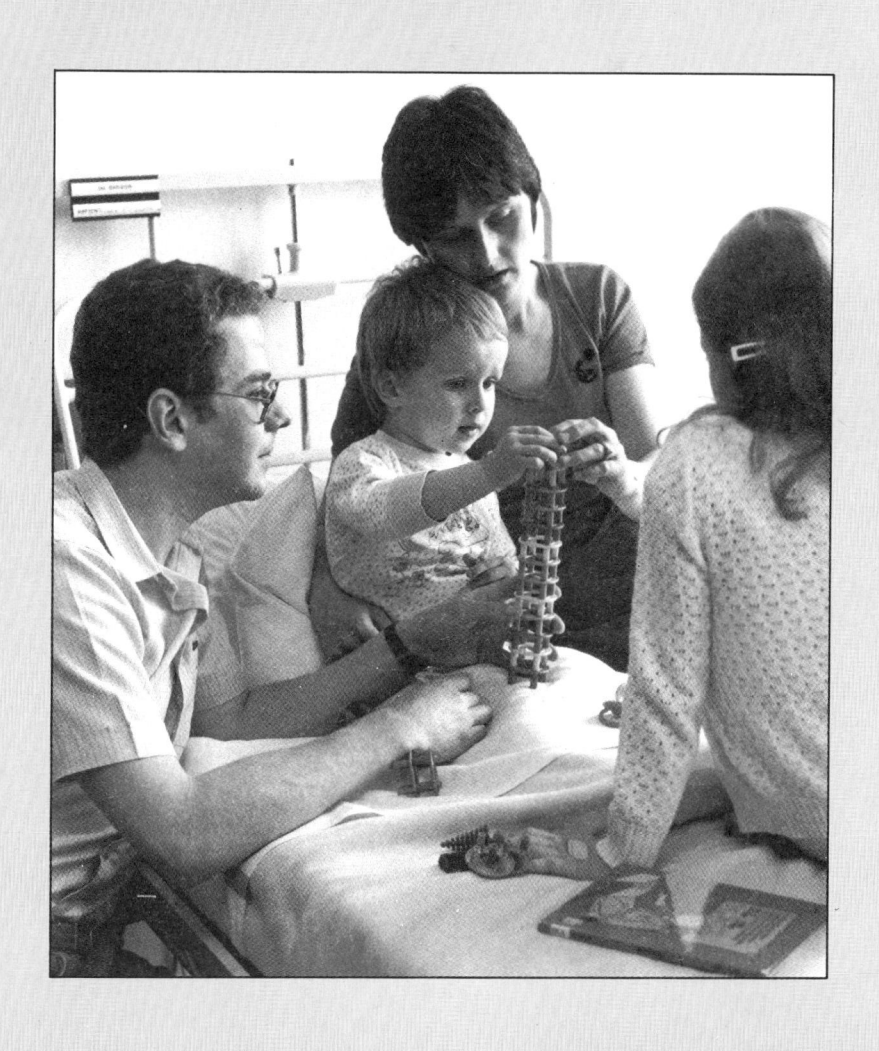

GENETICS

Of every 100 babies born 2 or 3 have serious physical or mental defects that can jeopardize their chances of survival or of leading normal lives. Many of these defects are hereditary, that is, caused by faulty genes or chromosomes passed on by the parents. Others arise through damage to the fetus during early development in the uterus. Some defects are due to a combination of both these factors. Examples of defects resulting from a combination of genetic and environmental factors are *spina bifida, congenital heart disorders, congenital dislocation of the hip, cleft lip and palate* and *club foot*.

Every normal body cell contains 46 chromosomes – 23 matching pairs. When the reproductive cells are formed, these pairs divide, so that egg or sperm each contain only 23 chromosomes. When egg and sperm fuse at fertilization, the new cell they form therefore again contains the full complement of 23 pairs, one member of each pair inherited from the mother and one from the father.

Strung out along the chromosomes are many hundreds of genes, forming a 'blueprint' that determines all body characteristics and functions. Each gene on one chromosome has a matching gene on the other chromosome of the pair. Gene action is described as dominant or recessive. The effect of the dominant gene normally overrides that of the gene on the other chromosome. Only if a recessive gene is present in both chromosomes will the feature it determines appear.

In this section the types of problems caused by faulty genes or chromosomes are described. **The unborn child** discusses other factors that may affect the baby before birth, while health problems developed during pregnancy, labour and the first week of life are covered in **Problems of the newborn child**.

▶**See also** Life and death; Appendices: Support groups and publications; Screening programme

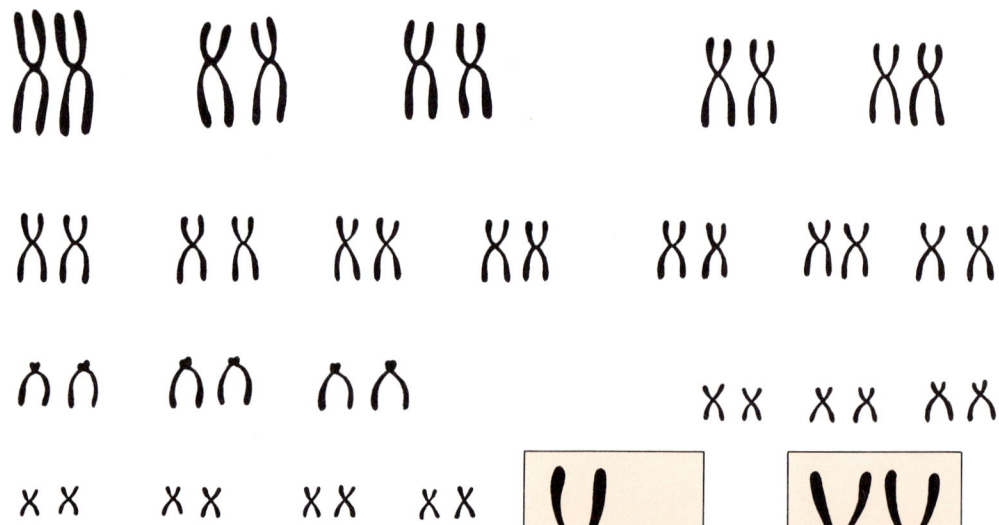

The 23rd pair of chromosomes determines sex. Women have two large indentical chromosomes known as X chromosomes. Men have one X chromosome and one, smaller, Y chromosome.

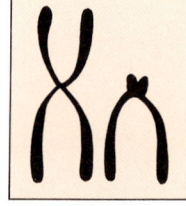

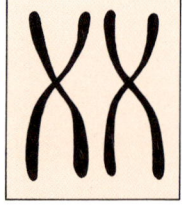

SINGLE-GENE DISORDERS

There are over 1,500 rare diseases that result from the action of one faulty gene. These are either dominantly inherited or recessively inherited disorders. A dominantly inherited disorder is one in which there is one abnormal dominant gene, present on only one of a pair of chromosomes. Because a child inherits only one chromosome of each pair from either parent, a parent who has the condition will not inevitably pass it on: the child has a 50 per cent chance of inheriting the chromosome with the normal gene. However, if the child does inherit the faulty gene, the action of the faulty gene will override that of the normal gene on the other chromosome of the pair, inherited from the other parent. The child, like the affected parent, has a 50 per cent chance of passing the condition on to his own children.

A faulty recessive gene rarely has any effect if it is present on only one chromosome of a pair; the normal gene on the other chromosome makes good the deficiency of its abnormal partner. Disease results if both chromosomes of a pair contain the abnormal gene. For this to happen, both parents must have the faulty gene. Each child born to them has a 25 per cent chance of inheriting both abnormal genes; or he may inherit only one abnormal gene or both normal genes, in which case he will be free of disease.

DOMINANTLY INHERITED DISORDERS

Tuberous sclerosis is a dominantly transmitted disorder that affects the skin and brain. There is a rash, resembling acne, on the cheeks, often coupled with patches of dark or pale skin on the trunk or limbs. Some affected individuals are mentally normal, but others may be mentally handicapped.

People suffering from **Huntington's chorea** develop psychiatric illness and abnormal body movements in middle or old age, although occasionally also in childhood. Tragically, those with a family history of this disorder do not know if they themselves suffer from it – and parents may pass it on to their own children before they become aware that they themselves are affected by it.

Achondroplasia is a form of dwarfism caused by a dominantly inherited bone disorder. Those affected can lead reasonably healthy lives, but have to cope with the psychological consequences of being very small. Although in some families one parent suffers from the same disease, more than 80 per cent of those affected have normal parents. In these cases what has happened is that the gene underwent a change, or mutation, when the sperm or egg was formed. Although the affected child can pass on the condition, the parents are unlikely to have another achondroplastic child, since the chances of a second such mutation occurring are very small.

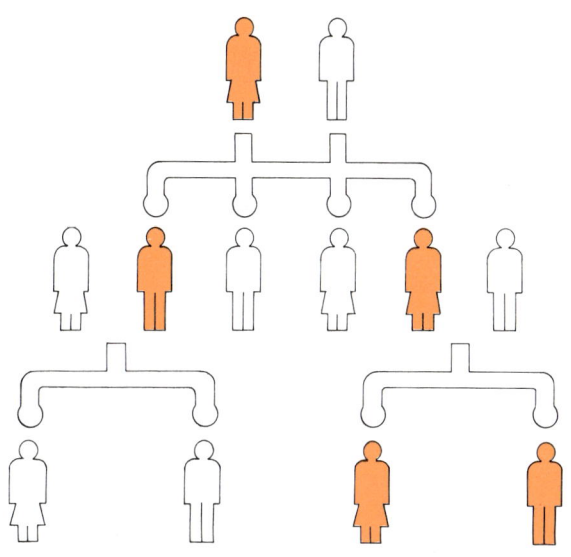

The tinted figures have inherited a faulty dominant gene. In the second generation, by chance one couple has two affected children, the other couple has two unaffected children.

RECESSIVELY INHERITED DISORDERS

One of the most common recessive disorders is *cystic fibrosis*. Another is *thalassaemia*, a disorder mainly affecting people from the Mediterranean and Middle and Far East. It prevents the normal formation of the oxygen-carrying blood pigment, haemoglobin. People who carry only one abnormal gene have minor and usually harmless changes in their blood: the disease is only seen in a severe form in people who inherit the recessive gene from both parents. *Sickle-cell anaemia* is a similar recessively inherited blood disorder almost entirely affecting people of African descent. There are screening programmes that can identify people who carry the gene and whose children would be at risk.

Phenylketonuria (PKU) is a rare recessive disorder, affecting only 1 in 10,000 babies. If it is not treated, PKU can result in mental retardation, often associated with convulsions. In most countries in the Western world newborn babies are given a blood test to detect the disease. If it is treated with a special diet within a few days of birth the child develops normally.

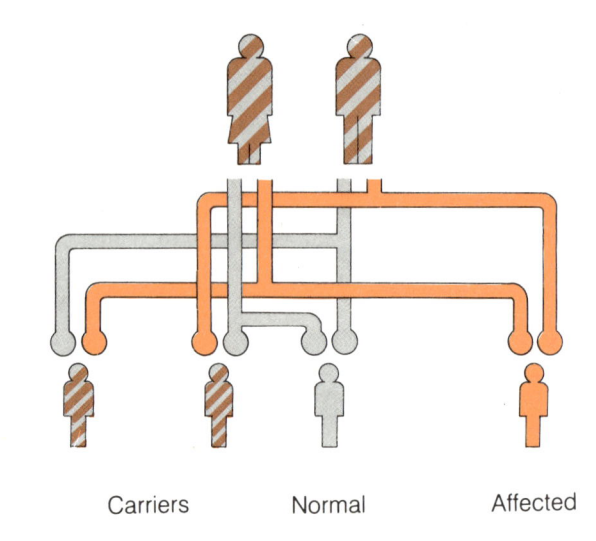

Carriers   Normal   Affected

Parents who are carriers can pass on a normal or an affected gene. Only children who inherit affected genes from both parents will be affected.

SEX-LINKED DISORDERS

A few disorders are carried by a faulty gene on one of the two sex chromosomes, nearly always the X chromosome. Disorders caused by a faulty recessive gene on the X chromosome, for example *haemophilia*, usually appear only in boys. The reason for this is that girls have two X chromosomes, and the effects of an abnormal recessive gene on one is usually counteracted by a normal gene on the other.

A girl who inherits the chromosome with the faulty gene will not be affected by the disease but her children have an equal chance of inheriting either the normal or the faulty gene.

In the exceedingly rare case of a girl inheriting a faulty recessive X chromosome from both parents, she will develop the disease. Boys, however, have only one X chromosome and when this chromosome has a faulty gene its effect cannot be counteracted as there is no equivalent normal gene on the Y chromosome. In this case, the boy will develop the disease. Also, because he has only one X chromosome, any daughters he has are bound to inherit it. Another disorder caused by an X-linked recessive gene is *Duchenne muscular dystrophy*.

CHROMOSOMAL DISORDERS

One in 200 children is born with a chromosomal disorder, of which *Down's syndrome* is the best known. These disorders are responsible for a high proportion of spontaneous abortions and deaths soon after birth. Some such disorders are caused by changes in chromosome structure, others by the presence of either too few or too many chromosomes. The risk of having a child with chromosomal abnormalities increases as the mother grows older. For a woman over 45 years old the risk of having a child with Down's syndrome is approximately 1 in 40; the risk of other chromosomal abnormalities is 1 in 70.

Several chromosomal abnormalities are due to a change in the number of sex chromosomes. **Turner's syndrome** which affects 1 baby girl in 2,000, is a condition in which there is only one X chromosome. Such a girl has an increased risk of a serious heart defect at birth; she will be short and usually infertile. Most fail to begin their periods. However, a few do, and their underlying abnormalities may not be detected until they reach adolescence or early adulthood.

About 1 in 1,000 baby girls is born with one extra X chromosome, so that she has the combination **XXX** instead of the normal pair. She has an increased risk of mental retardation and is often infertile. Some of these girls may be taller than average but otherwise appear quite normal.

Klinefelter's syndrome affects 1 in 1,000 newborn boys. In addition to the normal XY combination, there is an extra X chromosome. Some boys with this syndrome appear physically normal, others tend to develop enlarged breasts in adolescence and may have a female body shape. Some are infertile and may be mentally retarded.

A few boys are born with an extra Y chromosome, so that they have the combination XYY. They may be taller than average. Although it used to be believed that men with this chromosomal abnormality were particularly prone to criminal behaviour and psychiatric illness, recent research suggests that this may not be so.

DOWN'S SYNDROME

Down's syndrome, or Trisomy 21, affects 1 in 750 children. These children are born with an extra chromosome 21. This happens when the 21st pair of chromosomes in the egg, or less often the sperm, fails to separate completely. The egg or sperm therefore contain both members of the pair, so that the cell formed at fertilization contains three chromosomes 21 instead of the normal two.

A child with Down's syndrome has characteristic facial features: his eyes are widely separated and slant upwards and outwards, and the bridge of his nose is flat. There are a number of other identifying features, often including a single main crease on the palm of the hand instead of two. However, it is not always easy to diagnose a newborn baby as suffering from Down's syndrome. Occasionally neither the parents nor the doctors notice anything unusual. Babies with Down's syndrome behave much as other newborn babies although many seem quieter and more placid than usual. They are more likely to have internal problems. Almost half have a heart abnormality, commonly a *ventricular septal defect*. Some have a blockage in the bowel (duodenal artesia).

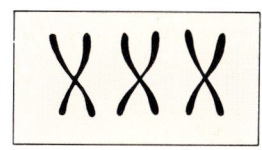

The extra chromosome of Down's syndrome is sometimes inherited from a parent who is a carrier but shows no abnormality. Genetic counselling can help to assess the chances of subsequent children inheriting this type of the syndrome. When a young mother has had one baby with Down's syndrome her chances of having another are low – approximately 1 in 100.

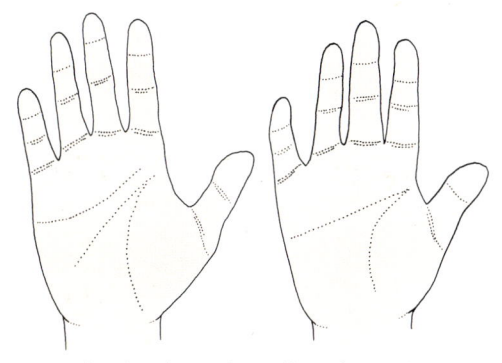

Some people who do not have Down's can have the characteristic palm crease pattern of the syndrome.

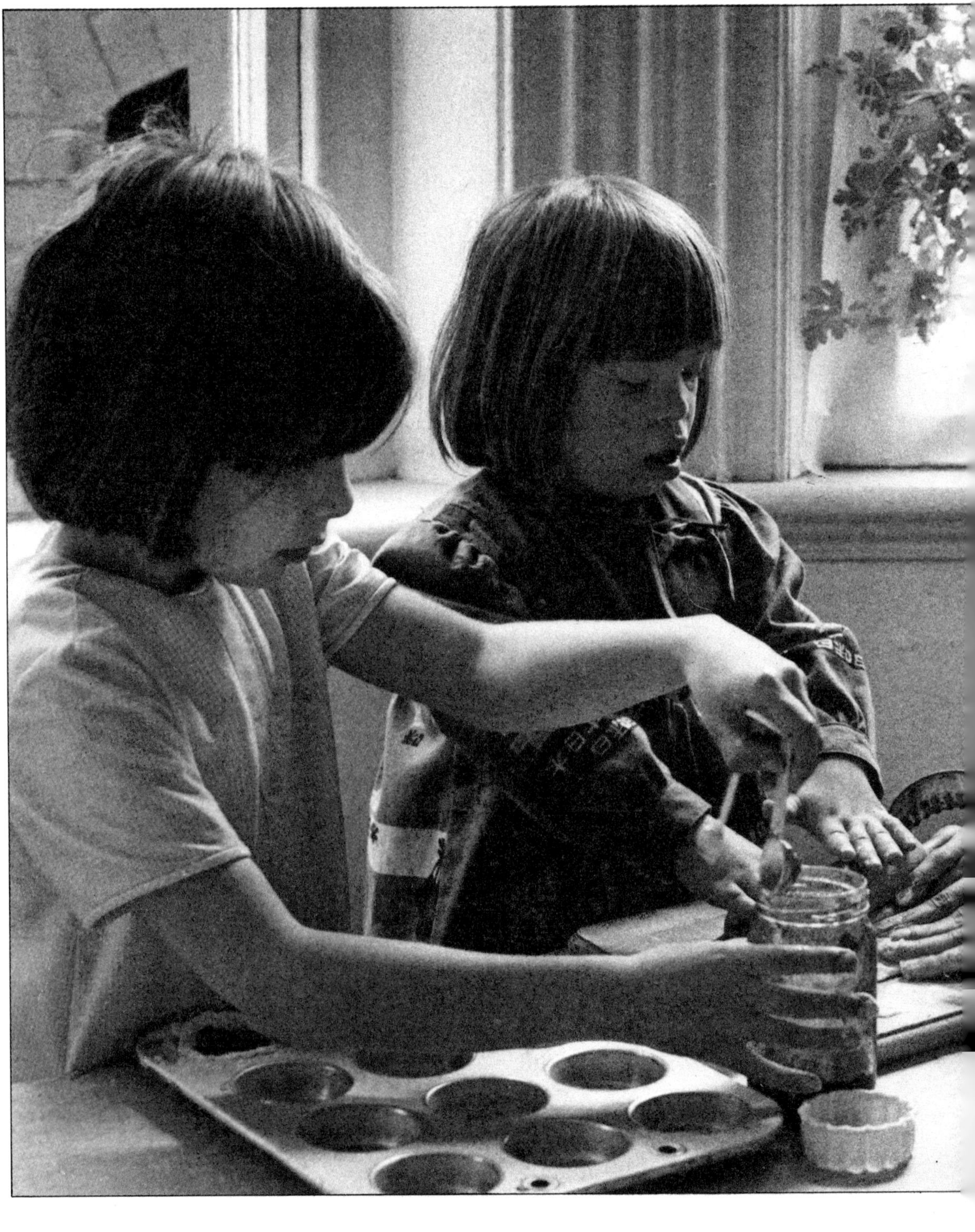

Most doctors talk with parents as soon as the features of Down's syndrome are recognized in the first few days after birth. A sample of the baby's blood is taken and the chromosomes analyzed to confirm the diagnosis. The decision on whether to operate on the heart and bowel if there are abnormalities is taken after discussion between doctor and parents. The child's situation is considered compassionately and realistically: the problems are discussed within the context of the family.

Even without severe physical complications, the diagnosis of Down's syndrome invariably comes as a shock to parents. If it is confirmed that your baby is suffering from Down's syndrome, you should talk to the medical staff and ask them about anything you want to know. They will be supportive and will do their best to answer your questions.

CARE

Children with Down's syndrome do learn to sit, stand, walk and use words, but they take longer than normal to achieve each skill. A parent can do a great deal to help a Down's child reach his full potential. Medical staff and support groups will give advice and help.

During their first few years, children with Down's syndrome tend to have more minor health problems than normal. They seem to suffer more frequently from colds and chest infections, and minor eye infections can also be troublesome. Their weight gain may be slow at first. Hearing and vision checks will ensure that short-term hearing impairments and squints are detected and dealt with.

Children with Down's syndrome benefit from pre-school nursery education and this enables assessment for the most suitable type of schooling. Following special school, an adult training centre can offer education in daily living and in acquiring manual skills for straightforward work. Even when they have grown to adulthood they will always need to live within a family or community setting.

A child with Down's syndrome responds to love and stimulation, and can become very much a full member of the family. Caring for her may be challenging and time-consuming, but also very rewarding.

PREVENTION OF GENETIC DISORDERS

Genetic counselling is a service offered to families with a history of genetic disorders, or to parents to whom a child with a genetic condition has been born. Your family doctor should be able to give you any information about it. The counsellor will explain the cause of the condition, and assess the chances of it recurring in subsequent pregnancies and being passed on to future generations.

If there is a high risk that a man might pass on an abnormal gene to his child, artificial insemination of his partner by donor (AID) may be carried out after careful counselling and discussion. Sperm is collected from a healthy, anonymous donor who is chosen for his similarity in appearance and intellect to the man himself. The sperm is injected into the woman's uterus around the time of ovulation.

Some genetic diseases can be diagnosed during early pregnancy by means of one of a number of antenatal tests. If a disease is detected the couple then have the option of an abortion. However, if for any reason a couple would not consider an abortion, these tests will not usually be offered.

ULTRASOUND

An ultrasound scan is a simple, painless technique. High-frequency sound waves are directed into the uterus from a probe placed on the mother's abdominal wall. The waves scan across the area and are reflected by the tissues of the uterus and of the fetus. The reflections are picked up by a receiver and converted into an image which is usually displayed on a television screen. In early pregnancy the scan is used to determine the stage of pregnancy and confirm the expected date of delivery. It may also be used to 'map' the position of the baby and placenta if an amniocentesis is planned, or to check the position of twins in the uterus. Some abnormalities of fetal structure can be detected by ultrasound early enough for an abortion to be considered.

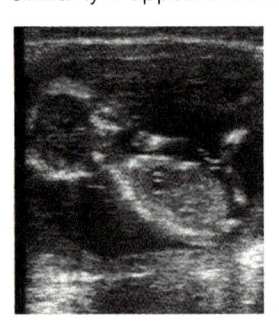

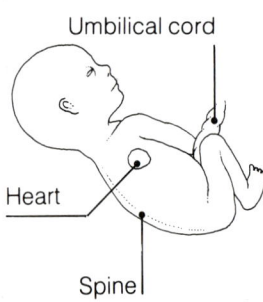

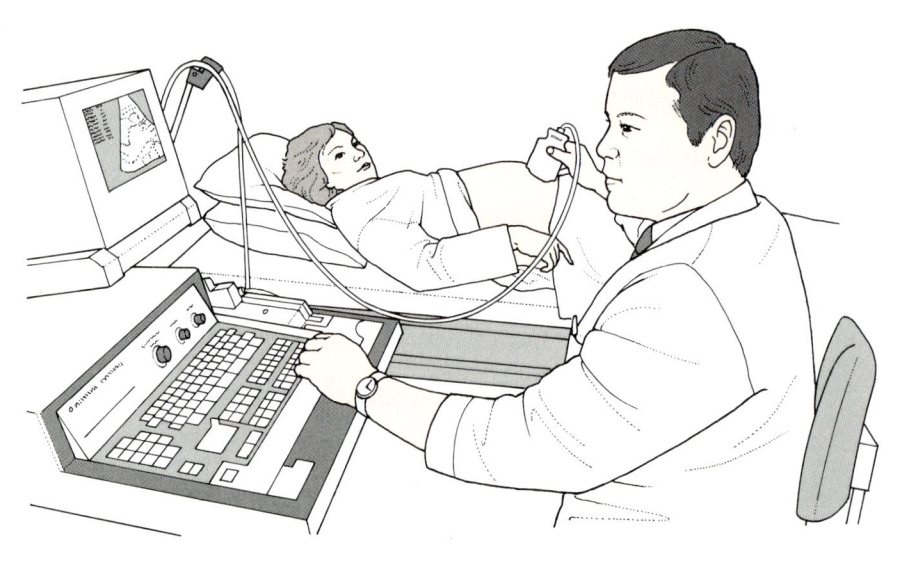

An ultrasound scan of a fetus about 14 weeks old gives a picture in which you may be able to identify the various parts of your baby's body.

AMNIOCENTESIS

Amniocentesis is a surgical procedure in which a sample of the amniotic fluid surrounding the fetus is taken for examination. The fluid contains fetal cells and the chromosomes of the fetus can be examined and disorders such as *Down's syndrome* can be diagnosed. The fluid can also be examined for a variety of biochemical substances. For example, a high level of alphafetoprotein may indicate *spina bifida*.

Amniocentesis is normally offered to women over the age of 38 who, because of their age, run a high risk of having a baby with Down's syndrome. It may also be offered to a woman who is very anxious about the outcome of her pregnancy, perhaps because she has had a previous Down's baby, or has a close relative with Down's syndrome.

Amniocentesis carries a small risk (approximately 1 per cent) of provoking an abortion, and is normally used only if the risk of serious disease outweighs the risk to the pregnancy. It carries a higher risk if there are twins, and in this care it is not usually advised.

If for any reason you would not consider terminating your pregnancy whatever the results of an amniocentesis, there is probably no reason to have one even if it is offered to you.

The abdomen is numbed with a local anaesthetic and a hollow needle is inserted to withdraw amniotic fluid. Amniocentesis is usually carried out in about the 15th to 16th week of pregnancy. There may be some bruising but the majority of women have no ill effects.

CHORIONIC BIOPSY

Chorionic biopsy is a relatively new procedure that is usually offered only to women whose children are known to be at risk of genetic disease. The test is performed at about the 8th to 10th week of pregnancy. A narrow instrument is inserted through the neck of the uterus. A few of the earliest fetal cells (which later develop into the placenta) are removed and analyzed for chromosomal and biochemical abnormalities. Chorionic biopsy allows earlier detection of abnormalities than does amniocentesis, and therefore earlier and safer termination of the pregnancy if necessary. The test is uncomfortable but not painful. It carries a risk of abortion of about 3 per cent.

FETOSCOPY

Fetoscopy is a highly specialized procedure that is not widely used. A hollow needle holding a telescopic probe and light is inserted into the uterus through the mother's abdominal wall. This enables the doctor to identify abnormalities of the baby's face or limbs, and to collect a sample of blood from the umbilical cord so that inherited blood disorders such as thalassaemia can be diagnosed. Fetoscopy carries a 3 to 5 per cent risk of abortion.

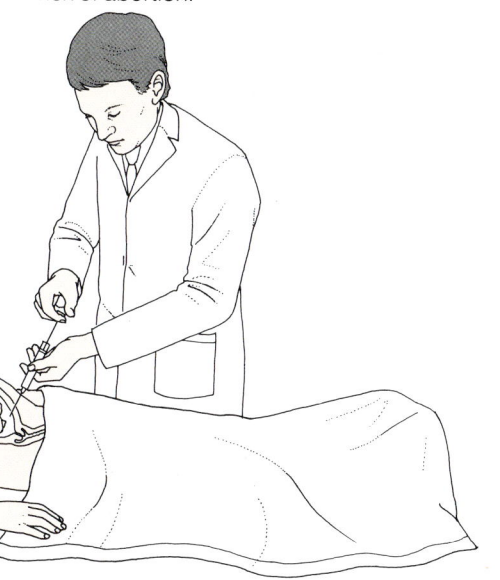

PROBLEMS OF THE NEWBORN CHILD

There are many sorts of problems that may affect newborn babies. The minor common ones like *rashes* and *birthmarks* are discussed in **The newborn child**. The serious but rare congenital diseases like *Down's syndrome* are discussed and explained in **Genetics**. In addition babies may need special care for problems that develop during pregnancy, or occur at birth or during the early weeks of life. These affect about 1 baby in 10, but as babies are remarkably resilient, with help the majority recover.

Even if your baby needs special care and is in an incubator, touching and fondling him whenever you can will lay the foundation for your growing relationship.

BABIES WHO NEED SPECIAL CARE
A baby may need special care as a result of:

o Illness of the mother (for example diabetes) which may affect the newborn baby (see **The unborn child**)
o Difficulties caused by *birth asphyxia* or *birth injuries*
o Low birthweight: less than 2 kg (4 lb 7 oz)
o Birth before 35 weeks of pregnancy
o Difficulty in breathing or continuing blueness after birth
o Problems that develop during the first week of life, such as marked *jaundice*, *fits*, infection or *feeding difficulties*
o *Rhesus incompatibility*
o Serious *congenital abnormality*

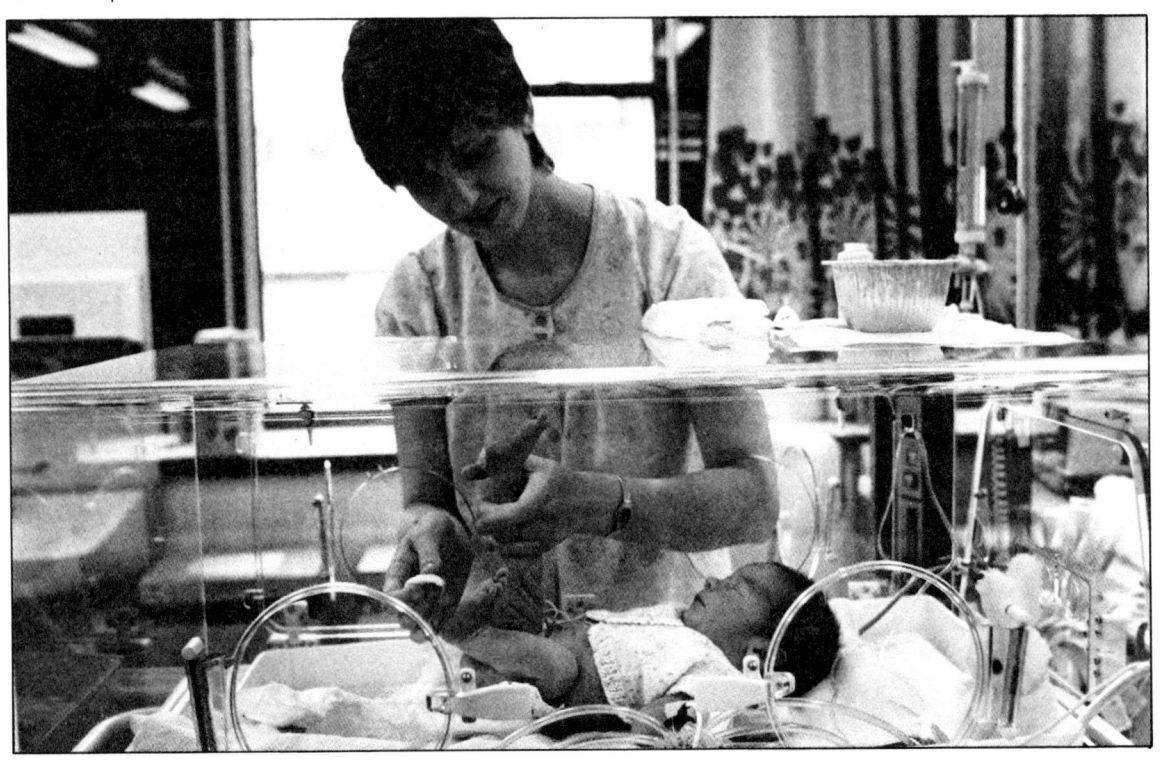

Special care

Most newborn babies who have health problems are looked after in special care baby units or neonatal units. Special care involves helping the baby to feed and keep warm. The baby can be given milk through a fine plastic tube passed through his nose down to his stomach. An incubator keeps the baby warm, and regular checks are made on his breathing, heart rate and temperature.

Intensive care

Most neonatal units in large hospitals have intensive care sections. These are for very small or very ill babies who need a mechanical ventilator to help them breathe and drip feeds into a vein to provide fluids and food. Monitoring devices are necessary so that the ventilator can be adjusted to the baby's needs and the baby receives exactly the right amount of oxygen.

Parents of a baby in an intensive care unit are faced with a bewildering array of equipment and technology, and they may feel they have nothing to contribute to their baby's care. But a premature baby needs just as much loving care as a healthy mature baby, if not more. If your baby is taken into an intensive care unit it is important for you to visit him as often as possible. Even if he cannot yet be taken out of the incubator you can still touch, soothe, stroke and talk to him, however sick he is. In fact he may respond better when lovingly handled, and you will find it easier to feel that he is really yours.

Perhaps the greatest anxiety is not knowing exactly what is wrong with your baby, how long he will have to stay in hospital and how he will progress when he is finally taken home. Do not hesitate to question the doctor until you understand your baby's condition and all its implications.

Whenever possible, your baby will be taken out of the incubator, so that you can hold him. He can be given expressed breast milk – the midwife will help with this. Ask the staff if you can help with changing and dressing him. Later, you can help with tube-feeding before the baby starts to breast- or bottle-feed. Gradually you should be able to do more so that, by the time your baby has recovered, you will have taken over the greater part of his care during your visits. This will make the baby's home-coming less stressful for you.

BIRTH ASPHYXIA

Lack of oxygen, or asphyxia, sometimes affects babies before or during birth because of a problem with the placenta or umbilical cord. Regular antenatal checks and monitoring the baby's heart and movements during labour help to detect whether he is receiving insufficient oxygen so that measures to prevent asphyxia can be taken, and if necessary a Caesarean section can be performed. Following birth, babies who have experienced asphyxia may be irritable and may dislike being handled; they may also have a shrill cry or difficulty in sucking and feeding. Severe asphyxia can affect all the body systems. Breathing may be affected. The baby may have inhaled mucus or *meconium* during birth, or may suffer from *respiratory distress syndrome*. Because the baby's kidneys are not working properly, fluid may accumulate in his tissues, causing swelling. He may suffer from *jaundice*.

At birth fluid will be quickly sucked out of the baby's air passages, and he will be encouraged to gasp and to begin spontaneous breathing. Some babies need extra oxygen to start breathing. The baby will be nursed in a cot or incubator with as little initial handling as possible. He may be fed by an intravenous drip at first, and if necessary given drugs to control irritability or *fits*.

Most babies recover well and after a few days may be fed and handled normally. However, severe asphyxia can result in permanent *brain damage*, causing fits, *mental handicap*, *hyperactivity* or *learning problems*, sometimes in addition to *cerebral palsy*.

BIRTH INJURIES

A baby may be injured during a difficult birth so that he needs to be watched for a while in a *special care* unit.

Bruising of his face may make him look very blue at birth, especially if it is the result of the cord being wrapped tightly around his neck or of being born face forwards. A baby born bottom first may have a very bruised bottom and genitals. All these bruises improve over a few days.

Nerve damage may be caused if a nerve is bruised or stretched during birth, creating temporary muscle weakness. During a forceps delivery, the nerve that controls the muscles of the face may be bruised and as a result the baby will move one cheek and one side of his mouth less than the other. This will be particularly noticeable when he cries. The nerve usually recovers spontaneously and the weakness disappears within a few weeks.

Erb's palsy is caused by the stretching or bruising of nerves in the root of the neck. The baby will hold his arm weakly by his side with the palm of his hand turned backwards. In most cases recovery takes place naturally.

Bone injuries occasionally occur during a difficult delivery. A fractured collar bone heals without treatment, although at first there may be a lump at the site where new bone forms. Sometimes a limb or one of the bones of the skull is fractured. A limb bone is rested by strapping or splinting it. Such fractures usually heal without treatment.

LOW-BIRTHWEIGHT BABIES

Some babies are small at birth because they are born before the pregnancy has run its full course of 37 to 42 weeks. A baby born before 37 weeks is called 'pre-term'. Others are smaller than usual in spite of the fact that they were born at the expected time. These babies are known as 'small-for-dates', 'light-for-dates' or 'dysmature'. A baby can be both pre-term and small-for-dates.

The term 'premature baby' was previously used for both, but the term 'low-birthweight (LBW) baby' is now used to refer to a baby weighing less than 2.5 kg (5.5 lb) at birth for whatever reason.

Some low-birthweight babies are perfectly healthy at birth, but they are, in general, more vulnerable than babies of average weight. Babies who weigh between 1.5 kg (3.5 lb) and 2.5 kg (5.5 lb) usually overcome their problems without difficulty, although they may need *special care*. Smaller babies usually need *intensive care*. Breathing difficulties are the most common problem of smaller babies and nearly all of them are self-limiting. They gradually disappear over the first few days or weeks of life. Other problems include temperature control, feeding difficulties and, for pre-term babies especially, *anaemia* and *jaundice*.

TEMPERATURE CONTROL

Pre-term babies have a limited ability to keep themselves warm, while small-for-dates babies tend to be long and thin and therefore have a large surface area compared to their volume, and so lose a lot of heat. Both will need extra warmth at first, usually in an incubator.

APNOEIC ATTACKS

If a baby is pre-term, the centre in the brain that controls breathing may still be too immature and breathing may stop. An apnoeic attack is when breathing stops for more than about 20 seconds. The baby may turn dusky or blue. Sometimes apnoeic attacks may be the result of an infection or a heart or lung problem. In this case the underlying problem is treated and the baby's breathing is encouraged by physical stimulation, such as stroking the soles of his feet, or by giving him a drug that stimulates breathing.

NECROTISING ENTEROCOLITIS

This serious illness, in which the bowel is damaged and inflamed, occurs in the 3 weeks after birth. Its cause is unknown. Any baby can suffer from it but it is more common in the smallest pre-term babies. The baby often vomits and may pass blood in his stools. Abdominal X-rays confirm the diagnosis. The baby's feeds are stopped for at least a week, and he is given nutrients by intravenous drip with antibiotics to combat possible infection.

Despite his apparent fragility you need not be afraid to handle your low-birthweight baby confidently, to wash, dress and play with him as you would a baby of normal birthweight.

ANAEMIA

Most of the iron stores a baby needs to make healthy red blood cells are transferred from the mother during the last 3 months of pregnancy. Babies who are born before 37 weeks do not therefore receive this iron. As a result they may develop anaemia during the weeks or months after birth. The condition is treated by giving the baby iron tablets from the time he is 1 month old.

Babies in intensive care have several blood samples taken to monitor their condition, and occasionally this can result in slight anaemia. If necessary these babies are given 'top-up' blood transfusions.

FEEDING DIFFICULTIES

A pre-term baby often cannot feed immediately after birth because his sucking reflex is not developed or because he cannot co-ordinate sucking and swallowing. His bowel may be too immature to move its contents along normally,

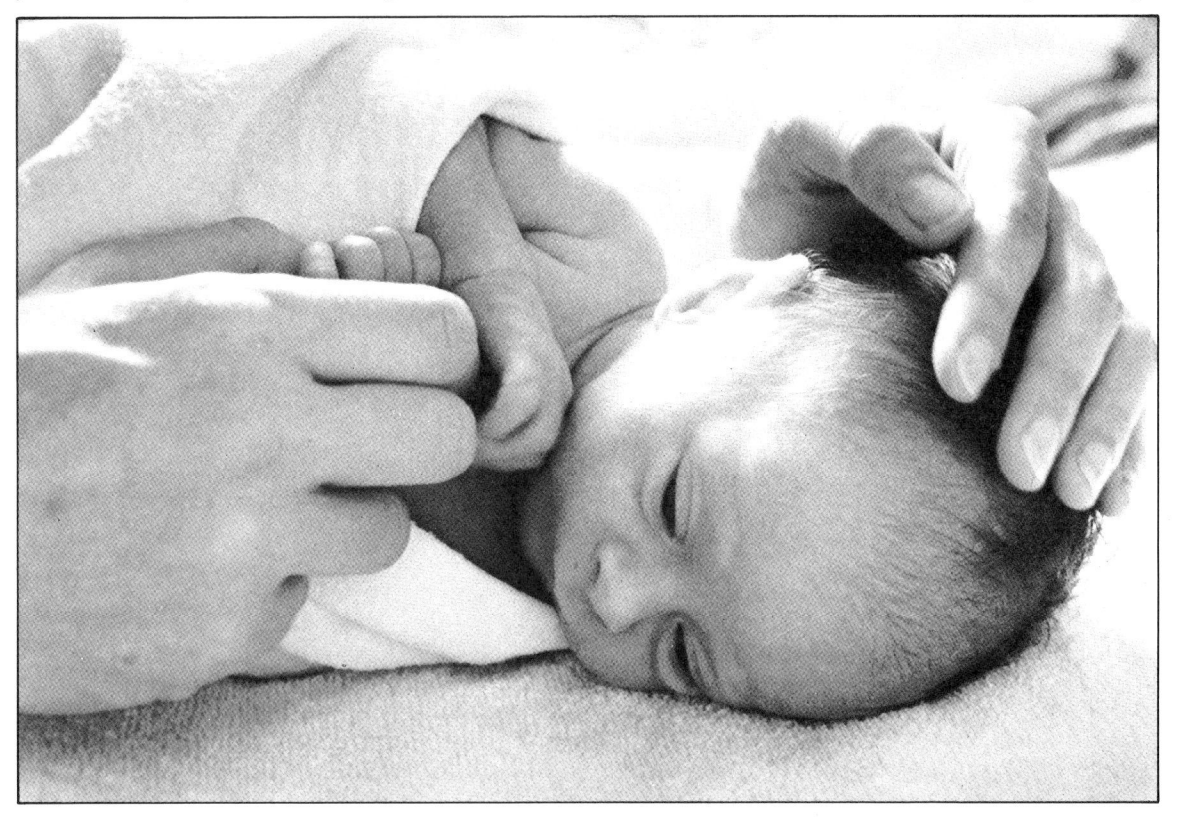

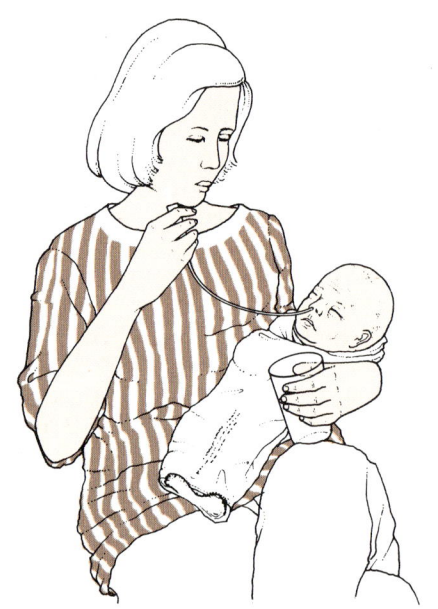

A nasogastric tube is inserted into one of the baby's nostrils and gradually passed into his stomach. When a baby is fed in this way a little glucose water is tried at first. If the baby tolerates this, small amounts of milk are given every hour and eventually larger feeds are given every 2 hours, then every 3 or 4 hours, as for a normal, healthy baby.

so that any milk he swallows stays in his stomach, which becomes swollen. For these reasons the baby may need an intravenous drip in the days after birth to ensure adequate intake of nutrients and fluids – a technique called total parenteral nutrition. Normal feeds are built up gradually. When the baby's condition is more stable, he may be fed through a nasogastric tube.

Pre-term babies' feeds are often built up to a higher total milk intake than those of full-term babies, to help them catch up. Some hospitals provide special low-birthweight formula milk in the early weeks, and all pre-term babies need vitamin drops.

EXTREME PREMATURITY

In the past babies born before 28 weeks of pregnancy hardly ever survived. With modern intensive care babies born before 28 weeks – even 24 or 25 weeks – can survive. However, because of the immaturity of the body systems, particularly the lungs, such babies tend to have repeated ups and downs in their condition.

Generally premature babies come through the newborn period well, pass their milestones normally, although rather later than the child born at term, and develop as any other child. Unfortunately the difficulties encountered by some of the smallest may be too great. About 1 in 10 babies weighing less than 1.5 kg (3.5 lb) at birth is likely to have a serious handicap such as *cerebral palsy*, *blindness* or *deafness*. For babies weighing less than 1 kg (2.2 lb) at birth the chance is about double. Even so, the majority of even the smallest surviving babies grow up fit and well.

RESPIRATORY DISTRESS SYNDROME

This difficulty is experienced by many pre-term babies because of the immaturity of their lungs. When a baby begins to breathe at birth the tiny air sacs, or alveoli, in the lungs have to be filled with air, and the first breaths require a great deal of effort. Once the alveoli are filled with air they are able to stay open due to surfactant, a substance produced by the body. A pre-term baby's lungs are immature and sometimes do not make enough surfactant so that the alveoli collapse each time the baby breathes out. This greatly increases the work of breathing: the baby's ribs protrude with each breath, he grunts when breathing out and he may even stop breathing altogether for a time. Extra oxygen is needed to prevent the baby becoming blue or dusky.

Very immature babies may suffer these breathing difficulties from the moment of birth. Others may have enough surfactant at first but then encounter difficulties several hours after birth as it becomes used up so that their breathing becomes distressed at this later time.

TREATMENT

The baby is kept warm in an incubator, and given fluids and food through an intravenous drip. Until the baby's lungs become able to make surfactant, his breathing will be supported, usually by giving extra oxygen, which can be fed into the incubator or put into a Perspex box placed over the baby's head. If more help is needed, the air/oxygen mixture is given under slight pressure, through a mask or a tube passed directly into the baby's windpipe. This technique is called continuous positive airways pressure (CPAP – pronounced 'seepap'). If the baby needs even more help, the physical work of breathing is done by a ventilator connected to a tube in the baby's windpipe.

Occasionally complications develop and breathing support has to be prolonged. One such complication is **pneumothorax**, a leakage of air from the lungs into the chest cavity around them. The air then has to be drained out through a tube passed between two ribs into the chest cavity. The tube is left in position until the air leak seals itself. Another complication is lung infection which is treated with antibiotics. Sometimes the lungs do not open properly and a condition known as **bronchopulmonary dysplasia** develops and continues for weeks or months. The baby will still need oxygen even when otherwise ready to leave hospital. He is likely to wheeze and cough more than others, but his lungs are likely to heal by the time he is 2 years old.

JAUNDICE

Red cells in the body are continually broken down, forming a yellowish-green waste product, bilirubin. Usually this is removed from the bloodstream by the liver, but if large amounts of bilirubin are being formed, or if the liver is working inefficiently, the level in the bloodstream will build up. Then the skin will look yellow and the urine will turn dark.

Some degree of jaundice is quite normal in newborn babies and affects about 80 per cent of pre-term babies. This 'physiological' jaundice develops because the liver is not yet working efficiently. The jaundice usually appears about the third day after birth.

A few babies become jaundiced within the first day of birth because of excessive breakdown of red cells, usually due to a blood group incompatibility.

A baby who is severely jaundiced may be treated by exposure to ultraviolet light (phototherapy) for several hours each day. Phototherapy can be given in an incubator or a cot and while she is being treated protective pads will be put over the baby's eyes.

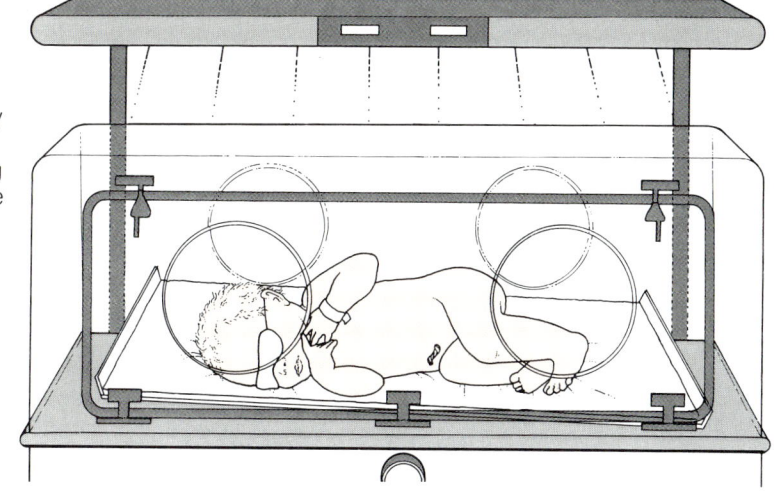

Infection, bruising and some inherited diseases can also cause jaundice in the newborn period. Occasionally 'breast milk jaundice' develops. This is quite harmless and if it happens to your baby there is no reason to discontinue breastfeeding. Other, much rarer, causes of jaundice during the first weeks are *hypothyroidism*, *hepatitis* and blockage of the bile duct.

Physiological jaundice usually needs no treatment. If a baby is severely affected he may be treated by phototherapy (exposure to ultraviolet light). Occasionally an exchange blood transfusion is needed when the bilirubin level is extremely high.

▶ **See also** The blood

RHESUS INCOMPATIBILITY

The Rhesus system is a blood-grouping system. About 80 per cent of people are Rhesus positive and the remainder are Rhesus negative. If the father is Rhesus positive, the mother Rhesus negative and their baby Rhesus positive, the baby in the uterus may be affected by 'incompatibility' between his blood and that of his mother. It begins when some of the baby's red blood cells leak into the mother's circulation. They stimulate her immune system to make antibodies against them, then these antibodies pass back via the placenta into the baby's blood, where they will destroy the baby's red blood cells.

First babies are rarely affected because usually red blood cells only enter a mother's circulation in any quantity at delivery. The mother thus 'sensitized' makes antibodies against Rhesus positive blood cells. A woman can also become sensitized as a result of a miscarriage or abortion. When sensitized, her antibodies may affect any subsequent Rhesus positive baby. However, for some reason that is not understood this does not always happen.

Rhesus incompatibility is now rare because mothers at risk are given an injection of a substance called Anti-D immediately after the birth of their babies and this prevents sensitization. Once a severely affected baby is born he will be watched carefully and if necessary treated by an exchange blood transfusion through a tube in the umbilical vein. At follow-up clinics Rhesus babies are carefully checked since they may develop anaemia during the early months of life.

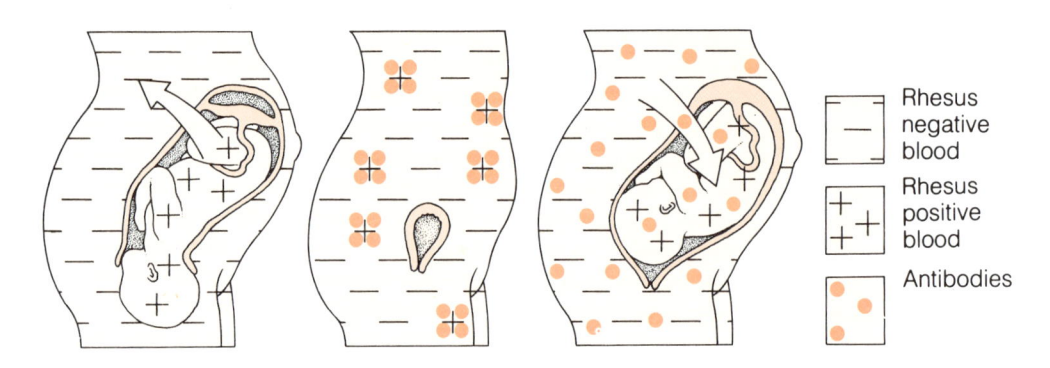

Antibodies to a Rhesus positive baby may be formed in a Rhesus negative mother's blood when the placenta separates during delivery and some of the baby's blood enters the mother's circulation. These antibodies can cross the placenta and damage the red blood cells of any subsequent Rhesus positive baby, although for some reason they do not always do so.

OTHER NEONATAL PROBLEMS

Besides *jaundice* there are other problems that may affect babies during the first weeks of life, or may only be noticed some time after birth.

Neonatal infection is unlike adult infection since babies cannot complain of a particular symptom such as a sore throat or pain when passing urine. So if they develop an infection, even a localized one, they show generalized signs such as going off their feeds, vomiting, lethargy or irritability. If your baby shows any of these signs you should tell your doctor. An examination may reveal the cause, but sometimes there is no obvious reason for the trouble. If the baby seems particularly ill, it may be necessary to admit him to hospital, where specimens of blood and urine can be taken for analysis.

Neonatal fits (also called convulsions) are more severe than the slight trembling of many babies when disturbed or handled. This jitteriness is usually normal, although it may be associated with a low level of glucose or calcium in the blood. It can be corrected by injection. Occasionally, however, a baby jerks one or more limbs, sometimes rolling his eyes and stopping breathing briefly. These fits need investigation by a doctor. There are a number of causes including *birth asphyxia*, *birth injuries*, infection (such as *meningitis*) or metabolic disease. The doctor will aim to identify and deal with the cause, if possible.

Bowel obstruction may be diagnosed if a baby vomits in an unusual way or brings up dark-stained fluid. Other signs are a swollen abdomen, lack of bowel action, or blood-stained stools. The obstruction may be the result of part of the bowel being narrow or not existing at all, or of the bowel becoming twisted after birth. If your baby develops any of these signs, call the doctor. After an examination the baby may be admitted to hospital. If there is an obstruction an operation is usually necessary to relieve it.

SPINA BIFIDA

Spina bifida is a condition in which the vertebrae of the baby are incompletely formed so that, in its more severe form, the spinal cord and its coverings, the meninges, are exposed. It is a defect resulting from a combination of genetic and environmental factors.

There are two types of spina bifida: spina bifida occulta and spina bifida cystica. Children suffering from spina bifida occulta have small defects in their vertebrae, mostly in the lower back. These defects rarely give rise to problems. A few children may have a tuft of hair, a pigmented spot or a fatty lump in the

When a child has a myelomeningocele his spinal cord protrudes, usually low on his back, and it may be exposed or covered with skin or membrane.

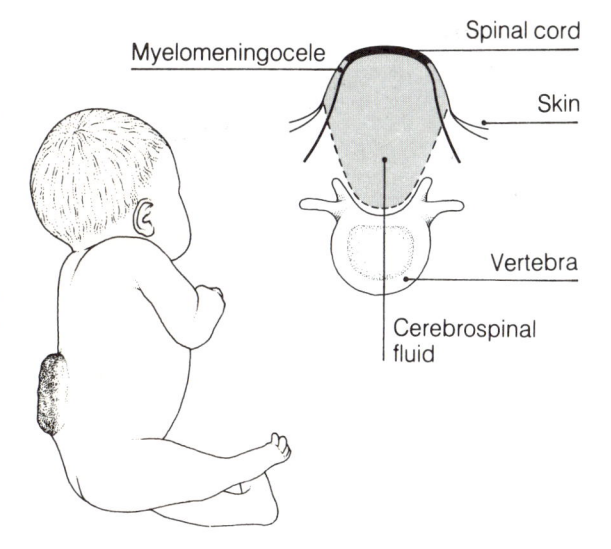

skin overlying the spinal defect. A small operation can usually make the skin look normal. In a very few cases, the underlying spinal cord has an abnormal structure that can cause problems in the child's control of his legs or bladder.

Children suffering from spina bifida cystica have more extensive defects in their vertebrae, and the spinal cord is involved. Approximately 1 baby in 200 is born with it and when a woman has had one such child her chances of having another rise to 1 in 20.

When only the membranes of the spinal cord protrude through the defect they form a sac filled with fluid called a meningocele. In this case the defect is usually covered with skin, the spinal cord is in its regular position and the nerves within it work normally.

When the cord itself protrudes it forms what is called a myelomeningocele. Sometimes the protruding cord may be covered by a combination of skin and meninges, giving it some protection. In the most severe form the skin is partially absent and the spinal cord nerve tissue is exposed. In this case the area may leak fluid and infection may occur, and *meningitis* results. Whether open or closed, the abnormal structure of the spinal cord leads to difficulties with the control of the lower limbs, bladder and bowel.

SYMPTOMS

A baby with spina bifida cystica may have paralysed legs with no feeling or reflexes. He may have or develop deformities in his legs such as *dislocated hip* or *club foot*. His bladder may not contract properly so that he will tend to dribble urine, and the back pressure of urine in his distended bladder may damage his kidneys and lead to urinary tract or kidney infection. His lower bowel may not contract properly, causing chronic constipation or uncontrolled defecation.

TREATMENT

In the meningocele type of spina bifida cystica an operation can repair the back defect to avoid any risk of rupturing the fluid-filled sac. Parents can then handle their baby with confidence.

For babies born with a myelomeningocele, the first step is immediate transfer of baby to a *special care* unit. The medical and surgical team will examine the baby carefully, and an operation will be advised for those with a good chance of doing well. Experiences since the 1960s have shown that babies with severe paralysis of the legs, a severely deformed and bent back, a very large head due to *hydrocephalus*, or another major problem such as *heart defect* or *birth asphyxia* will not do well with one or even several operations. These babies can be nursed in a hospital cot and given relief from any pain or distress. Because of their severe handicaps the majority die within 3 months of birth.

The decision on whether to operate is often difficult for everyone concerned. The doctor's aim is to help the parents appreciate any adverse factors affecting the baby, to explain what surgery may achieve, and its limitations, and to outline the probable future. The parents' feelings are paramount, and since the choice is between two courses which both have great problems, neither option can be a perfect solution. When the hospital team is fully aware of the parents' views a doctor member of the team suggests a course of action.

The main aim of surgery is to repair the skin, meninges and backbones as far as possible. The operation does not improve the function of the nerves. The paralysis remains. The doctors then watch carefully for any signs of meningitis, which is treated at once with antibiotics, or hydrocephalus.

After the baby goes home, follow-up visits will be to a special clinic for spina bifida. Here a team including surgeon, paediatrician, physiotherapist and social worker combine to help parents help their children.

Up to 70 per cent of children with spina bifida who survive to school age have intelligence within the normal range, and many attend normal schools. Some whose physical disabilities are more severe attend special schools for the physically handicapped.

▶**See also** Longstanding problems; Genetics

HYDROCEPHALUS

One complication of *spina bifida* cystica is that there may be an interruption of the normal flow of cerebrospinal fluid. The fluid may build up in the brain so that the baby's head becomes abnormally large. This condition is known as hydrocephalus. Of babies born with a meningocele, 10 to 20 per cent develop hydrocephalus. Some babies with myelomeningocele have hydrocephalus at birth and it subsequently develops in up to 90 per cent. Hydrocephalus also occurs without spina bifida. It is treated by draining fluid through a plastic tube, or shunt, from the brain to a blood vessel leading to the heart or from the brain into the abdomen from where it is easily absorbed.

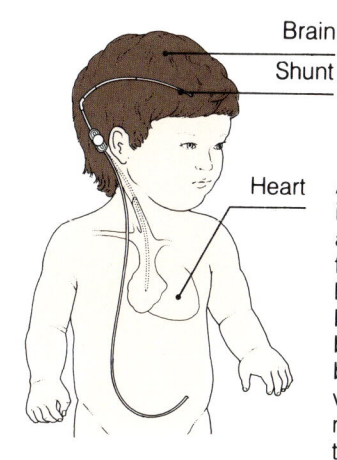

A permanently implanted fine tube with a one-way valve diverts fluid from the hydrocephalic child's brain. If it becomes blocked the child may become irritable or vomit and the blockage must be cleared or the tube replaced in hospital.

CLEFT LIP AND PALATE

About 1 in 700 newborn babies has a cleft or gap in the upper lip (previously called a 'hare lip'), in the palate or in both. The cause is unknown, although if there is a family history of the problem the chances of a baby being affected are far higher. The baby is usually normal in all other respects.

Cleft lips and palates are formed during the early weeks of pregnancy. The baby's face does not join up properly, but there is not necessarily any part missing. Surgery can correct the defects. The timing of the operation varies according to the needs of the particular baby: usually a lip is repaired when the baby is about 3 months old and a palate by one or two operations 6 to 12 months later. The baby will have to stay in hospital for up to 10 days for each operation.

If your child is born with one of these defects your first priority will be to establish good feeding. Babies with a cleft on one side of the lip usually feed well. Those with a cleft palate tend to find sucking difficult, but a nipple shield and teat may help. Often the simplest method is to express breast milk and use a

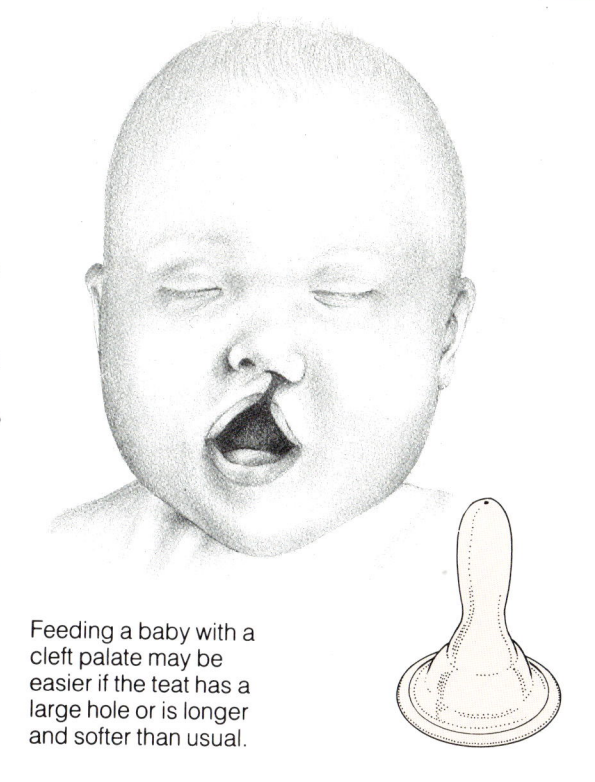

Feeding a baby with a cleft palate may be easier if the teat has a large hole or is longer and softer than usual.

spoon to feed the baby. With bottle-feeding, various types of teat can be tried. Whatever method you use, you will find it helpful to sit the baby up, and not to worry too much about some milk coming down his nose.

Try to avoid giving your baby a dummy during the months leading up to an operation, as after the surgery a dummy might damage the fine stitches in the lip or palate. Also avoid lying the baby on his tummy to sleep, because in hospital he will be nursed on his side to protect the operation site and it is easier if he is used to this position.

Babies with clefts are followed up at a cleft lip and palate clinic. They are more liable to develop ear infections so their hearing is checked regularly. They may also see a speech therapist to avoid speech problems: a baby's voice will sound nasal until the cleft palate is repaired. They should also be seen early by a dentist, since specialized dental work may be necessary to help teeth come through correctly.

CLUB FOOT

Club foot, known medically as talipes, is a malformation of the foot and ankle. A normal ankle joint can move in two ways: the foot can be bent down or up, and it can be turned inwards or outwards. During the first few hours after birth a baby's legs and feet tend to remain in the position they held in the uterus and the feet may appear to be deformed and at an angle. If gentle manipulation can move the foot to the normal position and also beyond it, this is called 'positional talipes'. In this case it needs no other treatment and disappears within a few days.

If a baby's foot cannot be moved into the normal position then he has a fixed club foot. His foot will usually be pointing inwards with toes down (talipes equinovarus); less commonly, and less severely, his foot will be bent upwards with the toes pointing outwards (talipes calcaneovalgus).

About 1 baby in 800 has fixed club foot, and of these about half have both feet affected. Although the cause is usually unknown it is more likely to affect a baby when a parent or sibling has the problem. The doctor will examine the baby carefully to make sure there is no evidence of nerve or muscle disease. Treatment depends on the severity of the condition but is usually started as soon as possible after birth. The baby's foot is gradually manipulated into a more normal position and strapped with adhesive tape. More than half of club feet are corrected in this way, but others need surgery.

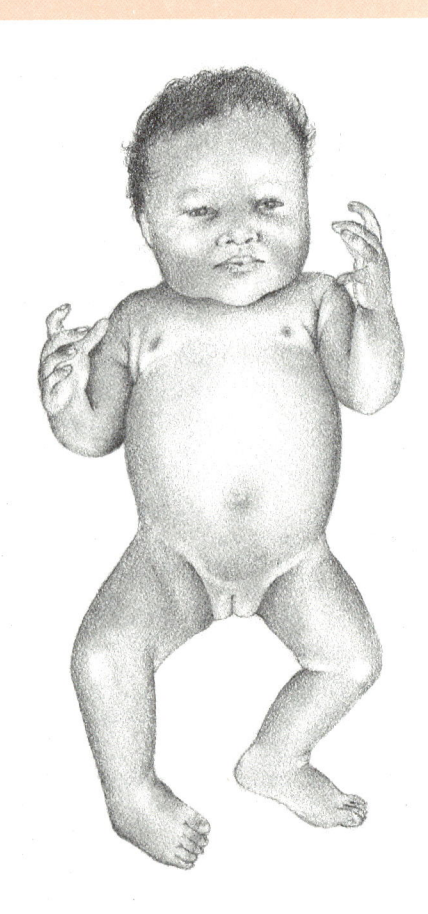

A baby who has a fixed club foot may need to wear special footwear at night in the final stages of treatment. This is essentially a pair of splints in the form of open-ended boots attached to a cross-bar.

ACCIDENT AND INJURY

Normal, active, curious, developing children are bound to have accidents and hurt themselves. Parents need to deal with all manner of injuries and also to interpret from their child's reaction how serious the situation is. This section describes the basics of hospital treatment for various injuries and what parents can do in the way of after-care. The first-aid actions you can take to treat minor injuries are described in **The sick child at home** in Part Two. What you should do in more serious and life-threatening situations is outlined in **Emergency actions** at the end of the book.

Going to hospital
Most children will have to go to hospital at some time because of accidental injury or some other emergency. Each year 1 child in 5 visits the casualty department of a hospital. The most common reasons are bruises, sprains, cuts and head injuries. Many also need emergency treatment for broken bones, burns, poisoning and near drowning. The majority are treated and can return home; only a small proportion are admitted to a ward.

If one person's condition is critical it has first claim on the time of the staff, hence the unpredictable wait for those less seriously injured. Many smaller hospitals do not have the facilities to deal with emergencies, and it is worth finding out in advance the location of the nearest hospital that is equipped to do so. Some larger hospitals have separate emergency departments for children.

If your child has to go to hospital for emergency treatment, you will probably feel shocked, frightened and possibly guilty. However, if you can stay calm, you will be able to give your child the support he needs and you will also be able to give the nurses and doctors essential information about the accident or injury. They will also need to know whether the child has any medical condition and whether he is receiving treatment for it. Wherever possible, parents are encouraged to hold their child, reassure him and comfort him. However, if you are distraught, it may be better for you to wait in a nearby room and allow the hospital staff to provide reassurance and bring you news.

After severe injury some children may be emotionally disturbed. Do not hesitate to seek help should problems arise.

▶**See also** Safety; Hospitals and the sick child; Counselling

Scalp wounds bleed profusely and may look more alarming than they really are. Blood loss, pain and fear may make your child vulnerable to shock if she has a scalp wound. A warm blanket, comfort and reassurance can help prevent shock developing.

SEVERE CUTS

Severe bleeding may be more dangerous for a young child than an adult. While an adult can lose up to a pint of blood without ill effects, in a young child, whose total blood volume is much less, heavy blood loss from a cut or wound leads to shock much more easily. In addition to blood loss there may be a great deal of damage to the body tissues from severe cuts and surgery may be necessary to correct the damage that has been done and to ensure proper healing.

IMMEDIATE CARE

If the injury is not serious, the nurse or doctor usually injects a local anaesthetic, cleans the wound thoroughly and closes it with stitches, metal clips, or adhesive strips. The doctor will also ask about *tetanus* immunization.

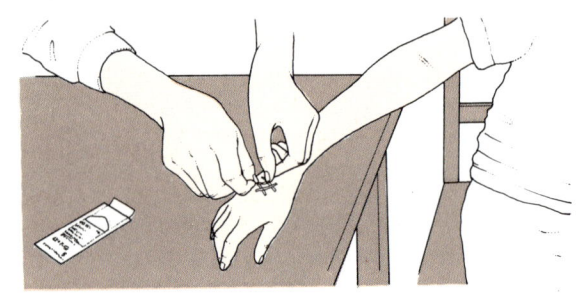

The edges of a severe cut must be held together either by stitches or skin closure strips if the cut is to heal properly. Strips may be used rather than stitches when the cut is straight and will not be stressed too much, by movement at the joint, for example.

A jagged-edged wound may need minor surgery to clean and neaten its edges so that it heals quickly with minimal scarring. Cuts on the face and other exposed areas may require more detailed attention from a plastic surgeon.

If the child's condition is critical, he will be operated on as soon as possible. While the surgeon examines the child, fluids may be given by *intravenous drip* to replace lost blood. His stomach may have to be washed out (*gastric washout*) before he is anaesthetized if he has eaten recently. The surgeon investigates the depth and extent of the wound, and then cleans and repairs each layer of tissue in turn. The child may be kept in hospital for several days so that staff can watch for infection and delayed shock.

AFTER-CARE

The wound is dressed and the doctor will advise you on caring for it and keeping it dry. The doctor will also tell you whether your child has to return to hospital to have any stitches removed. Larger wounds usually need checking and re-dressing by a nurse at a local surgery or hospital. The child should rest the injured part initially to encourage good healing. If underlying tissues such as muscles, tendons or ligaments were damaged, exercises supervised by a physiotherapist will help the child to regain movement and the strength of the injured part.

FRACTURES

If your child has an injury that causes pain, swelling and shock, and which makes it impossible for him to move the affected part, you should suspect a broken bone. You can take him to hospital yourself, unless the injury is to a leg or foot, in which case the child will find it difficult to move; or to the spine, pelvis or head, in which case moving the child may be dangerous. Call an ambulance instead.

At the hospital, an X-ray of the affected part will be taken to see whether the bone is in fact broken. If it is, various forms of treatment may be needed. Children's bones are still actively growing and after a break they usually heal quickly and well. However, the bones must be set correctly before they mend, or subsequent growth may magnify any small deformities and lead to permanent malformations.

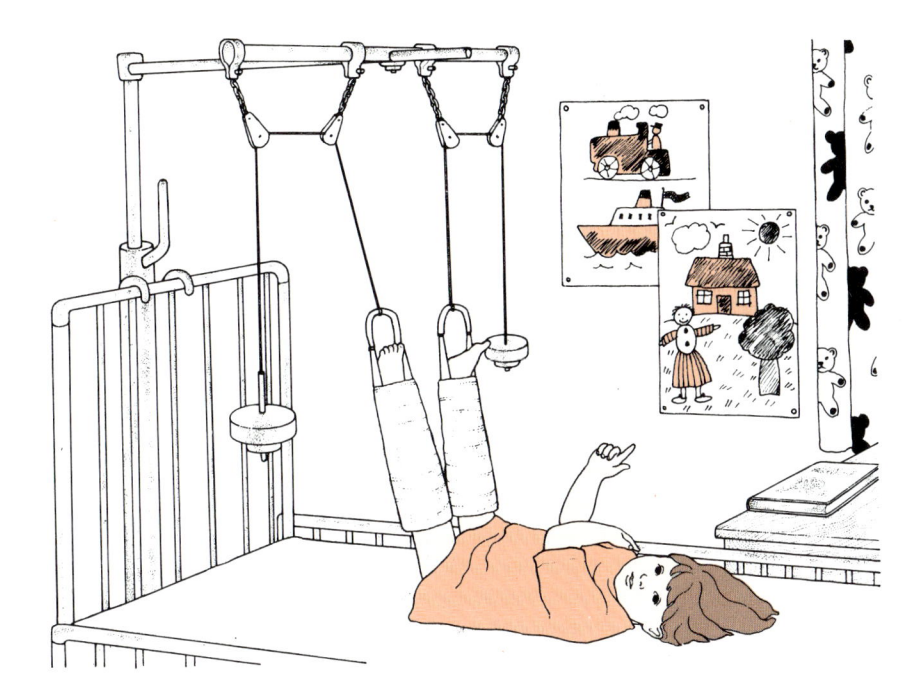

A child under 2 years old with one broken leg may have both legs put in traction. At this age the hip joint is very malleable and a balanced pull on both legs will prevent distortion.

IMMEDIATE CARE

For some fractures, plaster of Paris may be used to encase the injured part in the correct position for healing. This has the advantage that the child can become mobile and leave hospital relatively quickly.

For some types of fracture, the surgeon must operate to repair the bone. Metal pins and plates may be used as internal fixings. This is done under general anaesthetic.

The muscles near a fracture may go into spasm and pull the bone fragments out of alignment. Traction may be needed to counteract this. Weights are used to pull the muscles and bones into place. There are various positions for traction, depending on the part injured. For example, a child with a broken leg may lie on his back with the foot of the bed raised and his leg attached by a cord to hanging weights. Certain splints provide traction also.

AFTER-CARE

After a bad fracture it may be several weeks before the child is back to full activity. He may feel left out of home and school life. You have a vital role to play in talking, listening, understanding, and also in touching and handling your child as much as possible. Schoolwork, visits by friends and games that can be played with little movement will all help to keep him occupied. The physiotherapist will devise a set of exercises so that his healthy bones, joints and muscles do not waste and stiffen, and so that the injured part is gradually returned to full use. Encourage your child in his exercise programmes, both in hospital and afterwards.

If your child has plaster on:

○ do not allow it to become wet
○ inform the hospital if it cracks or breaks, or if the child complains of pain, tingling or numbness
○ keep the injured part raised as much as possible
○ with a young child, watch for small items pushed under the plaster

Listen to your doctor's advice about restricting the child's sports and games to allow gradual recovery. It may help to let him ignore some routine tasks, like bedmaking, in favour of important ones such as going to school.

DISLOCATIONS

A dislocated joint is one that has been torn apart or one in which a bone is not in its socket. A child with a dislocated joint will usually be in severe pain and will be unable to move the affected joint. If there is a dislocation, one of the bones may also be broken.

IMMEDIATE CARE

After initial X-rays and tests the doctor may give an anaesthetic, either general or local, and perhaps a muscle-relaxant drug. The dislocation is then manipulated and the bones are replaced in their correct position. The effects of this are often remarkable. A child who was screaming in pain from a dislocated shoulder may be going home happily a couple of hours later.

In some instances, the surgeon may need to operate on a dislocation to repair ligaments and other joint tissues.

AFTER-CARE

Care of children with dislocations is much the same as for *fractures*. Bruised muscles and tendons and torn ligaments take time to heal and you should follow the doctor's and physiotherapist's advice carefully. If a dislocated joint is rushed back into action too fast, the tissues may become slack and recurrent dislocation is likely: do not expect complete rehabilitation for some time.

▶**See also** Bones and joints

HEAD INJURIES

Although the damage involved in a head injury may look minor, there may be internal injury that does not become apparent for hours or even days. Blood vessels beneath the skull may have ruptured and as they leak the blood puts pressure on the brain. This is why a child with an apparently minor head injury may be admitted to hospital for a day or two for observation.

IMMEDIATE CARE

If your child injures his head, you should take him to a doctor immediately. If he has been unconscious (however briefly), or looks very pale, or has vomited or has had blood or fluid leaking from his nose or ear, he will almost certainly be admitted to hospital. The doctor may detect a possible skull fracture beneath a scalp wound; this also requires admission to hospital.

After an initial examination and X-ray, the child will be kept under close observation in the ward. The staff will check his blood pressure and watch for signs of brain or nerve problems such as fading consciousness. If the child has been vomiting he may receive fluids only, or be given an *intravenous drip*. If he stays well he will probably be allowed home after 24 to 48 hours.

If your child has suffered a major injury, the priorities are to ensure that his breathing and heartbeat remain steady, so he may be linked to various monitors and life-support machines in an *intensive care* unit. As he gradually improves, he will be moved to a children's ward and kept under observation.

AFTER-CARE

Internal head injuries may develop days after the original accident, so it is essential that you inform the doctor at once if your child becomes drowsy, or develops a headache or vomits. Your doctor will explain the significance of such danger signs, and many hospitals provide parents with a written list of what signs to watch out for following head injury so that problems developing after a child has left hospital can be dealt with swiftly.

BURNS AND SCALDS

A child with a severe burn needs urgent care in hospital. Some burned children have nightmares and may also develop behaviour problems or emotional disturbances as a result of pain and shock, and you may need professional help in coping with these.

IMMEDIATE CARE

The doctor's main aim is to maintain the child's vital systems. Burns on the neck or face, or inhaled smoke, may cause swellings in the mouth, throat or trachea. If these interfere with the child's breathing, a tube may be put down into his lungs or an opening made in the neck (tracheotomy).

A second priority is fluid replacement. Blood and body fluids leak from burned skin and into heat-damaged tissue. An *intravenous drip* will be set up to maintain fluid balance, and urine output may be measured by a catheter in the bladder. The intravenous fluids are likely to be continued for some time, and if burns cover a fifth or more of the skin area the doctor may recommend no food or drink by mouth until the child's condition has stabilized, usually after about 3 or 4 days.

AFTER-CARE

The child's room must be kept as sterile as possible, and parents are given masks and gowns to reduce the risk of airborne infection. In some cases, the burns may be left uncovered; in others they will be covered by special dressings. The child may have to be restrained from rubbing the burned areas, and burned limbs may be kept raised to minimize fluid loss and swelling.

You should touch and hold your child as much as possible, given the nursing restrictions.

A child with severe burns may also need skin grafts to replace scarred tissue. After initial care, he may therefore be transferred to a plastic surgery unit.

NEAR DROWNING

If your child has nearly drowned, he should see a doctor urgently. The doctor will want to know whether the incident took place in fresh water or sea water, whether the water was clean or polluted and whether the child needed any on-the-spot treatment such as mouth-to-mouth resuscitation.

The volume of water inhaled by a nearly drowned child may be negligible, but even a small amount poses several problems. The water is absorbed through the delicate airway linings into the bloodstream, where it dilutes the blood and causes red cells to burst open. Fresh water is much more dangerous than sea water in this respect. The burst red cells release their chemical contents into the blood and this may cause heart failure. Polluted water can cause a lung infection. Water may also have been swallowed.

IMMEDIATE CARE

If the child's breathing has stopped or is strained, he may need to be supported by a ventilator while his overall condition is checked. The staff will keep a close watch on the child's breathing, heart condition and blood composition. An *intravenous drip* may be set up to stabilize the blood's composition and prevent infection. The child may be given extra oxygen if lung damage is suspected.

Even an apparently healthy child may be admitted to hospital for a day or two in case an infection develops.

AFTER-CARE

Antibiotics may be prescribed following discharge from hospital. If your child cannot swim, lessons in swimming and water safety may help to prevent future accidents.

FITS

Most children who suffer a fit do not have *epilepsy*, but they should all see a doctor urgently. Certain information helps the doctor to assess how to treat a fit and investigate its cause, such as how the fit began and what the child did during it.

IMMEDIATE CARE

If the fit is still continuing the child will be prevented from hurting himself and closely watched. You should be on hand to provide reassurance when he recovers. If he has a high temperature, this will be brought down. He will also probably receive anticonvulsant drugs. If the fit is not caused by a high fever he will undergo several tests to discover the cause of a fit. He is likely to have a head X-ray and an *electroencephalogram* to record the brain's electrical activity. He may also have a *CAT scan* of the head. You may need to provide information on the family's medical history and on the child's previous fits or any fit-like behaviour, such as the occurrence of unresponsive periods during which he just stares into space.

AFTER-CARE

Most children who have a fit do not have another one. If the fit was due to fever, you should follow the doctor's advice about keeping your child's temperature near normal when he next develops a feverish illness.

POISONING

Fast action is vital when a child is suspected of consuming a poison, and you should take your child to hospital immediately. The staff will need as much information as possible: what was eaten, whether he definitely ate it, how much and how long ago. Take a sample of the suspected poison with you to hospital if possible. You may find some between your child's teeth.

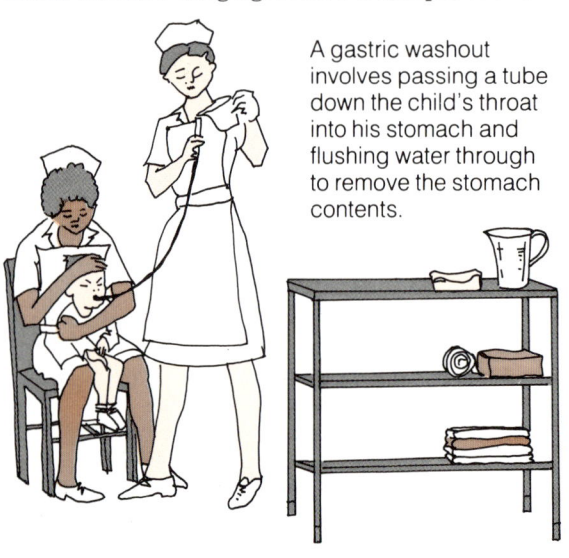

A gastric washout involves passing a tube down the child's throat into his stomach and flushing water through to remove the stomach contents.

IMMEDIATE CARE

Certain poisons can be measured in the blood, so a blood sample may be taken. A conscious child is likely to be given syrup of ipecacuanha to induce vomiting, provided the poison is not corrosive. If the syrup fails, another dose may be given. If this fails also, or if your child is unconscious, his stomach may be washed out (gastric washout). His condition is watched carefully. His breathing may need to be assisted by a ventilator.

Some poisons have specific antidotes, which the staff may give, depending on how much poison has been absorbed into the body.

Your child may be admitted to hospital for observation; most children go home the next day and show no further ill effects.

AFTER-CARE

The child should be given plenty of fluids and gradually returned to a normal diet.

INFECTION

An infectious disease is an illness that can be spread from one living organism to another. This organism need not be human but can be any kind of animal or plant. The cause, or agent, of the infection may be bacteria, viruses, parasites or fungi. Bacteria and viruses are microscopic organisms; many parasites and fungi are visible to the naked eye.

Infections may be spread in several ways: by direct physical contact, through saliva and mucus sprayed into the air as tiny droplets when an infected person talks or coughs, by contact with stools or urine, or by consuming contaminated food or drink. Following infection, there is a period of time during which the agent multiplies before symptoms appear; this is called the incubation period. Sometimes a person may harbour and spread infection but remain perfectly fit and well himself; such an individual is called a 'carrier'.

Bacteria

Bacteria are single-celled micro-organisms. Countless numbers of bacteria exist everywhere: in the air, on the ground, and on and in the bodies of living creatures, including humans. Each bacterial cell consists of genetic material surrounded by cytoplasm, enclosed in an outer wall called a cell membrane. They often have one or more thin whip-like tails, or flagella, which enable the bacteria to move rapidly. Some bacteria are spherical (cocci), others are rod-shaped (bacilli) or spiral-shaped (spirilli). Only a small proportion of bacteria cause disease. Antibiotic drugs are effective against many bacterial infections.

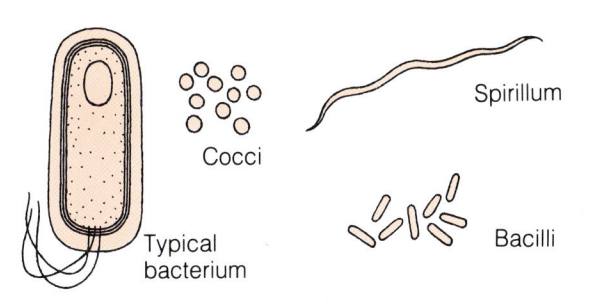

Viruses

Viruses are micro-organisms far smaller than bacteria. Indeed many of the bacteria that cause illnesses are themselves subject to diseases caused by viruses.

Basically a virus is a piece of genetic material surrounded, when outside other cells, by a protective coat of protein. Viruses have no metabolism of their own and can only multiply inside a living cell. Some viruses can exist in an inactive state outside a host cell for long periods, which aids their spread from one person to another.

No treatment will shorten the illnesses caused by most viruses. Antibiotics are ineffective and, except when there is also bacterial infection, there is no point in your child taking them for a viral infection. Viral infections give protection from further attacks from the same virus and vaccination can provide immunity against some viral infections.

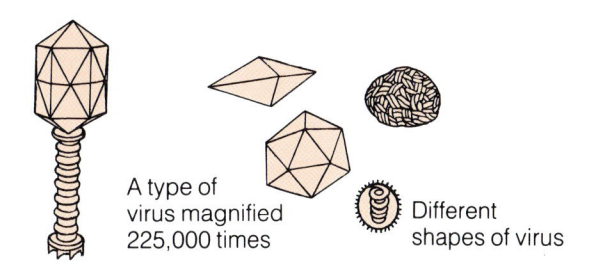

Parasites

These are animals that get their nourishment from other living organisms, which are called 'hosts'. They often cause their hosts to be diseased and sometimes even to die. Parasites that cause illness in humans may live on the skin or hair, or inside the body. Some are spread from other animals to humans since they need more than one host to complete their life cycle. Parasites vary in size from single-celled organisms such as some amoebae to tapeworms and roundworms, which can be more than 25 cm (10 in) long. The larger forms usually spread through their eggs.

Fungi

The term fungus encompasses mushrooms, toadstools, moulds, yeasts and similar organisms. There are many species of fungi that cause disease in humans and animals, usually on the skin, hair and nails, and on moist areas such as the linings of the mouth and of the vagina. Fungal infections usually spread as seed-like spores.

Thrush, the fungus candida albicans, is normally present in the body in small quantities, but if a child's resistance to infection is low, as it may be soon after birth or because of illness or following a course of antibiotics, the fungus may multiply and cause symptoms. These symptoms take several forms, depending on which part of the body is affected. Thrush in the mouth shows up as small white patches that can be rubbed off, exposing raw red areas of skin underneath. Thrush may also multiply in the vagina, causing a creamy white discharge, itching and possibly soreness; it rarely affects the penis. Vaginal thrush becomes more common in adolescence in girls who take a contraceptive pill. Thrush may also affect other areas.

▶**See also** Appendix: Drugs and treatments; Screening programme

IMMUNITY AND DEFENCE AGAINST INFECTION

Many infectious diseases are followed by lifelong protection against that disease, because the natural reaction to the infection creates defences, known as immunity, against a subsequent attack. This protection is set up by the body's immune system, and involves antigens and antibodies. Immunity is specific – an attack of chickenpox, for example, protects against future chickenpox but not against mumps, measles or other infections. However, diseases such as influenza and colds are caused by many different viruses. Although the body becomes immune to each individual cold or influenza virus, the viruses are continually evolving and another slightly different form will cause another infection.

ANTIGENS AND ANTIBODIES

Infecting organisms have antigens on their surfaces. An antigen is a protein molecule built into the skin or cell wall of the invader. It stimulates the white blood cells in the lymph glands of the body to produce antibodies which are also proteins. These antibodies are released into the bloodstream and react with the antigens and so destroy the invading bacteria or virus. Recovery from the infection follows. The immunity that is created relies on antibodies remaining in the body, or the antibody-producing cells being able to manufacture them quickly. In the case of a second invasion, the invaders are destroyed before they can multiply and cause symptoms.

When they are born most babies are immune to several viral diseases because antibodies pass through the placenta from the mother's bloodstream to the fetus. It is, for example, rare for an infant to develop measles during the first 6 months of life.

By the time a baby is 6 to 9 months old, most of the maternal antibodies will have disappeared and, unless immunized, he will then be susceptible to the infection.

OTHER BODY DEFENCES

The body has many other defences against bacteria and viruses. Whether an infection takes hold or not depends on how many of the invading organisms enter the body in the first instance, and how many succeed in thriving and multiplying. The skin, unless damaged by injury or disease, is an effective barrier. Many airborne micro-organisms are filtered out in the nose or caught in the mucus lining the airways. In the stomach, micro-organisms in food and drink are destroyed by stomach acid. If a virus or bacteria nevertheless gets into the circulation, it may be digested and destroyed by white blood cells and the spleen.

A person's general health is an important factor in the battle to overcome infection. Malnutrition is associated with a lowered resistance to many diseases, and stress may lessen a person's ability to fight off infection. If someone already has another disease, such as *diabetes*, this also reduces resistance.

COMMON CHILDHOOD INFECTIONS

DISEASE	CAUSE	INCUBATION	INFECTIVITY
INFLUENZA	virus	1 to 3 days	From just before the onset of symptoms for 5 to 10 days
MEASLES	virus	10 to 12 days	From several days before the rash appears until 5 days afterwards. However, if the child still seems ill, he is probably still infectious
MUMPS	virus	16 to 18 days	From several days before the child becomes unwell until the swellings have subsided; usually 10 days in all
CHICKENPOX (Varicella)	virus	14 to 16 days	From 1 day before the rash appears until the scabs have dried; dried scabs are not infectious
GERMAN MEASLES (Rubella)	virus	16 to 18 days	From a few days before the illness starts until a week after the rash appears
WHOOPING COUGH (Pertussis)	bacterium	7 to 10 days	From the earliest symptoms until 3 weeks after coughing spasms started
SCARLET FEVER	bacterium	2 to 4 days	From several days before the symptoms appear until the child recovers following antibiotics
ROSEOLA INFANTUM	virus	Uncertain, about 10 days	Not very infectious
GLANDULAR FEVER	virus	Uncertain, about 4 to 14 days	Not very infectious
HERPES B	virus	Persists for life once incubated	Infectious while the blisters last

IMMUNIZATION

When someone is given a vaccine, he reacts by producing antibodies in the same way as if he had suffered the natural infection, but in this case, suffering very few, if any, symptoms. This is because the vaccines used contain a weakened strain of the viruses or bacteria, or they contain only the antibody-stimulating part of the micro-organism and not the disease-causing parts.

For long-lasting immunity, usually more than one dose of vaccine is required. The first injection alerts the body's defences and stimulates the production of small numbers of antibodies over the following days. Further injections are necessary for full immunity to develop, and this protection sometimes needs to be reinforced by 'booster' injections given every 10 years or so.

For some diseases, immunity lasting only a few months can be created by giving a blood extract called gamma-globulin, which is rich in ready-made antibodies. Gamma-globulin is given, for example, to a child living in a household where someone has developed hepatitis, or to a young baby whose mother has developed measles or chickenpox.

IMMUNIZATION PROGRAMMES

There is no doubt that children should be protected against devastating diseases, such as polio, tetanus and diphtheria. Whooping cough can be dangerous, especially for young babies, and immunization is generally advisable. Measles vaccination is also recommended for children over 1 year of age; and it is sensible for all girls to be immunized against *German measles*. Children who live in residential homes may be offered vaccination against *influenza* although this has to be repeated every year and even then cannot give protection against every form of the disease. The mumps vaccine is usually reserved for adult men who have not had the disease.

Immunization is important not only to protect your own child against a specific disease, but also to protect other children and adults. When a high percentage of a community is protected, the disease cannot spread.

It is very important to keep a record of your child's vaccinations. As the years go by you may forget which immunizations various members of your family have had, and this information is often needed. For example, if a child has a bad cut or graze it is important to know whether he is fully protected against tetanus.

If your child has a feverish illness, it is usually sensible to postpone any immunization, although you should go ahead if he has minor snuffles but is otherwise well. Most immunizations, apart from polio, are given by injection of the vaccine.

TRIPLE VACCINE (DTP)

Diphtheria, tetanus and whooping cough vaccines are normally combined in one injection and are given at the same time as the polio vaccine. The side-effects are usually mild; if your child becomes fretful and slightly feverish 12 to 24 hours after immunization, a small amount of paracetamol will make him more comfortable. The injection site sometimes becomes swollen and red, and a small lump often develops under the skin, which may take some weeks to disappear. These symptoms may follow either the full triple injection or a diphtheria/tetanus injection without the whooping cough vaccine. They are not dangerous and are no reason to cancel the rest of the course.

WHOOPING COUGH (Pertussis)

Babies are susceptible to whooping cough from birth, since there is no transfer of immunity to this infection from a mother to her baby across the placenta. The disease can be particularly serious for young children, carrying a risk of persistent chest trouble, brain damage and even death. In epidemics of whooping cough, infected schoolchildren can spread the disease to their baby brothers and sisters who have not yet been immunized.

A full course of injections protects over 80 per cent of children and reduces the severity of the disease in those who still get whooping cough despite being immunized. There is a very slight risk that whooping cough immunization may be followed by a serious reaction, which can include brain damage. But for the vast majority of children, the benefits of immunization greatly outweigh such a risk. It has been estimated that about 1 in 300,000 children suffers brain damage after vaccination – a very much smaller risk than that of a serious reaction following whooping cough.

Certain children may be at increased risk of having an adverse reaction to whooping cough immunization – although this should not prevent them having other immunizations. For example, a child should not be vaccinated against whooping cough if he has had a severe reaction to a previous triple vaccine, such as persistent, high-pitched screaming or *fits* over the days following the immunization. If your child has had a previous fit or convulsion, *epilepsy*, or other disease of the brain, or if you or his brothers or sisters have had fits discuss the advisability of whooping cough vaccination with your doctor.

DIPHTHERIA
The basic course of immunizations gives long-lasting immunity.

TETANUS
The basic course is very effective in preventing tetanus, and immunity persists if a booster vaccine is given about once every 10 years. Some doctors prefer to give a booster vaccination to a child who has been injured, particularly if the injury occurred in dirty conditions.

MEASLES
This vaccine is usually given in the second year of life: it is less effective if given earlier. Side-effects, if any, are usually mild, and last only a day or two. The child may get a slight fever, with or without a rash, about a week after the inoculation, but there is no danger that the infection will spread to other children.

POLIO (Poliomyelitis)
This is the only common vaccine usually given by mouth. It not only stimulates the formation of anti-polio antibodies, but also increases the resistance of the gut to the infection. The basic course of three doses produces long-lasting immunity, but a booster dose is advised every 10 years or so. It used to be thought that polio vaccine taken by mouth was not effective for breastfeeding infants; this is not the case.

If your baby has diarrhoea, you should postpone the immunization, as the diarrhoea may interfere with the absorption of the vaccine.

GERMAN MEASLES (Rubella)
Girls should be immunized against German measles when they are about 11 years old. Even if you think that your daughter has had German measles already, it is wise for her to be immunized. Several infections produce symptoms identical to those of German measles – you can never be sure that a child has had German measles unless it has been confirmed by blood tests.

Your daughter may be mildly unwell about a fortnight after vaccination, with a slight fever and possibly a rash and swollen glands. However, there is no evidence that recently vaccinated girls can spread rubella to others.

TUBERCULOSIS (TB)
This immunization, called BCG, protects most children for at least 15 years. It is usually given before puberty. Your child will have a skin test that will show whether or not he has immunity. If he has not, he should be vaccinated. People of any age may be vaccinated if they have been in contact with a case of tuberculosis.

A small lump develops at the site of the vaccination about 2 to 6 weeks after the injection; it shrinks after about 2 months, leaving a small scar. If it weeps it should be covered with a dry non-waterproof dressing.

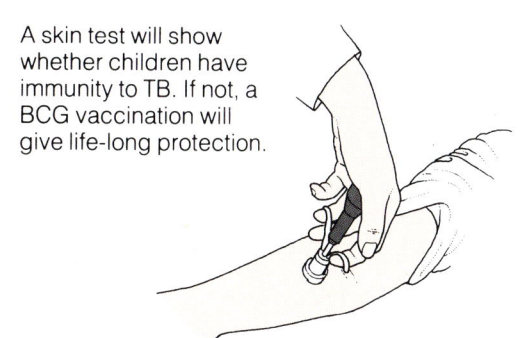

A skin test will show whether children have immunity to TB. If not, a BCG vaccination will give life-long protection.

INFLUENZA

Influenza (flu) is a very infectious viral illness. People with the infection may be only mildly unwell and may continue going to work or school, so it tends to spread rapidly throughout a neighbourhood. Although many people catch influenza each year, winter epidemics occur only every 2 or 3 years when a new strain of the virus appears in a particular country or area. An individual who has had influenza will become immune to that particular form of the virus, but will still be susceptible when a new strain appears.

SYMPTOMS

Many people use the term flu inaccurately to describe any short-lived feverish illness. Often a school-age child who is feeling unwell, achy and depressed is considered to have influenza.

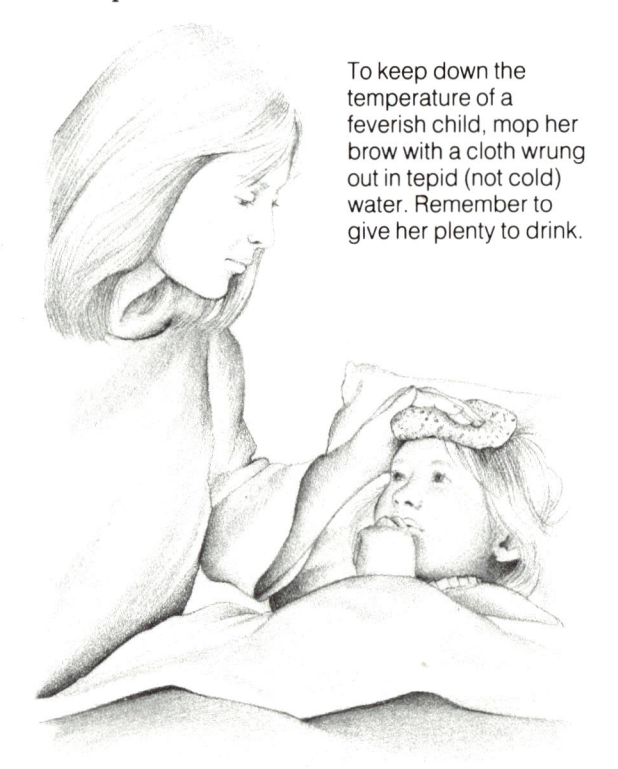

To keep down the temperature of a feverish child, mop her brow with a cloth wrung out in tepid (not cold) water. Remember to give her plenty to drink.

In fact, influenza is caused by a specific virus that has an incubation period of 1 to 3 days. The child may only be mildly unwell with a cold or a slight fever or may feel very ill indeed with a high fever, headache, painful muscles and attacks of shivering. He may also have a blocked nose and sore throat with a dry cough that causes soreness behind the breastbone.

Severe influenza tends to start suddenly with a rapidly increasing temperature that can reach 40°C (104°F). After about 3 or 4 days the fever subsides, although the child continues to cough and can feel weak for several more days. Children often cope with influenza rather better than adults. They nearly always make a straightforward recovery unless they have a chronic disease affecting the chest, in which case *bronchitis* or *pneumonia* are possible (but rare) complications.

TREATMENT

If your child has a bad attack of influenza he will probably want to stay in bed. Make sure that he rests and takes plenty of fluids. You can give paracetamol to bring down the temperature and ease the aches and pains. Consult your doctor

o if your child is less than 1 year old
o if he has a pre-existing illness such as *asthma* or *diabetes*
o if he does not improve after about 3 days

A child who is getting more chesty, with shortness of breath or pains in the chest on breathing, should also be seen by a doctor.

PREVENTION

The influenza vaccine protects an individual for about 1 year and is usually recommended only for a child who has a chronic lung or heart disease. The vaccine is usually given in late autumn or early winter. As it can only be prepared from existing forms of the virus it does not give protection against any new forms that may appear after its preparation.

MEASLES

Measles is a viral infection that affects the respiratory system and causes a rash. It is very infectious and is spread when an infected person sneezes or coughs. Measles has become much less common since immunization has been given widely.

SYMPTOMS

The child is usually ill for about a week. The illness begins like a bad cold and cough, and the child gradually becomes more feverish and unwell. In the early stages he may have sore eyes and he may dislike bright light. After a day or two many children develop Koplik spots, which look like grains of salt sprinkled on the inside of the cheeks at about the level of the back teeth. These spots are sometimes difficult to see but if they are there your child certainly has measles.

Around the third or fourth day, a rash begins to appear on the child's face. The spots are red and slightly raised, and they may join together, making the skin look blotchy. The child is by now likely to be very miserable and unwell, with a cough and a temperature of about 40°C (104°F). The rash, which is not itchy, spreads to the lower limbs in the next few days, by which time the child is usually starting to get better. After another couple of days the rash fades, leaving a brownish stain for a few more days.

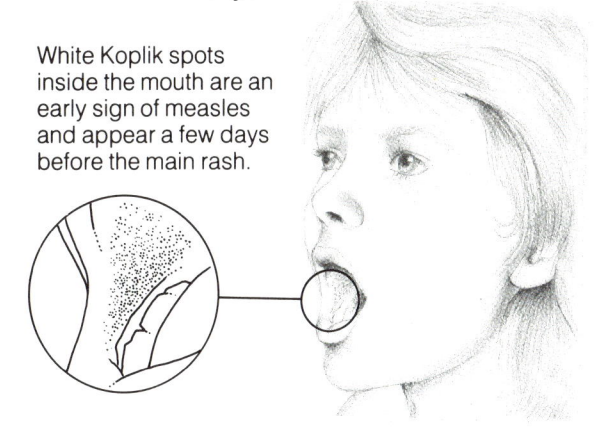

White Koplik spots inside the mouth are an early sign of measles and appear a few days before the main rash.

TREATMENT

If your child has measles he should be seen by the doctor. He will probably want to rest in bed or somewhere comfortable. There is no need to keep the room dark unless he finds that light hurts his eyes; being in a brightly lit room will in no way damage the eyes. Make sure that he has plenty to drink: warm drinks may soothe the cough. Proprietary cough medicines are not very effective. Paracetamol will help ease discomfort and will lower your child's temperature.

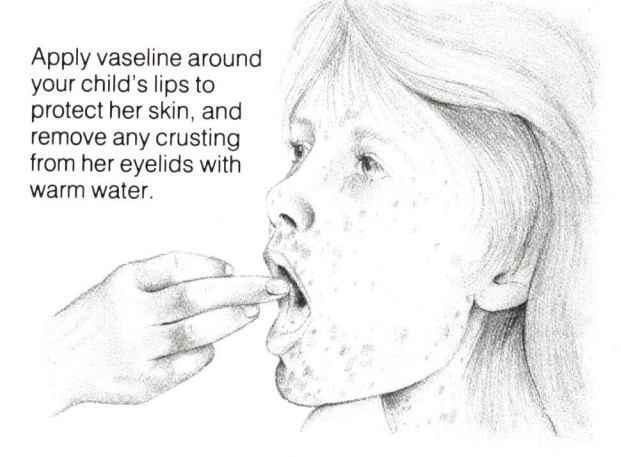

Apply vaseline around your child's lips to protect her skin, and remove any crusting from her eyelids with warm water.

COMPLICATIONS

The most common complication of measles is *Otitis media*. This is more likely to occur when a child has severe measles, or when a child has a history of ear infections. Your doctor will usually prescribe antibiotics for the treatment of otitis media.

Mild *croup* is a common complication of measles, and it may occasionally be severe, with a barking cough, hoarseness and noisy breathing. You should call your doctor if this happens. *Pneumonia* is another risk and should be suspected if your child is getting worse, instead of better, 2 to 3 days after the rash develops, and if he has increasing shortness of breath and a persistent cough. Very rarely *encephalitis* may develop.

MUMPS

Mumps is a viral infection of the salivary glands and is spread by droplets of saliva. It is fairly infectious, but not so infectious as *measles* or *chickenpox*. The salivary glands below and in front of the ear, known as parotid glands, are most usually affected, but sometimes the salivary gland below the jaw also swells up.

SYMPTOMS

Mumps produces very variable symptoms and it is not always easy to be sure that a child has the disease – a chubby toddler with mumps may just look as if he has a rather fat face. About one third of infected children are not unwell in any way, but still become immune to the disease. Unless you are certain your child has mumps – since, for example, a brother or sister had the infection 2 or 3 weeks previously – it is sensible to ask your doctor to confirm the diagnosis.

The child may be mildly unwell, feverish, and complain of pain around the ear, perhaps with discomfort on chewing. The next day, one or both of the parotid glands start to swell and become painful and tender. This swelling occurs on only one side in about a quarter of children with mumps. Usually one gland swells up first, followed by the other within a few days. The face returns to its normal shape and size within about a week.

Some children have a couple of days of stomach-ache and vomiting during an attack of mumps. This may mean they have an inflamed pancreas gland, so, if your child has these symptoms, you should consult your doctor.

TREATMENT

If your child has mumps, he may not feel particularly ill and may be quite happy to potter about the house. Paracetamol will ease the pain of the inflamed glands. Give him plenty to drink but avoid acid drinks such as fruit juices, which stimulate the flow of saliva and so cause pain.

COMPLICATIONS

The most feared complication of mumps is inflammation of the testes. This only rarely occurs in children. If it is going to happen in a child, it nearly always starts within 2 weeks of the first signs of the illness. The child becomes more feverish and unwell and the affected testis becomes swollen, painful and tender. Fortunately, it is unusual for both testes to be involved, and later sterility is very uncommon.

Meningitis and *encephalitis* are more common complications of mumps than of other viral infections. Up to 10 per cent of children with mumps are affected, but many only mildly – just enough to produce a severe headache. Meningitis or encephalitis may develop before the salivary glands swell, or with swelling, or after it, or even instead of it. The child usually has a headache, vomiting, dislike of light and perhaps drowsiness. If your child has these symptoms you should call your doctor. Admission to hospital may be necessary but children usually make a rapid and

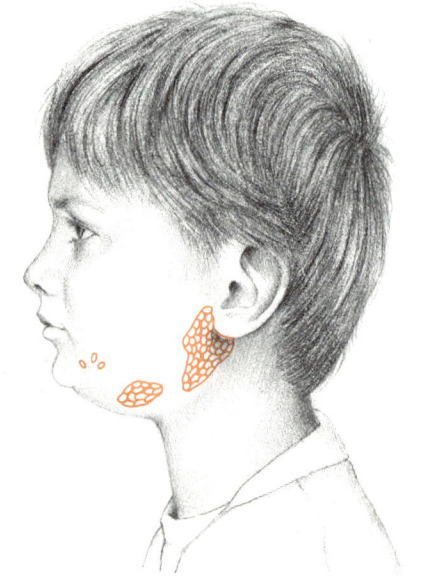

Swollen salivary glands make it painful to open the mouth or swallow.

CHICKENPOX (Varicella)

Chickenpox is a highly infectious disease characterized by an extremely itchy blistery rash. It is caused by a virus which also produces shingles. Shingles usually affects older people, but occasionally also affects children.

SYMPTOMS

Most children are only mildly affected by chickenpox. It often begins with the rash, although in some children this may be preceded by a day or two of feeling unwell. The child may run a slight temperature.

Chickenpox spots are red, and they become little fluid-filled blisters within a day of appearing. They usually show first on the trunk but within a couple of days they spread to the face, the scalp and the tops of the arms and legs. The spots gradually crust over and the crust then falls off within weeks, leaving a small whitish area that eventually blends with the surrounding skin. Spots usually come in crops over 3 or 4 days, so that on any one part of the body there may be new spots, blisters and older spots. Unless the spots have been badly infected, they do not leave a scar.

In a mild case of chickenpox there are so few spots and the child is so minimally affected that a doctor may be uncertain whether he has chickenpox or a few insect bites. Severely affected children, on the other hand, may have spots everywhere – including the mouth, genital area, eyelids and hands.

TREATMENT

If your child has the disease mildly and you are certain of the diagnosis, it is not necessary to consult your doctor; your child will almost certainly be better within a week or so. If he is unwell and distressed by the irritation and the rash is widespread, medical attention may be useful. Your doctor may prescribe antihistamines to ease the irritation.

Give your child plenty to drink. Paracetamol may help make him feel more comfortable, and will bring down a raised temperature. Calamine lotion may soothe the itchiness and irritation, but it is messy and its effects do not last very long. Most children do not feel ill enough to go to bed. Loose, soft cotton clothing will probably irritate the skin least. Cool baths may be helpful too.

COMPLICATIONS

The most common complication of chickenpox is secondary infection of the spots by bacteria, producing small boils. This secondary infection can be caused by scratching the spots with dirty fingernails, so keep your child's nails short and clean. Very rare complications of chickenpox include *pneumonia* and *encephalitis*.

GERMAN MEASLES (Rubella)

German measles is a mild respiratory illness, usually accompanied by a rash. It is a viral infection. It is nearly always very mild, but it has very serious implications for the unborn child of a pregnant woman. Young girls should therefore be allowed to contract the infection or should be immunized against the infection at puberty, and you should keep a child with suspected German measles at home, to avoid infecting anyone who might be pregnant.

SYMPTOMS

German measles usually starts with the same symptoms as a mild cold, with perhaps a slightly sore throat. The rash appears in a day or two, starting on the face and spreading down the trunk; it disappears within days. The spots of the rash are flat and pale pink; a severe rash may look like mild *measles*. The glands in the back of the child's neck may be swollen and tender.

TREATMENT

Apart from giving plenty to drink, no specific treatment is necessary. A child with German measles does not usually feel unwell.

COMPLICATIONS

It is rare for children to have complications from German measles, but teenagers may have swollen joints for a couple of weeks.

WHOOPING COUGH (Pertussis)

This debilitating respiratory illness is caused by bacteria, although some viruses can produce very similar symptoms. It is highly infectious, especially during the early stages, and is spread when an infected person coughs or sneezes. The severity of the disease varies. The vast majority of children with whooping cough recover completely, although the illness can last for 2 to 3 months. It is most dangerous for very young babies. Immunized children may get a mild form of the disease.

SYMPTOMS

Whooping cough begins with the symptoms of a cold: runny nose, runny eyes, cough and slight fever. Unless you know that your child has been in contact with someone with whooping cough, you probably will not suspect it at this stage.

Most coughs and colds are over in a couple of weeks, but the cough of a child with whooping cough becomes more persistent. Gradually, after about 2 weeks, the typical coughing spasms of whooping cough develop. The child coughs about 10 times in rapid succession while breathing out; this is often, but not always, followed by a crowing whoop as he gasps and breathes in again. Small babies may never develop the characteristic whoop but they sometimes have difficulty breathing in at the end of a coughing fit and may become very short of oxygen.

The number of coughing spasms varies from 2 or 3 a day to dozens each day. Sometimes spasms are followed by vomiting. All children find spasms exhausting, and young ones may become frightened. Many children do not seem to be particularly unwell between attacks, playing quite happily until the cough returns.

After some weeks, the number and severity of the coughing fits gradually decrease. Some children have recurring coughing fits for the next few months, whenever they get a cold.

TREATMENT

You should consult your doctor when you hear the characteristic whoop, or when your child's cough gets worse rather than better after a week or so and he develops longer, more frequent fits of coughing. Most children can be nursed at home but a young baby who needs constant nursing may be admitted to hospital.

Children tend to have fewer coughing fits if their attention is diverted by toys, books or television – but over-excitement may start them coughing again. If your child coughs and vomits when he eats a meal, try small portions of foods that are easily chewed and digested. Young babies with whooping cough will need to be fed again if they vomit soon after a breast- or bottle-feed, to make sure that they get enough fluid. Ask your doctor for advice on how to nurse a child with whooping cough.

Paracetamol will help reduce fever. Although the infection is bacterial, antibiotics do not have much effect unless the child develops a secondary infection of the lung. However, they may be effective in preventing the disease in young babies who are in contact with an infected child.

COMPLICATIONS

The complications associated with whooping cough can be quite severe, especially in very young children. The most serious are *encephalitis*, burst blood vessels in the brain, caused by a coughing bout, and lack of oxygen due to breathing difficulties. These can all lead to permanent brain damage; extremely rarely, they can cause death. There is also the risk of a secondary chest infection or even *pneumonia*, leading to permanent lung damage.

SCARLET FEVER

Scarlet fever is *tonsillitis* caused by a particular type of bacterium, accompanied by a rash. Several decades ago scarlet fever was a serious disease, but nowadays the bacteria seem to have become less virulent and penicillin can be used to treat the disease, so it is no more serious than any other streptococcal tonsillitis. Infection is spread by droplets of saliva, sometimes from individuals who harbour the bacteria in their throats but are not ill themselves.

SYMPTOMS

Scarlet fever symptoms vary a great deal from child to child. Many children are only mildly affected; they may have a slightly sore throat, a low fever, tender neck glands and a pink spotty rash. Occasionally they may have stomach-ache.

Sometimes a child has a more severe form of the disease, with a high temperature, a very sore throat and a fine red rash, looking rather like sunburn with goose pimples, covering most of the body. The child has a flushed face, often with a pale area around the lips. The tonsils become swollen and inflamed, with spots of pus on their surface, and after a few days the tongue becomes red and raw. The child's skin may start to peel a week or so after he has recovered, as it does after sunburn.

TREATMENT

Scarlet fever can be cured by a course of penicillin, or another antibiotic if your child is allergic to penicillin. If treated early enough, the illness will only last a week or less, so you should consult your doctor as soon as possible if your child becomes feverish and develops a sore throat accompanied by a rash. You can also give paracetamol to ease the sore throat and bring down the temperature.

COMPLICATIONS

Occasionally the bacteria may spread from the child's throat and cause *otitis media*, *sinusitis* or infected neck glands. *Rheumatic fever* or acute *glomerulonephritis* may also follow scarlet fever after a delay of up to 5 weeks, but complications of this nature are fortunately exceedingly rare.

ROSEOLA INFANTUM

This is a virus infection that commonly affects infants and toddlers. Its symptoms are similar to those of many other infections, including *urinary tract infections*, so your doctor may want to arrange for a urine sample to be tested.

SYMPTOMS

The child suddenly develops a high temperature, which continues for 3 or 4 days. He is likely to be somewhat irritable and listless, but perhaps not as unwell as might be expected with such a high temperature. He may have a slight cold. After a few days the fever subsides and the child develops a rash of pink, sometimes slightly raised, spots. The rash is more pronounced on the child's trunk than on his face. By the time the rash appears, the child is well, and the spots fade after a day or so.

TREATMENT

Consult your doctor if your child develops a high temperature with no other obvious symptoms, especially if he does not get better within 48 hours. If your child has roseola, paracetamol may bring down his temperature for a short while, but it soon goes up again.

COMPLICATIONS

On rare occasions, a child may have a *febrile convulsion* at the beginning of the illness as his temperature rises.

GLANDULAR FEVER (Infectious mononucleosis)

This common viral infection is usually associated with a fever, swollen glands and a sore throat. It is sometimes called the 'kissing disease' because it is most commonly transmitted through saliva passed on by contact between young people. The infection is seen most commonly in young people between the ages of 15 and 24 years old, but it also occurs in children between 5 and 14 years old, although rather less frequently.

SYMPTOMS

Glandular fever can produce many different symptoms. Young children usually remain fairly well, whereas teenagers tend to feel ill. They are usually feverish for a few days, before developing a bad sore throat with enlarged, tender lymph glands in the neck. Glands in the armpit and the groin may also become swollen.

The sore throat of glandular fever may make you suspect severe *tonsillitis*. You may only realize that your child has glandular fever when the initial sore throat continues for longer than expected or does not respond to treatment with an antibiotic.

Children and adolescents can return to school when the temperature and sore throat have subsided and they have been feeling better for a few days, usually 2 to 4 weeks after they first see the doctor. Teenagers may remain lethargic, depressed and easily tired for some weeks. They may even need to be reassured that they are not becoming mentally unbalanced.

TREATMENT

Your doctor will arrange a blood test, taken a week or so after your child first becomes unwell, to confirm the diagnosis of glandular fever. The child or young person will need to rest, but the vast majority make a complete recovery without medication.

HERPES INFECTION AND COLD SORES

Herpes simplex is a virus that causes sores around the mouth when it first infects a child. The infected child then becomes a carrier of the virus, but it usually lies dormant for most of the time. A minority of carriers suffer recurring crops of cold sores, or fever blisters.

HERPES SIMPLEX MOUTH INFECTION

A child who has a very sore, ulcerated mouth and is also feverish and ill almost always has a first infection of the *herpes simplex* virus.

The child's mouth may be only mildly sore, in which case the problem usually clears up in a few days. However, sometimes a child feels extremely ill and miserable and becomes reluctant to eat or drink because his mouth is so uncomfortable. Saliva drooling over his lips may spread the virus to the surrounding skin, causing more little blisters to develop. Despite the development of more blisters, the infection

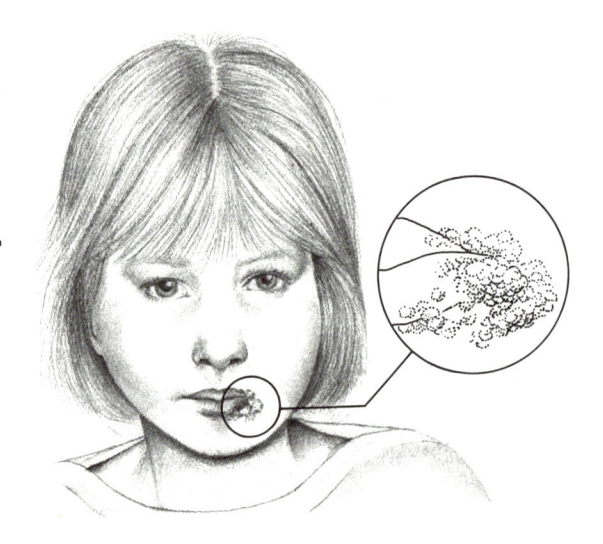

A little vaseline rubbed on the child's lips may ease friction between her teeth and sore mouth.

usually clears up in 10 to 14 days and the child feels well again. Occasionally the herpes virus, instead of causing a sore mouth, causes a sore red eye with little blisters around the eyelids.

Consult the doctor if your child develops a sore mouth and fever. The herpes virus is one of the few that can be treated effectively by drugs, although these are seldom necessary for children unless they are very unwell or have inflamed eyes. You may need advice on how to keep your child's mouth and lips clean, and also useful tips on how to give him enough fluids. He may find it easier to drink from a toddler's beaker with a spout, or through a straw. Ice cream and cold drinks are often easiest for a child to take.

COLD SORES

After the initial herpes infection, a child may later develop cold sores, most commonly around his lips and nostrils. These are provoked by various factors such as feverish illnesses (including colds), strong sunlight, stress and tiredness and injury to the skin. The child may have a few hours of itchiness and tingling at the site of the sore before little blisters develop. The blisters crust over after a day or two, and the sore usually heals in about 10 days. No treatment is necessary unless the cold sore starts to weep and spread after a few days. If this happens, consult your doctor; the cold sore may have become infected, in which case antibiotic treatment will be needed.

OTHER INFECTIOUS DISEASES

Tuberculosis (TB) is a bacterial infection most common in tropical countries. It usually affects the lungs, although it can attack any organ of the body. It is transmitted through droplets of saliva spread when an infected adult coughs: it is not possible to catch tuberculosis from a child with the disease. Your doctor may suspect TB if your child has a longstanding illness. A teenager with TB of the lungs may cough, but a child will not. The disease can be effectively treated with antibiotics that may have to be taken over months or years.

Toxoplasmosis is a rare infection caused by a protozoan, toxoplasma, that normally lives in the intestines of dogs, cats and other animals. It is caught by contact with infected animals or their droppings, or by eating infected, poorly cooked meat. The protozoan is able to pass from the blood of a pregnant woman to her fetus and may affect its development, although this is very rare. Treatment is with drugs.

Toxoplasmosis, along with several other uncommon infections transmitted by animals, can be prevented by good hygiene. Always wash hands, and ensure your child does, before touching food and eating. Wash and dry pet dishes and utensils separately from human ones. Do not let babies and toddlers play with pet food and drink, or crawl around in pets' feeding and toilet areas. Finally, while allowing the occasional pat or lick from the family pet, discourage more intimate contact such as kissing.

Bornholm disease (Epidemic myalgia) is a viral infection that is not uncommon among children. The child becomes unwell and may have severe muscle pain in the chest or abdomen, which is usually sharp and stabbing. The pain may be worse as the child breathes in. He will recover within a few days, although relapses sometimes occur.

Diphtheria is a serious bacterial infection that has been virtually eradicated in the Western world as a result of the routine immunization of all babies against it. Unfortunately, diphtheria is still prevalent in many poorer countries.

A child with diphtheria develops a sore throat, with a greyish film on his tonsils, and perhaps on the surrounding area. In severe cases, this is followed by inflammation of the heart muscles. The illness may last for many weeks, but can usually be treated by diphtheria antitoxin and antibiotics.

Malaria is spread widely throughout Africa, Asia and South America. People are infected when bitten by the female Anopheles mosquito which harbours the malaria parasite – a microscopic single-celled organism.

If your child becomes unwell with a fever, loss of appetite and perhaps vomiting, during or shortly after a trip to a country where the disease is prevalent, you should suspect malaria. Consult a doctor, and if you are back home, tell your doctor where you have been. If treated with anti-malarial drugs, the child will usually recover within a few days. The disease can recur but treatment is effective.

Fortunately, malaria can usually be prevented by taking tablets regularly from a week before a journey to a country where there is malaria. These should be continued until a month after returning home. Even if you spend only a few hours in a country where malaria is a risk, you should still follow this procedure. You should also use insect repellents and wear protective clothing covering the arms and legs when you are in a malaria zone.

Typhoid is a bacterial infection that occurs in many parts of the world where there are poor standards of hygiene. It usually affects older children and young adults, who gradually become more unwell and feverish, often complaining of a severe headache. Some children have diarrhoea but others may be constipated. There may be complications such as intestinal bleeding.

Immunization before travelling gives considerable protection, but care must also be taken to avoid contaminated food and drink.

If treated with antibiotics, most people recover from typhoid within a few weeks.

Cholera is a bacterial infection that is widely distributed throughout the world, affecting most parts of Asia and Africa. A child with cholera has profuse but painless watery diarrhoea and can lose a considerable amount of body fluid over a few hours. With effective replacements of the lost fluids, coupled with antibiotics, almost all those who get cholera recover.

Cholera vaccine before travelling is of limited value, and is no substitute for taking great care to avoid water or food that may be contaminated. The risk of cholera, typhoid and similar infections is small for travellers using the normal tourist facilities.

Poliomyelitis is a viral infection affecting motor nerves to the muscles. It is still common in many countries, although rare in the Western world. Initially, affected children experience symptoms similar to *influenza*, and many suffer no further ill effects. In more severe cases the nerve cells are affected causing pain and then paralysis, which may be permanent.

Immunization, routinely given and starting in infancy, will protect your child from infection.

Polio vaccine is usually given by mouth. If drops are put onto a sugar lump most children will take them happily.

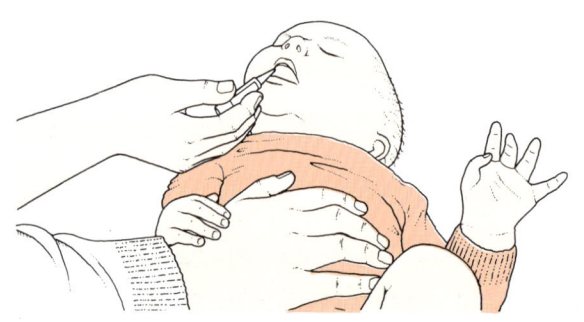

ALLERGY

Allergy means different things to different people. It is often used as a convenient, adaptable label to attach to any minor, unexplained episode of ill-health. However, for a person badly affected by *eczema* or *asthma*, allergy is a frustrating, occasionally disabling and generally distressing condition. For many doctors it poses the problem of perplexing symptoms and difficult diagnoses. The difficulties of diagnosing allergy lie in the variety of forms that it can take, in the many substances that can cause it, and in the effect that mood and stress can have in exacerbating symptoms.

Allergic reactions

Our bodies protect us from dangerous invading substances such as bacteria and viruses by making *antibodies*. In an allergy, antibodies are produced against a harmless substance such as animal hair or pollen. The provoking substance is called the allergen. The antibodies cause some cells in the body, known as mast cells, to release a chemical called histamine, which is responsible for most of the symptoms of the allergy. Why the body reacts in this way to harmless substances is not known.

This process does not happen on first exposure to the allergen. Initially the cells of the immune system recognize and memorize the allergen; this is called sensitization. On subsequent encounters, the immune system is ready to make antibodies against the allergen. When this happens, about 10 days after initial exposure, the person affected is said to be hypersensitive to the substance.

Breastfeeding is thought to lessen the likelihood of a child later developing allergies, or at any rate to reduce the severity of any allergy that does develop; it is not known exactly why this should be so.

Parents are sometimes too ready to suspect allergy, particularly food allergy, as a possible cause of their child's symptoms, but about 1 child in 20 does have a tendency to allergic reactions. The tendency seems to run in families and an affected child often has several allergies, such as asthma, eczema and *hay fever*. Such a child is said to be 'atopic'.

The way in which the allergy shows itself depends on which of the body's systems is affected. This in turn depends to some extent on how the allergen entered the body. It may contact the skin or eyes, or be swallowed, breathed in or injected.

Coping with allergy

Once a definite diagnosis of a specific allergy has been made, the best treatment is to avoid the allergen. This can sometimes be difficult. For instance, if your child needs a cow's-milk-free diet this means avoiding not only milk, butter and cheese, but also many foods containing a little milk, such as biscuits, cakes, gravies and even some breads. Also, children often do not understand why they must be served different foods from their family and friends. School meals present yet more problems, and even if your child does not eat school meals, you should make sure that his school is informed about any allergies. The diet must be taken seriously, and your doctor may help you to obtain the advice of a dietician on how to avoid dietary deficiencies.

ANAPHYLACTIC REACTION

Anaphylaxis is a sudden, severe, allergic reaction that is generalized over the entire body. It is unpredictable and may be due to something as apparently minor as a bee sting. Signs include:

1 Skin flush or rash, such as urticaria
2 Swelling of body tissues, particularly around the face and neck
3 Fast pulse
4 Difficulty in breathing, blueness of lips and skin
5 Collapse

The condition is a medical emergency and a doctor or ambulance should be called at once.

Drug treatment

Antihistamines are the drugs most often prescribed for allergies. They oppose the actions of histamine, the body chemical responsible for many allergic symptoms. Unfortunately they tend to make children rather sleepy and bad-tempered. There are newer antihistamines that cause fewer side-effects and are useful for hay fever, asthma and, to a lesser extent, eczema. Ask your doctor for one of the newer antihistamines if your child has not already tried one. Intal (sodium chromoglycate) and steroid medicines are also effective in blocking allergic reactions.

Desensitization

If a child is found to be allergic to just one substance, desensitization may be worth trying. Very small doses of the substance are injected, usually at weekly intervals, and the dose is gradually increased. It is a fairly hit-and-miss approach but gives some protection to 1 in 3 children treated, although the protection may fade afer several years. Young children usually dislike injections and the treatment is worth considering only if symptoms are severe. The doctor giving the injections will be alert for signs of a hypersensitive reaction.

SKIN TESTS

To confirm that your child has a particular skin allergy, your doctor may advise a skin test. A small drop of solution containing a possible allergen is placed on your child's skin, usually on his forearm. If a baby or young child is being tested the solution may be put on his back. A gentle prick is then made through the drop into the skin. Several potential allergens are usually tried at the same time, spaced out over the skin.

If there is an allergy, a weal appears at the site of the skin prick in about 10 to 15 minutes.
The solution used is weak, so that although it will produce a weal it will not cause any widespread or serious allergic reaction. Once the allergen responsible for the allergy has been identified, it can be used, in solutions of gradually increasing strengths, for a series of injections in the desensitization treatment described above.

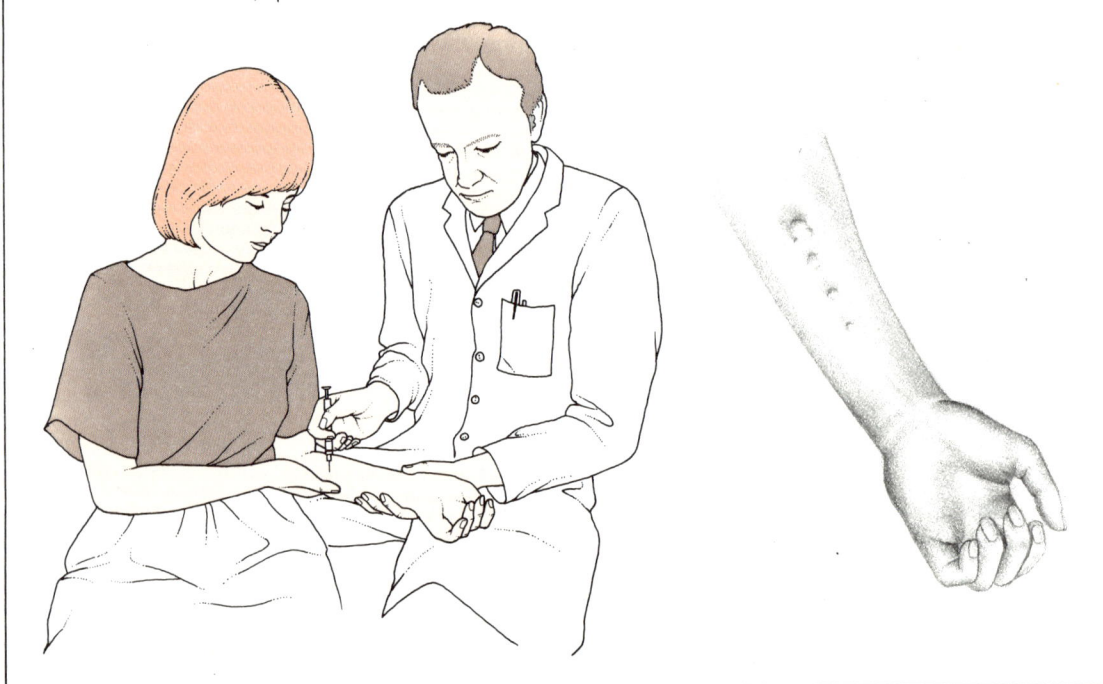

FOOD ALLERGIES

If a child is truly allergic to a food he will probably have both local and generalized reactions. The local reaction may consist of vomiting, colic, diarrhoea or blood in his stools. The generalized reaction can take various forms, including a general feeling of being ill, tiredness, weight loss, headaches or *migraine*, failure to grow properly, and possibly skin rashes such as *urticaria*. Occasionally a child may have a sudden, violent *anaphylactic reaction*.

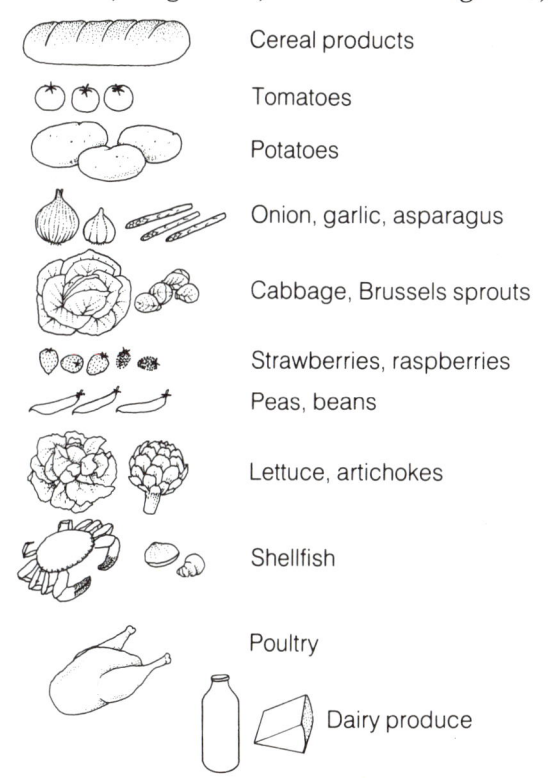

Cow's milk is by far the most common food allergen, especially amongst bottle-fed babies, but there are many others. A child usually reacts to a 'family' of foods: if he is allergic to one food in one of the groups listed opposite, he will usually be allergic to the other foods in the group as well.

The usual way of diagnosing a food allergy is by a combination of an exclusion diet and 'challenge tests'. The child is put on a diet that excludes the foods suspected of causing the allergy, and the suspected foods are then reintroduced one by one. If the food that is the cause of the allergy has been excluded, the symptoms should disappear; and they should return when the food is reintroduced during the challenge tests.

If a diagnosis of allergy to a particular food is made, your child should carefully avoid this food in future. However, children usually grow out of food allergies, so further challenges can be carried out every few years until it is found to be safe for your child to eat the problem food or foods again.

If your child's allergic symptoms are severe, it may be advisable for the challenge tests to be carried out in hospital. Sometimes a *biopsy* of are marked to see whether a particular food causes changes in the gut lining.

- Cereal products
- Tomatoes
- Potatoes
- Onion, garlic, asparagus
- Cabbage, Brussels sprouts
- Strawberries, raspberries
- Peas, beans
- Lettuce, artichokes
- Shellfish
- Poultry
- Dairy produce

SKIN ALLERGIES

The main allergic reactions affecting the skin are *urticaria* and *infantile eczema*. Skin rashes may also occur as a reaction to a drug, either used as a skin medication or taken by mouth. For example, an allergic reaction to the antibiotic amoxycillin may occur 10 days after taking the drug; it shows as a deep purple or red rash that disappears after 4 days.

Skin rashes can result from direct contact with an allergen: wearing clothes washed in certain soaps or detergents or jewellery made from particular metals may cause a rash. There is no clear distinction between irritant substances that affect the skin of anyone who touches them and substances that cause contact *dermatitis* only in sensitive people.

INHALED ALLERGENS

When a child with this type of allergy breathes in tiny particles of allergen, the linings of his nose and lungs become swollen and inflamed, causing coughing, sneezing and wheezing. When a child suffers from *hay fever* the nose lining swells. The allergen in this case is pollen. If the linings of the lungs are involved, the child will have the symptoms of *asthma*. It is often very difficult to tell whether wheezing is caused by infection or allergy, or by both. Probably the most common cause of permanently blocked noses and asthma is an allergic reaction to the house-dust mite, an eight-legged creature about the size of a pinpoint that lives in mattresses, feeding off the particles of skin we shed all the time. Allergy to house mites may be the reason many asthmatic children have attacks more frequently during the night. Bedroom dust can be reduced by using plastic foam mattresses or encasing standard mattresses in plastic covers, and exchanging blankets for continental quilts filled with man-made fibre rather than down.

Seasonal airborne allergens are easier to avoid. Air-conditioning may reduce the effects of airborne pollens in the spring and summer, and, if your child suffers in this way, you may discover that a seaside holiday poses fewer allergy problems than a holiday in the countryside, on a farm, for example.

Inhaled allergens make the susceptible child's eyelids swell and his eyes water.

Common airborne allergens include:

○ Animal fur, feathers, hair or skin flakes, producing symptoms throughout the year
○ House dust and house-dust mites, producing symptoms throughout the year
○ Tree pollens, producing symptoms in early spring
○ Grass pollens, producing symptoms in late spring
○ Mould spores producing symptoms throughout the summer
○ Other moulds producing symptoms during damp weather, in early spring and late autumn

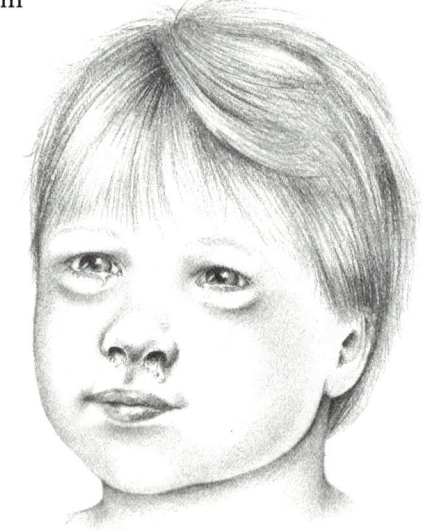

ALLERGY TO CHEMICALS AND DRUGS

Some medicines may cause allergic reactions:

○ Sulphonamides
○ Penicillin and many other antibiotics such as cephalosporins
○ Barbiturates
○ Salicylates
○ Vaccines such as antitetanus serum

If a drug does cause a reaction, this usually occurs more quickly if the drug is injected rather than swallowed.

Bee and wasp stings can also cause allergic reactions. Food additives such as antioxidants, preservatives and artificial colourings and flavourings may cause *asthma* or skin reactions such as *urticaria*.

CANCER

Childhood cancers are quite different from adult cancers. They tend to occur in different parts of the body, they look different under the microscope and they respond differently to treatment. Treatments develop quickly and there has been a much higher rate of cure for childhood cancers than for most adult cancers: 1 in 500 children under 15 years old develops cancer and of those 50 per cent can now be completely cured.

There are many distinct forms of cancer. In general, cancer occurs when cells in the body become out of control and multiply rapidly, producing more and more of that type of cell. The cells' normal functions are disrupted, and as their numbers increase they usually form a mass or a lump called a tumour. At first this lump stays in one part of the body but eventually some of the cancer cells (also called malignant cells) get into the bloodstream or lymph system and spread to other parts of the body, where they continue to multiply and cause damage. When cancer cells spread like this they are said to produce secondary tumours, or metastases, and are more difficult to treat.

The names given to the different kinds of cancer depend on where the original cells come from:

○ Leukemia originates in the bone marrow
○ Neuroblastoma originates in the nervous system
○ Hodgkin's disease and lymphomas originate in the lymph glands
○ Rhabdomyosarcoma originates in muscle tissue
○ Nephroblastoma, or Wilm's tumour, originates in the kidneys.
○ Osteosarcoma and Ewing's tumour originate in the bone

The cause of cancer in children is not known and it is unlikely that any one cause will be found to account for it. What is known is that cancer is not infectious, nor inherited, nor is it likely that the food you eat plays much part in causing it.

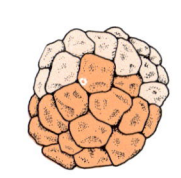

A cancer begins when a group of cells starts to behave abnormally, proliferating to form a growing tumour and invading the surrounding tissues. Eventually some cells may break away and spread to form a secondary tumour elsewhere.

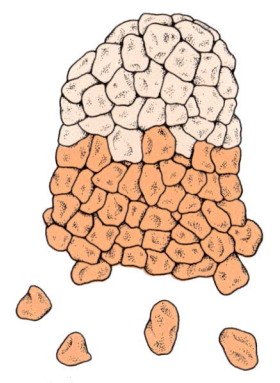

1 Bone tumours
2 Rhabdomyosarcoma
3 Hodgkin's disease
4 Non-Hodgkin's lymphoma
5 Nephroblastoma
6 Neuroblastoma
7 Miscellaneous
8 Brain tumour
9 Leukemia

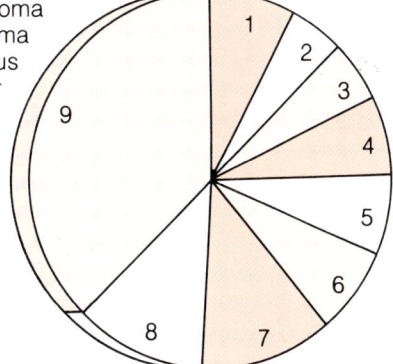

Cancer is rare in childhood, accounting for only about 1 per cent of the total annual number of deaths from cancer. Leukemia forms the highest proportion of childhood cancers.

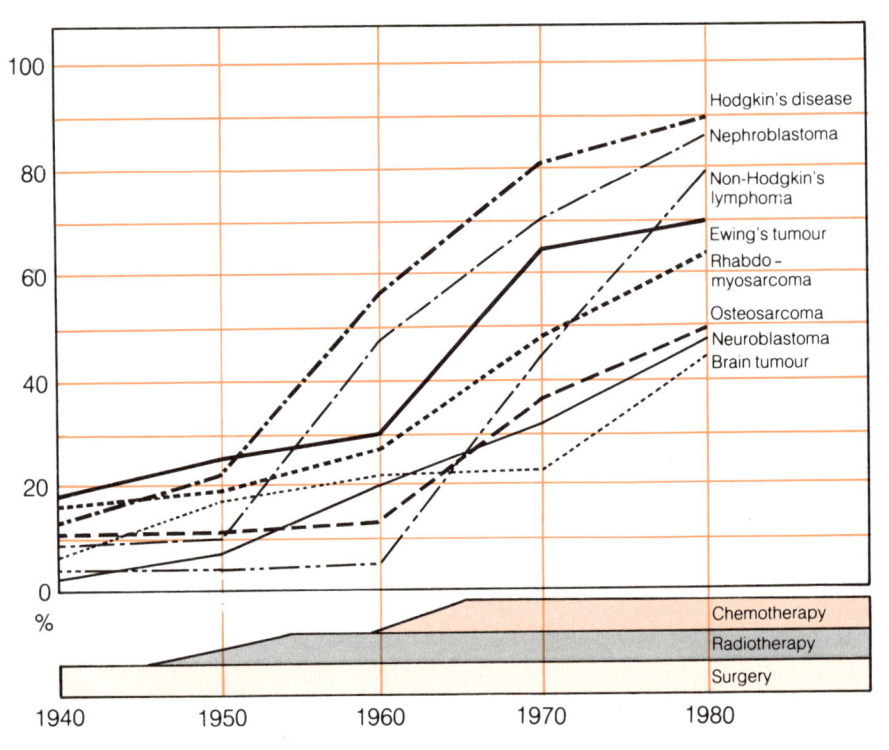

Changes in percentage survival rates with the development of various treatments.

Although the total number of children developing cancer has changed little in the last 40 years, the prospects for many of these children have improved dramatically with advances in the different therapies. The treatment by radiotherapy of leukemia (not shown) was not developed until much later than the treatment by radiotherapy of tumours.

Ewing's tumour and osteosarcoma are bone tumours

Parents' feelings

Great care is taken in making a diagnosis of cancer. Unfortunately it is not always possible to obtain a result immediately. Investigations may take a few days and your child may have to have further tests. If you are not told when the results will be known and exactly how they will be communicated to you, ask the doctor.

As a result of the painful feelings that you experience when first told your child has a cancer, various reactions may follow. You may feel guilty, believing that in some way you may have caused or failed to prevent the cancer. Be assured that there is no basis for these guilt feelings: there is nothing you could have done to prevent your child developing the disease. Family life may become tense and you may begin to quarrel with your partner more than usual. Feelings of anger may be great and directed against God, or the hospital, or the family doctor, or against your partner or your child. Many parents find that getting their feelings into the open and talking about their anger helps.

Some families prefer to cut off their usual social links. Many others would welcome the support of their friends but find that their friends do not know how to react and indeed need support themselves, rather than being able to offer it. Mutual frankness is important and often leads to mutual support.

It is also important to be frank with you child about his disease and treatment. His unexpressed fears and fantasies may be far worse than reality. If you can calmly and confidently exlain the truth and give your child time to express his fears, you will be gving him the best possible support. Remember that until he is at least 5 years old a child's major fear is not disease or pain but separation from his parents.

You will also need to be honest with your other children and to be aware of their feelings.

▶See also Life and Death; Appendices: Drugs and treatments; Support groups and publications

TESTS FOR CANCER

Each type of cancer behaves differently and needs slightly different treatment, but there are some general principles applicable to all forms of the disease.

When cancer is suspected, various tests are needed to make an accurate diagnosis and also to assess how advanced the cancer has become. This is called staging. The stage reached by the disease determines how much treatment is given. Since the treatment itself is quite dangerous, the minimum needed to cure the disease is used.

Blood tests indicate which type of cancer is involved, while physical examination and X-rays usually show where the tumour is. However, to be quite sure that the problem is a cancer, some of the suspect cells have to be examined under a microscope. Cells can be obtained by bone marrow aspiration, lumbar puncture or biopsy.

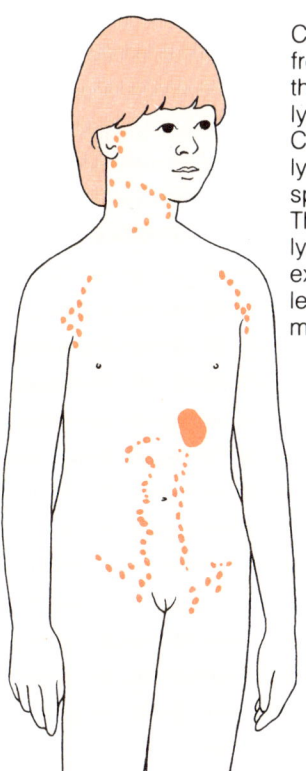

Cancer cells spread from the site of origin, through the blood and lymphatic circulation. Cancer arising near lymph glands may spread more easily. Those areas with a poor lymph supply, for example the brain, are less likely to metastasize.

BONE MARROW ASPIRATION
In this test, sometimes called marrow biopsy, a special needle is inserted through the skin and underlying tissue into the middle of a bone, and a small sample of marrow is sucked out. In young children the bone used is generally the shin bone; in older children the hip bone or one of the vertebrae in the lower back is used. Your child will probably be given a general anaesthetic or a heavy sedative. Sometimes the test can be done using local anaesthetic, but if this is used, the child may feel some discomfort as the needle is inserted and the marrow withdrawn. Often a *blood transfusion* is given at the same time as the bone morrow aspiration as this helps stop bleeding and generally makes the child feel better.

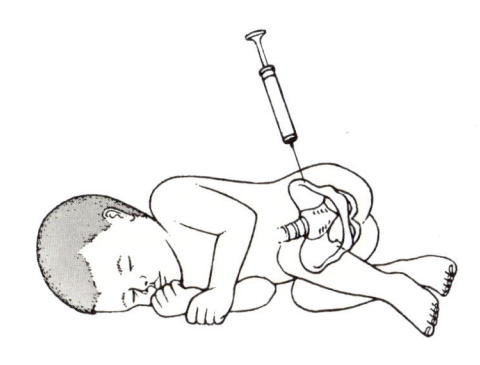

LUMBAR PUNCTURE
A sample of the fluid that surrounds the spinal cord can be removed for analysis by means of a *lumbar puncture*. In some cancers this procedure is also used to inject drugs into the fluid, as part of treatment.

BIOPSY
Many cancers affect the lymph glands, particularly those in the neck. If these glands are swollen and hard, but not painful, then they may be biopsied. A small sample of tissue is removed and examined under a microscope. Sometimes the lump suspected of being cancerous is itself biopsied or removed for examination.

TREATMENTS FOR CANCER

Once the diagnosis is certain, the paediatrician will discuss with you the treatment of the disease and its implications for the future. He may advise that your child should be admitted to a centre that specializes in the treatment of children's cancers. These centres are in constant touch with each other, so that any new treatment becoming available in one centre is swiftly communicated to the others. If you are in doubt about whether your child is having the most effective and up-to-date treatment, discuss the matter with the paediatrician or ask your family doctor to enquire on your behalf.

There are three main types of treatment: surgery, radiotherapy (X-ray therapy) and chemotherapy (treatment with drugs). These are sometimes used together and the exact combination of treatments depends on the type of cancer, the stage it has reached and the child's overall condition.

SURGERY
This is often the first line of treatment. It aims to remove as many cancer cells as possible. Although the tumour itself can be removed, some cancer cells may have spread in the bloodstream, so surgery alone is rarely adequate and is usually followed by radiotherapy or chemotherapy, or both.

CHEMOTHERAPY
Certain drugs, called cytotoxic agents, kill off cancer cells throughout the body. They are powerful and their side-effects need careful checking. Some can be given by mouth, others have to be injected – usually into a vein. It is essential that these drugs are given exactly as prescribed: if you find the dosages or instructions confusing or ambiguous, be certain to ask your doctor or pharmacist for clarification.

RADIOTHERAPY
Cancer cells, like other cells, can be destroyed by radiation. In radiotherapy, X-rays are focused on the tumour. Only cells in the treatment area are affected, so chemotherapy is usually needed as well to deal with cells that have spread to other parts of the body.

The radiotherapy machine is large and may be frightening for a child at first. Because of the danger of radiation, you will not be allowed in the radiotherapy room while your child is being treated, although it is often possible to talk through an intercommunication system. Radiotherapy is usually given daily for only a few minutes and courses may last between 2 to 6 weeks. Your child must stay perfectly still during exposure. Radiotherapy is completely painless but it does have side-effects.

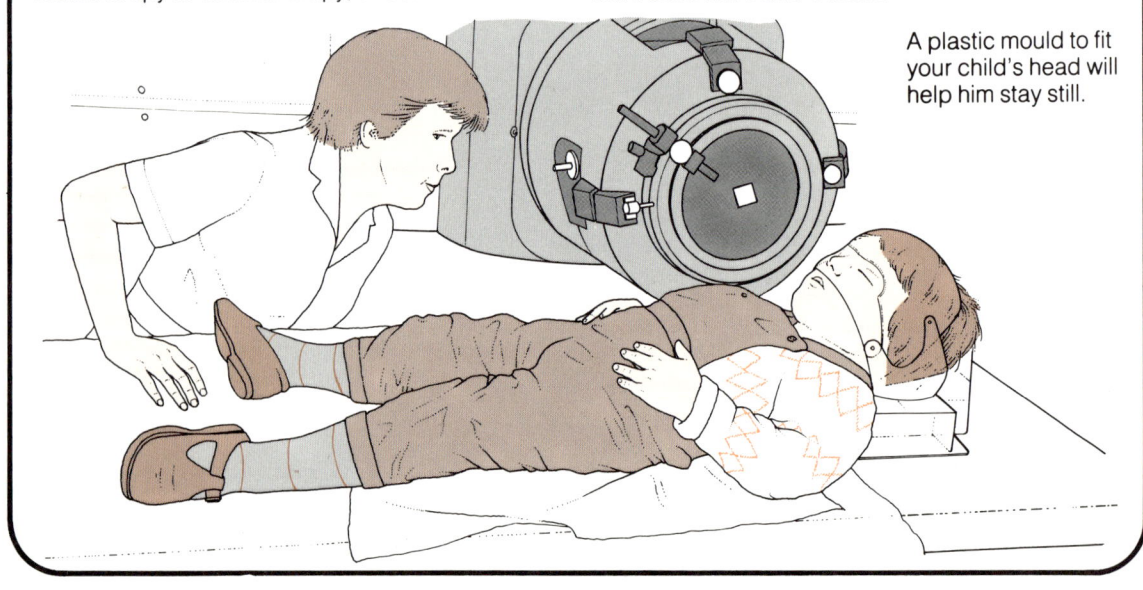

A plastic mould to fit your child's head will help him stay still.

CANCER

SIDE-EFFECTS OF TREATMENT

Cancer treatments do have several side-effects although the aim is always to give treatments in a way that maximizes their efficacy while minimizing any adverse reactions.

IMMUNO-SUPPRESSION
Both radiotherapy and chemotherapeutic drugs tend temporarily to dampen down or disable the body's normal defence system. This immuno-suppression means that the child's body cannot react effectively against infections, such as *measles* and *chickenpox*, which are not normally serious. It is, however, possible to give a child good protection against such infections with an injection of ready-made antibodies called gammaglobulins. This has to be given as soon as possible after the child has been exposed to an infection.

NAUSEA
Some drugs may cause nausea or vomiting. Radiotherapy given to the abdomen may also cause nausea. Drugs can be given before treatment which will help to prevent nausea and in most cases the nausea and vomiting pass of quite quickly.

BONE MARROW SUPPRESSION
Most chemotherapeutic drugs affect the bone marrow, which is responsible for making blood cells. As a result a child may suffer a lack of red blood cells which will cause *anaemia* and will require a *blood transfusion*. He may also suffer a lack of white blood cells which will further increase his risk of infection. A lack of *platelets* will lead to excessive bruising or bleeding and will require a platelet transfusion.

GROWTH AND FERTILITY
The production of hormones, for instance growth hormone, may be impaired by treatment. These can be replaced either by injections or tablets. If radiotherapy has been given to the testes or ovaries then the child's future fertility is likely to be affected. However, many children who completed courses of treatment have subsequently been able to have their own, and quite normal children.

LEUKEMIA

This is the most common cancer in children, but more than 50 per cent of children affected are permanently cured. The disease prevents normal maturation of cells in the bone marrow so that the marrow fills up with useless cells. In acute lymphoblastic leukaemia (ALL) the cells that do not mature properly are *lymphocytes*; in acute myeloblastic leukaemia (AML) they are *neutrophils*. Children suffer more often from ALL than AML.

SYMPTOMS

The useless cells in the bone marrow are continually trying to increase in number and this leads to pain in the bones. The leukemic cells crowd out normal bone marrow cells with the result that insufficient red blood cells are made; this causes *anaemia* and tiredness. Similarly, not enough platelets are made. This leads to excessive bruising or bleeding, often first noticed as small dots under the skin. Thirdly, not enough normal white blood cells are made, so infections cannot be dealt with in the usual way. Sometimes the symptoms come on over a few days; at other times they take many weeks.

DIAGNOSIS

Once leukemia is suspected your doctor will take a blood sample which may reveal that leukemic cells are spilling from the bone marrow into the blood; it will also show how anaemic your child is and how low the platelet count is. To confirm the diagnosis a *bone marrow aspiration* is carried out under local or general anaesthetic.

PROBLEMS, DISEASES AND DISORDERS

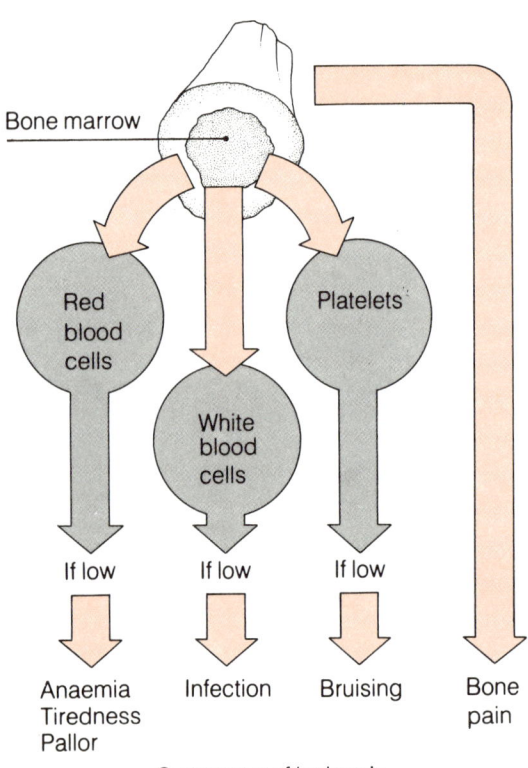

Symptoms of leukemia

- Bone marrow → Red blood cells → If low → Anaemia, Tiredness, Pallor
- Bone marrow → White blood cells → If low → Infection
- Bone marrow → Platelets → If low → Bruising
- Bone marrow → If low → Bone pain

The proliferating leukemic cells crowd out normal bone marrow cells so that the production of all types of blood cell is decreased and the symptoms typical of leukemia result.

TREATMENT

A *blood transfusion* treats the immediate problem of low level of red blood cells. The anti-cancer treatment consists of several drugs given according to a careful plan over 2 to 3 years. Within a few weeks of starting treatment your child may be virtually back to normal, and should be able to attend school and take part in all activities. This is a 'remission' and it shows that treatment is working; but there is a long way to go. If treatment is stopped your child will have a relapse and will be ill again within a month or two. Therefore drugs must be continued.

The anti-leukemia drugs given into a vein or taken by mouth do not penetrate the brain. To protect the brain from leukemia, radiotherapy is given to this area and a drug (called *methotrexate*) is administered via a *lumbar puncture* into the spinal fluid. The drugs may not reach cells in the testes, either, so the testes are usually biopsied to make sure there are no leukemic cells there.

Treatment can be painful and there are side effects, some of which are similar to the effects of leukemia itself. The bone marrow may be affected by the drugs so that red cells, white cells and platelets are not produced in adequate numbers. It is possible to give all three as a transfusion: red cells and platelets can come from a blood bank, but white cells must come from either the mother or the father. White cells are given only when the child seems unable to shake off an infection.

Both leukemia and its treatment deplete the child's white blood cells so that risk of infection is a particular problem throughout treatment. Antibiotics may be needed, and these are often given by means of an intravenous drip. However, it is neither possible nor wise to try to protect your child from all infections. If you think that your child may have been exposed to an infection, contact your family doctor or paediatrician immediately.

After treatment by drugs and radiotherapy to destroy all leukemic cells in the body, healthy bone marrow from a donor may be transplanted to your child's bones. It is essential that the bone marrow used for transplantation is compatible with the child's own marrow. Transplants are usually most successful if marrow from a brother or sister can be used, although only 1 in 4 siblings will have compatible marrow. Bone marrow banks are beginning to be built up and may be available for your child.

When treatment is finished, visits to the clinic will continue for some years, and your child's blood will be checked regularly. One year following the end of treatment your child can safely have 'live' vaccines or be exposed to *measles*, *chickenpox* and similar infections without special protection.

▶ See also The blood

HODGKIN'S DISEASE

Just as cells of the bone marrow can multiply uncontrollably to cause leukemia, so cells of the lymph gland can multiply to cause Hodgkin's disease. It can occur at any age, but develops most commonly in young adults aged between 15 and 30 years. Lymph glands may swell in the neck, under the arms, in the groin and in the chest. A child with Hodgkin's disease may also lose weight, have a fever, and sweat – especially at night.

To diagnose this disease a lymph gland is surgically removed and examined under the microscope. The stage that the disease has reached is then assessed by means of X-rays and blood tests.

Treatment is by chemotherapy and by radiotherapy, which is painless but, depending on the dose, may cause nausea and vomiting. Treatment may continue for 6 to 12 months. The outlook for most children is good.

NON-HODGKIN'S LYMPHOMA

Although this cancer, like Hodgkin's disease, has its origin in the lymph gland cells, its effects are rather different. There may be gland enlargement in the chest, neck or abdomen. To diagnose this disease various tests are carried out. These include *biopsy* of an enlarged lymph gland, X-rays, blood tests and *bone marrow aspiration*. Treatment consists of chemotherapy and of radiotherapy to the enlarged glands and to the head, to prevent the brain being affected by the cancer. More and more children are now surviving non-Hodgkin's lymphoma in good health for several years.

NEUROBLASTOMA

This is a tumour of the sympathetic nervous system, a part of the nervous system in the chest or abdomen. It usually affects children under 5 years of age. It occurs most commonly in the adrenal glands, which are situated just above the kidneys. This is a very rare form of childhood cancer.

SYMPTOMS

This tumour nearly always shows up as a lump, either in the chest or abdomen or in a site to which cancerous cells have spread. The symptoms depend on where the tumour is. A lump may be felt in the neck or abdomen when a child is being bathed or dressed. There may be lumps in the skin, or a lump may cause a protruding eye, or pains in the bones. Alternatively, the child may just be irritable and unwell.

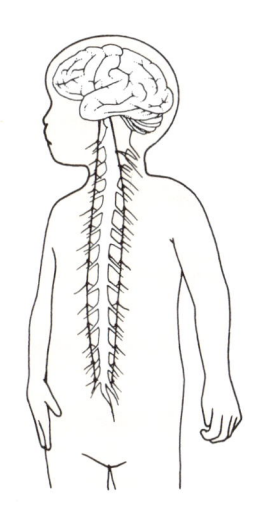

Neuroblastomas can arise anywhere within the sympathetic nervous system.

DIAGNOSIS

Before an operation is done certain tests are usually carried out so that the surgeon knows what to look for. Neuroblastomas produce substances called catecholamines which, when broken down by the body can be measured in the urine as vanillyl mandelic acid (VMA). A very high level of VMA in the urine indicates that the tumour is a neuroblastoma. If the tumour is in the adrenal glands, an X-ray of the kidneys will reveal its extent. A bone marrow aspiration will also be carried out to check whether the tumour has spread to the child's bone marrow.

TREATMENT

An operation is arranged to remove as much of the tumour as possible. After the operation, radiotherapy is given to the affected area to kill off any remaining cancer cells. This is followed by chemotherapy usually for 1 to 2 years. Whether the child recovers depends on the stage that the tumour has reached when treatment is started. Generally the outlook is poor – except for some very young children, usually under 1 year of age, who, even with widespread neuroblastoma and little treatment, appear to recover fully and spontaneously.

NEPHROBLASTOMA

This is a tumour of the kidney, also known as Wilm's tumour. It most commonly affects children aged between 1 and 5 years, and the majority can be cured. A child with this tumour may not be very ill, but the tumour can be felt as a lump in the abdomen. Sometimes the first sign is blood in the urine.

An *intravenous pyelogram* (IVP) will check that the lump in the abdomen is sited in the kidney. Surgery is the immediate treatment, except occasionally when the tumour is very large and has to be shrunk with drugs before it can be removed. The area where the tumour was sited then receives radiotherapy, and chemotherapy is given for between 6 months and 2 years.

The outlook depends partly on how far the tumour has progressed when diagnosed, and partly on the tumour cells themselves: the more like normal kidney cells they are, the more favourable the outlook.

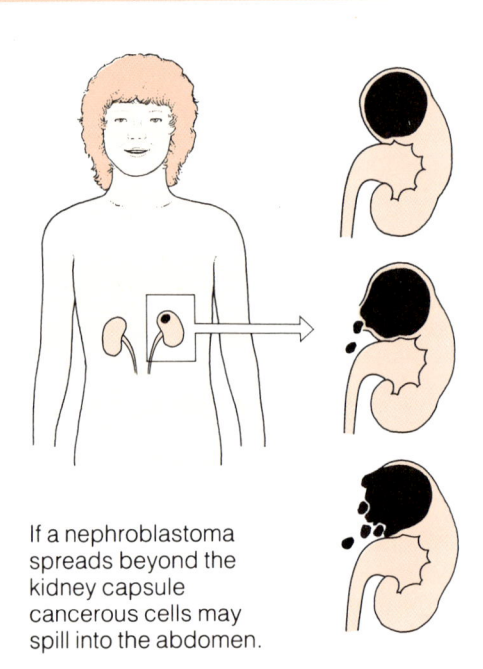

If a nephroblastoma spreads beyond the kidney capsule cancerous cells may spill into the abdomen.

RHABDOMYOSARCOMA

Rhabdomyosarcoma can occur at any age but it usually develops in children between 1 and 5 years old. It is a tumour of a certain type of muscle only. It most commonly occurs in the head and neck, particularly around the sinuses; the eye, where it may cause the eye to protrude; the muscles of the arms and legs; and the muscles of the bladder or vagina, where it can cause difficulty in passing urine or just form a lump.

After the initial tumour forms, its cells may spread to other parts of the child's body, such as lungs, liver, brain or bones.

The only way a diagnosis can be made with certainty is to examine a piece of tumour removed during an operation. Depending upon where the tumour is, various tests determine its extent and whether it has spread.

Treatment consists of surgery, where possible, plus radiotherapy to the tumour area. Drugs are also used and continued for up to 2 years. About 50 per cent of children with a rhabdomyosarcoma are alive and well 5 years after the condition is diagnosed. Some tumours, such as those in the eye, respond better to treatment than others.

BONE TUMOURS

Most lumps found in bones are not cancerous. They may be removed by surgery or they may be left untreated. There are two cancerous tumours that originate in bone; these are called Ewing's tumour and osteosarcoma.

Ewing's tumour usually causes swelling, vague pain and stiffness in the area where the tumour is – commonly in the thigh bone, pelvis, shoulder blade or shin bone. Children aged between 5 and 15 years are most often affected and many recover. The lump in the bone is biopsied to confirm the diagnosis, and further assessment consists of X-rays and blood tests. Treatment combines radiotherapy to the tumour site with chemotherapy using various drugs.

Osteosarcoma occurs most commonly around the knee and upper arm, and also requires biopsy and X-rays for diagnosis. Amputation may be necessary, or the bone with its tumour may be removed and an artificial bone inserted to preserve the limb. Powerful chemotherapy is also given.Treatment is developing rapidly and an increasing number of children are surviving the disease. The side-effects of treatment are still, unfortunately, unpleasant.

BRAIN TUMOUR

Tumours in the brain are amongst the most common that occur in children. Some are malignant and others are not. The latter are called benign tumours. It is where the tumour grows that is more important, as certain areas of the brain are vital for breathing or keeping the heart going. The most common malignant brain tumour is a medulloblastoma; this occurs at the back of the brain. There are, however, numerous other different types of tumour depending upon which type of cell has become malignant or has multiplied. Only 1 child in 5 with a malignant tumour recovers fully; others recover but with some permanent disability.

SYMPTOMS

Your child may vomit and have headaches and he may be unsteady when he walks if the tumour is in the back of his head. Headaches tend to be worse in the mornings and he may vomit without feeling very sick beforehand. One side of his body may become weak, and he may develop a squint quite suddenly or other visual problems. There may be changes in the child's mood and sometimes concentration falls off and his schoolwork may suffer.

TREATMENT

The most important treatment is by surgery and for many benign tumours this is successful. For malignant tumours it is also necessary to give radiotherapy. Chemotherapy is also used increasingly for certain tumours.

If your doctor suspects that your child has a brain tumour he will examine him carefully and take a *CAT scan*. This will reveal whether there is any abnormality in the brain, and if there is, its exact location.

CAT SCAN

CAT (computerized axial tumography) scan is a method of taking special X-ray pictures of soft body tissues, for example the brain. Pictures are taken of the area to be scanned from different angles by a camera in a rotating drum. A computer integrates these to give a detailed picture which can detect abnormalities such as tumours. Scanning is painless but a general anaesthetic may be given so that the child lies still during the procedure.

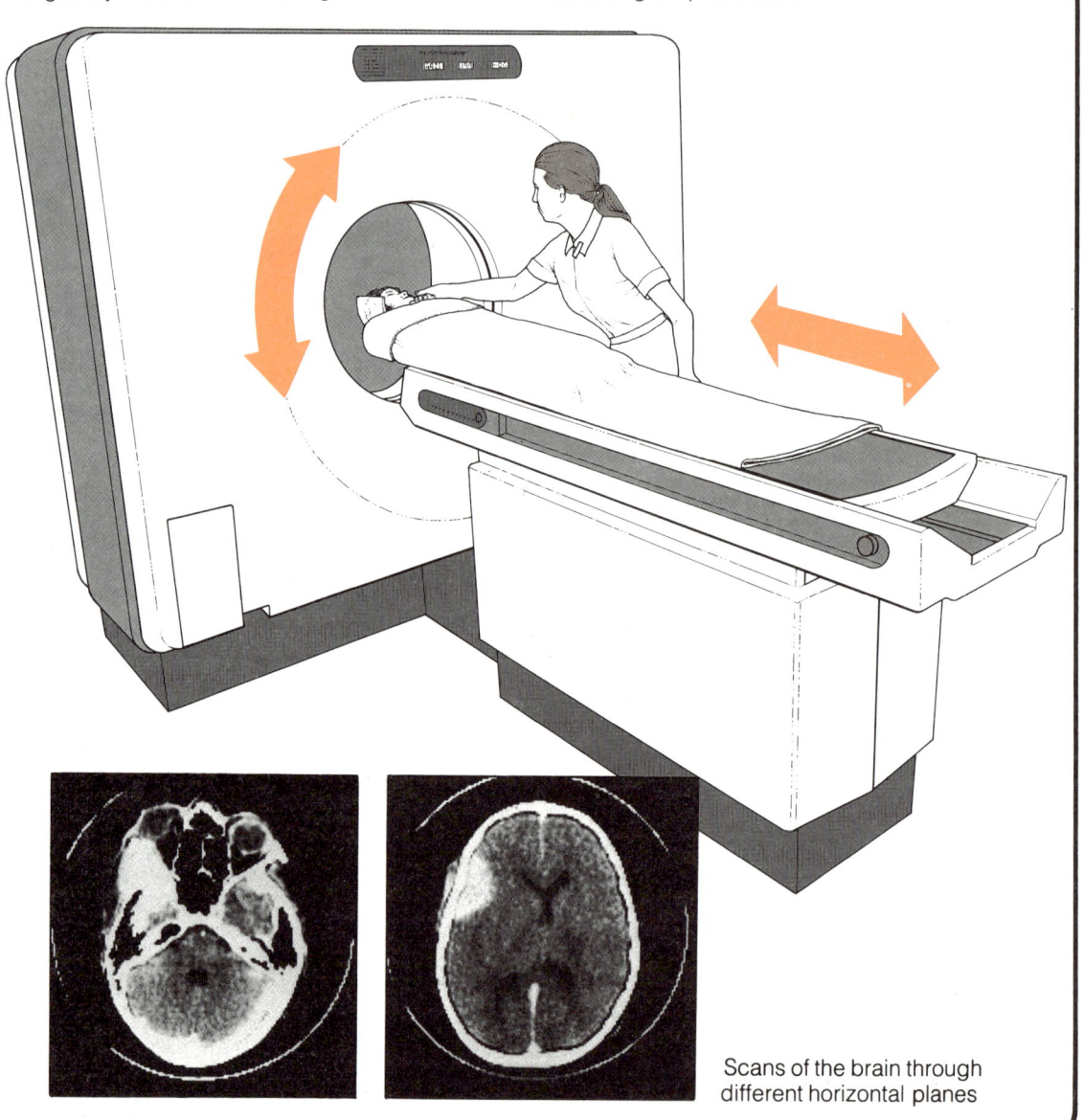

Scans of the brain through different horizontal planes

BEHAVIOUR AND DEVELOPMENT

Problems of behaviour usually arise for a combination of reasons. Some babies and children simply have more difficult temperaments than others – they may be harder to comfort, more irregular in their habits or more easily upset by changes. It may be especially hard for parents to feel confident with premature babies, or those with developmental problems. Many childhood problems run in families. Common examples include *bedwetting*, *phobias* and *psychosomatic symptoms* such as headaches or stomach-aches.

Different stages in a child's development bring with them different demands and problems. For instance, as children gain increasing independence at around 18 months or 2 years, they experiment with their ability to control their environment and their parents. Your child may behave badly simply to get your attention. If you are aware of his changing demands you can take steps to solve or avoid problems; when he craves your attention make sure that you have time to play with him every day and that you give him plenty of approval. All children need to feel secure in their parents' love and interest.

A child may appear to be 'naughty' because he is not yet able to understand the reasoning behind the various restrictions necessary for his safety – and for your peace of mind. When your child is very young, you will have to prevent him from doing many dangerous or undesirable things, while at the same time saying 'no' firmly. Gradually, as his language develops you can begin to give him simple explanations about the rules you have made and to negotiate with him. It is best to have as few rules as possible and to stick to them, so that you do not find yourself nagging all day about things that do not really matter, but have the energy to be firm about things that are important, such as wearing a seat belt in the car or not touching hot pans.

As your child grows older he will become increasingly responsive to any family tensions or problems that make you feel anxious or depressed. Very few families manage to avoid periods of emotional tension or practical difficulties about housing, finances or ill-health. If you explain the situation simply to your child and reassure him that you are trying to solve any problems, it will help him.

Problems can also be caused if parents tend to avoid dealing directly with their own differences by concentrating instead on their children. Either they involve their children by asking them in one way or another to take sides, or they may turn their attention away from each other and towards their children. Children can quickly learn to seek attention whenever they recognize tension between their parents.

Behavioural problems are usually an expression of distress. Your task is to try to understand what is causing the distress. Only when the source of a problem has been recognized and discussed can solutions be sought. However, if your child is in obvious distress or his problems persist despite your efforts to overcome them, you should seek advice from your doctor. He may be able to suggest further self-help, or he may suggest that you visit a specialist, such as a child psychiatrist or psychologist. Occasionally he may prescribe medicines, but these have limited uses.

COMFORT HABITS
Most children have a habit of some sort that their parents feel they should have outgrown. For example, 1 in 10 children still sucks his thumb by the age of 10 years. Most habits are fairly harmless and are best ignored, but one or two persistent childhood habits may need treatment.

Pre-school children

Most children have behavioural or emotional problems at some time. Understanding the needs of a baby or toddler takes time, and both children and parents have to be continually learning how to respond to each other's needs, adapting and adjusting as they change. As children grow up, they have to adjust to new situations and new demands on them, such as going to nursery school for the first time, facing the birth of a sibling or going into hospital.

From very early in life children may react by becoming angry and obstinate, by crying a great deal or by being very clingy. Intense reactions can be worrying, especially if it is your first child and you have no basis for comparison. Even if you have, remember that all children react differently.

You may feel upset or angry with your child and worry about the strength of your own feelings. You may feel that you are not coping well with the situation or that you are making it worse. Talking to other parents can help you to realize that your reactions, and those of your child, are normal, and that emotional or behavioural problems are common and generally resolve themselves in a short time.

It can be difficult to differentiate between the normal difficulties associated with growing up and problems for which you need professional help. In general, if you feel that you need help, you should ask for it. Talk to your doctor if:

○ your child is doing something that you think he should have grown out of some time ago
○ his problems last longer or seem more extreme than those of other children
○ the problem is such that it causes particular stress in the family, such as, for example, a toddler's sleeplessness
○ your child has a wide range of problems at the same time, such as tantrums, disobedience, soiling and unhappiness

SLEEPING PROBLEMS

The most common sleep problem is waking at night: 1 in 5 children still wakes regularly at the age of 1 year. Other difficulties may be about going to bed and settling to sleep in the evening; or children may want to come into their parents' bed during the night.

Most children have nightmares from time to time, and these are most frequent between the ages of 3 and 4 years, but nightmares are not a common cause of waking problems.

Sleeping difficulties are sometimes related to anxiety and a child's need for reassurance. They may also be related to the child's need to assert independence or the lack of a night-time routine for him.

If your child does cry after you have settled him, or wakes crying during the night, try not to pick him up but instead stroke him and talk calmly for a while.

Children vary in their sleeping patterns and in how easily they settle. Parents also vary in what they need and want. Coping with disturbed nights is one of the hardest jobs for parents and you may decide that you are happy, for example, to have a young child sleeping in your bed. If, however, you want to make changes in your child's sleeping habits, you may need to try various strategies and be patient while awaiting results.

Develop a consistent routine for settling your child at bedtime, and a regular time for going to bed.

Try encouraging your baby to go into his cot while still awake so that he gets used to falling asleep there. It is easy for babies to become accustomed to falling asleep on the breast or bottle or being rocked in your arms, but this makes them very dependent on you and may present problems when you want to wean them or to go out in the evening. Soothing routines such as patting, rocking the cot, crooning, or playing a musical box can be used instead. If you reduce little by little the amount of attention you give, your child will gradually get used to falling asleep without having to have you close by.

Rewards can be helpful for encouraging children to stay in their rooms during the evening or at night. You can also set up a chart onto which you put a star for every night that passes without intervention. The important part of a reward is the praise that goes with it and you may soon be able to rely on praise and appreciation alone.

▶ **See also** Day-to-day care

FEEDING PROBLEMS

Feeding problems are very common when children are young. These include reluctance or refusal to eat, being very finicky or difficult at meal-times, and eating between meals but never at meals. There are a few simple measures that may help to prevent or solve problems:

○ Establish a pleasant meal-time routine for your child early on
○ If your child is not eating well, try not to show that it worries you. Otherwise he may continue to refuse food purely in order to gain your attention
○ When you are introducing new foods into your child's diet, start with a very small amount given just before or with the food he is used to
○ It is never a good idea to force a child to eat: a battle is likely to make his refusal even more determined

Often what parents see as a feeding problem is not a problem at all. Appetites vary from child to child and from time to time, and some children just have naturally small appetites.

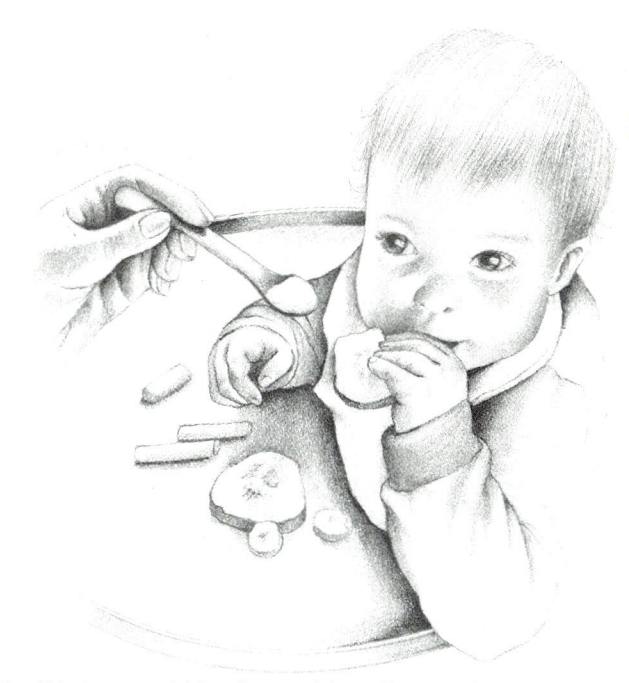

It will help to avoid feeding problems if you make meal-times relaxed, giving your child foods he likes and encouraging him to finger-feed.

A child's rate of growth naturally slows down in the second year of life and the child eats correspondingly less. If your child is putting on weight and growing normally and has a diet containing the basic nutrients, you need not worry about his eating habits.

Your own attitude to food may have a strong influence on your child – if your child sees that you do not eat or seem not to enjoy your food, he may copy you. He may also copy what you eat; so if you want your child to avoid sugary foods, for example, make sure that you are not eating them yourself.

Emotional factors play a large part in a child's attitude towards food; stressful atmospheres at meal-times, and his parents' anxieties about what and when he eats, can help to create eating problems. An older child may use food as a psychological weapon to assert his independence or 'punish' his parents; he may also turn to food for comfort. Obsessive dieting, or *anorexia nervosa* may occur in adolescence.

▶**See also** Feeding and diet

TANTRUMS AND BREATH-HOLDING

Most children have occasional temper tantrums, usually when they are 2 or 3 years old and at the age when they are beginning to try to exert control over their environment and assert some independence. A few toddlers also develop a habit, when in a temper, of holding their breath for so long that they may turn blue. This is alarming for an onlooker, but it is not dangerous.

You need sensitive judgment to deal with a tantrum successfully, since each tantrum is different and varies in intensity from another. Knowing your own child and what has triggered the tantrum means you should be able to tell whether the cause is essentially trivial, or the tantrum is in response to something deeper and far harder for the child to come to terms with. If the tantrum was provoked by your refusal to let him have his way, giving in may encourage him to have tantrums in future similar situations.

Sometimes you may be able to defuse a situation and distract your child through humour; or it may be enough to take the child away from the situation into another room until he has quietened down. However, if your child is deeply upset you should aim to hold him calmly during the tantrum, and reassure him with quiet and soothing talk. It can be terrifying for a small child to be in the grip of powerful emotions that he cannot yet control, and he needs your love and support.

When your child has a tantrum stay with him until he becomes calmer. Try to remain calm yourself; losing your temper will only make the situation more explosive and may prolong the tantrum.

HYPERACTIVITY

The energy of young children is amazing, and many parents are inclined to call their children hyperactive. However, true hyperactivity is rare, and only about 1 child in every 1,000 can be described as hyperactive. It is more common among boys than girls and is often associated with brain damage or developmental delay.

Sometimes a child's so-called hyperactivity may simply be his reaction to a family situation in which limits and rules have not been laid down. If you think your child is over-active, it may be worth considering this. You should also make sure that you are giving him enough attention, as his behaviour may simply be a plea for more of your time. Make sure, in addition, that he is getting enough exercise and time to run wild in open space.

If you think your child is more easily distracted than most children of the same age and may be hyperactive, try helping him to concentrate and slow down. For example, you could set a kitchen timer while he draws or plays a game to mark out a reasonable spell of sticking to one activity.

You may wonder if some particular food affects your child's behaviour. Current evidence about diet is conflicting, but many people including some doctors are convinced that cutting out certain foods and food additives is helpful. If you do decide to experiment with diet, get advice from your doctor, a dietician or a support group to ensure that it remains well balanced and that you are not excluding essential foods.

AUTISM

A child with autism is unable to communicate with his family or the rest of the world, although he may have average intelligence. He does not recognize his parents or other familiar people and does not communicate with words, gestures or facial expression. He may be silent, still and withdrawn or he may adopt strange postures or mutter unintelligibly; he may also on occasion be unpredictably violent. He will have difficulty with feeding and toilet-training.

Autism may be present from birth or it may develop in the first few years of a child's life. It affects about 1 in 3,000 children, and 5 times more boys than girls are autistic.

If autism is diagnosed, you will need specialist advice on caring for your child. You will probably be advised to involve yourself as much as possible with the child's activities so that he is forced to interact with you. Many doctors believe physical contact, holding and touching the child, will help him to become more responsive. The more attention, love and stimulation you can give him, the better his progress is likely to be. Some children recover from autism and are able to lead normal lives; others need special care for the rest of their lives.

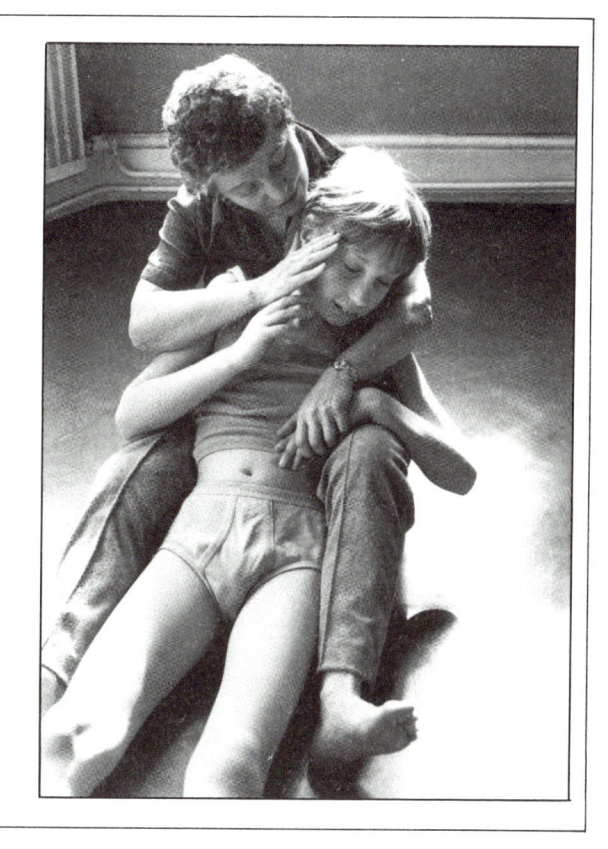

School-age children

Many of the normal problems that affect school-children, such as occasional bedwetting, fears and anxieties, defiance or sulks, are worrying if they become more intense, severe or persistent.

Persistent problems are usually the result of a combination of factors, including the child's temperament, difficulties in the family or at school, and ill health. Persistent misbehaviour is very often the result of educational problems, particularly *learning difficulties*.

Children from families whose members never argue may also have problems. If they do not learn to cope with arguments and how to settle differences within their families, they may have difficulty coping when such situations arise in the outside world, as they inevitably will.

FEARS AND ANXIETIES

It is very common for children to find some situations worrying or frightening. As children pass through different stages of development, they become frightened by different things, but gradually they learn to become less fearful.

Sometimes children are influenced by the fears of their parents. For example, the child who sees that an adult is frightened by a spider learns that spiders are something to be frightened of. Sometimes a bad experience with, for example, a dog makes a child fearful of all dogs. You can help by being sympathetic to your child's worries, while gently encouraging him, first just to look at, then gradually to approach the feared object in slow stages.

A child who is generally anxious or fearful about many different aspects of life, or who is still very clingy by the age of 4 or 5 years can be handicapped because he shies away from new situations and challenges. If your child seems more anxious than other children, you can help by listening to him talk about his worries while encouraging him gently to tackle new situations in stages. Sometimes a child's anxiety may be caused by his sensitivity to stresses in the family. If you are feeling particularly anxious or unhappy, you may unconsciously communicate this to your child.

Your child may be anxious about virtually anything, and some children are anxious about everything. If your child is so intensely anxious that it is affecting his concentration and sleep and generally hampering his ability to lead a normal life, then you should consult your doctor. Behaviour therapy or psychotherapy may be recommended and tranquillizers are occasionally prescribed for very anxious children. Many can also be helped by relaxation techniques.

SEPARATION ANXIETY

At some stage most children become anxious about being separated from their parents. Until they are 3 years old most children tend to be upset if they are not with very familiar people. Your child may cling particularly if he has had a period of enforced separation, such as going into hospital when you were unable to be with him all the time.

Families can be too close, and it is best to encourage your child to have a certain amount of separateness in order to learn to become an individual in his own right. Parents who are anxious about letting a child grow and experiment often find that he is anxious about separating and going to school.

A child who panics when separated from someone to whom he is close, usually his mother, but sometimes also a child or teacher to whom he has become close, may refuse to go to school. *School refusal* often occurs at points of major change for a child – the loss of familiar figures, starting school and changing schools.

PHOBIAS

The difference between having an anxious temperament and having a phobia is in part a matter of degree. Phobias are intense forms of anxiety that have a particular focus. Fears of animals and insects, which are most common among pre-school children, seldom arise after the age of 5 years. In school-age children, the most common fears are of specific situations such as being in the dark, going to the doctor or the dentist, having an injection or travelling in lifts. Children under 10 years old usually develop and lose phobias rapidly without the need for treatment.

RELAXATION TECHNIQUES

It is impossible to be both anxious and relaxed at the same time. So, if children can learn self-relaxation, physical symptoms of tension such as headaches or stomach-aches can be considerably reduced. The technique involves tensing up muscles and then deliberately relaxing them. Often the process must be repeated 2 or 3 times before the body is completely relaxed.

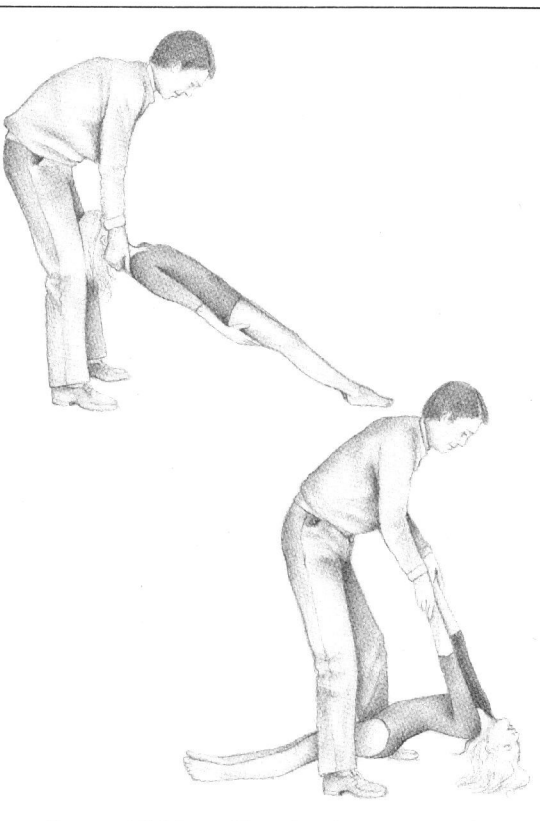

If your child first stiffens her body so that she can be supported (firmly) merely beneath her neck, she will have tensed all her muscles. If she then lets herself go loose and floppy this will demonstrate the difference between relaxation and tension.

From a position stretching as tall and straight as possible, tell your child to melt like an ice-cream, so that she gradually lets her muscles relax. Her body should flop towards the ground until she is a limp heap on the floor.

PSYCHOSOMATIC SYMPTOMS

The term 'psychosomatic' means mind affecting body. The mind affects the body, and vice versa, all the time. For example when children are upset, they cry, and when they are frightened, their hearts beat faster or they need to go to the toilet more often.

Virtually any physical symptom can be brought on by worry or upset, and psychosomatic problems represent the most common of all childhood disorders. For example, 1 in every 10 children suffers from aches for which there appears to be no physical cause. Stomach-aches and headaches are quite common when children experience separation anxieties, and can be symptoms of *school refusal*.

It may be hard for you to accept that your child's physical symptoms are stress-induced, and many parents fruitlessly seek a physical cause while ignoring the real problem. Many children who are anxious or who regularly suffer psychosomatic symptoms are helped by learning *relaxation techniques* which reduce tension and its physical symptoms.

TICS

A tic, a simple movement such as eye-blinking or head-jerking, can develop at any time between the ages of 2 and 15 years, but they develop most commonly around the age of 7 years. One in 4 children of this age suffers from a tic. They tend to run in families and are made worse by fatigue, excitement or anxiety. Although irritating, they are harmless.

Tics are usually transient and get better with time. They very often improve if the child can be kept free from tension or worries or if you can prevent him getting too tired. Trying to correct or stop the habit is only likely to make it worse, but if it does become very severe or persists for longer than a year you should consult your doctor.

LEARNING DIFFICULTIES AND DYSLEXIA

Dyslexia is a term used a great deal in relation to school-age children's language problems but there is confusion about exactly what dyslexia is, whether it exists at all, and how it should be assessed and treated.

Dyslexia is a very real condition: it refers to a child who has great difficulty in learning to read and write despite having normal abilities and adequate teaching. Frequent changes of school, poor quality of classroom teaching, lack of parental support and family stress are known to contribute to a written-language difficulty. However, despite good support and helpful circumstances at least 1 child in every 25 has some degree of dyslexia and 3 times as many boys as girls are affected.

It is generally accepted that dyslexia is a complex problem, and that its severity and symptoms may vary from one child to the next. Some psychologists and teachers prefer to use a term such as 'specific learning difficulty'.

If your child has learning difficulties, you may suspect he is dyslexic if:

o there is a family history of reading and spelling difficulties
o he has a pre-school history of speech and language problems
o he is slow in acquiring reading and spelling skills, while appearing to be just as able as his peers in other areas of achievement such as oral classwork, puzzles or games and language

o he shows a weakness in learning sequences, such as the days of the week, and in following long instructions
o he is confused over right and left directions

If you suspect a difficulty, ask your child's school to arrange an assessment by an educational psychologist. The child will be given tests to assess his general ability and discover his weaknesses. It will then be possible to decide whether he does, in fact, have a specific learning difficulty, how severe it is, its possible cause and what help is needed to remedy it.

Generally, children with specific learning difficulties can be educated in normal schools. However, they will need regular and specialist remedial teaching from an early age. Progress varies, depending on the child and his circumstances, but dyslexic children can, and often do, go on to have very successful school careers. Eventually many of these children manage to make up lost ground as far as their reading is concerned, although they may remain poor spellers.

▶See also Learning and school; Appendices: Who's who in the health service; The law and your child

A sample of writing by a young child with dyslexia shows characteristic letter reversals and mirror-writing, as well as writing one letter on top of another.

SUBNORMAL INTELLIGENCE

Mental subnormality or handicap is not the same as mental illness. It is the result of maldevelopment or malfunction of the part of the brain that controls intellect. This can be caused by chromosomal and genetic defects, as in *Down's syndrome* and *phenylketonuria*; influences on the unborn child such as maternal ill health, for example *German measles*, or maternal alcoholism; *birth injuries* and *birth asphyxia*; *thyroid deficiency* (cretinism) and severe *meningitis*, or *head injuries* and lead poisoning. Some children with *cerebral palsy* or *epilepsy* may also have mental handicap.

Intellectual ability depends not only on the structure of the brain but also on adequate nutrition, good physical health and an emotionally stable and stimulating environment. A child with limited potential may be helped to quite a degree if all these factors are taken into account.

A child who is considered educationally subnormal has an intelligence quotient of less than 85. A very few are severely affected and will be dependent on others throughout their lives. Most educationally subnormal children are only moderately so and can learn to live fairly independent lives, although they usually need to attend special schools and will need some kind of protected environment throughout their lives.

Some developmental and physical problems such as *dyslexia* or speech and hearing disorders may make a child appear less intelligent than he is in reality. Children who are suspected of being educationally subnormal are regularly assessed to confirm whether or not this is in fact the case.

Adolescents

Turbulent feelings are normal and common in adolescence. Nearly all adolescent problems arise from the difficulties faced in growing up, and although many adolescents have periods of moodiness or misbehaviour, it is not often that outside help is needed to deal with them.

An adolescent's problems may be partly inherited, and partly to do with his environment. An adolescent's success in achieving a healthy independence and in handling problems is the result of the way in which parents and teachers have encouraged or discouraged him and it is very much influenced by the way his family behave towards each other and deal with problems. However, the way in which the adolescent handles problems and reacts to them will also depend on his own personality and on how sensitive to stress he seems to be.

Common causes of emotional and behavioural problems are:

o severe family or marital tensions
o extremes of punitiveness, negligence, permissiveness or over-protectiveness of parents
o poor relationships with a parent
o a traumatic event, such as the death of someone close

These causes can profoundly affect a young person's development.

Some difficulties become more apparent or socially disabling in adolescence. These range from developmental problems such as *dyslexia* to physical problems such as *spasticity*, *epilepsy* or *diabetes*. Even relatively minor disorders such as *acne* or *short sight*, which others take in their stride, may affect an adolescent's self-confidence. Children who suffer from *mental retardation* have additional difficulties in adolescence as their social disabilities become more clearly handicapping. These children have a greater chance of developing psychiatric problems, but these problems will be quite different and distinct from their mental handicap.

If you are worried about your adolescent, discuss your concern with someone close to you and, if possible, also with your child. If he wants to be left alone you should respect this, but make it clear that you are available when needed and that, as a responsible caring parent, you will intervene if you feel that he is getting out of his depth.

If you find that you need outside help, you can approach your doctor, your child's teacher, an educational psychologist or a social worker. Any of these people may refer your child to a psychiatrist. The line between true psychiatric disorders and ordinary problems is not always clear. Whether or not a troubled adolescent will be advised to see a psychiatrist may

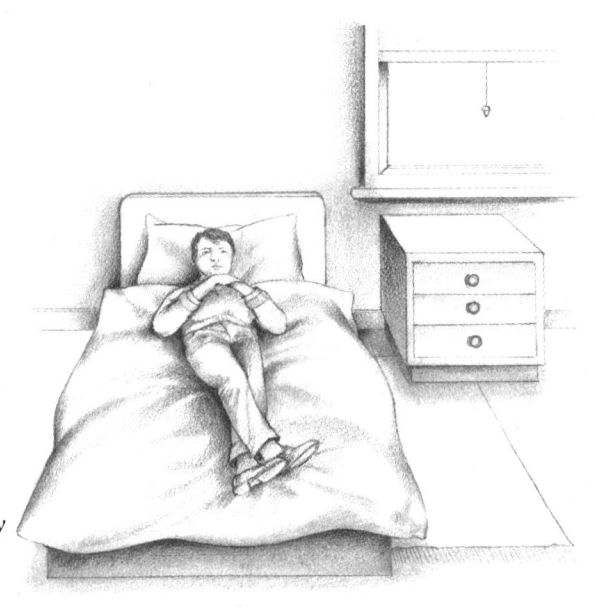

Parents often worry about the ever-increasing length of time adolescents spend with friends of whom they may or may not approve. However, these friendships give vital support to the child while he is making the gradual separation from the family. Much more a cause for concern is the child who seems socially isolated and so is forced into an unhealthy and continuing dependence on the family.

depend not only on the severity of the problem, but also on how your family, and perhaps your family doctor, perceive and handle it.

Psychiatric disorders are enormously varied in their nature and severity. About 10 to 15 per cent of adolescents need psychiatric help at some time. However, only a tiny proportion of these suffer from the kind of severe mental disorder in which they lose touch with reality, behave in a bizarre way or may need to be hospitalized. Even serious disorders such as *schizophrenia* can have quite different courses in different young people.

▶ **See also** The older child and adolescent

SCHOOL REFUSAL

Although school refusal is a problem among younger children also, it becomes more common in adolescence. About 5 per cent of all children see a psychiatrist for this reason.

School refusal is not the same as *truancy*, which has a different pattern and different causes. In school refusal a child may have headaches, stomach-aches, or other physical symptoms that prevent him going to school, or he may simply refuse to go. Although difficulties at school may precipitate the problem, children who refuse to go to school are usually frightened about *separation* from the family rather than about school itself, and they are often depressed, or anxious, or both. Sometimes, if there are family problems, the child may feel he has to stay at home to cope.

In this situation, your child's obvious distress will naturally distress you. The temptation may be to allow or encourage your child to avoid school, but this will only perpetuate the problem. If your child refuses to go to school, it is important to seek help quickly. The longer the difficulty persists, the harder it may be to overcome it; the child may well lose touch with schoolfriends and school activities and fall behind with his work, and these problems will reinforce his reluctance to leave the family. Professional help varies, but all approaches aim to give parents and their child whatever support is needed to cope more confidently with the return to school. If you agree, professional help may also involve liaising with the school.

ANXIETY STATES

In adolescence, the most common forms of anxiety are social phobia, an anxiety-laden shyness, and *school refusal*. Anxiety can be handicapping for the teenager, making it difficult for him to lead a normal social life.

Social phobia in some degree is almost universal in adolescence. You cannot force your child to be sociable, but you can boost his confidence and build up his self-esteem. You can also give him the opportunity to build up his social skills by making sure that you yourself have an active social life in which he is welcome, although not coerced, to join. Reassure him, too, that shyness is not his own personal affliction but affects almost everyone.

Sometimes, however, the teenager's phobia is so intense that it makes him withdraw from all social contact, even with people of his own age. If this happens, you should seek help. Therapy can teach the adolescent to relax and help him deal with the specific situations that are causing anxiety.

Misbehaviour is often a sign that a teenager is very anxious. Sometimes, too, anxiety may lie behind the recurrence of problems that occurred earlier in childhood, such as *bedwetting*. Problems may cause distress to you and your whole family, and you should seek professional help. Bad feelings within the family can create further anxiety for children.

DEPRESSION

Moments of sadness or tearfulness are perfectly normal among school-age children. Nevertheless, if your child cries a lot, seems generally miserable, has a poor appetite, sleeps badly and cannot concentrate, he is probably very upset about something and needs help in understanding what is wrong and perhaps guidance in putting it right. However, true depressive illness is very rare until adolescence and adulthood, and rarely causes the swings of mood and periods of misery that are common in adolescence.

However, if these periods of misery are so frequent, intense or prolonged that your adolescent becomes withdrawn and unable to cope with normal life at home and at school, you should consult your doctor. A few adolescents do develop depressive illnesses and need treatment. Some of these are teenagers who have a natural tendency to respond to stressful events with intense and prolonged sadness. Some, particularly where other members of the family have suffered from depressive illness, may become depressed for no understandable reason.

The symptoms of depressive illness include tears, withdrawal and lack of concentration, disturbance of sleep and appetite and, if the depression is severe, loss of weight. Your child may have physical symptoms such as headaches and stomach-aches, or vague feelings of being unwell that can be used by him to avoid school and other obligations. Depression, like *anxiety*, is sometimes the reason why an adolescent misbehaves. Very occasionally the depression may produce such severe mental disturbance that hospital admission is necessary.

It may help to understand your child's depression if you think of it in terms of an experience of loss – has he perhaps lost your attention or affection, or has some set-back or failure made him lose his own self-esteem or sense of purpose? Sometimes he may hardly seem to have been affected at the time of a particular loss, for example the death of a close relative or friend, but develops the symptoms of anxiety, or depression or a behavioural problem a year or so later. In such cases he may be showing signs of unresolved grief.

Although anti-depressant drugs do help some young people with depressive disorders, most psychiatrists prefer to use some form of therapy or counselling first.

SUICIDE AND SELF-INJURY

Attempted suicide, often by taking overdoses of drugs or cutting wrists, is not uncommon among adolescents. Actual suicide, however, is almost never carried out by children aged under 12 years, and is rare even in adolescence, although the rate increases as adulthood approaches.

If your child communicates thoughts or threats of suicide or reveals other forms of self-injury or self-neglect, this should always be taken seriously. However, such behaviour is quite often a response to circumstances rather than evidence of mental illness. You can help by encouraging your adolescent to express his despairing feelings; indeed, simply doing this will often meet his needs for care and attention so that he has less need for dramatic and dangerous ways of seeking them. This kind of behaviour is often described, pejoratively, as 'attention-seeking'. But in fact troubled young people do need and deserve attention, and perceptive and responsive adults can help them to seek it in more appropriate, less destructive ways.

▶**See also** Life and death; Appendix: Emergency actions

OBSESSIVE COMPULSIONS

Rituals and minor obsessions – a compulsion to avoid the cracks in the pavement or to have a special bedtime routine – are a common and normal part of childhood. Most adults, too, can understand the compulsion to check and recheck that the gas is turned off or that the house is locked. In rare cases during adolescence this type of behaviour becomes so exaggerated that it becomes disabling.

The adolescent with an obsessive-compulsive disorder has persistent thoughts which he cannot get rid of, or he may feel compelled to carry out certain acts which he knows are silly and unnecessary, but which, nonetheless, he cannot resist. The urge is so compelling that the repetitiveness of his behaviour can disable a child for hours, while he washes, arranges or rearranges clothes or follows some other ritual. It is easy for parents to be drawn into these rituals with the honest intention of attempting to help. However, if you do become involved in your adolescent's obsessive compulsion you will be unwittingly reinforcing his behaviour.

Therapy can help an adolescent to overcome obsessive compulsions. It usually involves his parents as well. If the obsessive child is very depressed or anxious, anti-depressant drugs may be prescribed. Most adolescents eventually recover, and although they usually remain rather over-conscientious and fastidious people, they rarely develop any serious mental illness.

ANOREXIA NERVOSA

Many adolescents, especially girls, become concerned about their weight and prescribe diets and exercise for themselves. This is not usually a cause for alarm. A few teenagers, however, have a quite unrealistic image of themselves as too fat, and develop an intense preoccupation with weight control, amounting to a phobia about gaining weight. Anorexia occurs mainly in adolescent girls and young women but it can affect boys.

Anorexics will go to elaborate lengths not only to achieve the desired weight loss, but to mislead people who might be concerned. They may exercise intensely, take laxatives, induce vomiting and wear baggy clothes. A girl who is anorexic will lose weight steadily and develop a growth of fine pale hair on her face and body. Her periods may stop, or may never start. The disorder can lead to severe illness and even, in extreme cases, death. If your child has anorexia nervosa she may need treatment in hospital where, with psychological assistance and control of diet, she will be helped to regain weight. Family therapy may play a valuable part in treatment.

A related condition, **bulimia nervosa** is characterized by 'binge' over-eating followed by self-induced vomiting.

However thin the anorexic girl, her self-image is still of someone who is 'too fat'.

PROBLEMS, DISEASES AND DISORDERS

CONDUCT DISORDERS

A conduct disorder is a term used to describe one of a variety of behavioural problems, from lying or stealing, to fighting, bullying, being mischievous and destructive, or simply being abusive. Young people who develop conduct disorders in adolescence have often been difficult children.

If you are faced with these sort of problem, try to find out the reasons for your child's behaviour. Some common-sense limit-setting and control may help but you will have to judge whether or not you need professional help to cope. In more severe disorders, such as setting fires or absconding from home, you should seek professional help.

Delinquency is a term which is often used to cover the whole spectrum of anti-social behaviour, although it is in fact a legal term and means law-breaking. You should be aware that occasional delinquent acts, such as stealing or truancy, are very common in adolescence, and do not mean that your child is headed for a life of crime.

Truancy is one form of delinquent behaviour. In contrast to *school refusal*, the truant has no particular anxiety about going to school. Indeed, he may very well go to school some days but not others, or walk out of school having registered.

ALCOHOL AND DRUG ABUSE

Children tend to imitate their parents in the use and misuse of alcohol and tobacco. If you lay down firm rules about drinking and smoking that are consistent with your own behaviour, your child should not become a heavy drinker or smoker. Regular heavy drinking and drunkenness can lead to delinquency if not to alcoholism, so encourage your children to recognize when they have had enough to drink. Tobacco is an addictive drug that can cause serious illness, so smoking should be discouraged.

Your best policy as a parent is to be alert to any unusual or inexplicable changes in your child's behaviour, and to be aware of what is going on in your own particular neighbourhood. It is important that you should know whether, for example, glue- or solvent-sniffing is a local habit among younger adolescents, and whether your child is associating with other young people who are unsupervised or generally misbehaving.

You should suspect your child of glue-sniffing if you notice personality changes, especially if they are at first short-lived, odd chemical odours or stains on his clothing, signs of skin damage and unexplained irritation around his nose and mouth.

Patterns of drug abuse change from time to time, with fashion and with what is commercially available. If your child is injecting drugs regularly you may notice injection marks, especially on his arms and legs, as well as personality changes and excited behaviour.

You should consult your doctor for advice and treatment about glue-sniffing and drug abuse. You should take emergency action if your child is trembling and sweating and has shallow breathing, has cold, clammy skin, and has a weak, fast pulse.

The social acceptibility of smoking makes it easy for parents, however unwittingly, to encourage it. Children are much more likely to smoke themselves if their parents do so and parents who are addicted smokers may understand how easy it is for an occasional cigarette to lead to a regular and unbreakable habit.

▶ **See also** Appendix: Emergency actions

PROMISCUITY

If an adolescent, particularly a younger adolescent, has frequent, casual sexual relationships, this is usually both a result and a cause of unhappiness. Regular sexual activity as part of a stable and mutually respecting relationship is not promiscuity, and there is a considerable difference, for example, between a 17-year-old behaving in this way and a 14-year-old who has casual sexual partners. The promiscuous adolescent needs understanding as well as parental control. If you are punitive or unsympathetic the young person is even more likely to turn to casually exciting, comforting and essentially immature promiscuous behaviour. If the behaviour continues, professional help may be advisable.

MENTAL ILLNESS

Severe mental illness is rare in childhood. However, there are a few serious psychiatric disorders that affect adolescents and that usually need a period of treatment in hospital. Some of these illnesses typically appear for the first time in adolescence.

SCHIZOPHRENIA

This term refers to a group of illnesses with quite specific and bizarre symptoms, which usually appear for the first time in late adolescence or early adulthood. The abnormality of brain chemistry thought to cause schizophrenia can be inherited.

Symptoms include delusional and often bizarre thinking. The adolescent may feel certain that he is under outside and usually malign influences. He may be convinced beyond all doubt that he is the object of special attention from complete strangers – a belief that is quite different from the feelings of self-consciousness that most adolescents experience. His thinking and speech may be disordered to the point of incoherence.

The adolescent who has suspected schizophrenia is usually admitted to hospital for confirmation of the diagnosis and treatment. A combination of drugs is usually given. The drugs used are powerful and have side-effects that often require their own medication. If your child has schizophrenia you will be given advice on now to help reduce the tension to which he will be particularly vulnerable. Although the illness may be lifelong or recurrent, substantial or complete recovery is also possible. It is well worth asking your doctor to put you in touch with a support group to avoid feeling helpless and isolated in this very stressful situation.

PSYCHOSIS

Psychotic illnesses are those which are so severe that thinking becomes seriously disturbed, as it does in *schizophrenia*. Very occasionally an adolescent may develop a psychotic depression and become convinced that he is worthless or that life is not worthwhile. Such irrational convictions, held with absolute certainty and tenacity, are known as delusions.

Psychosis can take an opposite form – manic illness – in which the affected person is extremely excited, talkative, restless, elated and generally 'high'. The elation can rapidly turn to irritability and anger, and often sadness seems not far below the surface. Some people have recurrent manic attacks, and others have both manic attacks and psychotic depression.

Psychosis can be controlled to a considerable degree by drugs. Close medical supervision will be necessary at the height of the illness.

▶See also Appendix: Support groups and publications

THE EYES

The eye focuses rays of light into a sharp image using its optical apparatus, the cornea and lens at the front of the eyeball. The image is focused on the retina, a highly specialized tissue that lines the inside of the eyeball. When the rays reach the light-sensitive cells, the rods and cones, in the retina, chemical reactions take place which generate nerve impulses. Cone cells work in plenty of light and detect colour. They are concentrated in an area called the fovea whose function is to permit detailed vision such as reading. Rod cells also function when there is only a very small amount of light, so they are used at night as well as during the day. They detect light and form a black and white image. The impulses from the rods and cones are refined and sent along the optic nerve to the brain. It is here that vision in the form that we understand it takes place: the images are processed and we perceive colour, shape, form, movement, shadow and distance.

Vision to the right of the object we look at is carried out in the left side of the brain, vision to the left of the object in the right side of the brain. This crossing-over of visual information takes place inside the skull, where the two optic nerves join together before passing to the visual centres at the back of the brain.

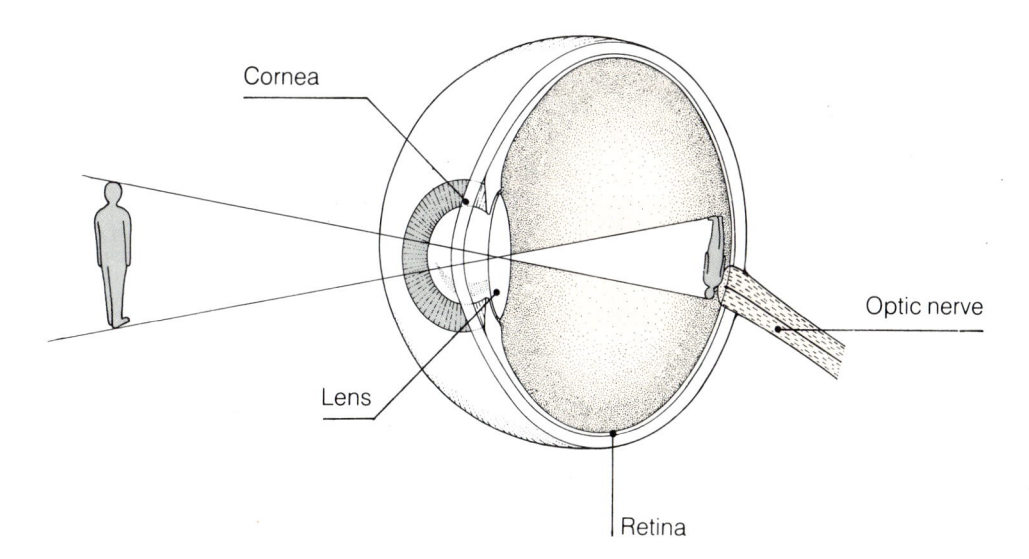

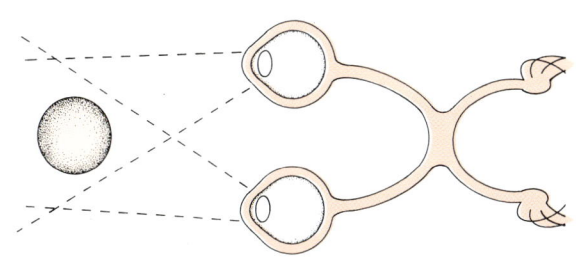

The brain co-ordinates the two slightly different views received from each eye to form one three-dimensioned image of the object being viewed.

If a blocked tear duct does not clear spontaneously, gently massage the corner of the eye against the side of the nose, pressing on the tear sac to break down the obstruction.

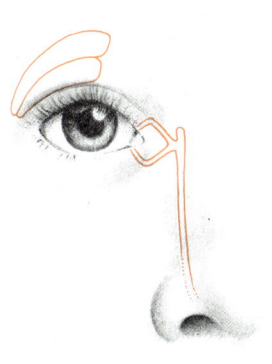

COMMON PROBLEMS

Eye pain or aching is hardly ever due to 'over-use' or 'strain'. There is no evidence that reading in poor light damages eyesight, although good light makes it easier to read. Tired eyes and headaches are more often caused by hunched shoulders while reading in poor light than by eyestrain. Insufficient sleep and spending time in smoky or stuffy rooms can also cause headaches and sore eyes. However, if your child complains of visual problems or seems unable to see clearly, you should report this to your doctor. Many visual changes are normal but early detection of eye disorders gives a better chance of successful treatment and cure. You should also consult your doctor if your baby's or child's eye has an unusual shape or colour, an odd-sized or odd-shaped pupil, or if the two eyes look different.

Colour blindness is not blindness to colours. The colour blind person simply perceives colour in a different way from other people. Brown, for instance, which is a mixture of reds and greens may require more red in it for a colour-blind person to perceive it as brown. Except when it occurs in association with a few extremely rare diseases, colour blindness does not affect other aspects of vision and is rarely important. In certain occupations, such as photography, colour blindness is a handicap.

Sticky and watering eyes in a newborn baby may be a result of blocked tear ducts. This common condition is not serious: the eye is not particularly red but it is sticky and watery, especially in windy weather or when the baby has a cold.

Red and sticky eyes may be caused by conjunctivitis, a bacterial or viral *infection* of the conjunctiva, the outer covering of the eye. It is one of the most common eye problems in childhood and is often caught by direct contact. If your child's eye is red, the lids stick together in the morning, and there is a discharge during the day, it is most likely that he has conjunctivitis. Conjunctivitis is not usually serious, but it should be seen and treated by your doctor.

Red and painful eyes may be caused by inflammation inside the eye or of one of the outer layers of the eyeball. Occasionally *conjunctivitis* also produces slight aching, but this is not severe. Consult your doctor if your child's eye is red and watery and he complains of pain like a piece of grit in the eye. He may have something in his eye that has to be removed.

Red and itchy eyes, with very little discharge or stickiness, are usually the result of some form of *allergy* or sensitivity affecting the eyes. If this is the case your child may also have other allergic symptoms, such as a runny nose or *eczema*. Your doctor will probably recommend eye drops.

Cysts and styes are usually caused by inflammation in the oil glands of the eyelids, which can cause stickiness. Although not serious they can be irritating and unpleasant to look at, so consult your doctor. The problem is usually treated by eye ointment or bathing with an eye lotion.

Photophobia is sensitivity to light. It is quite common in children. Consult your doctor if it is prolonged or if there are other symptoms, such as redness, stickiness, grittiness or itching of the eyes, or general ill health.

EYE INJURY
Any injury or possibility of injury to the eye or its surrounds, especially by a flying splinter of glass or metal, requires the urgent attention of a doctor. Go straight to your own doctor or to an eye specialist at the local hospital. It is never worth taking chances with eyesight: get medical attention without delay.

SQUINT

Squint is the most common major eye problem in childhood, affecting about 3 children in every 100. If a child has a squint, one eye looks in a different direction from the other. The medical term for this is strabismus. Squinting is common in the first few weeks of life, as a newborn baby's eyes do not work together all the time. However, if your baby still appears to squint by the time he is about 3 months old, consult your doctor.

CAUSES

Squint does not have one cause. Often there is a family history of squinting. The child may have *long sight*, illness may lead to the onset of a squint or there may be an underlying defect in the child's ability to use two eyes together. An eye that develops poor vision, for whatever reason, may also begin to squint. If one eye deviates persistently then that eye's image may be suppressed by the brain; the eye is then described as a lazy, or amblyopic, eye.

TREATMENT

In principle all squints are treated in the same way. The eye specialist first decides whether spectacles are necessary. If your child has a squint he is likely to be long-sighted and spectacles will make it easier for him to focus

Using a major amblioscope different images are seen through each eyepiece, but in normal vision these overlap. The adjustment needed to superimpose the images (a lion seen by one eye inside a cage seen by the other, for example) depends on the eyes' misalignment, and thus the degree of squint can be measured.

When one eye squints, patching the normal eye forces the child to use the squinting eye and is usually very effective in treating a squint. A major amblioscope (above) may sometimes be used in treatment.

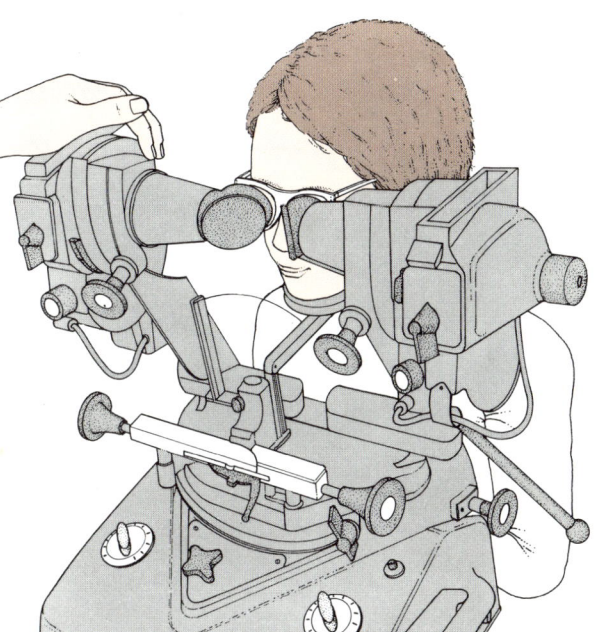

at close range, and thus discourage the squint. If only one eye squints persistently this often means that its vision is poor. The remedy is to patch the normal eye, so that the child is forced to use the lazy squinting eye. If the child is under 2 years old, wearing a patch almost invariably improves vision. It is often difficult for a child to accept an eye patch, but it should be worn for several hours a day.

Other forms of treatment, such as eye exercises, prism spectacles or eye drops, seldom succeed in curing childhood squints. If spectacles and patching are unsuccessful, your eye specialist is likely to recommend surgery. This aims to reposition the eyes so that they point in the same direction wherever the child looks. This is done by realigning the eye-moving muscles in the eye socket, increasing the effect of some and weakening others. The operation causes some pain and the child's eyes will be red and swollen for a few days afterwards. The chance of damage to the eyes is extremely small.

One child in 3 who has a squint operation requires another operation later. Treatment for squint continues throughout childhood and, even if the eyes are straightened by operation, the child should be seen regularly by an eye specialist.

> **DOUBLE VISION**
> Double vision in childhood may be the result of squint. You should take your child to the family doctor if he complains of double vision, even if it passes. It is rare for it to last a long time because a child is easily able to compensate for it by suppressing one of the images in the brain.

SHORT SIGHT

In medical terms, short sight, *long sight* and *astigmatism*, are known collectively as refractive error. Refractive error is not a disease. In most cases the eye itself is perfectly healthy but cannot form a perfectly focused image on the retina.

In short sight, also known as near sight or myopia, distant objects appear blurred, while near objects are seen clearly. If your child holds objects close or if he always wants to sit very near the television screen, he may be short-sighted. Many cases of short sight are picked up at school when a child is unable to see what is written on the blackboard. If you suspect that your child is short-sighted, ask your doctor to arrange for him to have an eye test.

Most short-sighted children achieve normal vision with the use of spectacles. During the growing years a short-sighted child is likely to become more short-sighted: his spectacles will need to be changed whenever distance vision becomes poor through them. A small child may need encouragement to wear spectacles.

Older children may prefer contact lenses for cosmetic reasons: wearing contact lenses can also improve the vision of a few children who have extremely short sight.

You should report any new visual symptoms that your short-sighted child develops to your optician or eye specialist.

LONG SIGHT

Long sight, also known as far sight or hypermetropia, is the normal condition of the eye in infancy. To bring a distant object into focus on the retina, the long-sighted eye needs to focus in the same way that a normal eye does for a near object. It is only in extreme cases that a long-sighted person is unable to see near objects clearly.

Long sight on its own does not often require treatment with spectacles. However, if it is associated with a *squint* then the squint may be treated by the use of spectacles.

TESTING FOR REFRACTIVE ERROR

In refractive errors images are not focused on the retina because the eyeball is an unusual shape, or because the focusing power of the cornea and lens is unusually strong (short sight), or weak (long sight), or the curvature of the cornea is irregular (*astigmatism*). The effects of the error can be compensated for by a lens placed in front of the eyeball.

An eye specialist or an optician can test for refractive error by looking into the eye. When children are young this requires the use of eye drops to prevent the eye from close-focusing and giving a false impression of short sight. The tester places various lenses in front of the eye and by observing the eye's reaction can estimate which type of lens neutralizes the refractive error of the eye.

Vision cannot usually be measured precisely until children can match letters. This is not normally before about 3 years of age. From this age a child should visit an optician regularly, every other year. Undetected and untreated visual defects may contribute to *learning difficulties*.

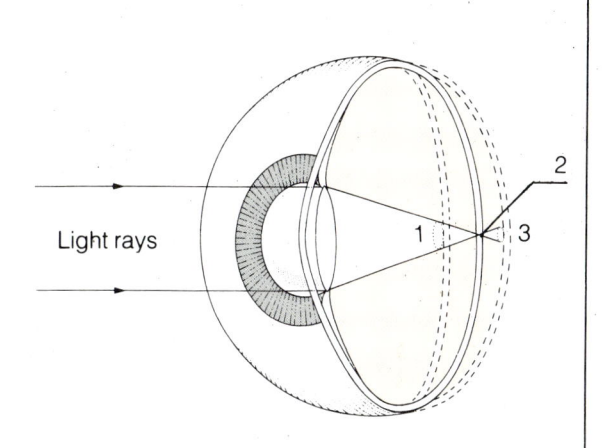

1 Position of retina in long site: image focused behind retina
2 Position of retina in normal vision: image focused on retina
3 Position of retina in short sight: image focused in front of retina

ASTIGMATISM

An astigmatic eye forms a distorted image on the retina because of uneven curvature of the eyeball. The cornea is often spoon-shaped with a horizontal curvature that differs from the vertical curvature. A child with astigmatism usually also has *short sight* or *long sight*.

If your child has eye problems and eye tests reveal astigmatism he will be prescribed spectacles with lenses that compensate for the irregular curvature of the eyeball. Occasionally children can be fitted with contact lenses for astigmatism, but if the cornea is imperfectly curved then there will be difficulty in wearing lenses.

In astigmatism either horizontal or vertical lines are unfocused. A cylindrical lens corrects this.

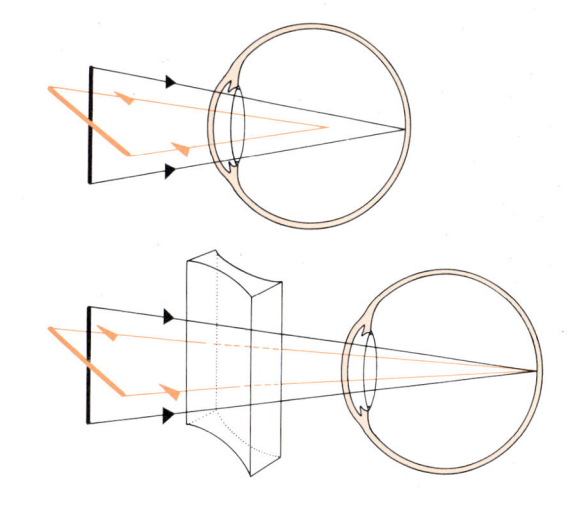

BLINDNESS

Many more children are partially visually handicapped than are blind. The chief cause of blindness is *congenital abnormality* of the eye, including cataracts, abnormalities of eye size or structural defects, where a part of the eye has developed faultily. These defects are not necessarily inherited; if an eye specialist considers that a child's visual handicap is hereditary he will refer the parents to a genetic counsellor.

SYMPTOMS

You may suspect blindness or partial-sightedness if your baby is not looking straight at you by the time he is a few weeks old. He may tend to look to one side, or be unable to look at you steadily or his eyes may wobble or shake when he tries to look at something. He may have a *squint*. If the visual problem is severe, even when awake he will not react when the light is turned on in a dark room.

DIAGNOSIS

If you suspect that your baby may have visual difficulties it is important to mention it to your doctor as soon as possible. The doctor will arrange for an optician to give him an eye test. If your doctor suspects a problem with vision your child will be referred to a specialist for further examinations. The eye specialist will ask you what you have noticed about your child's vision problem, and will also ask you for some details of your family history. He may need to carry out further tests using eye drops to open the pupil for detailed eye examination.

Some causes of blindness in childhood cannot be treated, but for those for which there is treatment it is usually best to start as soon as possible – hence the importance of early diagnosis.

CARE

The needs of a blind child are very much the same as those of other children. Try to avoid over-protecting and treating him with such extra-special care that he lacks physical

Encouraging a blind child to take part in activities that are exciting and present challenges will help him achieve the independence he will need in adult life, and also offer opportunities to enjoy the sense of freedom that his handicap may otherwise deny him.

contact. Indeed, physical contact is especially important for blind babies, to compensate for the loss of visual information about the world. For example, you can encourage your baby to feel your face and body. During the day put him where he can hear you.

If your child has some vision, you can encourage him to play with large bright toys as well as toys with textured surfaces and toys that make interesting noises. There is, however, no substitute for human contact and providing your child with plenty of opportunities for looking at faces.

The parents of a blind child often find that one parent feels partially excluded by the other, who becomes the 'expert', and it is important that both of you have plenty of contact with your child.

Brothers and sisters often want to help with the day-to-day care of a blind child, and to play

Modern technology has made it easier for blind people to train for a greater variety of jobs. Audiotyping is possible using a braille keyboard linked to a standard VDU. The printer provides a special braille printout.

with him. They should not be discouraged from doing everything they would do if the child were sighted: they should be allowed to fight, argue and play as normally as possible. Grandparents and other members of the family may not be confident about coping with a blind child and they may need encouragement to become involved.

It may be helpful to meet parents of children who have a similar condition, although it is important to remember that two children with a condition that has the same name rarely have the same problems. Talking to parents who have brought up a blind child will help you to realize that caring for a blind child is not nearly so frightening or worrying as you may have thought. Your family doctor and eye specialist can offer advice and provide information about support groups and local organizations such as special playgroups.

SCHOOLING

Many playgroups and kindergartens welcome blind children, but as a blind child grows older his education becomes more problematic. The particular type of education needed depends on a wide variety of factors: the degree of visual handicap the child suffers; any other associated handicaps that he has; whether parents can take him to a school some distance from home or whether transport has to be provided. Most important of all is the availability near to home of educational facilities for visually handicapped children. In recent years it has become more common for visually handicapped children to be educated at normal schools with other children. The more severe the handicap, however, the more specialized the facilities required and it may be difficult for a child to receive the best education possible at a local school.

For older children who are blind, residential schools may be the best form of education. This is often difficult for parents to accept, but a visit to the school is usually reassuring. One of the chief aims of education for visually handicapped children is to increase their mobility and independence, and parents can help greatly by joining in with the activities of the school.

▶See also Longstanding problems; Appendix: Support groups and publications

THE TEETH

Teeth begin to develop long before they appear in the mouth: the first stages in the development of primary, or first, teeth take place before birth. A child's first tooth usually appears when he is about 6 months old, although this varies from child to child. The first teeth to appear are incisors, followed by the primary molars and canines. A child at 2½ years usually has all 20 primary teeth.

Apart from their function in eating and speech, primary and permanent teeth are both important for the normal growth and development of a child's face. They affect a child's general appearance, and even young children may be self-conscious of, for example, front teeth that are discoloured or irregular.

Teething

When a baby is teething the gum over the emerging tooth may be red and sore, the corresponding cheek may be flushed and the baby may dribble more than usual. Sometimes an emerging tooth is covered for a short time with a small bluish swelling, caused by blood or, less often, fluid collecting in the gum tissue. These swellings usually disappear about two weeks after the tooth has completely appeared. If they upset your baby's feeding, you may need to get help from your dentist.

Many babies are irritable when they are teething. Some find that biting on a hard, smooth object like a (sugar-free) rusk or a plastic ring can relieve discomfort. If teething seems particularly painful, or goes on for a long time, you should take your baby to the doctor, who may prescribe a mild analgesic. Teething drops and solutions can be effective, but they may contain sugar and occasionally even local anaesthetic agents, so you should not give them to your baby frequently or over long periods of time.

There is no evidence that problems like diarrhoea or bronchitis are connected with teething. If your baby is suffering from such problems, the cause is not teething and he should be seen by a doctor.

Primary teeth
- 6 months: 1st incisors
- 7 months: 2nd incisors
- 18 months: canines
- 12 months: 1st molars
- 2-3 years: 2nd molars

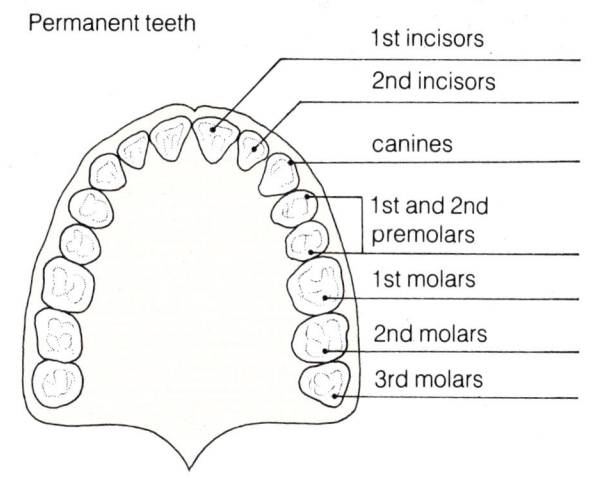

Permanent teeth
- 1st incisors
- 2nd incisors
- canines
- 1st and 2nd premolars
- 1st molars
- 2nd molars
- 3rd molars

Permanent teeth

When a child is about 6 years old his permanent, or second, teeth begin to appear. The first permanent molars develop in line behind the primary teeth farthest back in the mouth. They are often the first permanent teeth to appear and, because they do not replace primary teeth directly from below, they may be mistaken for part of the primary set of teeth. Permanent incisors, canines and premolars develop close to, and among, the roots of the primary teeth that they later come to replace. Gradually the roots of each primary tooth are absorbed, the tooth becomes loose and it falls out, usually without help.

A child normally has a set of 28 permanent teeth (not including his wisdom teeth) by the time he is about 13 years old.

Wisdom teeth

Third molars, or wisdom teeth, are the four permanent teeth that develop at the back of the mouth well after the other permanent teeth. They appear from about 17 years of age onwards. When there is insufficient space in the mouth for them to come through normally, they are said to be impacted. An impacted wisdom tooth may have to be extracted later in life. As wisdom teeth do not often cause problems before adulthood, their surgical removal is rarely necessary during childhood and adolescence. The decision on how to deal with problematic wisdom teeth is better delayed until the jaw is fully grown.

Structure

Both primary and permanent teeth have the same basic structure, although primary teeth are smaller and more widely spaced than permanent teeth and may also be whiter. Each tooth has a central core, or pulp, containing blood vessels and nerves. This is surrounded by a hard material, dentine, which forms the bulk of each tooth. The dentine forming the crown of each tooth is covered by a layer of enamel. Enamel is even harder than dentine and, unlike it, has no nerve supply. The roots of the teeth are covered with a bone-like material. This is attached to a series of short fibres holding each tooth root firmly within a socket in the bone of the jaw.

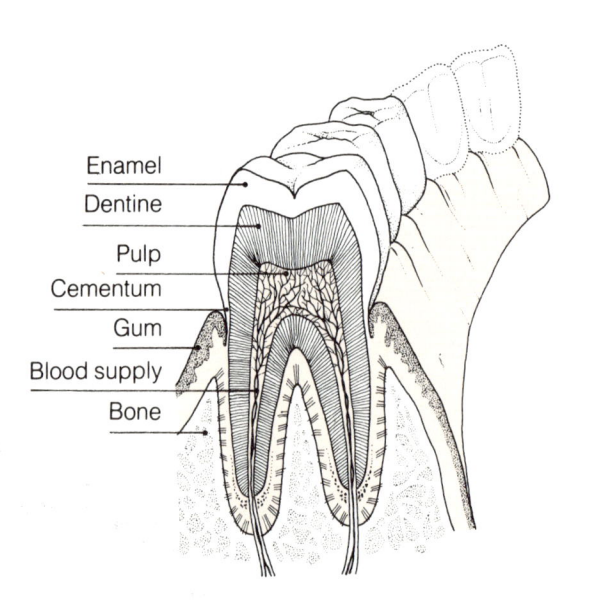

The supporting tissues of the tooth are made up of bone covered by gum. Healthy gums are firm and pale pink and surround each tooth with a tightly adapted cuff.

Prevention of tooth decay

Where water supplies are fluoridated the amount of tooth decay is strikingly reduced. Your dentist can tell you whether your local water contains adequate levels of fluoride, and will advise on fluoride supplements as drops or tablets if necessary. These are usually given from birth until about 13 years. Do not give more than the dose recommended, as an excess of fluoride can make teeth look mottled. Many toothpastes contain fluoride, which has a direct effect on teeth and also may have an indirect effect, as small amounts are swallowed. Tell your dentist if your child uses a fluoride toothpaste, as he will take this into account when recommending supplements. He may also apply fluoride agents directly to your child's teeth as a preventive measure.

Plastic fissure sealants can give great protection against decay. To be effective they must be applied as soon as possible after your child's permanent teeth come through.

Even though primary teeth are always replaced by permanent teeth, they should still be cared for scrupulously. Their decay may not only cause pain but may also interfere with the regular growth of permanent teeth. Primary molar teeth, which remain until a child is 11 or 12 years old, are particularly important. If they are lost or have to be removed prematurely owing to decay, adjoining teeth may fill the gaps into which permanent teeth should eventually emerge. As a result permanent teeth will be irregular and in order to correct them complicated treatment involving extractions and braces may become necessary at a later stage.

Oral hygiene is also important in preventing *sore and bleeding gums*.

▶See also Day-to-day care

TOOTH DECAY

Dental caries, or tooth decay, affects many children in the Western world, sometimes from a very early age. The resistance of a tooth to decay depends on various factors including the nature of the individual tooth, the rate of production and quality of saliva, and the level of fluoride in drinking water. A main factor in causing tooth decay is the frequency of eating sugary foods. By restricting these, together with effective teeth-cleaning with a fluoride toothpaste and regular visits to the dentist, much tooth decay can be prevented.

Plaque, a deposit on the teeth created from food particles, saliva and bacteria, acts with sugar to form acid. The acid begins by removing the mineral present in the tooth enamel. With further attack the enamel becomes roughened and stained, and breaks down so that the dentine is exposed. If unchecked, the decay proceeds to the pulp of the tooth, and the pulp may become inflamed and die. This in turn may lead to an abscess forming in the tissues surrounding the tooth.

Primary and permanent teeth both decay in the same way, but because primary teeth are smaller and have relatively larger pulps, their decay appears to be more rapid. The decay of very young children's teeth can be so fast and widespread that their primary teeth seem to have decayed before they have fully appeared.

This kind of decay is a particular risk if 'comforter' bottles and sweetened dummies are given to children to suck continually over any period of time.

SYMPTOMS

If your child complains of toothache, there is usually good reason and you should take him to the dentist promptly. Occasionally, as the enamel gets worn, teeth may become very sensitive, especially to changes in temperature, without any evidence of decay.

The earliest visible sign of tooth decay is an opaque white area where acid has removed the mineral in the tooth enamel. However, before you notice this your child may complain of discomfort following hot, cold or sweet foods and drinks. At this stage there may not be very much to see in his mouth and your dentist may take an X-ray to find out exactly what is wrong. If the decay is not treated, your child may begin to complain of a more severe and continuous ache.

In some cases children do not complain despite having obviously decayed teeth. The first sign of trouble may be a swelling, either of the gum around the tooth or, where the infection has spread further, of the child's face. Immediately you see a swelling, especially of your child's face, you should take him to the dentist (or to your doctor, if this is quicker).

TREATMENT

If your child complains of toothache mild analgesics will help to relieve the pain before you are able to take him to the dentist. If he has tooth decay, the dentist can often treat this in its early stages by drilling it out and filling the cavity left in the decayed tooth. A local anaesthetic may be necessary as dentine is very sensitive. When decay has reached as far as the pulp a root filling may be possible, or the tooth may have to be removed.

You must tell your dentist if your child has a heart condition as some methods of treatment might be dangerous for him.

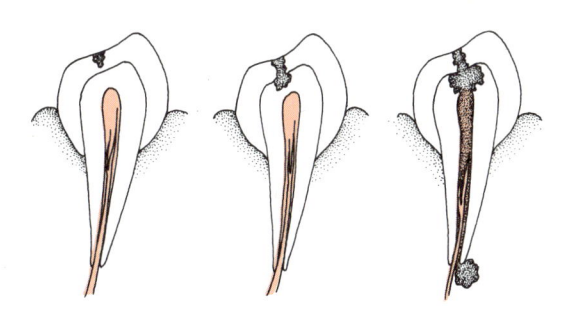

Acid first destroys tooth enamel and then attacks the dentine. If the decay continues untreated the pulp may become infected, the tooth may die and an abscess form.

SORE AND BLEEDING GUMS

The most common kind of gingivitis, or inflammation of the gums, is chronic gingivitis. This is caused by products of bacteria present in plaque affecting the gums, so that they become inflamed. Children's gums often suffer from mild inflammation but severe problems are rare.

If your child has gingivitis, his gums will be red and swollen. You will notice plaque accumulation on his teeth. His gums may begin to bleed easily, especially when his teeth are brushed. By brushing his teeth carefully and effectively, gingivitis should be relieved and prevented from recurring.

OVERCROWDED AND IRREGULAR TEETH

The way both primary and permanent teeth fit together may be disturbed by various factors. Primary teeth are often disturbed by dummy-, thumb- or finger-sucking. If your child continues one of these habits for a long time you may notice an 'open bite' where upper and lower teeth at the front fail to close together on biting. A more serious problem results when primary teeth, especially primary molars, have been taken out because of decay. This may lead to movement of neighbouring teeth so that permanent teeth do not have adequate space when they are ready to come through. Another common type of irregularity is where the lower teeth are too far forward or too far back in relation to the upper teeth. Orthodontic treatment aims to correct such problems.

A number of irregularities are at least partly inherited. All the same, successful prevention of dental decay makes many problems less complex and easier to treat.

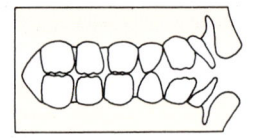

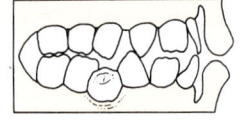

Open bite

Overcrowding

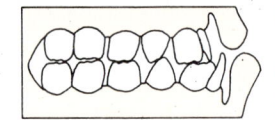

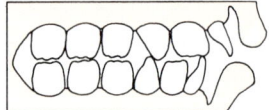

Irregular bites

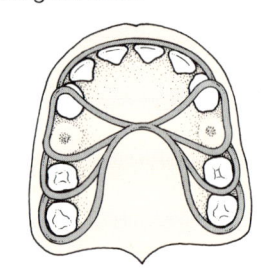

Irregular or overcrowded teeth may be corrected by extracting some teeth and using braces to move others into more regular positions.

INJURIES TO TEETH

Children often fall and damage their teeth. If your child has injured a tooth, you should take him to a dentist as soon as possible. Do not replace a primary tooth as this might damage the developing permanent tooth. However, a permanent tooth should be replaced in its socket as soon as possible, after rinsing the tooth and your child's mouth with cooled boiled water. If you are unable to replace the tooth, get your child to keep it in his mouth. Take him straight to a dentist who will splint the tooth into position and prescribe an antibiotic. If the tooth has been on the ground, *tetanus* immunization may also be necessary. Many reimplanted teeth are eventually lost, but they can function normally for several years.

THE EARS

The word ear is most often used to describe the ear flap, also known as the auricle or pinna, but the entire ear is a complex, delicate structure partly buried in the skull bone. It is made up of the outer, middle and inner ears.

The outer ear consists of the ear flap, which is a piece of cartilage, and the ear canal, or external auditory canal. The slightly curved canal leads into the eardrum. The middle ear starts with the eardrum, or tympanic membrane. The healthy eardrum is thin, pearly-grey and semi-transparent so that some of the structures behind it can be seen when a bright light is shone onto it. Behind the drum is an air-containing cavity with three small bones that transmit sound vibrations from the drum to the inner ear. The Eustachian tube runs from the middle-ear cavity to the throat, its main function being to equalize air pressure on each side of the eardrum. The inner ear is a complex series of fluid-filled chambers concerned with hearing and balance. They include the spiral cavity known as the cochlea and the semi-circular canals.

Protruding ears

There is a wide variation in the shape of the ear flap and many children have prominent ears. This does not affect hearing. You may be concerned that your child is being teased at school about his ears. A change in hairstyle is usually effective, but in an extreme case you may decide on a minor operation to improve your child's appearance. This is usually performed after the age of 6 years.

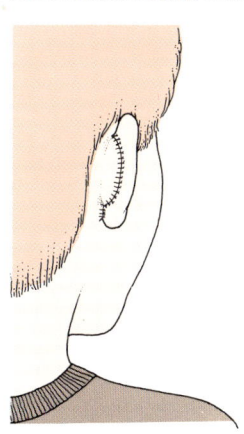

BAT EARS
Bat ears can be corrected by a simple operation. A strip of skin is removed from behind the ear and the two cut ends are rejoined so that the ear is pulled closer to the head. The operation is not usually performed until a child is at least 6 years old and his ears are fully developed.

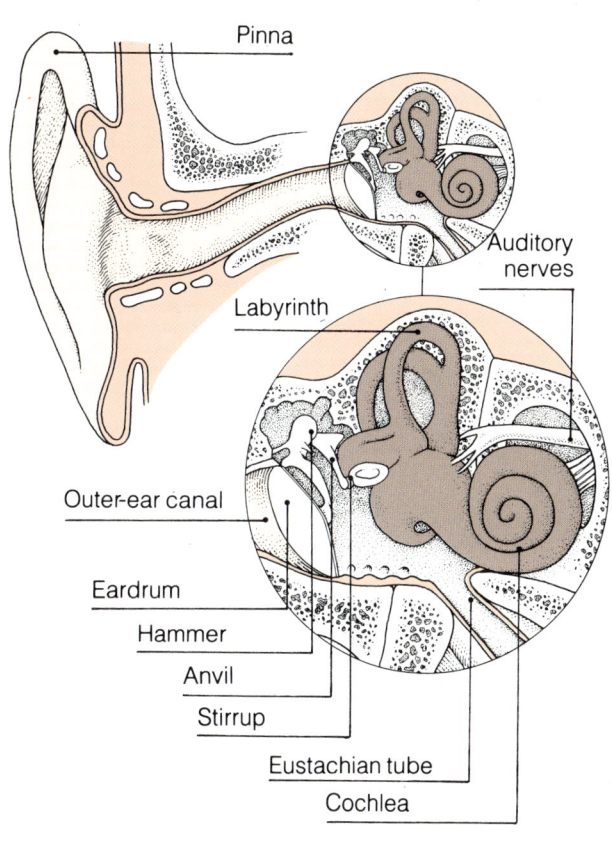

Flying

In aircraft, problems in the ear occur most commonly at taking off or landing. At these times the cabin pressure changes rapidly, and to ensure equalization of pressure on each side of the eardrum the Eustachian tube has to open. This is what is happening when your ears pop. If the difference in pressure builds up beyond a certain point it is not possible for the tube to open and air cannot enter the middle-ear cavity. The eardrum bends or stiffens, causing hearing loss and pain in the ear. Lowered middle-ear pressure is often followed

To relieve the discomfort caused by pressure change, make your child blow through her nose while you pinch it closed.

by the formation of fluid in the middle ear. If there is a sudden descent, the rapid change of pressure may rupture the eardrum.

Eating or sucking something stimulates swallowing and helps to open the Eustachian tube. When flying with a baby, breastfeed or offer a bottle on take-off and landing.

The problem is likely to be worse for a child with an upper respiratory infection such as a cold. It may be worth using a decongestant nasal spray or drops just before take-off and landing. If your child has had a recent bout of *hay fever*, he should take oral antihistamine before the flight.

Swimming
Inequality of pressure on either side of the eardrum is also a problem when diving underwater. There is some controversy about the effects of swimming on children with ear problems, but it seems common sense for your child to avoid swimming when he has an infection. If your child has a *perforated eardrum* any water that gets into the ear when swimming or washing is likely to cause *acute otitis media*.

Ear wax
Ear wax is a normal secretion from glands in the outer part of the ear canal. It helps to trap dust and other small particles and is then worked along the canal and out of the ear by the normal movements of the jaw. When it is first produced it is colourless and semi-liquid, but with time it darkens from yellow to brown, hardening at the same time.

The amount of wax the glands in the outer ear produce varies considerably from person to person. Usually the wax can be ignored or, if it builds up, it can be easily removed by gentle cleaning with a cotton-bud, if necessary first softening the wax with a little warmed olive oil. If produced in large quantities wax may form a plug that sticks in the ear canal causing irritation of the canal, or loss of hearing.

However, if your child's hearing is suffering you should seek medical advice. Syringing may be necessary to remove the wax. The doctor or nurse will flush out the ear canal with water warmed to body temperature. The wax comes out more easily if it has been softened by sodium bicarbonate ear drops given daily for a week beforehand.

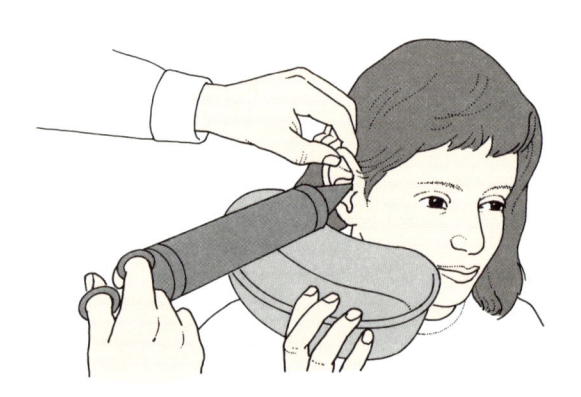

Syringing is most easily carried out with the ear flap pulled upwards and backwards to straighten the ear canal. The water can then be directed behind the wax to flush it out.

Dizziness
This is not a frequent symptom in children. However, a child who is unwell and feverish may describe a sensation of floating, blurring of vision, or unsteadiness on the feet. Such feelings can be triggered by a variety of causes. Dizziness alone rarely suggests that there is an underlying problem. Buzzing in the ear may be caused by wax obstructing the ear canal or by infection of the eardrum and middle ear.

▶**See also** The mouth, nose and throat

EARACHE

Pain in the ear is a common symptom that can be caused by several conditions. Children with sudden earache usually have *acute otitis media*. Other causes include a boil or skin infection in the ear canal (*otitis externa*); a cold with nasal catarrh that blocks the Eustachian tube; *glue ear*; a small object becoming lodged in the ear; or, in older children, the referred pain from a decaying upper molar tooth.

If your child has a severe earache it is very distressing both for him and for you, and it is important to seek medical advice without delay. If pus is being discharged from his ear he should see the doctor as soon as possible; a discharge may be a sign of inflammation in the ear canal or middle ear. Occasionally the discharge may be mixed with blood. This can indicate infection or injury; alternatively it may be a result of the child poking his ear because it irritates him.

You should carefully clean off any discharge without poking into the canal and give your child painkillers such as paracetamol.

A warm pad loosely applied to the ear may offer comfort; if the ear is hot and red outside, a cool, wrung-out flannel held to it can bring a little relief.

There is a commonly held belief that earache occurs most frequently at night, but there is little evidence to support this. However, pain can certainly seem worse to a child at night and he may become very distressed. A painkiller will help, but he will probably need extra holding and comforting as well.

A baby who has earache will seem obviously in pain, but because small babies cannot always localize pain he may not rub or pull the affected ear. It is only by examining the ear that your doctor can tell whether earache is causing the baby's distress.

By pulling the top of the ear up and back your doctor is able to see the whole canal. He will find it easiest to examine your young child's ear if you hold your child securely so that he stays still on your knee.

▶See also Accident and injury

BOILS IN THE EAR

Occasionally a hair follicle in the skin lining the ear canal becomes infected to produce a boil. You may not be able to see a boil in the ear canal from the outside, but your child will probably complain of earache or ear pains on chewing or when the ear is moved. When the boil comes to a head and bursts there may be a greenish-yellow discharge apparent from the ear canal.

A boil in the ear is seldom serious but it is often very painful. It may help to put a warm pad over the ear and you can always give your child a simple analgesic such as paracetamol until you can consult the doctor. He will carry out an examination to check the cause of the trouble, and in certain cases he may prescribe ear drops or a course of antibiotics. While symptoms persist keep the ear dry.

OTITIS EXTERNA

Otitis externa is inflammation, usually due to infection, of the skin lining the ear canal. Children who swim a lot may have a mild form of otitis externa, known as swimmer's ear. The infection causes inflammation and occasional discharge from the ear. Children with *eczema* are particularly susceptible to infection if water collects in their ears after washing or swimming.

Your doctor may take an ear swab to find out if there is infection, and if there is he will prescribe antibiotics. If the infection is mild, he may prescribe ear drops to be given at frequent intervals throughout the day. If there is a lot of discharge from the ear the doctor or nurse will mop out your child's ear canal using a probe covered with cotton-wool, and may then insert a ribbon of gauze soaked in a combination of liquid antibiotic and hydrocortisone drops. Do not try to mop out the ear yourself as you may damage the canal. If your child is in pain you can give an analgesic such as paracetamol.

If your child has otitis externa he should try to keep water out of his ears.

PERFORATED EARDRUM

Children occasionally suffer a perforated or ruptured eardrum, caused by an object poked down the ear canal or by the airborne pressure waves from a slap on the ear. The drum may also be ruptured as a result of infection of the middle ear or (intentionally) during ear surgery. The symptoms – if any – include slight pain, buzzing or other noises in the ear, and possibly a slight trickle of blood from the ear canal.

Surprisingly, a ruptured drum usually has little effect on hearing and heals by itself in a few weeks. If a persistently ruptured or heavily scarred drum is causing hearing difficulties your doctor may advise surgery to graft a new piece of tissue into place.

A clear or pale-yellow fluid issuing from the ear, possibly following a fall or blow to the head, indicates serious *head injury* and the child should be taken straight to hospital.

ACUTE OTITIS MEDIA

Otitis media is inflammation in the middle ear. A child who has had a cold or similar upper respiratory infection for several days may suddenly develop this, usually as a result of the infection spreading along the Eustachian tube.

Middle-ear infection is most common during the first few years of life, and remains common throughout the pre-school years. A child who has had one middle-ear infection will be prone to recurrent infection in the same ear, especially if the first attack was during the first 2 years of life. Also, a child is more likely to suffer recurrent otitis media when a parent or sibling has a history of the same problem.

Overall the condition is most frequent in the winter and spring, which coincides with the peak incidence of colds and similar respiratory infections in children.

SYMPTOMS

Pain is the main symptom of otitis media. Infection of the middle ear should be suspected if a baby is feverish, irritable or unwilling to feed. Vomiting and diarrhoea are also associated with middle-ear infection in young children, but are uncommon in older children. There may be discharge from the ear, accompanied by sudden relief from the pain.

Usually only one ear is affected, but there are many children who have infections of both ears at the same time.

TREATMENT
If your child has the symptoms of a middle-ear infection he should see your doctor as soon as possible. Meanwhile, give an analgesic to relieve pain and bring down fever. Your doctor will examine your child's eardrum and if it is inflamed may prescribe antibiotics. Intramuscular injections of antibiotics are occasionally necessary if the child's condition is severe. Decongestant antihistamine mixtures do not relieve the symptoms associated with acute otitis media. The pain usually ceases swiftly once treatment is given.

If pus builds up behind the eardrum, a small cut may be made in it to allow the pus to drain. This cut will heal naturally.

MASTOIDITIS
Mastoiditis is a complication, now rare, of acute otitis media. If infection spreads into the mastoid bone behind the ear, the child becomes obviously ill and has a fever. The area behind the ear will be extremely tender. There may also be discharge from the ear. This condition requires urgent medical treatment and possibly surgery.

Mastoid bone position

GLUE EAR

If the Eustachian tube becomes blocked, fluid accumulates in the middle ear behind the eardrum. The fluid is usually thick and sticky, hence the name glue ear. Enlarged adenoids may block the Eustachian tube or this may occur as a child recovers from *acute otitis media* in association with an upper respiratory infection such as a cold, or with nasal congestion caused by *allergy*.

Glue ear may persist for weeks or years. It prevents the eardrum and middle-ear bones from vibrating freely and thus may cause temporary deafness.

SYMPTOMS
The condition is usually detected because it causes hearing problems, discomfort or a 'stuffy feeling' in the ear. Earache is not usually a symptom. Glue ear is most common in children between 4 and 7 years old.

If your child has problems with hearing you may notice this at home, or it may be commented on at his playgroup or at school. If he has problems with schooling you should consider possible hearing difficulty.

TREATMENT
Glue ear is easily diagnosed by a doctor examining the ear. Treatment depends on the level of hearing loss and the stage the child has reached in speech and social development. Many children appear to recover spontaneously after a period of months or years. A short-term remedy is pinching the

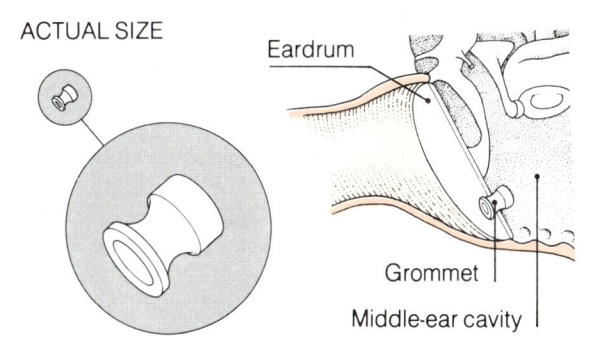

ACTUAL SIZE

Eardrum

Grommet

Middle-ear cavity

The grommet equalizes air pressure on either side of the eardrum and allows the middle ear to dry out. Until the grommet falls out naturally after 6 to 12 months your child may have to wear earplugs when swimming or bathing.

HEARING TESTS

When the screening tests carried out at routine *developmental checks* reveal a problem, more sophisticated tests are required. You will usually be referred to an ear, nose and throat specialist and audiologist.

AUDIOMETRY
Audiometry is usually only used after the age of 4 years, although it can be successful with younger children. An audiometer is an electronic instrument with headphones that delivers a single note at varying frequencies to each ear separately. Testing is conducted in a quiet room. The child is asked to place a brick in a box when he hears the tone. The audiometer records the frequencies that the child can hear and at what volumes, thus giving a complete hearing profile. The characteristics of the profile indicate which ear condition is causing the problem and which treatment might be suitable.

TYMPANOMETRY
A more sophisticated test for assessing middle-ear problems is tympanometry. Although the child may experience some discomfort, it is not a painful procedure. A tube within an earplug attached to a measuring instrument is put into the child's ear canal. A single note at a fixed frequency is delivered through the tube, and the pressure inside the canal is then varied by another attachment in the tube. Pressure changes alter the shape and stiffness of the eardrum, and yet another attachment in the tube

A child needs gentle encouragement at first to persuade him to put on the headphones necessary during audiometry tests.

Although some children dislike feeling the probe pushed into their ear, tympanometry can be carried out even on young children providing they sit reasonably still on a parent's knee.

nose and blowing out the cheeks which inflates the middle ear and temporarily improves hearing. Your doctor may prescribe antibiotics, especially in cases where glue ear develops after *acute otitis media*. If your child has a proven allergy or a history of *hay fever*, then your doctor may prescribe an antihistamine preparation in an attempt to reduce congestion in the middle ear and Eustachian tube. This is usually given by mouth. Remember that the antihistamine can make the child drowsy, while the decongestant may make him irritable. Decongestants can also be given in the form of nose drops but for no longer than 5 or 6 days because prolonged use may harm the lining of the nose. If you find your child dislikes nose drops and the distress caused is not worthwhile, stop giving them.

If the problem persists or recurs, your doctor will probably consider sending your child to an ear, nose and throat specialist. The specialist will test your child's hearing. He may advise an operation called myringotomy, in which a small incision is made in the eardrum and the fluid behind is sucked out. A grommet – a tiny silicone tube – is then inserted in the opening in the drum.

If adenoids are thought to have contributed to the glue ear, they are removed; tonsils are rarely removed as part of the treatment.

records the reflection of sound from the drum's surface. The reflections are recorded for various sound frequencies over a range of air pressures. This gives a profile of the response of the eardrum.

HEARING AIDS

A deaf child should be fitted with a hearing aid as soon as possible to avoid speech and learning difficulties.

The two main types of hearing aid used for young children are the body-worn aid, which is harnessed to the child's chest, and the post-aural aid, which is secured behind the ear. Both are connected to an earphone which fits tightly in the child's ear.

Although an older child may prefer a post-aural aid, because it is less obtrusive, for most young children a body-worn aid is more robust, and it also produces greater sound amplification than does a post-aural aid. So it is likely to be the first choice for children still at the stage where language is developing, as well as those whose deafness is severe. If speech is to develop normally a child must hear his own voice.

Your doctor will try to set your child's hearing aid at the lowest level at which he can easily hear conversation without giving a higher level of amplification than is necessary. If amplification is too high this may do further damage to hearing. Watch your child's reaction when he is wearing the aid and tell your doctor if you believe it is set too high or too low.

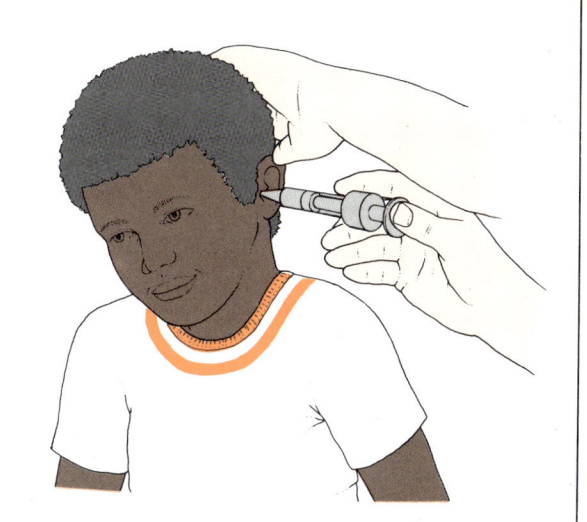

The earphone which receives sound must fit tightly into the child's ear. It will be made individually to fit him by taking an impression of his ear (above). The earphone is connected by a short plastic tube to the post-aural aid. This contains battery, microphone and amplifier in a light plastic case.

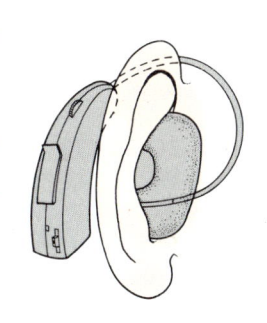

DEAFNESS

Deafness is a symptom, not a disorder. It can be partial or total, temporary or permanent, and it can be present at birth or it can develop later. It is a symptom of many ear diseases and hearing usually improves when the underlying problem is treated.

There are two major types of deafness. The first, conductive deafness, is the condition in which a mechanical fault prevents transmission of sound vibrations in the middle ear. Infections, excess ear wax and several other disorders can cause this type of hearing loss by restricting or immobilizing the eardrum or tiny middle-ear bones. The second type of deafness is perceptive. The fault may be in the cochlea in the inner ear, in the auditory nerve leading to the brain or in the brain itself. In general, perceptive deafness is more difficult to treat than conductive deafness.

About 1 baby in 10,000 is born deaf. Special attention is given to the hearing of babies born to mothers who had German measles during the first 3 or 4 months of pregnancy or who took certain drugs during pregnancy.

Deafness at any stage of life has enormous implications, but never more so than during the first few years when a child is learning to talk and listen. A child with poor or absent hearing is unable to listen to the speech of others – or to himself. The earlier hearing problems are detected, the sooner treatment can be started and the better the prospects. For this reason, if you suspect that your child is deaf or hard of hearing you should not hesitate to inform your doctor.

Conductive deafness is more common among younger children and, even without treatment, many conductive problems clear up by themselves. Many others are caused by mechanical problems which can often be completely cured by medical or surgical treatment so that the child can develop unhindered by the handicap.

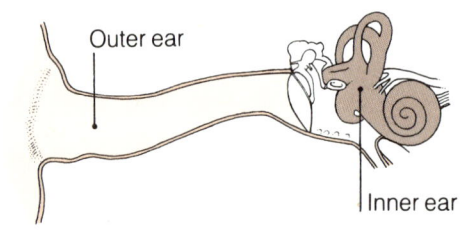

In conductive deafness a mechanical defect, usually in the middle ear, prevents the efficient conduction of sound from the outer ear to the inner ear.

WHEN TO SUSPECT DEAFNESS

Some deaf children are picked out by the developmental screening tests carried out on babies, toddlers and school-entry children. A substantial number are also detected because of parents' suspicions. Doctors work on the assumption that if you think your child has a hearing problem, this is the case until proved otherwise.

The deaf or hard-of-hearing child becomes amazingly adept at coping with, and therefore concealing, the problem. Using visual clues such as lip movements, gestures, facial expressions and directional glances, the child may appear perfectly normal until delayed speech development or *learning difficulties* arouse doubts.

You should be aware of the signs and clues that suggest hearing problems. For example:

o your child does not turn to someone speaking outside his field of vision
o he does not respond as expected to toys that make a noise
o he does not respond to significant sounds such as rustling sweet papers, the doorbell or the telephone
o he turns up the volume on the television or radio
o he ignores information shouted through from another room
o he tries to see your face when you speak, and keeps a close watch on your lips rather than making eye contact
o he seems unimpressed by unusual sounds such as sirens, aircraft or animal sounds
o he sometimes seems deliberately to ignore you, or responds only when you raise your voice, whether your tone is severe or not

COPING WITH DEAFNESS

Much can be done to help the child with longer-term or permanent deafness. Parents can help by becoming involved in specialized training such as lip-reading and sign language. It is important to speak clearly to your child, to avoid chewing or smoking as you speak and to make sure that he can see your face full on. Talk as much as you can to compensate for the isolation some deaf children feel. As your child grows older, explain the reactions of other people, and show your child how to persuade other people to help by speaking clearly.

Regular visits to the doctor may be advised, to monitor any change in the condition and to receive advice about new forms of treatment and new models of hearing aid. Many hard-of-hearing children attend ordinary schools and cope well with their education. Totally deaf children usually attend special schools with special teachers and equipment.

▶See also Early growth and development; Longstanding problems; Appendix: Support groups and publications

THE MOUTH, NOSE AND THROAT

Nature intended the nose for breathing and the mouth for eating and drinking, and each is well equipped for its function. The nasal lining's rich blood supply warms incoming air, and its mucus-producing glands humidify the air and trap airborne particles such as dust. The nasal hairs help to filter the air, while specialized nerve endings in the roof of the nasal cavity detect odours and provide us with our sense of smell.

The nasal passages continue backwards into the nasopharynx, above and behind the mouth. A raised ring of tissue, the adenoids, lies to the rear of the nasopharynx. This is small when children are young; it reaches a peak size when they are about 5 years old, and then gradually shrinks to disappear by puberty. Adenoids are composed mainly of lymph tissue and help to protect the body against infections.

The mouth has a tough, elastic lining. The tongue, cheeks and lips are muscular and help to move and compress food as the teeth chop and chew. At the back of the mouth, the digestive and respiratory passages come together to form the throat. The tonsils are on either side. Like adenoids, they are mainly composed of lymph tissue. Further down the throat the air and food passages separate again: the voice box (larynx) and windpipe (trachea) lead to the lungs, while the gullet (oesophagus) connects with the stomach.

In addition to all the other interconnected passages, air-filled sinus cavities branch from the nasal passages into the bones of the skull.

Teach your child to blow her nose by blocking first one nostril and then the other, so that she blows down one nostril at a time. Blowing down both nostrils at once may force mucus into the Eustachian tubes.

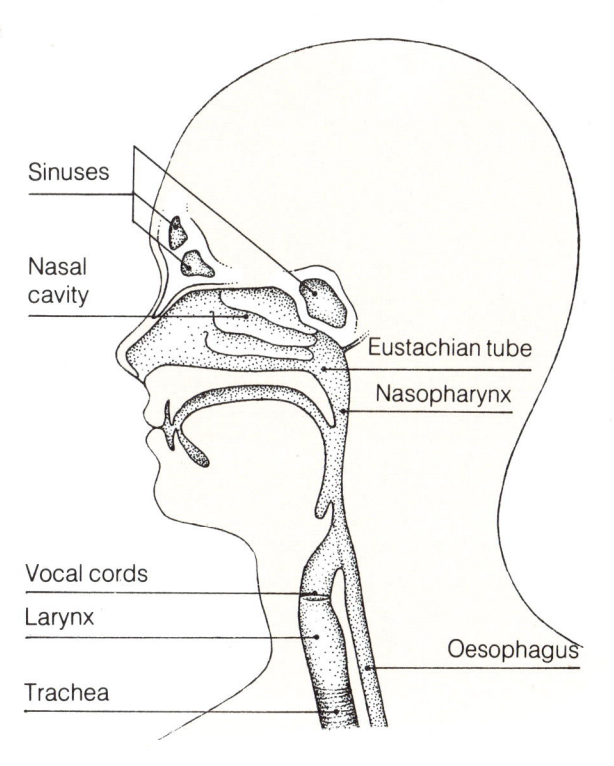

Sniffing and blowing
A child who sniffs usually has a cold. However, some children adopt sniffing as a habit. Occasionally there is an underlying problem such as enlarged adenoids, but usually the remedy is to teach your child to blow his nose correctly.

▶ **See also** Infection; The ears

COMMON PROBLEMS

The nose, sinuses, mouth, throat and ears form an interlinked system of air passages along which infection can easily spread. Children frequently and regularly suffer from such infections. Fortunately these are usually minor, such as *colds*. As their causes are not always known they are often referred to in general terms, as 'upper respiratory tract infections'.

Other problems common among children include mouth-breathing, catarrh, nosebleeds and mouth ulcers.

Mouth-breathing is particularly common when children are 4 to 5 years old. At this age both adenoids and tonsils reach their greatest size. If a child has *enlarged adenoids*, these may block his nose, forcing him to breathe through his mouth. Snoring is often associated with mouth-breathing and so is a night-time cough. Coughing is often the result of mucus accumulating in a child's throat, or of post-nasal drip, a drip from the back of the nose into the throat. Other causes of mouth-breathing are structural abnormalities of the nose, such as a *crooked septum*, or allergic conditions such as *hay fever*.

Catarrh is a word used to describe many problems including nasal congestion, a runny nose, a dirty nose, a cough due to the accumulation of mucus in the throat or any combination of these.

A child may have a clear, runny discharge from his nose as well as nasal congestion when he has a cold or hay fever.

A discharge which is yellow or green usually means there is a bacterial infection of the nose or sinuses, or both. This is often associated with infection of the adenoids. If a child, particularly a young child, has a discharge from only one side of his nose, he may have a small object stuck in his nostril. In this case the discharge may also have a peculiar smell – rather like the smell of blue cheese. You should consult your doctor.

Nosebleeds are hardly ever serious though they may look dramatic and be very upsetting for a child. The lining of the nose is thin and can be easily damaged. Its rich blood supply means that it can bleed profusely under the strain of a blow to the nose, or even of blowing the nose. If your child has persistent or recurring nosebleeds, consult your doctor. An operation may be necessary to cauterize the nasal lining in order to stop the bleeding.

An occasional nosebleed is easily treated by pinching the nostrils together for a few minutes.

Mouth ulcers are sometimes caused by a *herpes simplex* infection; aphthous ulcers are another common type. They occur mainly when children are aged 10 years and over. They are small painful patches with white or yellow centres and reddened edges, usually appearing on the lips, the insides of the cheeks and the edges of the tongue. They may persist for any time from a few days up to 2 weeks. They are uncomfortable but they nearly always heal of their own accord. To speed healing your doctor may prescribe either small steroid pellets for your child to hold against the ulcer, or a steroid-containing cream.

THRUSH

Thrush, also called moniliasis or candidiasis, is a fungal infection. Babies commonly have thrush infections in their mouths. Occasionally a child who is taking antibiotics develops thrush. The drug kills off the bacteria normally resident in the mouth – bacteria which keeps the fungus, also normally present, in check. If you suspect thrush, consult the doctor for an accurate diagnosis and advice on treatment. He will probably describe a mouthwash. Older children may be given lozenges to suck.

HALITOSIS

By far the most common cause of halitosis, or bad breath, is *tooth decay*: its remedy is simply to take your child to the dentist and to improve his oral hygiene. A second, often overlooked, cause is eating highly spiced or otherwise aromatic foods, such as garlic. During certain illnesses, for instance *tonsillitis*, a child's breath may be unpleasant but this should clear up after the illness. A few drugs tinge the breath with an odd odour; check with your doctor if you suspect this is the case. Do not be tempted to disguise bad breath with a mouthwash: there is nearly always an underlying cause that needs treatment.

COLDS

The common cold, or coryza, is a viral infection of the nose and throat causing nasal congestion, a runny nose, a mild sore throat and a feeling of general malaise. Most children get colds frequently, especially in the early school years. A child has about seven colds a year on average, and more if he or one of his siblings changes school. As children grow older they acquire more immunity. Babies' cold infections tend to spread to their ears or chest; older children's sinuses may be affected.

An uncomplicated cold lasts about a week and is best treated at home with plenty of fluids and simple analgesics such as aspirin, if necessary. Occasionally, when nasal congestion is severe, it is worth giving decongestant nose drops. However, you should not use decongestant drops for more than 5 to 6 days, since they can cause a rebound reaction and make the nose runnier than before.

A baby who catches cold may not be able to suck and feed properly. Try cleaning his nostrils with moist cotton-buds before feeding. If this does not help, your doctor may prescribe nose drops containing ethedrine; do not use these for more than 3 or 4 days. Applying a decongestant rub to the baby's chest or sprinkling the contents of a decongestant capsule on the cot sheet may also give some temporary relief.

HOARSENESS
A child may develop short periods of hoarseness when he has an ordinary cold. If they go on for a long time you should seek advice from your doctor. Singer's nodes – minute swellings on the vocal cords – are the commonest cause of hoarseness. They are usually due to over-use or abuse of the voice and need no treatment, other than trying to encourage the child not to shout so much. Another, much rarer cause is the presence in the larynx of papillomata. These are very small, benign, warty growths that may require surgical removal.

SORE THROATS AND TONSILLITIS

Sore throats vary a great deal depending on which part of the throat is affected, how badly, and whether the infection is bacterial or viral.

Mild sore throats usually last for only a few days and disappear without treatment. The majority of them are caused by viral infections, in which case antibiotics do not help. Your child will probably only appear a little miserable and may complain of a little soreness in his throat; a young child may complain that it is his mouth that hurts rather than his throat. The main treatment is to keep your child warm and rested, and to give him plenty of fluids and possibly an occasional analgesic such as paracetamol.

A child with bad tonsillitis is usually extremely unwell and wants to rest. He has a high temperature, sore throat, difficulty in swallowing and enlarged neck glands. His tonsils will be reddened and enlarged, often with a covering of pus. You should consult your doctor. The symptoms last for 3 or 4 days, although it may be a week or so before your child is back to normal.

Children usually have tonsillitis in their early school years although it can occur at any age. Many children have only 1 or 2 attacks but some have many more at frequent intervals. If your child suffers from frequent bouts of tonsillitis your doctor may want a specialist's opinion.

If a child has 3 or 4 bad attacks of tonsillitis each year for 2 years or more, most doctors would advise a tonsillectomy, an operation to remove the tonsils. If necessary the child's adenoids can be removed at the same time. A child usually remains in hospital for about 48 hours after the operation. Paracetamol helps to ease the pain.

When your child is allowed home, keep him indoors for the first few days and try to keep him away from other children for about 2 weeks so that he is less likely to catch infections while his throat is healing. He can eat normally and should have plenty to drink. If your child's throat starts to bleed or if you are worried about his condition, you should consult your doctor.

ENLARGED ADENOIDS
Enlarged adenoids usually shrink of their own accord. Removal of the adenoids by surgery (adenoidectomy) is, like tonsillectomy, performed much less frequently now than it was in the past. Your doctor is likely to consider it only if the enlarged adenoids appear to be involved in:

o persistent *mouth-breathing*, snoring and other associated problems
o recurrent or persistent hearing loss, caused by a condition such as *glue ear*, which interferes with schooling
o repeated *sinusitis* or *sore throats* that cause the child to miss school

Adenoidectomy itself is safe and effective, usually resulting in relief of the problem within days of the operation.

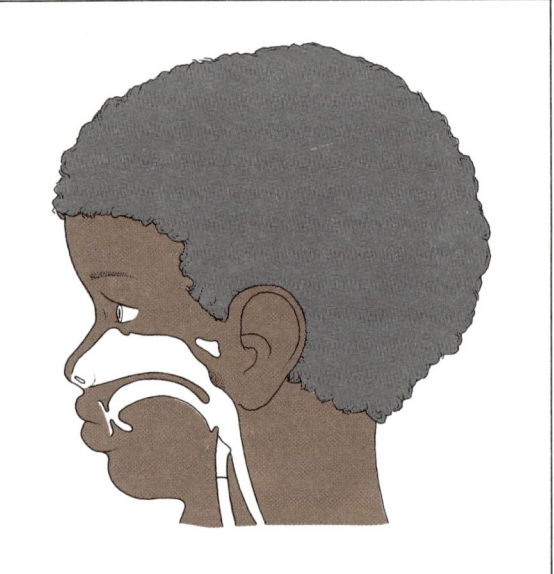

SINUSITIS

Sinusitis tends to follow a cold usually as a result of infection spreading from the nasal lining. The linings of the sinuses become inflamed and clogged with mucus. The main symptom is ache or pain over the affected sinus. It may be in the cheek region or the forehead. It tends to sharpen when the child bends forward or lies down; he may also have a fever, a green or yellow nasal discharge, watering eyes, and general tenderness over the affected area.

Mild sinusitis is very common and clears of its own accord in 2 to 3 days. Severe sinus infection in childhood is uncommon and your family doctor may advise decongestant medicines and prescribe antibiotics. The time-honoured remedy of steam inhalation often loosens mucus and allows the sinuses to drain more freely. Be very careful that a child who is inhaling does not scald himself with hot water. Your doctor may advise a minor operation to wash out your child's sinuses.

Sinusitis is uncommon before 3 or 4 years of age because the sinuses most often affected do not develop until then.

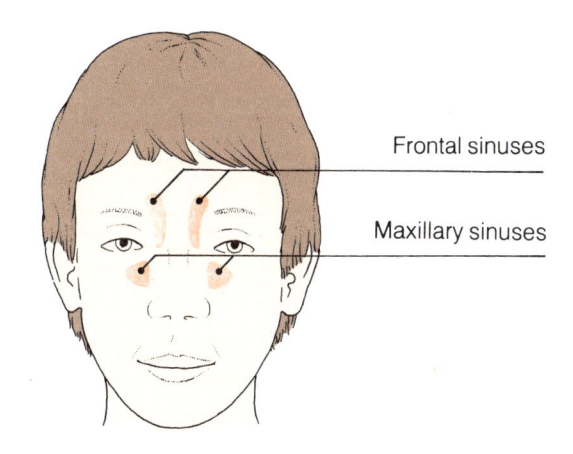

The maxillary and frontal sinuses are most easily infected because they connect directly with the nasal passages. If the maxillary sinuses become infected the child's face will hurt and he may feel as if he has toothache in his upper jaw. The pain may be increased when his teeth are tapped. Infection of the frontal sinuses causes pain in the forehead.

CROOKED SEPTUM

Occasionally a blocked nose in a child may be due to a structural abnormality within the child's nose. Most commonly this is when the septum, the cartilaginous wall between the nostrils, is not in its normal midline position. Most children with this condition manage without treatment, and in early adult life, when the nose has stopped growing, the need for surgery can be assessed. If, however, a crooked septum causes your child to have breathing problems or repeated attacks of *sinusitis*, your doctor may advise an operation to straighten it sooner.

Even if a child has a crooked septum her nose will not necessarily look crooked.

HAY FEVER

Hay fever is the most common form of *allergy* affecting the nose. It is caused by an allergic response of the tissues of the nose and eyes triggered by certain kinds of airborne pollen. The symptoms appear in spring and summer, especially in dry windy weather when the pollen count is high. There are other forms which occur all year round, and cause a constantly running nose. Sufferers may be allergic to one or more of a variety of things, including house dust and house dust mites, family pets and houseplants.

If your child has hay fever his nose and eye tissues will swell; the lining of his nose will produce excess mucus and his eyes will itch and become red, painful and watery. Rubbing the eyes will make them worse. He will sniff and sneeze and wheeze.

To avoid the symptoms your child should, as far as possible, steer clear of long grass and should sleep with the windows closed. Your doctor may prescribe antihistamines or a nasal spray containing steroids if the symptoms are bad or if your child is taking examinations.

DISTRESSED BREATHING AND STRIDOR

Extreme difficulty in breathing may be accompanied by a crowing noise on breathing in called stridor. Stridor has various causes: *croup*, *laryngomalacia* and *epiglottitis* are the most usual ones. Stridor can also occur if the child is choking on an inhaled foreign body. Severe breathing problems require urgent action and admission to hospital.

Croup is a barking cough. The term is also used to describe viral infections of the voice box. These are most common in children between the ages of 6 months and 4 years. The infection leads to swelling of the tissues lining the larynx, trachea and bronchi.

Initially the child has a slight cold and is mildy ill, but suddenly wakes in the night with stridor and distressed breathing. Try to be as calm and reassuring as possible. Creating a moist atmosphere for the child is the traditional remedy.

If the croup does not settle quickly, if your child's lower ribs are drawn in with each breath, or if his skin looks blue, then you should call an ambulance immediately. Very few children admitted to hospital with croup are likely to need anything other than close observation. However, a few develop increasingly severe symptoms, becoming drowsy and agitated, and may need their breathing difficulty relieved by a tube passed through the mouth into the windpipe.

Epiglottitis is an uncommon but potentially life-threatening infection. A child who was perfectly well rapidly becomes ill, suffering from severe stridor as the tissues of the epiglottis, a cartilage above the voice box, swell as a result of bacterial infection. If this happens you should call an ambulance at once. A doctor will confirm the diagnosis and your child will be will be admitted to *intensive care*, given antibiotics, and a breathing tube will usually be inserted into his windpipe until the danger period has passed.

Laryngomalacia, a congenital malformation of the larynx, may cause stridor in newborn and very young children. In this condition the larynx is very floppy and collapses when the child breathes in. Infants with laryngomalacia almost always recover by the age of 12 to 18 months and rarely need treatment, although if a cold develops the child may need to be admitted to hospital for observation.

▶ **See also** Appendix: Emergency actions

THE LUNGS

The lungs are two sponge-like structures which, together with the heart and main blood vessels, fill the chest cavity. Each lung is made up of smaller segments, or lobes; the right lung has three lobes and the left has two. The left lung is slightly smaller due to the position of the heart in the chest cavity.

The cells of the body need a continuous supply of oxygen. Oxygen is taken in through the lungs. The lungs are made up of very small cavities, or alveoli, lined with a thin membrane across which oxygen in the air can diffuse into a fine network of blood vessels. The oxygen is then transported around the body in the blood. At the same time carbon dioxide, the waste gas of the body, moves in the opposite direction in the blood, across the membrane and from there into the air sacs from where it is breathed out.

At birth, the lungs contain approximately 20 million alveoli, and the number rises to about 300 million by the time a child is 8 years old. The fine tubes or bronchioli from the alveoli join together, rather like the tributaries of a river, to meet eventually in a single, relatively large tub, or bronchus, which leads from each lung into the trachea, or windpipe.

Breathing

The alveoli act as reservoirs of air. If the transport of oxygen and carbon dioxide in and out of the blood is to continue for more than a few minutes, this air must be renewed by breathing. The diaphragm and chest wall muscles draw air into the lungs by increasing the size of the chest cavity. With this drawing in of air, the elastic tissues of the lungs are stretched and thus, when the diaphragm and chest wall muscles relax, air is forced out.

The rate and depth of breathing is carefully controlled by nerve endings in the blood vessels and brain which measure the levels of carbon dioxide and oxygen. If you need more oxygen, during exercise for example, or if the efficiency of the lungs is reduced by illness, the respiratory centre in the brain stimulates an increase in the rate and depth of breathing.

▶ See also Infection

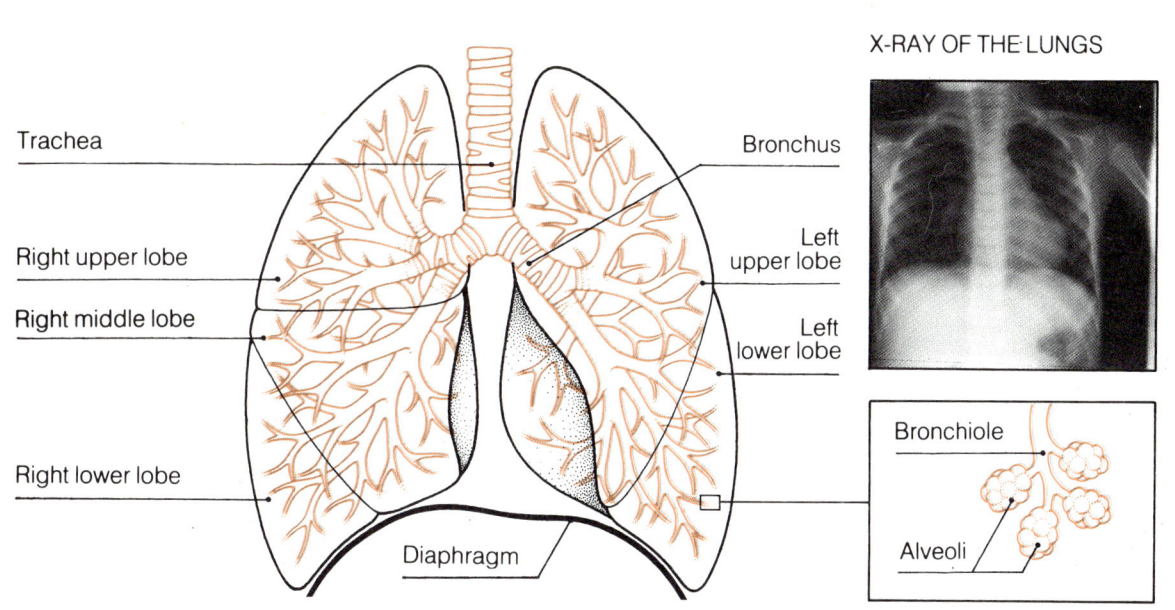

X-RAY OF THE LUNGS

COMMON PROBLEMS

Coughing is a defence response to irritation of the lungs. The thin, delicate membrane lining the alveoli is easily damaged by breathed-in dust, infectious organisms or irritant chemicals. They need and have a great deal of protection. The nose is lined with fine hairs which filter out many contaminants. The larger airways are also lined with millions of fine hair-like structures which help to waft irritants and mucus up out of the lungs. Mucus produced by cells lining the airways also helps keep them in good condition. Despite these mechanisms, dust, foreign organisms and irritant gases sometimes penetrate into the lungs, stimulating the cough. This reflex is also stimulated in order to clear accumulated secretions if the airways become infected.

Repeated coughing indicates an irritation of the airways caused by infection, for example *bronchitis*, *bronchiolitis* or *pneumonia*; or by a tightening of the muscles in the airways, as in *asthma*. It can also be caused by a small object, such as a peanut or a small toy, lying caught within the airways.

Chest pain is an occasional problem for children and can have a number of causes. Influenza-like illnesses often produce aches and pains in the muscles around the chest. These pass in a few days. Repeated coughing can itself temporarily damage muscle fibres, producing localized pain and often tenderness, which will wear off once the coughing has stopped. More obvious causes include physical damage to the muscles and ribs as a result of injury. If your child complains of pain following an accident he should see the doctor. Very rarely, pain in the chest on breathing and coughing is the result of the rupture or infection of a lung.

Wheezing, a whistling or semi-musical note, occurs when air rushes past a narrowing of part of an airway. By far the most common cause of wheezing is a tightening of the ring of muscles surrounding the airways, as in asthma. It can also be caused by an object lying within the airways or, rarely, by something pressing on the outside of the airway.

Your child may have to blow into a peak-flow meter to test lung efficiency. There are meters you can use at home.

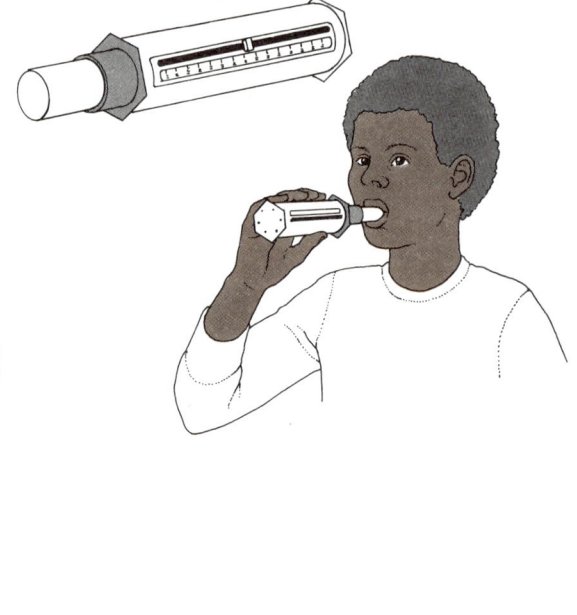

ASTHMA

In normal health the muscles surrounding the airways will tighten in response to a stimulus such as inhalation of cold air. In asthma this tendency is increased and is accompanied by swelling of the cells lining the airways and by the release of mucus.

Asthma is the most common long-term childhood disease. Between 15 and 20 per cent of all children are affected by asthma at some time. Every year 1 child in 10 has at least one attack of coughing and wheezing due to asthma. For the large majority the symptoms are relatively mild and settle with little, if any, treatment. Only about 1 child in 200 has chronic symptoms that are severe enough to interfere with his activities. However, a number have sufficient problems to prevent them from going to school or to stop them taking part in games from time to time. Most asthmatic children improve or appear to grow out of their asthma during adolescence, but for a few of them it returns in adult life.

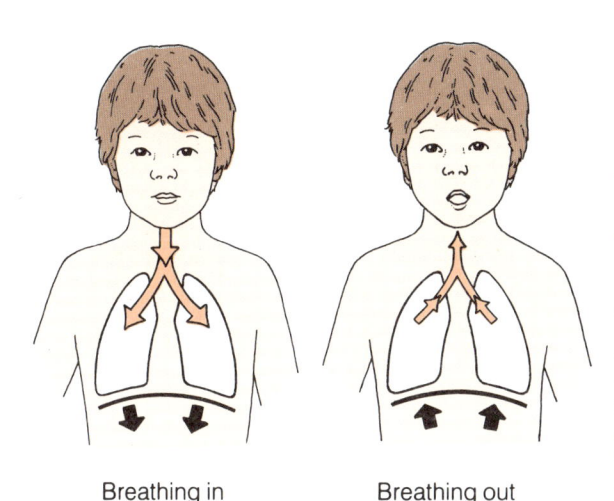

Breathing in   Breathing out

The child who has asthma finds breathing out during an attack more difficult than breathing in. Your child may find that if he sits with his arms resting on a table or the back of a chair his rib cage will be lifted and his chest muscles will be able to force air out more easily.

In a susceptible child, attacks of asthma may be brought on by viral infections including colds and sore throats, or by inhalation of pollens, animal furs and moulds to which the child is allergic, or by changes in weather conditions. Running about and breathing deeply in relatively cold dry air also tends to bring on asthma attacks, although in this case they usually settle within 10 to 15 minutes. Finally, asthma symptoms are more likely to be troublesome at times of stress.

SYMPTOMS

The pattern of illness varies from child to child. Some may cough, particularly at night or when running around, and this may be the only symptom. This represents the mild end of the spectrum. Most will have a tendency to wheeze and become breathless from time to time, particularly when they have colds. Some, but not all, will also have had *eczema, hay fever* symptoms and allergic skin rashes. Severe attacks of asthma may be accompanied by sweating, anxiety and a raised pulse. In very severe attacks, increasing breathlessness may turn the child's lips blue and his skin pale and clammy.

TREATMENT

Most children with asthma can be helped dramatically by taking bronchodilators – medicines that act directly on the smooth muscle around the airways, causing it to relax. Taken as tablets they give some relief within 20 to 30 minutes, but they are more effective and act within 2 to 3 minutes if inhaled as a mist from a nebulizer, as a powder, or, if your child is old enough, as a spray from an aerosol. Taken before strenuous games, they will also prevent wheezing and coughing developing and thus allow your child to take part in normal activities. If symptoms are particularly troublesome in the early hours of the morning, slow-release preparations of these drugs are available to help control the asthma throughout the night.

If bronchodilators do not control the symptoms, your doctor may prescribe Intal, another drug inhaled as a powder and taken regularly 3 or 4 times a day. It has a calming effect on the lungs, reducing the tendency to wheeze and cough, and acts only on the lungs with no unpleasant side effects.

If none of these drugs proves effective, your child may be given steroids to be inhaled, either as a powder or spray, 2 to 4 times a day. These reduce the irritability of the airways but may lead to *thrush* in the mouth. If your child is very badly affected, a 3- to 7-day course of steroid tablets may be prescribed, and should prove effective within 1 to 2 days. However, oral steroids have unwanted side-effects, particularly if taken continuously.

Desensitizing injections are usually disappointing but may help some children. *Acupuncture*, hypnosis, *homeopathy*, humidifiers and ionizers are of scientifically unproven value in asthma treatment.

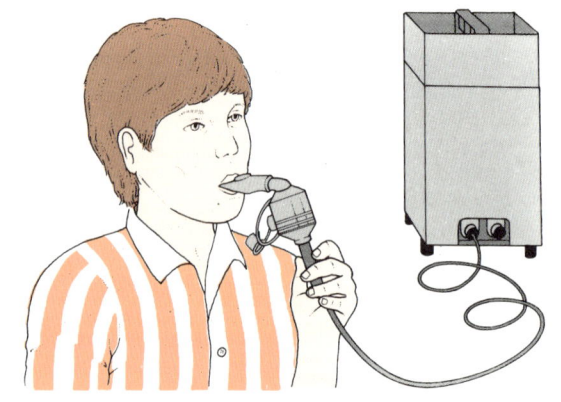

Bronchodilators can be inhaled as fine droplets produced by compressed air in a nebulizer.

▶ **See also** Longstanding problems; Allergy; Appendix: Drugs and treatments

ACUTE BRONCHITIS

Bronchitis is a common infection, mainly due to a virus affecting the larger airways. Your child may feel reasonably well, but may have a slight temperature and runny nose. The troublesome symptom is a frequent and often rattly cough, which tends to be worse at night, often waking the rest of the family. The symptoms generally settle within a few days. A cough suppressant, such as linctus codeine, may help your child to sleep better. If your child is having frequent and troublesome episodes of coughing, perhaps accompanied by wheezing, it is likely that he has mild *asthma* and anti-asthma drugs will help.

ACUTE BRONCHIOLITIS

Acute bronchiolitis is a viral illness that reaches epidemic proportions at some point during every winter. Those most affected are under 1 year old. The baby usually has a runny nose for a day or two, followed by a troublesome cough, rapid breathing, difficulty with feeds and often bubbling secretions at the mouth. In severe cases, babies may appear to have a blue tinge, due to insufficient oxygen in the blood.

If your baby has difficulty feeding, is having problems with breathing or looks blue you should contact your doctor urgently. Your doctor will probably arrange for your baby to be admitted directly to hospital, where oxygen can be given, and fluids, which are so important, can be given either through a fine stomach tube or *intravenous drip* if required. No drugs have been shown to alter the course of this illness, but most children are much better within 3 to 10 days and are able to return home. About 60 per cent of children who suffer in this way have sporadic *asthma* attacks during the following 2 to 3 years.

PNEUMONIA

Pneumonia may affect children at any age, although it is most common in the first year of life. It is a result of a bacterial or viral infection affecting the alveoli, with the result that part of the lung structure is blocked up with infected secretions and is therefore solid and airless.

SYMPTOMS

The first symptoms may be a runny nose or a high temperature and fast breathing. Your child will feel ill, have no interest in anything and may well look flushed. If the pneumonia is very extensive, his skin may appear grey and sweaty and he may make little grunting noises on breathing. He may or may not have a cough. If the pneumonia affects the outer surface of the lung, the infection may reach the pleural membranes that surround the lungs and line the ribcage, and each breath will therefore be painful.

TREATMENT

Children with relatively mild pneumonia can often be treated at home with antibiotics taken as tablets or syrups. Those more severely affected will need to be admitted to hospital for treatment. In hospital, antibiotics will be given by injection, intravenously or into the muscle and physiotherapy will be given to help clear the infected parts of the lungs. The child is usually much better within 2 to 3 days. Pneumonia does not recur.

If your child has more than one attack of pneumonia in a relatively short period of time, it may be because he has inhaled a nut or small toy. This causes an infection and produces pneumonia, which will clear after treatment with antibiotics but then recur. If an inhaled foreign body is suspected, it will probably be necessary to pass a tube down the airways, while the child is under anaesthetic, so that the object can be located and removed.

Some children, particularly babies and toddlers, regurgitate their feeds. Very occasionally the food at the back of the throat may spill over into the airways and, when inhaled, produce irritation and infection. This can happen to anyone but is particularly a problem for brain-damaged children who have difficulty co-ordinating swallowing and breathing. Very, very occasionally a child is born with a small tube connecting the gullet, or oesophagus, to the main airway, the trachea. In this case, food swallowed normally may trickle over into the trachea and cause choking. The condition is usually diagnosed with the help of X-rays.

BRONCHIECTASIS

This is a relatively rare condition in which some of the airways have been damaged and distorted, usually as a result of previous severe *pneumonia*, an inhaled foreign body, an underlying immune problem or, very occasionally, *measles*. As well as being distorted, the airways are often chronically inflamed and infected.

Your child may be fairly well in general but he will have a moist cough, often bringing up sputum (phlegm), particularly first thing in the morning. Occasionally the sputum will be blood-stained. You should take your child to the doctor, who will first try to discover whether there is an underlying cause, such as a foreign body, an immune disorder or even *cystic fibrosis*. Some cases of bronchiectasis are caused by a defect in the hair-like structures that line the airways.

To treat the bronchiectasis, your child will have to take antibiotics, probably for months at a time. The other and probably more important treatment is regular physiotherapy. You should also see that your child leads as active a life as possible: exercise will produce coughing, which helps to keep the lungs clear. He should avoid smokey atmospheres.

Provided there is no serious underlying problem, the condition tends to improve considerably as a child grows towards adolescence.

A physiotherapist will show you how to pummel your child's chest gently while she sits or lies in a position that helps to drain the affected areas of the lung most effectively. The child can then cough up the phlegm.

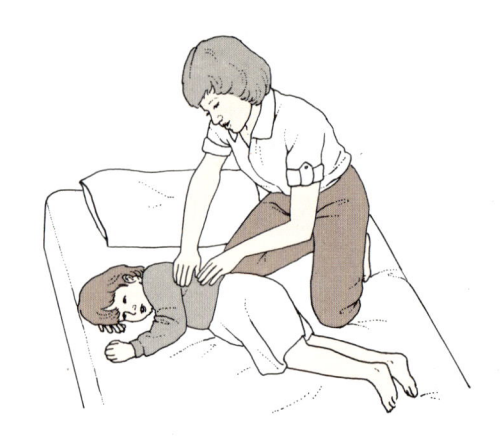

CYSTIC FIBROSIS

About 1 child in every 2,000 is affected by cystic fibrosis. It tends to run in families and a child's chances of being affected are far higher if others in the family have the disease. Until recently, few children with cystic fibrosis survived beyond their teens. Recently, with vigorous treatment, more children have been reaching adult life and in some instances survive until early middle age.

The primary problem in cystic fibrosis is that the mucus produced by the secretory glands is too thick. The three main areas most affected by this are the lungs, the digestive tract and the skin.

SYMPTOMS

A child with cystic fibrosis usually has chest symptoms within the first few months of life. The thick secretions of the glands in the airways cause infection with recurrent *pneumonia* and *bronchiectasis*. The child tends to have coughs, with chest infections at times. There may be characteristic changes in his fingertips, which swell to give 'clubbing'. He may also develop a barrel-shaped chest by the time he reaches his teens.

Thick secretions of the pancreas lead to pressure within it and its eventual destruction. Because the pancreas produces many of the enzymes necessary to break down food, the child will pass large, offensive stools containing massive quantities of protein and fat that have not been digested and absorbed. He will grow more slowly than normal and may have a distended abdomen.

Another symptom of cystic fibrosis is leakage of salt from the skin. In hot climates this is important as the salt loss may lead to a shock-like condition.

Other problems may arise. These include rectal prolapse, the protrusion of the rectal wall out through the anus due to the child's inability to digest food properly and the passage of large stools; gut obstructions particularly at birth; a mild form of *diabetes*, often developing in adolescence, due to the destruction of the pancreas; polyps in the nose; infertility, particularly in boys; and damage to the liver, which will be suspected if the child has *jaundice*.

TREATMENT

Cystic fibrosis cannot be cured although the symptoms can be alleviated. Chest problems are treated by antibiotics and physiotherapy twice or 3 times a day. The physiotherapy is very important and in order to help your child you will need repeated instructions from a skilled physiotherapist. Enzyme replacements, are usually given. They may be taken either as tablets immediately before a meal or, in the case of young children, as a powder scattered over their food. Your child will also need vitamin supplements.

THE HEART AND CIRCULATION

The heart lies behind the breastbone, roughly in the centre of the chest but extending to the left. It consists of two muscular pumps divided by a sheet of muscle called the septum. The pump on the right side of the heart sends blue de-oxygenated blood through the pulmonary artery to the lungs to pick up oxygen. Freshly oxygenated pink blood from the lungs returns to the left side of the heart and is pumped out from there to all parts of the body. The first part of this journey is through the aorta, the largest artery in the body which runs from the left side of the heart. It branches off into a network of blood vessels which carry the oxygenated blood to every cell in the body.

Each side of the heart consists of two compartments – the right atrium and the right ventricle, and the left atrium and left ventricle – linked by valves. Within the wall of the right atrium is a small, electrically active area called the sinus node, or pacemaker, where the beating of the heart originates. The sinus node discharges small pulses of electricity which spread over the surfaces of the right and left atria, and then pass down conducting fibres in the septum to spread out over the ventricles. These electrical impulses cause first the atria and then the ventricles to contract. When the heart muscle contracts, the internal volume of the compartment gets smaller so that blood is forced out. When the heart muscle relaxes, the internal volume increases in size, allowing blood to flow into the compartment.

Heart, or cardiac, muscle needs a lot of nutrients and oxygen in order to be able to function continuously. When the body is exercised or stressed, the heart responds by beating more quickly and forcefully, thus increasing its own needs. Like all other organs, the heart obtains its nutrients and oxygen from the blood. These do not come from the blood within the cavity of the heart, but from the coronary arteries, which branch off the aorta, run over the outside of the heart and penetrate the heart muscle.

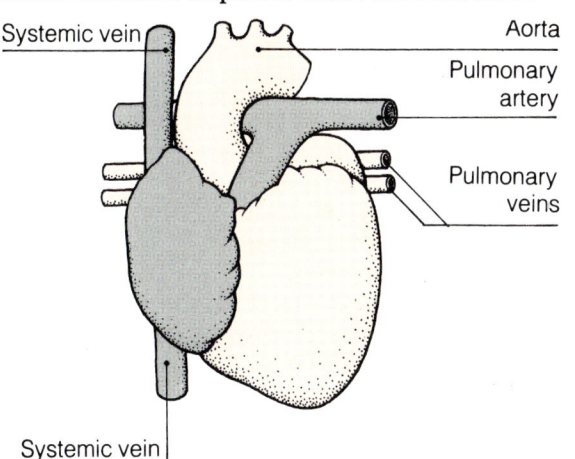

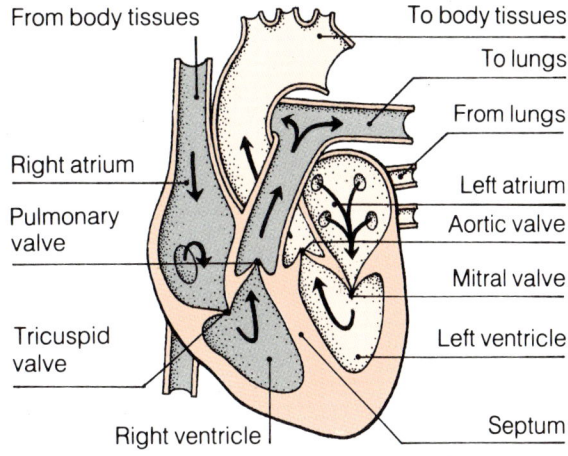

The pulse that you can feel in your wrist or temple is the wave of blood pumped along the arteries with each heartbeat. A normal pulse rate is about 130 beats per minute in a newborn baby, falling to about 70 beats per minute in an older child, although it can vary widely. The sounds that you can hear by placing your ear to someone's chest, and which are amplified by a stethoscope, are made by the closure of the heart valves. There are normally two of these sounds for each beat of the heart.

The arteries, which carry blood away from the heart, are tough, elastic-walled tubes built to withstand and absorb the surges of pressure with each heartbeat. Muscle tissue in the arterial wall can contract or relax to alter the bore of the artery, and in this way can control the distribution of blood to various parts of the body. Arteries divide, becoming smaller and smaller to form arterioles. These continue to divide until they become the smallest vessels, known as capillaries. Oxygen and nutrients from the blood diffuse through the thin-walled capillaries to be used by body cells, while carbon dioxide and wastes diffuse into the blood and are carried away.

The capillaries gradually join together and enlarge to become venules and then veins which finally join to form the 'great veins' or vena cava that return used blood to the right side of the heart. It is estimated that there are nearly 100,000 km (63,000 miles) of blood vessels in the body.

Heart murmurs

Heart murmurs are sounds made by the heart in addition to the normal sounds made by the closing of the valves. The majority of murmurs are 'innocent' and occur in normal hearts. *Significant murmurs* (which are the minority) mean that something is wrong with the heart.

Innocent murmurs are common in newborn babies as a result of changes in the circulation as the baby adjusts to life outside the uterus. They are also common in toddlers and young children. The heart is normal but the blood vibrates as it is expelled from the left ventricle into the aorta, making a noise that can easily be heard through a child's thin chest. At around the age of 5 years about 50 per cent of children have such innocent murmurs.

Heart rhythm

Abnormalities of the heart's rhythm, especially extra heartbeats, or ectopic beats, are also common in children. They are not a pointer towards heart disease and need no treatment. However, a rare condition called **supraventricular tachycardia** (SVT), which occurs in children with otherwise normal hearts, may need to be controlled by regular drug therapy. In this condition the child has bursts of a very fast heart rate (greater than 180 beats per minute); he will have palpitations, and will feel dizzy, breathless and weak. Like many conditions in childhood, SVT tends to improve with time.

Palpitations

These are feelings in the chest that make a child aware of his own heartbeat. They are normal after heavy exercise or a sudden fright, but can also occur when the child's heartbeat is abnormal. If the heartbeat is irregular, a child may be aware that his heart misses a beat or has extra beats. If your child has palpitations he should be examined by a doctor.

Breathlessness

Children who are excited and who have been exercising are naturally breathless. However, breathlessness can be a sign of a heart disorder or, more commonly, of a lung problem. A sustained breathing rate of 60 or more breaths a minute in a baby or 40 breaths a minute in a child is not normal. Nor is it normal to become breathless when walking, climbing a few stairs or running a short distance. If a baby continually pants for breath, even when asleep, and the panting becomes worse when he feeds or cries, then he may have a heart disorder. Babies with breathlessness often do not feed well and have to stop between mouthfuls to get their breath back.

Blueness

Poor circulation in the hands and feet, so that the extremities are bluish in appearance and feel cold to the touch, is very common when babies and children have become chilled. These temperature and colour changes are caused by sluggish circulation in the hands and the feet and are not a sign of an abnormal heart. Keeping your child's hands warm with gloves, and his feet warm with socks and boots will help to solve the problem.

▶See also The skin

INVESTIGATING HEART DISORDERS

If your doctor suspects that your child has a heart disorder, he will arrange for special tests to be carried out in hospital to find out exactly what the disorder is and how to treat it.

SIGNIFICANT MURMURS

Significant murmurs are caused by congenital abnormalities of the heart. They are usually due to blood flowing through holes in the septum or through valves that are narrowed. If there is the slightest doubt about whether a heart murmur is innocent or significant, arrangements will be made for a specialist to examine the child.

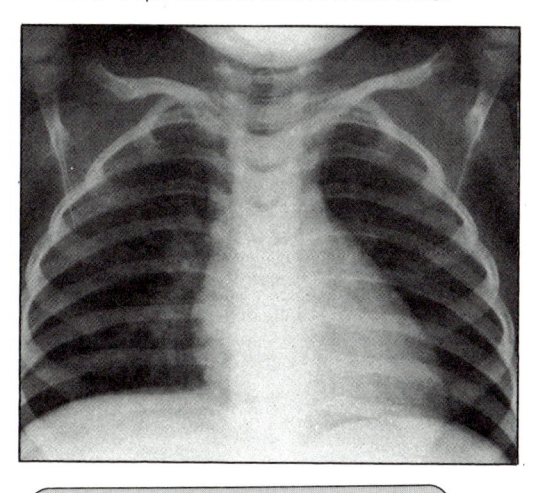

TESTS

o A chest X-ray gives the doctor a clear indication of the size and shape of the heart
o An electrocardiogram indicates the functioning of the heart
o An echocardiogram gives a picture of the heart produced by an *ultrasound* device that bounces sound waves off the heart and transforms them into an image on a screen
o Cardiac catheterization may be required before surgery. This investigation is carried out only in specialist heart centres and usually involves admission to hospital for a night or two. The child is given either a full general anaesthetic or sedation and a local anaesthetic. A small cut is made in the groin and a fine tube, or catheter is passed into a vein or an artery and up into the heart. It allows the doctor to measure the pressure in each heart chamber, to sample blood from the heart and so measure its oxygen content, and to introduce a special dye that shows up on X-ray

AN ELECTROCARDIOGRAM (ECG)

Electrocardiography is a way of monitoring the activity of the heart by making a recording, in graphic form, of the electrical impulses which initiate and control heartbeat. During the procedure, which is safe and painless, electrical leads ending in metal plates are placed on the child's wrists, ankles and chest to pick up and record the electrical changes. An electrocardiogram gives the doctor an indication of the relative sizes of the two halves of the heart and shows irregularities in its rhythm.

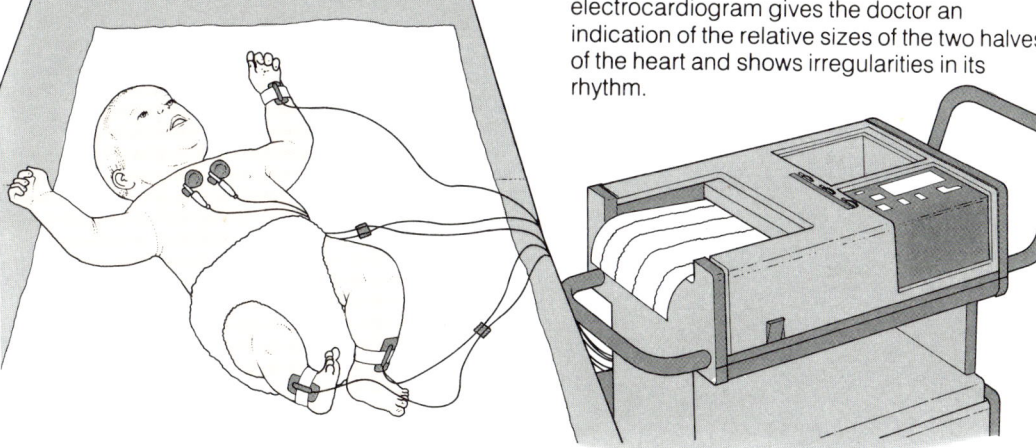

CONGENITAL HEART DISORDERS

Congenital heart disorders are a result of abnormal development of the heart while a baby is in the uterus, 3 to 8 weeks after conception. If something goes wrong early in this period, the disorder of the heart is likely to be severe. If it goes wrong towards the end of the period, the disorder is likely to be minor. About 8 babies in every 1,000 are born with a heart defect. There is no reliable test in pregnancy to detect such abnormalities, although with *ultrasound* scanning of the baby's heart before birth it is becoming possible. In most cases, the cause of the abnormality is unknown, although there may be a family history of similar heart problems. Occasionally abnormalities are caused by certain drugs, such as thalidomide, taken during pregnancy, or by an illness, such as *German measles*, that the mother has had while pregnant. However, most babies with congenital heart abnormalities are born to healthy parents who have no family history of heart abnormalities, and to mothers who have had no problems in pregnancy.

Congenital heart disorders vary widely in severity, and most affected children are healthy and active. Some children may need no treatment at all. For others, trouble from the abnormality may be anticipated in adult life, so the disorder is corrected by surgery during childhood. If possible the operation is delayed beyond infancy when the child will be better able to withstand surgery. A small number of babies have congenital heart disorders that are very severe and cannot be corrected by surgery. **Hypoplastic left heart syndrome**, for example, is a condition in which all the structures on the left side of the heart have failed to develop. Soon after birth the baby rapidly becomes blue and breathless. There is no surgical procedure to correct the abnormality, and the baby dies.

HEART SURGERY

Before admission to hospital for heart surgery it is usual for children to be given many of the necessary tests such as *cardiac catheterization*. A few further tests are done during the run-up to the operation. The child will be weighed and measured so that the amount of blood and fluid he is likely to need during the operation can be calculated. A blood sample will be taken so that blood of his own blood group can be made available. He may also be given a chest X-ray, an *electrocardiogram* and an *echocardiogram*

During the operation the child will be put on a heart-lung machine that takes over the child's circulation and breathing. The operation may last for several hours.

Following surgery the child will have to spend some time in the *intensive care* unit before he is moved to a ward where he will probably be given physiotherapy to teach him breathing exercises that will aid his recovery.

Most children who have major heart surgery will have previously spent a great deal of time in hospital undergoing tests and investigations. They are thus likely to be familiar with the hospital and the hospital staff, and may be less apprehensive about the operation than their parents.

If your child has to have major heart surgery it is inevitable that you will be anxious about the operation and its outcome. Do not hesitate to talk to the medical and nursing staff about your anxieties. They will be able to explain to you exactly what is involved both during the operation and in the recovery period.

The waiting time during the operation will probably be difficult and it may prove less nerve-racking if you can arrange to do something away from the hospital but to telephone in at regular intervals to find out how the operation is progressing. You can then be back with your child when he comes round from the anaesthetic, and may be able to help look after him while he is in hospital.

Ask the staff if you are not sure about any aspects of your child's after-care when the time comes to go home.

Ventricular septal defect (VSD) is often referred to as 'hole in the heart' and is the most common congenital heart disorder. A hole in the septum allows blood to flow through from the left to the right ventricle. This bloodflow produces a murmur which is often very loud. It can also be felt. Small VSDs cause no trouble. Moderate or large VSDs put a strain on the heart and cause breathlessness and sweating. About half of all VSDs close completely, usually by the time a child is 5 years old, and many others get smaller as the child grows. Surgery is necessary only when the hole is large, and is causing problems and is not getting smaller.

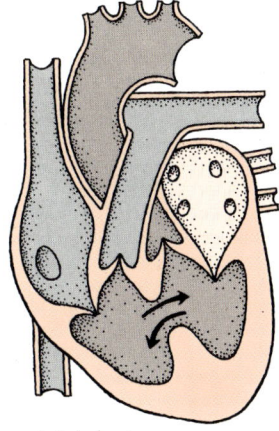

Ventricular septal defect

Atrial septal defect (ASD) is a hole in the septum that separates the left and right atria. There is a heart murmur, but an ASD very rarely produces any other symptoms in a child. If the hole is small it is left alone. If it is moderate or large, it is likely to cause trouble in adult life and an operation to repair it is therefore carried out in childhood.

Patent ductus arteriosus (PDA) is a condition in which the ductus arteriosus, an artery connecting the pulmonary artery and the aorta, which usually closes within a few hours of birth, fails to close. It has the same effect as a hole in the heart: if the artery is only partially open, the child has a heart murmur but no other problems; if the artery is completely open, the child may suffer breathlessness. Surgery to tie off the artery is a relatively simple and safe procedure.

Pulmonary stenosis is a condition in which a baby is born with a narrowed pulmonary valve so that it is difficult for blood to pass through. Even if the narrowing is severe it rarely causes illness, although the child will have a heart murmur, may be short of breath and tire easily. A mild narrowing is left untreated, while moderate or severe narrowings are usually widened by surgery in childhood to avoid illness in adult life.

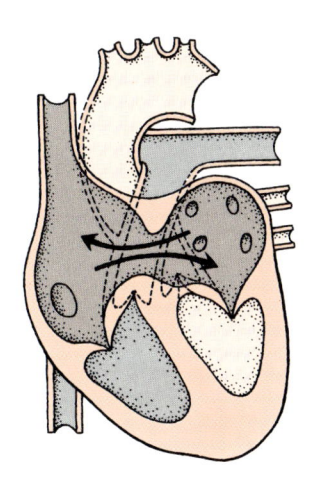

Atrial septal defect

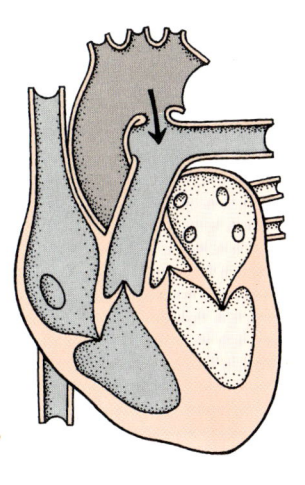

Patent ductus ateriosus

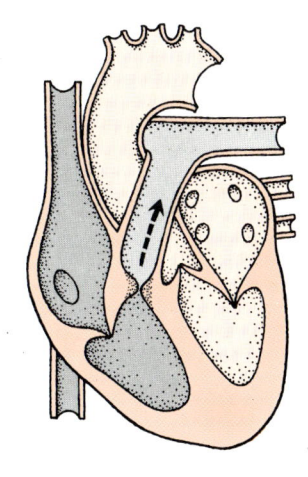

Pulmonary stenosis

Aortic stenosis is a narrowing of the aortic valve. It produces a heart murmur but, unless severe, rarely causes illness in childhood. It is treated by surgery in the same way as pulmonary stenosis. Children with moderate or severe narrowing of the aortic valve should not be allowed to take part in strenuous exercise or competitive sports.

Coarctation of the aorta is a narrowing of the aorta itself. If the defect is moderate or mild the child will be healthy but will have a heart murmur. If the narrowing is severe the child will be breathless and will sweat more than normal. An operation is carried out to cut out the narrowed segment of the aorta and join the ends together. This is usually done when the child is between 4 and 8 years old.

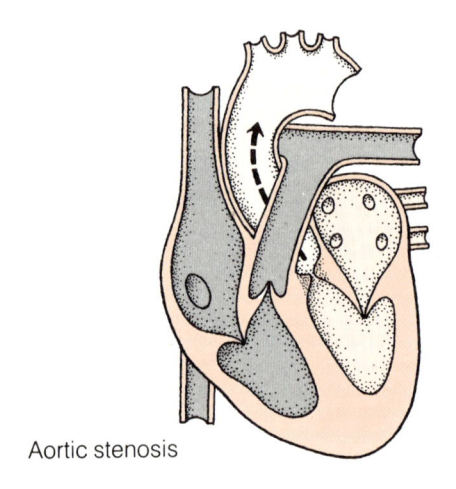

Transposition of the great arteries (TGA) is an uncommon disorder in which the aorta and pulmonary artery are in the wrong places. Soon after birth a baby with a TGA becomes very blue because pink oxygenated blood from the lungs is unable to reach the aorta and blue de-oxygenated blood from the body is unable to reach the lungs. As an emergency procedure, a hole in the atrial septum is created by inserting a tube into the heart via a vein. Major heart surgery is performed usually towards the end of the child's first year, to redirect the circulation of blood.

Fallot's tetralogy is another uncommon heart disorder in which the pulmonary valve and part of the right ventricle leading up to it are narrowed; there is also a large hole in the ventricular septum. An affected child usually begins to look blue during his first year of life and the blueness tends to get worse. An operation is normally carried out when the child is about 4 years old to close the hole and relieve the narrowing. Sometimes, however, increasing blueness makes earlier treatment necessary, and a 'shunt' operation is performed before full surgery can be carried out.

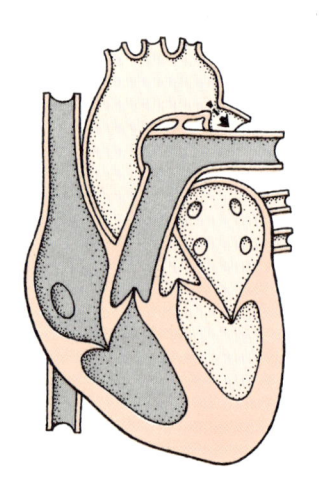

Aortic stenosis

Coarctation of the aorta

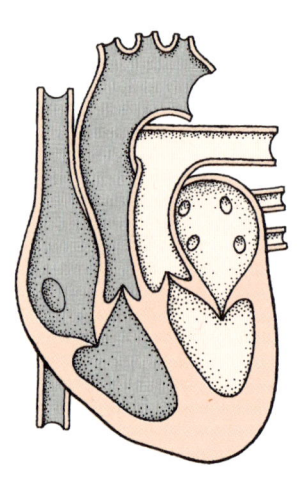

Transposition of the great arteries

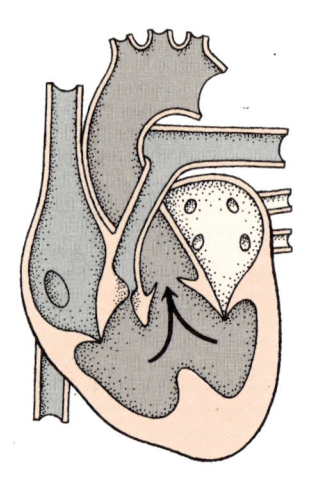

Fallot's tetralogy

CARING FOR YOUR CHILD

If your child has a heart disorder this does not mean that his heart is weak and that it is going to stop beating suddenly. You will need to take your child to hospital for a check-up occasionally and in some cases surgery may be recommended. Any breathlessness caused by a congenital heart disorder can be relieved by a number of drugs. They will not cure the disorder but will allow surgery to be postponed and sometimes avoided.

Ask your doctor exactly what limitations the child's condition imposes, and then encourage him to do everything possible within these limitations so that he leads as normal a life as he can. It is easy to become over-protective, and to allow your child to become difficult and demanding because you are afraid to discipline him in case he becomes upset.

TEETH
If your child has a heart disorder, no matter how minor, he should look after his teeth very carefully. Decaying teeth are a source of infection, and if your child has to have a filling or extraction this infection can pass into the bloodstream and cause damage to his heart. Regular brushing, adequate fluoride and regular visits to the dentist are important. You must notify your dentist that your child has a heart disorder: if your child needs fillings or extractions, the dentist will give him a dose of an antibiotic an hour beforehand.

IMMUNIZATION
Children with heart disorders are at no more risk from *immunization* than children without heart disorders, and it is even more important to protect them from illnesses such as *whooping cough* and *measles*.

EXERCISE
Your child's paediatrician or heart specialist will advise you on whether or not you should limit his activities. This is usually necessary only for children with *aortic stenosis*, who should avoid strenuous exertion and competitive sports. Otherwise there is no need to stop your child from taking part in all the usual childhood activities, or to treat him in any way differently from other children.

RHEUMATIC FEVER

Occasionally the heart muscle may be damaged later in life by infection or by drugs, and sometimes the heart valves can be damaged by rheumatic fever.

This is due to the body's response to an infection of the throat or *scarlet fever* caused by the streptococcus bacteria. Only a very few children with streptococcal infections go on to develop rheumatic fever. It is more likely to affect school-age children than babies or toddlers. Why they react like this to the bacteria is not known.

A week to a month after the initial infection the child develops a fever and a headache. His joints swell and become painful, he may have lumps under the skin around them and he may have a pink, blotchy, but not itchy, rash. Paracetamol helps to relieve the joint pains but you should also call your doctor. He will listen to your child's chest: a certain type of heart murmur suggests that the heart has become involved. If your child's heart has become inflamed, its inner lining and valves may suffer damage, which may be permanent. Your doctor will prescribe antibiotics to treat the infection.

Rheumatic fever used to be fairly common but it is now rare. However, it can still be dangerous and occasionally fatal. As rheumatic fever tends to recur, and as the risks of heart complications increase with each recurrence, most children who have had the disease are given antibiotics for the rest of their childhood. If your child has had rheumatic fever, make sure that any doctor or dentist treating him knows about it.

THE BLOOD

Blood has two basic parts: a clear fluid, called plasma, and the various cells that float in it: the red blood cells, white blood cells and platelets. The blood circulates around the body, supplying the tissues with oxygen and nutrients and carrying away waste substances. Most blood cells are made in the marrow inside certain bones, particularly the skull, spine and pelvis. Many of the chemicals in plasma, such as proteins, are made in the liver. A blood sample can be taken by a finger or heel prick, or from a vein using a syringe and needle.

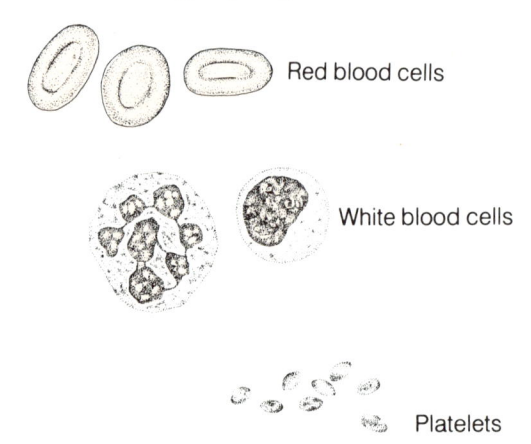

Red blood cells

White blood cells

Platelets

Red blood cells
Oxygen is carried from the lungs to the tissues by the red blood cells, or erythocytes. These cells are disc-shaped, and readily alter shape to squeeze through the body's smallest blood vessels, the capillaries. Each red cell contains about 600 million molecules of the oxygen-carrying protein haemoglobin. Haemoglobin contains iron and this gives the cells their red colour. The life of a red blood cell is about 120 days; when ageing, the cells are broken down in the liver, spleen and bone marrow. Much of the iron from their haemoglobin is stored for re-use. However, a little is lost, so an adequate supply of iron in a person's diet is necessary to maintain normal levels of haemoglobin in the blood – otherwise *anaemia* may result.

Vitamins such as folic acid and B_{12} are also needed for the development of red blood cells in the bone marrow.

White blood cells
There are many kinds of white blood cells but the three main types are neutrophils, monocytes and lymphocytes. All of these are important for defending the body against infection. Neutrophils and monocytes are made in the bone marrow and can move out of the blood vessels into the site of an injury or infection. Lymphocytes are made in the lymph nodes, the thymus gland and the spleen as well as in the bone marrow, and they move around all these areas. Without lymphocytes there is increased susceptibility to infections, particularly viral and fungal infections. There are two main types: T-lymphocytes, which are important in the control of viral and fungal infections; and B-lymphocytes, which produce antibodies in response to infection.

Blood clotting
Blood plasma contains a number of protein molecules that maintain a delicate balance, in the body's everyday wear and tear, between too much clotting (thrombosis) and too much bleeding (haemorrhage).

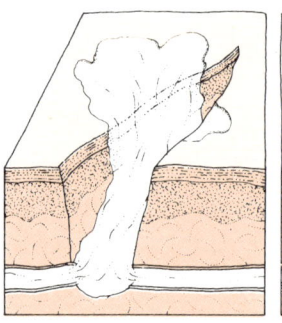

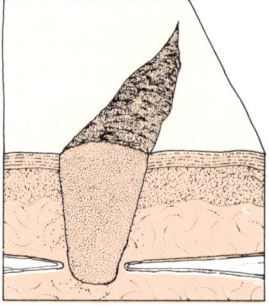

After an injury the damaged blood vessels contract down to restrict blood loss. Platelets, clumping around the wound, form a clot with strands of fibrin, produced by chemicals in the blood. This seals the wound and eventually forms a scab.

BLOOD GROUPS

Red blood cells carry *antigens* on their surfaces. Blood group is determined by the antigens which are present on red blood cells. The antigens of one person will interact with *antibodies* in the plasma of another person. There are several blood grouping systems within which these reactions occur. The ABO and Rhesus are the most important. In the ABO system a person is classified as AB, A, B, or O. The most common is O, which occurs in about 50 per cent of people. In each group the plasma carries antibodies relating to antigens that are *not* present: in blood group A there are anti-B antibodies, in B anti-A antibodies, in O anti-A and anti-B antibodies. So if, for example, blood cells of a group B person were given to a person of group A, they would be destroyed by the anti-B antibodies in the plasma. This would lead to a massive breakdown of the red blood cells in the circulation and possible kidney failure.

A person of group AB has neither A nor B antibodies and can receive blood of any group. However, as there might occasionally be problems, blood is normally matched exactly before any transfusion.

In the Rhesus system a blood group is either Rhesus positive or Rhesus negative. Antibodies will be produced to Rhesus positive blood introduced into a Rhesus negative person. This is *Rhesus incompatibility*.

There are approximately 5 times as many people who have Rhesus positive antigens as those who have Rhesus negative antigens.

The table above shows the antigens which are present on the cells of people with different blood groups. Group 0 is so called because there are no A or B antigens on its cells.

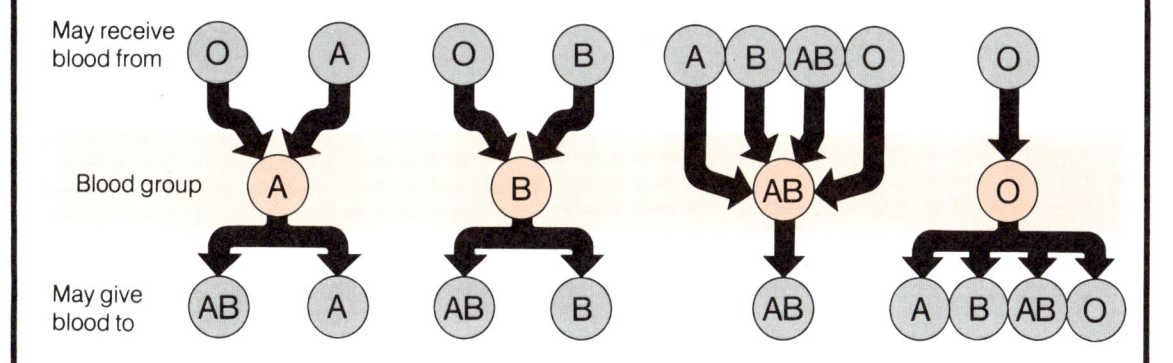

Antigen / Group	A	B	None	Rh+	Rh-
A Rh+	●			●	
A Rh-	●				●
B Rh+		●		●	
B Rh-		●			●
AB Rh+	●	●		●	
AB Rh-	●	●			●
O Rh+			○	●	
O Rh-			○		●

May receive blood from:
- A ← O, A
- B ← O, B
- AB ← A, B, AB, O
- O ← O

May give blood to:
- A → AB, A
- B → AB, B
- AB → AB
- O → A, B, AB, O

When a blood transfusion is to be given, the blood of recipient and donor must be carefully matched to make sure that antigens on the red blood cells of one person's blood will not be destroyed by antibodies in the plasma of the other. In the ABO system people whose blood is Group O (the most common) are known as universal donors. Their blood can safely be given to people of any other group. People in Group AB (the most rare) are universal recipients. They can safely receive blood of all other groups.

Platelets are necessary for blood to clot and plug gaps in the walls of small blood vessels. They play an essential part in the defence of the body against injury and in preventing bleeding and bruising. When there is an injury a soluble protein in the plasma, called fibrinogen, is chemically altered to an insoluble one, called fibrin, which forms a blood clot. During this process one protein is 'switched on' or activated and in turn triggers another one, in a series of up to a dozen different stages. Lack of any one of these proteins prevents clotting and so causes abnormal bleeding.

Bleeding and bruising
The normal toddler, in the process of learning to walk, is bound to have a few bumps and bruises. However, if the bruises seem unusually persistent, large and lumpy, if they appear without obvious explanation, or if your child seems to bleed profusely from the slightest knock, you should consult your doctor.

Most older children have a certain amount of bruising on their shins, particularly after games like football or hockey. Many children have the occasional *nosebleed*. However, these features are unusual:

o persistent or repeated bruising other than on the shins
o pinpoint freckle-like bleeding under the skin, especially on or around the neck and waist
o prolonged and repeated nosebleeds
o blood passed in the urine or stools, or loose, tar-coloured stools

If you think your child has a bleeding problem your doctor will need to know whether your family has a history of bleeding problems; when you first noticed the problem; exactly what sort of bleeding it is; where the common sites are; whether your child has had previous injuries or operations; and whether he takes medicines containing aspirin, as these can worsen any bleeding. With this information and the results of blood tests, your doctor should know whether there is a problem.

BLOOD TRANSFUSIONS

Blood transfusions are vital not only in treating blood diseases but also in replacing lost blood and plasma, for example during surgery and following accidents.

Before a blood transfusion a small sample of the patient's blood is taken to determine his blood group so as to avoid transfusion reactions. The blood to be transfused is then allowed to trickle into the patient's vein via a needle. Donated blood can be separated into its parts – the different cell types and plasma. The proteins in plasma can be concentrated and frozen for long-term storage. In this way clotting factors are prepared to treat patients with *haemophilia* and other clotting disorders. Blood transfusions are tedious (although not painful) for a young patient as he cannot move about freely. A fine tube is inserted into a vein on the back of the hand, wrist or forearm (or on the scalp of a baby) and taped in place. One-handed games, preferably with a companion, will help pass the time.

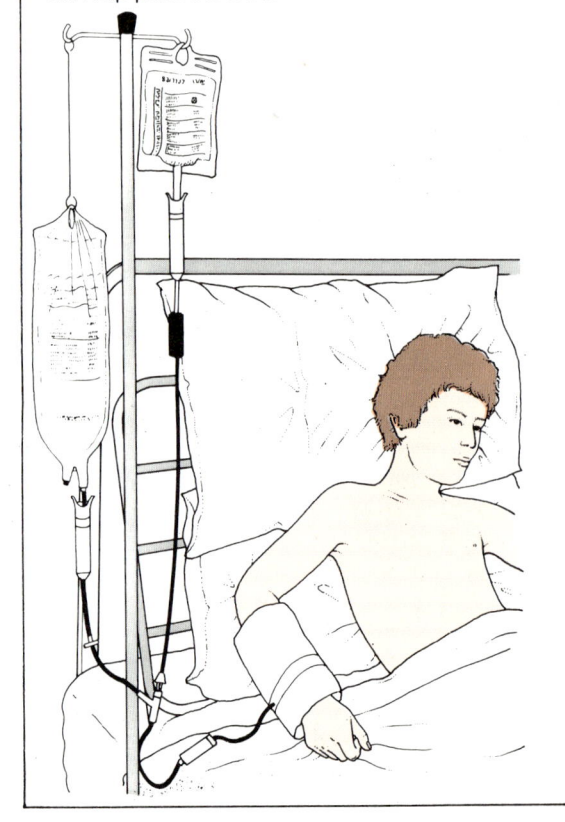

IRON-DEFICIENCY ANAEMIA

This is the most common form of anaemia. It is caused by lack of iron, which in turn prevents the production of enough haemoglobin for every red blood cell. This can be caused by insufficient iron in a child's diet. A poor and iron-deficient diet can cause iron-deficiency anaemia at any age, but a child who is growing fast needs to make plenty of red blood cells and under certain circumstances demand for iron may exceed supply. A newborn baby's stores of iron depend on his birthweight: small or premature babies tend to have low iron stores. The stores are used up during the fast growth period of the first year and extra iron is soon needed. This has to come from his diet. Iron is best absorbed from breast milk but premature babies become iron-deficient and anaemic even if fully breastfed unless they are given iron supplements.

Toddlers who are reluctant to take solids or to drink formula milk are likely to become iron-deficient. Another critical time is adolescence, when growth is rapid and girls, in addition, start menstruating.

Another cause of anaemia is poor absorption of iron from the diet. If a child has a condition such as *coeliac disease*, which prevents the bowel absorbing iron normally, he is likely to be anaemic.

Bleeding can also cause iron deficiency. Sudden, severe bleeding – often into the digestive tract – causes symptoms like faintness, vomiting and tar-coloured stools. Steady, slow loss of blood does not cause these dramatic symptoms but may, on the other hand, result in iron-deficiency anaemia. Parasites such as hookworms in the bowel are a cause of slow blood loss.

SYMPTOMS

Pallor and lethargy, blood in the stools or tar-coloured stools, nausea, vomiting and faintness may all be associated with iron-deficiency anaemia. The child may become breathless even on taking a minimal amount of exercise, and have a poor appetite.

An indication of anaemia is the colour of the underside of your child's eyelids. Pull down the lower eyelid and look at the colour of the mucous membrane underneath. If the eyelid lining is pale pink rather than red your child is probably anaemic.

TESTS AND TREATMENT

If your doctor suspects that your child is suffering from anaemia, he will take a blood test, which will show the concentration of haemoglobin in the red blood cells. Following the diagnosis he will try to find out the cause of the anaemia and will try to correct it – with advice about diet, for example. However, because the disease itself tends to diminish appetite it can be difficult to persuade a child, especially a toddler, to eat enough iron-containing food. Your doctor will almost certainly prescribe iron supplements, given as tablets to older children but as a liquid to younger ones. These are best taken through a straw and never mixed with a feed. Iron tends to discolour the teeth, so regular teeth-cleaning is particularly important. Iron supplements will turn a child's stools black.

A repeat blood test is necessary after a month or so, to check that the treatment is working. If there has been no improvement, further tests may be needed to look for other causes of iron deficiency. To build up the iron stores of your child's body, treatment will be continued for a couple of months after your child's blood has returned to normal.

PALLOR
Although children with anaemia tend to be pale and may be lethargic, in fact most pale, lethargic children are not anaemic. Skin colour is influenced by various factors, including pigmentation, whether the child is hot or cold, or has recently been exercising. Do not give a pale, tired child medicines such as iron without first consulting a doctor and having a blood test.

SICKLE-CELL ANAEMIA

Sickle-cell anaemia is caused by a defect in the structure of haemoglobin. The sufferer's haemoglobin carries oxygen to the tissues in the normal way, but after giving up its oxygen tends to solidify within the red blood cells so that eventually the cells become deformed and sickle-shaped. These cells have a shorter life than normal, so that the child who has sickle-cell anaemia becomes short of red blood cells.

This is a condition that is inherited. Both parents will be 'carriers' of the sickle-cell gene. The gene is most common in people of African origin, of whom 1 in 1,000 is affected. It is also found in Asian and Mediterranean peoples. Genetic counselling and antenatal diagnosis are available for couples at risk of having an affected child.

The affected baby may develop problems in the first few months after birth. Sickled red cells block up small blood vessels causing pain and fever. The hands and feet of young children may swell, and older children may have pains in the back, limbs and abdomen. A child may also have a pneumonia-like problem and the ability of his kidneys to concentrate urine may be upset. Episodes of illness may be triggered by chills, infections or an anaesthetic – or they may have no obvious cause.

Current research aims to find ways of avoiding these episodes of illness, but no proven method as yet exists. A good diet and good hygiene help children with sickle-cell anaemia lead normal lives. Infections should be treated promptly; keep your child warm and in any illness encourage him to drink plenty of fluids to reduce strain on the kidneys. Blood transfusions are only needed in the event of worsening anaemia, in preparation for an anaesthetic or, occasionally, to treat a severe episode.

▶See also Genetics; Appendix: Support groups and publications

THALASSAEMIA

Thalassaemia is an inherited disease common among people of Middle and Far Eastern origin. The disease reduces or totally destroys the body's ability to produce healthy haemoglobin. It exists in many forms. The most severe form is known as alpha thalassaemia, in which no haemoglobin is made. A fetus with alpha thalassaemia cannot survive. In other forms there is a mild deficiency of haemoglobin causing symptoms not unlike those of *iron-deficiency anaemia*.

The form called beta thalassaemia major is a serious disease in which half of the haemoglobin is missing. After the first few months of life a child with beta thalassaemia major develops severe anaemia, fails to grow, has bone deformities due to over-developed bone marrow, particularly noticeable in the face and skull, and suffers general ill-health.

To treat a child with beta thalassaemia major regular transfusions of red blood cells are given every 4 to 6 weeks. As these have to be continued for life, the child's body will eventually become overloaded with iron and damage may result to his heart and other organs. In order to rid the body of excess iron so that overload can be delayed a drug is given by injection.

The chances of a child suffering from thalassaemia and surviving into adulthood are small but are gradually increasing. Genetic counselling and antenatal diagnosis are available for parents at risk of having a child with certain forms of thalassaemia.

▶See also Genetics; Appendix: Support groups and publications

HAEMOPHILIA

Haemophilia is one of a group of conditions in which there exists abnormality of a blood plasma factor essential for blood clotting. Haemophilia is inherited and affects boys. Approximately 1 boy in 14,000 has a serious, lifelong disorder with spontaneous bleeding. Boys with mild haemophilia suffer only after severe injury or surgery.

SYMPTOMS

Usually only severe haemophilia causes problems. It is recognized when a child learns to walk and suffers bumps and falls. It may be diagnosed earlier because of a family history of haemophilia or because of bleeding after circumcision. The first symptoms are often large, lumpy bruises and pain in the ankle, knee and elbow joints as a result of bleeding into the joints.

TREATMENT

Although haemophilia is a lifelong disease, with prompt treatment an affected child can grow and develop normally without permanent damage to joints. If your child is haemophiliac, register him with a recognized haemophilia centre which will provide him with an identity card carrying details of his blood group and his exact clotting-factor abnormality. You can also discuss problems of education and your child's career with the staff of the centre. Schooling may often be missed because of joint bleeds. Adjustments in lifestyle may be necessary to avoid troublesome bleeds.

The mainstay of treatment is the prompt replacement of the missing clotting factor at the first sign of bleeding. This is done by injection into a vein. As your child grows, you will be able to treat him in this way at home. Because the life of most of the clotting factors in the body is short (up to 48 hours) it is not possible, except in special circumstances, to give continuous replacement therapy to prevent bleeds altogether. Clotting factors are made from blood. There is a risk that some blood used may be infected by Acquired Immuno-deficiency Disease (AIDS). However, the chances of a child acquiring the infection from clotting factors is very low.

Physiotherapy is also important in treatment. After a bleed into a joint, the muscles very easily become weak and need strengthening to prevent possible further bleeding.

▶ See also Appendix: Support groups and publications

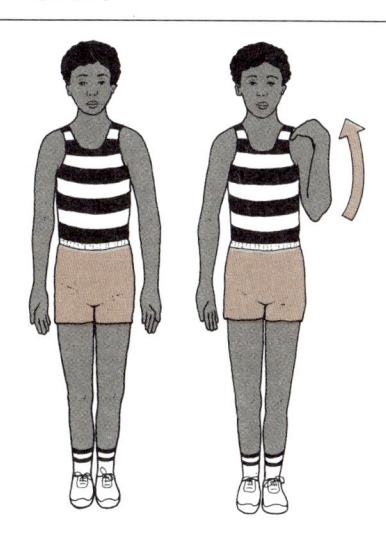

A physiotherapist will instruct your child in a programme of exercises for stretching and strengthening his muscles and joints. He should only do the exercises chosen for him. If you think he may have an injury, consult your doctor before continuing.

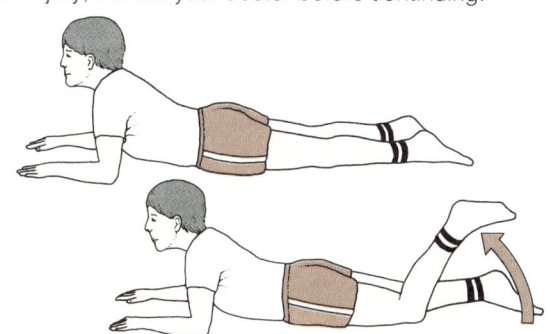

OTHER BLOOD DISORDERS

Besides *haemophilia*, *sickle-cell anaemia* and *thalassaemia*, genetic inheritance is also reponsible for two conditions, both causing *anaemia*, in which the red blood cells are faulty. These are G-6-PD and spherocytosis. Another disorder, aplastic anaemia, affects the blood-forming bone marrow.

G-6-PD is a red cell enzyme that may be lacking as the result of an inherited condition. It is found in many millions of people. Children with low G-6-PD levels are well most of the time, but they are at risk of sudden breakdown of red cells and consequent anaemia if they take certain chemicals and drugs, such as sulphonamides and some antimalarial drugs. In the most severe type of deficiency, occurring mostly among people of the Mediterranean region, anaemia can also be triggered by eating broad beans.

A child who suffers from this condition can lead a normal life. He will recover from the sudden breakdown of red cells but he may need a blood transfusion if his anaemia is severe. If your family is affected so that you suspect your child might suffer, you should ask the doctor for a list of medicines and chemicals to be avoided.

Spherocytosis is an inherited blood disorder where the red blood cells are spherical rather than disc-shaped and they cannot change shape easily to squeeze through small capillaries. They tend to get held up in the circulation through the spleen, which then destroys them. The condition can cause anaemia and jaundice in the newborn baby. The child's spleen is removed, usually after the age of 5 or 6 years, and this helps cure the anaemia. A child with spherocytosis leads an entirely normal life, although he may suffer jaundice if he has an infection. Very occasionally his bone marrow stops working and he may need a transfusion. Otherwise the only treatment necessary is extra folic acid which can be taken as pills.

Aplastic anaemia, also called bone marrow failure, is a rare disease in which there is deficient production of all types of blood cell. Lack of red cells results in anaemia, low platelet levels lead to bleeding and bruising, and serious infections may occur due to lack of white blood cells. These symptoms also occur in *leukaemia* and other forms of *cancer* but the conditions can be distinguished by a bone marrow test. Sometimes a particular drug can cause serious bone marrow failure, but most cases of aplastic anaemia in childhood are 'idiopathic' – that is, the cause is unknown.

The disease has a high risk of death from bleeding or infection, although occasionally children seem to recover spontaneously. If someone in the family, usually a brother or sister, has the same white blood cell type then a *bone marrow transplant* may be attempted.

Thrombocytopenic purpura means excessive bruising due to lack of platelets in the blood. Its most common form is idiopathic thrombocytopenic purpura (ITP), a condition where for an unknown reason a previously healthy child begins to bruise easily. Sometimes ITP follows an illness such as *chickenpox* or *German measles*. A blood test shows that the platelet level is low but the rest of the blood is normal. Although a child may look terribly bruised the majority who suffer recover within weeks or months without any treatment. Some children can have low platelet levels for several years and yet still recover. Provided that a child does not have bleeding from his nose or gums (mucous membrane bleeding), no treatment is necessary after the first few weeks – he only needs to avoid potentially injurious games and sports. If his platelet level remains low and bleeding problems continue, the doctor may advise a course of intravenous immunoglobulin or steroid tablets. If the condition has not cleared up in 6 months the doctor may advise an operation to remove the spleen.

THE DIGESTIVE SYSTEM

The digestive tract is essentially one long tube running through the body. The tube has several main parts, each designed for a certain job. The mouth chews and mixes food with saliva. The gullet, or oesophagus, propels the chewed food to the stomach and prevents its return. The stomach pummels the food into smaller pieces and adds acid and enzymes to break it down chemically. The small intestine, or duodenum and ileum, adds more enzymes and absorbs any useful nutrients through its wall into the bloodstream. The large intestine, or colon, absorbs water and compacts the undigested waste. The rectum stores this waste and the anus is the opening through which the waste is excreted from the body. The entire tract, and its associated glands and organs, such as the liver and gall bladder, make up the digestive system.

Liver and gall bladder
The liver is made up of sponge-like tissue that accommodates a huge blood supply. It receives this supply partly from the heart, and partly from the intestine, second-hand. It is this second-hand, nutrient-laden blood that gives the liver its role as the filter and regulator of nutrients, enzymes and other substances in the bloodstream.

The liver is also a gland, secreting green-pigmented bile down the bile duct to the small intestine. The gall bladder, which sits just under the liver, acts as a temporary reservoir for bile and discharges its contents soon after a meal is eaten. Bile is an important digestive juice, particularly for breaking down foods with a high fat content.

Swallowing
After food has been chewed and broken up into small soft pieces, it is pushed in a lump to the back of the mouth by the tongue. At the top of the oesophagus there is a valve-like mechanism called the upper oesophageal sphincter, which relaxes and allows the lump of food to enter the oesophagus; at the same

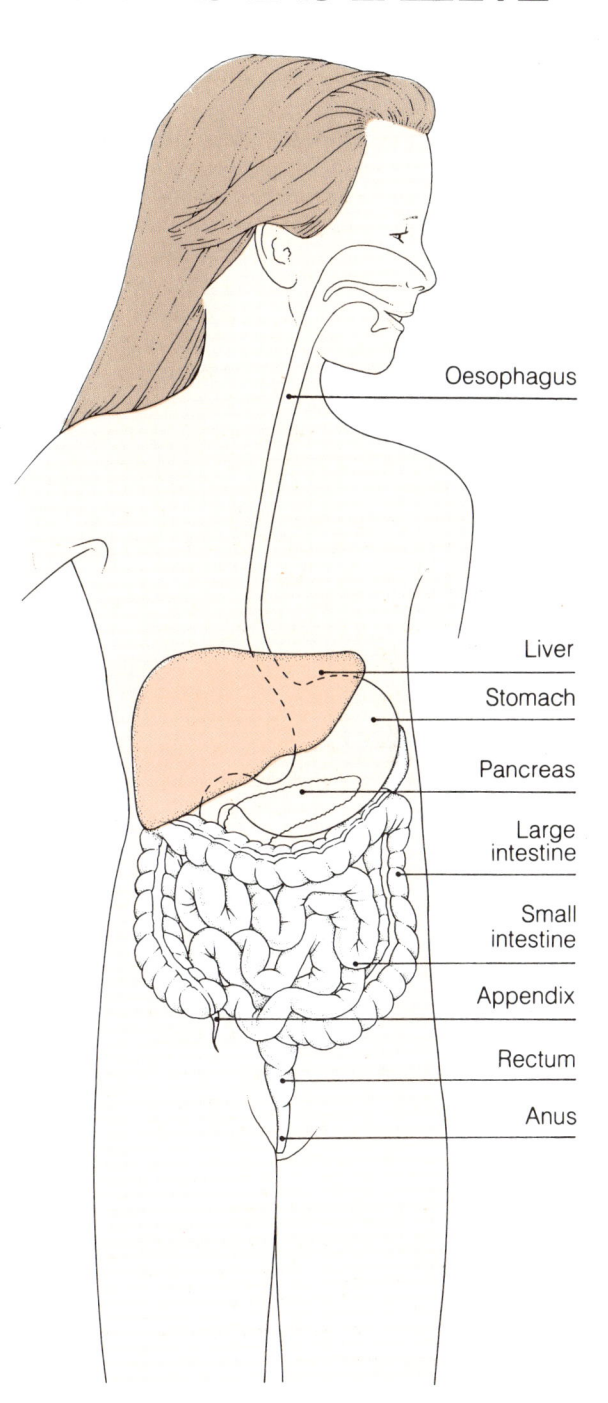

time the top of the trachea is closed to prevent the lump going into the lungs. The food is propelled down the oesophagus to the stomach by waves of muscle contraction, known as peristaltic waves.

Digestion
Food must be converted into soluble nutrients before the small intestine can absorb it. In fact digestion starts in the mouth, where the salivary juices begin to break down the starch in food. In the stomach, hydrochloric acid and another enzyme, pepsin, are secreted to digest proteins. The pancreas pours a variety of enzymes into the duodenum. These enzymes break down proteins, fats and carbohydrates. Bile salts, secreted by the liver, help to make fats soluble in water. Food is further broken down at the lining of the gut in the small intestine, where more enzymes complete the digestion of nutrients before they are absorbed through the intestinal wall into the bloodstream.

Defecation
The outflow of waste matter is controlled by two rings of muscle through the anus, known as the inner and outer anal sphincters. When the rectum is full and distended, a nervous reflex known as the ano-rectal reflex comes into play and the sphincters relax; the rectum then contracts, expelling its contents.

By the age of about 2 years most children have achieved *bowel control*. However, about 3 children in 100 do not achieve control by this age. Their problems are usually that they

o continue to open their bowels in inappropriate places after training has started. This may be because training started too soon, or it may the child's way of exerting control or of responding to tension in the family
o start soiling again after they have achieved bowel control, very likely as a result of stresses at home
o hold back bowel motions for some reason and develop *constipation*

If your child has not achieved bowel control by 4 years you should consult your doctor.

TESTS FOR DIGESTIVE DISORDERS

A barium meal enables X-ray pictures of the upper part of the digestive tract to be taken. The child must fast for 4 hours, then drink a palatable liquid containing barium, a chemical visible on X-ray. As the liquid is digested, X-rays are taken and reveal any abnormalities.

To obtain X-ray pictures of the lower part of the digestive tract, the bowel is first completely emptied. An enema containing barium is then given. X-rays taken while the fluid is in the gut reveal any abnormalities.

VOMITING

Babies regurgitate, spit back (posset) or forcefully vomit their feeds for many reasons, including inadequate winding, coughs and colds, overfeeding and stress at home. Possetting is common. More seriously, vomiting can be caused by an infection such as *gastroenteritis* or *meningitis*; but there are usually other signs of illness.

Occasionally effortless vomiting of relatively unchanged food may be associated with a *hiatus hernia* - a weakness at the lower end of the oesophagus. Projectile vomiting, where the returned food shoots out, may be associated with an obstruction of the stomach outlet, as in *pyloric stenosis*. If your baby has severe, prolonged vomiting he risks dehydration, and needs urgent medical help.

When a child is older, vomiting tends to be associated with disease, although travel sickness is another possibility. Physical obstruction of the digestive tract or inflammation inside the abdomen, as in acute *appendicitis*, may cause vomiting and abdominal pain.

Infections, particularly *tonsillitis* and *pneumonia*, are another cause. Hormonal and *metabolic disorders* may give rise to vomiting.

You can buy drugs to suppress nausea and vomiting, known as anti-emetic drugs, from your pharmacist. However, few doctors would recommend that you should use them, except for travel sickness, since vomiting is normally a symptom of an underlying problem that should be found and treated.

TRAVEL SICKNESS
If you have a child with a tendency to travel sickness, give him no more than a light meal some time before you set off and provide snacks such as dry biscuits and barley sugar, and cold water to drink. Avoid fizzy drinks. Encourage your child to recognize the symptoms of impending sickness and to tell you in time. Your doctor may prescribe drugs, but for most children it is an occasional rather than a chronic problem and therefore it does not justify giving medicine just in case.

ABDOMINAL PAIN

Pain in the abdomen may be either recurrent, in repeated bouts, or acute, when a severe pain starts suddenly.

RECURRENT ABDOMINAL PAIN
If your child has abdominal pain that recurs for no obvious reason, he may be unusually sensitive to distension or contractions of the intestines, or his intestines may contract particularly strongly.

He may also be suffering from stress and anxiety and may be asking indirectly for your attention, help and guidance. The problem occurs mainly in school-age children. The pain tends to be colicky and worse after a meal. The child often has *constipation*, alternating with loose stools. If your child has this type of abdominal pain, make sure his diet contains enough fibre. Consult your doctor if your child has recurrent abdominal pain coupled with symptoms such as weight loss, fever, rashes, joint pains and swelling, or mouth ulcers.

ACUTE ABDOMINAL PAIN
A sudden attack of severe abdominal pain is alarming for a child, and for his parents. However, the cause may be simple and short-term; a severe attack of wind, for example, can cause acute pain that passes quickly.

If the pain persists, or becomes worse, or if your child develops other symptoms such as vomiting, diarrhoea or blood in his stools or urine, you should consult your doctor. It will help your doctor if you can tell him whether the pain is constant or whether it comes in colicky spasms, with your child feeling fairly comfortable between them.

Causes of acute abdominal pain are many and varied. There may be problems in the digestive tract, the kidneys, the urinary tract or the sex organs. Some abdominal pains are the result of diseases elsewhere in the body, such as *pneumonia*, *meningitis* or *diabetes*. Viral *gastroenteritis* (gastric flu) can also cause quite severe pain.

HIATUS HERNIA

The oesophagus passes through a hole in the diaphragm, the large sheet of muscle dividing the chest and abdomen, and joins the stomach just below the hole. In hiatus hernia, part of the stomach protrudes through the hole in the diaphragm and into the chest. As a result the normal valve-like mechanism at the junction of the oesophagus and stomach cannot work properly, and so the stomach's contents are easily regurgitated up the oesophagus and into the mouth. Hiatus hernia may develop at any time, most commonly in the first weeks of life.

SYMPTOMS

If your baby has a hiatus hernia he will usually begin to regurgitate feeds in the first week after birth. Regurgitation occurs during, after and between feeds. Later the pattern is for solid feeds to be kept down and liquid ones to be vomited. The vomit may be blood-stained. You should consult your doctor.

If the regurgitation is mild and infrequent, your baby is likely to grow out of the condition by the age of 12 months. More severe regurgitation, however, needs treatment, as it otherwise may lead to pain, poor growth, chest infections and ulceration of the lower oesophagus. There is also the risk that the baby will inhale the vomit.

TREATMENT

If the regurgitation is mild and your baby is otherwise healthy and thriving, your doctor may be able to advise you on measures you can take to alleviate the problem. Usually all that you need to do is nurse your baby in an upright position and thicken his feeds with cornflour or other thickening agents.

A proportion of babies who are severely affected get better at around 12 to 18 months when they spend more time walking and being upright, and when their diet changes to mainly solid foods. As the oesophagus grows in length this also helps to relieve the problem. However, these children may later have occasional problems when, for example, they develop coughs.

If your child still has recurrent bleeding or persistent chest infections at the age of 18 months, surgery may be necessary to repair the hiatus hernia.

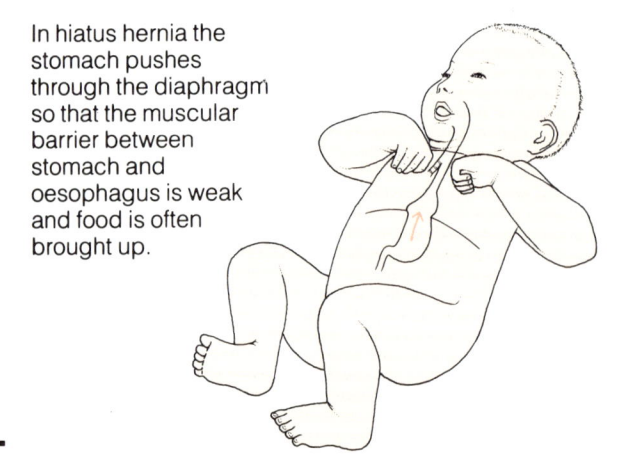

In hiatus hernia the stomach pushes through the diaphragm so that the muscular barrier between stomach and oesophagus is weak and food is often brought up.

PYLORIC STENOSIS

If the muscular tissues at the outlet from the stomach are thickened so that the outlet is blocked, this is known as pyloric stenosis. The stomach's contents cannot pass normally into the intestine with the result that they are vomited back. A baby with pyloric stenosis vomits after each feed. His vomiting will become increasingly copious and forceful, often shooting several feet. Initially he will be irritable and hungry but will not be gaining weight; he will gradually become dehydrated, miserable and lethargic.

The disorder usually becomes noticeable a few weeks after birth, but may appear sooner or, indeed, much later.

Consult your doctor as soon as you realize your baby is vomiting persistently. Meanwhile feed your baby rather more often than usual, but give smaller amounts of food at each feed.

An operation will be carried out to relieve the obstruction to the stomach's outlet by dividing the enlarged muscle tissue. If your baby is dehydrated and malnourished then he will have to be fed via a drip before surgery can be carried out. Recovery is usually rapid and most babies are out of hospital and on their way to full recovery 5 days after the operation.

The cause of pyloric stenosis is unknown. One baby in 500 suffers from it and far more boys than girls are affected. It also runs in families. A boy who is the baby of a mother who was herself affected has a 1 in 5 chance of developing pyloric stenosis.

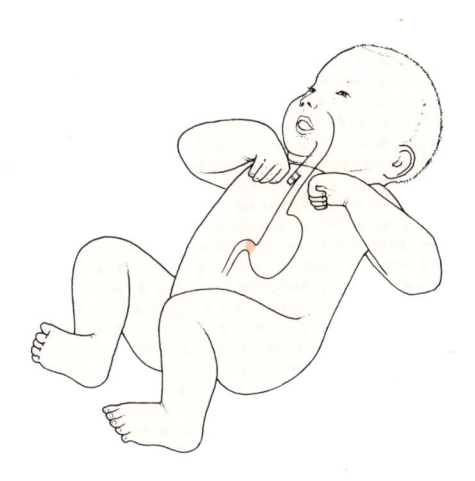

Thickened walls at the stomach exit mean that even strong contractions cannot force the milk through and it may be vomited instead.

MECKEL'S DIVERTICULUM

While a baby is in the uterus, there is a connection between the intestine and the umbilical cord through the navel. The intestinal end of this connection sometimes persists after birth as a little sac attached to the small intestine. Alternatively the sac, or diverticulum, may remain attached to the navel. This is known as Meckel's diverticulum and is present in about 1 person in 50. Mostly it causes no trouble, but occasionally complications such as *intussusception* or *volvulus* may cause colicky pain, bleeding from the anus and vomiting. The diverticulum must then be surgically removed.

PEPTIC ULCER

As food enters the stomach it is mixed with digestive juices that include dilute hydrochloric acid. If the stomach produces too much acid this may lead to inflammation of the stomach lining (gastritis), or even to a raw, exposed sore or ulcer in the lining of the stomach or of the duodenum. Stomach and duodenal ulcers are both known as peptic ulcers. Although they are more common in adulthood, children can suffer from them, especially if there is a family history of indigestion or ulcers.

A child with peptic ulcer will complain of pain in the upper abdomen or lower chest, especially after spicy meals, long periods without food and at night. Occasionally he may vomit blood.

You should consult your doctor if your child has these symptoms. He will probably arrange for your child to be given a *barium meal* to show up the ulcer. Sometimes a further test, known as endoscopy, is necessary. A long, flexible viewing tube is passed down your child's oesophagus so that the doctor can see inside the stomach. If your child is young, this may be done under a general anaesthetic; older children usually need only have sedation.

If there is an ulcer your child will be given drugs to aid its healing and to reduce acid production. Your doctor will give you advice on what your child should and should not eat. Aspirin, which can sometimes cause bleeding from the stomach or intestine, should be avoided completely.

INTUSSUSCEPTION AND VOLVULUS

These are two disorders in which the intestines become entangled. In intussusception, one part of the intestine telescopes into an adjacent portion, so as to lie inside it. This stimulates the muscular activity of the intestine and more and more of the intestine becomes intussuscepted. A child suffering from this has severe, colicky abdominal pain. Later he may vomit and pass watery, bloodstained stools. His abdomen may become distended.

Intussusception can occur at any age but on the whole affects children between the ages of 3 and 9 months. It may follow *gastroenteritis* or an *upper repiratory infection* which has produced enlarged glands in the abdomen. Diagnosis is confirmed by a *barium enema* and in some cases the enema itself may untangle the gut. However, an operation is usually necessary.

Many portions of the intestine move about as food is propelled through them. If a loop of intestine twists on itself, not only will it block the passage of its contents, but it may also cut off its blood supply, possibly leading to gangrene of the affected loop. This twisting is termed a volvulus. The symptoms are severe colicky abdominal pain and vomiting. Treatment is by operation.

HENOCH-SCHONLEIN PURPURA

This is a disease that may cause abdominal pain and blood in the stools. The body has an allergic reaction to an ordinary throat infection, about 10 days after the initial disease. Besides pain, caused by swellings in the intestines, the child has swollen joints and raised purple blotches (purpura) on his skin – usually worse on the buttocks and the backs of the legs. If your child has these symptoms you should consult your doctor.

MESENTERIC ADENITIS

There are infection-fighting lymph glands in the intestinal tract and its blood supply, and so it is an important organ of the immune system. During any infection, even if the digestive system is not directly affected, the lymph glands may become swollen. This disorder, known as mesenteric adenitis, may cause abdominal pain. It nearly always occurs in conjunction with an infection, such as *tonsillitis*, elsewhere.

It may be difficult for a doctor to be certain whether your child's abdominal pain is due to mesenteric adenitis or to another problem, such as *appendicitis*. He may advise admission to hospital for a period of observation. However, it is unusual for pain caused by mesenteric adenitis to last for much longer than 36 to 48 hours.

APPENDICITIS

The appendix is a finger-sized dead-end tube situated at the junction of the small and large intestines, in the lower right side of the abdomen. If it becomes blocked by a kink, or by a lump of faecal matter or a mass of *threadworms*, it may become inflamed: this is known as appendicitis. If left untreated, the appendix may eventually burst, leaving a perforated appendix.

Appendicitis may occur at any time; it is rare in very young children, but becomes more common in adolescence. If you suspect that your child has appendicitis you should consult your doctor. The disease progresses rapidly, and a child who is in normal health may have a burst appendix within 8 hours, in which case he will require an emergency operation.

SYMPTOMS

An older child with appendicitis commonly complains of colicky pain around the navel, which then becomes constant and moves to the right. The child may lose his appetite, vomit, be constipated and develop a fever. Later he may have diarrhoea, a higher fever, and pain on any movement, especially on coughing.

A younger child has very vague symptoms. He will tend to be irritable, unco-operative and restless. If your doctor presses your child's abdomen carefully, he may be able to detect right-sided tenderness.

TREATMENT

After an operation to remove the appendix, your child will probably need an *intravenous drip* to replace fluid and nutrients into the bloodstream, and a *nasogastric tube* to suck off any fluid from the stomach for 1 or 2 days. He will probably be given analgesics during the first 24 hours after the operation to relieve pain. After the first couple of days he will be able to begin to eat normally.

Your child will be encouraged to move around as soon as possible. Most children recover from appendicectomy very quickly and are allowed home after about 3 to 5 days.

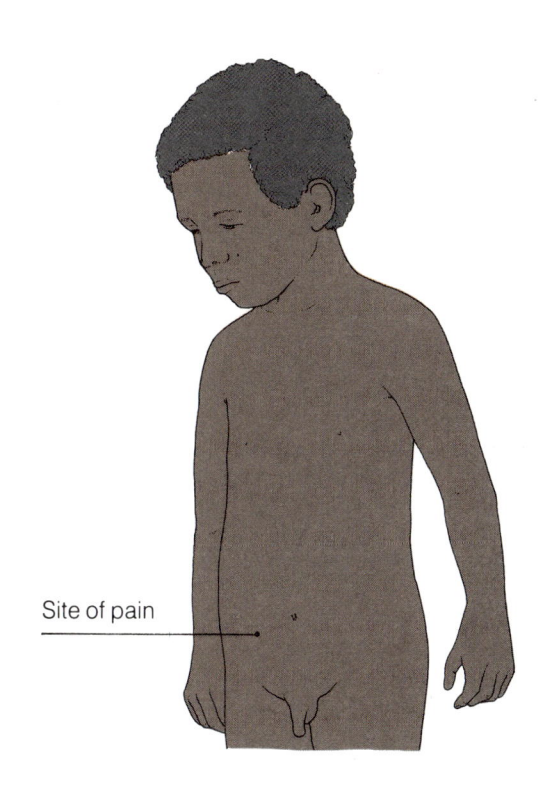

Site of pain

The child may first be aware of an inflamed appendix only as a vague feeling of discomfort around the navel. Gradually the pain may become continuous, and grow worse. Usually it becomes localized in the lower right-hand side of the abdomen. If peritonitis has developed the child's abdomen will feel hard and rigid and so tender he cannot bear you to touch it.

PERITONITIS
The peritoneum is the membrane lining the abdomen and covering the organs within it. Peritonitis is inflammation of the peritoneum which may result when a part of the digestive tract is ruptured, as, for example, when an appendix bursts. Symptoms are severe abdominal pain, vomiting and fever. Immediate surgery is necessary: Emergency action is vital.

DIARRHOEA

Diarrhoea may be defined as the passage of loose or watery stools 4 or more times daily.

Because diarrhoea increases the loss of fluid from the body, it may lead to dehydration. A short-lived attack usually does little harm, but if diarrhoea persists the severe dehydration can be life-threatening to a child.

If you have a small baby who has diarrhoea, you should seek the help of your doctor as soon as possible. Meanwhile, you can give the baby cooled boiled water but avoid other feeds. If your child is over 1 year old, consult your doctor if there is no sign of the diarrhoea settling after 36 hours. Never give medicines to control diarrhoea except on a doctor's advice.

Constipation may sometimes be accompanied by involuntary diarrhoea, also known as overflow or spurious diarrhoea. Although the rectum is full of hard faecal matter, liquids may leak past and dribble from the anus, giving the impression of diarrhoea.

TODDLER DIARRHOEA

Mild diarrhoea is fairly common in children who have been weaned but are under 4 years old. Children with this 'toddler diarrhoea' are well and thriving although they may pass several loose, mucousy stools each day, which contain undigested food remnants such as peas and carrots.

FOOD POISONING

Sudden diarrhoea, vomiting, abdominal pain and distension may be the result of eating food contaminated by bacteria such as salmonella. Foods that are at risk of being contaminated are poultry and cooked meats which are eaten cold, or rewarmed but not thoroughly heated through.

Most episodes of food poisoning, particularly in older children, are short-lived and require little treatment. However, if your child's diarrhoea is profuse or bloody, or if his vomiting or abdominal pain is severe, you should consult your doctor.

In some parts of the world precautions must be taken against infections such as *typhoid*, *cholera* and *infectious hepatitis* which can be contracted from contaminated food and water.

▶ **See also** Safety

GASTROENTERITIS

An infection of the digestive tract causing diarrhoea is known as gastroenteritis. In most children, the infection is viral in origin; the commonest cause is rotavirus. Summer diarrhoea, on the other hand, is more often due to bacteria. Most episodes of gastroenteritis last only 3 to 4 days.

You should consult your doctor if your baby or young child shows no signs of improving after 2 or 3 days. Your doctor will probably advise treatment with oral dehydration solutions (ORS). These consist of glucose and salt provided as powder to be made up with sterile water and they help to prevent dehydration and to maintain the body's balance of fluids and minerals. If you are breastfeeding your baby, continue to do so while you give ORS. Otherwise, children should be given no milk or solids until 24 hours after the start of treatment. If symptoms worsen or the diarrhoea reappears when you restart feeding, consult your doctor.

LACTOSE INTOLERANCE

Lactose intolerance may be an inherited condition or, more commonly, it may be caused by diseases of the intestinal lining.

Lactose, a natural sugar present in milk and milk-containing foods, is broken down in the digestive tract by the enzyme lactase into two sugars, glucose and galactose. These sugars are then absorbed by the intestine. A child who has lactose intolerance has no lactase enzyme. The undigested lactose draws water from the intestinal wall and so causes diarrhoea. The lactose passes to the large intestine and is fermented by the bacteria there, producing abdominal distension, pain and wind. The child has acid, frothy stools.

If you have a baby with lactose intolerance your doctor may prescribe an infant-formula milk that does not contain lactose. If an older child suffers from lactose intolerance, reduce the amount of milk he drinks.

COW'S MILK INTOLERANCE

Many conditions have been blamed on reactions to cow's milk, including *asthma*, *eczema*, *urticaria*, *colitis* and *migraine*. These claims extend to *colic*, general irritability, hyperactivity, fatigue and learning difficulties. The facts are less certain, and there is no sure way of showing whether milk is in any way responsible or not.

However, some digestive disturbances are undoubtedly due to cow's milk intolerance. One takes the form of diarrhoea, with or without blood or mucus. The diarrhoea may be intermittent, with loose unformed stools that contain undigested food remnants. A more serious reaction is severe diarrhoea with symptoms like *ulcerative colitis*. Children who have bad diarrhoea may lose weight and become generally ill.

Vomiting can also be caused by cow's milk intolerance; it usually occurs within an hour of eating or drinking dairy produce. Abdominal pain due to sensitivity to cow's milk varies from child to child: it may be mild and vague or severe and colicky, but it always occurs shortly after feeding.

If your child reacts to cow's milk in this way, you should consult your doctor. He may suggest excluding cow's milk from your child's diet. For a baby, you can use a specially formulated soya-based milk. For older children, you will need expert dietetic advice to make sure that their diet is nutritionally adequate.

▶ **See also** Allergy

COELIAC DISEASE

If a child suffers from coeliac disease the germ protein in wheat, known as gluten, causes him intestinal problems. It is thought that, following contact with gluten, the intestinal lining is damaged by a reaction of the immune system. As a result, there is a marked reduction in the absorptive area of the intestinal lining, which leads to malabsorption of many essential nutrients from the diet.

For no known reason the disease is more common in some areas of the Western world than others. For example, it is quite common in parts of Ireland, fairly rare in Switzerland, and rare in England and the United States. It tends to run in families, and is nearly always detected in early childhood.

Gluten is a protein found in some cereals, particularly wheat and rye. Corn, rice, sago and tapioca are gluten-free. Wheat-based cereals contain gluten, as do bread, biscuits, cakes and pasta (unless they are made with gluten-free flours).

SYMPTOMS

The majority of sufferers show symptoms before the age of 2 years although the condition can begin later. There may be diarrhoea and vomiting but, more usually, the first signs are loose, bulky, greasy or frothy stools that are difficult to flush away. Other signs include abdominal distension, loss of appetite, poor growth, muscle wasting, apathy, irritability and delayed development.

Older children may not show these symptoms. They may instead develop *anaemia*, or they may be small or slow to mature.

TREATMENT

If it is confirmed that your child is suffering from coeliac disease he will be put on a gluten-free diet. Once on the diet his symptoms will disappear and the damaged intestine will heal. The advice of your doctor and of a skilled dietician is essential to obtain the best possible diet. They will give you a list detailing gluten-containing and gluten-free foods. You should be aware that many prepared and packaged foods contain gluten in the form of fillers and additives.

ULCERATIVE COLITIS AND CROHN'S DISEASE

These conditions cause long-term inflammation of the intestine. In ulcerative colitis, the inflammation is restricted to the colon, whereas Crohn's disease may affect any part of the digestive tract from mouth to anus. Both can start within a few weeks of birth, but in most cases begin around 8 to 10 years of age. The causes of both conditions are unknown.

Inflammation and ulceration of the intestines causes bloody diarrhoea. A child has abdominal pain, especially before passing motions, and intermittent fever; he also loses his appetite and becomes lethargic. Some children also have recurrent mouth ulcers, joint swellings and pain; raised red lumps in the skin, sore eyes and back pain.

A child suffering from Crohn's disease, in particular, may have symptoms that are very difficult to pin down, with only occasional abdominal pain and loss of appetite; in puberty he may grow slowly but have few other signs.

If your family doctor suspects that your child has either of these conditions he will refer him to a hospital specialist. Several investigations will be necessary including blood tests, X-rays of the digestive tract and an *endoscopy*. The conditions are treated by drugs, but in severe cases surgery may be required to remove badly affected portions of intestine. A *stoma* may also be necessary.

CONSTIPATION

There is a wide variation in normal bowel habits; some children open their bowels 2 or 3 times daily, others only once every few days. Constipation is the infrequent passage of hard, compact stools. Infrequency alone is not cause for concern; there is more cause for worry if a child's regular bowel habits change so that his motions become less frequent, harder, and more difficult to pass. He may be constipated and have overflow *diarrhoea*.

Breastfed babies digest and absorb all their milk and so usually pass infrequent, small motions. This is not constipation.

CAUSES

Constipation sometimes occurs with or just after an illness, particularly a feverish one. This is usually because the child has eaten less food while ill or taken insufficient fluid. The bowels should return to normal as the child begins to eat a full diet.

Occasionally a bowel disorder, such as *appendicitis* or *Hirschsprungs's disease*, underlies constipation. If this is so, there are usually other signs of illness, and a doctor should be consulted.

Another possible cause of constipation is *anal fissure*. Passing stools causes the child pain, so he holds back. The motions stay in the bowel where more water is absorbed from them, making them even harder, and a vicious circle is set up.

In some young children, constipation may have an emotional rather than a physical cause. Over-zealous potty training or anxiety about having to pass a motion every day can contribute to the problem. Some children are frightened of sitting on the potty or toilet, and some are worried when they see 'parts of their body' falling out. Some children will not use school toilets and may develop constipation as a result. In addition, your child may be using constipation as a weapon in the battle towards independence, or he may be asking for attention, especially if you started toilet-training early or had many battles over it.

PREVENTION AND TREATMENT

The digestive tract is designed to work on a bulky, fibre-rich diet that leaves bulky, soft stools. Make sure that your child's diet includes enough fibre-rich foods, such as wheat-based cereals, wholemeal bread, fruit and vegetables. If he is constipated, avoid giving him regular laxatives as his bowel may become unable to function properly without them. They are useful, however, as a short-term measure while an underlying disorder is treated, provided you ask your doctor's advice about a suitable laxative to choose.

If your child's rectum is grossly distended with impacted faeces, your doctor may recommend an enema. A liquid that stimulates defecation is drained into the rectum and your child will need to hold it in for a short period of time so that his bowels will discharge as much of their contents as possible. Usually, however, a course of laxatives to keep your child's bowels open while he becomes used to new toilet habits suffices.

PILES

A pile is an enlarged or varicose vein just inside the anus. The presence of piles usually indicates many years of *constipation* and straining to pass stools. For this reason, piles are common in adults but very rare in children.

Avoiding constipation by ensuring that your child eats a diet rich in fibre prevents piles developing. If they have already developed, avoiding constipation will prevent them from becoming worse.

A few children have prominent veins under the skin near the back passage. These are usually not piles but a form of birthmark. They require no treatment, other than avoiding constipation.

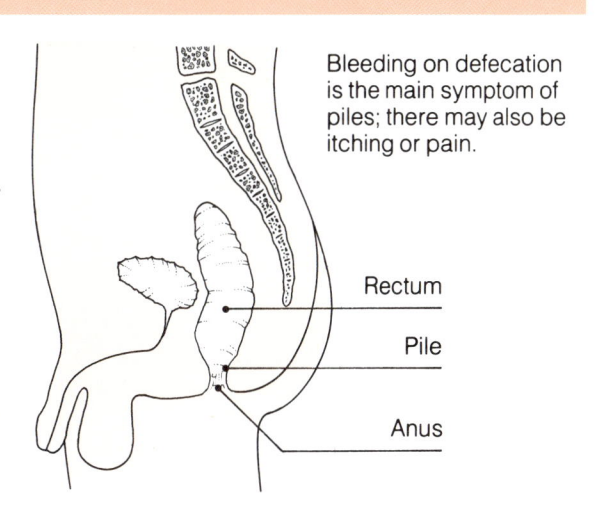

Bleeding on defecation is the main symptom of piles; there may also be itching or pain.

Rectum

Pile

Anus

ANAL FISSURE

This is a split in the lining of the anus. It is common at any age and is usually a result of *constipation*. When there is a fissure it is intensely painful to try to open the bowels, and sometimes there is a bloody streaking on the surface of the stools. Because of the pain, a child with an anal fissure tries to avoid bowel actions, and remains or becomes constipated again and a vicious circle is set up.

If the pain is severe, you can help your child by giving him a hot bath and a gentle laxative, sufficient to ensure a bowel action at least once a day. If these measures fail, consult your doctor who may advise deliberate over-stretching of the muscles around the anus under anaesthetic. This should allow the fissure to heal. Unfortunately recurrence is common.

HIRSCHSPRUNG'S DISEASE

The contents of the intestines are propelled along by waves of muscular contraction called peristalsis. Normal peristalsis depends on a normal nerve supply to the intestinal muscle. Hirschsprung's disease is a very rare *congenital abnormality* in which the nerve supply to some of the large intestine is absent. This means that the intestine is unable to contract and relax and as a result is much narrower than normal. Hirschsprung's disease may make a baby unwell within a few days of birth, by delaying the passage of stools and causing the baby's abdomen to swell.

If the disease is less severe, the problem may show up later as a very obstinate form of *constipation*. In this case, the child may have swelling, especially of the upper part of the abdomen, and the abdomen may have a taut, drum-like feel because he cannot pass wind normally.

If Hirschsprung's disease is suspected, several tests may be carried out, including a bowel pressure test by means of a little tube introduced into the back passage.

Treatment depends on the length of intestine involved. A colostomy may be advised. This is an operation to remove the part of the bowel causing the problem and to create an artificial opening, or stoma, in the abdominal wall. Waste matter passes into an attached bag. The colostomy may be temporary and a later operation may reconnect the bowel to the anus.

WORMS

It is very common for children to suffer from threadworms. These worms look like very tiny pieces of white thread. They live in the digestive tract and the females emerge at night through the anus to lay their eggs on the surrounding skin; this causes the child irritation and disturbed sleep. Reinfection tends to occur because the child scratches his bottom and then subsequently puts his fingers to his mouth, swallowing more eggs. Threadworms are also highly infectious within

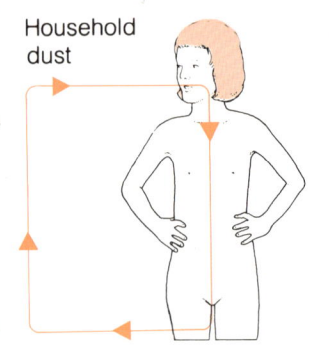

Household dust

Change your child's sheets and underclothes often to prevent reinfection with threadworms. Wearing pyjamas makes it less likely that she will scratch her skin directly and transfer eggs to her fingers.

a family because eggs get into the household dust. In girls, threadworms can enter the vagina and urethra, causing irritation, vaginal discharge and pain on passing urine.

If you suspect your child has worms, you should consult your doctor for treatment. A drug that has a laxative effect is used to treat threadworms. There are several preparations available, which can be given in single doses or several doses at daily or weekly intervals. Whatever treatment your doctor prescribes, you must make sure that all members of the family are treated at the same time. You must all be very careful to wash your hands and brush your nails before meals and after going to the toilet. A bath first thing in the morning helps to remove from the skin any eggs that have been deposited in the night.

JAUNDICE

The yellow skin colour characteristic of jaundice is caused by raised levels of the pigment *bilirubin* in the blood. Jaundice is usually the most conspicuous sign of a sick liver. If a child is suffering from jaundice, the yellow colour appears first in the whites of the eyes and then on the face, before spreading down the body. The child may not feel particularly unwell but he will be miserable, lethargic and will lose his appetite.

Jaundice is very common in newborn babies; in this case it almost always represents liver immaturity rather than liver disease.

However, babies whose jaundice persists for more than 3 weeks and who have abnormally pale stools need special tests to diagnose the cause. Most have neonatal hepatitis, liver inflammation due to infection or inherited disorders of the body's chemistry. Sometimes no cause can be found. Babies with neonatal hepatitis usually make a good recovery.

A few babies have scarring and blockage of the main bile duct, **biliary atresia**, which prevents bile from leaving the liver. This used invariably to be fatal, but surgery can now be used to help the bile drain.

Jaundice occurring for the first time when a child has been previously healthy is usually due to *infectious hepatitis*.

▶See also Problems of the newborn child

INFECTIOUS HEPATITIS

The virus that causes infectious hepatitis, hepatitis A, is most prevalent where sanitary conditions are poor. Children in developing countries catch hepatitis, recover and acquire immunity at an early age. In more privileged countries, outbreaks are scattered and may involve whole families and affect all ages. The virus is spread by faecal contamination of fingers.

After an incubation period of up to 40 days a child with infectious hepatitis loses his appetite and has stomach pains, diarrhoea, fever and headache. At least half of the children affected have very mild, often unrecognized symptoms. Then *jaundice* appears; and as it does, so the earlier symptoms fade. The jaundice seldom lasts longer than 2 weeks and there is usually complete recovery.

TREATMENT

Your doctor should have no difficulty in recognizing infectious hepatitis, especially if there is a local outbreak. Tests are not necessary unless there is doubt about the cause, or unless the course of the jaundice is unusual or protracted. As with many viral illnesses, there is no specific treatment and your child must rest and drink plenty of fluids. In general he is usually the best judge of when he is ready for more activity and a fuller diet. The infectious phase of the disease precedes the jaundice, and children are no longer infectious 2 weeks after the jaundice appears. Your doctor may recommend a protective injection for some of your child's contacts. You will need to take special precautions to prevent infection spreading within the family. The lavatory pan and any pot your child uses should be cleaned frequently with an antiseptic lavatory cleaner. Keep your child's towel separate and use a special towel to dry his crockery and cutlery.

HEPATITIS B

Another type of viral infectious hepatitis, hepatitis B, is fairly rare in the Western world. Some groups, such as drug addicts and homosexuals are particularly at risk, as are children of mothers who carry the active virus.

CHRONIC INFECTIOUS HEPATITIS

This disease usually affects adolescent girls. It is caused by a reaction of the immune system against its own liver cells. This causes either an unusual attack of suspected infective hepatitis or slowly evolving hepatitis almost without symptoms. A liver *biopsy* is necessary to diagnose the problem.

Steroid drugs suppress the inflammation and stop the liver becoming scarred. Fortunately, a child's liver has considerable powers of recovery.

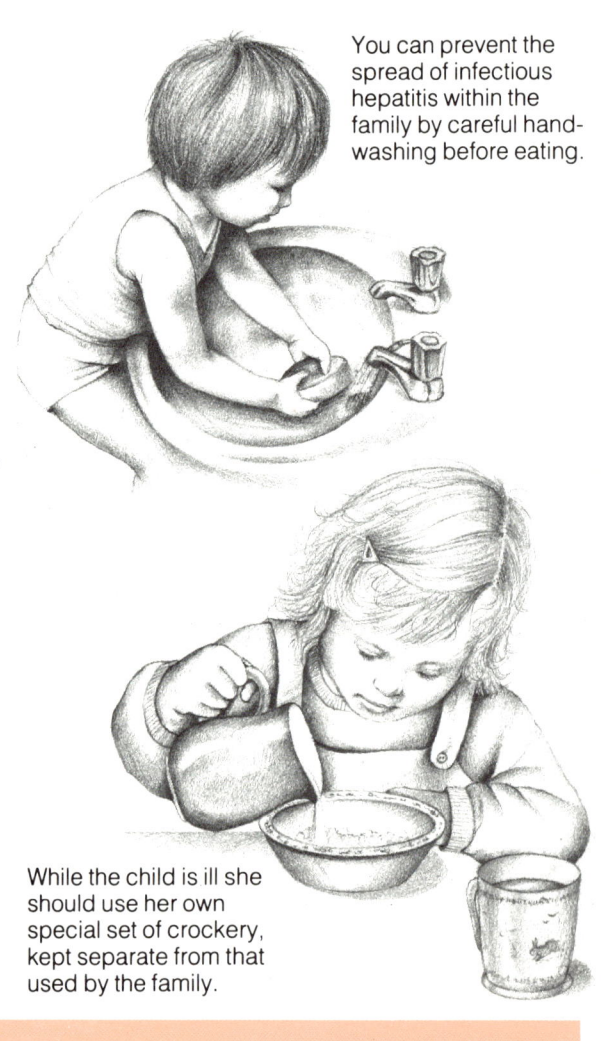

You can prevent the spread of infectious hepatitis within the family by careful hand-washing before eating.

While the child is ill she should use her own special set of crockery, kept separate from that used by the family.

OTHER LIVER DISEASES

There are some rare liver disorders that may come to light because your child has prolonged *jaundice*; or because your doctor finds that he has an enlarged liver, or because a sick liver has been discovered through blood or some other tests.

Wilson's disease is a rare, inherited disease in which the body stores abnormally large amounts of copper, which slowly damages organs – notably the liver and, at a later stage, the brain. Children are unlikely to show any symptoms before they are 6 years old. This can be effectively treated with drugs.

Cirrhosis is a disease in which the liver is severely scarred and its function disrupted. It is not always accompanied by *jaundice*. It is very rare among children, partly because their livers have such good powers of recovery and partly because they do not usually drink significant quantities of alcohol – the major cause of cirrhosis among adults. A gross excess of vitamin A sometimes causes cirrhosis.

THE KIDNEYS, BLADDER AND GENITALS

The urinary tract is made up of the kidneys, ureters, bladder and urethra. In the female, the urinary and genital tracts are quite separate. The female urethra is very short and opens just in front of the vagina. In the male the urethra is much longer than in the female. It opens in the tip of the penis and it is used for the passage of semen as well as of urine.

The urinary tract
The two kidneys lie in the abdomen on either side of the spine at waist level, where they are well protected by the lower ribs and the back muscles. The kidneys' function is to maintain the chemical composition of the body. The body obtains its energy from the nutrients contained in food and the nutrients are carried to body cells by the blood. Waste products from the body cells are then carried in the blood to the kidneys. Each kidney contains about a million nephrons, each of which consists of a glomerulus, or filter, and a fine draining tube.

Waste products and excess water are drained off from the kidneys through a tube called a ureter to the bladder.

The bladder acts as a reservoir for the constant trickle of liquid from the kidneys. When the bladder is full, its muscular walls contract to expel the liquid through a valve or sphincter into the urethra. From there it passes out of the body as urine.

Kidney function in newborn babies is limited, and a newborn baby given an unsuitable diet will suffer from an accumulation of toxic chemicals in the body. Breast milk, or a modified cows' milk preparation, provides a baby with sufficient energy and water without overworking his kidneys. By the time a baby is about 4 months old, his kidneys will have matured enough to cope with the waste products from a more general diet. Bladder function in newborn babies is automatic, and control is not achieved until 2 to 3 years of age.

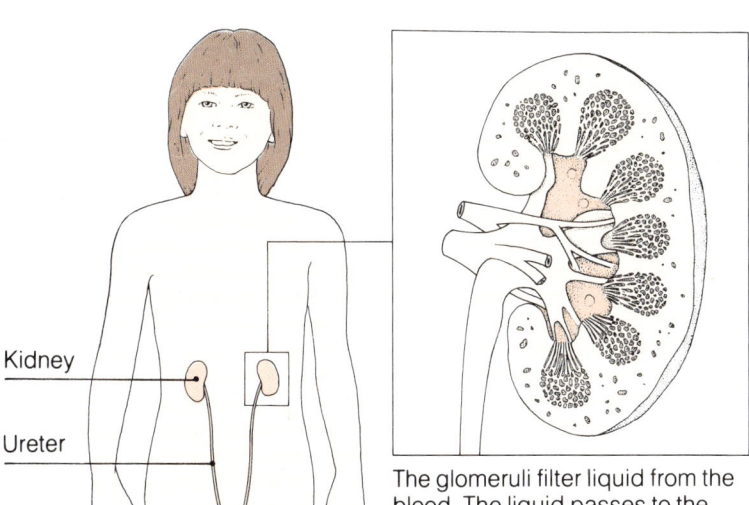

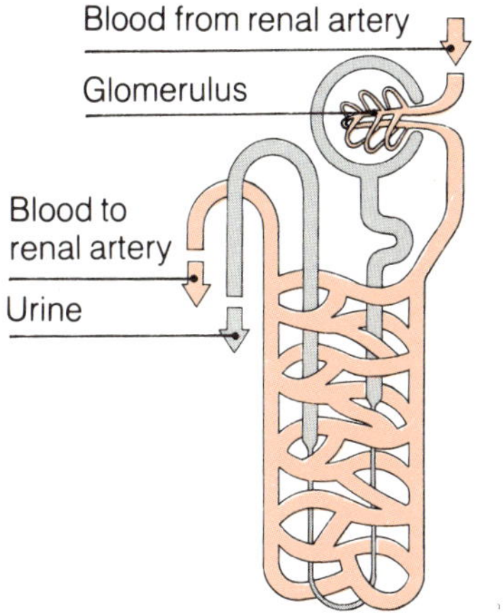

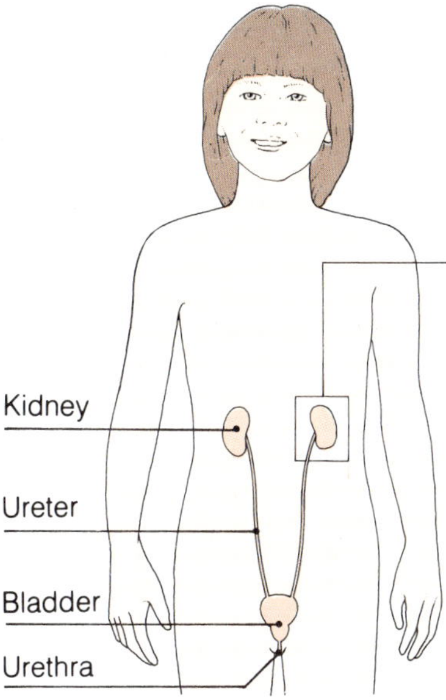

The glomeruli filter liquid from the blood. The liquid passes to the central part of the kidney, the medulla, along a thin tube surrounded by blood vessels. Any nutrients are reabsorbed into the blood. The remaining liquid, containing waste products, drains into the ureter and thence to the bladder.

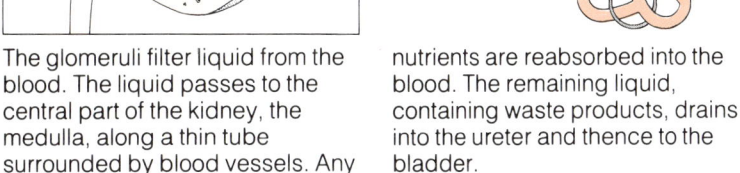

A few children are born with abnormalities of the urinary tract. Unfortunately, serious kidney disorders can go unnoticed until considerable damage has occurred. If a child has suspected kidney disease a blood test will often detect a problem. Symptoms such as poor appetite, nausea or vomiting, poor weight gain or growth, abdominal pain, fever or headaches are occasionally caused by disease of the kidneys. If your child has these symptoms, you should consult a doctor.

The reproductive system
The reproductive, or genital, system consists of paired glands that produce sex hormones and germ cells (egg and sperm cells), and the associated system of tubes and channels necessary for the transmission of the germ cells, and for the sexual act of insemination.

The male sex glands are the testicles or testes; they lie in the scrotal sac and produce sex hormones and sperm. The mature sperm pass through a very fine tube, the vas, to enter the urethra close to its junction with the bladder. Surrounding the urethra at this point are the prostate glands. The secretion from these and other glands together with sperm, form a fluid called semen or seminal fluid.

The female sex glands are the ovaries. They are situated in the lower part of the abdominal cavity and produce sex hormones and egg cells, or ova. The ova pass along the Fallopian tubes to the womb, or uterus, the neck of which leads into the vagina.

In the very early development of the embryo the male or female sex glands start high up in the abdomen. During development, they gradually move down into the pelvis. The ovaries remain there but the testicles leave the pelvis through the inguinal canal, and from there they pass across the front of the pelvic bone to enter the scrotal sac. This takes place

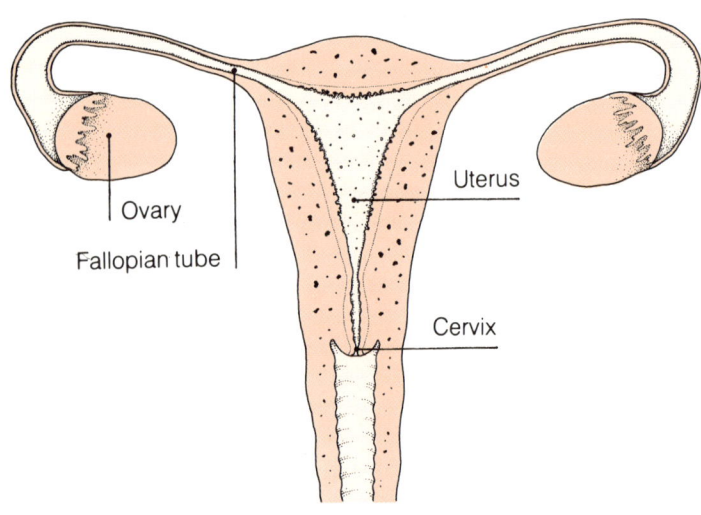

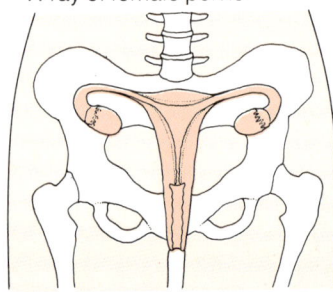

Ovary
Fallopian tube
Uterus
Cervix

Vulva of a young girl

X-ray of female pelvis

The female urethra is short and is positioned closed to the anus, so that infection can easily reach the bladder. The vagina leading to the uterus lies behind the urethra so the reproductive and urinary tracts are quite separate.

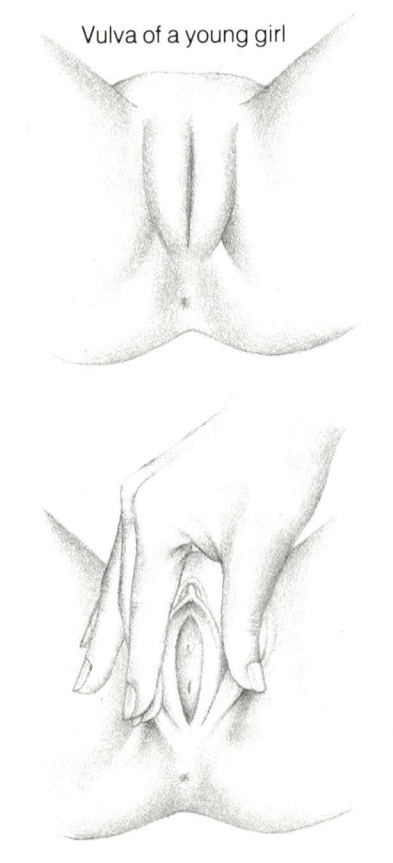

THE KIDNEYS, BLADDER AND GENITALS

in the last month or two before birth, so if a baby is born very prematurely his testicles may not have entered the scrotum.

Sometimes the sex of a newborn child is not immediately obvious. The reasons for this are complex, and investigations have to be carried out as soon as possible after birth to determine the genetic sex of the child and the exact type of genital structures and sex glands that are present.

A child's sex glands are immature: they do contain ova or the elements necessary to produce sperm but they do not produce very much hormone. As puberty approaches they become much more active; hormone production rises and the physical and emotional changes that are typical of puberty and adolescence will occur.

▶ **See also** The older child and adolescent

CIRCUMCISION

The foreskin protects the underlying delicate skin of the head of the penis. The foreskin of a newborn baby is usually tightly stuck to his penis and cannot and should not be pulled back.

After birth the foreskin gradually separates from the head of the penis and becomes fully retractable. If, by the time the child is 3 or 4 years old, it is still not possible to retract his foreskin, or if infections of the foreskin occur, then circumcision, or removal of the foreskin may be advised.

Attitudes towards circumcision vary widely between people of different countries, cultures and religions. The operation is carried out under general anaesthetic, although newborn boys are sometimes circumcised for religious reasons without anaesthetic.

Circumcision is a major operation when a boy is older.

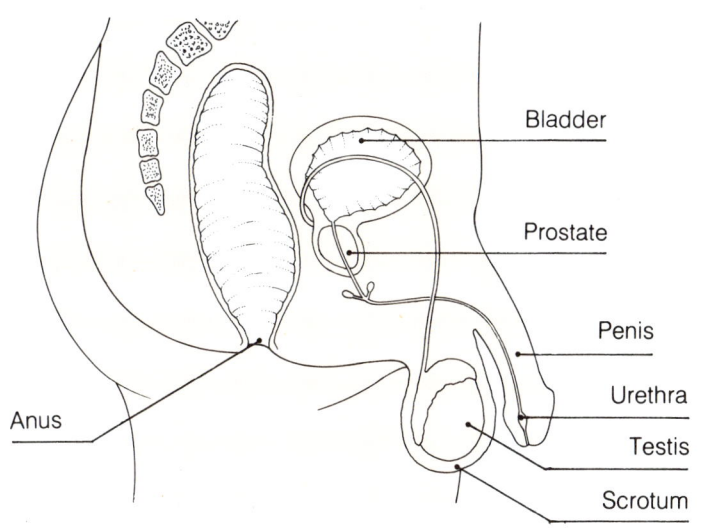

The sperm-producing male testicles lie outside the body within the scrotum. This is because sperm cannot develop normally at body temperature. A boy whose testicles remained undescended would probably be infertile as an adult. The long male urethra acts as a barrier to germs, making boys much less susceptible to bladder infection than girls.

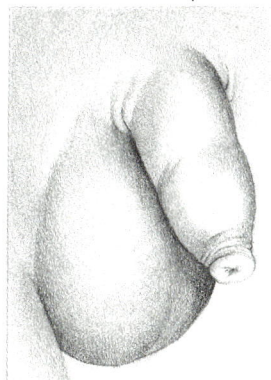

Uncircumcised penis

Circumcised penis

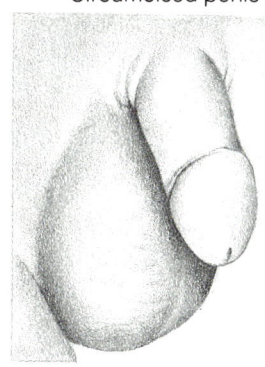

KIDNEY FAILURE

If the filtering power of the kidneys has been reduced to the point where changes in the chemical balance of the body begin to affect health, this is described as kidney or renal failure. Many kidney diseases can lead to kidney failure. Overall, however, kidney failure is rare in childhood.

A child with kidney failure will be given a special diet to limit his intake of protein, phosphorous and other salts. He will be prescribed drugs to treat any accompanying high blood pressure. If the kidney failure continues or worsens dialysis or a kidney transplant will be necessary.

Dialysis is a means of taking over the function of the kidney – clearing waste products from the body and regulating the balance of water and chemicals in it – by machine. There are two forms of dialysis: peritoneal dialysis and haemodialysis. Haemodialysis can be carried out on a kidney machine in the child's own home. In peritoneal dialysis a tube is inserted into the abdominal cavity and a special fluid is introduced which bathes the abdominal organs. Waste products seep from the abdomen into the fluid, which is continually sucked out and replaced.

KIDNEY TRANSPLANT

Kidney failure can be treated for some years either by dialysis or by replacing the diseased kidney with a healthy one donated by another person. The donor may be a person who has recently died, in which case the kidney must be removed within 30 minutes of death; or preferably, the donor may be a living person, usually a relative. The kidney cannot be stored for more than 24 hours.

As with any transplant, there is a risk that the recipient's body will identify the implanted organ as 'foreign' and will reject the new tissue. To minimize this risk, the tissues of the donor and recipient have to be carefully matched: centralized records help to facilitate the matching of donor and recipient from country to country. A limited number of further transplants can be attempted if one donated kidney fails.

Dialysis may have to be carried out 2 or 3 times each week. During haemodialysis on a kidney machine, blood from an artery in the child's arm is led through a needle and along a fine tube to the machine. Here, waste products are filtered out and the blood is returned through another tube and needle to a vein in the arm. To make insertion of the needle easier, a permanent arteriovenous shunt is made in the child's arm by joining a suitable artery and vein together.

NEPHRITIS

Glomerulonephritis is a rare inflammation of the glomerular filters of the kidney. There are various types of glomerulonephritis. The one that most commonly affects children is acute nephritis which occurs between 1 to 3 weeks after an *infection* caused by streptococcus bacteria. The bacteria do not damage the kidneys directly; it is the *antibodies* that the body produces to destroy the bacteria that attack the glomerular filters, causing them to swell. The filtering capacity of the kidneys is reduced so that too much salt and water are retained in the body causing swelling, especially around the eyes, and a rise in blood pressure. Both kidneys are always involved.

Kidney failure can occur but is uncommon. A child suffering from acute nephritis is treated with antibiotics and given medicines to control blood pressure. Admission to hospital is often required. If kidney failure does result then *dialysis* will be necessary for a week or two to allow the kidneys to recover.

Blood is usually seen in the urine for a few weeks, and it can return from time to time, especially during unrelated virus infections. This does not mean that the kidney inflammation is worse. Almost all children recover fully without long-term damage, although their urine may be found to contain blood and protein for up to a year.

NEPHROTIC SYNDROME

Very occasionally, the glomerular filters in the kidneys are damaged so that they leak protein from the bloodstream into the urine. Water accumulates in the tissues and causes swelling, or oedema. The condition is called nephrotic syndrome.

The main symptom of nephrotic syndrome is slow swelling, especially of the face. The disorder usually responds to steroid medicines. It often recurs but most children eventually grow out of it. A child with nephrotic syndrome is vulnerable to infections. Any such child who appears at all ill, but especially with fever, abdominal pain, vomiting or diarrhoea, should see a doctor.

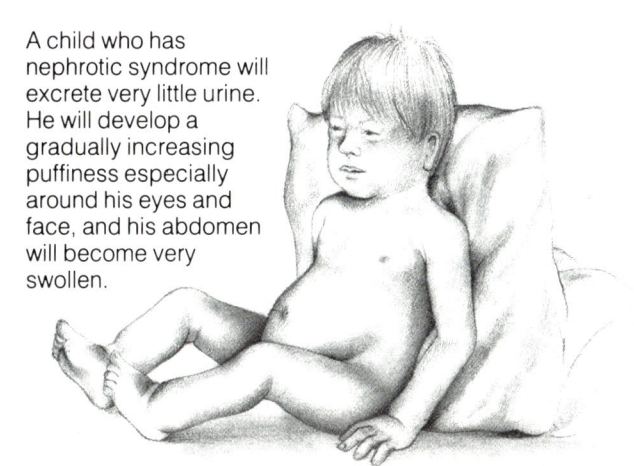

A child who has nephrotic syndrome will excrete very little urine. He will develop a gradually increasing puffiness especially around his eyes and face, and his abdomen will become very swollen.

POLYDIPSIA

Healthy kidneys adjust the amount of urine produced according to the intake of fluid. Damaged kidneys may produce too much urine for the amount of fluid taken in, depriving the rest of the body of water and causing thirst. Excessive thirst is called polydipsia. Drinking a lot is usually a result of habit rather than disease but if your child appears to drink excessively it is worth arranging for his urine to be tested to ensure that there is no kidney disease. Tests will also show whether he has any other conditions such as *diabetes*.

ENURESIS (Bladder incontinence)

By the age of 2 years most children are aware when they have full bladders. *Bladder control* during the day is usually achieved by children when they are between the ages of 2½ and 3½ years, and by the time they are 5 years old most children can empty their bladders even when they are not full.

If your school-age child has accidents during the day as well as wetting his bed at night (nocturnal enuresis), concentrate on *toilet-training* before tackling bedwetting. If he dribbles all the time, or if there are symptoms of *urinary tract infection*, then see your doctor. He will probably check whether there are any abnormalities of the urinary tract. Enuresis is rarely due to infection or abnormality.

Bladder training involves encouraging your child to learn bladder control. This is best done during the school holidays and can be introduced as a game, with a wall chart to be filled in each day. Your child should carry around an alarm watch, clock or kitchen alarm, set to go off every hour. When it goes off he should attempt to empty his bladder. Increase the period by 15 minutes each day, building the intervals up to 4 hours. An accident one day means reducing the time period the following day. If this procedure fails, try again during the next school holidays.

BEDWETTING

Dryness at night is usually achieved between the ages of 3 and 4 years. Approximately 1 in every 7 children of 5 years of age and 1 in every 14 children of 10 years of age regularly wet the bed. By the age of 15 years only about 1 child in 100 suffers from bedwetting. It is more common among boys than girls.

If your child wets his bed he needs your patience, support, encouragement and good humour. Enuresis is not due to laziness or naughtiness, so your child should not be scolded for a wet bed, even though daily washing of bed linen may make staying good-humoured difficult. Certain strategies may help in coping with the problem: protect the mattress with a rubber sheet; wake your child to pass urine when you go to bed if it does not upset him; and limit his drinks before bedtime.

Bedwetting is best managed just by encouragement and patience until the child is about 9 years old and able to co-operate with bladder training using a buzzer alarm. Used properly, buzzer alarms work for the majority

The buzzer alarm system consists of two pads which, when wet, complete an electrical circuit and cause a bell or buzzer to sound. The two pads, separated by a flanelette draw sheet, are placed on top of the mattress, with the child's ordinary sheet over them. When the child starts to urinate, The alarm should be in such a position that the child has to get out of bed to switch it off and use the pot.

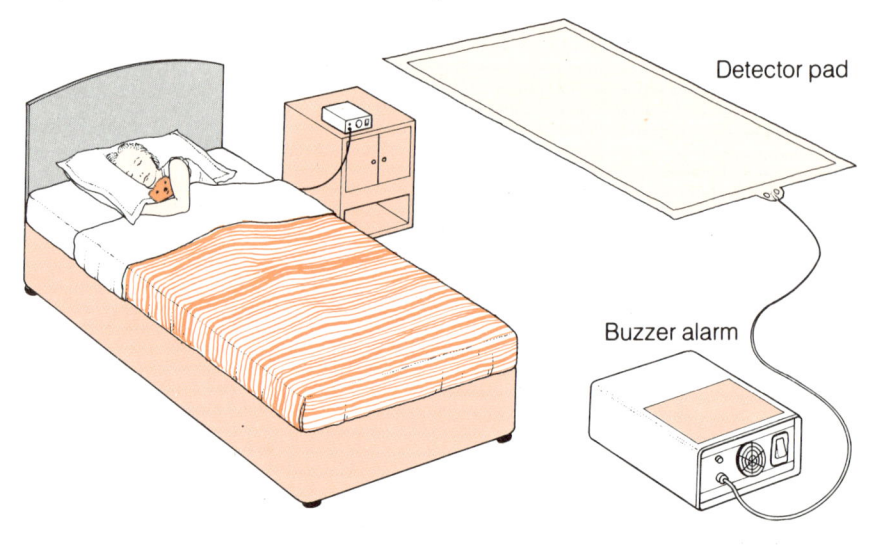

of children with the problem; most consist of mesh sheets placed under the bed sheet and wired to a battery alarm, but one type can be fitted to the child's pants and is connected to an alarm pinned to his pyjama top. When he begins to wet the bed the alarm sounds and wakes him. In this way he should come to associate bladder emptying with waking, so that in due course waking precedes the bladder emptying. Some children sleep deeply and may require medicines that lighten sleep as well as acting on the bladder. On the whole, however, medicines are not particularly useful in curing bedwetting.

URINARY TRACT INFECTIONS

Infection of the urinary tract is common in childhood. Most infections are caused by germs from the bowel that enter the urinary tract through the urethra. Because the female urethra is shorter than the male, urinary tract infection is about 5 times more common among girls than boys. Some children are born with an abnormality of the urinary tract which can predispose them to infection, and in order to prevent further problems such an abnormality should be detected and the infection treated as early as possible. If your child has a urine infection your doctor will probably recommend an investigation to ensure there are no abnormalities of the urinary tract. An intravenous pyelogram will reveal whether or not this is so.

Your child will be prescribed an antibiotic to cure the infection. In the few children with an abnormality of the urinary tract, corrective surgery may be necessary. However, some children have a mild abnormality that disappears as they get older. They will be prescribed an antibiotic, to be taken at bedtime, to prevent reinfection.

When your child has had a urinary tract infection it is more important than ever to keep his bowels regular, as *constipation* may interfere with emptying the bladder. Make sure that he drinks plenty of fluids to encourage frequent emptying of his bladder. Two visits to the lavatory just before bedtime should ensure that his bladder is empty during the night.

It is important to teach girls to wipe from front to back after defecation so that faeces are not brought into contact with the opening of the urethra.

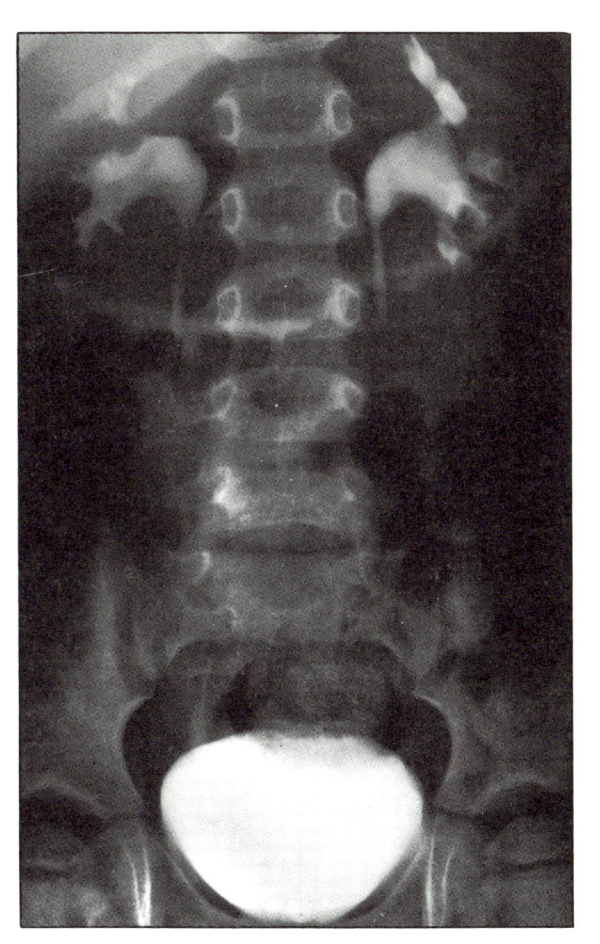

An intravenous pyelogram is a means of examining the kidneys and urinary tract. A solution visible on X-ray is injected into a vein and travels in the bloodstream to the kidneys from where it is excreted. As it moves through the urinary tract, a series of X-rays will show any abnormalities.

VAGINAL DISCHARGE

From the age of about 2 years onwards many girls develop an inoffensive, white or creamy-yellow discharge from the vagina, which may or may not cause itching. There are many possible causes such as infections due to *thrush* which can follow a course of antibiotics; *threadworms*; or *dermatitis*, which can be caused by bath oils and salts, scented soaps, or nylon pants. Sometimes the girl's vaginal lining is inactive, and therefore easily infected: a short course of hormone treatment may be advised. Antibiotics are usually unnecessary.

A blood-stained vaginal discharge is much less common and may be the result of the child pushing some small object, such as a bead or paper clip, into her vagina. If your child has a blood-stained discharge you should take her to the doctor for a full investigation. She may need an anaesthetic in order to remove a foreign body.

VULVOVAGINITIS

Girls sometimes complain of redness, soreness and itching of the vulva and vaginal entrance, often made worse because they scratch.

If your child complains of itching at night, the most likely cause is *threadworms*, which sometimes creep forward from the anus into the vagina and can cause intense irritation.

Vulvovaginitis may also be the result of an infection, perhaps because the child has not yet learned to wipe herself from front to back after defecating. Occasionally an allergy to wool or nylon underpants or to a bath additive may be the cause and, more rarely still, a foreign body inserted into the vagina by a young child.

URETHRAL VALVES

Some boys are born with urethral valves. These are very delicate little flaps of tissue situated high in the urethra just below the exit from the bladder. They obstruct the flow of urine from the bladder into the urethra. The range of severity is wide. If the abnormality is severe, it may be picked up in late pregnancy by *ultrasound*. Babies produce urine before birth and, if the bladder outflow is blocked, the bladder, ureters and kidneys will be distended by the back pressure of urine. At birth the baby will dribble urine rather than pass a good stream, and he may have some *kidney failure*. Milder cases may not be recognized for weeks, months or sometimes even years, until symptoms such as failure to grow, urine infections or extreme slowness in emptying his bladder become apparent. The valves are removed under general anaesthetic by means of an instrument passed up the urethra.

HERNIA

A month or so before birth a boy's testicles descend from the pelvis into the scrotum. As each testicle descends it draws down in front of itself part of the filmy lining of the abdominal cavity. This lining then lies in front of the testicle in the scrotum, part of it forming an enclosed sac. The channel between the abdominal cavity and the sac in front of the

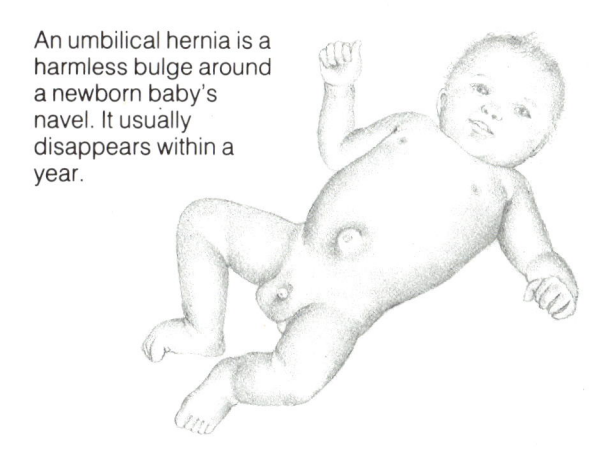

An umbilical hernia is a harmless bulge around a newborn baby's navel. It usually disappears within a year.

testis usually disappears spontaneously. If the channel does not disappear, fluid is able to pass down it into the sac, causing a hydrocele. If the persisting channel is quite wide, a loop of bowel may drop through, causing a hernia.

Once it has appeared a hydrocele is usually noticeable all the time. It is a soft, painless swelling around the testicle and may increase in size as the day goes on. A hernia, on the other hand, appears as a lump in the groin, or groin and scrotum, when the baby cries or strains. It is said to be reducible if the lump disappears when the baby stops crying, or if it can be made to disappear by gentle massage. If it cannot be made to disappear it is said to be irreducible. A reducable hernia may cause discomfort; an irreducible lump causes pain.

If your child has a hernia in the groin or scrotum he will need urgent treatment. Even if the hernia is completely reducible there is still a risk that his bowel may become obstructed. The younger the child the more likely this is to happen. Treatment consists of an operation to replace the protrusion and to close off the channel. If the child has an irreducible hernia his legs will be raised in the air for an hour or so to encourage the hernia to reduce in size before the operation.

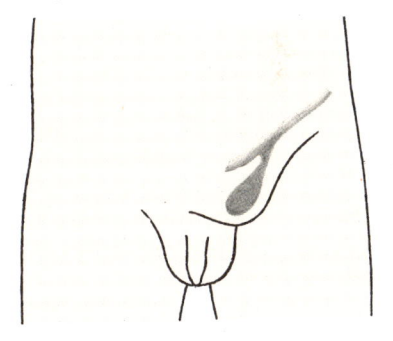

Inguinal hernias may develop in boys, causing a bulge in the groin. An operation is always needed because of the risk of bowel obstruction.

HYDROCELE

A hydrocele forms when the channel between the abdominal cavity and the scrotal sac persists after the testicles have descended. Fluid from the abdominal cavity causes a persistent soft swelling in the sac.

A hydrocele that is noticeable shortly after birth often disappears without treatment within 12 months. If it does not, an operation may be recommended to draw off the fluid and to remove part of the sac so that fluid can no longer collect there. Occasionally hydrocele may appear for the first time in an older boy. In this case an operation is necessary because a late-developing hydrocele may mean that the testicle is abnormal or infected, or that there is *torsion of the testicle*.

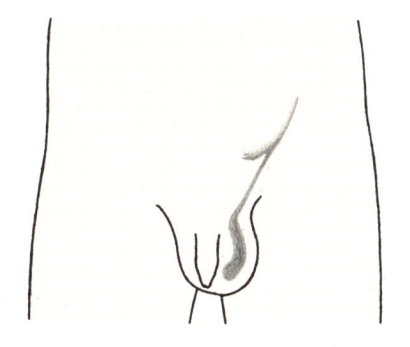

The channel connecting the abdominal cavity to the scrotum begins to close at birth and is normally completely obliterated during the first year of life. If it remains a hydrocele may form.

UNDESCENDED TESTICLE

When a baby boy is born one or both testicles may not be in the scrotum. In a premature baby an undescended testicle may well come down without treatment over the next few months. This can also happen when a baby is born full-term with undescended testicles, but it is less likely.

Until *puberty* a boy's testicles may be withdrawn from the scrotum by involuntary muscular action, especially when he is nervous or cold. This is normal and is not to be confused with an undescended testicle, which cannot be coaxed into the scrotum at any time.

An undescended testicle may not develop normally. An abnormally positioned testicle is more prone to accidental damage or *torsion*. Therefore, if the testicles are not in the scrotum, an operation called orchidopexy is usually carried out when the boy is between the ages of 1 and 3 years.

Rarely a child may be born with one testicle completely undeveloped, and in this situation he may be offered a false implant. This is usually left until he is older, partly to avoid the necessity for several operations to increase the size of the false testicle as the boy grows.

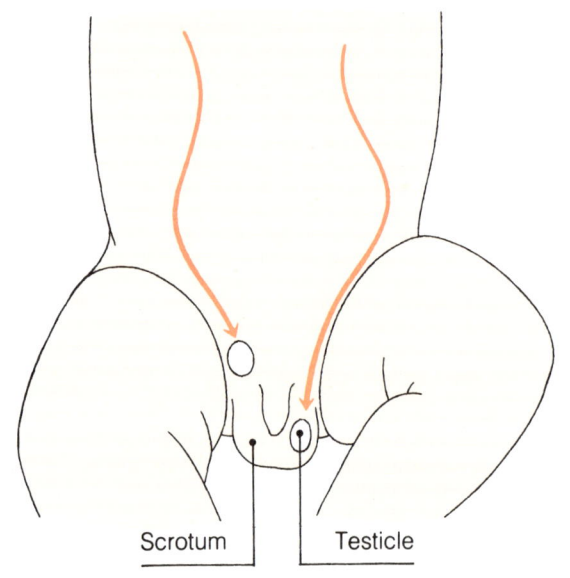

The testes normally develop in the abdomen and descend into the scrotum about a month before birth. The operation to bring an undescended testicle into the scrotum is straightforward and the child may only need to spend 1 or 2 days in hospital. Any swelling or discomfort can be relieved by giving the child a scrotal support and, if necessary, an analgesic.

TORSION OF THE TESTICLE

If the internal sheath in which each testicle is enclosed is too loose, the testicle can twist out of its normal position. Such twisting, or torsion cuts off the blood supply to the testicle, with a consequent risk of damage. Torsion usually happens either to newborn boys or to those over 8 years old, but it can occur at any age. It causes severe pain in the testicle, groin and abdomen, usually accompanied by vomiting. An operation is urgently needed and must be carried out within 6 hours of the onset of pain to straighten the testicle and fix it in position. To prevent the same problem arising with the other testicle, both will probably be stitched into position at the same time.

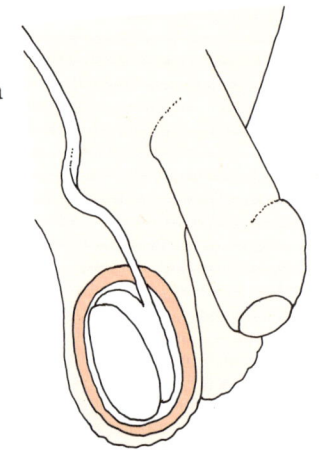

If a testicle can move within its sheath it may twist, kinking the veins that normally take blood away from the testicle and making it swollen and painful. It may untwist spontaneously but operation is always necessary to prevent recurrence.

HYPOSPADIAS

Normally a boy's urethra opens almost at the tip of the penis, and the foreskin surrounds it. Hypospadias is the condition in which the urethra opens at some other point on the rear shaft of the penis or even in the perineum. Sometimes the shaft of the penis is also relatively short on the underside, producing a downward curvature called chordee. A mild degree of hypospadias is extremely common, and it can run in families. Treatment is usually deferred until a child is 3 or 4 years old, although occasionally the urethral opening may need to be enlarged a little at birth. This can be done without anaesthetic.

Surgical repair is necessary in all but the mildest cases of hypospadias. This is normally carried out before the child is of school age. Sometimes an abnormal urethral opening reappears soon after repair, necessitating a further operation. The problem is solved once the child can pass a good forward stream of urine. Sexual intercourse and insemination will be normal in adult life.

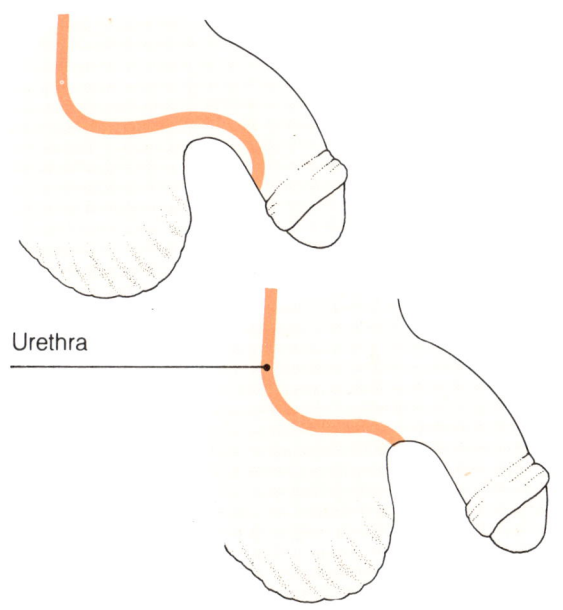

Mild hypospadias may not require treatment, but if the urethra opens far from the tip of the penis an operation is necessary to correct the abnormality.

SEXUALLY TRANSMITTED DISEASES (STD)

Diseases usually transmitted by intercourse or intimate sexual contact between adults – STD or venereal diseases (VD) – do occur in children, although very rarely.

There is little risk of a baby being born with a sexually transmitted disease. A routine test for syphilis is performed at the first antenatal visit. If there is infection, early treatment of the mother with antibiotics will remove any danger to the baby. If gonorrhoea is contracted by the mother during pregnancy, the baby's eyes may be infected during birth. However, the disease is usually recognized and treated. If genital herpes is active at the time of birth, *Caesarean section* protects the baby.

Full sexual intercourse is not necessary to infect somebody with a sexually transmitted disease and a child may be infected by someone who already has a disease by contact – anything from innocent but intimate play to sexual abuse.

Sexually transmitted diseases may become much more of a problem when children enter *puberty*. If adolescents are promiscuous they are at greater risk of contracting gonorrhoea, genital herpes, non-specific urethritis (NSU), pubic lice, syphilis and acquired immune deficiency syndrome (AIDS).

If your child has a rash, swellings or sores around the genital area, or any unusual discharge from the penis or vagina, he or she should be seen by a doctor. Encourage your children to be aware of the risks and to seek advice and treatment if they think they may be infected or have been in contact with anyone who may be infected.

GLANDULAR DISORDERS

Endocrine glands secrete hormones, chemicals that are essential for the normal control and functioning of many body processes, particularly growth, development, energy utilization and reactions to stress. The main endocrine glands are the pituitary, thyroid, adrenals and sex glands (ovaries or testes). In addition, the pancreas, besides manufacturing digestive juices, has within it special islands of cells that make hormones and so is in part an endocrine gland.

Each gland has a control system. In overall control of all endocrine activity is a small area of the brain called the hypothalamus. Hormone-like chemicals from the hypothalamus pass to the pituitary gland, the endocrine system's 'master' gland. This is about the size of a marble and situated at the base of the brain, just behind the eyes. The chemicals from the hypothalamus control the release of hormones from the pituitary which pass into the bloodstream. Each pituitary hormone controls the activity of an endocrine gland, causing it to secrete its own hormones. The levels of these hormones in the blood are detected by the hypothalamus, thus setting up a feedback loop that regulates endocrine secretions. Normal production of the hormones is essential for growth and development, including puberty.

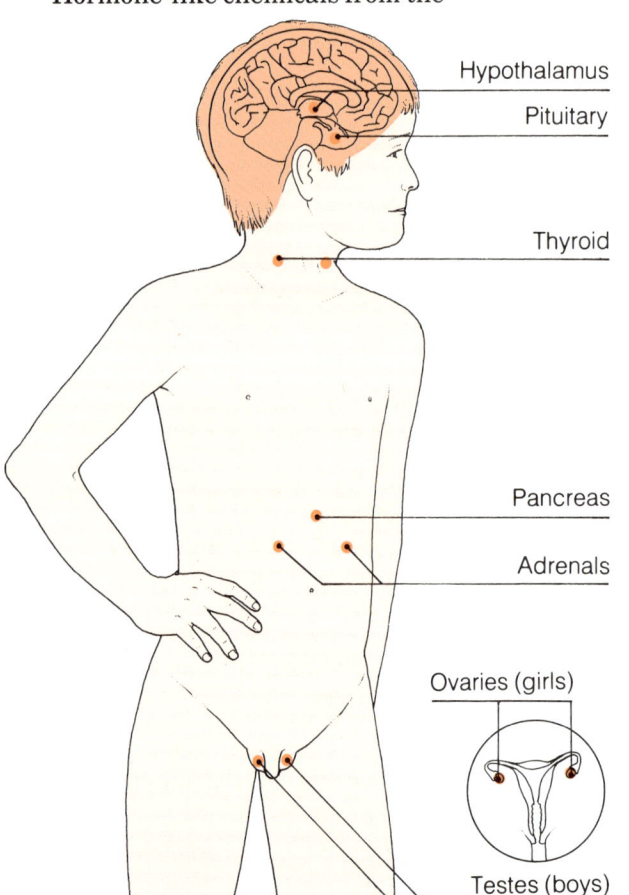

GLANDS AND HORMONES

PITUITARY
Under control of chemical messages from hypothalamus. Regulates many aspects of growth and development.

THYROID
Controls speed at which chemical processes occur in body.

PARATHYROID
Controls level of calcium in blood.

PANCREAS
Regulates glucose level in blood.

ADRENAL CORTEX
Regulates chemical balance of body. Affects protein and carbohydrate metabolism. Influences sexual development.

ADRENAL MEDULLA
Prepares body for action by controlling heart rate and blood pressure.

TESTES
Maintains secondary sexual characteristics.

OVARIES
Produce secondary sexual characteristics and prepare uterus for pregnancy.

The pancreas

The body, and in particular the brain, depends on a carefully regulated fuel supply of blood sugar. Blood glucose is the more exact term, because other sugars (such as table sugar, or sucrose) are converted into glucose by the body. Glucose enters the bloodstream by two routes, either from recently digested foods containing carbohydrates or from glycogen (an insoluble starch-like substance made from chains of glucose molecules) in the liver.

In normal health the body keeps its blood glucose level steady within narrow limits, despite variations in food intake and the energy needed by the body. The pancreas makes two hormones, insulin and glucagon, which play vital roles in this process.

The pancreas lies across the back of the abdomen, just below the stomach. The bulk of the pancreas produces digestive juices; the remainder is concerned with blood glucose control. This part is made up of thousands of cell clumps, or islets, visible only under a microscope. The islets continuously secrete insulin into the bloodstream, usually at a low rate but at a higher rate after meals, especially those rich in carbohydrate. When blood insulin levels are high, blood glucose is able to enter body cells and can be used for energy, growth and repair. Any glucose that is surplus to immediate requirements is directed into the liver for storage as glycogen. Blood glucose levels fall as a result of both these processes.

Whereas insulin is responsible for replenishing fuel reserves in times of plenty, glucagon is produced in times of scarcity in order to mobilize these stores. It causes blood glucose to rise when the body suffers low food intake, illness or injury.

Growth and maturation

Monitoring a child's *growth rate* is the best long-term test of his good health. Normal growth and maturation depends on the body's hormone production as well as on adequate nutrition and happiness. In the Western world, children rarely eat so little as to impair their physical growth but their emotional environment is also important. Children who are starved of affection fail to grow well, because the emotional stresses involved suppress normal hormone production. When they have happier surroundings, their growth returns to normal. In addition some childhood diseases can interfere with growth and development. A longstanding disease may affect eventual body size, but most diseases only have a temporary effect and any lost growth is subsequently recovered.

Sex hormones from the ovaries or testes are responsible for physical maturation at puberty. Not all children grow and mature at the same age. Some are full-grown by 14 years of age while others may go on growing into their early twenties. Such variations in growth are often reflected in the timing of puberty. For example, a tall child who starts showing signs of puberty at the age of 10 years is probably simply an early maturer. A girl of 15 years who is smaller than her peers, but who has normal breast and pubic hair development, may well not start her periods for some time and yet be perfectly normal. On the other hand, a child who is very tall and not showing any signs of development is much more likely to have a problem, as his growth and development are clearly out of step.

▶ **See also** The older child and adolescent

METABOLISM

The chemical processes that keep the body going are known as metabolism. The overall metabolism of the body is governed by hormones secreted by various glands which are under the control of the pituitary gland.

It is by the process of metabolism that food is broken down into a form the body can use, and energy is produced, to be either used or stored for use at some future time. The speed at which these processes occur depends on the body's energy needs at any particular time, and also on the person's age. The 'basal metabolic rate' is a measure of the energy needed to keep the body 'ticking over' in a resting state. This is low in a newborn baby, rises to a peak in about the second year of life and then falls slowly until adolescence. It remains at this level throughout early adult life.

STATURE AND GROWTH PROBLEMS

A child may be short for several reasons. Short parents tend to have short children. Some children mature late and, while their contemporaries are growing rapidly at *puberty*, they will appear short – until their growth spurt happens.

If you are worried about your child's growth rate, you should consult your doctor sooner rather than later; any previous measurements of your child's height may be very helpful. Your doctor will probably want to take two accurate height measurements 3 months apart, so that your child's rate of growth can be calculated. He may also arrange an X-ray of your child's wrist to gauge his bone maturity. If your child's bones are immature compared with his chronological age, then his short stature is probably the result of a disease or disorder. Further investigations will be carried out to discover what the problem is. These investigations usually involve measuring particular hormone levels.

As well as producing hormones to stimulate other endocrine glands, the pituitary also produces growth hormone. A baby born with a deficiency in this hormone will not grow as expected and the problem is usually recognized within his first few years. The problem may also develop later in life. If a child has a deficiency of growth hormone, he is small but otherwise normal.

Radiotherapy to the head can damage the pituitary gland so that a child who has had to have this treatment for *cancer* may have a deficiency of growth hormone.

To treat the deficiency, growth hormone is given by injection. During the treatment, which may continue until after adolescence when normal growth ceases, the child is regularly measured and tested.

A child who appears very tall for his age in comparison with his peers may be entering puberty early; following adolescence the differences usually even out.

A child with tall parents may be growing very tall. Although it is not usually advisable, it may be possible in some cases to limit a child's final height by bringing on puberty early with hormone injections. However, attempting to prevent a tall child becoming very tall may lead to difficulties.

▶ **See also** Early growth and development

THYROID PROBLEMS

The thyroid gland in the neck makes the hormone thyroxine. Lack of thyroxine, or hypothyroidism, may be caused either by disease in the thyroid gland itself or by disease of the pituitary gland which controls it. It leads to several problems: slow growth, constipation, dry skin and hair, a general slowness in motion and thought, and a tendency to feel cold. If your child has problems that make you suspect he may be suffering from hypothyroidism you should consult your doctor, who will probably send your child to a specialist. If the diagnosis is confirmed by tests your child will be prescribed thyroxine tablets. As a rule, these will be needed for life. The dose will be controlled by monitoring your child's *growth rate* and by checking his bone maturation by means of X-rays.

A deficiency of thyroxine during the first 2 or 3 years of life may lead to **cretinism**, or developmental and mental retardation.

Excessive production of thyroid hormone, or hyperthyroidism, is rare in childhood. It may cause *behavioural problems*, and schoolwork may fall off as concentration becomes poor. The disorder is more common in girls, and they are likely to be tall as well. Treatment is with an anti-thyroid drug.

ADRENAL PROBLEMS

The two adrenal glands produce the hormones cortisol and aldosterone as well as sex hormones.

Cortisol is important for the maintenance of normal blood glucose levels – it has the opposite effect to *insulin*. Too much of this hormone makes a child short, rather fat and hairy, and liable to bruise easily.

Aldosterone affects the salt and water balance in the body. Some children are born with a lack of this hormone and become very ill unless treated with a salt-retaining hormone within a few days of birth.

The sex hormones – mainly androgens (testosterone) in boys and oestrogens in girls – are partly responsible for the rapid growth that occurs at *puberty*, as well as for the development of underarm and pubic hair. It is possible for too much sex hormone to be produced before birth and this may make it difficult to tell whether a baby is a boy or a girl. When a child is older, a tumour of the adrenal gland may cause over-production of sex hormones and this generally causes masculinization, with the early appearance of underarm and pubic hair and acne.

Adrenal glands

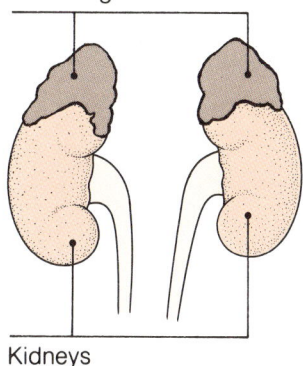

The adrenals are a pair of glands that lie on top of the kidneys. The inner part of each gland, the medulla, secretes adrenaline and noradrenaline, the hormones that prepare the body to deal with stress. In the outer part, the cortex, steroid and sex hormones are produced.

Kidneys

NON-DIABETIC HYPOGLYCEMIA

Hypoglycemia means too little glucose in the blood. It is a rare problem for children who do not suffer *diabetes*. However, if your child has fits or a period of unconsciousness, you should take him to your doctor who will arrange a check for hypoglycemia. Recurrent hypoglycemia needs detailed tests in hospital.

There are several possible causes of recurrent non-diabetic hypoglycemia: inherited problems of glucose storage in the liver; inherited defects in the complex chemical pathways that turn other body fuels into glucose; or imbalance of the various hormones that regulate the body's energy utilization.

DIABETES

Diabetes mellitus, often called sugar diabetes, is the most common hormonal problem that children suffer. The islets of the *pancreas* become progressively and irreversibly scarred. Why this happens is not clear, but research indicates that certain children, perhaps partly because of the genes they carry, react to events such as ordinary viral infections by activating their immune system to attack their own pancreatic islets. The scarred pancreas cannot make enough insulin and the child's blood glucose levels rise while his body cells are starved of energy.

About 1 child in 800 develops diabetes, usually in adolescence. The symptoms often appear over a few days or weeks but, at this point, irreversible damage has already been done to the pancreas.

SYMPTOMS

When a child has diabetes excess blood glucose 'overflows' from the kidneys so that extra water is needed for excretion. The presence of sugar in the urine is an important clue in the diagnosis of diabetes. The child becomes excessively thirsty, passes more urine than normal, wakes in the night to go to the toilet and may revert to bedwetting. Because his body cannot get enough energy, the child loses weight, becomes listless and is also vulnerable to infections, especially *boils*. Girls may develop vulval *thrush*.

If your child has these symptoms you should take him to the doctor, who will carry out urine and blood-glucose tests. It is important for diabetes to be recognized and treated as soon as possible. If the disease progresses untreated, the body loses control of its blood-glucose system and has to burn fat in order to release energy. The waste products from this process, ketones, are potentially poisonous. If they accumulate the child will become very ill with dehydration, heavy breathing, vomiting and abdominal pains. If still untreated, this state, diabetic ketoacidosis, can give way to *coma* and *shock* requiring emergency hospital treatment.

TREATMENT

The mainstay of diabetic treatment is the replacement of the missing insulin. It has to be given by injections, as insulin taken by mouth is destroyed in the gut. A few days after beginning treatment a diabetic child will experience a dramatic transition back to good health and from this point onwards his health will depend on insulin injections.

The longer-term success of diabetic treatment depends on the interest, skill and participation of the child and his family. If your child has diabetes, both he and you will be asked to attend the diabetes clinic regularly for check-ups, adjustment of insulin dosage and reviews of diet and exercise – all of which influence control of the disorder. The doctors, nurses and dieticians treating him act as trainers and managers, teaching and encouraging both you and him. Children as young as 6 years old cope well with injections and their administration and even younger ones learn to help. Diabetes is a life-long disorder and its control requires considerable effort on the part of your child and family. But it is not a conspicuous condition and diabetics do as well as others at school, in work and in sport. Your child can look forward to a fruitful adult life, including having children.

LOSS OF CONTROL

Diabetic children are bound to get common illnesses, and these may upset the control of the disorder. Despite eating less, your child's blood glucose level may rise and his body may revert to the dangerous process of burning fat. Resist any temptation to reduce insulin dosage when your child is ill. It is also important to ensure that your child has an adequate carbohydrate intake and to monitor blood glucose levels closely. Your diabetes clinic team will have discussed these strategies with you in advance, and you will have been given a telephone number for prompt help.

HYPOGLYCEMIA

Children with diabetes tend to suffer hypoglycemia – which means having too little glucose in the blood – after missed snacks, unusually strenuous exercise or an accidental overdose of insulin. Hypoglycemia, also called a 'hypo' or insulin reaction, can occasionally start quickly but there are usually warning signs such as faintness, sweating, sickness, headache, bad temper and double vision. Each diabetic has his own hypo pattern and it is important that family, friends and teachers all know the significance of the symptoms and what they should do. Glucose tablets, sugar or a sweet drink given promptly will rapidly correct most hypos. Your child should always wear an identity disc or bracelet when out of the house, stating that he is diabetic, and he must carry an emergency supply of glucose. Some children carry an injection of glucagon for emergency use; this is guaranteed to correct even the most severe hypo. An unrecognized hypo can lead to loss of consciousness.

▶**See also** Appendix: Support groups and publications

GLANDULAR DISORDERS

BLOOD AND URINE TESTS

You or your child will have to carry out tests regularly to monitor blood-glucose levels and thus see whether treatment is effective. The diabetes clinic will provide a finger-pricking or thigh-pricking gadget and blood-glucose test strips, with or without a portable blood-glucose meter. Children of all ages have been found to accept a regular schedule of finger or thigh pricks. Usually they enjoy understanding more about their diabetes and seeing the resulting blood-sugar measurements charted. The target for most children is to keep the majority of blood-glucose readings within a specified range.

Urine tests are simple but unfortunately they only detect glucose overflowing through the kidneys, and by the time this is happening the child's blood-glucose level is already twice as high as normal. In the main, urine tests are being replaced by direct blood-glucose measurement.

To collect a blood sample the pricking gadget is placed against one thumb and a button that releases a needle into it is pressed by the other. The drop of blood is put on the test strip and the resulting colour of the strip is matched against a chart to give a blood-glucose reading.

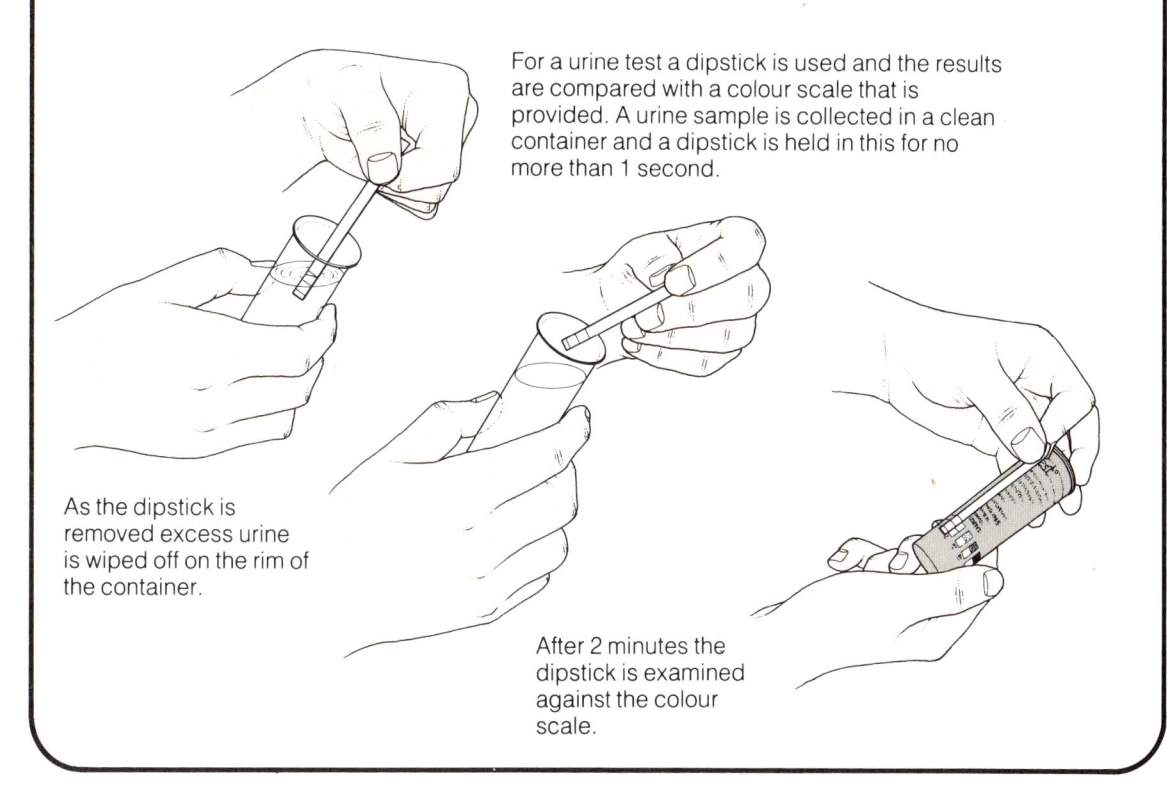

For a urine test a dipstick is used and the results are compared with a colour scale that is provided. A urine sample is collected in a clean container and a dipstick is held in this for no more than 1 second.

As the dipstick is removed excess urine is wiped off on the rim of the container.

After 2 minutes the dipstick is examined against the colour scale.

SELF-TREATMENT

DIET
Your child's diet should be based on good, balanced nutrition – but it should also include carbohydrate control. You must be selective about carbohydrate-rich foods, choosing those rich in fibre which release their sugars slowly during digestion. The gradual flow of sugars into the bloodstream is easier for the diabetic's body to handle, and the injected insulin has a better chance of controlling it efficiently. Very sugary food, such as chocolate or sweetened drinks, causes an uncontrollable surge of blood glucose that overflows into the urine.

Diabetic clinics recommend a simple scheme for measuring daily carbohydrate intake, and by following this your child's intake and his insulin dose can be balanced and can be kept relatively stable. There are illustrated manuals to explain this system.

There are no restrictions on high protein or high fat foods other than general dietary recommendations.

The diabetic's diet is generally healthy for everyone. A child will soon accept a change in his diet, especially if the entire family joins in. Dieticians will help you to develop a varied and acceptable menu, usually in the pattern of three main meals and three snacks per day to ensure that blood glucose levels are kept steady.

Diabetic children cannot cope with erratic or missed meals. Regular injections must be matched by regular meals. However, there is a certain flexibility, and your child can have more to eat on active days and vice versa. You will soon discover that life does not have to be totally dominated by the clock – insulin injection and breakfast can both be delayed on Sundays or holidays, for example.

INSULIN
The hormone insulin is either extracted and purified from the pancreas glands of pigs, or made by bacteria which have been genetically engineered to produce insulin identical to the human version. Both types are safe and effective for children to use.

Two main classes of insulin are made: clear insulins, which act quickly and have a short duration (6 to 8 hours); and cloudy insulins, which are active over a longer period (18 to 24 hours). Mixed injections of clear and cloudy insulins can be used, tailored to suit your child. The doctor chooses the most suitable insulin and works out dosages and when these should be injected. You and your child are taught how to prepare the correct insulin dose, how to mix clear and cloudy insulins in the same syringe if necessary, and how to inject.

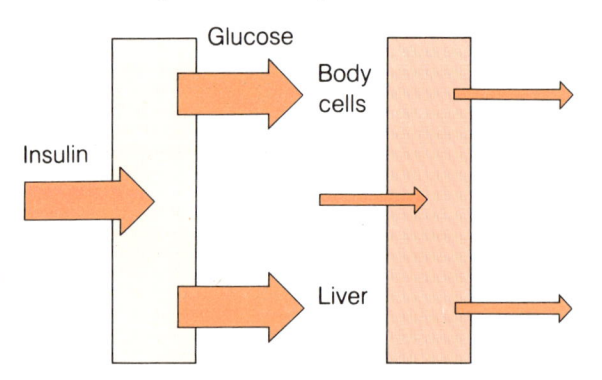

Insulin, secreted by the pancreas, enables the body cells to absorb glucose from the blood, for energy. It also acts on the liver, enabling it to store glucose in the form of glycogen. Insulin therefore lowers the level of glucose in the blood.

INJECTIONS
Insulin is injected into the fatty layer just under the skin. With practical instruction you will soon become adept at handling the bottles, syringes and needles. The exact timetable of injections depends on each individual, but a common pattern is one dose 15 to 20 minutes before breakfast and a second dose before the main evening meal.

A few diabetics use portable battery-powered pumps to inject insulin continuously under the skin. This often gives better control of the diabetes, but it is not yet a practical alternative for most children.

Injections of insulin are remarkably pain-free and do not require a precise aim. A youngster can soon become adept at injecting himself.

GLANDULAR DISORDERS

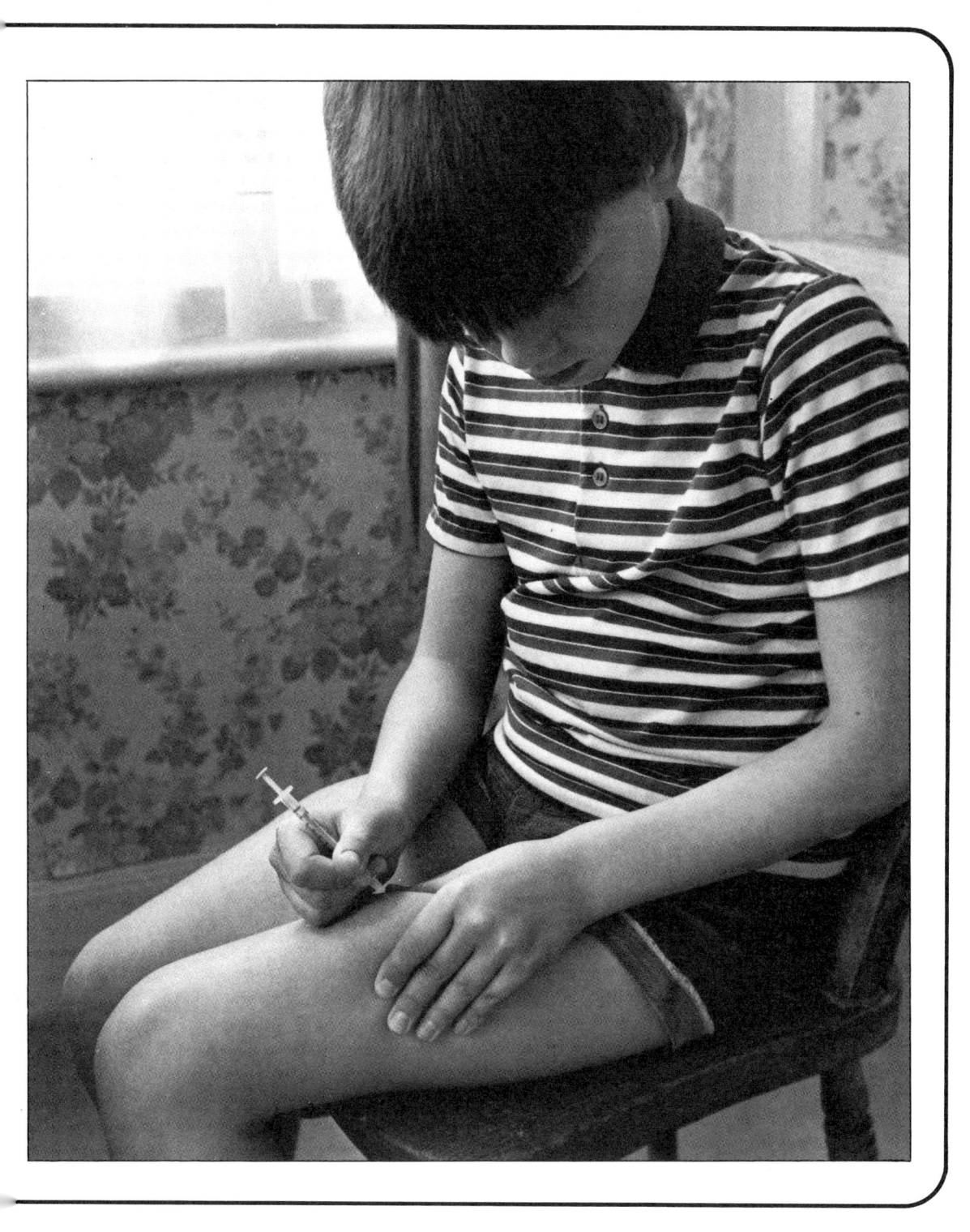

THE BONES AND JOINTS

The bony skeleton is the supporting framework of the body and a protective surround for vital organs such as the brain, spinal cord, heart and lungs. It also works as a system of levers against which the muscles of the body can act to produce movement.

The final size and shape of a person's skeleton in adulthood depends on both inherited and environmental factors. Between the sexes the most obvious differences are in the size of the bones – male bones are usually bigger – and in the shape of the pelvis, which is wider and shallower in a woman to allow for the passage of a baby during delivery.

Bones are very strong, but weigh relatively little because they are not solid. In children, the cavities in the long limb bones and other flat bones such as the skull are filled with marrow in which blood cells are produced. Bone is a living tissue and has a remarkable capacity to regenerate and repair itself.

For adequate bone growth, it is important that a child has enough of two nutrients. One is calcium, obtained from dairy products and vegetables; the other is vitamin D, obtained from sunlight and some oily foods. Without vitamin D the body tissues cannot utilize calcium properly.

Sports training
If your child is involved in competitive sports or takes part in sports training, you should be aware of the possibility that there may be strain on his bones and joints. You can best protect your child by making sure that his trainer or coach is professionally qualified, and by taking seriously any aches and pains that develop.

You may be able to treat minor sports injuries yourself, but you should seek medical advice if in doubt. *Fractures* to bones are often the result of accidents during sports.

Small cracks in the bone may not even show up on an X-ray. Such stress-fractures will be painful as long as exercise continues, but with rest will soon heal.

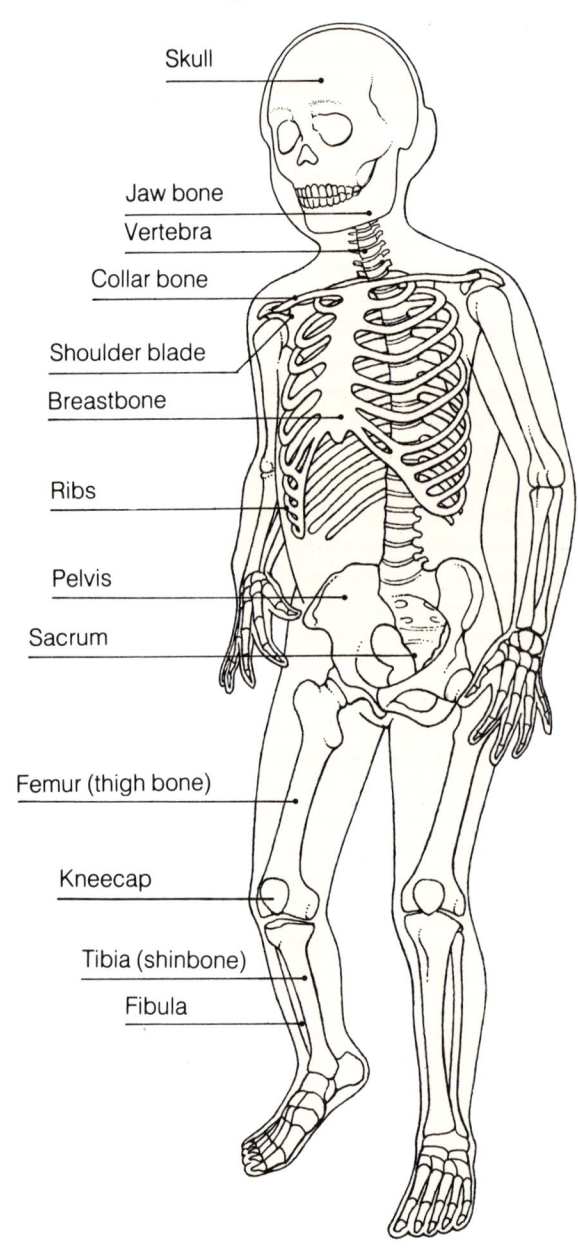

COMMON PROBLEMS

Minor variations in the skeleton's structure are common and usually of no importance; the presence of extra rudimentary ribs is one example. The same bone can vary considerably in shape and alignment between one person and another, and most of the variations are quite normal. Variations in the bones of the leg, the femur and tibia, can cause bow legs, knock knees and intoeing as a child grows.

Bow legs and knock knees are common conditions. They are the result both of inherited skeletal shape and of the moulding of the bones that takes place while the baby is in the uterus. A newborn child is normally slightly bow-legged, and by the age of 3 years most children are slightly knock-kneed. By the time a child is 7 years old, his legs will have reached their adult position. The majority of healthy children with bow legs and knock knees improve spontaneously without the aid of special footwear, braces or exercises.

If a child is extremely bow-legged or knock-kneed, or if only one leg is affected, it is more likely that an underlying bone disorder is the cause. Even if this is the case, effective treatment is usually available.

Intoeing, or 'pigeon toes', in an older child is caused by one or a combination of three factors: a foot that turns inwards at the toes, the inward twisting of the lower part of the shinbone or the inward rotation of the upper part of the thighbone. Most children with pigeon toes grow up with normal foot posture.

Given the confined space in which the fetus grows, it is not surprising that a newborn baby's feet are often bent. If they cannot be gently moved back into a normal position – if the foot is fixed in an abnormal position – the baby has a *club foot* and will need treatment by an orthopaedic surgeon.

Flat feet may appear to be a problem for babies because the arches of their feet are filled in by fat. As they grow, the mature arch emerges and the final shape of the arch depends on inherited factors. You need only consult a doctor if your child's flat feet are painful.

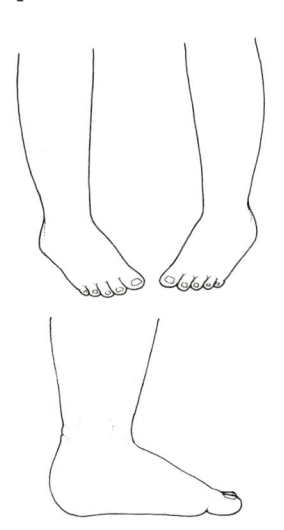

A young child's pigeon toes usually correct themselves with age. If you are worried that this is not so, consult your doctor.

A toddler's feet may look flat but this is usually quite normal. For healthy feet, encourage your child to spend at least part of the time barefoot.

Poor posture may be the result of the way the muscular, skeletal and nervous systems interact, as well as of inherited, cultural and psychological factors. Posture does not begin to become permanent until a child has reached the age of about 10 years.

If your child's posture is poor you are unlikely to achieve much by telling him to stand up straight if he does not want to – but you can encourage him to take up swimming or trampolining, both of which tend to improve posture. However, sports which develop one side of the body more than the other may be responsible for some back problems which may develop later in life.

It is quite important for children to carry packs or bags across their backs rather than on one shoulder. Over the years carrying on one side of the body only can affect posture.

A painful back is rarely the result of poor posture, although older children may well develop backache as a result of slouching. When backache does occur, it is more likely that an underlying cause is responsible for both bad posture and discomfort. If your child has persistent back pain seek medical advice.

THE ALEXANDER TECHNIQUE

Small children naturally adopt well balanced, upright positions. As they grow older the tendency is to adopt potentially harmful positions, pulling shoulders up and head back and slumping when sitting. The Alexander technique is a method of improving posture by developing the correct relationship between head, neck and back and therefore the position of the spine. The body is placed in position by a therapist and guided through everyday movements. Eventually position and movements can be adopted without help.

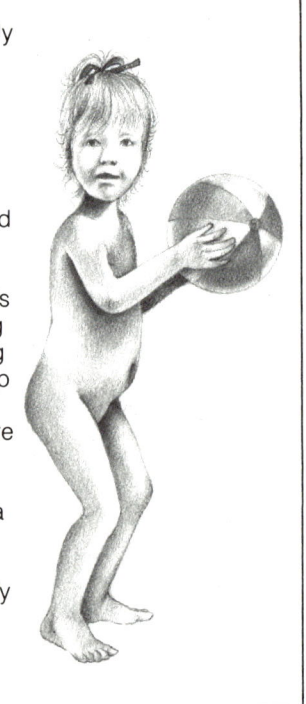

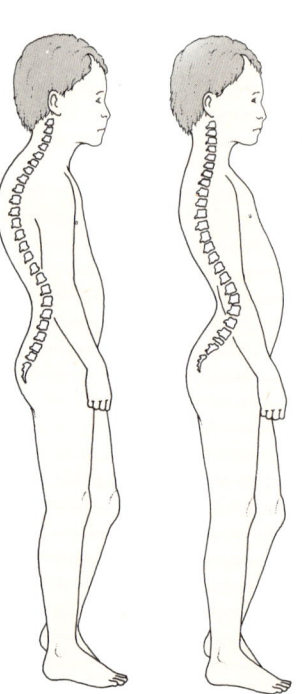

If your child stands with an exaggerated forward curve of the upper part of the spine (kyphosis) or backward curve of the lower spine (lordosis), this is unlikely to have serious consequences although it may not look very attractive.

Leg pains are a common childhood complaint. Pains that are in both legs and occur between the ages of 4 and 8 years old have been described as 'growing pains'. The discomfort is felt deep in the thigh or lower leg. Pain at night may be bad enough to wake the child, even though he has no fever or limp and is unable to identify any specific areas of pain. Physical growth is not painful, and just why the pains occur is not known. Comforting and calm reassurance may be all that your child needs. If pains persist check with your doctor to confirm that there is no underlying problem.

There may be a particular reason why your child is feeling anxious – for example, he may have just started school – and in this case the pain may be an expression of this anxiety.

The pains are far more likely to be caused by an underlying problem if they occur in one rather than both legs, or if there are other symptoms, such as joint swelling. When older children and teenagers complain of leg pains there is often an underlying problem.

CONGENITAL DISLOCATION OF THE HIP (CDH)

Many of the bone and joint problems of childhood involve the hip joint. This ball-and-socket joint is the largest in the body. The round head of the thigh bone, or femur, fits into a socket in the pelvis. Normal growth and development of both the head of the thigh bone and its socket depend on their proper juxtaposition. If they do not fit together properly, as in congenital dislocation of the hip, your child should be treated to correct this as early in childhood as possible, so that the joint can go on to develop normally.

If the head of the thigh bone is not inside the socket of the hip joint, the hip is said to be dislocated. When the head can be manoevred out of the socket it is said to be unstable.

Approximately 7 out of every 1,000 newborn babies have dislocation or instability of the hip. Girls are more often affected than boys. It is more likely to happen where there is a family history of the problem, in a first pregnancy when the uterus is unstretched and the baby has been cramped, or when the baby has been in an unusual position in the uterus, as in a breech presentation.

Some dislocated or unstable hips would probably correct themselves without any intervention but this cannot be known in advance and all are treated. This involves splinting the baby's thighs to keep them apart and to hold the ball of the hip joint in its socket. The splint is worn continuously (although it can be removed for washing). As the baby grows, the hip joint becomes stabilized and after a few months the splint can be removed. Despite the awkward appearance, the splint causes the baby no discomfort. Early treatment is very successful and, even if delayed until a child is 1 or 2 years old, is usually effective for most children. The remainder need surgery.

Rarely dislocations of the hip may not be evident at birth but the child has a noticeable limp when he learns to walk. He will probably need surgery, followed by several months with his legs in plaster casts.

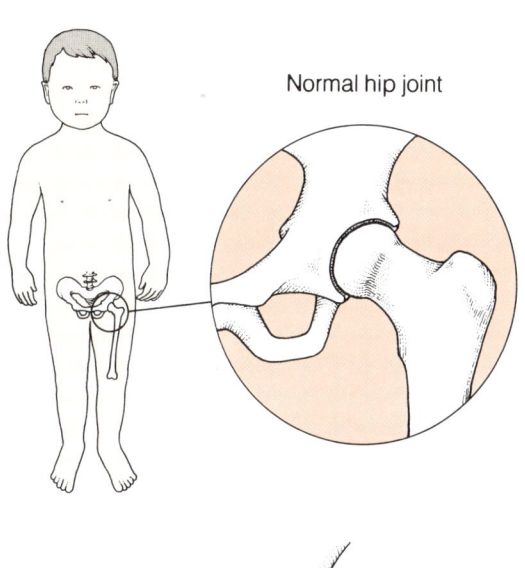

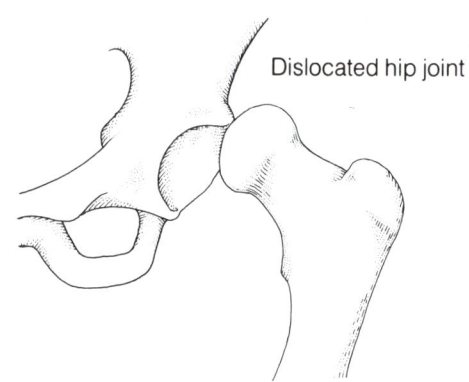

In the normal hip joint the round head of the femur fits securely into a socket in the pelvis. Sometimes the socket does not develop properly and is shallow and the head of the femur lies outside it.

CLICKY HIP
During the routine examination of a newborn baby's hips the paediatrician manipulates the thighs, and in a few babies the hip gives a snapping 'click'. Although most clicks are probably to do with ligaments and so are not important, a baby with a click hip will usually be monitored to ensure that the hip is not dislocated.

IRRITABLE HIP

Otherwise known as observation hip or transient synovitis, this is a common cause of a sudden limp in children under 10 years old and usually less than 6 years old. Boys are more frequently affected than girls. The precise cause is unknown, but it is thought that the hip joint may have been briefly inflamed, possibly after injury or *viral infection*. The hip is painful to move.

A child with an irritable hip recovers after a few days' rest. If you suspect your child has the problem you should consult your doctor since an X-ray of the hip is important, both when the symptoms first appear and 3 months after recovery, to exclude the possibility of other conditions. Minor relapses soon after the first episode are common, but children rarely have long-term problems.

PERTHES' DISEASE

Perthes' disease affects approximately 1 in every 5,000 children between the ages of 4 and 10 years old. Boys are more often affected than girls. Its cause is unknown.

Over a period of up to 4 years the head of the thigh bone collapses and fragments, then knits together and grows again. In 15 per cent of children with this condition both hips are affected. A child with Perthes' disease has a limp. Hip movements are painful although the pain may not be severe and may seem to originate in the knee. It is difficult to distinguish Perthes' disease from *irritable hip* without the aid of X-rays.

In mild cases, children recover spontaneously. If the head of the thigh bone is more severely affected and is at risk of permanent deformity, orthopaedic surgery may be necessary to ensure that the bone is securely contained within the socket of the hip.

SLIPPED FEMORAL EPIPHYSIS

Epiphysis is the name of the growing end of a long bone such as the thigh bone, or femur. Until growth is complete, the epiphyseal growth centre remains separated from the neck of the bone by a band of cartilage. In general, despite the fact that all the weight of the body is being transmitted through the hip joint, the head and neck of the thigh bone remain stable. Sometimes, however, the upper femoral epiphysis can literally slip off the neck of the femur. This condition affects more boys than girls, normally between 11 and 16 years. About 7 children in every 100,000 have the disorder, and in 20 per cent of these both hips are affected. A child with slipped epiphysis develops a sudden limp and has a sore hip or may feel pain in the knee.

Children who are very overweight seem to be more susceptible to slipped femoral epiphysis. About 1 child in 4 has both hips affected.

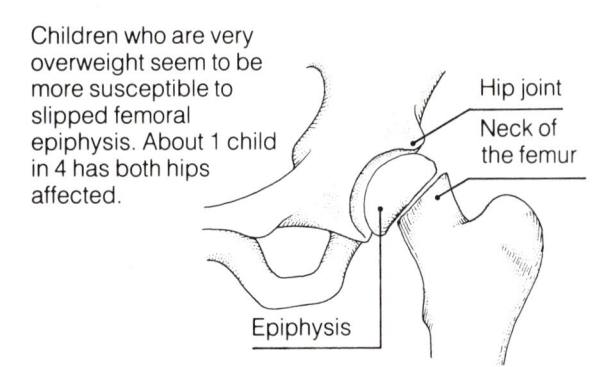

Treatment is by an operation to return the displaced femoral head to its proper position, where it is held in place by metal pins. When healing is complete, the pins are removed, and the long-term results are usually excellent.

SCOLIOSIS

Scoliosis is a distortion of the spinal column, in which the spine bends to one side and may be twisted. Scoliosis usually develops in children, mainly girls, over the age of 10 years. In this case the cause is unknown. There are other forms; for example, it can be present at birth, as a result of the position the baby held in the uterus, when it usually corrects itself spontaneously. Scoliosis at birth may also be due to malformations of the vertebrae, which is more difficult to correct, and children with *cerebral palsy* are at risk of developing a scoliosis because of unequal muscle action on the spine.

It is important for scoliosis to be diagnosed early in adolescence because, with the rapid growth spurt that occurs at this time the deformity, if uncorrected, may quickly become more severe. It may affect the child's general health too, making him breathless and more vulnerable to chest infections. Screening for scoliosis is usually a part of routine health checks of schoolchildren.

If a spinal curvature is detected the child will probably be referred to a specialist who will see the child at regular intervals to monitor the progression of the curvature.

Not all curvatures of the spine require treatment but where severe scoliosis is not improved by physiotherapy, or a spinal brace, corrective surgery may be necessary. The treatment is lengthy and is undertaken in special centres where new techniques are continually being developed.

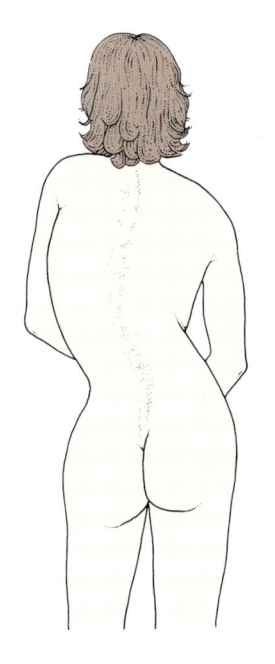

Curvature of the spine can be seen most easily from the back or by asking the child to bend forward and let his arms hang freely. If scoliosis is allowed to progress untreated it may rapidly increase during the adolescent growth spurt and result in a grossly hunched back.

The operation aims to straighten the spine by fusing the vertebrae. Before surgery traction is applied so that the child's spine is straightened as much as possible and the back muscles can adapt to the new position. After the operation a plaster jacket must be worn for several months. When this is removed a brace is usually necessary for a further period.

▶ **See also** Appendix: Screening programme

OSTEOMYELITIS AND SEPTIC ARTHRITIS

Bacterial infection of the bone, or osteomyelitis, and bacterial infection of a joint, or septic arthritis, are neither as common nor as threatening as they once were. The symptoms are swelling and extreme tenderness over the affected area accompanied by a high fever. Treatment is by antibiotics, in high doses. These are usually given intravenously for 1 or 2 weeks and then orally until the infection has cleared completely. If the child shows no improvement after 48 hours of treatment, pus may have to be removed from infected joints or bones under a general anaesthetic.

RICKETS

The rigidity of bone depends on *vitamin D*. If a child is deficient in this vitamin, or if its activity within the body is impaired, the child will develop rickets. Bones affected by rickets, or rachitic bones, are soft and may bend and even crack under the child's weight, causing considerable postural deformities. These changes are usually reversed by taking extra vitamin D.

Vitamin D is manufactured by the skin from sunlight, and is also present in oily foods such as fish and fish oils, butter and eggs. Although in the past it was common amongst undernourished children, particularly those who lived in industrial areas with little sunlight, today it is rare.

In the Western world, rickets is most commonly seen among dark-skinned children whose families adhere to a strict vegetarian diet and who are not given a regular vitamin D supplement. Rarely children who eat a mixed diet may develop rickets because of a defect in the body's absorption or utilization of vitamin D, but this is rare. Treatment is with high doses or special modifications of the vitamin.

▶ See also Feeding and diet

Young children with rickets may be severely bow-legged, while adolescents are more likely to develop *knock knees*.

OSGOOD SCHLATTER DISEASE

Osgood Schlatter disease is a painful enlargement of a point on the upper shinbone, the tibial tubercle, that is aggravated by exercise and kneeling. It is more likely to occur in athletic children over 10 years of age and probably starts with a minor injury. The condition disappears when childhood growth is complete.

If your child suffers in this way he will find that cutting down on exercise will diminish the discomfort, but some children prefer to bear the pain rather than stop all participation in sporting activities.

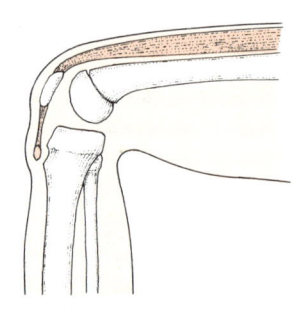

Damage to the cartilaginous growing end of the shin, where the kneecap is attached, may cause pain. This resolves when the bone hardens.

JUVENILE RHEUMATOID ARTHRITIS

A whole variety of medical problems may lead to inflammation of the joints in children. *Glandular fever*, *infective hepatitis*, *German measles* (especially in teenage girls) and even some type of *virus* causing the common cold are all well-recognized causes of temporary arthritic illnesses in children. An arthritis affecting several joints is particularly likely to follow dysentery-like illnesses in which bloody diarrhoea, fever and abdominal pain are features.

Juvenile rheumatoid arthritis, also known as juvenile chronic arthritis or, more commonly, as Still's disease, does not usually follow this course. It is more persistent, affecting joints for at least 3 months. Roughly 1 in every 1,500 children is affected, and the disorder usually occurs between the ages of 1 and 3 and 8 and 12 years. Twice as many girls as boys suffer from it. Although the joints are most commonly affected, other parts of the body, including the eyes, may be inflamed.

Despite the name given to this disorder, many doctors do not believe that it is a juvenile form of rheumatoid arthritis.

SYMPTOMS

The illness develops most frequently with swelling and discomfort of one or two joints only, usually the knee, ankle or elbow. Often joints are only slightly painful, despite swelling, and the swelling may or may not be accompanied by fever and general lassitude. In other cases several joints are affected and the finger joints are often involved. Some children, usually younger ones, are very ill with high fever although they may not have joint inflammation initially. In this case a rash may develop and is most obvious where the skin has been rubbed or subjected to pressure from clothing. Eventually most of these children develop obvious swelling of the joints.

TREATMENT

Children with suspected juvenile rheumatoid arthritis are usually admitted to hospital for investigative tests and treatment.

A child with juvenile rheumatoid arthritis only has to rest in bed during periods of active joint inflammation and fever, when weight-bearing is very painful. He will need physiotherapy to maintain full movement of the affected joints. Splints may be used to make sure the inflamed joints keep their correct positions while at rest. Once the child is able to move about, physiotherapy in the form of exercise is an important part of treatment, as it maintains and increases mobility as much as possible. Painkilling drugs that also reduce joint inflammation are prescribed.

Juvenile rheumatoid arthritis is usually a self-limiting illness that eventually clears up permanently, although it may take years to do so. Even when it does not clear completely, impairment of mobility and joint function is rarely severe.

If your child has arthritis problems in her hands she may need 'gauntlets'. Worn during the day, and removed only when she exercises her hands, they offer firm support and help to prevent the loss of correct functioning. At night her hands will be supported on 'night-paddles'.

THE SKIN AND HAIR

Skin is made up of two layers: the epidermis, or surface layer, and below it the dermis. Its average thickness is 2 mm (1/12 in) but on areas such as palms of hands and soles of feet the epidermis particularly is much thicker than usual. Beneath the skin lies subcutaneous fat.

The cells in the lowermost part of the epidermis are continually dividing and working their way to the surface. On the way, they fill with a hard substance called keratin and then die, so the skin you see and touch is made up of dead cells.

The dermis contains the fibrous elastic tissue that gives strength and elasticity to the skin. It also contains lymph vessels, nerve endings, muscles, hair within hair follicles, sweat glands and oil or sebaceous glands. In a young child, the sebaceous glands are small and virtually inactive, so that the skin is not greasy. At *puberty*, the sebaceous glands enlarge under the influence of male hormones, which are present to some extent in girls as well as in boys. The glands then begin to produce their greasy secretion, called sebum. The duct along which sebum flows from the gland normally opens into a hair follicle, allowing the secretion to reach and lubricate the hair and the skin's surface.

Around 1 in 10 cells in the basal layer of the epidermis is a pigment-producing cell, or melanocyte. These cells produce melanin, the skin pigment. Everyone has roughly the same number of melanocytes, whatever the colour of his skin, but the melanocytes in darker-skinned people manufacture more melanin.

Moles are small highly pigmented areas of skin. They are extremely common, and mostly appear in childhood or adolescence. A child usually has 20 or so scattered over the body, but some children have more.

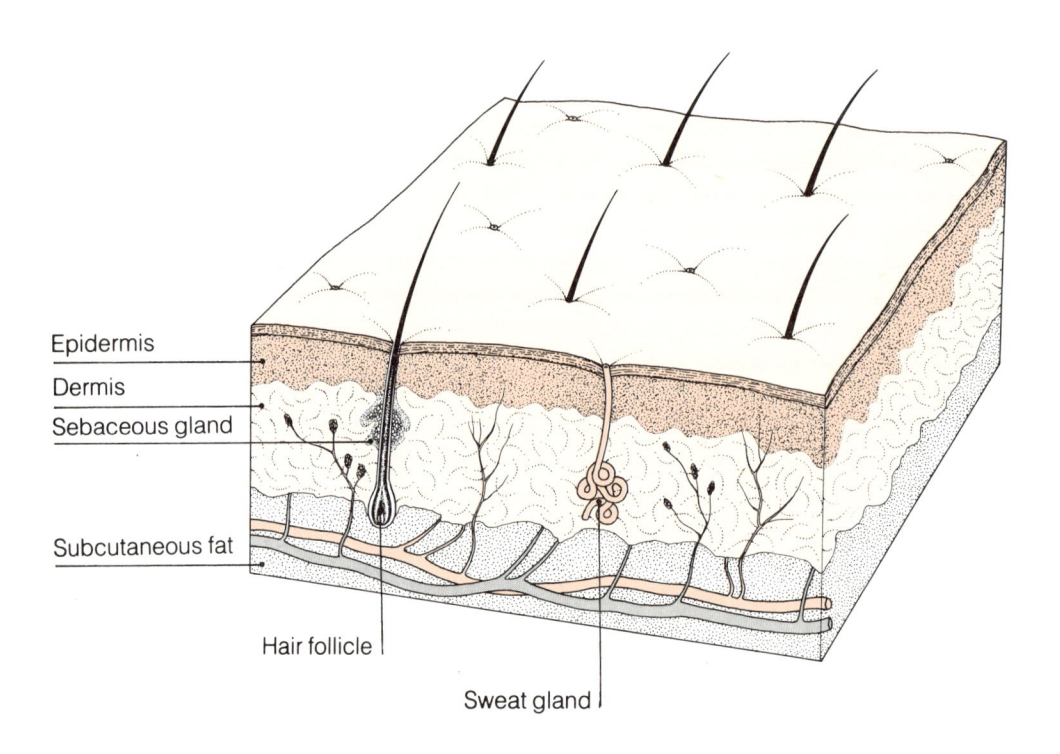

THE SKIN AND HAIR

SKIN DRYNESS
Prolonged soaking in water tends to dry out skin. If a child already has dry skin, frequent baths will further dry his skin and increase its permeability, allowing minor irritants such as soap and traces of detergent in clothing to damage it.

GREASY SKIN
Greasy skin is a special problem during adolescence when the glands which produce the skin's natural oil become more active. Normal washing should be sufficient, with a special tar soap if the skin is very oily.

There are different types of moles, varying in colour from brown to black. They usually appear on the face, neck and back. Some are hairy, some are flat and some are raised. Although moles in adults occasionally become malignant, moles in children hardly ever do so. However, if your child's moles suddenly start to increase in size, or bleed, or crust over, it is wise to consult your doctor.

Function of the skin
The skin has many important functions:
o It protects the underlying tissues from the cold, heat, wind, sun, chemicals and injury
o It is fairly waterproof, so it keeps body fluids in and other fluids out
o Skin helps to regulate body temperature. When the body is overheated, in a fever for example, the evaporation of sweat helps to cool it. The subcutaneous fat beneath the skin insulates the body and helps to conserve heat
o The nerve endings in the skin recognize touch, pain, heat and cold
o Certain waste substances, ucha s urea, are excretedin sweat through the skin
o *Vitamin D* is synthesized in the skin

Hair
By about the 5th to 6th month of pregnancy, the fetus is covered with a fine layer of delicate hairs. This layer is lost before birth except for the hairs on the scalp, and the eyebrows and eyelashes, which become coarser and stronger. Shortly after birth a new growth of downy hair covers the baby's body.

STRETCH MARKS
Stretch marks, at first red, then fading, are caused by weight gain that extends the skin beyond its elastic limit. They may develop on the breasts, buttocks and thighs of adolescent girls.

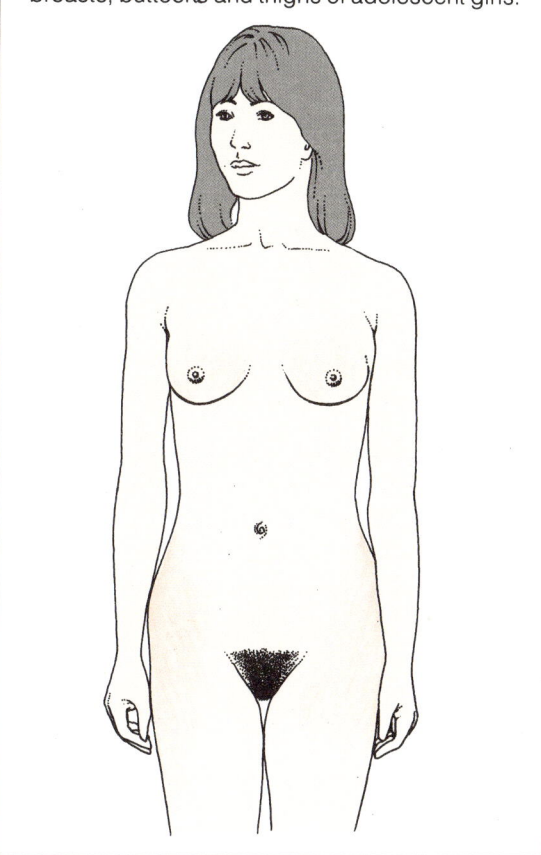

At puberty, further coarse hairs develop in the pubic region, under the arms and on the face and chest of boys. There are about 100,000 hairs on the average human scalp; every day about 50-100 hairs are shed but they are continually being replaced.

Hair colour is dependent on special melanin granules contained within melanocytes, in the hair. Black hair has plenty of pigmented granules while pure white hair has no granules at all. Blonde hair has a smaller number of granules and they contain less pigment than the granules contained within black hair.

COMMON PROBLEMS

There are many minor skin conditions affecting children from birth to adolescence, some of which you can treat using common sense and common remedies.

Most babies suffer from *nappy rash* and many adolescents have mild *acne*, although sometimes both these problems can be severe and very troublesome. Many children have dandruff, and boils at some time or another, and the majority will get *sunburn* in hot sunny weather and *chapped skin* in cold weather.

Itchy skin may be caused by *skin dryness*, and this may be the sole cause. Alternatively it may be the a result of a skin eruption such as *eczema*, *hives* or *psoriasis*, either present or about to form. *Scabies* results in intense itchiness, and *threadworms* result in itchiness around the anus.

Rashes in children are usually short-lived and of no significance to health.

Do not try to treat rashes, patchy irritation or skin discoloration yourself with medicines bought over the counter, since these may make the condition worse or trigger a different skin reaction that masks the original problem.

An unexplained rash should be shown to your doctor. It may be a sign of a *viral infection*.

Dandruff is the name given to small scales of skin flaking from the scalp. Its cause is unknown. Some children are susceptible to dandruff, but the condition can usually be kept under control by regular use of a medicated shampoo. Follow the instructions on the label carefully, but do not expect an instant cure.

If the dandruff does not go away consult your doctor. It may be helpful to try different shampoos.

Boils are *bacterial infections* of the skin around hair follicles. The skin becomes reddened and sore and over a few days swells and fills with pus. After about a week, most boils burst of their own accord; some may disappear without bursting.

Most boils need no treatment, although hot compresses may help to relieve pain and may encourage the boil to burst. It is important to keep the skin around the boil clean; covering it with a dressing helps to prevent spreading the infection to others. If the boil is in an awkward place, such as the ear, your doctor may be able to lance it by making a small cut that allows the pus to drain away. You should also consult your doctor if your child has a persistent boil or recurrent boils; occasionally recurrent boils are a sign of *diabetes*.

SUNBURN

Distributed evenly throughout the skin are special cells, the melanocytes, which contain a pigment melanin. The amount of melanin the skin contains varies from person to person. Fair skins contain much less than darker skins. Melanin also protects the skin from sunburn, which is why fair-skinned people burn more easily than dark-skinned people.

The ultra-violet rays of the sun stimulate the melanocytes to produce more pigment, darkening the skin and at the same time protecting it against sunburn. If melanin is allowed to build up by sunbathing for short periods, the skin will gradually tan without burning. Too much sun too quickly will burn the skin before it has had time to build up a protective layer of melanin. Babies and young children whose skins are unaccustomed to the sun, are easily burned. Remember that:

○ Fair-skinned, fair-haired and red-haired children are most sensitive
○ A child whose skin is used to exposure to the air and sunlight – as a result of running

THE SKIN AND HAIR

around naked in the garden – will be less sensitive
o The sun is most likely to burn between 10 am and 2 pm, although this may not be the hottest time of day
o The sun can burn through a thin cloud layer
o You do not have to feel hot to be burned – wind keeps you cool but does not reduce the sun's burning power

The problem usually arises on holiday: be especially careful for the first few days. Ideally, you should introduce your young child's skin to strong sun in stages, starting with a few minutes' exposure and building up gradually by 30 minutes each day. Use hats, longsleeved shirts and sunscreen creams to protect his skin at other times. Sunburn can vary from a mild redness to a severe reaction with blisters. To treat mild sunburn apply calamine lotion. Keep your child out of the sun for a few days. If there are blisters and other symptoms, you should take your child to a doctor.

Over-exposure to the sun's rays can also cause *sunstroke*.

A child will neither show nor feel the signs of sunburn while he is being exposed to the sun – the pain comes later. The sun's rays reflected off water are especially powerful, so it is sensible to make sure your child wears a tee-shirt while bathing to protect his arms and shoulders.

▶See also The sick child at home

INFANTILE SEBORRHOEIC DERMATITIS

This condition usually develops within the first 3 months of life, often in the first few weeks. It affects a baby's scalp or nappy area, including the groins, and sometimes also the armpits, neck and the area behind the ears. Occasionally the rash spreads over the baby's trunk and face. The skin is red, weepy and scaling, particularly in the skin folds. The rash is not itchy. Its cause is not known.

If your baby has infantile seborrhoeic dermatitis wash and thoroughly dry his skin, and use a bland, non-irritant soap. Avoid putting plastic pants over his nappies as these increase the likelihood of the rash becoming infected. The rash rarely distresses the baby. If there are signs of infection such as pus-filled spots, consult your doctor.

Babies who have infantile seborrhoeic dermatitis seem to have a slightly greater risk of developing *infantile eczema* later.

Cradle cap may appear alone or be part of infantile seborrhoeic dermatitis.

ECZEMA (Dermatitis)

Eczema is sometimes called dermatitis. It is characterized by red, itchy, inflamed skin. There are several forms of eczema. If your child suffers from any form he should be seen by your doctor.

At least 3 children in every 100 develop eczema, which invariably starts in infancy and is called **infantile eczema**. Breastfeeding may delay the onset of infantile eczema, but the condition does occur when babies are breastfed, sometimes even before they are weaned.

Eczema tends to improve as a child gets older; about 50 per cent of affected children are free of their eczema by the age of 6 years and most of them by 15 years.

The healthy skin of children with eczema is

commonly rather dry, and some children inherit a tendency to have eczema and also to have *dry skin*.

SYMPTOMS

Infantile eczema is an itchy rash that usually appears when a baby is between 3 months and 2 years old. The face and scalp are common starting points for the eczema, and it spreads to the backs of the arms and fronts of the legs. Within months of its first appearance, the eczema spreads to the child's inner elbows and knees, the lower buttock folds, and areas subject to friction such as the neck, wrists and ankles. The backs of the hands are another common site. Dark-skinned children may have areas of slightly scaling, pale skin on the face.

The child will rub and scratch in response to the itchiness and thus encourage *bacterial infection*. If your child is troubled by infantile eczema and is distressed, you should consult your doctor for advice and treatment.

TREATMENT

The exact part played in eczema by allergy to foods is not known. However, there is no doubt that eggs and milk make some children's eczema much worse, so it may be worth a trial period of eliminating them from your child's diet. It is also possible that the eczema in some instances is linked to inhaled allergens such as house-dust mites.

The mainstays of traditional treatment are skin creams, bath oils, tar and tar-impregnated bandages. If you feel that the treatment you are giving is not working, consult your doctor, since there are alternative drugs and medications to choose from.

It is best for any clothes worn next to the skin to be made of cotton. If your child's eczema is very bad, you might consider buying gloves or mittens for him to wear at night, so that he does not damage his skin too much by scratching in his sleep.

A child with eczema should avoid contact with anyone who has *herpes simplex* (cold sores). If he has either active or latent eczema he may develop a widespread eruption of cold sores that can be serious and require special treatment.

Forefoot eczema is itching, burning, dryness and cracking of the skin under the big toe, which spreads to the other toes and the whole underside of the forefoot. The skin between the toes is unaffected, unlike *athlete's foot*. This form of eczema is usually caused by wearing synthetic footwear, which allows little permeability and moisture absorption.

Contact eczema or dermatitis may be caused by irritants or by an allergy. A common example of contact eczema caused by irritation is *nappy rash*. A child with generalized eczema is particularly likely to suffer skin irritation from soap, detergents and the friction of clothing.

A baby may have irritant eczema around his mouth caused by a combination of dribbling saliva, lip-licking and rubbing.

▶ **See also** Allergy; Appendix: Support groups and publications

DRY SKIN

Children often have dry skin without any other disorder. A very dry skin may be inherited. The most common form is known as ichthyosis vulgaris: about 1 in 300 children suffers from it. The child has dull scaling skin, except on his face, and elbow and knee-bends, it tends to improve as he gets older. Children with ichthyosis may also have a tendency to *asthma*, *eczema* and *hay fever*. The dryness is usually worse in winter so encourage your child to wear warm clothes and to avoid getting cold.

Aqueous creams help to soothe dry skin. Your child should keep washing to the minimum necessary for comfort and hygiene and should use superfatted soaps or bath oils. Cotton clothes will help to minimize skin irritation and cotton gloves will protect your child's hands from cracking or chapping. Your doctor may prescribe creams containing urea, a natural waste-product of the body, as urea helps the skin to hold water and thus makes it more supple.

Hot dry air in centrally heated houses also tends to make skin dry and itchy. You can moisten the dry air by using a humidifier or by putting a bowl of water over each radiator in the house.

▶ **See also** Allergy

URTICARIA (Nettle rash or hives)

This is a short-lived, itchy red rash characterized by raised, flesh-coloured patches called weals. It is very common and most people experience at least one attack in a lifetime. Attacks may last for a day, a week or even a few weeks. The first time an attack occurs you should take your child to the doctor, who may prescribe an antihistamine drug. Subsequent attacks may require only calamine to reduce the itchy discomfort. More severe attacks may involve swelling of the lips, eyelids, genitalia, tongue or larynx.

Urticaria may be caused by *infection* or allergies to drugs or foods, but many attacks have no known cause. It is one of the allergic reactions found when children have other allergies.

▶ **See also** Allergy

IMPETIGO

This is a *bacterial infection* that mainly affects children, and tends to spread from one to another rapidly. Blisters, which may be quite large, form and then quickly dry and crust; they appear most commonly on the face. If you suspect impetigo, consult your doctor within a day or so.

The treatment is first to remove the crusts, which are infected by bacteria, with a salt and water solution or a weak antiseptic. You should then apply a prescribed antiseptic or antibiotic cream. Following this the impetigo should clear within about 5 days, with no scarring of the skin. While the attack lasts, the affected child should avoid skin contact with other people and you should keep his bedding, flannels and towels separate. Scrupulous hygiene is important to prevent a recurrence. If the attack is widespread, a course of antibiotics may be prescribed.

In newborn babies, impetigo sometimes appears as a widespread, tender, scald-like rash that is accompanied by a fever. Your doctor may prescribe antibiotics and in some cases your baby may be admitted to hospital for a few days.

CHILBLAINS AND CHAPPED SKIN

When the skin becomes cold, the small arteries constrict to reduce the bloodflow to the skin. This is part of the body's natural reaction to save heat. If the nerves that control small-artery constriction do not work properly, chilblains may develop.

Chilblains chiefly affect the hands and feet, and occasionally the ankles, backs of the legs and nose. In cold weather most of the skin on these areas turns pale and perhaps numb, but there are also scattered red, sore, itchy lumps, which subside as the skin becomes warmer.

Chilblains are not a serious problem, but they can be painful. The best remedy is to prevent the susceptible skin from becoming cold. Make sure that your child wears warm dry loose-fitting gloves and socks under generously fitting, waterproof footwear. Change gloves or socks if they become damp. Encourage your child to avoid scratching since this further irritates and breaks the skin. A warm bath or physical activity in a warm place helps to restore the skin's circulation.

The reduced blood supply to cold skin can also cause chapping, or dry, cracked, sore areas, usually on the fingers, hands and lips. On cold days, lip-salve can be helpful. If your child's skin chaps easily make sure that he dries himself thoroughly after bathing, swimming or playing with water.

WARTS AND VERRUCAS

Warts are caused by a *virus* that infects the epidermal skin cells. They are very common, particularly on the fingers and soles of the feet, as well as on the knees and face. Almost all children's warts disappear spontaneously within 3 years and many are gone within months. They are not usually painful; if they are, there is probably an additional *bacterial infection*. Because warts do tend to disappear spontaneously, many folk remedies may appear to be effective in curing them.

Although common warts are not normally painful, plantar warts, or verrucas, on the soles of the feet are often painful because of the pressure put on the affected area.

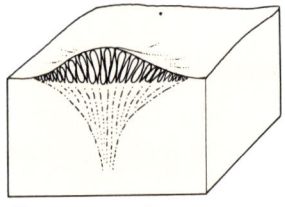

Common wart

Verruca

If your child has a wart or a verruca you should consult your doctor. Many anti-wart preparations are available but if you use one you must follow the instructions carefully. These preparations should be applied to the wart area only, because they can irritate and inflame normal skin. For hand, elbow or knee warts your doctor may recommend a peeling agent, which is applied with a brush at night for up to 10 weeks. Plantar warts are usually overlaid with hard skin that should be pared with an emery board or nail file used for this purpose only, before you apply an anti-wart preparation.

There is some evidence that covering a verruca is ineffective in preventing the spread of the viral infection

ACNE

Acne is a result of overactive sebaceous glands that produce too much of their oily secretion, sebum. When the sebum cannot discharge from the hair follicles as normal, it accumulates and leads to spots and pimples.

The sebaceous glands are stimulated to overactivity by the male hormone testosterone, and during puberty and the late teens, the level of testosterone rises in girls as well as in boys. Mild acne is so common during adolescence that it is considered part of normal growing up.

If your child develops acne well before puberty – especially before he is 5 years old – you should take him to your doctor. Children who have the problem when very young tend to

THE SKIN AND HAIR 289

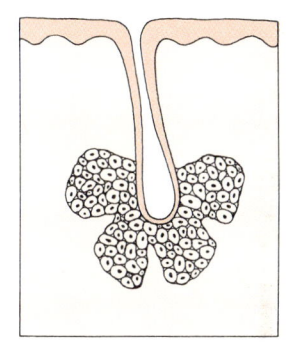

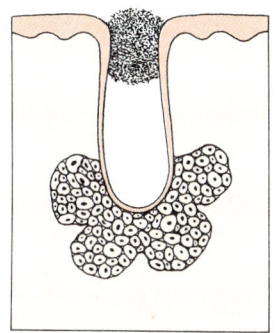

Normal sebaceous gland | Open blackhead | Spot

A spot develops when the opening of a follicle becomes blocked by excess sebum and dead cells, forming a blackhead. Sebum cannot escape and builds up within the blocked follicle, with the result that the follicle may become inflamed and a red spot appears. Sometimes the spot becomes septic.

grow out of it, but they may have a more severe form of acne during adolescence. The first sign is often greasiness of the child's scalp and skin. Next, blackheads and whiteheads develop: these are plugs of sebum blocking the hair follicles. Then pimples, pustules and cysts may erupt over the face, upper chest and back.

Some adolescents have very little acne, while others suffer badly; some have it in their early teens, others a few years later. For some girls it is worse just before a period. The majority of sufferers grow out of the condition by their early twenties.

A skin disorder such as acne can be a problem at the best of times. To the adolescent, who is gradually developing his or her self-image and who is usually ultra-sensitive to looks and appearance, acne can be devastating. It can cause mental anguish, self-imposed social isolation and a great deal of embarrassment. Reassurances that 'it's just part of growing up', while well-meant and true, are rarely very helpful.

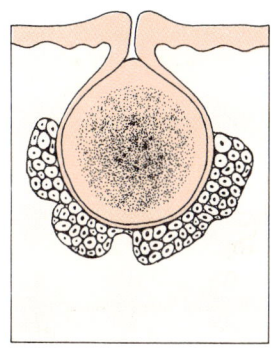

TREATMENT

The acne sufferer can do a certain amount to minimize or control the condition. Personal hygiene and washing are important: hair and skin should be kept as clean as possible. Spots should never be picked or squeezed. Make-up and cosmetics ought to be those intended for greasy skin, and they should be used sparingly. Sunshine often improves the condition, but there is no scientific evidence that diet helps to prevent or improve acne. If your child's acne seems very bad or if it is causing deep distress, encourage a visit to the doctor. Several drugs have been developed in recent years that help certain types of acne. Some decrease sebum production; in some cases antibiotics may be prescribed and will stop bacterial infection and small spots flaring into large, angry pustules or cysts that may leave permanent and unsightly scars.

▶ **See also** The older child and adolescent

INSECT BITES

Flea bites from human, bird, cat or dog fleas show as groups of itchy small, red, flat spots or patches, each with a central small blister. Other insects that bite include bed bugs, mosquitoes and dog lice; their bites look similar to flea bites.

Hypersensitive children may have a more severe reaction to insect bites; itching, blisters, pimples and weals may appear over their buttocks, lower limbs and possibly elsewhere. The child usually scratches the bites and *bacterial infection* of the bite is common. Usually only one child in a family shows the reaction, which tends to recur in the summer for a few years. Calamine lotion may help to soothe itching.

HEAD LICE (Nits)

Head-scratching suggests that your child has head lice. There may be a skin infection over the nape of his neck. Although hairs on a child's head may be infested by the insects, scalp skin is tough and so any itching and scratching usually show up over the neck.

Head lice are caught by direct head contact with another child who has them and are nothing to do with the cleanliness of your child's hair – in fact it is thought that lice may thrive particularly well in clean hair. If you look closely at your child's infested hair, you will be able to see a few head lice and many nits, or egg capsules, sticking to the hairs like grains of salt. Unlike *dandruff*, which can be brushed away easily, nits are firmly attached to hairs. The eggs are laid where the hair emerges from the scalp, so if the nits are close to the scalp this means that the infestation is recent, but if they spread up the hair this means that your child has probably had nits for some time.

TREATMENT

As head lice are very easily passed from child to child, it is important that you report them to your doctor, who will inform the local health authority. All your child's contacts at home and school will be checked, and treated if necessary.

Your doctor may prescribe a special shampoo that should be rubbed into the wet scalp, left for 5 minutes, and then rinsed off. Your child's hair should then be combed thoroughly with a stiff fine-toothed comb. The treatment must be repeated a week later because more lice will have hatched out by that time. Some doctors prefer to prescribe a lotion; this is applied to the scalp, allowed to dry, and the child's hair is shampooed and combed 12 hours later. Haircutting is never necessary.

SCABIES

This infestation by tiny insect-like mites shows up after an incubation period of 4 to 6 weeks. The female mites burrow through the surface layer of the skin and deposit their eggs as they move. The eggs reach maturity in 21 days and a new cycle begins. Scabies is passed from person to person through close physical contact.

The burrows are just large enough to be visible and are usually between the fingers and toes, on the fronts of the wrists, backs of the elbows, in the armpits and on the buttocks. The mites may be even more widespread on a baby's skin, sometimes with firm pimples over the trunk or small blisters over the palms and soles. The condition may cause *eczema*, *impetigo* or *urticaria*.

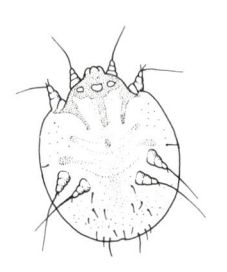

The mites that cause scabies cannot survive for long away from human skin. Even if clothes and bedclothes cannot be laundered, if they are left unused for more than 4 days they will be free from infestation.

TREATMENT

The characteristic symptoms of scabies infestation is intense irritation, especially at night. Your doctor will prescribe a lotion to be applied twice.

Normally, the first application is in the evening and the second the following morning. Alternatively, some lotions are applied once and left on for 12 hours.

Your whole family will need treatment. Change and launder all bedding. Your child's skin may be itchy for up to 14 days after treatment, but if you treat scabies exactly as advised, it should be cured.

OTHER SKIN AND HAIR PROBLEMS

Among other problems affecting the skin are molluscum contagiosum, ringworm, psoriasis, pityriasis rosea, Raynaud's disease and alopecia areata.

Molluscum contagiosum is a wart like *virus infection* common in both babies and children. Pearly pimples, each with a central depression, appear singly or in groups over the buttocks, trunk and face. They are harmless and will disappear spontaneously within a year or so without treatment.

Ringworm and athlete's foot is a *fungal infection* that may affect skin or nails. Scalp ringworm and foot ringworm, or athlete's foot, are common in children. The fungal growths tend to form rings on the skin, with raised scaly edges.

Ringworm can be caught from other people, from animals or from the soil. Ringworm caught from cattle looks bright red and inflamed; ringworm from cats and dogs looks less red but if it infects the scalp it causes areas of hair loss, as well as some hairs breaking off. You should consult your doctor for treatment.

Psoriasis is a long-lasting skin condition of unknown cause. It is rare in children under 2 years old. It usually takes the form of a rash of small, silvery, scaly spots that appear abruptly, often a few weeks after *tonsillitis* or a similar infection. The rash can last for a period of time up to 3 months but it then fades; however, it often recurs. It is not infectious and does not affect general health.

If your child has psoriasis he should see a doctor, although there may be no need for treatment. Bland ointments or coal-tar applications may be prescribed. Natural sunlight or ultra-violet light from a sunlamp usually helps to clear the rash, but ultra-violet lamps should only be used under medical supervision; they may provoke a return of the psoriasis. You should also take care the child does not become sunburnt.

Pityriasis rosea is an infection thought to be caused by a virus and lasts about 6 weeks. It occurs most commonly in winter, in older children. The first sign is a red area called the herald patch. A few days later, other red spots or patches appear, with scaling round their edges. They appear particularly over the trunk, sometimes following the line of the ribs round to the back. They may be itchy, especially after a bath. No treatment is needed, except for a lotion such as calamine to relieve any itching.

Raynaud's disease is a rare disease in young children; it tends to occur in adolescents or young adults, mainly women. The small arteries supplying the skin with blood seem to become extra-sensitive to cold. They constrict under the slightest provocation and the skin, usually of the fingers and toes, becomes pale, possibly bluish, and numb or tingling. The cause of this arterial spasm is not clear. When the spasm ends the skin's blood circulation returns and this can be painful. As a preventive measure the sufferer's hands and feet should be kept warm and dry.

If you have an adolescent child who has Raynaud's disease, suggest that he wears loose fitting gloves, shoes and socks, and that he might wear fingerless mittens indoors.

Very rarely a drug may be prescribed to keep the arteries open, or an operation recommended to cut the nerves that stimulate the artery constriction.

Alopecia areata means hair loss in patches. It tends to run in families but the cause is unknown. Usually one or two completely bald patches appear over the scalp, although any part of the body may be affected. The patches may have an irregular outline to start with. It is very rare to lose hair from the whole of the scalp. If there are only a few patches of hair loss, your child's hair is likely to regrow in a year or so. If your child has alopecia, consult your doctor.

THE BRAIN, NERVES AND MUSCLES

Your brain generates, controls and integrates almost everything you do. It receives information from the various sense organs – eyes, ears, nose, tongue, skin, joints, muscles and others – along sensory nerves, so that it is aware of what is going on both outside and inside the body. It sorts, organizes and stores this information as necessary. It decides which actions are appropriate, then sends out messages along motor nerves to the 600 or so muscles in the body that control movement and posture. The brain is also the seat of consciousness, the organ of thinking, learning, behaviour, language and emotion. Besides these 'higher' functions it also controls vital functions such as breathing.

The brain and spinal cord together make up the central nervous system. They are well protected within the skull and spine. The peripheral nervous system consists of nerves that run from the brain and spinal cord to all other parts of the body. The nerve cell, or neurone, forms the basic unit of the system and is capable of transmitting tiny electrical impulses that form a nerve message. There are about 100,000,000,000 neurones in the brain, and each one of these connects with some 1,000 neurones elsewhere in the body.

The bulk of the brain is made up of the two cerebral hemispheres, right and left, where the higher functions of the brain take place. Below is the brainstem, which connects the hemispheres to the spinal cord and which is concerned with basic life processes such as heartbeat. Attached to the rear of the brainstem is the cauliflower-like cerebellum, which controls body posture and some types of movements.

The brain and spinal cord are bathed by cerebrospinal fluid, which is produced in the fluid-filled cavities or ventricles within the brain. The fluid circulates by passing out through the brainstem to bathe the outside of the brain and spinal cord and is then absorbed by veins in the membranes, or meninges, surrounding the brain.

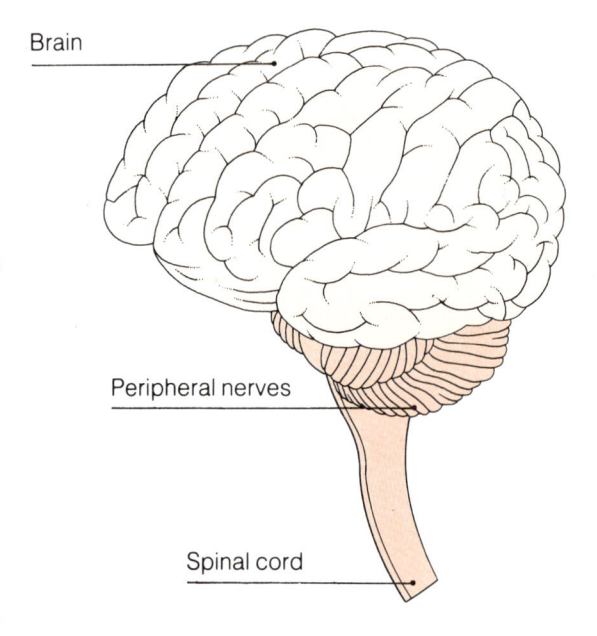

Motor nerves carry messages to muscles, instructing them how much to contract, how forcefully and how quickly. There are three major types of muscle in the body: voluntary, involuntary and cardiac muscle. Voluntary muscle is largely under conscious control and forms the muscles that move the skeleton. Involuntary muscle makes up the bulk of the digestive, urinary and other internal organs. It works largely automatically without conscious instruction. The heart is composed of cardiac muscle.

Every movement a person makes depends on a three-stage process. First, the area of the brain that controls movement in that part of

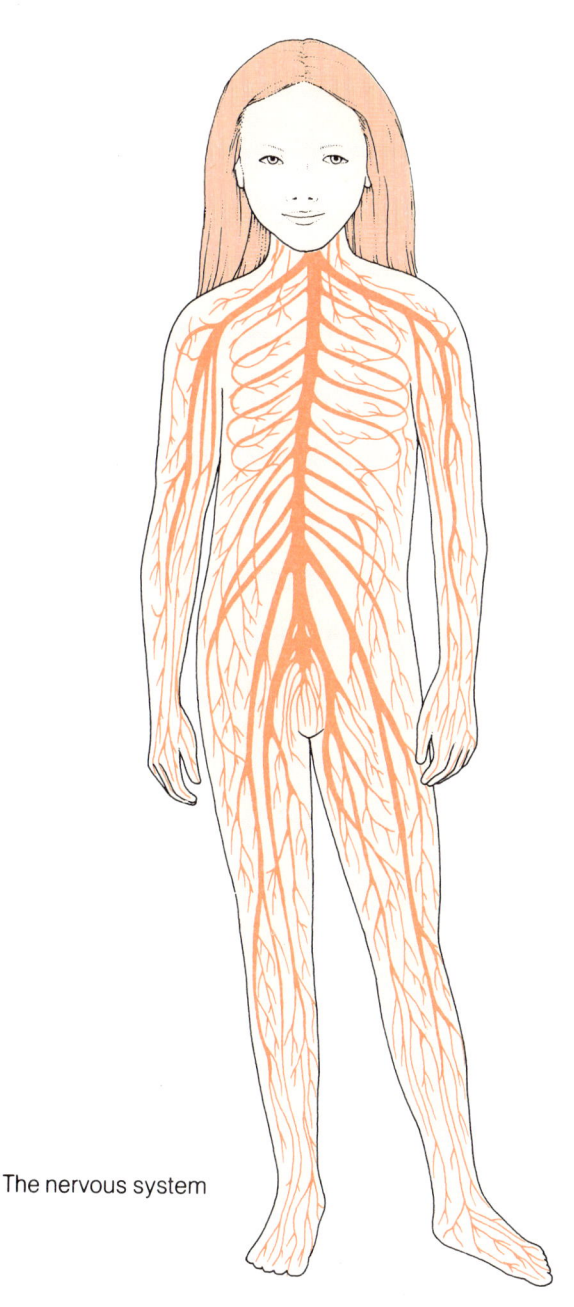

The nervous system

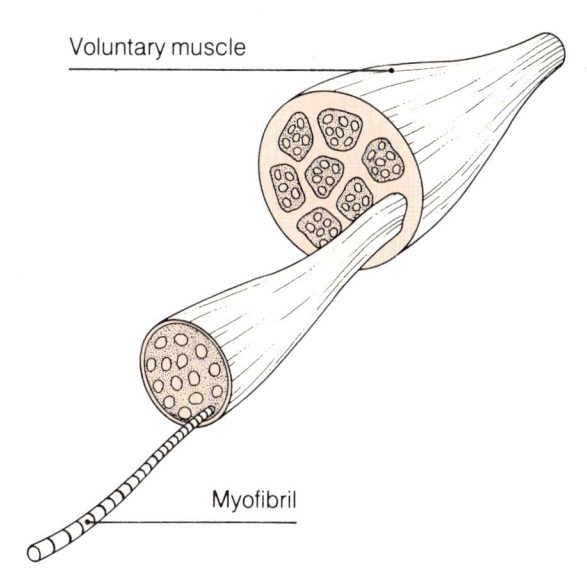

Voluntary muscle

Myofibril

Voluntary muscle is made up of bundles or sheets of long, thin muscle cells or myofibrils. It is also called 'striped muscle'.

the body must be functioning properly. Secondly, the motor nerve that carries the messages must be intact and working. Thirdly, the muscle itself must be healthy and able to contract when stimulated. So, for example, when a doctor is investigating paralysis, he must carry out observations and tests to deduce which part of the system is at fault before diagnosis and treatment are possible.

Headaches

Children as well as adults have occasional headaches. Provided that your child's headaches are mild, short-term, infrequent and do not occur in conjunction with other symptoms, they can probably be accepted as minor annoyances rather than as indications of illness. Give your child paracetamol if necessary.

Headaches that are more severe, frequent or long-lasting may be due to a variety of causes but the majority are either tension or *migraine* headaches. Tension headaches generally affect older children, but they can even affect pre-school children. They are usually felt at the front and sides of the head and they tend to occur at times of stress. Take steps to reduce stress if you can identify the situations that cause it. Most children who are particularly susceptible to tension headaches can be helped by being taught *relaxation techniques*.

A child with *astigmatism* or *long sight* may suffer mild but persistent headaches that increase when he has to concentrate on close work. The right spectacles should solve the problem. Headaches due to *sinusitis* are usually easy to recognize because they accompany respiratory infections and your child will feel that the affected sinuses are tender when you put pressure on them. High blood pressure is a very rare cause of a child's headache, but a doctor will usually measure the child's blood pressure to make sure this is normal.

If *meningitis* is the cause of a headache, the child will also have a stiff, painful neck. The headache caused by a *brain tumour* is usually worse in the mornings and is associated with vomiting. Unlike a tension or migraine headache, it worsens progressively and other symptoms such as unsteadiness will appear.

Fainting

A fainting attack, also known as a syncopal attack, may occur at any age throughout childhood, although it is particularly common during adolescence.

Faints are due to a reflex that slows the heart rate and reduces the amount of blood returning to the heart, and thus the supply to the brain, causing loss of consciousness. In some people this reflex is very sensitive, and they are prone to fainting.

A child cannot faint when lying down – he will either be sitting or standing. Common causes include: standing still for a long time in the heat; an emotional upset caused by, for example, an unpleasant event or the sight of blood; a painful experience; a blood test; and mass hysteria, such as may occur at a rock concert. Characteristically, the child feels weak and light-headed, the colour drains from his face and he slumps slowly to the ground and lies unconscious. If left lying down, the child will start to recover very quickly, usually after a few seconds. His head should be at the same level as or lower than his legs. He should not be allowed to sit or stand up until he is fully recovered.

Recurrent faints can sometimes raise the suspicion that a child may be suffering from *epilepsy*, but the circumstances in which the attacks occur and the sequence of events during the attack are usually distinctive. Recurrent fainting attacks, although a nuisance, do no harm. You can help your child by working out which situations precipitate faints and by trying to avoid them in future. Drug treatment is of no benefit.

Cramps and stitches

Cramps are sudden, painful and involuntary muscle spasms. Reduced bloodflow to a muscle, as a result of sitting in an awkward position for example, can cause cramp, partly because the muscle is deprived of oxygen and partly because lactic acid, formed in the muscle during exertion and normally removed by the blood, builds up within it. The familiar 'stitch' which every child knows is simply cramp in a rib muscle.

Cramp sometimes occurs during prolonged and vigorous exercise because lactic acid builds up in the muscle more quickly than it can be removed by the blood. The 'warm up' exercises that athletes perform before any serious exertion are designed to stimulate the circulation and to ensure that the muscles have a good blood supply.

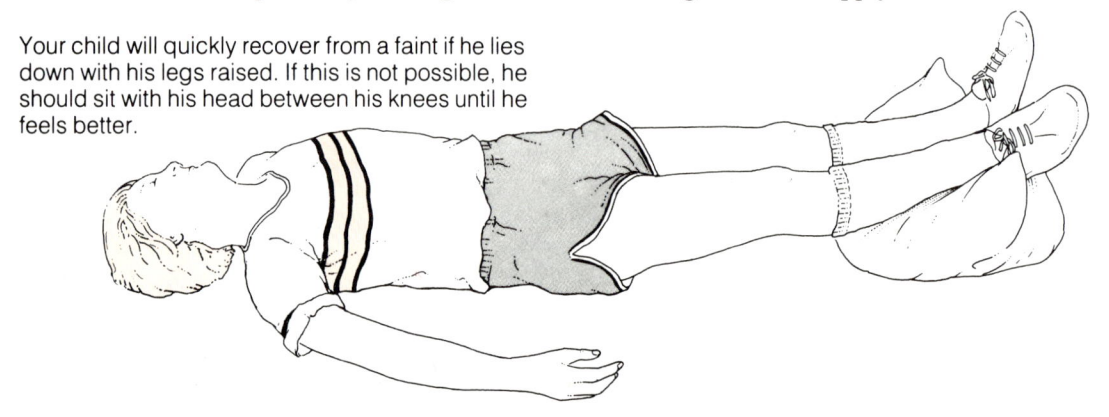

Your child will quickly recover from a faint if he lies down with his legs raised. If this is not possible, he should sit with his head between his knees until he feels better.

Cramps often strike at night, usually in the calf or toes, and may develop because the child has been lying awkwardly so that the circulation to a limb has been obstructed. However, cramps often seem to occur spontaneously and for no apparent reason, and although they may be very painful they are not a sign of any disorder. Teach your child how to get rid of the cramp by forcibly straightening his affected muscle. If the cramp is in the calf he should get out of bed and stand, forcing his heel hard down on the floor so that the muscle relaxes. If the cramp is in his fingers or toes he should forcibly uncurl them. Massaging the affected part for a few minutes until the pain has abated will restore the circulation and reduce the risk of cramp recurring.

Swimming in cold water can cause cramp, because the bloodflow to the skin and peripheral muscles is reduced in order to prevent the body losing too much heat. Your child should not swim after a heavy meal because blood is diverted to the intestines to aid digestion, and this further depletes the blood supply to the peripheral muscles and increases the likelihood of cramp. However, if the water is warm and the child has only had a light meal, cramp is unlikely to be a real risk.

Clumsiness

Children vary in their natural physical agility and manual dexterity. Between 5 and 15 per cent of children are noticeably clumsy and appear to lack physical co-ordination. Such children may have difficulty with tying shoelaces, doing up buttons, eating tidily or tackling puzzles, but they seldom have any other developmental or physical problems.

Confidence is often as much of a problem as any lack of co-ordination. If you think your child is clumsy, give him opportunities to develop physical skills such as hand-eye co-ordination and sense of balance. Encourage him first to practise tasks that he can manage easily, and then introduce others which are more challenging and which may previously have defeated him. Help him to become more aware of his own body, by pointing out which parts of his body are involved in a particular action, for example.

Some children go through clumsy phases, especially boys in adolescence when for a time their rapidly growing bodies may seem to outstrip their ability to control them.

▶**See also** Early growth and development

Building towers of bricks with both hands at the same time will help to improve physical co-ordination. Guessing which tower will fall down first adds excitement to the exercise.

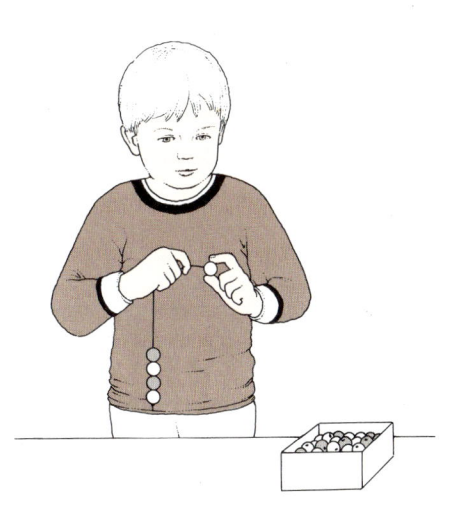

Threading beads on a string will help a clumsy child to concentrate on precise actions. Different coloured beads can be used to create different patterned chains and this will make the activity more fun.

MIGRAINE

Migraine is one of the most frequent causes of recurrent headaches and about 4 per cent of all school-age children suffer from it at some time. There is a strong tendency for migraine to run in families.

SYMPTOMS

In a typical attack the headache, which may or may not be one-sided, is accompanied at the start by nausea, often leading to vomiting. The child looks very pale and may sweat excessively. When the child vomits his headache is a little relieved, but both headache and vomiting continue for some hours. The child probably feels better after a few hours' rest in a darkened room.

A few children may also experience dizziness, double vision, pins and needles or weakness down one side of the body or a temporary inability to speak. They may also see flickering lights before their eyes either just before or as the headache begins.

Younger children may have attacks of migraine with little sign of a headache. The attacks often take the form of recurrent episodes of vomiting and stomach-ache during which the child appears very pale. This condition may be described as periodic syndrome or cyclical vomiting. Many of the children who are affected have more typical migraine attacks when they are older.

TREATMENT

Children who have only very occasional mild attacks of migraine require no particular treatment except bedrest until the attack has worn off. If your child has more severe attacks, the doctor may prescribe drugs to relieve both the nausea and the headache. It is important for your child to take these tablets as soon as an attack begins, so that he does not vomit them up before they are absorbed into the system.

If your child suffers from frequent, severe attacks of migraine, the symptoms may be relieved if he cuts out cheese, chocolate or citrus fruits from his diet. He may also benefit from learning *relaxation techniques*.

▶ **See also** Appendix: Support groups and publications

FITS AND CONVULSIONS

A child having a fit or a convulsion falls unconscious, goes stiff and then jerks all over. Fits are due to uninhibited overactivity of the neurones in the brain, which interrupts the brain's normal working for a short time. Fits and convulsions are called non-*epileptic* when they have no external cause. Febrile fits, for example, are triggered by a sudden rise in body temperature caused by an infection.

By far the most common non-epileptic fits in childhood are febrile convulsions. About 4 per cent of all children have at least one febrile convulsion. They occur almost exclusively in children aged between 6 months and 5 years and happen most often during the second year of life. There is usually a tendency to convulsions in the family.

The convulsion is usually over in a few minutes and the child will then probably sleep for an hour or so. If you are alone with the child, stay with him while he is having the fit to make sure he does not hurt himself, but as soon as he is calm, call a doctor.

Because very prolonged febrile convulsions can cause *brain damage*, intravenous drugs are usually given to stop a febrile convulsion that has lasted for more than 15 minutes. After a first febrile convulsion a child, especially if very young, will probably be admitted to hospital for a day or two for observation. It is particularly important to make sure that the symptoms are not those of developing *meningitis*.

About 1 child in 4 who has had one fit will have recurring febrile convulsions. You can minimize the risk of recurrence by checking your child's temperature whenever he appears hot or ill. If his temperature is high, remove his clothing and give a sponge bath with tepid water. Give paracetamol and check his temperature periodically. If febrile convulsions recur despite these measures, your child may need regular medication. About 1 child in 50 who has had a febrile convulsion will go on to have true epileptic seizures. In most cases, although febrile convulsions are upsetting they have no lasting ill effects and very rarely occur after a child is 6 years old.

A child may also have convulsions shortly after a *head injury* or during an illness such as meningitis or *encephalitis*. Newborn babies are prone to convulsions if they have been deprived of oxygen before birth or if they have had breathing difficulties immediately after delivery. They may also have convulsions if the level of calcium in their blood is low. Children with *diabetes* who are receiving a little too much insulin may have convulsions because their blood sugar is falling dangerously low.

▶ See also Appendix: Emergency actions

EPILEPSY

Epilepsy affects about 6 school-age children in every 1,000. It tends to run in families. *Fits and convulsions* are termed epileptic when they are recurrent and have no obvious external cause. Various types of seizure may occur and sometimes a child will have more than one type. The most common type of epileptic seizure is known as a 'grand mal' or 'major' seizure.

SYMPTOMS

With grand mal epilepsy there is often no warning before the start of an attack. The child suddenly falls unconscious to the ground, and may stiffen before his body and limbs begin to jerk rhythmically. The child may pass urine and froth at the mouth during this stage. After a few minutes the convulsive movements settle and the child passes into sleep for an hour or so. He may be wakened during this period. After the sleep, the child wakes fully recovered.

Focal epileptic seizures usually produce rhythmic jerking of one hand and arm, which may spread to involve the leg and face on the same side. The child does not usually lose consciousness but a seizure of this type may be followed by weakness of the affected arm for an hour or two afterwards.

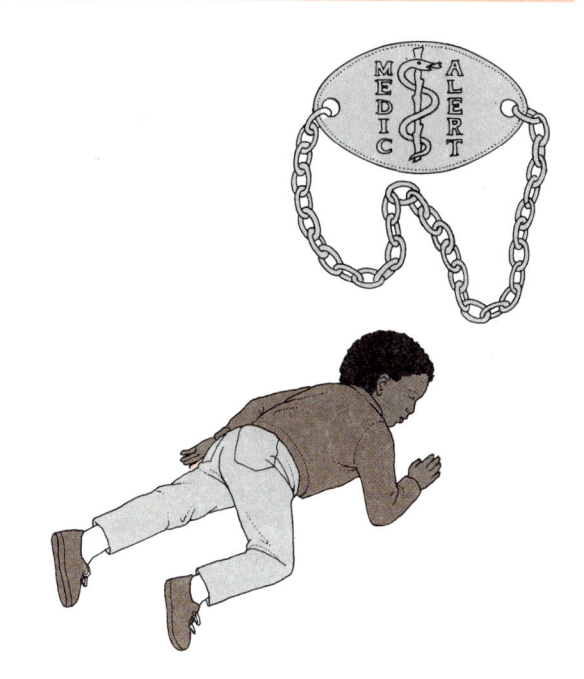

In case your child has a fit when on his own and away from home it is wise to arrange for him to wear a special bracelet or tag that will inform a stranger or passerby that he has epilepsy. The telephone number of the organization issuing the bracelets is also on the tag and the staff will give relevant medical information about your child to anyone contacting them.

Psychomotor seizures can produce very odd symptoms. Usually the child goes into a trance-like state for a minute or two, perhaps walking about, talking nonsense, doing things out of context or appearing frightened. Chewing or sucking movements are common during an attack. A child old enough to describe sensations experienced during the attack may tell of objects appearing too big or too small, dizziness, hearing voices or seeing faces, feelings of sadness, fear, or familiarity of surroundings never seen before. The attack passes off after a few minutes but the child may want to sleep for a while afterwards.

A child who goes blank for a short period is said to have had an absence seizure. Usually the child does not fall or move during the attack. A special kind of absence seizure, known as 'petit mal', consists of attacks lasting only 10 to 15 seconds but perhaps occurring many times in one day.

Myoclonic seizures take the form of sudden, shock-like jerks which may involve the whole body and cause the child suddenly to drop heavily to the floor. Infantile spasms are a special kind of seizure and usually occur in the first year of life.

If your child has had a seizure the doctor will consider other possible causes, such as a febrile fit, *fainting*, a *temper tantrum*, a nightmare, infantile *colic* or *breath-holding* before diagnosing epilepsy. After listening to your description of your child's attacks, the doctor may arrange for an electroencephalogram.

TREATMENT

If your child has epilepsy his activities should be restricted as little as possible. For obvious reasons he should not cycle in traffic, but he may swim provided that there is a responsible adult at hand. The majority of children with epilepsy attend ordinary schools and do well there. Discipline should be the same as for any other child and there is usually no risk that ordinary reactions of frustration or anger will bring on an attack. When your child is older and goes out alone he should be encouraged to wear a specially engraved bracelet: this will inform anyone trying to help during a fit that he has epilepsy.

AN ELECTROENCEPHALOGRAM (EEG)

Epilepsy alters the normal electrical activity of the brain in a characteristic way. The typical abnormal patterns can be detected by means of an electroencephalogram. Metal electrodes are attached to the child's head with a special glue and a moving pen records the impulse in graphic form. The procedure is painless and harmless.

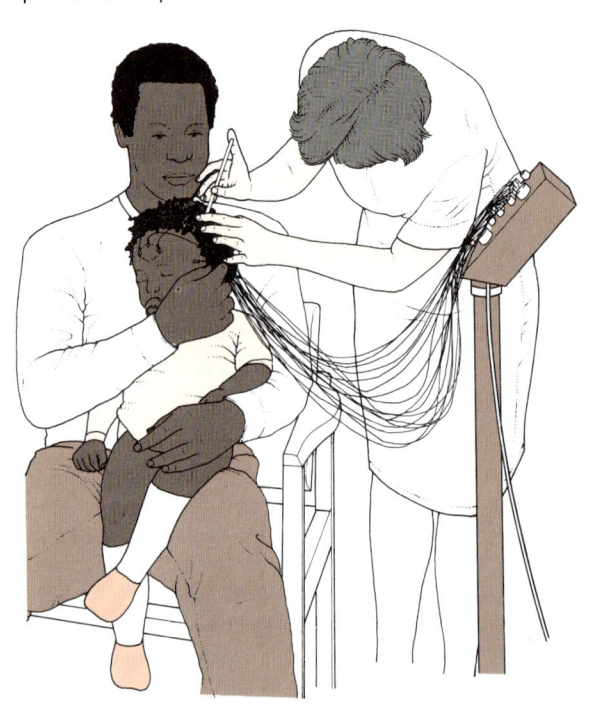

If you are with a child having a fit, you should remain calm and place him in the *recovery position* to make sure that his breathing is not obstructed. On no account force anything between his teeth as this may interfere with his breathing or break his teeth. On recovery from a fit many children are confused and need the security of a calm, friendly adult's presence. Most fits cease spontaneously after a few minutes, but you should seek medical help immediately if any fit lasts more than 10 minutes.

Many children with epilepsy require regular drug treatment over a period of several years to prevent or reduce the frequency and severity of the seizures. The drugs used are powerful and they do have side-effects. They may, for example, cause mood changes. Ask your doctor to describe to you the likely side-effects of any drugs he prescribes for your child.

Despite drug treatment some children continue to have seizures, although these will usually be reduced in frequency and severity. However, for the majority of children, seizures stop completely after a period of treatment, and children are able to discontinue treatment when they have not had a fit for a year or two. Many children simply grow out of epilepsy.

▶ See also Longstanding problems; Appendices: Support groups and publications; Drugs and treatments

MENINGITIS

Meningitis is caused by *bacteria* or *viruses* that enter the cerebrospinal fluid surrounding the brain and spinal cord and infect the brain membranes, the meninges. Bacterial meningitis is considered a medical emergency: early treatment often but not always brings about a complete cure, whereas delay may result in some *brain damage* or even death. Fortunately bacterial meningitis is rare.

A child can develop meningitis at any age, although the disorder is often more serious for babies and young children. Because they cannot explain that they have a headache or neckache and may not develop a stiff neck in the early stages, meningitis is suspected if a baby or young child is clearly unwell and if there appears to be no definite cause for his illness. Older children complain of headache and neckache, feel sick, look flushed and run a temperature, go off their food, become irritable and want to lie down and sleep. They may turn their heads away or shield their eyes from bright light. Sometimes meningitis can cause *convulsions*, and the *fontanelle* of a baby who is affected may bulge because inflammation increases the pressure of cerebrospinal fluid within the meninges.

If you find that your child holds his neck stiffly and resists having it bent forward call your doctor at once. The doctor will arrange admission to hospital, where a *lumbar puncture* will be carried out in order to obtain a sample of cerebrospinal fluid for laboratory analysis. If bacterial meningitis is confirmed, your child will be given antibiotics, usually intravenously at first. Antibiotic treatment is continued for 10 days. It is followed by a period of check-ups and hearing tests to ensure that the meningitis has not caused brain damage.

Meningitis can also be caused by viruses. This form of meningitis is more common but fortunately less severe. The symptoms are much the same as for bacterial meningitis except that the child may not become drowsy. Irritability, headache, sickness, temperature and neck stiffness all occur. In this case analysis of cerebrospinal fluid obtained by a lumbar puncture will show that there is inflammation but no sign of bacteria. Affected children usually make a spontaneous and full recovery without any specific treatment.

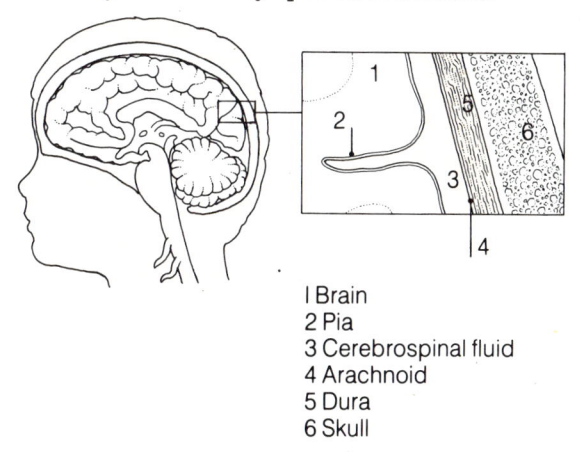

1 Brain
2 Pia
3 Cerebrospinal fluid
4 Arachnoid
5 Dura
6 Skull

Three sheets of tissue surround the brain and spinal cord. The outer, toughest layer, is called the dura. Between the two inner layers, the pia and the arachnoid, is a space filled with cerebrospinal fluid. If this fluid becomes infected the membranes will become inflamed and meningitis will develop. A sample of fluid, withdrawn by lumbar puncture, can be analyzed to confirm the diagnosis.

POLYNEURITIS

Polyneuritis is inflammation of the nerves in the legs, trunk, arms and head that carry messages to the muscles and relay feelings of touch and pain. It is a rare condition. The cause is not fully understood but it usually seems to be an inflammatory reaction in the nerves to some infection elsewhere in the body. It can sometimes follow influenza, measles, glandular fever, colds and other viral infections. It can occur at any age after the first year of life.

The first symptom is weakness in the muscles of the legs, and this may be accompanied by pins and needles or numbness in the hands and feet. The affected child will be unable to walk or stand but will not feel particularly ill. The muscle weakness worsens over the next few days and involves the trunk and arms as well as the legs. Often the muscles in the face are affected on both sides so that the child cannot close his eyelids properly and smiling is impossible. Some children have only partial weakness, others become severely paralysed.

You should consult your doctor at once if your child shows the first signs of polyneuritis. It is imperative that he is admitted to hospital for observation while the weakness is progressing as, in a small number of children, the muscles used for breathing become involved. If breathing is difficult, a ventilator is used for a while. After a few days the weakness progresses no further, and after 2 or 3 weeks strength gradually starts to return to the weakened muscles. Recovery may take many months but is usually complete provided that physiotherapy is carried out during this time. You may have to make special arrangements for your child's schooling until he has fully recovered.

ENCEPHALITIS

Encephalitis strictly means inflammation of the brain from any cause, but it is usually due to a virus infection. Viruses, such as *herpes simplex*, may attack the brain directly; or the brain may have an inflammatory reaction to a viral infection elsewhere in the body, such as *measles*, *chickenpox* or *German measles*.

Whatever the cause, a child with encephalitis becomes ill with increasing drowsiness and headache. *Convulsions* are common and may be generalized or affect just one part of the body. Weakness and stiffness of one side or of the whole body may develop. Difficulty in emptying bladder and bowels is a common feature. The drowsiness often progresses until the child is in a coma.

Treatment depends on the cause and symptoms present. Special antiviral drugs are available to help combat herpes simplex but they are ineffective on any other virus. Cortisone can help in some types of

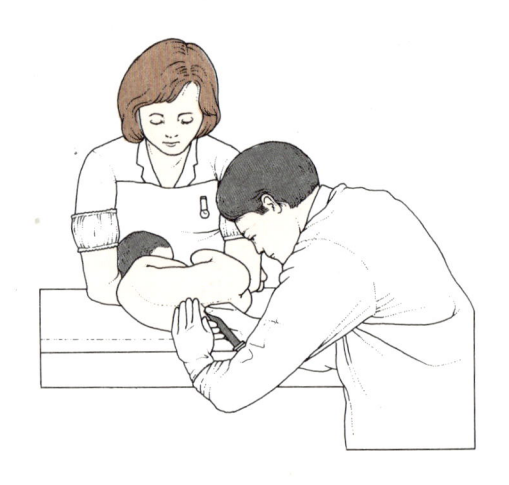

A lumbar puncture can help to diagnose encephalitis. A needle is inserted between two vertebrae in the lower spine and cerebrospinal fluid is withdrawn through a needle. Hold a young child's limbs securely to reassure him and to prevent him moving.

encephalitis by reducing inflammation. Convulsions can usually be controlled by drugs. A child in a coma has to be fed intravenously or by a tube into the stomach. Nursing care will prevent chestiness and pressure sores, and physiotherapy is given to reduce stiffness in the limbs.

Most children recover gradually and continue to do so for at least a year. However, encephalitis does carry a risk of *brain damage*.

A few very severe cases of encephalitis may be fatal.

CEREBRAL PALSY

The term cerebral palsy literally means muscle paralysis whose cause is in the brain. More precisely, cerebral palsy can be defined as a disorder of posture or movement which is permanent, although sometimes changing in character. Anything that damages the growing brain may cause cerebral palsy. In many cases, it seems that for unknown reasons the brain has not developed normally during the early stages in the womb. Cerebral palsy may also be due to an infection such as *German measles* in pregnancy; shortage of oxygen to the baby's brain during late pregnancy or labour; or to severe illnesses in the first weeks of life. Cerebral palsy may also result from brain damage in the first few years of life, for example from injuries to the head or *meningitis*. The *brain damage* that causes cerebral palsy, however severe, does not get worse once it has occurred; nor, unfortunately, is it likely to improve, since dead nerve cells cannot regenerate.

Cerebral palsy is not a single condition: the brain may be damaged in a number of ways, and the resulting disabilities will vary in severity depending on how badly the brain was damaged and which part of it was affected. Thus there are several types and in each type severity may range from a trivial disability to severe handicap. Also, children whose main handicap is mental retardation may have problems of movement and posture, although doctors will often disagree about whether the term cerebral palsy can be used in these instances. Because the term itself is not very precise, it is impossible to say exactly how common cerebral palsy is, but estimates vary between 1 and 4 out of every 1,000 children born in the Western world.

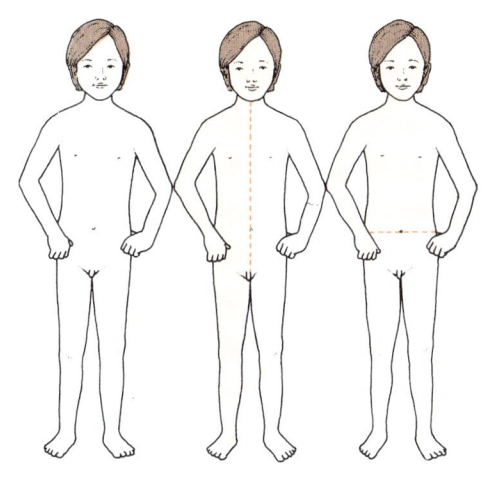

In the most severe form of cerebral palsy all four limbs are paralysed and the condition is known as quadriplegia. In hemiplegia one side of the body is paralysed. If the legs only are affected the condition is known as paraplegia.

Spasticity is the most common type of cerebral palsy. It means stiffness of the muscles. This makes it difficult for a child to bend his limbs or his trunk. It is caused by loss of the control mechanisms in the brain that normally maintain muscle tone at the correct level. Spastic muscles feel strong but are actually weak because they cannot be accurately controlled. In spastic hemiplegia only one side of the body is affected; in spastic diplegia all four limbs are affected, but the legs more so than the arms; and in spastic quadriplegia all four limbs are equally affected. Paraplegia means that only the legs are involved; however, this is more likely to occur in cases of spinal-cord damage than in cerebral palsy.

A child with athetosis is afflicted by continuous movements of the trunk and limbs, with strange postures of the hands and facial grimaces. Speech is often severely affected and he may also suffer hearing loss. In this form of cerebral palsy intelligence may not be affected despite severe physical disability.

Children with ataxia have very poor balance, so that there is often a long delay between starting to walk holding on and learning to walk alone. There may be some tremor of the hands with poor co-ordination. Eye movements may be abnormal.

Children with cerebral palsy often have other handicaps as well; whatever caused damage to the parts of the brain that control movement may also have affected thought processes, speech, sight and hearing. About a half to two-thirds of children with cerebral palsy have some degree of mental handicap; some may have a *squint* or another eye defect; and a much smaller number have *epilepsy* or some degree of *deafness*. Poor feeding and constipation are common problems. Arms or legs affected by spasticity may be somewhat shorter than normal and may chill easily and develop *chilblains*. If a child has severe cerebral palsy he will be unable to amuse himself and may therefore be irritable and demanding of attention.

SYMPTOMS

Young babies, except those with spastic hemiplegia, do not always show typical signs of cerebral palsy immediately; they appear months or even years later. Often the first signs are floppiness, poor head control and refusal to suck, perhaps with a general lack of interest in the surroundings, and little spontaneous movement. All the normal milestones are delayed. A parent may say that the baby does not 'feel' right when handled. The diagnosis can still be difficult even when parents and paediatrician are alerted because the baby is known to have suffered one of the potential causes of cerebral palsy.

If you have cause to be worried about your child's development you should insist on seeing a paediatrician with experience of childhood handicap.

TREATMENT

There is no cure for cerebral palsy and no effective medical treatment. Drug treatment rarely helps although there is one that will occasionally reduce spasticity and make a child easier to handle; and of course drugs may be needed to treat epilepsy.

Orthopaedic surgery has a small but important role. The surgeon sometimes divides tendons to prevent deformities or even dislocation of joints, particularly of the hip. The surgeon can also lengthen tendons that have become contracted. The most common operation is lengthening of the heel cord of a child who has spastic hemiplegia and whose heel cord is so tight that he can walk only on tiptoe. Surgery can help a child to walk better but it is unlikely to enable a child to walk who has not previously been able to do so.

A child with severe cerebral palsy may need a wheelchair, and even a very young child can operate an electric wheelchair or other type of electric transporter. An occupational therapist can advise on this and other aspects of equipment and can also assist your child in learning to cope with daily activities such as feeding, dressing and play.

A speech therapist should see all children with severe cerebral palsy, since they may have serious difficulties in communication. The muscles that control speech may be so affected that your child cannot produce intelligible words or even sounds; and if the control of hand movements is also very impaired, your child will not be able to point, gesture or write. In such instances your child may be wrongly judged to be mentally handicapped and you should seek expert assessment. Modern technological aids such as computers have a very special place for these children: they make it possible for them to fulfil more of their potential and to communicate with others.

A child with mild cerebral palsy may have normal intelligence but may not be able to control her movements in a normal manner. Physiotherapy and encouragement will help her gain her full potential and understand her limitations so that she will be able to cope with and enjoy life.

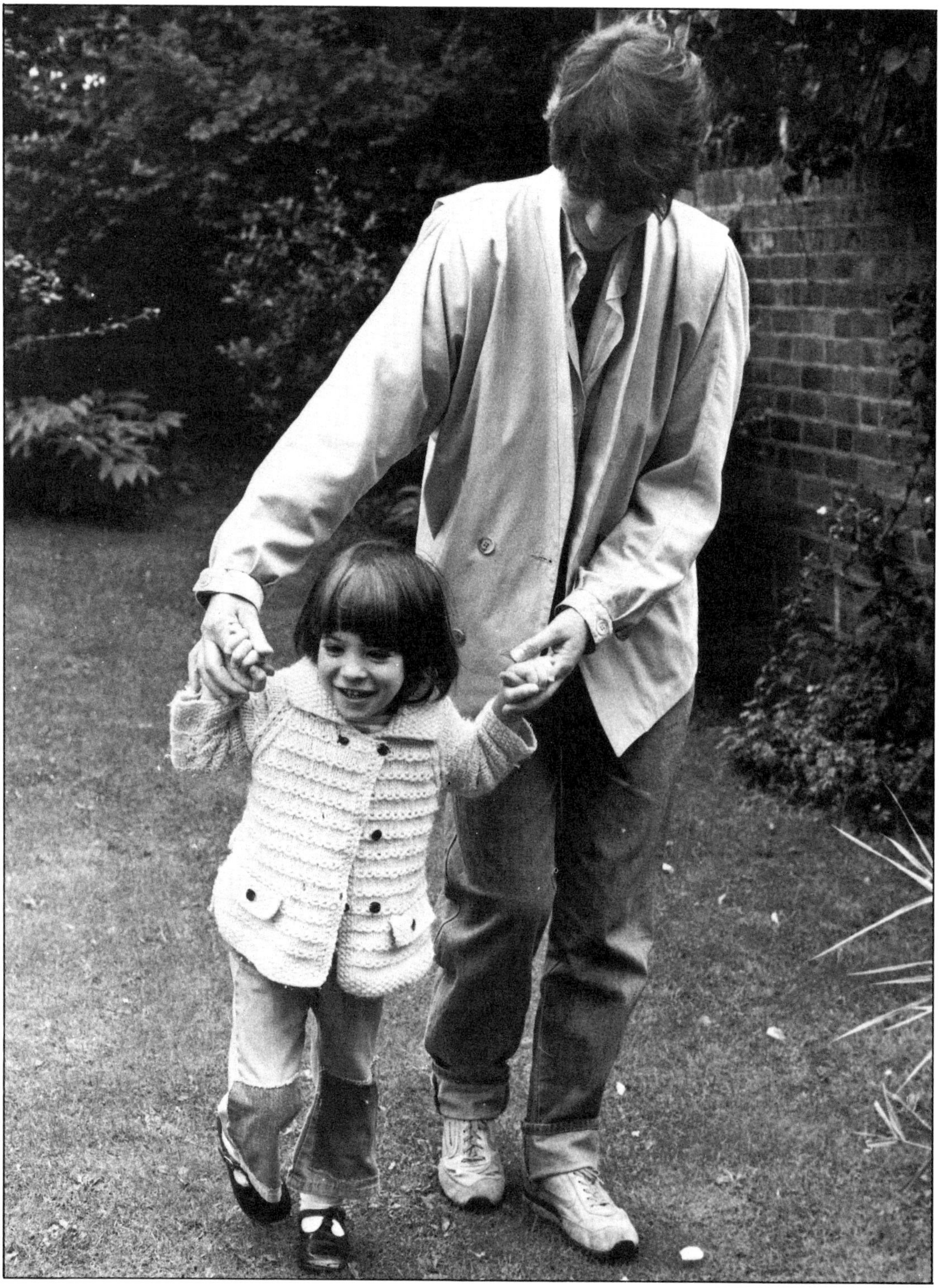

Children with spastic hemiplegia generally progress well. Their development is not very much delayed and they can usually attend ordinary schools, although they may have a variety of learning problems and minor practical difficulties. The same applies to children with mild spastic diplegia. A child with moderate athetosis or ataxia may not walk until the age of 5 or 6 years, or even later in a few instances. Children with severe quadriplegia, diplegia or athetosis may never walk without support and are likely to require special schooling.

> ▶**See also** Longstanding problems; Appendices: Support groups and publications; The law and your child

MUSCLE DISEASES

The term myopathy is applied to any disease of the muscles in which either structure or their function is abnormal. A dystrophy is a form of myopathy in which there is progressive deterioration with increasing wasting and weakness. There are numerous rare myopathies and dystrophies.

The most common muscle disease of childhood is **Duchenne muscular dystrophy**, named after the French physician who first described the disease in 1861. This affects boys almost exclusively and is found in about 1 in every 3,000 boys. It is hereditary, although there may not be a family history of the disease. Parents of a boy found to have muscular dystrophy should always seek expert genetic counselling. There is no cure for the disease.

Research is progressing rapidly towards diagnosing muscular dystrophy in early pregnancy, so that an abortion can be offered to a mother who is carrying an affected child.

A boy with muscular dystrophy is late in walking, but his parents may only gradually realize that he is slower and weaker than his peers. He is clumsy and falls often, cannot run properly and has difficulty with stairs. His gait is waddling and he may walk on his toes. He is unable to stand upright directly, but does so by 'walking' his hands up his thighs. Fat is deposited in the leg muscles, so that they look surprisingly large and bulging in view of their obvious weakness.

The weakness progresses steadily and the boy is usually confined to a wheelchair by his early teens. His respiratory muscles become weaker and he is unlikely to survive long.

A similar but milder disorder is known as **Becker muscular dystrophy**.

> ▶**See also** Longstanding problems; Genetics; Appendix: Support groups and publications

HYPOTONIA

Hypotonia, or floppiness, is when the muscle tension of a baby at rest is less than normal, so that the baby feels like a rag doll when handled. This can occur when a baby is very sick or premature and in conditions such as *Down's syndrome*.

Floppiness in a very young baby can be a sign of brain injury and other signs of *cerebral palsy* may develop later. It may also signify other brain disorders often associated with mental handicap. There are also some rare disorders of the muscles and nerves that cause hypotonia but do not affect the brain.

The description 'floppy infant' is usually reserved for babies in whom the cause of the floppiness is not so obvious. In some instances, investigations reveal no cause for the floppiness and the baby develops normally.

BRAIN DAMAGE

Brain cells can be damaged either by injury or by lack of oxygen, during a difficult birth, for example, or through *infection*. The cells in some parts of the brain are more easily damaged than others. Damaged cells may become more 'irritable' than normal cells so that they fire off electrical impulses more readily. This is why *fits* sometimes develop after brain injury.

Brain cells, unlike other body cells, once destroyed do not regenerate. However, this is partly compensated for by the fact that brain cells are more 'plastic' in their function than other body cells. If one part of the brain is damaged its function can often be taken over by another part, and the younger the victim, the more readily this happens. Thus although brain damage is irreversible a child may be encouraged, to a certain extent, to cope with loss of brain function.

Many children who suffered brain damage as a result of *birth injury* are severely physically handicapped. They can benefit from attending special schools where constant supervision and attention in a carefully devised programme will help them develop greater awareness of their own bodies and surroundings.

LIFE AND DEATH

In the West, death in childhood is now less common than at any time in history, and as a consequence the death of a child, however young, has a more devastating effect on his family than ever before. The grief of parents after their child has died is often mixed with anger and guilt. Many parents feel bitter or angry at the 'unfairness' of losing their child, or self-reproachful about their inability to prevent the death.

Men and women often have different ways of coping with the death of their child. Unless the couple can talk to each other freely about their feelings, tensions and misunderstanding may come between them. Most mothers, sooner or later, want to talk about the death. Fathers, on the other hand, often feel, at least initially, that they must be 'strong' and contain their grief in order to support their partners and cope with the administrative procedures that are required. Later they may plunge into their work and find it difficult to talk about their feelings so that the mother believes that she alone really cared about their child. Couples often experience sexual tensions as part of their reaction to bereavement, each partner withdrawing into him- or herself.

The importance of mourning
You may feel that you must put on a brave face after bereavement, often for the sake of your other children, but you will need to work through your grief and express your feelings about your child's death before you can begin the process of recovery. Parents who do not go through this mourning process risk emotional problems later on. They may become depressed and withdrawn; their marital relationship may be disturbed, or even break down altogether. Because they have not truly come to terms with their loss, they may have difficulties in their relationships with their other children, particularly with a surviving twin or with children born subsequently. They may be over-anxious and protective of them or, occasionally, reject or even abuse them.

To mourn your child you have first to accept the reality of the loss. This may be easier if you were able to be with him when he was dying, to hold him after death and help with laying out. The pain of grief from a death following an accident, for which you are entirely unprepared, can be so overwhelming that you may find it difficult to believe that it has happened. However painful it is, go with your partner or with a friend to see your dead child, to touch him and caress him. By doing this you will confront the reality of your loss.

It is very helpful to talk about your child's death with those who love you. This is the time to call on the help of friends, minister and doctor. Avoid sedatives and hypnotics, if possible, or use them for only a short time. Talking, crying and sharing are what help. It can be especially comforting to talk to someone who has come through the same experience, and it is often helpful to contact a self-help organization which will put you in touch with parents who have been similarly bereaved.

The time will come when the pangs of grief are less acute, although feelings of bereavement can persist for well over a year and be especially intense at times like Christmas or the anniversary of your child's birth or death. Bereavement counselling can help you work through your grief: if you are finding it very difficult to come to terms with your loss, ask your doctor to put you in touch with a professional counsellor or psychiatrist.

The death of a handicapped child
When a child dies who has been a special problem to rear, because of severe handicap, you may feel great grief. A child who has been especially dependent on you is often especially close, too, and the pain of grief is directly related to the degree of attachment. The sympathy of friends may be tempered with remarks which you may find hurtful, such as 'He's better off dead – it was no life for him.' In spite of the relief that your child is no longer suffering, your pain will be great.

THE DEATH OF A BABY

Grief after the loss of a young baby is no different from the grief which follows the loss of any loved person. Even if your baby is stillborn, or dies very soon after birth, he will have been a part of your life from conception onwards, and is a person whose loss you will need to mourn.

In addition you may experience physical symptoms; your arms may ache for your baby or you may imagine that you hear him cry. It will help to have a photograph of your baby to keep. It will also help to hold a funeral which the whole family can attend. Distress for a mother may be exacerbated when she produces milk even though her baby has died. She may for a while have very negative feelings towards other young babies.

After a time you may feel ready to have another child, but it is best not to embark on a pregnancy until you can accept your loss with sadness but equanimity. If you have not mourned, you may regard your next baby as a replacement for the child who died instead of seeing him as a child in his own right.

MISCARRIAGE AND ABORTION

Most miscarriages occur in the first few weeks of pregnancy, but even at this early stage, many parents feel a profound sense of loss. A miscarriage late in pregnancy is a true bereavement.

Some screening tests may be carried out during pregnancy and reveal a severe defect in the fetus. Even though you may choose to have an abortion following a positive result, you will still need to recognize your loss. There may also be pressing psychological reasons for choosing to have an abortion and you will come to this decision with advice from professionals. Guilt associated with this choice is understandable but unjustifiable.

The attitudes of medical staff, friends and relations may make it harder for parents to express their grief after an abortion, but it is best for you to acknowledge this grief in order to recover from the loss.

As with any other bereavement, the healing process is helped by acceptance of your loss. Seeing your baby, even if he is in an early stage of development or malformed, can help; but showing an aborted or miscarried child to parents is not common hospital practice and therefore has to be requested before an abortion or during a miscarriage. It may also help you to hold a funeral, although you may encounter frustrating administrative difficulties if you wish to bury a baby who is below the age of legal viability.

STILLBIRTH

There is a painful 'emptiness' about stillbirth. You will have come through the months of pregnancy, anticipating the birth of your child – only to find you do not have a child. These feelings are made worse if your baby is quickly removed after the birth and you do not see or hold him. Without real memories of your baby, there is no real person to mourn and recovery is difficult. Ask to see, hold and name your baby, and to take a photograph so that you are able to remember him. Even if he is severely deformed, you may well be surprised that the reality is not as bad as you had feared, and without seeing him you may continue to imagine the worst.

Anger is often felt after stillbirth. It will help to talk to the medical staff about what went wrong, and to express and work through your anger with them. You may feel shunned and isolated when you return home, and even carry a sense of shame. At this time you should draw on the support of family and friends. You should expect your recovery from a stillbirth to take at least as long as recovery from the death of a baby who has lived for a short time. If you need help, ask your doctor to put you in touch with a counsellor and support group.

▶See also Family life; The unborn child; Counselling; Genetics; Appendix: Support groups and publications

COT DEATH

The term 'cot death' was first used in the 1950s to describe sudden and unexpected death of babies in their cots. Cot deaths are not a new problem, but have become more prominent as other causes of death in infancy have become rarer. Post mortem examinations of babies who died unexpectedly sometimes reveal medical reasons for the death. Often, however, no adequate explanation can be found, and such deaths are described medically as Sudden Infant Death Syndrome (SIDS), or as unexplained cot deaths. For some of these deaths there may be partial explanations, for example a mild *infection* may have contributed, but in others no recognizable disease is evident.

CAUSES

Although rare, cot deaths are the most common kind of infant death in the Western world after the first week of life. Of children under the age of 2 years who die suddenly for no obvious reason, the majority are between 1 and 8 months, with a peak incidence at 2 to 3 months. Boys seem to be more vulnerable than girls. Most cot deaths occur during the winter months.

BABIES AT INCREASED RISK
o Premature and low birthweight babies, twin babies and babies born after a short interval between pregnancies
o Babies of young mothers with several children
o Babies of mothers who smoked in pregnancy
o Cot deaths are more common in bottle-fed than in breastfed babies
o It has been suggested that a very small proportion of cot deaths may be due to an allergic reaction following inhalation of cows' milk, but this theory has been neither proved nor disproved

Sudden infant death can, however, occur to first babies in families living in favourable circumstances, to babies who were breastfed and whose mothers do not smoke.

There are probably many different causes of cot deaths. These may include sudden overwhelming infections, overwhelming *allergic reactions*, *metabolic disorders* and inability to regulate breathing properly. It seems likely that in many cases death is not due to any single cause but is the result of a variety of factors. For example, it may be that a slight infection has a fatal effect on a child who is passing through a vulnerable stage of development or who has an undetected abnormality.

There is no specific advice on preventing cot death but for some babies the risk may be less if normal health care advice is taken: do not smoke, breastfeed your baby if possible, and make sure your baby does not get too hot or too cold. Look out for early warning signs of illness. It is also worthwhile monitoring your baby's weight, as failure to gain weight may sometimes indicate unsuspected illness.

Although some babies die suddenly and inexplicably with no warning signs at all, in others there have been preceding minor symptoms of illness, including unusual drowsiness, excessive crying, an altered character to their cry, unusual quietness and reluctance to feed, irritability or sweating. It must be emphasized that the vast majority of children who show these commonly occurring symptoms do not suffer cot death. But they may be danger signals that something is amiss and that the baby needs close observation. In a very few cases, parents recall an earlier episode when their baby stopped breathing for a while (apnoea) and turned blue. If your baby has an episode of apnoea, he should be examined by a paediatrician since there is often a treatable reason.

COPING WITH COT DEATH

The untimely death of a child at home, where you feel wholly responsible, is a devastating tragedy. Whatever reassurances you are given, you are likely to feel that in some way you were to blame. You may go over and over the event in your mind to see whether there was anything you did or failed to do which can have led to it. You may blame yourself or feel angry with a doctor or health visitor who may have recently seen the baby; if you were out at the time of death you may feel guilty, and the babysitter who was left caring for your baby may blame him- or herself. No one is guilty or to be blamed.

This is a time when you will need comfort and practical help from relatives and close friends. You will be involved with officials when the death is reported. A post mortem may be required legally. Ask your doctor to give you a detailed explanation of the post mortem findings. When the first shock is over, arrange to talk to a paediatrician, to ask questions and seek advice about future children. Many parents find it helps to talk to someone who has come through a similar experience, and there are organizations for parents who have suffered the loss of a baby as the result of a cot death.

The chance of the tragedy recurring is remote. Most couples who have suffered one unexplained cot death have afterwards brought up a healthy family. When any subsequent children are born, you will need extra support from your doctor and health visitor. You should also ask your doctor to arrange for a paediatrician to examine your baby, discuss his needs and decide if anything can be done to relieve your own inevitable anxiety during the first crucial months.

▶ **See also** Appendices: Support groups and publications; The law and your child

THE DYING CHILD

Families now are less familiar than ever before with the experience of coping with mortally ill children. At the same time many have abandoned religious faith which may have helped make some sense of such events. If a child has a fatal illness and the adults in his world find it so painful to talk to him openly and honestly about his illness that they try to avoid all communication, he will have no support in coping with his fear of death and uncertainty about the future. For the child, this new isolation can be more painful than the illness itself. It can lead him to mistrust parents, doctors and nurses, which can hinder treatment and add psychological symptoms to his physical ones.

FACING UNCERTAINTY AND DEATH

Modern treatments of conditions once generally fatal, for example *leukaemia*, may put unbearable stress on the whole family by lengthening the period when the outcome for the child is uncertain. Even though remission and even cure is more likely, the price that is paid may be high in terms of psychological ill health within the family. This is particularly so when the child suffers pain from the disease itself or when the treatment is unpleasant or painful.

A child with a terminal illness may have years of valuable life ahead in which to develop, enjoy himself and achieve. It is the task of everyone around him to help him live, in the full sense of the word, until he dies. It is best for him if he is told from the start that he has a serious illness – different from those he had before which lasted a few days – and that this one may go on for a long time. Gradually you will let him know, in answer to his questions, that he may not get better, although the doctors are working hard to try to get him well again or make him feel comfortable. At some stage, perhaps after someone he knows with the same disease has died, he will ask if he is going to die, or his behaviour may change so that you will be aware that this thought is preoccupying him.

All the evidence is that families who communicate openly and sensitively about the possibility of death become closer and cope better with the pain it engenders. Finding the words to be honest and yet keep hope alive is one of the most challenging tasks. Keeping close, cherishing and being warm, yet not becoming over-protective and stifling is another. You have to find ways of acknowledging what is happening to your child and somehow making it acceptable to him.

Even when the hope of a cure has to be relinquished and death must be faced, your child will depend on you to comfort him and help him cope. Dying is rarely, if ever, painful, and you should reassure your child that it will not hurt, and that he will not be alone.

Older children sometimes feel they have to protect their parents and this may prevent them from seeking the help they themselves need. They need to know that your sadness is because you will miss them, but that there is nothing for them to fear: all their pain will be at an end. It is important for the child to have the chance to say goodbye to everyone he loves and he may want to cry together with them.

Families who do manage to support their fatally ill children through their last illness find a sense of achievement that helps to mitigate the pain of loss and sustains them through their mourning.

As well as coping with their own feelings about their dying child, parents have to cope with the reactions of brothers and sisters to the situation. Your apparent inability to control what is happening may make your other children feel insecure and confused, and it is important that they see you making ultimate decisions. They may have feelings of failure. Your concern for your dying child may make them feel that they matter less, and they need confirmation that this is not so. If they are old enough, discuss what is happening openly. A sibling of a dying child may develop *behavioural problems* or suffer from severe *depression*. He should see the family doctor who will refer him to a child psychiatrist.

The strains on the family of a child's life-threatening illness are sometimes unendurable. To help your child die with dignity and serenity you, too, will need help – someone, whether family or friend, religious adviser, doctor or member of the hospital staff, to whom you can talk. Mourning begins when you realize that death is likely. Resist the instinct to become detached when this realization comes, and instead try to draw closer to your dying child. This can be difficult, so do not hesitate to get expert help if necessary.

▶ See also Family life; Counselling

SUICIDE

Suicide of children under 14 years old is very rare (1 in 800,000 per year). Even in adolescence, although suicide gestures and threats have become more frequent, they are rarely fatal. Most adolescent suicide is caused, as it is in adults, by mental distress of the kind that occurs usually only in *depressive illness* or in *schizophrenia*. It may unfortunately be the first manifestation of such an illness.

The suicide of a child imposes a burden of guilt upon the whole family. Grandparents may know of mental illness in the family and may feel guilty that they have passed on 'bad genes'. Siblings may feel responsible, as though they have somehow driven the child to kill himself. There may be a temptation to keep the event secret, for fear of stigma and blame by society.

This is an event when help from an experienced family therapist with knowledge of mental illness should be sought. It is especially important if there are young children in the family who may be sensitive to what is not said and react in subtle ways which can be damaging to their development. If the members of your family can be open with each other and seek to help each other bear feelings of guilt and helplessness, then you can emerge from your grief strengthened.

▶ See also Behaviour and development

PART FOUR

APPENDICES: RESOURCES

WHO'S WHO IN THE HEALTH SERVICE

The Department of Health and Social Security (DHSS) and the Department of Education and Science (DES) in the United Kingdom are the two ministries involved in the provision of services for children. The health, education and social services interlink, as many of the problems that children have need the support of professionals from different services. For example, a child with *cerebral palsy* may need medical care from the family doctor, paediatrician and physiotherapist; the social services make sure that family support is provided; and the education authority makes special educational provision.

General practitioners
Your general practitioner (GP) is your family doctor. A GP provides a 24-hour service every day of the year, and can always arrange for your child to be seen if it seems necessary, whatever the hour.

Although GPs are self-employed, family

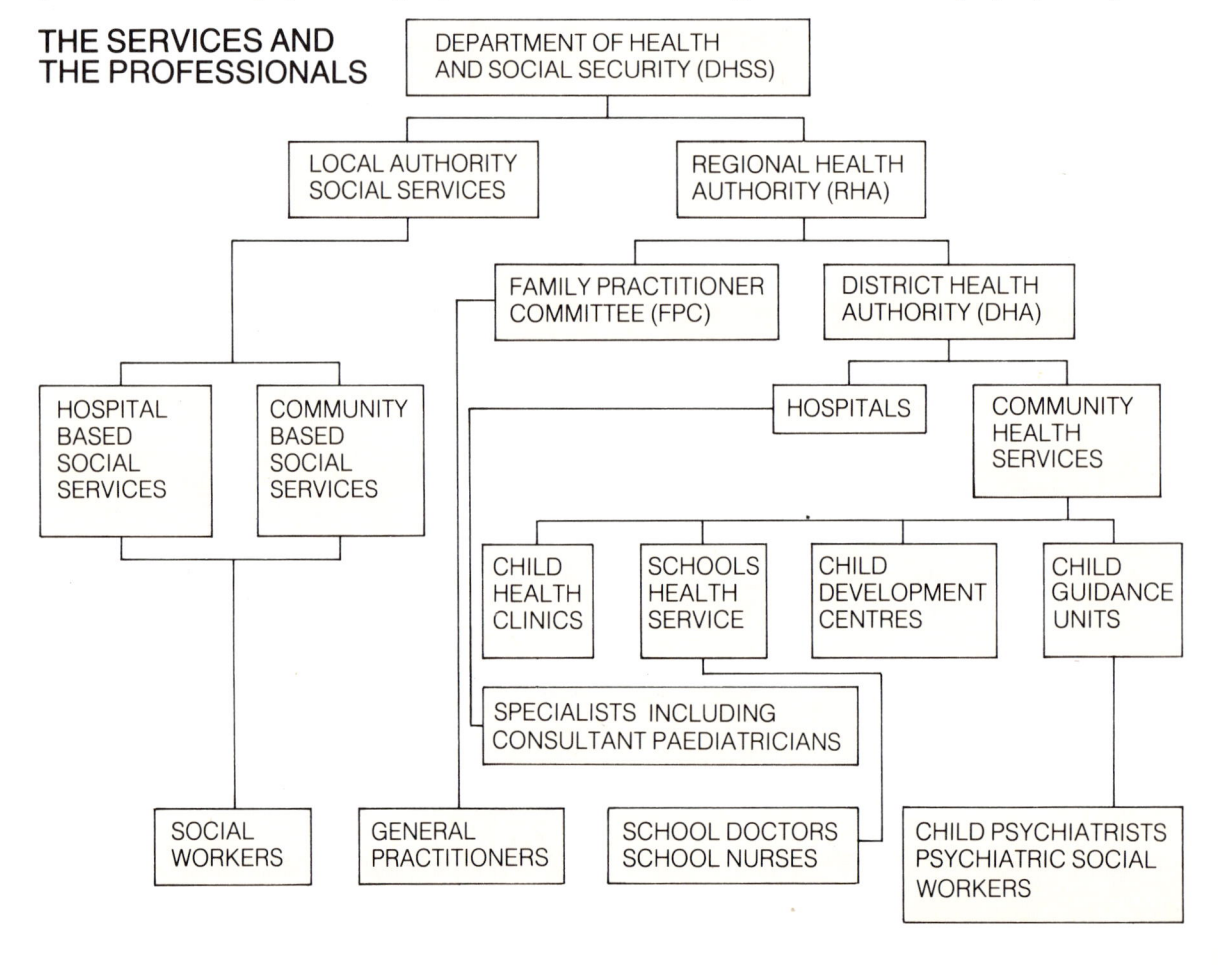

THE SERVICES AND THE PROFESSIONALS

- DEPARTMENT OF HEALTH AND SOCIAL SECURITY (DHSS)
  - LOCAL AUTHORITY SOCIAL SERVICES
    - HOSPITAL BASED SOCIAL SERVICES
    - COMMUNITY BASED SOCIAL SERVICES
      - SOCIAL WORKERS
  - REGIONAL HEALTH AUTHORITY (RHA)
    - FAMILY PRACTITIONER COMMITTEE (FPC)
      - GENERAL PRACTITIONERS
    - DISTRICT HEALTH AUTHORITY (DHA)
      - HOSPITALS
      - COMMUNITY HEALTH SERVICES
        - CHILD HEALTH CLINICS
        - SCHOOLS HEALTH SERVICE
        - CHILD DEVELOPMENT CENTRES
        - CHILD GUIDANCE UNITS
        - SPECIALISTS INCLUDING CONSULTANT PAEDIATRICIANS
          - SCHOOL DOCTORS SCHOOL NURSES
          - CHILD PSYCHIATRISTS PSYCHIATRIC SOCIAL WORKERS

practitioner committees make sure that they conform to reasonable health care standards. In addition to this local control any doctor in clinical practice in Britain must be registered with the General Medical Council (GMC). The GMC investigates complaints about a doctor's conduct and can stop a doctor from practising.

If you have any difficulty in registering with a general practice you can telephone or write to your local family practitioner committee: the town hall or your local library will give you the address. The committee will allocate you to a doctor near your home. If you are dissatisfied with your family doctor, you can change simply by enrolling with another practice. If you have a complaint about your GP, write to your local family practitioner committee.

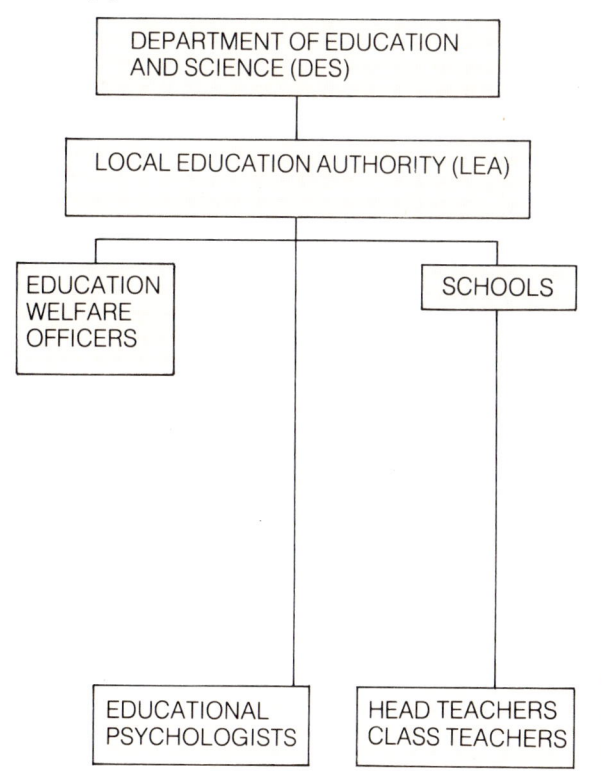

```
┌──────────────────────────────┐
│ DEPARTMENT OF EDUCATION      │
│ AND SCIENCE (DES)            │
└──────────────┬───────────────┘
               │
┌──────────────┴───────────────┐
│ LOCAL EDUCATION AUTHORITY (LEA) │
└──┬────────────────────────┬──┘
   │                        │
┌──┴──────┐          ┌──────┴──┐
│EDUCATION│          │ SCHOOLS │
│WELFARE  │          │         │
│OFFICERS │          │         │
└─────────┘          └────┬────┘
                          │
          ┌───────────────┴──────────┐
   ┌──────┴──────┐          ┌────────┴──────┐
   │EDUCATIONAL  │          │HEAD TEACHERS  │
   │PSYCHOLOGISTS│          │CLASS TEACHERS │
   └─────────────┘          └───────────────┘
```

Consultants

Your child may be referred to a consultant paediatrician, or specialist, for a second opinion, or for help when your child needs specialized services not available in general practice, such as X-rays. In hospital a consultant heads a medical team consisting of a senior registrar, or registrar (who may deputize for the consultant), senior house officer and house officer. The nursing staff are under the senior nursing officer. The wards are staffed by a sister (charge nurse if male), state registered nurses (3 years' training) and state enrolled nurses (2 years' training). Student nurses are training to be SRN and pupil nurses are training to be SEN.

Consultant paediatricians usually work in hospitals but in some areas they also work in local clinics and schools. They are salaried employees of the national health service.

If you have a complaint about a consultant paediatrician, other members of hospital staff or about administrative negligence you should write to the senior administrator of the hospital or alternatively to the district administrator of the health district.

Clinical medical officers

Senior clinical medical officers (SCMOs) and clinical medical officers (CMOs) are doctors working outside hospitals in the community health services. In most areas they work from child health clinics and schools.

The community health services are run by the district health authorities and are responsible for the prevention of illness in their districts. They run clinics such as family planning and child health clinics. They are responsible for immunizations.

Child development centres are run by either the hospital or the community health services. They assess any child with a handicap or delayed development and provide ongoing supervision and care if this is judged to be necessary.

Health visitors

Nurses who have trained in community health care are known as health visitors. A health visitor has a particular responsibility to

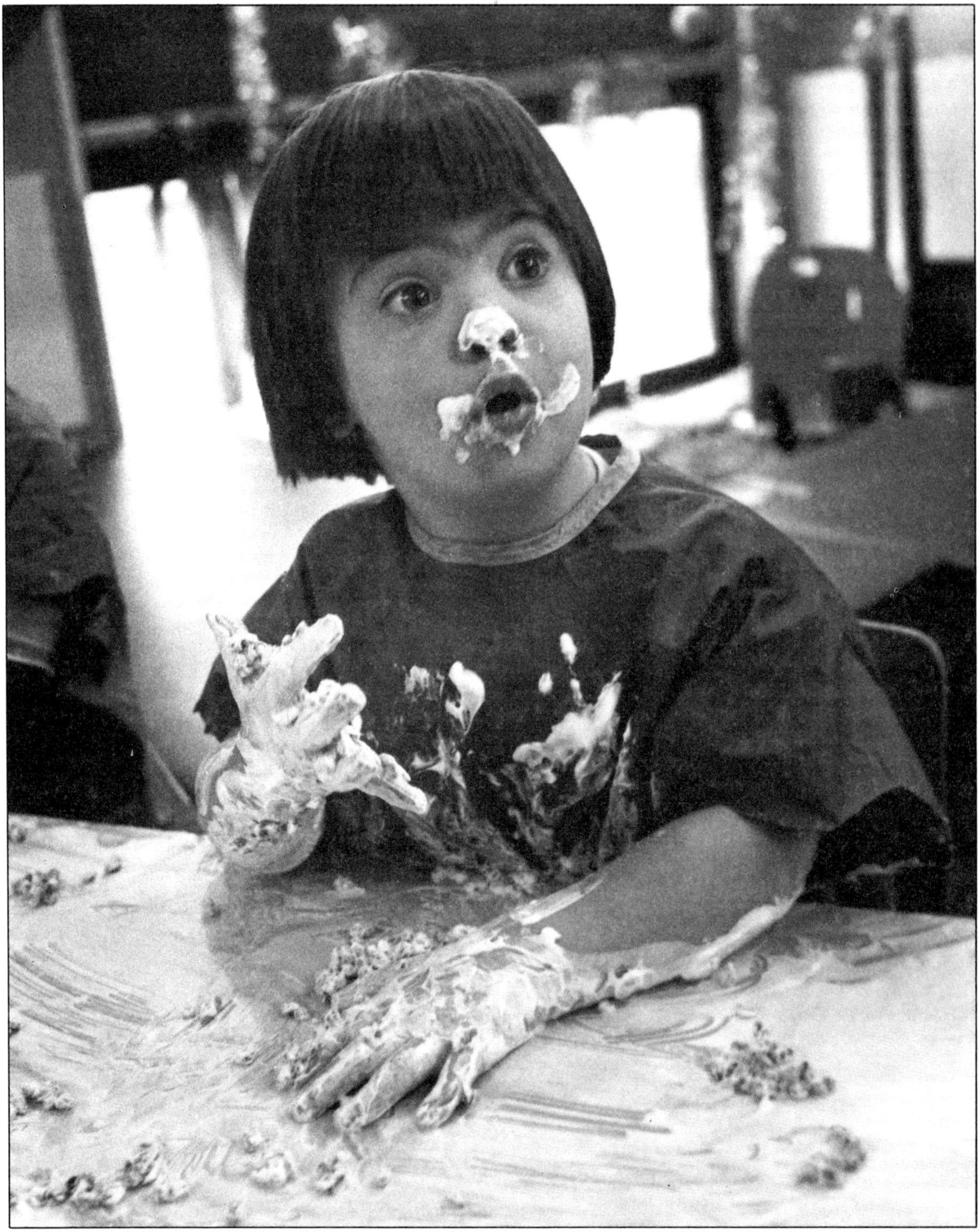

monitor the growth and development of all the pre-school children in a particular area. She will be based with your local child health clinic, or in some cases with your general practitioner's group practice. She will come to visit you at home, either when you are pregnant or shortly after your baby is born and will advise you on any problems that you may have, for example, in feeding, bathing or changing your child. Your health visitor is also a local expert on children's facilities and activities and will be able to tell you the whereabouts of local playgroups, one o'clock clubs and nurseries. If you move and want to contact your health visitor in a new district you can find out who she is by telephoning the community health services for the district in which you now live.

If you have a complaint about a health visitor, write to the director of nursing services for the district health authority or to the district administrator.

School nurses

A school nurse is a qualified nurse with additional school nursing training. Her role is to work with the teachers and school doctor to ensure that your child is physically well and therefore able to benefit from being at school. She carries out sight and hearing tests and arranges for children to be seen by the school doctor when necessary. School nurses are also involved in arranging programmes of health education for children.

If you have a complaint about a school nurse, write to the director of nursing services for the district health authority in which you live.

Educational psychologists

These are specialists in the ways in which children and young people develop and learn. In most parts of the country, educational psychologists are required to have a teaching qualification and also an honours degree in psychology and a postgraduate qualification in education psychology.

If your child has a longstanding handicap, the joint support of the education, health and social services is essential for your family.

Many educational psychologists work not only in schools but also in child guidance units which are run by local education authorities to help with the psychological problems of schoolchildren. They may also work in child development centres. Educational psychologists see children referred by teachers in school but will also see your child if you feel there is a problem. The head teacher of your child's school can make an appointment or you can telephone the school psychology service via your local education authority.

Education welfare officers

There is no nationally prescribed training for education welfare officers but they often have experience in school nursing, social work or teaching. Education welfare departments vary in different parts of Britain but in general education welfare officers are responsible for monitoring children's attendance at school and are also involved in the management of child abuse in school-age children.

Social workers

Social workers are answerable to the local authority and they work in hospitals or in the community. They are alerted if families are having specific problems for example, with housing, and help out directly or by putting them in touch with other professionals. Social workers also have a statutory responsibility to manage cases of suspected child abuse. Psychiatric social workers work with psychiatrists in child guidance units.

The social services run pre-school nurseries for children and also keep registers of approved childminders. A social worker may therefore be able to give you information about day-care facilities for your pre-school child.

If you want to talk to a social worker, your local town hall will give you the address and telephone number of your nearest social services office. Most parts of the country run a system of emergency cover 24 hours a day so that even at night in an emergency you should be able to get hold of a social worker.

If you have a complaint about a social worker, write to the director of social services for the area in which you live.

THE LAW AND YOUR CHILD

In the United Kingdom parliament and the courts have avoided defining parents' rights and duties precisely and have instead concentrated on the principle that in the event of any dispute the child's welfare is the first and paramount consideration. If you have any conflict or anxiety over rights and duties as a parent, you should seek legal advice.

There are some general principles laid down in law. Parents must protect, maintain and educate their children and must also show affection and interest. Broadly speaking, they must care for their children. In return, they have certain rights: the right to have their children living with them, the right to consent to their medical treatment, adoption or emigration, the right to administer their property and the right to dispense appropriate discipline. In addition, parents have a broad sweep of authority to control their children's lives as part of caring for them: they have the right to choose their clothes, books, toys and the time they go to bed, for example.

The parents of a legitimate child share these rights and duties equally. Either parent may exercise any of the parental rights independently, provided the other parent has not expressed disapproval. If the parents are unable to agree on a particular issue, either can ultimately take the matter to court. After a divorce, the court usually makes orders clarifying how parental rights and duties are to be shared in future.

Where an illegitimate child is concerned, however, all parental rights and duties rest with the mother, although the father is entitled to apply for custody of or access to the child and may also be liable for maintenance if an affiliation order is obtained against him.

Children in care

The role of the state in safeguarding children's welfare usually rests with local authorities. Children may either be 'committed' to the care of a local authority or 'received' on a voluntary basis. Local authorities must legally accept a child into voluntary care if, for example, he has no parent or guardian, is abandoned or lost, or if his parent or guardian is permanently or temporarily prevented 'by reason of mental or bodily disease or infirmity or other circumstances from providing for his proper accommodation, maintenance or upbringing'. If the local authority intervenes, this must be necessary in the interests of the child's welfare. While it is the duty of the local authority to keep a child in care as long as necessary for his welfare, the authority also has a duty to try to return the care of the child to a parent, guardian, relative or friend if this will not interfere with the child's welfare.

Children may be committed to care by a court. This is usually done by a juvenile court under the Children and Young Persons Act, in which case it must be done for one of several specific reasons. The child must be guilty of a legal offence; or he must be beyond his parents' control; or he must be neglected, ill-treated or exposed to moral danger; or his education must be suffering. In addition, the court must decide that the child is in need of care and control which he is unlikely to receive unless taken into care.

Once a child is in care, the local authority must promote his welfare and must take into account his feelings and wishes and give them careful consideration. A parent's rights and duties are inevitably affected while a child is in care. A local authority may pass a resolution vesting parental rights and duties in themselves if, for example, the parents are dead or unfit or if the child has been in voluntary care for 3 years or more. If your child is in care and you want to challenge a resolution giving the local authority parental rights, you should seek prompt legal advice.

Education

A parent has a legal obligation 'to cause every child of compulsory school age (5 - 16 years) to receive efficient full-time education suitable to his or her age, ability and aptitude, either by regular attendance at school or otherwise'. Local education authorities in turn have a duty to enforce this obligation. Truancy is not an offence as such, but a parent may be prosecuted for failing to comply with a school attendance order, and persistent truancy may result in proceedings to take the child into care.

Detailed legislation governs the role of a local education authority. Authorities have various duties and discretions. These include, for example, the duty to comply with a parent's choice of school unless to do so would 'prejudice the efficient provision of education for the efficient use of resources'. They also have an obligation to establish an appeals procedure against admission decisions.

Providing for children with special educational needs is another duty of local education authorities under the 1981 Education Act. This category includes children with significantly greater difficulty in learning than the majority of children of the same age, and children with a disability that prevents or hinders them from using the educational facilities normally provided in schools. The authorities are obliged to identify such children and to educate as many of them as possible in ordinary schools with whatever additional help is needed. Many districts have special facilities for children from around the age of 2 years.

Some children, usually those with severe and multiple difficulties, may need special schooling. When special schooling is suggested an assessment procedure involving an educational psychologist and a doctor is laid down under the Education Act. Assessments are carried out in child assessment or development centres. Assessment is a continuous process and when the child is between $13\frac{1}{2}$ and $14\frac{1}{2}$ years old, he must be fully reassessed.

Parents can request an assessment and their views will be taken into account. They can discuss schooling recommendations with an officer of the local education authority and visit any school before a final decision is made for their child.

Nurseries and childminders also come under the supervision of local authorities. Childminders are defined as people who are paid to take children under the age of 5 years into their homes for 2 or more hours a day. A childminder must register with the local authority by law: the authority may inspect the childminder's home to make sure that it complies with regulations, and penalties may be incurred for looking after children in breach of regulations.

Health

The law relating to children's health is much less specific than that relating to education. However, some areas are clearly defined. For example, parents have the right to consent to medical treatment on behalf of children under 16 years old and remain responsible for them while they are in hospital. The law also states clearly that once a child is 16 years old he can give consent to any medical treatment, in which case parental consent is redundant. The validity of any consent given by a child of under 16 years old is not specifically dealt with by statute but is generally regarded as depending upon the ability of the child to understand the issues involved. However, a doctor always encourages parental involvement.

If a parent withholds consent for medical treatment or requires treatment that may not be in the child's best interests, the state may legally intervene after making the child a ward of court. This is because the state has a legal right and duty to safeguard a child's welfare. However, in practice this rarely happens.

Cot death

After *cot death*, the coroner has a legal duty to arrange a post-mortem examination and to make enquiries into the circumstances surrounding the death. This usually means that the police are asked to visit the bereaved parents, which may be a shock for them, but it in no way implies that they are to blame.

ADOPTION AND FOSTERING

Adoption and fostering are both means of enabling children to enjoy life in a family when they cannot be cared for by their own parents. However, there are important differences between adoption and fostering. Adoption is a legal process. The court makes an adoption order and a child becomes legally yours. Fostering is essentially a temporary arrangement for looking after someone else's child in your own home.

At present there are very few unwanted babies in the United Kingdom. Adoption agencies are now mainly trying to find families for older children. These children vary widely. Some are emotionally disturbed; others are mentally or physically handicapped; some are of different racial origins. They have one thing in common – they want to be part of a family. Adoption can be very successful, yet there are many more children who could be adopted than families willing to do so.

Foster homes are needed for children of all ages for short or long periods during a family crisis. Some children will continue to be visited by their own parents. There are also special schemes in which foster parents may give children special preparation to move into another family on a more permanent basis; others care for difficult teenagers or handicapped children. These foster parents receive extra training and local authority support and are often paid a salary.

In Britain, both single people and married couples can adopt. They must be at least 21 years old. Adoption and fostering agencies also have their own rules about whom they will accept. British Agencies for Adoption and Fostering (BAAF) provides a list of all the adoption agencies in Britain.

If you would like to be a foster parent, you can apply to a local authority. You can make a private arrangement, but if you do this you must inform the local authority.

Adoption and fostering agencies will want to study you carefully in order to find out which child would be right for you. They will usually arrange several meetings for you and the child to get to know each other before you decide whether you can live together. A social worker will visit to advise and support you when the child comes to live with you and will continue to visit if you are fostering. Most agencies will be available to help after adoption if you are having problems.

The experience of being an adoptive or foster parent is different from bringing up your own children and it will help you to to talk to other adoptive and foster parents. There are groups which provide information, education and support. Ask your social worker about these. BAAF provides a list of books and leaflets.

It is much the best for an adopted child, even if he comes to you as a baby, to be told by you that he is adopted. If you do not tell him, he will almost certainly find out anyway. Start with a simple but truthful story when he is a toddler and gradually provide more information as he grows. When you adopt an older child you have to learn to live together and to get used to each other's different habits and ways of doing things. Your child may still have loyalties to his first parents; he may also have been badly hurt by them. You may be confronted by all sorts of difficult behaviour and you may need help to cope with it.

British Agencies for Adoption and Fostering
11 Southwark Street
London SE1 IRQ
01 407 8800

National Foster Care Association
Francis House
Francis Street
London SW1
01 828 6266

CHILD ABUSE

In the last 20 years, concern has arisen about children who are damaged either physically or emotionally as a result of treatment within their own families, particularly treatment by their parents. Accidents are common in childhood and it has only recently been recognized that some accidents are caused by care-givers rather than by the impulsive actions of children themselves.

In the United Kingdom the attitude is that if parents cannot help abusing their children, the community should intervene. Action can be taken to protect a child against abuse if:

o a parent physically chastises or punishes a child to such a degree that the child has recurrent fractures or bruises; or a child is so persistently neglected that he may be physically injured or become ill
o a child fails to grow or thrive because of emotional rejection that cannot be overcome
o a child's physical health is neglected because his parents do not use or accept essential medical treatment, particularly in instances where there is some evidence of treatable disability or handicap
o a child is emotionally rejected, victimized or misused to such a degree that his potential is severely affected, as shown by his behaviour at school or by the severe restriction of his life
o a child is being sexually misused or abused. A child is sexually abused if he or she is involved by an adult in sexual activities that he or she is not old enough to understand, or to consent to, and which breaks the community taboos and expectations. Sexual abuse is probably 3 times more likely from within the family or circle of trusted adults than by strangers

When intervention is necessary, there are prescribed procedures to be gone through. If there is concern that a child has been abused, someone of experience, often a hospital paediatrician, will ask the parents what explanation they have, for example, for the bruises or fractures that their child has had, or for the severe growth problem. Parents will be informed that because of concern for their child and his well-being, a case conference will be arranged to discuss how best to help the family. The case conference involves all the professionals in the community who know the family: family doctor, health visitor, teachers, social workers. The police may be involved at this stage.

Fortunately professionals now have a very great deal of discretion, enabling them to work together for the benefit of children and their families, and ensuring that they get the help that they need. Generally speaking actions are avoided that would make matters more difficult for the family, but obviously in some situations if an injury is severe or life-threatening, then action has to be taken to protect the child and to prevent the family situation from getting worse.

Parents are invited to a meeting after the case conference to discuss their views of the situation and to hear what recommendations were made. These may be that a social worker or child guidance clinic should offer the family help. If there is sufficient concern, it may be considered necessary for the child to stay in hospital or go to a foster home while the situation is sorted out. As a last resort, it may be recommended that the child is taken into long-term care.

National Society for the Prevention of Cruelty
   to Children (NSPCC)
1 Riding House Street
London W1
01 580 8812
   24-hour service:
67 Saffron Hill
London EC1
01 242 1626

Parents Anonymous
24-hour service:
01 668 4805

SUPPORT GROUPS AND PUBLICATIONS

The following list gives the names and addresses of organizations which are in some way concerned with the health and welfare of children and their families. Although the address given in each case is that of the central office of the organization concerned, in most cases branches exist all over the country. The central office will be able to tell you the address of any branch in your particular area.

The list is broken down into three sections. The first of these covers general organizations such as the National Children's Bureau which, as well as giving advice themselves, can often direct people who approach them to the appropriate helping organizations.

The second section deals with family life and problems. Some of the organizations listed deal with matters which at some time or another are likely to concern every family, such as family planning, pregnancy or education. Others exist to help the family in time of special need or crisis brought about, for example, by poverty, illness, bereavement or family break-up.

The third section lists support groups which will be helpful for the family whose child has a chronic illness, handicap or disability. In these groups people who have lived with a particular problem such as allergy, leukemia or mental handicap can share their experiences and use their common knowledge to support each other.

Even if you cannot find within this list an organization which seems to deal with your particular problem, it is still well worth your while to approach a more broadly based organization for help. Many organizations can offer advice on a wide range of problems. Even though no specific support group is listed under 'arthritis', for example, other organizations listed under the general heading of *Physical handicap*, such as the Lady Hoare Trust, would be able to offer help in this area.

GENERAL ADDRESSES

Citizens Advice Bureau
See local telephone directory

Exploring Parenthood
Omnibus
39 North Road
London N7
01 607 7021

London Youth Advisory Centre
26 Prince of Wales Road
London NW5
01 267 4792

National Children's Bureau
8 Wakley Street
London EC1V 7QE
01 278 9441

National Council for Voluntary Organizations
26 Bedford Square
London WC1B 3HU
01 636 4066

National Youth Bureau
17 Albion Street
Leicester LE1 6GD
0533 538811

Share Community Ltd
Alexander House
140 Battersea Park Road
London SW11
01 622 6885
(Have information bank on self-help groups)

FAMILY LIFE AND PROBLEMS

Accidents and emergencies
British Red Cross Society
9 Grosvenor Crescent
London SW1X 7EJ
01 235 5454

Parents Anonymous
See local telephone directory
or telephone: 01 668 4805
(24-hour service)

The Samaritans
See local telephone directory

National Society for the Prevention of Cruelty to Children
1 Riding House Street
London W1P 8AA
01 580 8812
(See also local telephone directory)

Adoption and fostering
British Agencies for Adoption and
Fostering (BAAF)
11 Southwark Street
London SE1 1RQ

The National Foster Care Association
Francis House
Francis Street
London SW1
01 828 6266

Alcoholism
Accept
Western Hospital
Seagrave Road
London SW6 1RZ
01 385 2481
(Community centres for education,
prevention and treatment)

Al-Anon Family Groups UK and Eire
61 Great Dover Street
London SE1 4YF
01 403 0888

Alcoholics Anonymous
See local telephone directory

Alternative medicine
Society of Teachers in the Alexander
Technique
10 London House
266 Fulham Road
London SW10 9EC

The British Acupuncture Association
and Register
34 Alderney Street
London SW1V 4EU
01 834 1012

The British College of Naturopathy and
Osteopathy
6 Netherhall Gardens
London NW3
01 435 7830

The British Homeopathic Association
27a Devonshire Street
London W1
01 935 2163

The British School of Osteopathy
1-4 Suffolk Place
London SW1
01 930 9254

Breastfeeding
La Leche League
PO Box 3424
London WC1V 6XX

National Childbirth Trust
9 Queensborough Terrace
London W2 3TB
01 221 3833

Children's homes and children in need
Children's Society
Old Town Hall
Kennington Road
London SE11 4OD
01 735 2441

Dr Barnardo's
Tanner's Lane
Barkingside
Essex
01 550 8822

National Children's Homes
85 Highbury Park
London N5 1UD
01 226 2033

Save the Children Fund
157 Clapham Road
London SW9 OPT
01 582 1414

Contraception
British Pregnancy Advisory Service
Austy Manor
Wootton Wawen
Solihull B15 6DA
05642 3225
(Head office will send list of branches)

Brook Advisory Centre
233 Tottenham Court Road
London W1P 9AE
01 580 2991

Death in the family
Compassionate Friends
Mrs Jill Hodder
5 Lower Clifton Hill
Bristol 8
0272 292778

The Foundation for the Study of
Infant Deaths
4 Grosvenor Place
London SW1X 7HD
01 235 1721

National Organization for the Widowed
and their Children (CRUSE)
126 Sheen Road
Richmond
Surrey
01 940 4818

Stillbirth and Perinatal Death
Association
Argyll House
29-31 Euston Road
London NW1 2SD
01 833 2851

Drug abuse
Drugs Information and Advisory
Service Ltd
111 Cowbridge Road East
Canton
Cardiff
0222 26113

Families Anonymous
88 Caledonian Road
London N1 9DN
01 278 8805
(Self-help group for addict's relatives)

Release
1 Elgin Avenue
London W9
01 603 8654

Education
Advisory Centre for Education
18 Victoria Park Square
London E2 9PB
01 980 4596

British Association for
Early Childhood Education
Montgomery Hall
Kennington
London SE11 5SW
01 582 8744

National Association for Gifted
Children
1 South Audley Street
London W1Y 5DQ
01 499 1188

Hospitals
The Patients Association
Room 33
18 Charing Cross Road
London WC2H 0HR
01 240 0671

National Association for the
Welfare of Children in Hospital
Argyll House
29-41 Euston Road
London NW1 2SD
01 833 2041

Legal Advice
Children's Legal Centre
20 Compton Terrace
London N1 2UN
01 359 6251

Family Rights Group
619 Manor Gardens
London N7
01 272 7308

Marriage guidance
National Marriage Guidance Council
Little Church Street
Rugby CV21 3AP
0788 732441
(See also local telephone directory)

Miscarriage
Miscarriage Association
Dolphin Cottage
4 Ashfield Terrace
Thorpe
Nr Wakefield
West Yorkshire WF3 3DD
0532 828946

One-parent families
Gingerbread
35 Wellington Street
London WC2 E7BN
01 240 0953

National Council for One-Parent
Families
255 Kentish Town Road
London NW5 2LX
01 267 1361

Playgroups and play
Children and Youth Action Group
Victoria Chambers
16/20 Strutton Ground
London SW1
01 222 0261

Pre-school Playgroups Association
Alford House
Aveline Street
London SE11 5DH
01 582 8871

Toy Libraries Association
Wyllotts Manor
Darkes Lane
London EN6 5HL
0707 44571

Poverty
Child Poverty Action Group
1 Macklin Street
London WC2 5NH
01 405 5942

Family Service Units
207 Old Marylebone Road
London NW1 5QP
01 402 5175

Pregnancy
Association for Improvements in
Maternity Services (AIMS)
163 Liverpool Road
London N1 0RF
01 278 5628

Maternity Alliance
59-61 Camden High Street
London NW1 7JL
01 388 6337

National Childbirth Trust
9 Queensborough Terrace
London W2 3TB
01 221 3833

Safety
Royal Society for the Prevention of
Accidents
The Priory
Queensway
Birmingham B4 6BS
021 233 2641

Safety in Playgrounds Action Group
85 Dalston Drive
Manchester M20 0LQ

Step-families
Step-families
Mavis House
Mavis Lane
Trumpington
Cambridge

Twins
The Twins Clubs Association
Pooh Corner
2 Steele Road
London W4
01 994 1660

SPECIFIC ILLNESSES AND HANDICAPS

Allergy
Action Against Allergy
43 The Downs
London SW20 8HG
01 947 5082

Allergy Support Service
c/o Chris Dowsett SRN
Little Porters
64a Marshalls Drive
St Albans
Herts
0727 58705

Anorexia
Anorexic Aid
The Priory Centre
11 Priory Road
High Wycombe
Bucks
0494 214341

The National Information Centre for
Anorexic
Family Aid
Sackville Place
44/48 Magdalen Street
Norwich NR3 1JE
0603 21414

Asthma
Asthma Research Council
12 Pembridge Square
London W2 4EH
01 229 1149

Ataxia
Friedreich's Ataxia Group
12c Worpleston Road
Guildford
Surrey
0483 503133

Autism
National Society for Autistic Children
276 Willesden Lane
London NW2
01 451 3844

Blindness
Royal National Institute for the Blind
224 Great Portland Street
London W1N 6AA

Brittle bones
Brittle Bones Association
63 Byron Crescent
Dundee DD3 6SS
0382 87130

Cancer
Cancer Information Association
Gloucester Green
Oxford OX1 2EQ
0865 725223

National Society for Cancer Relief
30 Dorset Square
London NW1
01 402 8125

Cerebral palsy
Association of Parents and Friends
of Spastics
19 Ardmory Avenue
Glasgow G3
041 647 5933

The Bobath Centre
5 Netherhall Gardens
London NW3 5RN
01 794 6084

Spastics Society
12 Park Crescent
London W1N 4LQ
01 636 5020

Cleft Lip
Cleft Lip and Palate Association
Hospital for Sick Children
Great Ormond Street
London WC1
01 405 9200 extension 316

Coeliac Disease
Coeliac Society
PO Box 181
London NW2 2YA

Cystic Fibrosis
Cystic Fibrosis Research Trust
Alexandra House
5 Blyth Road
Kent BR1 3RS
01 464 7211

Deafness
National Deaf Children's Society
45 Hereford Road
London W2 5AH
01 229 9272

Royal Association in Aid of the Deaf
and Dumb
27 Old Oak Road
London W3 7HN
01 743 6187

Royal National Institute for the Deaf
105 Gower Street
London WC1E 6AH
01 387 8033

Diabetes
British Diabetic Association
10 Queen Anne Street
London W1M 0BD
01 323 1531

Down's syndrome
Down's Children's Association
Quinborne Centre
Ridgacre Road
Quinton
Birmingham B32 2TW
021 427 1374

Dyslexia
British Dyslexia Association
Church Lane
Peppard
Oxfordshire RG9 5JN
04917 699

Dyslexia Institute
133 Gresham Road
Staines
Middlesex
81 59498

Eczema
National Eczema Society
Tavistock House North
Tavistock Square
London WC1H 9SR

Epilepsy
British Epilepsy Association
New Wokingham Road
Wokingham
Berks RG11 3AY
03446 3122

National Society for Epileptics
Chalfont St Peter
Bucks SL9 0RJ
02407 3991

Haemophilia
Haemophilia Society
PO Box 9
16 Trinity Street
London SE1 1DE
01 407 1010

Heart disorders
The Association for Children with
Heart Disorders
11 Millthorne Avenue
Clitheroe
Lancs

Children's Chest Circle
Tavistock House North
Tavistock Square
London WC1H 9JE
01 387 3012

Hyperactivity
Hyperactive Children's Support Group
59 Meadowside
Angmering BN16 4BW
09062 6172

Ileostomy
Ileostomy Association
Amblehurst House
Chobham
Woking
Surrey
09905 8277

Kidney disorders
British Kidney Patient
Association
Bordon
Hants
04203 2021

The Renal Society
Miss G. Blick
64 South Hill Park
London NW3
01 794 9479

Leukemia
Leukemia Society
Mrs J. Pankhurst
Hamlyns View
St Andrews Road
Exeter EX4 2AF

Liver disease
Liver Disease in Children (LDC)
The Michael McGough Foundation
against Liver Disease in Children
PO Box 494
Western Avenue
London N3 0SH

Mental illness
National Association for Mental Health
(MIND)
22 Harley Street
London W1N 2ED
01 637 0741

British Institute of Mental
Handicap
Information and Resource Centre
Wolverhampton Road
Kidderminster DY10 3PP

National Elfrida Rathbone
Society
Greenwich Project
Unit 11 Block 1
Woolwich Dockyard Industrial
Estate
Woolwich Church Street
London SE18
01 855 9312

Royal Society for Mentally Handicapped
Children and Adults (MENCAP)
123 Golden Lane
London EC1Y 0RT
01 253 9433

Metabolic Diseases
Research Trust for Metabolic Diseases
in Children
9 Gerard Drive
Nanthill
Cheshire
0270 626834

Migraine
British Migraine Association
178a High Road
Byfleet
Weybridge
Surrey KT14 7ED

Migraine Trust
45 Great Ormond Street
London WC1 3HD
01 278 2676

Muscular dystrophy
Muscular Dystrophy Group of
Great Britain
Nattrass House
35 Macaulay Road
London SW4 0QP
01 720 8055

Neurofibromatosis
Mrs T Green
14 Willow Way
Shuffield on Loddon
Basingstoke
Hants
0256 8824482

Phenylketonuria
National Society for
Phenylketonuria and
Allied Diseases
26 Towngate Grove
Mirfield
West Yorkshire WS14 9JF

Phobias
Phobic Trust
Mrs Vanna Gothard
25a The Grove
Coulsden
Surrey CR3 2BH
01 660 0332

Physical handicap
Disabled Living Foundation
380-384 Harrow Road
London W9 2HU
01 289 6111

Lady Hoare Trust for Physically
Handicapped Children
7 North Street
Midhurst
Sussex
073 081 3696

Royal Association for Disability and
Rehabilitation (RADAR)
25 Mortimer Street
London W1N 8AB
01 637 5400

Shaftesbury Society
2a Amity Grove
London SW20 0LJ
01 946 6634

Society for the Sexual and Personal
Relationships of the Disabled (SPOD)
286 Camden Road
London N7 0BJ
01 607 8851

Voluntary Council for Handicapped
Children
National Children's Bureau
8 Wakley Street
London EC1V 7QE
01 278 9441

Polio
British Polio Fellowship
West End Road
Ruislip
Middlesex HA4 6LP
08956 75155

Psoriasis
Psoriasis Association
7 Milton Street
Northampton NN2 7JG
0604 711129

Rheumatism and arthritis
British Rheumatism and Arthritis
Association
6 Grosvenor Crescent
London SW1X 7ER
01 235 0902

Rubella
Deaf/Blind Rubella Children
61 Senneleys Park Road
Northfield
Birmingham
021 475 1392

National Association for Blind-Deaf
and Rubella Handicapped Children
311 Gray's Inn Road
London WC1X 8PT
01 278 1000

Schizophrenia
Schizophrenia Fellowship
79 Victoria Street
Surbiton
01 390 3651

Sickle-cell anaemia
Sickle Cell Society
c/o Brent Community Health Council
16 High Street
London NW10 4LX
01 961 2028

SUPPORT GROUPS AND PUBLICATIONS

Spina bifida
Association of Spina Bifida and
Hydrocephalus
22 Upper Woburn Place
London WC1H 0EP
01 388 1382

Spinal injuries
Spinal Injuries Association
183 Royal College Street
London NW1
01 485 4227

Speech impairment
Association for All Speech-Impaired
Children
347 Central Market
London EC1A 9HN
01 236 6487

Tay sachs
The Tay Sachs and Allied Diseases
Association
17 Sidney Road
Barkingside
Ilford
Essex
01 550 8989

Thalassaemia
Thalassaemia Society
107 Nightingale Lane
London N8
01 348 0437

Vaccine-Damage
Association of Parents of Vaccine-
Damaged Children
2 Church Street
Shipston-on-Stour
Warwickshire CV6 4AP
0608 61595

WORLD WIDE

Helping organizations and
support groups similar to these
listed above exist in most
countries in the Western world
and can be contacted through the
relevant Department of Health.

Australia
Department of Health
McKell Buildings
Rawson Place
Sydney 2000
New South Wales
217 6666

Department of Health
State Health Building
147-163 Charlotte Street
Brisbane 4000
Queensland
224 0515

Public Health Promotion Services
Saving Bank Buildings
158 Rundle Mall
Adelaide 5000
South Australia
218 3211

Health Department of Western
Australia
Curtis House
60 Beaufort Street
East Perth 6000
Western Australia
328 0241

Health Commission of Victoria
555 Collins Street
Melbourne 3000
Victoria
616 7777

New Zealand
The Director General
Department of Health
P.O. Box 5013
Wellington
New Zealand

South Africa
The Director General
The Department of Health and Welfare
Private bag X63
Pretoria 0001
Transvaal
South Africa

PUBLICATIONS

Apart from the books on
childcare and child health that
are available in any number of
bookshops, useful books and
publications on specific aspects
of health education available
from:

Child Poverty Action Group
1 Macklin Street
London WC2 5NH

Health Education Council
78 New Oxford Street
London WC1A 1AH

National Children's Bureau
8 Wakley Street
London EC1V 7QE

Directories are available which list
support groups and organizations:

*The King's Fund Directory of
Organizations for
Patients and Disabled People*,
compiled by Kathy Sayer,
published by King Edward's
Hospital Fund for London

DRUGS AND TREATMENTS

A medicine is a substance which can cure or prevent disease, replace vital substances that the body lacks or suppress or relieve symptoms.

With all drugs there is a potential benefit and a potential risk. Drugs used for minor complaints generally have obvious benefits and negligible risks otherwise most of us would prefer to put up with the complaint. For more serious diseases more powerful drugs are required and the risk of adverse reaction is usually higher, but well worth taking. With potentially lethal conditions like cancer, the benefit/risk ratio becomes a major consideration. Often some unwanted side-effect, such as loss of hair, has to be accepted to gain the benefit.

Adverse reactions to drugs take many forms. Some happen to everyone; some affect only certain people, such as those with liver disease or the very young; some are individual and unpredictable depending on our own special make-up and some are allergic in nature.

Drugs often have two names, a general name and a proprietary or brand name which the drug company gives its product. For example, the painkiller, paracetamol, is also called Calpol, Paldesic or Panadol depending on which drug company makes and markets it.

The following is a list of some of the drugs used to treat sick children. Some examples of proprietary names are given in italics after the general name of the drug. The facts are taken from the British National Formulary (BNF) (1984).

Infection
Drugs against bacterial infections Penicillins: benzylpenicillin, phenoxymethylpenicillin, cloxacillin, flucloxacillin, ampicillin, amoxycillin; cephalosporins: cefuroxime, cefotaxime; aminoglycosides: gentamicin, neomycin; erythromycin; sodium fusidate; sulphonamides: co-trimoxazole (*Septrin, Bactrim*); tetracyclines may be given to treat acne; chloramphenicol is reserved for serious illnesses like meningitis; isoniazid, rifampicin and streptomycin are among the antibiotics against tuberculosis (TB); ampicillin, co-trimoxazole, nitrofurantoin and nalidixic acid are among the antibiotics used in urinary tract infection.

Drugs against fungal infections Nystatin; griseofulvin, amphotercin or ketoconazole for more serious infection.

Drugs against viral infections At the present only very few viral diseases (herpes simplex and herpes zoster) can be treated with anti-viral agents like acyclovir.

Drugs against malaria Chloroquine; primaquine; proguanil hydrochloride; pyrimethamine.

Drugs against worms Piperazine for threadworms and roundworms.

Cancer
Cytotoxic drugs Actinomycin D; cyclophosphamide; mercaptopurine; methotrexate; prednisolone; vincristine. These act by poisoning the cancer cells. Side-effects are varied and may be troublesome.

Breathing disorders
Bronchodilators Salbutamol (*Ventolin*); terbutaline (*Bricanyl*); ipratropium bromide (*Atrovent*); Aminophylline; theopohylline. These act to widen the tubes in the lung to ease breathing and are of particular value in asthma. Adrenalin by injection is occasionally used for serious allergic problems.

Corticosteroids These are powerful and often life-saving drugs with many beneficial actions. They have many side-effects. When given by inhalation their side-effects are reduced. Inhaled steroids used in asthma include beclomethasone dipropionate (*Becotide*); betathasone valerate (*Bextasol*)

Prophylaxis (preventive treatment) of asthma Sodium cromoglycate (*Intal*) works by interfering with the allergic reaction. It is given by inhalation.

Antihistamines Promethazine hydrochloride (*Phenergen*); trimeprazine tartrate (*Vallergan*); chlorpheniramine maleate (*Piriton*). These modify the allergic response. Drowsiness is a side-effect.

Cough medicine Codeine linctus, paediatric (suppressant); simple linctus, paediatric (expectorant). These aim to encourage the cough (expectorants) by loosening the sputum, or to suppress the cough (suppressants).

Heart and kidney disorders
Some conditions, for example hypertension or oedema, that is a build-up of water in the tissues, can be caused by malfunctioning of either the heart or the kidneys and the same drugs may be used in treatment.

Heart tablets These usually mean digoxin which is an extract of poppy seeds. Nausea, vomiting and visual disturbance are some of the known side-effects.

Diuretics Thiazides (*Hygroton*); frusemide (*Lasix*); spironolactone. These drugs are used to increase water excretion from the kidneys.

Beta blockers These include propranolol (*Inderal*) and are also used in the treatment of raised blood pressure.

Digestive disorders
Antacids Aluminium hydroxide; magnesium salts; sodium bicarbonate. These settle the stomach and they may be given to infants for regurgitation. *Infant Gaviscon* is one of the many proprietary products specially prepared for children which are often mixtures of all three.

Antispasmodics Drugs in this category include dicyclomine hydrochloride (*Merbetyl*). They reduce spasm in the muscle wall of the bowel and may be prescribed to help treat colic.

Antidiarrhoeal drugs It is usually *not* necessary or appropriate to use drugs to stop diarrhoea in children. Paediatric kaolin mixture may be given to absorb the water in the motion and give it substance. Drugs like diphenoxylate (*Lomotil*) and loperamide (*Imodium*) can cause excessive sedation in children.

Laxatives These may work by either increasing the faecal bulk or stimulating the intestine, softening the faeces, drawing water into the bowel or providing local lubrication. Bulk-forming drugs: bran; ispaghula husk; methyl cellulose; sterculia. Increasing the bulk of faecal mass stimulates the bowel to start contracting more strongly. Stimulant laxatives: bisacodyl (*Dulcolax*); cascara; castor oil; danthron (*Dorbanex*); senna (*Senokot*). Faecal softeners lubricate or soften the faeces thus easing their passage. Osmotic laxatives: these include lactulose (*Duphalac*) and draw fluid into the bowel so making the faeces softer. Their action is gentle.

Glandular disorders
Hormonal preparations used for treating glandular disorders include: insulins – for diabetes; thyroxine – for hypothyroidism; corticosteroids – for adrenal disease; oestrogens and progesterone – for menstrual disorders and contraception; testosterone – for hypogonadism; growth hormone – for short stature; vasopressin – for diabetes insipidus.

Corticosteroids Betamethasone; dexamethasone; hydrocortisone; prednisolone; triamcinolone. Given in supra-physiological amounts steroids suppress the disease process. They block the body's defence mechanisms and thus reduce inflammation, delay scar formation, are anti-allergic, are anti-cancerous and interfere with antibody production. They may be used in the treatment of asthma, skin allergies and allergic shock, rheumatoid arthritis, rheumatic fever, ulcerative colitis, Crohn's disease, nephrotic syndrome and leukemia.

Adverse reactions include: increased susceptibility to infection; behaviour change; increased appetite and obesity; hairiness; more rarely, raised blood pressure and sugar in urine; prolonged continuous administration can stunt growth. It is important that doctors and dentists know if your child is on steroids: he should carry a special card.

Skin disorders

In the treatment of skin conditions the substance in which the drug is applied is often as effective as the drug itself. Lotions cool the skin and have to be applied frequently. In a lotion the drug is either dissolved or suspended in water. An example is calamine lotion, used in the treatment of itching. Creams can act as the vehicle for antihistamines, antiseptics, antibiotics, antiviral agents and steroids. Ointments are greasy and are usually resistant to water. An example is zinc and castor oil ointment.

Keratolytics These are skin treatments that act to remove thickened layers of skin. They include creams containing salicylic acid and coal tar.

Steroids These are very helpful in the treatment of a wide range of skin conditions. Examples are: hydrocortisone (mild); clobetasone butyrate (*Eumovate*) (moderate); betamethasone (*Betnovate*) (potent); clobetasol propionate (*Dermovate*) (very potent).

Brain and nerve disorders

Sedatives and stress-releasing drugs These are undoubtedly helpful at times but regular use must be avoided. Chloral elixir, paediatric; dichloralphenazone (*Welldorm*); promethazine (*Phenergan*); trimeprazine (*Vallergan*) nitrazepam (*Mogadon*); diazepam (*Valium*).

Drugs for bedwetting Amitriptyline hydrochloride (*Tryptizol*); imipramine hydrochloride (*Tofranil*). The tricyclics are used to treat depressed adults. They have a limited place in treating of bedwetting. One of the many side-effects is behaviour disturbance.

Drugs for motion sickness Hyoscine; dimenhydrinate (*Dramamine*); promethazine hydrochloride (*Phenergen*). Usually they should be taken ½ hour before the journey. All can cause drowsiness, dried mouth and may result in blurred vision.

Analgesics (pain killers) Paediatric dispersible paracetamol (*Calpol, Panadol, Paldesic*); paracetamol elixir, paediatric. Paracetamol is used for mild to moderate pain. For severe pain there are many effective drugs available on prescription.

Anti-convulsants These drugs help to control fits or epilepsy. There is wide individual variation in the response to different drugs and the severity of the side-effects, so your doctor may well need to try different ones before the optimum benefit is achieved. The drugs of choice for the different forms of epilepsy are: sodium valproate (*Epilim*); carbamazepine (*Tegretol*), phenytoin (*Epanutin*) – for tonic-clonic (grand mal) or partial (focal) seizures; ethosuximide (*Zarontin*), sodium valproate (*Epilim*) – for absence seizures (petit mal); clonazepam (*Rivotril*) – for myoclonic spasms.

SCREENING PROGRAMME

This chart indicates the major screening procedures carried out in the United Kingdom and the approximate times at which they take place. They are not all routine in every area; some may not take place at all, or their timing may vary depending on the area and its population [*]. There is also variation from country to country although most countries in the industrialized world would carry out the majority of the procedures.

ANTENATAL
(See **The unborn child; Genetics**)

At about 12 weeks of pregnancy or on booking at clinic if later: blood test from mother to detect *spina bifida* in fetus; also *rhesus incompatibility* and maternal syphilis

At about 16 weeks of pregnancy: *amniocentesis* to detect *Down's syndrome* in fetus. The test is done when mother is over 38 years or a previous child has Down's. Other chromosomal abnormalities can also be detected

NEONATAL
(See **The newborn child**)

At birth: *blood test from umbilical cord to detect *sickle-cell anaemia* and *thalassaemia* when these are risks

2nd day: physical examination to detect, for example, *congenital heart defects*, *congenital dislocation of the hip* and *undescended testes*

At about 1 week: heel prick to test baby for *phenylketonuria* and *hypothyroidism*

PRE-SCHOOL
Children undergo at least 3 checks after their postnatal checks and before they go to school. Their general development is monitored throughout this period.
(See **Early growth and development**)

At about 6 weeks: repeat examination of hips and testes

6 to 8 months: *hearing* and *vision*

15, 18 months or 2 years: developmental testing

3 to 4 years: physical and developmental testing including hearing, vision and *teeth*

SCHOOL-AGE
Children undergo a medical and developmental check at school entry (5 years) including vision and hearing tests. Vision is tested regularly until at least 11 years and teeth are examined by a dentist. At some time after 11 years they have a general examination, including in particular a check for *scoliosis*.

IMMUNIZATIONS
(See **Infection**)

The programme is standard throughout the United Kingdom.

3 months: *diphtheria/pertussis/tetanus* and *polio* (or diphtheria/tetanus and polio)

5 months: second injection

10 to 12 months: third injection

15 months: *measles*

4½ to 5 years: Diphtheria/tetanus and polio booster

10 to 14 years: *Rubella* (girls)

At about 11 years (or newborn or at about 5 years in some areas*): *Tuberculosis* (BCG)

EMERGENCY ACTIONS

Most accidents that happen to children are minor and cause only scratches, scrapes and bruises which can be dealt with easily following basic first-aid procedures as described in Part Two: **The sick child at home**. You can reduce the chances of many accidents by taking safety precautions, some of which are outlined in Part One: **Safety**.

If your child is in a life-threatening situation, there is invariably no time to consult books or to ask for advice. Immediate action may be necessary to preserve life or minimize injury so you should read this appendix in order to understand which emergency actions are required in each situation – and why. You should also make sure you are familiar with the fastest way to summon the emergency services and to obtain expert help.

Organizations such as the British Red Cross Society, the St John Ambulance and St Andrew's Ambulance Association run first-aid courses that combine theoretical exercises with practical instruction. Every household should have at least one person trained in first-aid procedures: this is especially important for families with babies or young children.

AIMS OF EMERGENCY ACTION

Emergency measures should be quick, simple and directed towards: preserving life; preventing the child's condition from worsening; and, in some cases, helping the child to recover.

In serious emergency situations the order of priorities is:

1 Remove child from immediate danger (or vice versa)
2 Maintain breathing and heartbeat
3 Check for and treat severe *bleeding*
4 Deal with severe *burns*
5 Make a conscious child comfortable or put an unconscious child into a suitable position (usually *recovery position*), and watch for signs of *shock*
6 At first opportunity, get medical help

EMERGENCY ABC

A = Airway Ensure that child's mouth, throat and windpipe are unobstructed and that he has access to fresh air
B = Breathing Ensure that child is breathing; if necessary give artificial respiration (your exhaled air still contains plenty of oxygen)
C = Circulation Ensure that child's heart is beating and the blood circulation is reasonably intact; if necessary, restore heart or maintain circulation by *heart massage*

HOW TO CALL THE EMERGENCY SERVICES

Exactly when you contact the emergency services depends on whether others are nearby to help you. If you are alone and no one can be attracted by shouting and signalling, urgent first aid is a priority before you summon help. If there are others, someone else should at once take care of contacting the emergency services.

o The quickest solution, and whenever there is any doubt, is to make a 999 call on the nearest telephone (these calls are free). Try to remain calm and answer the questions asked so that an ambulance and other appropriate help can be dispatched as soon as possible
o In some less urgent situations a telephone call to the local hospital or your family doctor may suffice. (Make sure these important numbers are clearly displayed near your telephone.) Explain the situation clearly and act quickly on the advice given.
o For some emergencies, such as suspected poisoning, it may be more appropriate to take a fully conscious child to the nearest hospital accident and emergency department by car. Check ahead by telephone first. Do not attempt this with a drowsy child as he may collapse or vomit and endanger his life
o In rural areas where the nearest ambulance may take some time to arrive, advice may be given by telephone. If you can, write down this information to ensure it does not get forgotten or mixed up in the heat of the moment

CONTENTS

Appendicitis and other acute conditions of the abdomen
  see **The digestive system**

Anaphylactic shock   341

Artificial respiration   332

Asphyxiation   332

Back injury
  see *Neck and spine injuries*

Bleeding   334

Breathing stopped   332

Broken bones   335

Burns   337

Chemical burns   337

Chest injuries   336

Choking   334

Coma   339   340

Concussion   340

Convulsions   340

Dislocations
  see **Accident and injury**

Drowning   334

Drug abuse see *Poisoning*

Electrical shock   337

Electrical burns   337

Eye injury
  see **The sick child at home**

Fits   340

Foreign bodies in ears and nose
  see **The sick child at home**

Fractures
  see *Broken bones*

Head injuries   339

Heart massage   333

Heartbeat stopped   333

Intoxication   341

Medical shock   336

Neck injury
  see *Neck and spine injuries*

Poisoning   341

Pulse stopped   333

Recovery position   333

Scalds   337

Shock   336

Spine injury
  see *Neck and spine injuries*

Suffocation   332

Unconsciousness   339

ASPHYXIATION

In asphyxia, the body's tissues cannot obtain enough oxygen to survive; neither can they get rid of carbon dioxide, which quickly builds up to poisonous levels. (Lack of oxygen alone is called anoxia.) The brain in particular is susceptible to lack of oxygen and carbon dioxide build-up, and will begin to suffer damage after only 3 to 4 minutes.

Delivering oxygen to body tissues depends on: unobstructed airways to the lungs; renewal of air by the movements of breathing; and a beating heart plus intact circulation to send oxygenated blood around the body. Interference with any of these processes can cause asphyxia. Possible causes include:

o being confined in a small airtight space where oxygen is soon used up
o an object such as a plastic bag or pillow over the nose and mouth (suffocation)
o obstruction of the main airway by an object (*choking*) or by swollen tissues (after an insect sting, for example)
o external constriction of the airway, usually in the neck (strangling)
o replacing air in the lungs by water (*drowning*) or by a gas other than oxygen
o paralysis or physical restriction of breathing movements (including *chest injuries*)
o copious blood loss from a severed artery or main vein
o severe asthmatic attack

1 Remove child from danger: take off plastic bag or cut strangling cord
2 Check his condition. Signs of asphyxia include: pale or blue skin, particularly around face and lips; weak, shallow breathing (or none at all); weak pulse (or none at all); *unconsciousness*
3 Check that his airway is clear. If it is obstructed, act as for *choking*
4 If breathing is absent or erratic give *artificial respiration*
5 Examine for pulse, and if you are certain this is absent give *heart massage*
6 *Call emergency services*. If child's breathing and pulse are strong and regular, place him in the *recovery position*, keep him warm to prevent *shock*, and give reassurance. Do not give food or drink. Transport child to hospital for further treatment and checks

ARTIFICIAL RESPIRATION

1 Observe child's chest movements and place your ear near his mouth to hear and feel moving air. If breathing has stopped child will almost certainly be unconscious
2 Lay child on his back and tip his head back by pressing his forehead down and lifting his chin or neck. Make sure that there is nothing obstructing his nose, mouth or throat
3 Take a deep breath, cover child's nose and mouth with your mouth, and blow gently until you see his chest rise. For bigger children, pinch child's nose shut and cover his mouth with yours, then blow

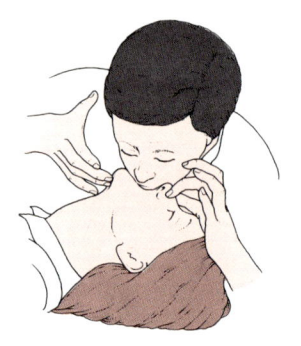

4 Remove your mouth to take another breath and watch child's chest fall
5 Repeat 3 times rapidly to reinflate lungs and provide initial supply of oxygen. Check for pulse as in *heart massage*
6 Continue to repeat at a rate a little faster than your own breathing rate. Continue until child breathes regularly for himself
7 Ensure that child is seen by a doctor

EMERGENCY ACTIONS

HEART MASSAGE

1 Feel for child's pulse in the carotid arteries on either side of the larynx (voice box). If his heartbeat has ceased, child will be pale, grey or blue and his pupils will be dilated. It is dangerous to attempt heart massage if heart is still beating

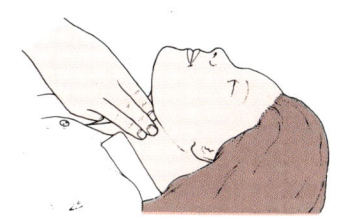

2 Lay child on his back and ensure that his airway is open (see *artificial respiration*: 2)

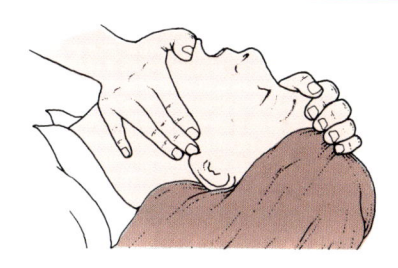

3 For a baby, push down lightly on lower part of the breastbone with your arm straight, using two straight fingers, at a rate approaching 2 compressions per second; for a child, use the heel of your hand, at a rate of just over 1 compression per second. After 15 compressions give two breaths by *artificial respiration*

4 Check pulse and breathing. If pulse is absent, repeat steps 3, 4 and 5 until it returns

5 Ensure that child is seen by a doctor

RECOVERY POSITION

The recovery position is used when a child has strong regular breathing and pulse but is unconscious or semi-conscious. It stabilizes the body and limbs, allows easy breathing, and ensures that vomit will not obstruct the airway.

Do not use recovery position if you suspect a broken neck or spine (see *neck and spine injuries*) unless the child's breathing is threatened.

Babies and small children are easily placed in position; for a larger, heavier child lying on his back follow the steps below. See also *unconsciousness*.

1 Loosen clothes and remove spectacles. Put child's nearest arm under his buttock and his other arm across his chest. Cross farthest leg over nearest one

2 Roll him towards you, cupping and protecting his head

3 Straighten his head, far arm and far leg, and bend his nearest arm and leg upwards

4 Keep child warm and check breathing and pulse every few minutes. Do not leave him until expert help arrives

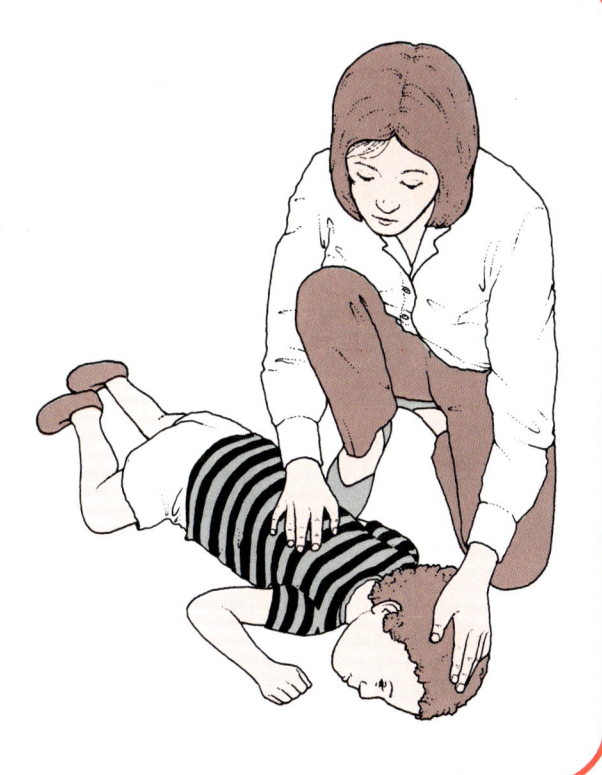

CHOKING

In most cases a child's natural cough reflex will dislodge any airway obstruction. Do not slap the back of a coughing child since he may suddenly gasp and suck the object farther in. If coughing becomes very weak or ceases, if breathing is weak or erratic, or if there are signs of *asphyxiation* you must act quickly.

1 Clear child's mouth by sweeping your finger around and hooking out any obstruction. For a small baby use your little finger
2 Hold a baby upside down and strike between his shoulder blades 3 or 4 times
3 With a bigger child, place him face downwards on your knee and strike between his shoulder blades
4 As a last resort, sit child on your knee with his back to you and put your arms around him. Using two fingers of each hand placed between his navel and breastbone, press sharply inwards and upwards to force air out of the lungs and hopefully blow out the object. Ensure that child is seen by a doctor after this manoeuvre
5 If child becomes unconscious, give *artificial respiration*

DROWNING

Get child out of the water as quickly as possible, but also begin *artificial respiration* as quickly as possible – even in the water if you can support child. Although water may block the upper airway, very little enters the lungs so do not waste time trying to remove it. Ensure child is seen by a doctor since there is a possibility of lung infection.

BLEEDING

Bleeding is serious if bright-red arterial blood spurts or gushes from a wound. This is because the normal small-artery constriction and blood-clotting mechanisms cannot cope with such a major loss. This type of bleeding must be controlled quickly otherwise blood pressure falls, circulation to the heart and brain diminishes, and child may go into *shock*.

1 Check child's airway, breathing and heartbeat and act as necessary (see *artificial respiration* and *heart massage*)
2 Control flow of blood using direct pressure
3 Call emergency services

Internal bleeding is also serious but may be difficult for a person without medical training to diagnose. The first sign of it is usually *shock*. Seek help if you suspect it.

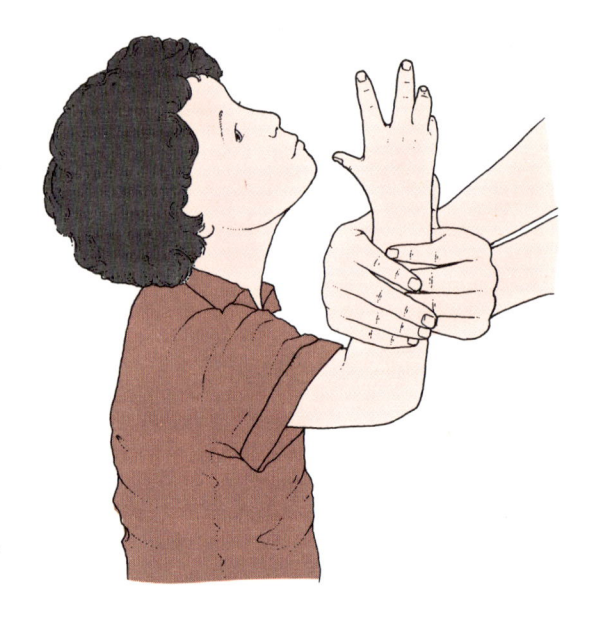

BROKEN BONES

The bones of a baby or toddler are still hardening and so are relatively flexible and elastic. As a child's small body is also fairly light, this means that fractures caused by falls are uncommon. Broken bones in this age group are most likely to be caused by falls from a table or highchair.

As a child becomes older, more daring and more active, his bones also become more brittle and the likelihood of a break is greater. Broken limbs are painful but rarely life-threatening, although they may be serious if the head, neck, or ribs are involved (see *head injuries* and *neck and spine injuries*).

Unless the child has a simple fracture that does not affect his mobility and does not involve his head, spine or ribs, you should not move him unless his life is in danger, for example from fire or obstructed airway. Movement may worsen his condition.

A dislocation occurs when the bones in a joint become disengaged. It is often difficult to distinguish dislocations and fractures but emergency treatment is the same.

In a break or dislocation the part is usually misshapen (compare it with the other, uninjured side of the body if possible), swells quickly and is extremely painful. There may well be other problems such as wounds and internal injuries.

Call emergency services as soon as possible.

1 Check child's airway, breathing and circulation and act as necessary (see *artificial respiration* and *heart massage*)
2 Cover any open wounds (see *bleeding*) but do not apply pressure to wounds near the site of the break
3 If child's condition is stable, immobilize the broken part with soft padding such as coats, scarves, cushions or crumpled paper. Remove belts, jewellery or shoes or any other items that may constrict swelling
4 Do not move child, but keep him warm, comforted and reassured until emergency help arrives
5 If you have to move child, the broken bone must be immobilized and secured in the most comfortable position. Put an arm in a sling or strap it to the side of the body; splint a leg to its partner with something stiff, like a piece of wood, between. Use whatever materials are to hand. Ensure that the injured part is well padded and secure but not too tightly strapped

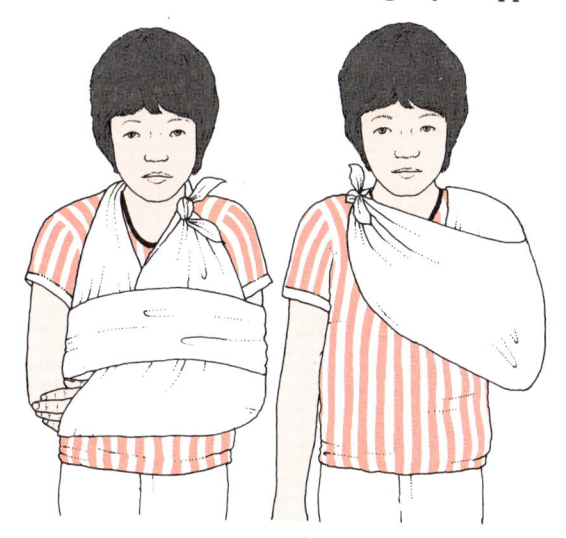

6 Do not give food or drink since this will delay administration of a general anaesthetic if it is needed in hospital

CHEST INJURIES

A chest injury may threaten life if it prevents the movements of breathing, in which case *artificial respiration* must be started at once.

Another serious type of chest injury is penetration of the rib cage or back, allowing air into the space between the lungs and the lining of the chest cavity. The injury can develop into a 'sucking wound', in which breathing sucks air in and out from around the lungs through the wound, while the lungs themselves collapse and become ineffective. Breathing is shallow and rapid, blood-stained liquid may bubble from the wound and the child may be in *shock*. *Asphyxia* is likely unless immediate action is taken.
Call emergency services.

1 Seal wound immediately, using the palm of your hand or a clean cloth
2 Support child in a half-sitting position, leaning towards the injured side so that wound is encouraged to seal from inside
3 Cover wound with a clean dressing to ensure an airtight seal. Be prepared to treat child for *shock* and give *artificial respiration* if necessary

NECK AND SPINE INJURIES

The brain or spinal cord may be damaged by a blow that fractures the skull, or a sudden movement that whiplashes the neck, or a fall that wrenches the back; once this happens, the nerves take a long time to mend. There is also a possibility of spine injury damaging the nerves that control breathing.

Neck and spine injuries are indicated by pain or by insensitivity, numbness, inability to move parts of a limb or the whole limb, a feeling of being 'cut in half' and possibly loss of bowel or bladder control.

Call emergency services, and if possible tell them the nature of the injury so that a special spinal stretcher can be provided.

Do not move child unless his life is in danger. If he really must be moved, support his head, neck and back as carefully as possible, maintaining their relative positions. Otherwise, keep child as still as possible.

SHOCK

Medical shock, as opposed to electrical shock, is caused by the failure of the circulation to deliver enough blood to the heart and brain. It is rarely caused by fright or pain. Signs of shock include pale, cold, clammy skin; faintness and nausea; shallow breathing and rapid pulse; and possibly tiredness, yawning, delirium and *unconsciousness*. Be prepared for signs of shock after any serious accident.

1 Check child's airway, breathing and circulation (see *artificial respiration* and *heart massage*)
2 Deal with the cause of the shock, such as severe *bleeding* or *burns*
3 *Call emergency services*
4 Loosen constricting clothing. If child is *unconscious* place him in the *recovery position*. If he is conscious raise and support his legs above his head to reduce the work of the heart. Do not move child if you suspect neck or back injury (see *neck and spine injuries*)
5 Keep child warm and reassured. Moisten his lips with water if he complains of thirst. Check breathing and pulse every few minutes. Do not leave him until expert help arrives

ELECTRICAL SHOCK

An electrical shock passing through the body can stop or interrupt heartbeat and the movements of breathing, and can also burn body tissues, particularly beneath the skin at the point of contact. Do not touch a child in contact with electricity. Switch off the current or break the contact by pushing child or source of electricity away with a non-metallic, dry object like a wooden chair.

1 Check child's breathing and circulation (see *artificial respiration*)
2 *Call emergency services*

There may be very little injury on the skin's surface following an electrical burn but the tissue beneath may be severely damaged. Show it to a doctor at once.
See *burns and scalds*.

BURNS AND SCALDS

Burns can be caused not only by fire, but also by contact with hot objects, chemicals, electricity and by friction. Scalds are caused by hot liquids and steam. In both burns and scalds, heat expands the blood vessels beneath the skin so that plasma, the clear liquid part of the blood, escapes. In burns, plasma collects in a blister or, where the skin has been burnt off altogether, it leaks from the exposed raw area. In scalds, fluid loss takes place under the skin.

Loss of fluid may lead to *shock*; burns that may not be considered serious in adults should be treated as very serious in children because they have less fluid to lose.

Generally, a burn or scald requires emergency attention when:

○ its area is larger than 2.5 cm (1 in) square
○ or it is deep and leaves the surface charred and greyish-white in appearance, whatever its skin area
○ or it is on the face, a joint or other crucial part of the body, even though it may not be large

If you are in any doubt as to whether a burn or scald needs urgent medical attention go at once to your doctor or to hospital.

CHEMICAL BURNS

Many chemicals found in the home can cause severe burns. Hold the affected area under cold running water at once and for at least 10 minutes while removing contaminated clothing carefully. *Call emergency services.*

CHILD ON FIRE

If your child's clothes or hair catch fire the immediate and urgent priority is to extinguish the flames, and to prevent further damage to body tissues. *Call emergency services* as soon as possible but note that 1 and 2 are top priority.

1 If child is on fire, put out the flames, making sure the flames fan away from the child's head: douse with lots of cold water; or smother the flames with a heavy blanket, or similar large item of non-synthetic material; or smother the flames with your body by lying closely on top of child
2 Put child into a cold bath or hold the injured part of the body under cold water for at least 10 minutes
3 Remove any clothing soaked in hot water or fat as soon as the affected area is under water. But do not pull off clothing if this will damage the skin and introduce the risk of infection
4 Remove carefully from the affected area any items that might constrict swelling, such as watches or shoes
5 Protect injured area with a clean light dry dressing or wrap child in a clean dry sheet. Do not use fluffy material or adhesive dressings and do not apply ointment, grease or creams of any kind. If fluid leaks through, add another dressing rather than changing the first. Do not break blisters: they protect raw areas beneath from infection
6 Give lots of comfort. Fluid loss may lead to *shock*: give a conscious child sips of water to help replace fluid loss

BURNS IN THE MOUTH

Drinking very hot liquids, breathing very hot air or swallowing corrosive chemicals can burn the mouth and throat.

If child is in great pain or has difficulty in breathing:

1 *Call emergency services*
2 Give reassurance to prevent panic
3 Give frequent sips of cold water
4 Loosen or remove any items around neck and chest that might restrict breathing
5 Be prepared to treat *shock* and to deal with *unconsciousness* or *asphyxiation*

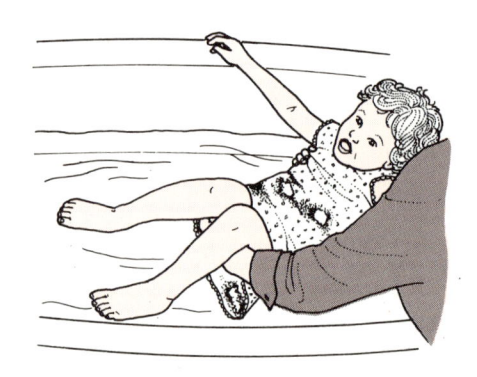

HEAD INJURIES

Small children's heads are relatively large and heavy compared with their bodies, which makes them 'top heavy'. Coupled with a toddler's unsteadiness or an older child's adventurous nature, this makes head-first falls a frequent occurrence. The face and scalp have a rich blood supply and bleed easily, but the bones of the young skull are soft, flexible and unlikely to break.

The problem with serious head injury is that damage may only become apparent hours later. There may be bleeding inside the skull that compresses the brain tissue, with potentially serious consequences. It is advisable to act sooner rather than later and take the child to hospital or obtain emergency help if you are suspicious.

At the time of injury these signs require emergency attention:

o clear, straw-coloured or bloodstained fluid
o bloodshot eyes
o broken facial bones
o injury or swelling around the mouth, jaw or neck that may obstruct the airway
o *unconsciousness*

In addition, signs requiring medical attention may appear up to 3 days after the injury:

o nausea and/or vomiting
o loss of memory
o paleness
o dilated pupils
o drowsiness or unconsciousness

If child's general alertness and condition deteriorate rapidly, or he appears to fall asleep and cannot be roused, *call emergency services*.

UNCONSCIOUSNESS

There are literally dozens of causes of unconsciousness. Sometimes the reason is obvious, such as falls or *fits*; sometimes the cause is obscure. Even if the child recovers in a few seconds, he should see a doctor as soon as possible.

1 Remove the cause of unconsciousness, if possible
2 Check child's airway, breathing and circulation (see *artificial respiration* and *heart massage*)
3 Control severe *bleeding*.
4 *Call emergency services*
5 Place child in the *recovery position* and keep him warm with coats or blankets. Do not move him if you suspect neck or back injury.
6 Deal with minor injuries. Check breathing and pulse every few minutes. Gather relevant information (such as medical history). Do not leave him until expert help arrives – he may recover and need reassurance

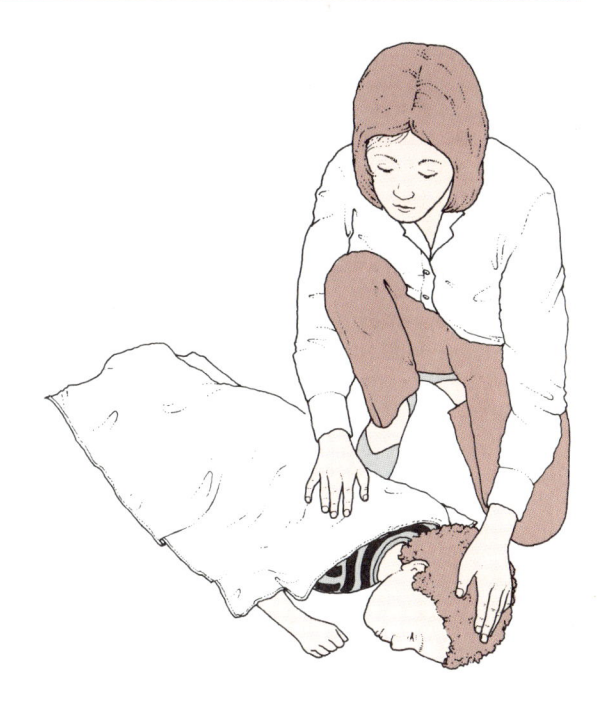

CONCUSSION

Concussion is a temporary loss of consciousness due to jarring of the brain by a blow on the head or to the base of the spine. The child may be panting and pale with a rapid, weak pulse. However, as with other *head injuries*, signs may appear some time after the original incident that indicate concussion. These include:

o noisy breathing
o fever
o slow pulse
o unequal pupils
o weakness or numbness

Unconsciousness may follow rapidly. If such signs appear, *call emergency services*.

FITS

There are several causes of fits – see **Brain nerves and muscles**: *Fits and convulsions*. In young children, up to 4 years old, most fits are febrile – caused by the high temperature of a fever interfering with the brain's function. Febrile fits are therefore usually associated with infection. Other causes of fits are *epilepsy* and *poisoning*.

Once the likely cause of a fit is established, treat as below. For a first fit which is short and where the child regains consciousness, contact a doctor quickly for advice. For a first fit which lasts for more than 3 minutes or where there is *unconsciousness*, whatever the suspected cause, *call emergency services*.

Febrile fits include temperature above 39°C (102°F), twitching muscles, rolling eyes, rigidity, breath-holding, frothing at the mouth.

Gently cool child. Remove upper clothes and sponge arms with tepid water. If child is conscious give paracetamol.

Epileptic fits are of several types. Most serious is a major seizure, which includes rigidity, noisy breathing or cessation of breathing, twitching and convulsive, jerky movements, frothing at the mouth, loss of bladder and/or bowel control and unconsciousness.

Move objects out of the way so child cannot harm himself. Loosen clothing. Do not restrain child or force anything into his mouth.

Diabetic hypoglycemia (low blood sugar) coma may resemble a fit. The child feels faint and acts 'drunk'; he becomes pale with rapid pulse and shallow breathing; his limbs tremble; he loses consciousness.

If you know child is diabetic and probably hypoglycemic, give him something sweet (chocolate, sugar, sweetened drink) before he loses consciousness. Arrange medical examination to review diabetic control.

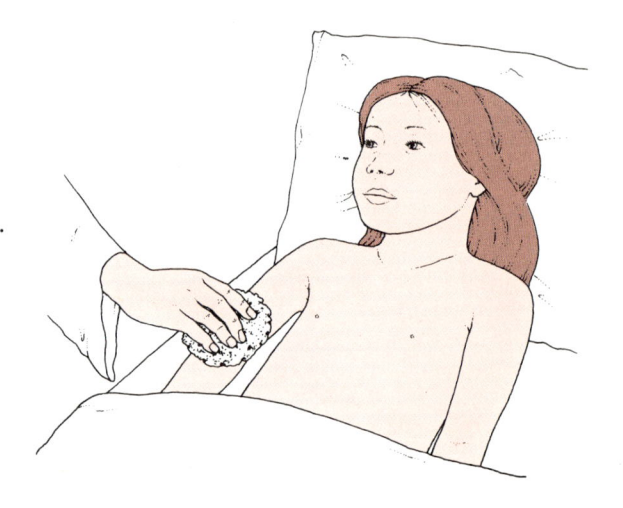

POISONING AND INTOXICATION

Babies and young children are forever putting things in their mouths, and children like to experiment with the taste and texture of 'food'. The list of potential poisons is enormous and, unless such substances are kept out of reach, the likelihood of a young child swallowing one is high. It is best to regard anything that is not accepted food and drink as a possible poison. Even everyday food or drink may be dangerous: one measure of neat spirits can kill a small toddler, as can an eaten cigarette.

However, emergency hospital treatment for suspected poisoning is frightening, particularly for a child, and to be avoided if possible. So be sure the substance is poisonous, and be reasonably sure it has been swallowed. All the same, if in any doubt, take action.

Signs vary with the poison and time since it was consumed. They include some or all of:

o delirium or odd behaviour
o *fits*
o *unconsciousness*
o diarrhoea
o abdominal pain
o headache
o breath smells of poison
o signs of burns or rashes around the lips, or mouth, or on fingers

1 Check child's airway, breathing and circulation (see *artificial respiration* and *heart massage*). Wipe the mouth free of any poison before giving artificial respiration
2 If the poison is strongly acidic or alkaline, give sips of water or milk to dilute it. Do not induce vomiting
3 Remove contaminated clothing and wash contaminated skin
4 Identify likely poison, and if possible obtain sample. If child is conscious, take him to hospital at once, taking sample as well
5 If child loses consciousness, *call emergency services*

ANAPHYLACTIC SHOCK

This is a massive, possibly life-threatening allergic reaction to a food, drug or even insect sting. Signs appear rapidly and include:

o signs of medical *shock*
o vomiting
o difficulty in breathing, possibly with swollen face, mouth or throat
o swellings elsewhere in the body
o rapid pulse

Take pulse for 1-2½ minutes as necessary. To confirm pulse is abnormal you may want to take it for longer. Normal pulse rates (number of beats per minute) are:

0-1 years	100-140
1-5 years	80-120
5-15 years	70-110
15 years+	60-80

Treat as for poisoning but if child's condition deteriorates or he becomes unconscious *call emergency services*.

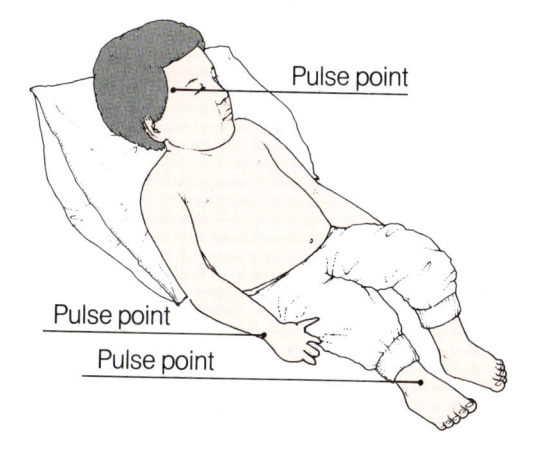

INDEX OF SYMPTOMS

This index can be used to lead you to some of the disorders discussed in this book that might be responsible for a particular symptom. Where the symptom itself is discussed, the page reference is given. It is not intended and should not be used as a guide to diagnosis: if you are worried about a symptom that your child has, consult your doctor.

Abdominal pain 243
    appendicitis 247
    Bornholm disease 163
    food allergy 167
    food poisoning 248
    Henoch-Schonlein purpura 246
    infectious hepatitis 253
    intussusception and volvulus 246
    lactose intolerance 249
    mesenteric adenitis 246
    peptic ulcers 245
    psychosomatic pain 186
    ulcerative colitis and Crohn's disease 250
Abdominal swelling
    coeliac disease 250
    cystic fibrosis 226
    Hirschsprung's disease 252
    intussusception and volvulus 246
    nephroblastoma 176
Appetite loss 97 99 190
    anaemia 228
    aplastic anaemia 240
    coeliac disease 250
    depression 190
    infectious hepatitis 253
    jaundice 253

Bleeding, excessive 236
    aplastic anaemia 240
    haemophilia 239
    leukemia 173-4
    thrombocytopenic purpura 240
Blocked or runny nose 216
    allergy 168
    colds 217
    enlarged adenoids 218
    hay fever 220
    influenza 156
    sinusitis 219
Blood in stools
    aplastic anaemia 240
    food allergy 167
    intussusception and volvulus 246
    lactose intolerance 249
    thalassaemia 238
    ulcerative colitis and Crohn's disease 250
Blood in urine
    nephritis 259
    nephroblastoma 176
    urinary infection 261
Blurred or distorted vision 198
    astigmatism 199
    migraine 296
    short sight 198
Bones, pain in 276
    leukemia 173
    neuroblastoma 175
    osteomyelitis 279
    sickle-cell anaemia 238
    tumours 177
Breathlessness 228
    anaemia 237
    congenital heart disorders 231-2
    see also **The Lungs** 221-6
Breathing difficulty 220
    asthma 223
    bronchiolitis 224
    croup 220
    epiglottitis 220
    laryngomalacia 220
    pneumonia 225
Bruising, excessive 236
    aplastic anaemia 240
    haemophilia 239
    Henoch-Schonlein purpura 246
    leukemia 173-4
    thrombocytopenic purpura 240

Colic *see* **Abdominal pain**
Cough 222
    allergy 165
    asthma 223
    bronchiectasis 225
    bronchiolitis 224
    bronchitis 224
    cystic fibrosis 226
    influenza 156
    inhaled foreign body 222
    measles 157
    pneumonia 225
    sinusitis 219
    whooping cough 160

Diarrhoea 248
    appendicitis 247
    cholera 164
    coeliac disease 250
    food allergy 167
    food poisoning 248
    gastroenteritis 248
    infectious hepatitis 253
    lactose intolerance 249
    ulcerative colitis and Crohn's disease 250
Dizziness 208
    migraine 296
    otitis media 210

Earache 209
    otitis externa 210
    otitis media 210
    referred pain from decayed tooth 205
Eyes: red and itchy or watery
    allergy 196
    hay fever 220
    red and painful
    foreign body 196
    inflammation 196
    styes 196
    red and sticky
    conjunctivitis 196
    sticky and watering
    blocked tear duct 196

Faintness 294
    anaemia 237
    emotion or pain 294
    hypoglycemia 270
    standing in hot conditions 294
Fever 89 98
    appendicitis 247
    bronchitis 224
    chickenpox 159
    glandular fever 162
    herpes simplex 162
    Hodgkin's disease 175
    infectious hepatitis 253
    influenza 156
    juvenile rheumatoid arthritis 281
    measles 157
    meningitis 299
    mumps 158
    osteomyelitis 279
    otitis media 210
    pneumonia 225
    rheumatic fever 233
    roseola infantum 161
    scarlet fever 161
    septic arthritis 279
    sickle-cell anaemia 238
    tonsillitis 218
    typhoid 164
    whooping cough 160

Fits 141 296
  birth asphyxia 135
  encephalitis 300
  epilepsy 297
  high temperature 296
  hypoglycemia 270
  meningitis 299

Genital rash, swellings or sores
  sexually transmitted disease 265
Glands, swollen
  glandular fever 162
  Hodgkin's disease 175
Groin, swelling in
  hernia 263

Hair loss
  alopecia areata 291
  ringworm 291
Headache 293
  astigmatism 199
  brain tumour 177
  encephalitis 300
  hypoglycemia 270
  infectious hepatitis 253
  influenza 156
  long sight 198
  meningitis 299
  migraine 296
  rheumatic fever 233
  sinusitis 219
  tension 293
  typhoid 164
Hearing difficulty
  conductive deafness 213
  glue ear 211
  perceptive deafness 213
  wax in ear 208
Hip, painful
  irritable hip 278
  Perthes' disease 278
  septic arthritis 279
  slipped femoral epiphysis 278

Itching 284
  chilblains 287
  eczema 285
  forefoot eczema 286
  insect bites 289
  pityriasis rosea 291
  scabies 290
  threadworms 252
  urticaria 287
  vulvovaginitis 262

Joints, painful
  juvenile rheumatoid arthritis 281
  septic arthritis 279
  ulcerative colitis and Crohn's
    disease 250
  See also **Knee, painful**

Joints, swollen
  haemophilia 239
  Henoch-Schonlein purpura 246
  juvenile rheumatoid arthritis 281
  rheumatic fever 233
  septic arthritis 279
  ulcerative colitis and Crohn's
    disease 250

Knee, painful
  juvenile rheumatoid arthritis 281
  Osgood Schlatter disease 280
  slipped femoral epiphysis 278

Mouth-breathing 216
  allergies 168
  crooked septum 219
  enlarged adenoids 218

Nausea *see* **The Digestive system**
  239-52
  anaemia 237
  low blood sugar 270
  meningitis 299
  migraine 296

Pallor
  anaemia 237
  leukemia 173
  thalassaemia 238
Photophobia 196
  measles 157
  meningitis 299

Rash 33 284
  allergy 167
  chickenpox 159
  eczema 285
  German measles 159
  infantile seborrhoeic dermatitis
    285
  measles 157
  rheumatic fever 233
  roseola infantum 161
  scarlet fever 161
  See also **Itching**
Retarded growth
  coeliac disease 250
  cystic fibrosis 226
  emotional deprivation 267
  lack of pituitary growth hormone
    268
  thalassaemia 238
  thyroid problems 268

Sleep disturbance 180
  anxiety 180
  depression 190
Small stature
  achondroplasia 127
  Turner's syndrome 129

Sneezing
  allergy 168
  hay fever 220
Sore mouth 216
  cold sores 163
  gingivitis 206
  herpes simplex 162
Sore throat 218
  colds 217
  German measles 159
  glandular fever 162
  influenza 156
  scarlet fever 161
  tonsillitis 218
Stomach-ache *see* **Abdominal pain**
Stools, blood in *see* **Blood in stools**
Stools, bulky
  coeliac disease 250
  cystic fibrosis 226

Thirst, extreme
  diabetes 270
  polydipsia 259
Tiredness
  anaemia 237
  coeliac disease 250
  diabetes 270
  leukemia 173
  thalassaemia 238

Urination, excessive
  diabetes 270

Vaginal discharge
  dermatitis 285
  threadworms 252
  thrush 152
Vomiting
  anaemia 237
  appendicitis 247
  brain tumour 177
  food allergy 167
  food poisoning 250
  hiatus hernia 244
  intussusception and volvulus 248
  lactose intolerance 249
  meningitis 299
  migraine 296
  pyloric stenosis 244

Weight loss
  anorexia nervosa 191
  depression 190
  Hodgkin's disease 175
Wheezing 222
  allergy 168
  asthma 223
  hay fever 220

INDEX

Abdominal pain **243**
  see also Stomach-ache,
  Index of symptoms
Abdominal swelling *see* Index of
  symptoms
Abnormal movement *see* Athetosis
  see also Index of symptoms
Abortion 86 88 133 **307**
Absence seizures 297
Absent periods *see* Amenorrhoea
Abstract thinking 73 82
Accident and injury 12 89 **145-50**
  burns and scalds 149
  fits 150
  fractures 146-7
  going to hospital 145
  head injuries 148
  minor injuries 102-5
  near drowning 149
  poisoning 150
  prevention of **52-9**
  severe cuts 146
  dislocations 148
Aching muscles *see* Influenza
Achondroplasia 127
Acne 284 **288**
Acupuncture 122 **123** 224
Acute bronchitis 124 156 222 **224**
Acute bronchiolitis 222 **224**
Acute otitis media 157 161 209
  210 212
Adenoids 212 215 216 **218**
Adolescence 11 71 73 **80-6** 117
  behavioural problems of
    188-191
  emotional maturity 81-4
  physical development 80-1
  sexual activity 85-6
Adoption and fostering 317
Adrenal glands 266
  problems of **269**
Alcohol 193
  during pregnancy 24
Alexander technique **276**
Allergens **165-8** 223 286
Allergic rhinitis *see* Hay fever
Allergy 37 39 **165-8** 196 212 220
  223 286 287
Alopecia areata **291**
Alternative therapies 90 **122-4**
Amblioscope 197
Amenorrhoea 80 191
Amniocentesis 133
Amniotic fluid 23
Anaemia 173 **237** 250
  in the newborn 136 137

Anaesthesia 111
  during labour 26
Anal fissure 251 **252**
Anaphylactic reaction 104 **165**
Anorexia nervosa 182 **191**
Antenatal care **25-6**
Antenatal diagnosis **132-3** 238
  305
Antibiotics **93** 122 149 151 152
  see also Drugs and
  treatments
Antibodies 33 140 152 **165** 234
  235 259
Antidepressant drugs 190
  see also Drugs and
  treatments
Antiemetic drugs 243
  see also Drugs and
  treatments
Antigens 152 235
Antihistamines 166 212 287
  see also Drugs and
  treatments
Anxiety 49 180 184
  in adolescence 81
Aortic stenosis 232 233
Apgar score 27 28
Aplastic anaemia 240
Apnoeic attacks 136 306
Appendicitis 92 243 246 **247** 251
Appetite 181
  loss of 97 99 190
  see also Index of symptoms
Arthritis *see* Juvenile
  rheumatoid arthritis
Artificial insemination 132
Asphyxia *see* Birth asphyxia
Astigmatism 198 **199** 293
Asthma 92 117 122 124 165 168
  222 **223** 224 249 286
Ataxia 303
Athetosis 303
Athlete's foot 286 **291**
Atrial septal defect 231
Audiometry 212
Autism 124 **183**

'Babbling' 68
Backache 276
Bacteria **151** 152 154
  see also Infection
Bad breath *see* Halitosis
Barium enema 242 246
  meal 242 245
'Bat' ears *see* Ears, protruding
Becker muscular dystrophy 304

Bedwetting 11 13 **50** 179 189 **260**
Behaviour and development **60-71**
  80-6 179-94
Behaviour therapy 184
Behavioural problems 10 50 78 79
  268 310
  alcohol and drug abuse 193
  anxiety states 189
  conduct disorders 193
  depression 190
  hyperactivity 135 183
  fears and anxieties 184-5
  feeding problems 181
  in adolescents **188-93**
  in pre-school children **179-83**
  in school-age children **184-7**
  learning difficulties and
    dyslexia 186
  mental illness 194
  obsessive compulsions 191
  promiscuity 194
  psychosomatic symptoms 186
  school refusal 189
  sleeping problems 180
  subnormal intelligence 79
  suicide and self-injury 190
  tantrums and breath-holding
    182
  tics 186
Bereavement 119 190 306
  see also Death, Grieving
Bile 241
Biliary atresia 253
Bilingual families 68
Biopsy 112 167 171 177
Birth **27**
  asphyxia **135** 141
  examination 29-31
  injuries 32 124 **136** 141
Birthmarks 32
Bites and stings 104
Bladder **255** 261
  control 45 260
Black eye 105
Blackhead 289
Bleeding 146
  and iron deficiency 237
  excessive 236 239 240
  see also Index of symptoms
Blindness 25 66 138 **200-2**
Blisters 102
  see also Index of symptoms
Blocked or runny nose *see*
  Catarrh
  see also Index of symptoms
Blocked tear duct 196

Blood **234-6**
  disorders 237-40
  groups 139 **235**
  pressure 112
  tests 113 171 237 250 270
  transfusions 171 174 236
  see also Rhesus
    incompatibility
Blood in sputum see Bronchiectasis
Blood in stools see Index of symptoms
Blood in urine see Index of symptoms
Blueness 228
  see also Index of symptoms
Blurred vision 198
  see also Index of symptoms
Boils **284**
  in the ear 209
Bonding 13 68
Bones
  deformities see Index of
    symptoms
  injuries 136
  pain see Index of symptoms
  tumour 177
  see also Fractures
Bone marrow
  aspiration 171 175
  transplant 175
  tumour 173-4
Bones and joints **274-81**
'Booster' injection 154
Bornholm disease 163
Bottle-feeding **36-8**
Bow legs **275**
Bowel **241-2**
  changes in illness 97
  control 45 242
  obstruction 141 226
  problems **243-53**
Brain, nerves and muscles **292-305**
Brain damage 154 **305** 296 299 301
  tumour **177** 294
Breast development 80
Breastfeeding 28 **36-8**
  and allergies 165
'Breastmilk jaundice' 140
Breath-holding **182** 299
Breathing 221
  changes in illness 97
  difficulty 88 138 **220**
  see also Index of symptoms
Breathlessness 228
  see also Index of symptoms
Breech presentation 24
Bronchiectasis **225** 226
Bronchiolitis see Acute
  bronchiolitis
Bronchitis see Acute bronchitis
Bronchodilators 223
Bronchopulmonary dysplasia 139

Bruises **103**
Bruising, excessive 236
  in the newborn 32 136
  see also Index of symptoms
Bulimia nervosa 191
Bullying 69 193
Burns and scalds 52 54 **149**
  first aid for **103**

Caesarean section 24 25 26 135
Candidiasis see Thrush
Cancer **169-78** 268
Car safety 53
Cardiac catheterization 229 230
Cardiology 106
Caries see Tooth decay
'Carriers' of disease 151 23
CAT scan 150 177 **178**
Cataract 200
Catarrh 211 **216**
Cephalhaematoma 32
Cerebral palsy 135 138 188 279
  301-4
Challenge tests 167
Change, response to 12 14 18 19
  70 179 184
Chapped skin 284 **287**
  see also Dry skin
Chemotherapy 172 173 175 176 177
Chest pain **222**
  see also Bornholm disease
Chickenpox 152 151 **159** 301
Chilblains **287** 302
Child abuse 319
Child guidance clinics 76 119
Childminders see Substitute
  care-takers
Cholera 59 **163** 248
Chorionic biopsy 132
Chromosomal disorders **128-9** 187
Chromosomes 126
Chronic illness see Longstanding
  illness
Circulation see Heart and
  circulation
Circumcision **257**
Cirrhosis 254
Cleanliness see Hygiene
Cleft lip and palate 30 37 **143**
'Clicky hip' 275
Clotting **234**
Club foot 31 142 **144** 274
Clumsiness **295**
Coarctation of the aorta 232
Coeliac disease 237 **249**
Colds 121 123 152 216 **217**
  in the newborn 33
Cold sores 162 **163**
Colic 122
  see also Abdominal pain,
    Three-month colic

Colostomy 252
Colostrum 36 37
Colour blindness 196
Coma 270
Comfort habits 49 179
Complementary medicine see
  Alternative therapies
Compulsions see Obsessive
  compulsions
Conductive deafness **213-4**
Confusion 96
Congenital abnormalities 24 25
  26 **141-4**
  of bowel 252
  of eye 200
  of heart 25 **230-3**
  of hip 31 35 **277**
  see also Genetic disorders
Conjunctivitis 196
Constipation 35 123 242 248
  250-1 252 261
  see also Index of symptoms
Contact dermatitis 167 **286**
Contact lenses 198
Continuous positive airways
  pressure 139
Contraception **85-6**
Contraceptive pill 86 152
Contusion see Bruises
Convulsions see Fits
  see also Febrile
    convulsions
Co-ordination 50
Cot death **308-9**
Cough 88 93 122 **222**
  suppressant 224
  see also Index of symptoms
Counselling **119-21** 190
Cradle cap 33 285
Cramp 58 **294**
Cranial osteopathy 124
Cretinism 35 268
Crohn's disease **250**
Crooked septum 216 **219**
Croup 92 123 157 **220**
Cuts and grazes 102
  severe **146**
Cycling 52-3
Cystic fibrosis 127 225 **226**
Cytotoxic drugs 172
  see also Drugs and
    treatment

Dandruff **284**
Dark urine see Jaundice
Dating (cancer) 85
Day nurseries see Nurseries
Day-to-day care **43-51**
  bladder and bowel control
    45
  bedwetting 50

care of the teeth 45
play and activity 50
sleep 48-9
stress and relaxation 50-1
warmth and clothing 47-8
washing and hygiene 43-5
Deafness 25 66 138 **213-4** 303
Death in the family **19-21 306-10**
Decongestants 33 212 217 219
  see also Drugs and
    treatments
Deep-breathing techniques 51
Defecation 242
Delinquency 193
Delirium 105
Demand feeding 37
Dental caries *see* Tooth decay
Dental hygiene 45
Depression **190** 310
  see also Psychosis
Dermatitis 33 124 262 **285**
  see also Contact dermatitis
Dermatology 106
Desensitization **166** 224
Development
  see Behaviour and
    development
Developmental checks 30-1 35 **60** 93
Dexterity 61
Diabetes 112 114 117 152 188 226 259 **268** 284 297
  see also Maternal diabetes
Dialysis 258 259
Diarrhoea 88 93 122 **248** 250
  see also Index of symptoms
Diet 36 **40-2**
  diabetic 272
  during pregnancy 24
  food exclusion 124 167 183 249 250 286 298
Dieting, excessive 191
Digestion 242
Digestive system **241-54**
  disorders of **242-54**
Diphtheria 112 155 **163**
Diplegia 302
Disability **115-8** 302-4
Discharge
  from ear 209 210
  from eyes 196
  from nose 216 219
  from genitals *see* Index of
    symptoms
Dislocations **148**
  see also Hip
Divorce 15 **16-18**
Dizziness 105 **208**
  see also Index of symptoms
Doctors
  in hospital 107 111

specialist referral 93
  see also Family doctor
Down's syndrome 30 **129** 133 187 304
Dressing 64
Drinking *see* Alcohol
Drowning, near 55 57 **149**
Drowsiness 96
  see also Index of symptoms
Drugs
  abuse 124 193
  allergy 168
  during pregnancy 25
  see also Medicines
Drugs and treatments 326-8
Dry skin *see* Skin, dry
Duchenne muscular dystrophy 128 **304**
Dyslexia 78 **186-7** 188
Dysmaturity *see* Low-birthweight
  babies

Eardrum, perforated 208 **210**
Ears **207-14**
  boils in 209
  discharge from 209-10
  disorders of **208-14**
  drops 101 210
  earache 209
  glue ear 211
  hearing aids 213
  hearing tests 212
  injuries 105
  insect in 105
  perforated eardrum 210
  'popping' 207-8
  protruding 207
  wax in 208
Earache 122 **209** 210
  see also Index of symptoms
Early growth and development **60-79**
  developmental checks 60 62-3
  dexterity 61 64
  emotional and social
    development 68-71
  growth 64-5
  hearing 66
  language development 68
  physical skills 61
  sexuality 71
  vision 67
Echocardiogram 229 230
Ecological therapy 124
Ectopic heartbeats 228
Eczema 123 124 165 210 223 284 **285-6**
Educational psychologist 78-9 119 187 188
Educationally subnormal children 79

  see also Mental retardation
Electric shock 55
Electrocardiography 229 230
Electroencephalogram 150 **298**
Emergency actions **330-41**
Emotional and social development **68-71** 81-3
Emotional deprivation 267
Emotional problems *see*
  Behavioural problems
Encephalitis 157 158 297 **300**
Endocrine glands **266-7**
Endocrinology 106
Endoscopy 250
Enema 251
Enuresis 260
Epidural anaesthesia 26
Epiglottitis **220**
Epilepsy 79 117 188 294 296 **297- 9** 302
Erb's palsy 136
Examinations 77
Exchange transfusion 140
Exclusion diet *see* Diet
Eustachian tube 207 208 210 211 212 215
Evening colic *see* Three-month
  colic
Ewing's tumour 170 **177**
Eyedrops 101
Eyes **195-202**
  astigmatism 199
  blindness 200-2
  common problems 196
  infections in the newborn 33
  injuries 105 196
  long sight 198
  short sight 198
  squint 197
  tests 199
  see also Index of symptoms
Eye blinking 186

Facial pain *see* Index of
  symptoms
Facial swelling *see* Index of
  symptoms
Fainting 88 **294** 298
  see also Index of
    symptoms
Falls 52 54
Family doctor **88-93** 119 121 188
  appointments system 92 93
  changing your doctor 90
  choosing a doctor 89
  confidentiality 92
  home visits 92
Family life **10-21** 68
  coping with family

problems 12
death in the family 19-21
decision-making 12
divorce 16
sibling rivalry 14
single-parent family 15
substitute care 13
with disabled children 115
Family therapy 121 191
Farm safety 58
Fathers as care-takers 68
Fears 49 69 **184-5**
of separation *see*
Separation anxiety
Febrile convulsions 89 161 **296**
Feeding and diet **36-42** 64
in infants 37-9
see also Diet
Feeding problems **181-2**
in the newborn 37 137
Fetoscopy 133
Fetus, development of 22
see also Intrauterine growth
Fever 89 **98** 105
see also Index of symptoms
Fibre 42 251
Fireworks 57
First aid **102-5**
Fits 88 96 135 150 **296** 297
in the newborn **141**
see also Index of symptoms
Flat feet 275
Flea bites *see* Insect bites
'Floppy' babies *see* Hypotonia
Fluoride supplements 204 205
Focal seizure 297
Fontanelle 30 299
Food additives 168 183
Food allergy 39 **167**
Food fads 42 181
Food poisoning **248**
Foot care 47
Forceps delivery 25 32
Forefoot eczema **286**
Fractures 144 274
Friendships 69 71
Fungal infections 151 **152** 217

G-6-PD 240
Gallbladder 241
Gamma-globulin 154
Gastric flu *see* Gastroenteritis
Gastroenteritis 243 **248** 246
Gastroenterology 106
Genes **126-33**
Genetics **126-33**
chromosomal disorders 128-9
Down's syndrome 129-31
genetic counselling **132** 200 238 304
genetically inherited

disorders **127-33 238-40**
prevention of genetic
disorders 132-3
sex-linked disorders 128
single-gene disorders 127-8
Genitals **255-7**
herpes 26
itching *see* Index of
symptoms
rash, swellings or sores
see Sexually transmitted
disease
German measles 112 153 155 **159-60** 281 300 301
during pregnancy 25 213 230
Gestational diabetes *see*
Maternal diabetes
Gingivitis **206**
Glands, swollen *see* Index of
symptoms
see also Endocrine glands
Glandular disorders **266-73**
Glandular fever 153 **162** 281
Glomerulonephritis 161 **259**
Glucose 114
Glue ear 209 **211**
Glue-sniffing 193
Gluten sensitivity *see* Coeliac
disease
Grand mal seizure 297
Grazes *see* Cuts and grazes
Greasy skin *see* Skin, greasy
Grieving 18 19 **20 306**-10
after divorce 16
Groin, swelling in *see* Hernia
Grommet 211 212
'Growing pains' 276
Growth **64-6 80-1** 182
in uterus 25
monitoring 66
predicting 65
problems **267-8**
spurt 81
Gums, sore and bleeding 206
Guthrie test 35

Haematology 106
Haemophilia 128 **239**
Haemorrhoids *see* Piles
Hair *see* Skin and hair
Halitosis **217**
Handicap *see* Disability
Hare lip *see* Cleft lip
Hay fever 165 168 212 216 **220** 223 286
Headache 88 186 **293-4**
see also Index of symptoms
Head injury 148 210
Head-jerking 186
Health visitor 89 119
Hearing 66

aids 213
difficulty 211 **213-4**
profile 212
tests 212
see also Index of symptoms
Heart and circulation **227-8**
congenital defects 25
142 **230-3**
disorders **229-33**
investigation 229
murmurs 29 30 35
228 229 233
surgery 230
Heartbeat irregularities 228
Heat exhaustion 105
Heat rash 33
Heatstroke 105
Height, prediction of 65
Hemiplegia 302 303
Henoch-Schonlein purpura 246
Hepatitis *see*
Infectious hepatitis
Hernia **262-3**
see also Hiatus hernia
Herpes B 153
Herpes simplex **162** 216 301
Hiatus hernia 243 **244**
Hip
congenital dislocation 31
35 142 **278**
irritable **278**
painful *see* Index
of symptoms
Hirschsprung's disease 251 **252**
Histology 106
Hives *see* Urticaria
Hoarseness 215
Hodgkin's disease 170 **175**
Holidays 58-9
Home nursing **94-105**
Homeopathy **122-3** 224
Homework 76
Hormone treatment 173 262
Hormones 266
Hospitals and the sick
child **106-10** 145
Humidifiers 224
Huntington's chorea 127
Hydrocele 263
Hydrocephalus 142 **143**
Hygiene 98
in the newborn 28 **43-5**
Hyperactivity 135 **183**
Hypersensitivity 165
Hyperthyroidism **268**
Hypnosis 222
Hypoglycemia **269-70**
Hypoplastic left heart syndrome 230
Hypospadias **265**
Hypothalamus 266

Hypothyroidism 140 **268**
Hypotonia **304**

Ichthyosis 286
Idiopathic thrombocytopenic
  purpura **240**
Imagination, development of 72
Immune system 152
Immunity **152** 234
Immunization 25 35 59 93 102 112
  146 **154-5** 233
Immunoglobulin 240
Impetigo **287**
Incontinence see Enuresis
Incubator 135 136 139
Independence, learning 10 68 70
  71 82 118 179 180
Induction of pregnancy 26
Infantile eczema 167 **285**
Infantile seborrhoeic dermatitis
  34 **285**
Infection 93 99 **151-3** 259 287
  bacterial 152 160 161 163
    220 233 248 259 279 284
    286 287
  common 153
  in the newborn 33 43
  defence against 152
  fungal 152
  parasitic 151
  prevention of 154-5
  viral 93 151 153 223 224
    248 278 281 284
  See also Immunization
Infectious diseases **156-64**
  Bornholm disease 163
  chickenpox 159
  cholera 164
  diphtheria 163
  German measles 159
  glandular fever 162
  herpes and cold sores 162-3
  influenza 156
  malaria 164
  measles 157
  mumps 158
  poliomyelitis 164
  roseola infantum 161
  scarlet fever 161
  toxoplasmosis 163
  tuberculosis 163
  typhoid 164
  whooping cough 160
Infectious hepatitis 59 140 248
  253-4 281
Influenza 152 153 **156**
Inherited disorders see
  Genetically inherited
    disorders
Injections 91 **112**
Injury see Accident and injury

Insect bites **291**
Insulin 269 271 272 **274**
Intellectual development **72-3**
Intelligence assessment 78
Intelligence quotient 79 189
Intelligence tests 79
Intensive care **135** 136 150
  222 232
Intrauterine growth, poor
  25-6
  see also Smoking
Intravenous drip 139 140 148
  151 226
Intravenous pyelogram 178
Intussusception 247 **248**
Iron-deficiency anaemia 237
  see also Anaemia
Iron supplements 237
Irritability 88
Itching 284
  see also Index of symptoms
ITP see Idiopathic
  thrombocytopenic purpura

Jaundice 226 **253** 254
  in the newborn **32** 135 136
    139-40 253
Jealousy see Sibling rivalry
Joints **274**
  disorders of **277-81**
  painful see Index of
    symptoms
  swollen see Index of
    symptoms

Kidneys, bladder and genitals
  255-7
Kidney
  disorders 256 **258-9**
  failure **258** 259 262
  transplant 259
  tumour of see
    Nephroblastoma
Klinefelter's syndrome 129
Knee, painful see Index of
  symptoms
Knock knees **275**
Koplik spots 157

Labour 26
Lactose intolerance **249**
Language development 50 60 **68**
  see also Speech
Lanugo 22
Laryngomalacia **220**
Law and your child 316
Laxatives 191 251
  see also Drugs and
    treatments
'Lazy eye' see Squint
Learning and school **72-9**

assessment of intelligence
  78-9
intellectual development 72
learning and reasoning 72-3
learning difficulties 78
moral development 73
special needs 79
stress at school 76-7
Learning difficulties 78 79 135
  184 **186-7** 199 249
  and deafness 214
  see also Dyslexia
Leg pains 276
Left-handedness 64
Leukemia 170 **173-4**
Life and death **306-10**
  cot death 308-9
  death of a handicapped
    child 306
  dying child 309-10
  importance of mourning 306
  miscarriage and abortion
    307
  suicide 310
Light-for-dates see Low-
  birthweight babies
Limp see Index of symptoms
Liver **241**
  damage 226
  disorders **253-4**
Long sight 197 **198** 199 293
Longstanding illness 109 **115-21**
Low-birthweight babies **136**
Lumbar puncture 112 171 174 299
  300
Lungs **221**
  problems 222
Lying 193
Lymph glands 152 170 175
  see also Mesenteric
    adenitis
Lymphoma 175
  see also Hodgkin's disease

Malaria 59 **164**
Malignancy see Cancer
Malnutrition 152
Manipulation 124
Manual dexterity see Dexterity
Massage 51
Mastoiditis 211
Masturbation 71 85
Maternal diabetes 26
Maternal toxemia see Toxemia
Maturation 81
  see also Growth
Measles 112 152 153 155 **157** 225
Meckel's Diverticulum **245**
Medical procedures 111 **112-4**
  barium enema and meal 242
  bone marrow aspiration 171 175

blood pressure 112
blood tests 113 171 237 250 270
injections 112
stool tests 114
urine tests 114 270 271
X-rays 114
see also Operations and Hospital Procedures
Medicines 93 **99-101**
see also Drugs and treatment
Medulloblastoma 177
Memory 73
Meningitis 141 142 158 294 **299**
Menstruation 80
see also Amenorrhoea
Mental illness **194** 310
Mental retardation 25 135 187 188 268 301
see also Disability
Mesenteric adenitis **246**
Metabolic disorders *see* Glandular disorders
Metabolism 96 **267**
Microbiology 106
Middle-ear infection *see* Acute otitis media
Migraine 124 167 249 **296**
Milia 33
Milk intolerance *see* Lactose intolerance
Misbehaviour *see* Behavioural problems *see also* Index of symptoms
Miscarriage 25 **307**
Moles 282-3
Molluscum contagiosum **291**
Mongolian spots 32
Mongolism *see* Down's syndrome
Moral development **73**
Moro reflex 31
Mourning *see* Grieving
Mouth, nose and throat **215-20**
Mouth ulcers 99 162 **216**
see also Index of symptoms
Mouth-breathing 216
see also Index of symptoms
Moving house 12 18 19
Mumps 152 153 **158**
Murmur *see* Heart murmur
Muscle **292-3**
diseases **303**
spasms 294
tumour *see* Rhabdomyosarcoma
Muscular dystrophy 128 **304**
Myopia *see* Short sight

Nail-biting 50
Nappy rash **33** 284 286
Nasal polyps 226

Nasogastric tube 138 247
Naturopathy 122
Naughtiness 179
Nausea *see* Index of symptoms
Navel, infection of 33 43
see also Umbilical hernia
Neck, pain in *see* Index of symptoms
Necrotising enterocolitis 137
Neonatal care **27-35**
problems **134-44**
Neonatal units *see* Special baby care units
Nephritis **259**
Nephroblastoma 170 **176**
Nephrology 106
Nephrotic syndrome **259**
Nerve damage 136
Nerve deafness *see* Perceptive deafness
Nervous system 31 170 175 **292-3**
tumour *see* Neuroblastoma
Nettle rash *see* Urticaria
Neuroblastoma 170 **175**
Neurology 106
Neurosurgery 106
Newborn child **27-35** 47
see also Problems of the newborn child
Nightmares 49 180 299
Nits *see* Head lice
Nose **215**
blowing 215
disorders of **216-20**
objects pushed up 105
Nosebleeds 216 236
Nosedrops 101
Nurseries 13 117
Myopia *see* Short sight
Nail-biting 50
Nappy rash **33** 284 286
Nasal polyps 226
Nasogastric tube 138 247

Obesity **42**
Obsessive compulsions **191**
Obstetrics 106
Occupational therapists 117
Oedema 259
Oncology 106
Operations **111**
Ophthalmology 106
Orchidopexy 264
Orthopaedics 106
Osgood Schlatter disease **280**
Osteomyelitis **279**
Osteopathy 122 124
Osteosarcoma 170 **177**
Otitis externa 209 **210**
Otitis media *see* Acute otitis media

Outpatient clinics **107**
Overprotection 10 12 52 57
and heart disorders 233
of disabled children 115
Overweight *see* Obesity

Paediatrics 106
Pain 96
relief 98 123
Pallor *see* Index of symptoms
Palpitations 228
Paraplegia 301
Parasites 151
Parenteral nutrition 138
Parenting styles 68
Patent ductus arteriosus 231
Pathology 106
Peak-flow meter 222
Peer group identification 71
Peptic ulcer **245**
Perceptive (nerve) deafness 66 213
Perforated eardrum **210**
Perinatal mortality rate 22
Periods, absent *see* Amenorrhoea
Peritonitis **247**
Perthes' disease **278**
Pertussis *see* Whooping cough
Pets 55 57
Phenylketonuria 35 128
Phobias 179 **185**
Photophobia 196
see also Index of symptoms
Phototherapy 139
Physical skills **61-4**
Physiological jaundice 139
Physiotherapy 51 117 146 226 239 303
Piaget, Jean 72
Pigeon toes **275**
Piles **251**
Pill, *see* Contraceptive pill
Pins and needles *see* Index of symptoms
Pityriasis rosea **291**
Placenta 23 25
Plantar wart *see* Verruca
Plaque 205 206
Plastic surgery 149
Play 50 69
Playground safety 56
Playgroups 13 74
Pneumonia 112 156 157 160 222 **225** 226
Pneumothorax 139
Poisoning 52 55 56 **150**
Poisonous plants 56
Poliomyelitis 59 155 **164**
Polydipsia **259**
Polyneuritis **300**
Port wine stains 32

Possetting 34
Posture 276
Pre-eclampsia *see* Toxemia
Pregnancy **22-6**
  teenage 86
  tests 86
Prematurity 25 29 37 135 **136-8** 237
Preschool children **60-9** 72
  problems **180-3**
  see also Day-to-day care
Pre-school experience 74
Prescriptions 93
Problems of the newborn child **134-44**
  anaemia 137
  apnoeic attacks 136
  birth asphyxia 135
  birth injuries 136
  bowel obstruction 141
  cleft lip and palate 143-4
  club foot 144
  extreme prematurity 138
  feeding difficulties 137-8
  hydrocephalus 143
  intensive care 135
  jaundice 139-40
  low-birthweight babies 136-7
  necrotising enterocolitis 137
  neonatal fits 141
  neonatal infection 141
  respiratory distress syndrome 138-9
  rhesus incompatibility 140
  special care 134-5
  spina bifida 141-2
  temperature control 136
Projectile vomiting 97
Promiscuity 85 **194**
Psoriasis 124 284 **291**
Psychiatrist 119 179 188
Psychiatry 106
Psychologist 117 179
Psychomotor seizures 298
Psychosomatic disorders 123 179 **186**
Psychosis 194
Psychotherapy 90 119 120-1 184
Puberty **80** 282 288
Pulmonary stenosis 231
Pyloric stenosis 243 **244**

Quadriplegia 301

Rabies 59 104
Radiology 106
Radiotherapy 172 173 174 175 176 177
Rashes **284**
  in the newborn 33
  see also Index of symptoms
Raynaud's disease **291**
Reading difficulties 78
Reasoning 72
Rebelliousness 15 82
Rectal prolapse 226
Refractive errors 198
  testing for 199
Regressed behaviour 70
Relationships
  ability to form 60
  after divorce 18
  with care-takers 13
  with parents 10 29
  with peers 50 69
  with step-parents 15
Relaxation techniques 51 184 **185** 186 293
Remarriage 15 16
Remedial teaching 186
Reproductive system **256-7**
Resistance to disease 152
Respiratory distress syndrome 135 **138**
Respiratory diseases **222-6**
Resuscitation 28
Retarded growth *see* Stature and growth problems
Rewards 14 181
Rhabdomyosarcoma 170 **176**
Rhesus incompatibility **140**
Rheumatic fever 161 233
Rheumatoid arthritis *see* Juvenile rheumatoid arthritis
Rheumatology 106
Rickets **280**
Ringworm 55 **291**
Rituals 191
Road safety 53
Roseola infantum 153 **161**
Routine, importance of 43 49 50 181
Rubella *see* German measles

Safety 12 **52-9**
  holiday and travel 58-9
  in the home 54-5
  on the road 53
  out of doors 56-7
Salmon patches 32
Salmonella poisoning *see* Food poisoning
Scabies 284 **290**
Scalds *see* Burns and scalds
Scalp wounds 145 148
Scaly skin *see* Index of symptoms
Scanning *see* CAT scan
Scarlet fever 153 **161** 233
Schizophrenia 189 **194** 310

School *see* Learning and school
School-age children **69-71 73-9**
  problems **184-7**
Scoliosis **279**
Screening procedures 35
Screening programme 000
Sebaceous gland 289
Seborrhoeic dermatitis *see* Infantile seborrhoeic dermatitis
Seizures *see* Fits
Sensitization 165
Self-esteem 189
Self-injury 190
Self-image 70
Self-help groups 115 183
  see also Support groups and publications
Separation anxiety 10 49 69 186 189
Separation of parents 15 16
Septic arthritis **279**
Sex differences 82
Sex education 71 85
Sex-linked disorders **128**
Sexual activity in adolescence 85
Sexual development 71 80
Sexual stereotypes 82
Sexually transmitted disease 85 86 **265**
Shingles 158
Shivering *see* Index of symptoms
Shock 270
Shoes 48
Short sight **198** 199
Shyness 189
Sibling rivalry 14 19
Sick child at home **94-105**
  care and comfort 98-9
  fever 98
  fluids and food 99
  games and entertainment 94-5
  giving medicines 100-1
  pain relief 98
  rest 98
  skin care and cleanliness 99
Sickle-cell anaemia 128 **238**
Single-parent family 15
Sinuses 215 216
Sinusitis 124 161 **219** 293
Skin and hair 152 **282-91**
  acne 288-9
  alopecia areata 291
  boils 284
  chilblains and chapped skin 287
  dandruff 284
  dry skin 34 283 284 286

see also Index of
  symptoms
eczema 285-6
greasy skin 283
hair loss 291
head lice 290
impetigo 287
infantile seborrhoeic
  dermatitis 285
insect bites 289
itchiness 284
rashes 284
scabies 290
spots 286
sunburn 284-5
stretch marks 283
urticaria 287
warts and verrucas 288
see also Rashes
Skull deformities *see* Index of
  symptoms
Skull fracture 148
Sleep needs 48
Sleep patterns 48 181
Sleeping problems 11 13 49 119
  180-1 190
  see also Index of
    symptoms
Slipped femoral epiphysis **278**
Small-for-dates babies 26 34 136
  see also Low-birthweight
    babies
Small stature *see* Stature and
  growth problems
  see also Index
    of symptoms
Smoking 193
  during pregnancy 25
Sneezing *see* Index of symptoms
Sniffing 215
Social development 69
Social phobia 189
Social services 115 117 119
Social skills 189
Social worker 188
Solitary children 71
Solvent sniffing 193
Spasticity *see* Cerebral palsy
Speech 62 **68** 79 214
  therapy 117 303
Special baby care units 26 **135**
  136 142
Special educational needs 79
Special school 79 117 131 187
Spectacles 197 198 199
Spherocytosis **240**
Spina bifida 24 29 **141-2** 143
Spine, curved *see* Scoliosis
  see also Index of symptoms
Sports injuries 52 57 274
Spots 289

in the newborn 33
  see also Index of symptoms
Sprains and strains 104
Squint 67 **197** 200 302
Stature and growth problems **268**
  see also Growth
Stealing 193
Step-parents **15**
Steroid drugs 240 254
  see also Drugs and
    treatments
Still's disease *see* Juvenile
  rheumatoid arthritis
Stillbirth **307**
Stings *see* Bites and stings
Stitches **294**
Stoma 250 **252**
Stomach-ache 186 189 190
  see also Abdominal pain
Stools 34
  blood in *see* Index of
    symptoms
  bulky *see* Index of symptoms
  tarry *see* Anaemia
  tests 114
Stork's beak marks *see* Salmon
  patches
Strains *see* Sprains and strains
Strawberry marks 32
Streptococcal infection 233 259
Stress 12 50 70 76 185
  and asthma 223
  and lowered resistance 152
Stretch marks 283
Stridor 97 **220**
Styes 196
Subnormality *see* Mental
  retardation
Substitute care-takers **13** 68
Sudden Infant Death Syndrome *see*
  Cot death
Suffocation 55
Suicide **190 310**
Sunburn 58 102 **284**
Sunstroke 58 105 285
  see also Heatstroke
Support groups and publications
  320-5
Supraventricular tachycardia 228
Surgery 172 173
Swallowing 241
  pain on *see* Index of
    symptoms
Sweating 45
  see also Index of symptoms
Symptoms, Index of 342-3

Talipes *see* Club foot
Tantrums 15 69 119 **182** 298
Teenage pregnancy 86
Teenagers *see* Adolescence

Teeth 30 **203-4** 233
  care of **45-7 204-5** 233
  decaying **205**
  injuries to **206**
  overcrowded and irregular
    206
Temperature 96 97
  control in newborn 136
Tension *see* Stress
Terminal illness **309**
Testes, or Testicles 30
  inflammation of 158
  painful *see* torsion of
  swollen *see* Hydrocele
  torsion of 262 **264**
  undescended **264**
Tetanus 59 **102** 112 146 155
Thalidomide 230
Thalassaemia 127 **238**
Thirst, extreme *see* Index of
  symptoms
Thoracic surgery 106
Thought disorders *see*
  Schizophrenia
Threadworms **252** 262 284
Three-month colic 38
Throat, sore **218**
  see also Index of symptoms
Thrombocytopenic purpura 240
Thrush **217**
  oral 33 34 37 152 224
  vaginal 33 34 152 270
Thumb-sucking 49
Thyroid problems **268**
Tics 50 186
Tiredness *see* Index of symptoms
Toilet-training **45** 61 251 260
Tooth decay 205 209 233
  prevention of 204
Toothache 205
Tonsillectomy 218
Tonsillitis 161 162 **218** 246
Tonsils 215 **218**
Torsion of the testicle 262 **264**
Toxemia 24 25
Toxocara 55
Toxoplasmosis 163
Toy libraries 117
Tracheotomy 149
Traction 147
Tranquillizers 184
Transfusion *see* Blood
  transfusion
Transplant, kidney 258
Transposition of the great
  arteries 232
Travel sickness **243**
Travelling 58
Triple vaccine 154
Trisomy 21 *see* Down's syndrome
Truancy 189 **193**

Tube feeding 135
Tuberculosis 112 155 **163**
Tuberous sclerosis 127
Tumour 169
  benign 177
  of bone 177
  of bone marrow 173-4
  of brain 177
  of lymph glands 175
  of kidneys 176
  of muscle 176
  of nervous system 175
  see also Cancer
Turner's syndrome 129
Twins 24
Twitches 96
Tympanometry 212
Typhoid 59 164 248

Ultrasound scanning 25 **132** 230 262
Ultraviolet light 139 291
Umbilical cord 23 27 28 44
Umbilical hernia 263
Unborn child 22-6
Unconsciousness 88
Undescended testicle **264**
Unsteadiness *see* Index of symptoms
Upper respiratory tract infections **216** 246
Urethral valves **262**
Urination, excessive, *see* Diabetes
Urinary tract 255
  abnormalities 256
  infection 161 260 **261**
Urine 97
  dark *see* Jaundice
  tests 114 270 271
Urology 106
Urticaria 33 167 168 284 **287** 290
Uterus 22

Vaccination *see* Immunization
Vaginal deodorants 45
Vaginal discharge *see* Index of symptoms
Vaginal thrush *see* Thrush
Vegan diet 42
Vegetarian diet 42
Venereal disease *see* Sexually transmitted disease
Ventilation of newborn 135 139
Ventilator 149
Ventouse extraction 32
Ventricular septal defect 129
Vernix 22 28
Verrucas **288**
Viruses **151** 154
  see also Infection
Vision 67
  problems *see* Eye disorders
Vitamin D 280 283
Vitamins 24 41
Volvulus 245 **246**

Vomiting 34 88 93 97 **243**
  self-induced 191
  See also Index of symptoms
Vulvovaginitis **264**

Waking at night 49
Warts **288**
Washing and hygiene *see* Hygiene
Wax in the ear **208** 213
Weaning 39
Weight loss 190 191
  see also Index of symptoms
Wheezing 88 **222**
  see also Index of symptoms
Wilm's tumour *see* Nephroblastoma
Wilson's disease 254
Wisdom teeth 202
Whooping cough 153 154 **160**
Who's who in the health service 312-5
Womb *see* Uterus
Working parents 13
Worms **252**

X-rays **114** 137 146 148 150 177 205 229 250

Yellow fever 59
Yellow skin *see* Index of symptoms

ACKNOWLEDGEMENTS

Frances Lincoln Limited would like to thank Anthea Sieveking for the photographs; Will Giles, Edwina Ridell and Elaine Anderson for illustrations; and Venner Artists, Andrew Macdonald and Lindsay Blow for additional artwork; Wordsmith typesetting; and Michael Burman for the colour reproduction.

Also, thanks to Elizabeth Fenwick for the Index and much editorial assistance; and Radius for the paste-up. For advice and help: Priscilla Alderson; Molly and Kitty Anderson; Armour Pharmaceutical Company Limited; Ben Berryman; Aela and Sue Bregman; Jago Brown; Ben Caplin; Dr Paul Carmen; Millie and Norma Cohen; Charlie, Sophie and Daniella Cox; Judy Dodds; John, Annabel and Max Fraser; Alison Freegard; Vivienne, Katie and Joe Gordon; Sarah Gregory; Victoria Gregory; Kathy Henderson; Amelia Hill; Dr Beve Hornsby; Dr Sue Jenkins; Ben John; Susan Kennedy; Dan Killian; Berry Mayall; Claudine Meissner; Fenella Merrilees; James, Alison and Guy Naftalin; Hartley and Lloyd Pack; Gil Parker; Nigel Partridge; Deborah Raphael; Angela Royston; Gaye and Jolyon Rubinstein; Hannah Schneebeli; Katherine and Karin Slater; Roger and Emily Spencer; Polly and Daisy Staniford; Louise Templeton; Louise Tucker; Spike and Angela Watson; Zoe Webber; pupils and staff of Brookfield School London; pupils and staff of Chorley Wood College for Girls; the Harley Street Clinic; Hornsey Rise Health Centre; pupils and staff of Queen's School, Bushey; pupils and staff of Queen Elizabeth II School, Paddington; patients and staff of the Child Health Department, University Hospital, Nottingham; the James Wigg Practice, Kentish Town.